THE CAMBR

EARLY CHRI

VC

CHRIST:
Through the Nestorian Controversy

The Cambridge Edition of Early Christian Writings provides the definitive anthology of early Christian texts, from ca. 100 CE to ca. 650 CE. Its volumes reflect the cultural, intellectual, and linguistic diversity of early Christianity, and are organized thematically on the topics of God, Practice, Christ, Community, Reading, and Creation. The series expands the pool of source material to include not only Greek and Latin writings, but also Syriac and Coptic texts. Additionally, the series rejects a theologically normative view by juxtaposing texts that were important in antiquity but later deemed "heretical" with orthodox texts. The translations are accompanied by introductions, notes, suggestions for further reading, and scriptural indices. The third volume focuses on early Christian reflection on Christ as God incarnate from the first century to ca. 450 CE. It will be an invaluable resource for students and academic researchers in early Christian studies, history of Christianity, theology and religious studies, and late antique Roman history.

MARK DELCOGLIANO is Associate Professor of Theology at the University of St. Thomas, Minnesota. He is the author of *Basil of Caesarea's Anti-Eunomian Theory of Names* (2010), and has published numerous journal articles as well as translations of Basil of Caesarea, Athanasius of Alexandria, Didymus the Blind, Gregory of Nyssa, and Gregory the Great.

THE CAMBRIDGE EDITION OF EARLY CHRISTIAN WRITINGS

The Cambridge Edition of Early Christian Writings offers new translations of a wide range of materials from ca. 100 CE to ca. 650 CE, including many writings that have not previously been accessible in English. The volumes will focus on selected themes and will include translations of works originally written in Greek, Latin, Syriac, and Coptic, together with introductions, notes, bibliographies, and scriptural indices to aid the reader. Taken together they should greatly expand the range of texts available to scholars, students, and all who are interested in this period of Christian thought.

THE CAMBRIDGE EDITION OF

EARLY CHRISTIAN WRITINGS

VOLUME 3

CHRIST:
Through the Nestorian Controversy

EDITED BY

Mark DelCogliano

University of St. Thomas, Minnesota

CAMBRIDGE
UNIVERSITY PRESS

Shaftesbury Road, Cambridge CB2 8EA, United Kingdom

One Liberty Plaza, 20th Floor, New York, NY 10006, USA

477 Williamstown Road, Port Melbourne, VIC 3207, Australia

314–321, 3rd Floor, Plot 3, Splendor Forum, Jasola District Centre, New Delhi – 110025, India

103 Penang Road, #05–06/07, Visioncrest Commercial, Singapore 238467

Cambridge University Press is part of Cambridge University Press & Assessment, a department of the University of Cambridge.

We share the University's mission to contribute to society through the pursuit of education, learning and research at the highest international levels of excellence.

www.cambridge.org
Information on this title: www.cambridge.org/9781107693326

DOI: 10.1017/9781107449640

First published 2022
First paperback edition 2024

A catalogue record for this publication is available from the British Library

ISBN 978-1-107-06213-9 Hardback
ISBN 978-1-107-69332-6 Paperback

Contents

PART III: TRADITIONS OF PRO-NICENE CHRISTOLOGY

PART IV: CONTROVERSY OVER NESTORIUS

Notes on Contributors

Anthony Briggman is Associate Professor of Early Christianity at Candler School of Theology, Emory University. He translated the selections from Irenaeus of Lyons's *Against Heresies*. Professor Briggman would like to acknowledge that his translation of Irenaeus is the result of a joint translation project shared with his graduate students Sarah Bogue, Brian Gronewoller, Brendan Harris, Micah Miller, and Devin White.

Dexter Brown is a doctoral student in the Departments of Classics and Religious Studies at Yale University. He translated the selection from the *Ascension of Isaiah* with Aaron Michael Butts.

Aaron Michael Butts is Associate Professor in the Department of Semitic and Egyptian Languages and Literatures at the Catholic University of America. He translated the selections from the *Odes of Solomon*. He also translated the selection from the *Ascension of Isaiah* with Dexter Brown.

Matthew R. Crawford is Associate Professor and Director of the Research Program in Biblical and Early Christian Studies in the Institute for Religion and Critical Inquiry at the Australian Catholic University. He translated Cyril of Alexandria's *Second and Third Letters to Nestorius*, his *Letter of Reunion to John of Antioch*, and his *First and Second Letters to Succensus*; and Nestorius's *Second Letter to Cyril of Alexandria*, his *Letter to John of Antioch*, and his *First Letter to Celestine of Rome*. He also translated the selections from John Cassian's *On the Incarnation of the Lord against Nestorius* with Thomas L. Humphries.

Mark DelCogliano is Associate Professor of Theology at the University of St. Thomas. He translated the *Gospel of Peter*; the selections of the *The First Letter of Clement*, of Ignatius of Antioch's *Letters*, and of the *Epistle to Diognetus*; the Greek and Latin *Fragments* of Paul of Samosata; the selections of the *Tome to the Antiochenes* and of Hilary of Poitiers's *On the Trinity*; Athanasius of Alexandria's *Christological Letters to Epictetus, Adelphius, and Maximus*; Apollinarius of Laodicea's *Recapitulation*, his *Letter to the Bishops in Diocaesarea*, his *Synodical Tome*, his *Fragments of Letters to Dionysius, Serapion, Terentius, and Julian*, his *Fragments of Other Writings*, and his *Fragmentary Writings against Diodore and Flavian*; Basil of Caesarea's *Letters* 261 *and* 262 and his *Homily on the Holy Birth of Christ*; the Greek and Latin fragments of Theodore of Mopsuestia's *On the Incarnation of the Lord against the Apollinarians and Eunomians*; Leporius's *Statement of Amendment*; the first book of John Cassian's *On the Incarnation of the Lord against Nestorius*; Nestorius's *Second and Third Letters to Celestine of Rome*; and the selections from *Acts of the Council of Ephesus*.

Emanuel Fiano is Assistant Professor of Syriac Studies at Fordham University. He translated the Syriac *Fragments* of Paul of Samosata.

Thomas L. Humphries is Associate Professor of Philosophy, Theology, and Religion at Saint Leo University. He translated the selections from John Cassian's *On the Incarnation of the Lord against Nestorius* with Matthew R. Crawford.

Ellen Muehlberger is Professor of History at the University of Michigan. She translated Aphrahat's *Demonstration* 17: *On the Son*; the *Selected Fragments* of Diodore of Tarsus; and the Syriac fragments of Theodore of Mopsuestia's *On the Incarnation of the Lord against the Apollinarians and Eunomians*.

Michael Papazian is Professor of Religion and Philosophy at Berry College. He translated the Armenian *Fragments* of Paul of Samosata.

Andrew Radde-Gallwitz is Associate Professor of Liberal Studies at the University of Notre Dame. He translated the selections from Justin Martyr's *First* and *Second Apologies*; Gregory of Nyssa's *Oration on the Savior's Nativity*; Augustine of Hippo's *On Eighty-Three Different Questions. Number 80: Against the Apollinarians* and his *Letters* 137 and 219; and Proclus of Constantinople's *Homily on the Holy Virgin Theotokos*. Professor Radde-Gallwitz would like to thank Margaret M. Mitchell for her helpful feedback on his translation of Gregory of Nyssa.

Paul S. Russell is Lecturer in Theology at St. Joseph of Arimathea Anglican Theological College. He translated the selections of Ephrem the Syrian's *Hymns on Faith*.

Jared Secord is an Academic Strategist at the University of Calgary. He translated the selections from Tertullian's *Apology*, from his *On the Flesh of Christ*, and from his *Against Praxeas*.

Melissa Harl Sellew is Professor Emerita of Classical and Near Eastern Studies at the University of Minnesota. She translated the *Treatise on Resurrection*.

Bradley K. Storin is Associate Professor of Religious Studies at Louisiana State University. He translated the selections from Tatian's *Address to the Greeks* and from Origen's *On First Principles*; Apollinarius of Laodicea's *Letter to Jovian*, his *First Letter to Dionysius*, his *On the Faith and the Incarnation*, and his *On the Body's Union with the Divinity in Christ*; Gregory of Nazianzus's *Letter* 101 *to Cledonius* and the selections from his *Poems*; and Ibas of Edessa's *Letter to Mari the Persian*.

Vasilije Vranic is a priest in the Serbian Orthodox Church in Washington, DC and a Visiting Fellow in the Center for the Study of Early Christianity at the Catholic University of America. He translated Eusebius of Dorylaeum's *Protest*, and Theodoret of Cyrrhus's *Exposition of the Orthodox Faith*, his *Refutation of the Twelve Anathemas of Cyril of Alexandria*, and the epilogue to his *Eranistes*.

Francis Watson is Professor in the Department of Theology and Religion at Durham University. He translated the *Epistle of the Apostles*.

Acknowledgments

Planning for what became volumes 3 and 4 in the Cambridge Edition of Early Christian Writings (CEECW) series began in 2012 when Andrew Radde-Gallwitz asked Ellen Muehlberger, Bradley K. Storin, and me to join him in editing a new series of thematic anthologies of early Christian texts. A scholar cannot have hoped for more knowledgeable, hard-working, and generous collaborators. Each of us brings a truly complementary set of skills, expertise, and perspectives to this project, making each volume of the series far greater than the sum of its parts. So first of all I thank my three collaborators, Andy, Ellen, and Brad, for their tireless efforts in the countless hours spent bringing this volume to completion, with painstaking attention to detail, with patience when progress was slow, with support for me when times were tough, and always, always, with plenty of good humor: thank you, my dear friends.

No less do I thank all those who contributed translations to this volume: Anthony Briggman, Dexter Brown, Aaron Michael Butts, Matthew R. Crawford, Emanuel Fiano, Thomas L. Humphries, Michael Papazian, Paul S. Russell, Jared Secord, Melissa Harl Sellew, Vasilije Vranic, and Francis Watson. Thank you for collaborating with us as your translations went through the multi-stage checking and editing process, which I realize could seem overly scrupulous at times. It was a thrill for me to be able to work closely with you on both the nuts-and-bolts and the finer points of your introductions and translations. To those who joined the project early on, thank you for your patience with me in the years it took to get your work into print. To those who joined the project at the eleventh hour, thank you for squeezing this project into your busy schedule on such short notice and yet producing such top-notch work.

Along the way several others have also made this volume possible through their sharing of advice, expertise, and time, by giving feedback, checking translations, helping crack difficult passages, providing unpublished work, and so forth: Pauline Allen, Lewis Ayres, John Behr, Matthew R. Crawford, Philip Michael Forness, Margaret M. Mitchell, Alex Pierce, Richard Price,

Corey Stephan, Francis Watson, Robin Darling Young, and Kevin Zilverberg. Your assistance has been an immense help to me: thank you.

A special thanks to Hilary Gaskin at Cambridge University Press for encouragement and advice with this large and complex project that took longer to complete than any of us anticipated, as well as to Hal Churchman, her assistant, Lisa Carter, our content manager, and Mary Starkey, our copy-editor. This volume has benefited immensely from their efforts and attention to detail.

And finally to Amy, Iris, and Richard: I simply cannot find the words to say how grateful I am to you, my three true loves.

Note on the Texts and Translations

Our translations have been produced in consultation with published editions and, in some cases, with manuscripts. Bibliographical information for the editions used can be found in the introduction to each translated text. The numeration of each work follows that of the editions from which we have translated. Numbers in the text with no surrounding brackets indicate chapter or paragraph divisions. In the case of texts with subdivisions or multiple numbering systems, the major chapter division is indicated in bold, followed by the subdivision in regular type with a full stop. Where bracketed numbers in bold appear, these indicate page numbers in a printed edition or folio numbers in a manuscript codex.

When a text quotes earlier material, references are provided in the notes with the following format: first, the series and number within the series or the abbreviation used for the critical edition, followed by a colon; then, the page number of the edition and, after a comma, the line numbers (if any); and finally the editor's name. For example, if Basil of Caesarea's *Against Eunomius* 1.12 were to be quoted, the reference would be: Basil of Caesarea, *Against Eunomius* 1.12, 32–35 (SChr 299: 214 Sesboüé). In some cases, as in this example, the line numbering in the critical edition is tied to the subdivisions of the work itself, not to the pages of the edition.

Psalms are cited according to the Septuagint numbering and versification, with the numbering of the Masoretic text in parenthesis. Note that in many English translations of the Psalms, the versification differs from the Septuagint and Masoretic text because the psalm heading is not included in the verse numbering.

All dates in the volume are CE unless otherwise noted.

The following conventions are used in the translations:

[]	Editorial supplement within a text by the translator to improve the sense
<...>	Lacuna within a text
<aaa>	Conjectural emendation by the text's editor to fill a lacuna

* * *	Transition from one document or major section to another
* * *	Intentional omission of material from the translation

Abbreviations

ACO	Acta Conciliorum Oecumenicorum
Apollinaris	Hans Lietzmann (ed. and trans.), *Apollinaris von Laodicea und seine Schule: Texte und Untersuchungen* (Tübingen: Mohr Siebeck, 1904).
CACSS	Corpus apologetarum Christianorum saeculi secundi
CCSG	Corpus Christianorum, Series Graeca
CCSL	Corpus Christianorum, Series Latina
CEECW	*Cambridge Edition of Early Christian Writings*
CPG	Clavis Patrum Graecorum
CSCO	Corpus Scriptorum Christianorum Orientalium
CSEL	Corpus Scriptorum Ecclesiasticorum Latinorum
Ep.	*Epistula*, *Epistle*
GCS	Die griechischen christlichen Schriftsteller
GCS n.F.	Die griechischen christlichen Schriftsteller, Neue Folge
GNO	Gregorii Nysseni Opera
LXX	Septuagint
Nestoriana	Friedrich Loofs (ed.), *Nestoriana: Die Fragmente des Nestorius* (Halle: Max Niemeyer, 1905).
PG	Patrologiae Cursus Completus, Series Graeca
PL	Patrologiae Cursus Completus, Series Latina
PO	Patrologia Orientalis
SChr	Sources chrétiennes

Series Introduction

The literary legacy of the early Christians is vast and spans multiple linguistic traditions. Early Christians used the written word in many ways: they sent letters, staged dialogues, reported revelations, gave advice, defended themselves, accused others, preached homilies, wrote histories, sang hymns, hammered out creeds, interpreted texts, and legislated penances – just to list the most common examples. They did these things in Greek, Latin, Syriac, and Coptic; while countless Christians would have used other languages, such as Armenian, these four are the medium of the vast majority of our surviving texts. For each text that has survived, there is a unique story. Some became part of educational curricula for Christians in medieval Byzantium, Basra, and Bologna; some were recited or sung liturgically; some were read in private devotions; some lay at the core of later theological debates such as the European Reformations in the sixteenth century or the Ressourcement movement in twentieth-century Catholicism; some suffered a literary death, being buried in the sands of Egypt only to be discovered again, quite by accident, in the past century. The question of how these works have been received over the centuries is undoubtedly important, but their later interpreters and interpretations ought not to overshadow their original significance and context.

The Cambridge Edition of Early Christian Writings offers a representative sample of this diverse literature in seven thematic volumes: *God*, *Practice*, *Christ: Through the Nestorian Controversy*, *Christ: Chalcedon and Beyond*, *Creation*, *Community*, and *Reading*. While no series of this kind can be comprehensive, these themes allow the reader to understand early Christianity in its full intellectual, practical, ritual, and communal diversity. The theme and the selection of texts are thoroughly discussed in each volume's respective introduction, but certain principles have guided the construction of all seven volumes. Our goal has been neither to narrate the establishment of orthodox or normative Christianity as this has been traditionally understood nor to champion its replacement by another form of Christianity. Instead, we have opted to let each text speak with its own historical voice and authority, while aiming to expand the number and range of early Christian texts available to English speakers. Because of this, many of these texts are translated into English here for the first time, while all others have been translated anew. We have combined magisterial works with neglected ones in order to show the diversity and interconnectedness of Christianity in its formative period. We are neither reproducing a canon of classics nor creating a new one. We make no claims that the included works are aesthetically or intellectually superior to other texts we have excluded. Some well-known classics have been omitted for simply that reason: they are readily accessible and widely read. Others are too lengthy and do not bear excerpting well. In some cases, we have judged that attention to a single work by an author has led to an unfortunate neglect of other works of equal or greater value by the same author. In such cases, we are taking the opportunity to cast our spotlight on the latter. In sum, by no means have we felt constrained by previous lists of "must-reads" in our own selections.

We have sought to produce translations that are literal – faithful to the original language's meaning and, when possible, syntax. If a meaningful term appears in the original language, we have aimed to capture it in the translation. At the same time, we have aimed to produce intelligible and attractive English prose. At times the two goals have conflicted and prudential judgments have been made; as part of a team of translators, we are fortunate that we have not had to make such decisions alone. Every translation that appears in our volumes has gone through a rigorous multi-stage editorial process to ensure accuracy as well as readability. We hope that this painstaking collaborative process ensures the reliability and consistency of our translations. As a team, we have come to see the value – and indeed the necessity – of such collaborative work for the academic study of early Christianity's rich library of texts.

Andrew Radde-Gallwitz
Mark DelCogliano
Ellen Muehlberger
Bradley K. Storin

Introduction

An anthology on the vast topic of "Christ" is a fool's errand. No single volume, no matter how large it is, can cover everything or satisfy everyone. Yet one can be ambitious. Indeed, the anthology compiled for this project turned out to be so large that it became impractical to publish it in a single volume. So this volume has a companion: *The Cambridge Edition of Early Christian Writings*, volume 4: *Christ: Chalcedon and Beyond*. Though physically separate, the two volumes belong together and are intended to be used together. In fact, together they encapsulate the editor's vision for the study of Christology in the formative centuries of Christianity.

It is not the aim of these volumes to give a comprehensive or definitive account of early Christian reflection on "the full sweep of the Son's existence," as Peter W. Martens has admirably expressed it,

> beginning with his pre-existent state, eternally begotten from God the Father, to his role in the creation of an invisible and visible cosmos, his modes of ministry in the human race, especially in Hebrew saints like Moses and the prophets, his embodiment in Mary and the many details of his ministry as relayed in the gospels, through his death, resurrection and ascension, his ongoing ministry in the world, and his eschatological activities which would culminate when he handed over the kingdom to the Father.[1]

While all these topics – and more – appear in the texts in these volumes, some delimitation has necessarily been made. The focus of these volumes, then, is on Christ as God incarnate. For it was this remarkable claim above all that sparked so much early Christian reflection on – and debate over – Christ.

These volumes include only non-biblical texts, though of course the Bible itself is profusely cited in the early Christian texts selected for them.

1 Peter W. Martens, "The Development of Origen's Christology in the Context of Second and Third Century Christologies," in Ronald E. Heine and Karen Jo Torjesen (eds.), *The Oxford Handbook on Origen* (Oxford: Oxford University Press, 2022), 355–372.

This selection is intended to be as wide and diverse as possible in terms of theological perspective, ideological commitment, language of composition, geographical origin, literary genre, and so forth, but at the same time also focused enough to give a sense of the various traditions of thought that developed about Christ in early Christianity, whether or not these traditions were deemed orthodox or heretical by contemporaries or later generations. A primary goal of these volumes is, then, to give readers a sense of the full scope of the Christological options that developed in early Christianity. At the same time the texts chosen provide coverage of the primary debates over Christ and illustrate how the development of Christological doctrine often proceeded polemically by the clarifying of positions in response to the criticisms of opponents. Thus many of the texts chosen for these volumes are "in conversation" with one another, whether by way of endorsement, development, or contestation. Texts have often been chosen for inclusion in these volumes because of their intertextual features, which highlight the "conversational" nature of Christological development.

These volumes include texts that range from the late first century to the early eighth century. They thereby not only span a much wider chronological range than can be found in other sourcebooks on Christology, but also have the intended consequence of de-centering the Definition of Faith promulgated at the Council of Chalcedon in 451, which stated that in Christ the divine and human natures were united unconfusedly, unchangeably, undividedly, and inseparably. The early story of the development of Christological doctrine should not be read through the lens of this Definition, with a retroactive Chalcedonian standard being imposed on pre-Chalcedonian authors and texts. Nor should it be assumed that the concerns and issues that animated Christological debate at Chalcedon were shared by earlier generations. The present volume therefore gives voice to the Christological concerns of these earlier generations on their own terms. Indeed, it was from these various streams of reflection on Christ going back to the first century that different traditions of Christological thinking developed in the third and fourth centuries, and from them too the pro-Nicene Christological developments of the fourth and early fifth centuries emerged. It is true that some theologians and documents from this period were later appropriated as advocates of Chalcedonianism *avant la lettre*. But presenting them in this volume in the context of preceding and contemporary reflection on Christ allows their peculiar perspectives to sound out more distinctly, making it obvious that the Chalcedonian reception of these figures is really a selective appropriation of a Christological landscape that was far richer and more diverse in actuality.

The extended chronological range has also been deemed necessary in order to demonstrate that Christological reflection did not end in 451 with the Chalcedonian Definition, the immediate prelude to which opens the next volume (CEECW 4). Notwithstanding its achievements, the Council of Chalcedon was extremely controversial, fomenting strains of Christological thinking opposed to its settlement, whose criticisms later led even diehard Chalcedonians to admit its weaknesses. Thus, it became the impetus for centuries of further reflection on Christ and theological development. The story of the reception of Chalcedon is as important as the story of any other period before 451 not only because it was decisive in shaping the ways in which Chalcedon was understood and passed on to subsequent generations, but also because of the constructive and innovative Christological contributions made in this period, which are of intrinsic value despite the general neglect they have received by students and scholars alike. For these too have had a profound influence on Christological doctrine until the present day.

So far this introduction has deliberately used vague expressions like "reflection on Christ" to describe that key feature of the texts that merits their inclusion in these volumes. But now it is time for some specification. At the heart of early Christian reflection on Christ lies the question of identity: Who is Jesus? Indeed, in one gospel Jesus himself puts this very question to his closest disciples: "But who do you say that I am?" (Matt 16:15). But there was no easy answer to this question; or rather, there were many possible, plausible, or viable answers in the early centuries of Christianity. The question of Christ's identity was furthermore bound up with the unfolding of that identity in history, namely, what Christ did and experienced during his earthly existence, what Christ does now in the church (especially how Christ is present and active in the sacraments), and what Christ will do when the eschatological age dawns. Just as the ancient Israelites and Jews came to know their God by his repeated interventions in their history – that is, by what he did for them – so too it was for the early Christians: what Christ did and does and will do teaches who Christ is.

This sort of reflection on Christ is already evident in the earliest writings about Christ available to us, writings later canonized as the New Testament. The letters of Paul, and those attributed to him by the earliest Christians, contain numerous accounts of who Christ was, such as the so-called

Philippians Hymn (Phil 2:6–11). Furthermore, Paul's view that Christ's death and resurrection were absolutely indispensable for understanding Jesus had massive influence on later generations of Christians. The centrality of Paul for early Christian reflection on Christ was one reason that later generations of Christians called him simply *the* Apostle.

The gospels also engage in reflection on Christ, but in a narrative mode. Recall Simon Peter's reply to the aforementioned question posed by Jesus: "You are the Christ, the Son of the living God" (Matt 16:16) – a strong Christological affirmation indeed! The gospels became the primary resources through which early Christians processed the unveiling of Christ's identity in history, since the gospels recount his life from birth to death and resurrection and beyond. Several events in the life of Christ narrated in the gospels became privileged sites for pondering the precise details of his identity: his birth from Mary, his baptism by John, his miracles, his ignorance, his hunger, his thirst, his suffering, his crucifixion and death, his resurrection from the dead, and his ascension into heaven. When reflection on Christ later entered into more technical debates, such as over the status of his knowledge or the mechanics of his willing, other events and episodes from his life were equally scrutinized.

The question of identity was always linked with what we might call the question of constitution: What is it that makes Christ the incarnate Son of God, the incarnate Word of God? In other words, once a theologian entertained a particular view about who Christ was, the issue became explaining what sort of constitution Christ had to have in order to ensure that identity. In time, when the age of the ecumenical councils dawned, discussions about Christ became more technical and refined, accounts of Christ more precise and nuanced, and debates over Christ more heated and divisive than they had been in earlier centuries. These councils sought to define the contours of Christ's identity and constitution with greater clarity, though not without violent controversy, vociferous resistance, and lamentable schisms within Christianity that have lasted until the present day. The seeming resolution of one issue only opened the door to others, each of which in turn required correction. And then the process inevitably began anew.

The fundamental conceptual problem of the incarnation was the concurrence in Christ of divinity and humanity, whose properties are, at least apparently, contradictory. For example, how can Jesus be both eternal and temporal, both immortal and have died on the cross? To claim so without further qualification risked nonsense for most early and late antique Christians. These volumes of course do not intend to solve this conceptual problem as such by highlighting a single answer to it, but rather to provide the reader with the range of answers given in the early centuries of the church in a broadly chronological order. Though this introduction is not the place for a full account of the history of attempts to provide a resolution to this fundamental problem, in keeping with the "fool's errand" nature of these volumes, a thumbnail sketch of that history is provided in the next paragraph.

Some of the earliest approaches to solving the conceptual problem included denying the reality of either the divinity or the humanity, making Christ actually the one but in some sense not really the other. These accounts took various forms, as seen in texts of CEECW 3 Parts I and II, and even III. Another strand of the earliest Christian thinking on the issue, however, affirmed the reality of both the divinity and humanity in Jesus, that is, as constituent parts of his individual identity. By the time we get to the texts in CEECW 3 Part IV and CEECW 4 Parts I and II, the understanding of Christ that theologians of the era believed to have been articulated in the Nicene Creed provided a common benchmark for all subsequent Christological development and debate: Christ was constituted of a fully divine nature and a fully human nature (save for sin). This pro-Nicene solution, however, created a new problem: how to conceptualize Christ, the incarnate God, as the single agent of salvation while constituted of two distinct and perfectly intact natures with seemingly contradictory properties. Accordingly, approaches to Christ in this period can be described as tending toward "unitive" or "dualistic" accounts, namely, those that emphasized the oneness or unity of Christ (however defined) or those that stressed his twoness or duality (however that was defined). For example, "miaphysites" held that a single nature (*mia physis*) resulted from the union of the two natures from which Christ was constituted. In contrast, "dyophysites" held that Christ's two natures (*dyo physeis*) perdured intact even after the union. But neither "miaphysite" nor "dyophysite" were monolithic categories, and there was a host of variations under these two broad headings. Furthermore, one could advocate for a unitive or dualistic approach to Christ in other terms than "nature," such as "person," "hypostasis," "activity," and "will." Of the major Christological schools that developed, the "Nestorian," the Miaphysite, and the Chalcedonian, each was as firmly committed to the pro-Nicene tradition as the others, and all had both unitive and dualistic elements in their peculiar Christologies, combined of course in different ways. Each of their positions had its strengths and weaknesses, its true insights and blind spots. Each of these schools was also volatile in its own way, since their individual trajectories of development veered (or perhaps self-corrected) in response to a variety of influences and underwent a process of bringing a more fine-grained precision to their Christologies. This thumbnail sketch is of course a gross oversimplification, but it is hoped that it exposes some of the key dynamics at work in Christological development in the period covered in this volume.

The following survey of the terrain covered in the present volume places each text in its historical and theological context and highlights its salient features. The purpose of this survey is (1) to help the reader see where each of the texts translated in this volume fits into the larger story of reflection on Christ, (2) to assist the reader in determining which texts are best suited to her or his interests, and, above all, (3) to clarify for the reader the interrelationships among the texts and the conversations happening between them. While the survey here is necessarily panoptic, the reader should know that the translation of each text is preceded by its own individual introduction that in short compass provides a biographical sketch of the author, a fuller account of the historical and theological context of the text, and a brief survey of the text's contents or key points. In the following survey, the titles of texts translated in this volume are in boldface the first time they appear. The order in which the texts are discussed is not necessarily the order in which they appear in the volume (which is broadly chronological).

PART I: THE BEGINNINGS OF CHRISTOLOGY

Part I contains a number of second-century texts that present reflection on Christ in a variety of genres: heavenly visions, gospel narratives, dialogues between Christ and his disciples, confessions of faith, letters, apologies, poetry, theological essays, exegetical tracts, and anti-heretical treatises. All these texts address, each in its own way, the key features of Christ's identity, his mission and purpose, his relation to the heavenly realm inhabited by God the Father and the angels, as well as the meaning and implications of his earthly life, passion, death, resurrection, and ascension into heaven. The texts in Part I therefore testify to the rich diversity of approaches to Christ in the earliest stages of Christianity. While it is difficult to establish precise dates for most of these texts, in general they date to the second century. In this period there were numerous possibilities for affirming that Jesus Christ was human and divine, and the earliest Christians availed themselves of diverse ways of conceptualizing this core belief. None of the positions on Christ found in these texts was deemed by later Christians to be a satisfactory account of Christ, though some of them remained viable options for centuries and a few even served as the basis or at least the impetus for later developments.

The first three texts in Part I are today classified as "pseudepigraphical," that is, "falsely attributed" to their authors, who are typically biblical personages. Such works thus evoke a scriptural ambiance and have a scriptural "feel" to them. The selection of the ***Ascension of Isaiah*** translated here recounts the prophet Isaiah's upward journey through the heavens where he encounters Christ, who is described in "angelomorphic" terms, that is, as a kind of angel or being who assumes an angelic form. ***The Gospel of Peter*** narrates the passion, crucifixion, and resurrection of Jesus in a way that emphasizes his real suffering and heroism – and features a walking and talking cross. It affirms Jesus as Lord, Son of God, King of Israel, and Savior of human beings, but not as Christ or Messiah. ***The Epistle of the Apostles*** records a purported dialogue on Easter morning between Jesus and his disciples in which Jesus answers questions put to him by his disciples in preparation for their future mission. The letter also includes a confession of faith about Jesus.

The next three texts belong to the corpus of writings known as the Apostolic Fathers, a collection of works first associated with one another in the seventeenth century because traditionally the authors of these texts were believed to have personally known or been otherwise formatively influenced by one of the twelve apostles of Jesus Christ. The selections of ***The First Letter of Clement*** translated here spell out the ethical implications and obligations of Christ's advent, suffering, death, and resurrection for the Christian community in its quest for peace and harmony. The selections from the ***Letters*** of Ignatius of Antioch affirm the embodied reality of Jesus in his human descent from David, his birth from Mary, as well as in his suffering, death, and resurrection, against those who denied their reality. Such people viewed Christ as a divine being who only seemed or appeared to be a human being in an illusory manner without being so in reality. Later Christians would call this view "docetism" because it attributed to Jesus only an "appearance" (in Greek, *dokein*) of embodied existence, not the true reality of incarnation. The ***Epistle to Diognetus*** is an early Christian apology in epistolary form that explicates the role of Christ in God's plan of salvation.

In the above-mentioned *The First Letter of Clement* there are several examples of the early Christian use of *testimonia*, passages from the Hebrew scriptures that are applied to Christ in an effort to interpret and arrive at a fuller understanding of his life, death, and resurrection. This common practice merits further explanation. The earliest followers of Jesus, all Jews, in the aftermath of the resurrection, tried to make sense of Jesus by scouring their scriptures. An instance of this approach is seen in Paul's remark that through Christ the veil over the (Hebrew) scriptures is removed and the Christ hidden therein made manifest.[2] Accordingly, early Christians reflecting on Christ saw the Hebrew scriptures, which later became the Christian Old Testament, as a key resource for understanding Christ. They believed Christ to be present and active in the Old Testament, whose narrative was but the first part of a single story of salvation that culminated in Jesus Christ. This engagement with the Hebrew scriptures is apparent in the earliest writings about Christ, such as Paul's letters and the gospels; it is also found in early Christian texts coeval with the biblical texts like *The First Letter of Clement*; and the application of Old Testament *testimonia* to Christ is found in many texts from the first Christian centuries, including some of the other texts translated in this volume.

The authors of the next group of texts are today classified as "Apologists" because they penned defenses of Christianity in response to the Roman persecution of Christians and to dispel widespread Roman misconceptions about their beliefs and practices. These defenses included accounts of God and Christ as well as critiques of traditional Roman culture. This volume contains selections from Justin Martyr's ***First* and *Second Apologies*** (dated to the early 150s) and from Tatian's ***Address to the Greeks*** (written a decade or more after Justin's *Apologies*). These texts identify Jesus Christ with the Word (*Logos*) of God, whom they understand to have been brought into existence by God to be the intermediary between the utterly transcendent God the Father and the material creation so that God could make and administer the world through him. It was the Word of God who thus became incarnate in Jesus Christ. This way of thinking about Jesus is now known as "Logos theology." While later Christians became dissatisfied with Logos

2 2 Cor 3:13–16.

theology because of a perception that it flirted with ditheism, conceptualizing Christ as the incarnate Word of God became standard. Furthermore, Justin contends that the events that occurred in connection with Jesus' life, death, and resurrection, as well as the history of the church after him, were foretold by the Jewish prophets. Thus, the match between ancient prophecy and recent events was proof for Justin that Jesus is the incarnate Son of God, the incarnate Logos.

The selections from the ***Odes of Solomon*** translated here illustrate reflection on Christ in early Christian poetry. These highly allusive poems identify Jesus, the Messiah, with the Son of God and explore the significance of his birth from a virgin, crucifixion, and resurrection.

The next two texts stem from the milieu of Valentinian Gnosticism. The ***Treatise on Resurrection*** is a didactic epistle that contains a brief exposition on the true meaning of resurrection. The treatise highlights Christ's salvific work, teaching that his defeat of death by resurrection enables those who believe in him to experience the true resurrection, namely, a spiritual transformation. The ***Ptolemaic Theology*** is a mid-second-century account of a Valentinian exegesis of the prologue of the Gospel of John. Here the prologue is interpreted as the revelation of the generation of the Ogdoad, the first eight Aeons, in a series of four conjugal couples: Father and Grace, Only-Begotten and Truth, Word and Life, and Human Being and Church.

Part I concludes with selections from Irenaeus of Lyons's ***Against Heresies*** from the late second century. Writing against opponents of various stripes, Irenaeus articulated a profoundly influential account of Christ, in which Jesus Christ is identified as the one and the same Word and Son of God now incarnate, as human as we are human (excepting sin) and as divine as the Father is divine. Irenaeus recapitulates and indeed advances upon the proto-orthodox traditions of Christological reflection that preceded him and became the harbinger of the dominant strands of Christological reflection that would follow.

PART II: DEVELOPING CHRISTOLOGICAL TRADITIONS

The texts in Part II illustrate the beginning stages of the gradual establishment of Christological standards. This part contains several third- and fourth-century texts that showcase the traditions of Christological reflection that were developing in the Latin, Greek, and Syriac milieux. This period witnesses to the emergence of a widespread set of beliefs about Christ as well as the initial development of a technical theological vocabulary for speaking about Christ, though of course these were not shared by all. Most of the authors of the texts presented here had a formative influence on subsequent generations in their respective traditions.

The Latin tradition is represented by two figures. Excerpts from three writings of Tertullian written between ca. 197 and the early 210s are included. In his early ***Apology***, continuing the apologetic tradition found also in Justin and Tatian, he offers a range of proofs for his traditionalist Roman audience in support of the Christian belief that Christ was both human and divine, emphasizing the plausibility and reasonableness of such a belief. ***On the Flesh of Christ*** is a defense of the reality of Christ's human body, sufferings, and death against different strains of docetism taught by the followers of Marcion, Apelles (a disciple of Marcion), and Valentinus, all of whom were thought to deny the reality of Christ's flesh in some way. In ***Against Praxeas*** Tertullian takes on the monarchians, whose view of Christ, he claimed, resulted in "patripassianism." In other words, the monarchians identified God and Christ, and the result of this, according to Tertullian, was that the Father experienced the sufferings experienced by Christ – an implication rejected as a blasphemous impossibility by Tertullian. In this treatise he offers an account of the incarnation that attempts to uphold the divine immutability of Christ. In the course of his writings Tertullian developed a technical vocabulary for discourse about Christ that would prove to be enormously influential on the later Latin tradition. The second work of Latin theology that appears in this part is ***On the Trinity*** of Hilary of Poitiers, written around 360. In the selection in this volume Hilary refutes the "Arian" idea that the Son is by nature inferior to the Father simply because of the incarnation. He affirms that in the incarnation God lowers himself to the human condition without ceasing to be fully God, and that Christ's expressions of weakness or ignorance must be attributed to his human nature, not taken as proof of his lesser divinity.

The Greek tradition is represented by Origen of Alexandria and Paul of Samosata. In the selection from ***On First Principles*** translated here, likely written between 220 and 230, Origen investigates what he takes to be not yet clear in the ecclesiastical proclamation about Christ. This proclamation maintained an anti-monarchian distinction of the Father and Son, the preexistence of Christ, his becoming human while remaining divine, and an anti-docetic insistence upon the true humanity of Christ and the reality of his human experiences, especially his suffering and death. In inquiring into these teachings further, Origen presents Christ as the "God-human being" and conceives the incarnation as the Word of God taking on flesh through the intermediary of the soul of Christ. The Antiochene bishop Paul of Samosata was condemned and deposed for heresy in the 260s. ***Selected Fragments*** of Paul are presented in this volume. Paul's views are difficult to reconstruct because of the fragmentary nature of the evidence. He appears to have viewed the incarnation as an instance of the Word's indwelling of a human being, an instance that was qualitatively akin to its presence in all righteous human beings, but with a permanence and completeness unlike all others. By the early fourth century Paul's teaching was routinely regarded as resulting in a Christ who was a "mere human being" who was "adopted" by God as his Son. Later Christians would pillory these positions as "psilanthropism" (a term based on the Greek for "mere human being," *psilos anthrōpos*) and "adoptionism." In the fifth century, Paul would be viewed as a precursor to Nestorius.

The Syriac tradition is represented in Part II by Aphrahat and Ephrem the Syrian. The early to mid-fourth-century Aphrahat's ***Demonstration 17: On the Son*** is a response to objections imagined to be raised by Jews about Christian beliefs about Jesus, that they call someone who is only a human being "God." In the selections from the ***Hymns on Faith*** that appear in this volume, which were probably written in the 360s, Ephrem addresses the issue of the limits of human knowledge when it comes to divine topics such as Christ's divinity and his incarnation. Ephrem also deals with the "Arian" argument that Christ's knowledge, which the gospels present as inferior to the Father's, suggests his ontological subordination to the Father. He counters that this inferior knowledge is explained by the Son having assumed human nature.

PART III: TRADITIONS OF PRO-NICENE CHRISTOLOGY

Part III presents several texts from pro-Nicene writers of the late fourth and early fifth centuries. The pro-Nicene alliance started to emerge in the 350s, through the efforts of Athanasius of Alexandria and then of Basil of Caesarea and others, when the Nicene Creed, promulgated in 325 and interpreted according to a Trinitarian logic and doctrine articulated by its chief proponents, gradually became the basis for consensus in the

Trinitarian debates of the era. These pro-Nicene efforts reached an apogee at the Council of Constantinople in 381, when a revised version of the Creed was issued and imperial legislation subsequently enforced the pro-Nicene doctrine of the Trinity. In late antiquity the original version of the Nicene Creed was known as the creed of 318 fathers and the revised version as that of 150 fathers, referring to the purported number of bishops who assembled at the first and second ecumenical councils in 325 and 381. Today they are called the Nicene Creed and the Nicene-Constantinopolitan Creed.

Both versions of the Creed, however, are quite laconic on the subject of the incarnate Christ, simply affirming that Jesus Christ, the Son of God, "became incarnate" (*sarkōthenta*) and "became human" (*enanthrōpēsanta*) to save humanity. Accordingly, most pro-Nicene accounts of Christ in the late fourth and early fifth centuries attempt to explain *inter alia* precisely what "becoming flesh" and "becoming human" meant. At the same time, most of these pro-Nicene authors were refuting various strains of "Arian" Christology, such as that of the Heteroousians (or Eunomians) or the Homoians, or other currents of thought whose sources are hard to determine. But since pro-Nicenes themselves espoused a range of Christological positions, with some opting for a more unified approach to Christ (stressing the single subjectivity of Christ) whereas others maintained a more dualistic perspective, they also engaged in polemics with each other. All the pro-Nicene theologians represented in this part laid the foundations for centuries of further Christological debate and development, whether later deemed touchstones of orthodoxy or fountainheads of heresy – even though the later Christological traditions that developed did not agree as to who should be placed in which category.

The selection of the ***Tome to the Antiochenes*** penned by Athanasius of Alexandria and others in connection with the Council of Alexandria in 362 offers a precious snapshot of the Christological issues under debate at the time. Several of the affirmations made in the *Tome* reappear or are debated in other writings from this period: that the Word did not indwell Christ in the same manner that he dwelt in the prophets, but he really became a human being, taking flesh from Mary, for the redemption and salvation of humanity; and that the incarnate Word is one and his divinity and humanity should not be divided into separately acting and experiencing agents. Athanasius's three ***Christological Letters to Epictetus, Adelphius, and Maximus***, written between 360 and 374, confront a wide range of

Christological aberrations that had been reported to him. As some of these positions are inconsistent with others, it seems likely that Athanasius is dealing with a hodgepodge of Christological views rather than a cohesive Christological system, though he describes some as "Arian." In response, Athanasius affirms that the divine Word became incarnate without any change to his divine properties. He repeatedly emphasizes the single subjectivity of the incarnate Word, insisting that the humanity, its properties, and its experiences *belong to* the Word, making them his own. The Word acts and experiences in a twofold manner, divinely and humanly, and yet he remains a single individual. The *Letter to Epictetus* in particular was later esteemed as a monument of Christological orthodoxy at the Councils of Ephesus and Chalcedon as well as by Cyril of Alexandria.

Several writings of Apollinarius of Laodicea are included in this volume: ***Recapitulation***, ***Selected Letters***, ***On the Faith and the Incarnation***, ***On the Body's Union with the Divinity in Christ***, ***Fragments of Other Writings***, and the ***Fragmentary Writings against Diodore and Flavian***. Apollinarius exemplifies the unitive approach, stressing the absolute unity of divinity and humanity in Christ, whom he called one person (*prosōpon*), one hypostasis, and "one incarnate nature of God the Word." Intending to avoid any dualistic subjectivity in Christ, he conceptualized the incarnation as the Word assuming human flesh or a human body through an integrative union and thus eliminated the humanity's rational soul from the Christological compound, with the Word of God effectively taking the place of Christ's human power of self-determination. His opponents seized on this precise point as the chief defect of his teaching, inasmuch as they claimed he attributed a defective humanity to Christ. Because Apollinarius so emphasized the identity of the Word and Jesus, it permitted him, for example, to speak of Christ's flesh as "heavenly" and same-in-substance with God precisely on account of the union. The technical term for such an understanding is *communicatio idiomatum*, "a sharing of properties." But this led his opponents to accuse Apollinarius of teaching that the flesh of Jesus had descended from heaven, even though Apollinarius himself denied it. The numerous translations presented in this volume allow the reader to hear Apollinarius speaking in his own voice, his views for the most part set within their own argumentative context and not subjected to the polemical conjectures and distortions of his opponents. One of Apollinarius's interlocutors was Diodore of Tarsus, whose approach to Christ was more dualistic than his. The ***Selected Fragments*** of his translated in this volume illustrate how he could speak of Christ as if he were two separate entities, "the seed of David" or "the one from Mary," and "God the Word."

In ***Letters* 261 and 262**, from the 370s, Basil of Caesarea confronts several Christological opinions he takes to be deviant, including one that held that Christ's body was "heavenly." In the course of refuting the deviant opinions, he provides a sketch of his own Christological views. His ***Homily on the Holy Birth of Christ***, also from the 370s, is a commentary on selected verses of the infancy narrative in Matthew 1:18–2:11, which includes reflection on the incarnation. Here Basil conceives of the incarnation as God's presence in human flesh, in a human body that is just like ours, but in a unique way unlike his intermittent presence in the prophets. Basil affirms divine immutability even in the incarnation, explaining that the Word was not diminished or changed when he came to dwell among us.

In the 380s the tide turned definitively against Apollinarius when Gregory of Nazianzus and Gregory of Nyssa began to write against him. The former's ***Letter* 101 *to Cledonius*** and ***Poems* 1.1.10–11** demonstrate Gregory's anti-Apollinarian polemics in two different genres: letter and verse. Against Apollinarius Gregory affirms that Christ was fully divine and fully human with body, soul, and mind as he lays out a Christological vision that was to have profound influence on subsequent generations of Christians. *Letter* 101 later became another monument of Christological orthodoxy, and in it Gregory's famous (and often misquoted) dictum appears: "For what is not assumed is not healed, but what is united to God is saved." Though Gregory of Nyssa wrote works specifically against Apollinarius, the Laodicean bishop is not in his sights in his ***Oration on the Savior's Nativity***. In the course of commenting on the Matthean infancy narrative (much as Basil had done) Gregory addresses various objections to the doctrine of the incarnation: If this intervention was providentially necessary, why was it delayed in human history? If evil and death were conquered by Christ, why are they still so powerful? Isn't the incarnation out of character for God, who is perfect and incorruptible?

Diodore's protégé Theodore of Mopsuestia's ***On the Incarnation***, from the late 380s or early 390s, is directed against both Eunomians and Apollinarians. This work survives only in fragments, which have been arranged in their original order as far as can be determined. In this work Theodore expounds a Christology that is very much a work in progress. He attempts to work out the categories, concepts, and contours with which to articulate his dualistic understanding of Christ, which he expresses in dyophysite ("two natures") terms: in Christ there is a union of two distinct, intact, and complete natures (humanity and divinity) in a single person. Theodore speaks of God indwelling in Christ "by good pleasure" and goes to great lengths to elucidate what he means by that. He teaches that Christ can be called "Son of God" (by grace) because of his conjunction with the Word (who is Son of God by nature).

The pro-Nicene Christological dynamics found in the Greek East were also found in the Latin West, which is represented here by selected writings of Augustine of Hippo and a dossier of texts connected with Leporius. In ***On Eighty-Three Different Questions. Number 80: Against the Apollinarians*** from 396 Augustine engages in anti-Apollinarian polemics. In ***Letter 137*** from 412 he defends the incarnation as the Word's assumption of a human being and answers pagan objections to this belief, namely, that it posits that the ruler of heaven was confined in the tiny body of an infant and underwent the ordinary experiences of a human being. In ***Letter 219*** from about 420 – the first document in the Leporius Dossier – Augustine reports how he persuaded the monk Leporius to abandon his Christological dualism in favor of a more unitive pro-Nicene Christology and provides a succinct summary of his Christology. There are two more documents in the Leporius Dossier. The first is Leporius's ***Statement of Amendment***, in which he demonstrates his abandonment of his earlier Christological opinions and outlines his corrected Christological views, articulating his reasons for holding them. He admits that his former views had the unintended consequence of positing two Christs and adding a fourth person to the Trinity. He now views the incarnation as a mixture of divinity and humanity without confusion or detriment to either nature, a mixture in which the properties of each nature are shared by the one Christ, the incarnate Word, who is the subject of all the human experiences of Jesus in respect of his humanity. The third document in the Leporius Dossier is the first book of John Cassian's ***On the Incarnation of the Lord against Nestorius***, from late 429 or early 430. Here Cassian depicts Leporius as a kind of Nestorius before Nestorius, attributing his Christological errors to his adherence to the teaching of Pelagius.

The final selection in Part III is Theodoret of Cyrrhus's ***Exposition of the Orthodox Faith***, probably from the 420s. The first section of this work summarizes the doctrine of the Trinity, against unnamed opponents, most likely "Arians" of his era, perhaps some sort such as Heteroousians, and here Theodoret recapitulates the central pro-Nicene teachings about the

Trinity articulated in the fourth century and in particular by the Cappadocian Fathers. The second part of the work is devoted to Christology. The focus of this section is the mode of union between the humanity and divinity in Christ, teaching that in the incarnation two different substances have been united in a conjunction to create a single new entity, which he calls a person. He also deals with the problem of reconciling the omnipresence of the Word with the constraints of the human body assumed in the incarnation and rejects Christologies which conceive the incarnation as a blending or confusion of the divine and human natures, or which speak of the Word changing into the body or the body becoming divine. As this work illustrates the concerns of pro-Nicene Christology on the eve of the controversy over Nestorius, it is a fitting conclusion to Part III.

PART IV: CONTROVERSY OVER NESTORIUS

Of the six parts of CEECW 3 and 4, this one is the most compressed in time. The texts translated here were written over a period of less than twenty years, from about 428 to around 447. All of them are connected in some way with the controversy over Nestorius and have been chosen to illuminate the Christological positions and political machinations of the two main factions.[3] One was headed by Cyril of Alexandria, who had allied himself with Celestine of Rome against Nestorius of Constantinople. Their opponents were the "Easterners" (so called because they came from the Roman diocese of Oriens or "East") led by John of Antioch; their chief theological authority was Theodoret of Cyrrhus. While the Easterners eventually repudiated Nestorius, their Christological differences with the party of Cyril endured.

Soon after Nestorius became bishop of Constantinople in 428, a dispute erupted between two groups in the imperial capital over the propriety of the titles Theotokos ("bearer of God") and Anthropotokos ("bearer of the human being") for the Virgin Mary. Neither term was novel, the former having entered Christian usage in the early fourth century and the latter in the late fourth century. In an attempt to resolve the issue, Nestorius rejected both terms and advocated instead Christotokos ("bearer of Christ"). In several of his documents contained in this part he rehearses

3 The introductions to the individual texts narrate the progression of this controversy in greater detail.

his reasons for preferring this title. But this did not quieten the dispute as he had hoped. At some point, a layman named Eusebius, later the bishop of Dorylaeum, harangued Nestorius in defense of the title Theotokos while the Constantinopolitan bishop was preaching in church. Shortly after this, he issued a formal ***Protest*** against Nestorius, a public denunciation of his views. In this document he accused Nestorius of reviving the doctrines of Paul of Samosata, mentioned above, whose teaching by the 420s was universally considered indisputably heretical. Because of his interventions Nestorius now found himself at the center of the dispute he had tried to resolve.

News of the controversy in Constantinople soon spread throughout the East. It made its way to Egypt, over whose church Cyril of Alexandria presided. In two letters intended for Egyptian audiences written in early 429, he touched upon the Christological issues roiling Constantinople, rejecting Nestorius's position though without naming him. One of these letters, his *Letter to the Monks of Egypt*, reached Constantinople and upset Nestorius, whom everybody knew was the object of Cyril's rebuke. Reports of Nestorius's annoyance reached Cyril, and in the face of the unabated controversy in Constantinople, he wrote directly to Nestorius for the first time, justifying his *Letter to the Monks of Egypt* and announcing that his concern for Nestorius's orthodoxy was shared by Celestine the bishop of Rome (with whom Cyril was in regular contact).

In early 430 Cyril wrote his ***Second Letter to Nestorius***, in which he for the first time engages directly with the Christological issues raised by Nestorius's teaching. Here he explicates the Christological statements of the Nicene Creed of 325 and introduces his conception of the "hypostatic union" of the divine and human natures in Christ, which, he teaches, results in a single subject to whom can be attributed all the actions, experiences, and sayings of Jesus Christ, both those human and those divine – the doctrine of *communicatio idiomatum*. The Council of Ephesus in 431 and the Council of Chalcedon in 451 would give formal approval to the *Second Letter to Nestorius*, securing its status as a monument of Christological orthodoxy. In response to this letter Nestorius wrote his ***Second Letter to Cyril***, in which he summarizes his Christological teaching in a way that highlights his differences from Cyril. Toward the end of the same year, 430, bishop Proclus of Cyzicus (he became bishop of Constantinople in 434) preached a ***Homily on the Holy Virgin Theotokos*** in defiance of his archbishop Nestorius, who was present in the audience. In the homily he unequivocally defends using the title Theotokos for the Virgin Mary, as it safeguarded the union of the divine and human natures in Christ the incarnate God.

Cyril's attempts to form an alliance with Celestine prompted Nestorius to write ***Three Letters to Celestine of Rome*** over the course of about a year, from late 429 to late 430, to try to win the bishop of Rome to his cause. These letters not only provide a clearer picture of the theological issues at stake at this early stage in the controversy, but also illuminate the political aspects of the dispute. Celestine never responded to these letters, but he was in communication with Cyril, who wrote to the bishop of Rome seeking a judgment on the question of whether it was necessary to sever communion with Nestorius. Cyril also provided Celestine with a dossier of Nestorius's writings. By mid-430 at the latest Celestine had tasked his archdeacon Leo (the future bishop of Rome) with evaluating them. Leo in turn requested John Cassian to examine the texts of Nestorius and produce a document to advise Celestine and the Roman church about the matter. In his ***On the Incarnation of the Lord against Nestorius*** Cassian firmly rejected Nestorius's position. As the first Latin text to assess Nestorius's theology, this treatise had a profound influence on subsequent perceptions of Nestorius in the Latin West. In August 430 a synod met in Rome under Celestine that formally condemned Nestorius. Celestine then wrote to Nestorius for the first time, informing him of the Roman synod's decision against him and ordering him to recant his views or be deposed. Celestine also wrote to Cyril about the synodal decision against Nestorius, prompting Cyril to hold a synod in Alexandria that also condemned Nestorius. Cyril then wrote his ***Third Letter to Nestorius***. Unlike his *Second Letter to Nestorius*, this letter was not a personal communication but intended to reflect the consensus that had formed against Nestorius's views, and to spell out in greater detail the Christological dogmas to which the bishop of Constantinople must adhere. In the *Third Letter* Cyril explains the Christology of his *Second Letter* in more detail, also touching upon its implications. To the letter Cyril appended Twelve Anathemas (or Twelve Chapters) which summarized his position as forthrightly as possible and deliberately excluded Nestorius's teachings as viable. Both this letter and Celestine's were delivered to Nestorius on November 30, 430.

In early December 430 Nestorius wrote his ***Letter to John of Antioch*** in an attempt to garner his support against the alliance of Cyril and Celestine. He expressed his willingness to confess the Theotokos so long as its possible heretical meaning was rejected. He also forwarded Cyril's *Third*

Letter to Nestorius along with its Twelve Anathemas. This turned out to be a shrewd move. For John and the Easterners were appalled by the Twelve Anathemas, which they viewed as smacking of the heresies of Apollinarius, Arius, and Eunomius. In response, Theodoret of Cyrrhus, the preeminent theologian among the Easterners, wrote his ***Refutation of the Twelve Anathemas of Cyril of Alexandria***. (Andrew of Samosata wrote another refutation of the same.) In the months before the Council of Ephesus in 431, then, Cyril's views as expressed in the Twelve Anathemas were under as much suspicion by the Easterners as Nestorius's were by Cyril and his allies. The upcoming council was intended to be an examination of both bishops.

But the Council of Ephesus was a debacle from its opening session on June 22 until its dissolution in October – see the introduction to ***Acts of the Council of Ephesus*** for details. The selections from this council translated in this volume begin with proceedings of the ***First Session*** on June 22 chaired by Cyril, at which Nestorius was deposed. The acts include a florilegium of twenty-five excerpts from the writings of Nestorius, compiled to highlight his most distinctive and, to his opponents, his most damning teachings. The proceedings of the ***Session of the Counter-Council of the Easterners*** on June 26 chaired by John of Antioch is also translated, which provides insight into the political dimensions of the council. At this session Cyril and his ally Memnon of Ephesus were deposed. At the ***Sixth Session*** on July 22 a "Nestorian" creed attributed to Theodore of Mopsuestia was presented because some Lydian Christians hoping to return to orthodoxy from heresy had been "tricked" into signing it. This creed teaches that the human nature of Christ, conceptualized as a distinct subject conjoined to God the Word, shares in the titles of Son and Lord, as well as the honor and worship properly belonging to them, in virtue of his conjunction with God the Word. As such, it is a succinct statement of "Nestorian" Christology. In July Nestorius wrote his ***Letter to Scholasticus the Eunuch of Emperor Theodosius*** in response to slander about him being circulated in the imperial capital. Here he reiterates his acceptance of the term Theotokos, as long as it is paired with Anthropotokos, and rails against Cyril's Christology because it attributes change, suffering, and even death to God the Word. This letter provides the best insight into Nestorius's own thinking in the midst of the council. In early August the Eastern delegation wrote a letter to Emperor Theodosius in response to his sacra (imperial letter) accepting the depositions of Nestorius, Cyril, and Memnon. This ***Report of the Easterners Written in Response to the Sacra Delivered by Count John*** offers a rare glimpse into the Christology of those opposed to Cyril: though they were willing to make Christological affirmations that amounted to a repudiation of Nestorius, they were unwilling to drop the charge that Cyril's Twelve Chapters were tainted with Apollinarianism. This *Report* includes one of the earliest statements – if not the earliest statement – of the so-called double consubstantiality of Christ, the idea that Christ is both same-in-substance (*homoousios*) with the Father and same-in-substance with all humanity. The ***Letter of John of Antioch and Others to Rufus of Thessalonica*** from October is another letter of the Easterners in which they justify their deposition of Cyril and Memnon and provide insight into their understanding of their opponents' Christology. The selections from the acts of Ephesus conclude with the ***Homily of John of Antioch***, also from October. Here John bids farewell to his supporters and urges them to remain steadfast in the authentic Christological faith they hold, which John concisely summarizes and contrasts with his opponents' views. In the end, the Council of Ephesus did nothing to resolve the Christological issues that had pitted Cyril and his allies against Nestorius and his supporters, apart from securing agreement that Nestorius should be deposed. Rather, the council only exacerbated the divisions between the Cyrilline party and the Easterners led by John of Antioch.

It took nearly two years for a compromise to be reached, in 433, when both factions agreed to a statement of faith known as the Formula of Reunion. The Formula was actually a slightly modified version of the statement of faith contained in the *Report of the Easterners Written in Response to the Sacra Delivered by Count John*, from August 431, with its double consubstantiality clause. Cyril quotes the Formula of Reunion in his ***Letter of Reunion to John of Antioch***. Along with Cyril's *Second Letter*, this letter would be endorsed as a Christological standard at the Council of Chalcedon (and at subsequent ecumenical councils), associated with the work of the Council of Ephesus even though it was written two years afterward. In the *Letter of Reunion* Cyril also clarifies his Christological positions against critics accusing him of heresy. One of these critics was Ibas of Edessa, who in his ***Letter to Mari the Persian*** gives an account of the Council of Ephesus and the reconciliation between Cyril and John in 433 in a way that disparages the Alexandrian bishop quite harshly. The *Letter* of Ibas later became quite infamous as one of the so-called Three Chapters.

Cyril's reunion with John led some of his supporters to wonder whether it amounted to a departure from his earlier views or even a capitulation to the "Nestorian" Easterners. One such partisan was Succensus of Diocaesarea, who voiced such concerns to Cyril. In response Cyril wrote his ***First and Second Letters to Succensus*** between 434 and 438. In the first letter Cyril identifies Diodore of Tarsus and Theodore of Mopsuestia as the sources of Nestorius's teachings, initiating a long trajectory of condemning these two pro-Nicene theologians of an earlier generation who died in the peace of the church. In the same letter Cyril addresses how one ought to speak of the "two natures" of Christ, the incorruptibility of Christ's flesh, and the proper interpretation of his own writings – all subjects that would continue to be debated for centuries. This letter contains one of Cyril's usages of the famous phrase "one incarnate nature of the Word" (*mia physis tou logou sesarkōmenē*), which later became the hallmark of the miaphysite movement. The second letter responds to a series of questions posed by an unnamed Easterner on the issue of what the words "flesh" or "become incarnate" mean and what they imply about how one should use the language of "nature" with respect to Christ. This letter could almost be regarded as the charter of the miaphysite movement that would crystalize after the Council of Chalcedon.

Part IV concludes with the epilogue of the ***Eranistes*** of Theodoret of Cyrrhus, which sums up the three dialogues of the treatise on, respectively, the immutability of the Word, the manner of union between the Word and the human nature in Christ, and the impassibility of the Word qua God in the union of the two natures in the incarnation. Written around 447, it is a fitting résumé of the dyophysite Christology of the Easterners before controversy was renewed soon thereafter, this time over Eutyches.

A feature in the texts surveyed in this part must also be noted. It is a feature also found in the texts in CEECW 4. The Nestorian controversy marks the beginning of a new method of theological argumentation in the Christological debates (though there were precedents before this time). It is the so-called argument from authority. Participants in the Christological debates, no matter what side they were on, were concerned with fidelity to the authoritative figures of earlier generations. To be considered as departing from these authorities and engaging in the development of doctrine, which was routinely called "novelty" or "innovation," was tantamount to being charged with heresy. Accordingly, theologians in this period strove above all to be traditional, to affirm what the "fathers" had previously taught.

Such arguments took two interrelated forms. The first was recourse to certain statements of faith, and especially creeds, as irreformable touchstones of orthodoxy. By the early fifth century everyone agreed that the Nicene Creed (whether the original creed of 325 or the version issued in 381) was the authoritative document par excellence (apart from scripture). Christological developments were therefore often presented as nothing more than clarifications of the Nicene Creed. Over time certain documents were identified as particularly helpful explanations of the pro-Nicene faith encapsulated in the Nicene Creed: Athanasius's *Letter to Epictetus*, Gregory of Nazianzus's *Letter* 101 *to Cledonius*, Cyril of Alexandria's *Second Letter to Nestorius* and *Letter of Reunion to John of Antioch*, the Tome of Leo, the Chalcedonian Definition, and other synodal definitions and documents.

The argument from authority took another form: direct quotations from the works of the authoritative men of the past ("church fathers"), often collected into florilegia. Many theologians and councils from the fifth century onward included such florilegia in their texts to prove that whatever they were teaching had the approbation of tradition, that what they were teaching was nothing more than what approved church fathers had taught. Sometimes the patristic quotations are presented as self-evident justifications for the position endorsed by the theologian; on other occasions some exposition is provided to demonstrate how the excerpt confirms the position of the theologian. Florilegia of counter-testimonia were also produced: a theologian might compile excerpts from notorious heretics to prove that his opponent's views were nothing more than the recrudescence of some already-condemned heresy. Regrettably, most of these florilegia have been excluded from the translations in the interests of space, but several have been included to demonstrate this method of argumentation.

A CATALOGUE OF HERETICS

In all the parts of this volume the authors of the texts frequently make reference to those whose views they disagree with or are writing against. Such opponents are typically labeled "heretics" and their Christological views are deemed aberrant or erroneous or even dangerous. Of course, this was all a matter of perspective. For example, dyophysites of the Church of the East revered Theodore of Mopsuestia, the Interpreter, as they called him, as the champion of orthodoxy, whereas Chalcedonians reviled him as one of the Three Chapters and the inspiration of Nestorius's heresy. In this section, to avoid repetition in the footnotes, a brief catalogue of the pre-fifth-century "heretics" is provided, listing those most frequently mentioned in the texts in this volume. The focus here is on how these figures were viewed by early and late antique Christians, not necessarily what they may or may not have actually taught, insofar as their teaching is recoverable by modern scholarship.

The encounter between **Simon Magus** and the apostles Philip and Peter is recorded in Acts 8. In early Christianity many apocryphal traditions developed around Simon, who was depicted as a sorcerer, a rival Christ, the cause of the first persecutions of Christians in Rome, and the archetypal heretic. The term "simony" is derived from Simon's actions in Acts 8:18–25.

Several Jewish Christian groups were identified as "Ebionites" in early Christianity, purportedly founded by one **Ebion**. These sects were reported to have lived according to the Jewish law, rejected the writings of the apostle Paul, and regarded Jesus as an ordinary human being (psilanthropism). The name Ebionite was actually derived from the Hebrew word for "poor" and referred to the poverty of the group, rather than a founding figure named Ebion, who is a heresiological invention.

Valentinus was a Christian philosopher from Alexandria who moved to Rome between 136 and 140, where he taught until his death around 165. Later generations of Christians considered him the fountainhead of an influential variety of Gnosticism and credited him with docetic views about Christ. Texts from the Valentinian school included in this volume are the *Treatise on Resurrection* and *A Ptolemaic Theology*.

Marcion came from Pontus to Rome in 140, but only four years later was expelled from the church for his dualistic views. He taught that Jesus had revealed a new and unknown God, his Father, the good God who sought to destroy the evil God of the Old Testament, who was seen as the imperfect and flawed Creator, the God of the Jews, the Lawgiver, and the Judge. Later generations of Christians routinely accused Marcionites of espousing a docetic Christology.

The early third-century **Sabellius** was a proponent of monarchianism or modalism (also called Sabellianism) which stressed the "monarchy" ("single rule") or the oneness of God to avoid any hint of ditheism or tritheism. Monarchians saw the Father, Son, and Holy Spirit as three manifestations of the single God or three modes in which the one God appeared or was revealed to humanity in salvation history. Opposition to monarchianism became a feature of orthodox thinking from the middle of the second century onward.

Paul of Samosata, a bishop deposed for Christological heresy in the 260s, became widely regarded as teaching adoptionism or psilanthropism. Selected fragments of Paul of Samosata are translated in this volume.

Mani (also known as **Manichaeus**) was from southern Mesopotamia and died a martyr in 276. He was the founder of a Christian sect that espoused a radical dualism of light and darkness. Later generations of Christians frequently accused Manichaeans (also called Manichees) of teaching a docetic Christology.

Arius was an early fourth-century presbyter in Alexandria whom later generations of Christians depicted as teaching that the Son was inferior to the Father and in fact a creature made by God. His dispute with his bishop, Alexander, over the relationship of the Father and Son sparked the decades-long "Arian" controversy. It was Arius who was the impetus for the Council of Nicaea in 325, and thereafter opposition to Arianism became a key feature of any theology that claimed allegiance to Nicaea. Later generations considered "Arian" Christology defective because of its unwillingness to distinguish between Christ's human and divine attributes and its implication that the Son could not unite humanity to God.

Marcellus of Ancyra was deposed for heresy in 336, though he lived into the 370s. His theology was driven by a concern to preserve the unity of God at any cost, understanding God as a unitary divine monad that mysteriously expanded into a triad (namely, the Word and Spirit) without losing its essential oneness and indivisibility. For Marcellus, the Word could only be called "Son" in the proper sense at the incarnation. Marcellus was viewed as a reviver of a form of Sabellianism, and opposition to him became a hallmark of pro-Nicene theology. A disciple of Marcellus, **Photinus of Sirmium**, was deposed for heresy in 351. In his own day and long afterwards he was considered by some as an adoptionist and by others as a monarchian.

In the second half of the fourth century **Eunomius**, the quondam bishop of Cyzicus, was the leader of the Heteroousians (also called Eunomians) who taught that the Father and Son were "different-in-substance" (*heteroousios*). Opposition to Heteroousian theology became a touchstone of the pro-Nicene movement from the 360s onward. Pro-Nicenes rejected Eunomius's Christology on two grounds. First, since they interpreted Eunomius as affirming that the Son was created, they took him to be implying that the Son was inherently mutable and thus naturally suited to life in the body but incapable of effecting salvation. Second, noting that Eunomius did not distinguish between Christ's human and divine attributes, they accused Eunomius of denying that Christ had a human soul, which they understood to result in a confusion of the distinct properties of his humanity and divinity.

Macedonius was bishop of Constantinople until 360. An anti-Arian Homoiousian during his lifetime, he came to be considered by later generations of Christians as the founder of the Macedonians, whose denial of the divinity of the Holy Spirit provoked the First Council of Constantinople in 381.

The pro-Nicene **Apollinarius of Laodicea** (d. ca. 392) was condemned during his lifetime for Christological heterodoxy. Later generations of Christians typically accused him of teaching the elimination of the rational soul from Christ's humanity to avoid any dualistic subjectivity in Christ and the descent of the flesh of Jesus from heaven. Several writings of Apollinarius are translated in this volume.

A CHRISTOLOGICAL VOCABULARY

In the course of the first eight centuries of Christianity, a number of conceptual models were put forward at various stages to explain how Christ was the incarnate Son of God. Old models which later Christians judged to be deficient were replaced by new ones aiming to resolve the issues once and for all. Each of these conceptual models had a technical vocabulary associated with it, frequently overlapping with the technical vocabulary of other conceptual models, without the terms always being used in precisely the same sense. Accordingly, theologians in the various Christological traditions gradually developed Christological lexicons to express their understanding of the incarnation. Each tradition had a preference for certain conceptual models and terms, and they attempted to refine the meaning of these terms and hone precision in their usage over time through debate. By the end of the period covered in these volumes a rich technical vocabulary for speaking about Christ was firmly in place for the various Christological traditions.

One benefit of including texts spanning over 600 years in CEECW volumes 3 and 4 is that the development of this technical vocabulary can be traced. For this reason considerable effort has been made in these volumes to translate key technical terms consistently across texts, at least when the terms are used in a technical sense. Consistency in translation, however, has not been elevated to an unbending rule. So if the usage of a particular author has warranted a different translation, the term has been translated accordingly. The following paragraphs survey the key terms for which an attempt has been made to offer a consistent translation in these volumes.

Terms for the incarnation that use the root "flesh" (e.g. *sarx* in Greek, *caro* in Latin, *basrā* in Syriac) have been translated in a way that preserves this root, or at least signifies it with the Latinate *-carn-* root. Examples include "incarnation," "incarnate," "enfleshment," "enfleshed," "became incarnate," "become flesh," "made flesh," and so forth. Terms that fall into this category are the Greek *sarkōsis*, *ensarkōsis*, and *sarkōthenta*; the Latin *incarnatio* and *incarnatus*; and the Syriac *besrānuṯā*, *mḇasrānuṯā*, and *meṯbasrānuṯā*. Other terms for the incarnation use the root "human" (e.g. *anthrōpo-* in Greek, *homo/humanus* in Latin, *bar[ʾ]nāšā* in Syriac, *rōme* in Coptic). These terms are likewise translated in a way that preserves their root, such as "became human," "made human," and so forth. Terms that fall into this category are the Greek *enanthrōpeō*; the Latin *homo factus*; and the Syriac *eṯbarnaš*. Abstract nouns with this root, such as the Greek *enanthrōpēsis* and the Syriac *meṯbarnšānuṯā*, have been rendered with "humanification."

The Nicene *homoousios* is translated with "same-in-substance." The Latin equivalents *eiusdem substantiae* and *consubstantialis* and the Syriac equivalent *bar kyānā* are translated in the same way. When the Greek term *hypostasis* is used in a technical Christological sense it is simply transliterated. Its Syriac equivalent *qnoma* is rendered by the same transliteration (when the text is a Syriac translation of a Greek original). The phrase *kath' hypostasin*, which literally means "according to hypostasis," is frequently rendered with "hypostatically" or "hypostatic," depending on the context. The standard translation of the Greek *prosōpon*, the Latin *persona*, and the Syriac *parṣopā*, when used in a technical Christological sense, is "person." The Greek term *synapheia* is translated "conjunction," and its verbal cognates based on *synaptō*, "conjoin."

The three Greek terms *theotokos*, *christotokos*, and *anthrōpotokos* are also simply transliterated. These titles, which respectively mean "bearer or birthgiver of God, of Christ, or the human being," refer to Mary, the mother of Jesus, but each encapsulates a particular view of the incarnation. The Latin equivalents are rendered with the Greek transliterations: *theotocos*, *dei genetrix*, and *partrix dei* for Theotokos; and *genetrix hominis* and *genetrix*

Christi for the other two terms. The Syriac equivalent for Theotokos, *yāldaṯ alāhā*, is also rendered with the Greek transliteration.

The four Chalcedonian adverbs are translated, when possible, as adverbs: "unconfusedly" (*asugchutōs*), "unchangeably" (*atreptōs*), "undividedly" (*adiairetōs*), and "inseparably" (*achōristōs*). The adjectival forms of these are also rendered similarly when possible.

The Greek term *oikonomia*, whose Latin equivalent is *oeconomia*, is translated by "economy" or "divine plan" when the term is used to refer to God's plan for salvation. A related term with a similar meaning is the Latin *dispensatio*, "dispensation."

Two circumlocutions were used in Greek in reference to Christ. The phrase *allo kai allo*, which consists of two neuter singular pronouns joined by the conjunction "and," was used to describe the position that Christ consists of two different "things" (substances or natures). This phrase is typically rendered by "one thing and another" or something similar. The expression *allos kai allos*, which contains two masculine singular pronouns, was used to describe the position that Christ consisted of two distinct persons or subjects. This expression is typically rendered by "one and another" or something similar.

A FINAL WORD: THE MYSTERY OF CHRIST

Many of the texts in this volume contain some sort of acknowledgment that the incarnation is ultimately a mystery whose full comprehension is beyond the capacities of the human intellect. Such a viewpoint was not the exclusive preserve of any single Christological tradition – it is found in all of them. One might think that this shared belief in the ultimate incomprehensibility of the incarnation would have made early Christians engaged in Christological debate more tolerant of differences in approach and opinion. Sadly that was not the case. Rather, respect for this mystery and recognition of what could and could not be known and said about the incarnation was deemed an essential feature of any theological account of Christ. As Theodoret of Cyrrhus memorably remarked, "We confess that we do not have a clear understanding of the truth – indeed, that is a significant part of the victory" (*Exposition of the Orthodox Faith* 17). Indeed, the errors of "heretics" were often attributed to a failure to respect this mystery. Attempting to explain the unexplainable, it was thought, inevitably led to heresy.

And so, in the many pages of this volume containing early Christian texts that in one way or another attempt to explain Christ as God incarnate there is an underlying current of apophaticism or unknowing, along with an assumption that the subject of inquiry would prove ever elusive, ever beyond the grasp of the human mind. For most of the theologians in this volume the divine–human Christ was in the final analysis not a problem to be solved, however much ink they spilled on that endeavor, but a person to be contemplated, to be experienced, and to be loved in the midst of a community of believers on the quest for salvation. It was in the service of this quest that so much reflection on Christ, so much inquiry into his identity and constitution, was set down for posterity.

PART I

The Beginnings of Christology

I

Ascension of Isaiah 6–11 (Ethiopic Version)

Introduction and Translation by
Dexter Brown and Aaron Michael Butts

INTRODUCTION

The *Ascension of Isaiah* imagines Isaiah's tour of the seven heavens, the descent of Christ through the divine realms in the form of an angel, and the death of the prophet at the hands of King Hezekiah's wicked son, Manasseh. This enigmatic work falls into two main parts: the martyrdom of Isaiah (chapters 1–5) and the vision of Isaiah (chapters 6–11). There is no consensus about the date, composition, or provenance of the *Ascension of Isaiah*. A 1996 monograph on the text stresses the unity of the work and locates it in the second century CE, probably in Syria.[1] This all, however, remains disputed.

The entire text of the *Ascension of Isaiah* likely once existed in Greek, but the only extant Greek text is a papyrus, probably from the fifth or sixth century, which preserves 2.4–4.4 with lacunae. A Latin codex preserves 2.14–3.13 and 7.1–19 (=Lat[1]), and there are also smaller fragments in Coptic. Fortunately, the entire text of the *Ascension of Isaiah* survives in Classical Ethiopic (Gəʿəz). The Ethiopic translation was likely made from Greek sometime during the Axumite period (fourth century–ca. 900). The earliest Ethiopic manuscripts, however, date from a much later time; in fact, the complete Ethiopic text is first found in manuscripts probably from the fifteenth century. Thus, though the Ethiopic version is an invaluable witness to the *Ascension of Isaiah*, it must be stressed that there is a large chronological gap between the Ethiopic version, as we now have it, and its Greek *Vorlage*, not to mention the linguistic and cultural distance between the two.

1 Jonathan Knight, *Disciples of the Beloved One: The Christology, Social Setting and Theological Context of the Ascension of Isaiah*, Journal for the Study of the Pseudepigrapha Supplement Series 18 (Sheffield: Sheffield Academic Press, 1996).

In addition to the *Ascension of Isaiah*, two related texts should be noted here that are useful for reconstructing the original text: a work in Latin (=Lat^2) and Slavonic (=Slav), which is based on the second part of the *Ascension of Isaiah* (6.1–11.40); and the Greek *Prophecy, Martyrdom, and Apocalypse of Isaiah* (sometimes called the *Greek Legend of Isaiah*), which contains a shorter account of Isaiah's heavenly journey and martyrdom.

The selection translated here consists of the account of Isaiah's vision of the heavenly realms (chapters 6–11). The text is notable for its elaborate angelology. As Isaiah traverses the seven heavens, he encounters increasingly glorious and more numerous angels, brighter lights, and more splendid praise. When the prophet climactically reaches the seventh heaven, he even momentarily sees the "great glory" of God. Throughout his ascension, the glory of the angels that Isaiah encounters is meticulously described and ranked. Scholarship on the vision has focused especially on the description of Christ in angelomorphic terms. In the seventh heaven, Isaiah sees Christ transform and become "like an angel," whom the prophet worships (9.30–31). Isaiah also encounters the enigmatic "angel of the Holy Spirit," who is likewise worshiped (9.33–36). Of particular Christological interest is the fact that the lord and the angel of the Holy Spirit join in worshiping God (9.40).

This translation is based on the edition of the Ethiopic version of the *Ascension of Isaiah* published by Lorenzo Perrone and Enrico Norelli, "Ascensione di Isaia profeta: Versione etiópica," in Paolo Bettiolo et al. (eds.), *Ascensio Isaiae: Textus*, Corpus Christianorum Series Apocryphorum 7 (Turnhout: Brepols, 1995), 1–129. We have occasionally emended the text, but not all emendations have been noted here.

TRANSLATION

The Vision that Isaiah, Son of Amoz, Saw

6, 1. In the twentieth year of the reign of Hezekiah, king of Judah, Isaiah, the son of Amoz, and Josab, the son of Isaiah, came to Hezekiah in Jerusalem from Gilgal. 2. Isaiah sat on the king's bed. They brought a throne for him, but he did not want to sit on it. 3. When Isaiah began to discuss the word of faith and righteousness with King Hezekiah, all the rulers of Israel, the eunuchs, and the king's advisors were sitting. There were also forty prophets and sons of prophets there; they had come from the surrounding areas, the mountains, and the plains when they heard that Isaiah was coming to Hezekiah from Gilgal. 4. They came to welcome him and to hear his words, 5. and that he might lay his hand upon them, that they might prophesy, and that he might hear their prophecy. They were all before Isaiah. 6. When he discussed the words of righteousness and faith with Hezekiah, they all heard a door that had opened and the voice of the Spirit.[2] 7. The king called all the prophets and all the people who were there, and they came. Micah, the elderly Ananias, Joel, and Josab were sitting on his right. 8. When they all heard the voice of the Holy Spirit, they bowed down on their knees and praised the lord of righteousness, the exalted one who is in the exalted world, the one who sits on high, the holy one, the one who takes rest among the holy ones. 9. They gave praise to the one who had, in this way, granted humanity a door in a strange world. 10. As he was speaking through the Holy Spirit while they all listened, he became silent. His mind was taken from him, and he could not see the men standing in front of him. 11. His eyes were open, his mouth was silent, and the mind of his flesh was taken from him. 12. However, he was still breathing, for he was seeing a vision. 13. The angel who had been sent to show him [the vision] was not of that firmament, nor was he one of the glorious angels of this world, but he came from the seventh heaven. 14. The people who were standing by, except for the circle of prophets, thought that the holy Isaiah had been taken up.[3] 15. The vision that he saw was not from this world, but from the world hidden from the flesh. 16. After Isaiah had seen this vision, he recounted it to Hezekiah, to Josab, his son, and to the other prophets who had come. 17. The officials, the eunuchs, and the people did not hear it, apart from Samnas, the scribe, Jehoiakim, and Asaph, the record keeper, for they were doers of righteousness, and they had the fragrance of the Spirit. The people did not hear it, since Micah and Josab, his son, had led them out when the wisdom of this world had risen from him as if he had died.

7, 1. The vision that Isaiah saw, he told Hezekiah, Josab, his son, Micah, and the other prophets. 2. It was this: When I prophesied according to the message that you heard, I saw a splendid angel. He was not like the splendor of the angels that I would frequently see, but he had a great splendor and rank, such that I am unable to describe the splendor of this angel. 3. I saw as he took me by the hand, and I said, "Who are you? What is your

2 See Rev 4:1. 3 That is, they thought that Isaiah had died.

name? Where are you bringing me?" For the strength to speak with him had been given to me. 4. He said to me, "When I have led you up the ascension and I have shown you the vision for which I have been sent, then you will understand who I am, but you will not know my name, 5. for you must return to this flesh. You will see where I am bringing you, for I have been sent for this purpose."

6. I rejoiced because he had spoken to me gently. 7. Then he said to me, "Do you rejoice because I have spoken to you gently?" He said, "You will see how one greater than me will speak with you gently and peacefully, 8. and you will see the Father of this greater one because I have been sent to explain all this to you."

9. We ascended, he and I, to the firmament, and there I saw Samael and his hosts. There was a great battle therein, and the words of Satan, and they were envying one another[4] 10. – as above, so also on earth, for the form of that which is in the firmament is here on earth. 11. I said to the angel, "What is this envy?" 12. He said to me, "It has been like this since the world came to be until now, and this battle [will continue] until the one whom you shall see comes and destroys him."

13. Then he brought me above the firmament – this is heaven. 14. There I saw a throne in the middle, and there were angels on the right and left of it. 15. The angels on the left[5] were not like the angels standing on the right, but those on the right had more splendor. They all offered praise with one voice. The throne was in the middle, and they praised it, while those on the left [offered praise] after them. Their voice was not like the voice of those on the right, and their praise was not like the praise of those [on the right]. 16. I asked the angel who was guiding me, "To whom is this praise sent?" 17. He said to me, "It was sent to the glory of the seventh heaven for the one who takes rest in the holy world and for his beloved, from where I was sent to you."

18. Again he brought me to the second heaven. The height of that heaven is like that from heaven to earth to the firmament. 19. I saw there, as in the first heaven, angels on the right and on the left, a throne in the middle, and the glory of the angels in the second heaven. The one who was sitting on

4 The text is possibly corrupt. Lat[1] reads, "and the angels of Satan were envious of each other."

5 The text is likely corrupt, lacking "the angels on the left," which is supplied here from Lat[1].

the throne in the second heaven had more splendor than all [of them]. 20. There was great splendor in the second heaven, and their glory was not like the glory of those in the first heaven. 21. I fell down on my face so that I might bow down to him, but the angel who was guiding me did not let me. Instead, he said to me, "Do not bow down to a throne or an angel from the six heavens, from where I was sent to guide you, until I tell you [to do so] in the seventh heaven,[6] 22. because your throne, your garments, and your crown, which you shall see, reside above all the heavens and their angels." 23. I rejoiced greatly since, at their end, those who love the exalted one and his beloved will ascend there by the angel of the Holy Spirit.

24. He brought me to the third heaven, and similarly I saw those on the left and on the right, a throne there in the middle, and one sitting [on it]. But no mention of this world was made there. 25. I said to the angel who was with me, since the splendor of my face was changing as I was ascending each heaven, "The vanity of that world is not named here at all." 26. He replied, "On account of its weakness, it is not named at all. But nothing done there is hidden." 27. I wanted to learn how it is known, but he replied, "When I have brought you to the seventh heaven, from where I have been sent, which is above these, then you will know that nothing is hidden from the thrones, from those who reside in the heavens, or from the angels." The praise that they offered and the splendor of the one sitting on the throne were great, and the angels on the right and on the left had more splendor than the heaven below them.

28. Again he led me to the fourth heaven. The height from the third to the fourth heaven exceeds that from earth to the firmament. 29. There again I saw those on the right and those on the left, and the one who was sitting on the throne was in the middle. There too they were offering praise. 30. The glory and splendor of the angels on the right was greater than those on the left. 31. Again the splendor of the one who was sitting on the throne exceeded that of the angels on the right, while their splendor exceeded that of those below.

32. He led me to the fifth heaven. 33. Again I saw those on the right and on the left, and the one who was sitting on the throne had more splendor than those of the fourth heaven. 34. The splendor of those on the right exceeded [that of] those on the left, from the third to the fourth.[7] 35. The splendor of the one on the throne was greater than the angels on the

6 See Rev 19:10, 22:8–9. 7 The text is possibly corrupt.

right, 36. and their glory had greater splendor than the fourth heaven. 37. I praised the one who is not named and the unique one who dwells in the heavens, whose name is not known by any flesh, who has thus given splendor to each heaven, who makes the splendor of the angels great and the splendor of the one who sits on the throne greater.

8, 1. He led me still farther up into the air of the sixth heaven, and I saw glory such as I had not seen in the five heavens as I ascended. 2. The angels were greatly splendid. 3. The glory there was holy and wonderful. 4. I said to the angel who was guiding me, "What am I seeing, my lord?" 5. He said, "I am not your lord but your equal."[8] 6. Again I asked him, "Why not an equal of angels?" 7. He said to me, "From now on, from the sixth heaven upwards, there are no longer those on the left, nor a throne residing in the middle, but [they have their order][9] by the power of the seventh heaven, where the one who is not named dwells along with his chosen one, whose name is not known – none of the heavens can know his name, 8. because he is the only one whose voice all the heavens and thrones answer. Now, I have been empowered and sent to bring you here so that you may see this glory. 9. You will see the lord of all these heavens and these thrones 10. being transformed until he is like you in appearance and in form. 11. So I will tell you, Isaiah, that no one who will return into the flesh of that world has seen or ascended or understood what you have seen and what you must see, 12. because you must come here by the lot of the lord, by the lot of the tree. The power of the sixth heaven and its air is from there." 13. I extolled my lord in praise because I will come here by his lot. 14. He said to me, "Hear this also from your equal: When, by the angel of the Spirit, you have ascended here from a strange body, then you will receive the garment that you will see, and you will see a set number of other garments residing [there]. 15. Then you will be equal to the angels in the seventh heaven."

16. He brought me up to the sixth heaven. There were none on the left and no throne in the middle, but all had one appearance, and their glory was equal. 17. It[10] was given to me. I offered praise with them, along with that angel too. Our praise was like theirs. 18. All of them named there the

8 See Rev 19:10, 22:8–9.

9 The text seems to be corrupt; some such phrase should probably be supplied on the basis of Lat[2] and Slav.

10 The antecedent of this pronoun is unclear: Is it "appearance"? Or "glory"? Or perhaps more circuitous for "I was allowed to offer praise … ", that is, "It was given to me to offer praise … ".

primal Father, the beloved, Christ, and the Holy Spirit – all with one voice. 19. It was not like the voices of the angels in the five heavens. 20. It was not like their speech, but there was a different voice there, and there was abundant light there. 21. Then, when I was in the sixth heaven, I likened those lights that I had seen in the five heavens to darkness. 22. I rejoiced and praised the one who has granted such lights to those who await his promise. 23. I implored the angel who was guiding me that from this time forward I should not return to the world of flesh. 24. Thus, I will tell you, Hezekiah, Josab, my son, and Micah, that there is abundant darkness here. Abundant darkness indeed. 25. The angel who was guiding me knew what I was thinking. He said, "If you rejoiced over these lights, how much more will you rejoice in the seventh heaven when you see the lights where the lord is, along with his beloved, from where I have been sent – he who will be called Son in the world. 26. The one who will be in the passing world has not been revealed, nor the garments, nor the thrones, nor the crowns, which reside [there] for the righteous who believe in that lord who will descend in your likeness, because the light there is great and wonderful. 27. Now, as for your not returning to the flesh, your days are not yet completed for coming here." 28. When I heard [that], I grew sad. He said to me, "Do not be sad."

9, 1. He led me to the air of the seventh heaven, and then I heard a voice saying, "How far should this one who dwells among the strangers ascend?" I was afraid and trembling. 2. He said to me as I trembled, "Another voice, which was sent, has come forth from there, and it says that the holy Isaiah is allowed to ascend to here because his garment is here." 3. I asked the angel who was with me, "Who prevented me? Who allowed me to ascend?" 4. He said to me, "The one who prevented you is the one on whom the glory of the sixth heaven is. 5. The one who allowed you is your lord God, the lord Christ, who will be called in the world Jesus but whose name you are unable to hear until you ascend from this flesh of yours."

6. He brought me up to the seventh heaven, and I saw there a wonderful light and angels without number. 7. There I saw all the righteous from the time of Adam. 8. There I saw the holy Abel and all the righteous. 9. There I saw Enoch and all those who were with him, who were stripped of garments of the flesh, and I saw them in the garments of above,[11] and

11 That is, heavenly garments (cf. Rev 3:4–5).

they were like angels, who were standing there in great glory. 10. However, they were not sitting on their thrones, and their crowns of glory were not upon them. 11. I asked the angel who was with me, "How have they taken garments, but they are not on thrones with crowns?" 12. He said to me, "They do not take crowns and magnificent thrones now – but they see and know which thrones and which crowns are theirs – until the beloved descends with the appearance in which you will see him descend. 13. The lord who will be called Christ will descend at the end of days. After he has descended and takes on your appearance, they will think that he is flesh and a human. 14. The lord of that world will stretch out through the hand of his son,[12] and they will bring their hands down upon him and crucify him on a tree without knowing who he is. 15. Then his descent, as you will see, will be hidden even from the heavens, so that it is not known who he is. 16. When he robs the angel of death, ascends on the third day, and remains in that world for five hundred and forty-five days, 17. many of the righteous, whose spirits will not have taken garments until the lord Christ ascends and they ascend with him, will ascend with him. 18. Then they will take their garments, thrones, and crowns when he has ascended to the seventh heaven."

19. I said to him what I had asked him in the third heaven.[13] 20. He told me that everything done in that world is known here. 21. While I was speaking with him, one of the angels who was standing [there], more glorious than the glory of that angel who had brought me up from the world, 22. showed me [some] books. The books were not like the books of this world. He opened them, and there was writing there. They were not like the books of this world. They were given to me, and I read them. The deeds of the children of Israel were written there – the deeds which you know, my son, Josab. 23. I said, "Truly, the things done in the world are not hidden in the seventh heaven!"

24. I saw there many garments, thrones, and crowns. 25. I said to the angel who was guiding me, "Whose are these garments, thrones, and crowns?" 26. He said to me, "Many from that world will receive these garments after having believed in the word of that one who will be called what

12 The text is not entirely clear. Alternatively, it could be emended to: "stretch out his hand against his son."

13 See 7.24–27 above.

I have told you, and they will keep them and believe in his cross – they reside here for them."[14]

27. I saw standing one whose glory surpassed all – his glory was great and wonderful. 28. Seeing him, all the righteous ones, whom I saw, as well as the angels came to him. Adam, Abel, Seth, and all the righteous ones first approached and bowed down to him. All of them praised him in one voice. I was praising him along with them, and my praise was like theirs. 29. Then all the angels approached, bowed down, and praised him. 30. He was transformed, and he became like an angel. 31. Then the angel who was guiding me said to me, "Bow down to this one!" I bowed down and offered praise. 32. The angel said to me, "This is the lord of all glory, whom you have seen."

33. While I was still speaking, I saw another glorious one, who resembled him. The righteous ones approached him, bowed down, and offered praise. I offered praise along with them. His glory was not transformed into their appearance. 34. Then the angels approached and bowed down. 35. I saw the lord and the second angel, and they were standing. 36. The second one, whom I saw, was on the left of my lord. I asked, "Who is this one?" He told me, "Bow down to him because this is the angel of the Holy Spirit, who is upon you and who has spoken to other righteous ones."

37. I saw a great glory after the eyes of my spirit had been opened.[15] I was unable then to see, as was the case with the angel who was with me and all the angels whom I had seen bowing down to my lord. 38. However, I saw the righteous with great power seeing the glory of that one. 39. My lord and the angel of the Spirit approached me and said, "See, it has been given to you to see God, and, on account of you, power has been given to the angel with you." 40. I saw that my lord and the angel of the Spirit bowed down, and the two of them praised God together. 41. Then all the righteous approached and bowed down. 42. All the righteous and the angels approached and bowed down. All the angels offered praise.

10, 1. Then I heard the voices and praises that I had heard in the six heavens, which I had heard when I was ascending there. 2. All this was being directed to that glorious one, whose glory I was unable to see, 3. but I was hearing and seeing his praise. 4. The lord and the angel of the

14 That is, the garments, thrones, and crowns are here for people who have believed.

15 See John 12:41 (and also Isa 6:1–6).

Spirit were hearing and seeing everything. 5. All the praise that was being directed from the six heavens was not only heard but seen. 6. I heard the angel who was guiding me say to me, "This is the exalted of the exalted ones, who dwells in the holy world and takes rest among the holy ones,[16] who is called Father of the lord by the Holy Spirit through the mouth of the holy ones." 7. I heard the voice of this most exalted one, the Father of my lord, saying to my lord, Christ, who is called Jesus, 8. "Go out and descend through each of the heavens. You will descend through the firmament and that world until the angel in Sheol, but you will not go to perdition. 9. You will resemble the form of everyone in the five heavens. 10. You will be careful to resemble the appearance of the angels of the firmament as well as the appearance of the angels who are in Sheol. 11. None of the angels of that world will know that you are lord with me of the seven heavens and of their angels. 12. They will not know that you were with me when with the word of the heavens I called you along with their angels and lights, exalting you to the sixth heaven so that you would judge and destroy the judges, angels, and lords of that world as well as the world that is ruled by them 13. because they denied me and they said, 'We are alone. There is no one except for us.' 14. Afterwards, you will ascend from the lords of death to your place, without being transformed in each of the heavens, but in glory you will ascend and reside at my right hand. 15. Then the judges and hosts of that world will bow down to you." 16. I heard this great praise as he was commanding my lord.

17. In this way, I saw my lord go out from the seventh heaven to the sixth heaven. 18. The angel who led me from this world was with me, and he said to me, "Understand, Isaiah, and make sure to see the transformation of the lord and his descent." 19. I saw that, when the angels of the sixth heaven saw him, they praised and worshiped him because he was not transformed into the appearance of the angels there. They praised him, and I praised him with them. 20. I saw that, when he descended into the fifth heaven, he resembled those who were in the fifth heaven according to the appearance of the angels there, and they did not praise him because his appearance was like theirs. 21. Then he descended into the fourth heaven, and he resembled the appearance of the angels there. 22. When they saw him, they did not praise or worship him because his appearance was like

16 See Isa 57:15.

their appearance. 23. Then I saw him descend into the third heaven, and he resembled the appearance of the angels in the third heaven. 24. Those who guard the gates were asking him for the key, and the lord gave it to them so that he would remain unknown. When they saw him, they did not praise and worship him because his appearance was like their appearance. 25. Then I saw him descend into the second heaven. Then he gave the key there because those who guard the gates were seeking it, and he gave it to them. 26. I saw when he resembled the appearance of the angels in the second heaven, and they saw him, but they did not praise him because his appearance was like their appearance. 27. Then I saw him descend to the first heaven. There he gave the key to those who guard the gates, and he resembled the appearance of the angels who were at the left of that throne. They did not praise or worship him because his appearance was like their appearance. 28. As for me, no one questioned me about the angel who was guiding me. 29. Then he descended into the firmament where the judge of this world resides. He gave the key to those who were at the left, and his appearance was like theirs. There they did not praise him, but in envy each of them was fighting because there is there an evil power and envy over minutiae. 30. I saw when he descended, and he resembled the angels of the air. He was like one of them. 31. He did not give them a key because each one of them was plundering and afflicting the other.

11, 1. After this, I looked, and the angel who had spoken with me and who had guided me said to me, "Understand, Isaiah, son of Amoz, because it is for this that I have been sent by God." 2. I saw a woman from the family of the prophet David, whose name was Mary. She was a virgin, and she was betrothed to a carpenter, whose name was Joseph. He was from the seed and family of the righteous David, from Bethlehem of Judah. 3. He was coming by his lot. Having been betrothed, she was found to be pregnant, and Joseph the carpenter wanted to leave her. 4. The angel of the Spirit appeared in this world, and so Joseph did not leave Mary, but he guarded her. He did not reveal this matter. 5. He did not approach Mary, but he kept her as a holy virgin, even though she was pregnant. 6. He did not reside with her for two months. 7. After two months, Joseph was in the house along with Mary his wife, but both of them were alone. 8. It happened when they were alone that Mary looked with her own eyes and saw a young child, and she was amazed. 9. After being amazed, her womb came to be like it was previously without pregnancy. 10. When her husband, Joseph, said to her, "What is causing you amazement?" his eyes were opened, and he saw the child. He praised God because the lord came by his lot. 11. A voice came to them that they should not tell this vision to anyone. 12. Word of this child was being spoken in Bethlehem. 13. Some were saying, "Mary, the virgin, gave birth not having been married for even two months." 14. Many others were saying, "She did not give birth, a midwife did not go up [to her], and we have not heard cries of pain."[17] They were all blind to him. None of them believed in him, and they did not see where he was from. 15. They took him, and they came to Nazareth of Galilee. 16. I saw, Hezekiah and Josab, my son, and I say to the other prophets who are standing [here] that he was hidden from every heaven, every judge, and every lord of that world. 17. I saw that in Nazareth he was suckling like a child, and as was customary he was suckling, so that he was unknown. 18. When he grew up, he was doing great miracles and wonders in the land of Israel and in Jerusalem. 19. After this, the adversary grew jealous, and he brought the children of Israel upon him, when they did not know who he was. They led him to the king, they crucified him, and they brought him down to the angel in Sheol. 20. In Jerusalem, I saw them crucify him on a tree, 21. and after three days he was raised and remained for [some] days. 22. The angel who was guiding me said to me, "Understand, Isaiah!" I saw when he sent twelve apostles, and he ascended. 23. I saw, and he was in the firmament, and he was not changed according to their appearance. All the angels of the firmament as well as Satan saw him, and they bowed down. 24. There was great sadness there as they were saying, "How did our lord descend upon us, and we did not understand the glory that was upon him, which we [now] see is found upon him from the sixth heaven?" 25. He ascended to the second heaven, and he was not changed, but all the angels who are on the right and left, with the throne in the middle, 26. were bowing to him and praising him. They were saying, "How was the lord hidden when he was descending, and we did not understand?" 27. In this way, he ascended to the third heaven, and in this way they praised him and spoke. 28. So also it was in the fourth heaven and the fifth, and in this way they spoke. 29. However, there was one glory, and from it he was not transformed. 30. I saw when he ascended to the sixth heaven, and they bowed to him and worshiped him, 31. but in all the heavens the praise increased. 32. I saw how he ascended to the seventh heaven, and all the righteous and

17 See *Acts of Peter* 24.

all the angels praised him. Then I saw that he sat to the right of that great glory, whose glory I have told you that I was unable to see. 33. I saw that the angel of the Holy Spirit sat to the left. 34. The angel said to me, "Isaiah, son of Amoz, let me save you[18] because these matters are great, for you have observed that which no one of flesh has observed. 35. You will return to your garment until your days are complete, and then you will come here." 36. I saw these things.

Isaiah spoke to all those who were standing before him, and they offered praise. He said to Hezekiah, the king, "I have spoken these things. 37. The end of this world 38. and all this vision will be complete in the last generation." 39. Isaiah made him swear that he would not tell the people of Israel these words and that he would not allow anyone to write [them] down. 40. Then they will read them. As for you, be in the Holy Spirit so that you receive your garments, thrones, and crowns of glory, which reside in the seventh heaven. 41. On account of these visions and prophecies, Samael, the Satan, sawed the prophet Isaiah, son of Amoz, in two through Manasseh. 42. Hezekiah gave all this to Manasseh, his son, in the twenty-sixth year of his reign. 43. Manasseh did not remember, and he did not place it in his heart, but having submitted to Satan, he was destroyed.

Completed here is the vision of the prophet Isaiah, son of Amoz, along with his ascension.

18 The text is possibly corrupt.

2

The Gospel of Peter

Introduction and Translation by Mark DelCogliano

INTRODUCTION

The *Gospel of Peter* is one of many non-canonical gospels produced in the early centuries of Christianity. Only a fragment is extant, containing an account of the trial, passion, death, resurrection, and ascension of Jesus. While having numerous parallels with the passion narratives in the canonical synoptic gospels, the *Gospel of Peter* departs from them in significant ways, such as by exonerating Pontius Pilate, by blaming Herod Antipas for the crucifixion of Jesus, and by making those soldiers who were guarding Jesus's tomb witnesses of the resurrection. Most famously, the narrative features an enormous walking and talking cross. Scholars continue to debate whether the *Gospel of Peter* used one or more of the synoptic gospels as sources or was written independently of them by utilizing common sources. While the dating of the *Gospel of Peter* has been a heavily contested issue, the majority of scholars assign it to the years 150–190, making it one of the earliest non-canonical gospels to survive.

The *Gospel of Peter* preserves an example of narrative Christology that both complements and diverges from the four canonical and other non-canonical gospels. It affirms Jesus as Lord, Son of God, King of Israel, and Savior of human beings, but not as Christ, Messiah, or other titles found in other gospels. It has long been considered to present a docetic Christology, primarily on the basis of the Lord's apparent lack of pain during the crucifixion (10), his being forsaken by his "power" at the moment of death (19), and his death seemingly being downplayed by saying that he was "taken up" (19). But these passages have also been interpreted as offering weak proof for a docetic Christology, and other parts of the text affirm the real suffering of the Lord, his heroism in the face of it, and his actual death. The *Gospel of Peter*, then, is an early text whose Christology is difficult to categorize and shows the breadth of concerns that met early narrators of the passion.

This translation is based on the edition of Paul Foster, *The Gospel of Peter* (Leiden: Brill, 2010), 198–204.

TRANSLATION

1, 1. ... But none of the Jews washed his hands, neither Herod[1] nor one of his judges. And since they were unwilling to wash, Pilate stood up. 2. And then Herod the king ordered that the Lord be taken away when he said to them, "Do to him what I ordered you to do."

2, 3. Now standing there was Joseph,[2] the friend of Pilate and of the Lord. And knowing that they were going to crucify him, he went to Pilate and requested the body of the Lord for burial. 4. And Pilate sent a message to Herod and requested his body. 5. And Herod said, "Brother Pilate, even if someone had not requested him, we ourselves would have buried him, precisely because Sabbath is dawning. For it is written in the Law, 'Do not let the sun set on the executed.'"[3] And he handed him over to the people before the first day of their feast of the unleavened bread.

3, 6. Now those who took the Lord[4] kept shoving him[5] as they sped along, and they kept saying, "Let us drag the Son of God since we have authority over him." 7. And they draped him in purple and sat him on the judgment seat, saying, "Judge justly, King of Israel." 8. And one of them got a crown of thorns and put it on the Lord's head. 9. And others standing there kept spitting in his face, and others struck his cheeks. Others kept jabbing him with a reed, and some were scourging him, saying, "With this honor let us honor the Son of God."

4, 10. And they got two criminals and crucified the Lord in the middle of them. But he remained silent as if having no pain at all. 11. And when they erected the cross, they wrote down, "This is the King of Israel." 12. And after putting his garments in front of him, they divided them up and cast lots for them. 13. One of those criminals, however, scolded them, saying, "We are suffering in this way because of the crimes we committed;

1 Herod Antipas.
2 Traditionally, this figure has been identified as Joseph of Arimathea.
3 See Deut 21:22–23. 4 Reading *kyrion* instead of *kyriou*.
5 Reading *auton* instead of *autōn*.

but this one[6] who became Savior of human beings, what harm has he done to you?" 14. And since they had become angry with him, they ordered that his legs not be broken, so that he might die in torment.

5, 15. And it was midday, and darkness gripped all Judaea. And they grew concerned and anxious that the sun would set while he was still alive. [For] it is written for them, "Do not let the sun set on the executed." 16. And one of them said, "Give him gall with vinegar to drink." And after mixing it they gave it to him to drink. 17. And they fulfilled all things and brought the sins on their head to perfection. 18. Many people were going around with lamps, thinking that it was night, and they fell. 19. And the Lord cried out, saying, "My power, the power, you have forsaken me." And after he said this he was taken up. 20. And at the same hour the curtain of the temple in Jerusalem was torn into two.

6, 21. And then they pulled the nails out of the Lord's hands and set him upon the earth, and all the earth was shaken and there arose a great fear. 22. Then the sun began to shine, and it was found to be the ninth hour. 23. And the Jews rejoiced and gave his body to Joseph so that he might bury it, since he was one who saw all the good things he did. 24. And after he had received the Lord, he washed him and bound him in a linen cloth and brought him into his own tomb, called the Garden of Joseph.

7, 25. Then the Jews and the elders and the priests, realizing what evil they did to themselves, began to beat themselves and say, "Woe to our sins! The judgment and the end of Jerusalem is at hand!" 26. But I was grieving together with my companions, and since we had been wounded in mind we went in hiding. For we were being hunted by them as if we were criminals and as if we were planning to set the temple on fire. 27. And moreover, in addition to all these things we were fasting and were sitting, mourning and weeping night and day until the Sabbath.

8, 28. Now when the scribes and Pharisees and elders gathered together with one another after hearing that all the people were murmuring and beating their breasts, saying, "If these greatest signs happened at his death, behold how just he was!" 29. the elders became afraid and went to Pilate, beseeching him and saying, 30. "Let us have soldiers so that I may guard his burial place for three days, to prevent his disciples from coming and stealing him, and the people from thinking that he has risen from the dead

6 Reading *houtos* instead of *houtōs*.

and doing us harm." 31. Pilate let them have Petronius the centurion and soldiers to guard the tomb. And the elders and scribes went to the burial place with them. 32. And after they rolled a large stone down toward the centurion and the soldiers, all who were there together placed it at the door of the burial place. 33. And they made seven seals and once they had pitched a tent there, they stood guard.

9, 34. Now early as the Sabbath dawned a crowd came from Jerusalem and its environs to see the sealed tomb. 35. But during the night in which the Lord's day dawned, while the soldiers were guarding it two by two on every watch, there had been a loud voice in the heaven, 36. and they saw the heavens opened and two men of great splendor descending from there and approaching the tomb. 37. And that stone which had been placed at the door rolled away on its own and in turn gave access. And the tomb opened, and both the young men entered.

10, 38. So then, when the soldiers saw this, they woke up the centurion and the elders – for they were also present keeping guard. 39. And while they were reporting what they had seen, again they saw three men exiting the tomb: two of them supported the one, and a cross followed them. 40. And the head of the two reached all the way to heaven, but that of the one being led out by them went beyond the heavens. 41. And they heard a voice from the heavens saying, "Have you preached to those who are fallen asleep?" 42. And an answer was heard from the cross, "Yes."[7]

11, 43. So then, those people started to plot with each other to go off and make these things clear to Pilate. 44. And while they were still pondering this, again the heavens were seen to be opened and a certain human being descended and entered into the burial place. 45. When they saw these things, the centurion and his unit rushed at night to Pilate, abandoning the tomb that they were guarding, and reported all the things that they had seen, greatly upset and saying, "Truly he was God's Son." 46. In reply Pilate said, "I am clean of the blood of the Son of God, and this seemed good to us." 47. Then they all approached him and began to beseech and urge him to order the centurion and the soldiers to repeat nothing of what they had seen. 48. "For it is better," they said, "for us to become liable for the greatest sin before God than to fall into the hands of the Jewish people and be stoned." 49. So then, Pilate ordered the centurion and the soldiers to say nothing.

7 An allusion to the harrowing of hell.

12, 50. Now at dawn on the Lord's day Mary Magdalene, a disciple[8] of the Lord, who was afraid because of the Jews since they were burning with wrath, had not done at the Lord's tomb what women were accustomed to do for their beloved dead. 51. Taking her friends with her, she went to the tomb where he was placed. 52. And they were afraid that the Jews might see them, and they were saying, "Since we were not able on that day on which he was crucified to weep and beat ourselves, let us do these things right now at his tomb. 53. But who will roll away for us the stone placed at the door of the tomb, so that we can enter and sit beside him and do what is necessary? 54. For the stone was large, and we are afraid of anyone seeing us. But if we are unable, let us place at the door what we are bringing in memory of him. We shall weep and beat ourselves until we reach our home."

13, 55. And when they arrived, they found the tomb opened. And when they approached it, they stooped down there and saw there a certain young man sitting in the middle of the tomb, handsome and clothed with a splendid robe. He said to them, 56. "Why did you come? Whom do you seek? Not that one who was crucified? He has risen and gone away. But if you do not believe, stoop down and see the place <...>[9] because he is not [here]. For he has risen and gone away to the place from which he was sent." 57. Then the women became afraid and fled.

14, 58. Now it was the final day of the unleavened bread, and many were leaving, returning to their home since the feast was over. 59. But we, the twelve disciples of the Lord, wept and grieved. And each one, grieving because of what had happened, returned to his home. 60. But I, Simon Peter, and Andrew my brother took our nets and went off to the sea. And with us was Levi of Alphaeus whom the Lord ...[10]

8 In Greek, *mathētria*, the feminine form of *mathētēs*.

9 A few words in the text are corrupt here.

10 The text breaks off at this point.

3

The Epistle of the Apostles

Introduction and Translation by Francis Watson

INTRODUCTION

The Latin title, *Epistula Apostolorum*, was suggested by Carl Schmidt, the first editor of this previously unknown work. In chapter 2 eleven apostles are indeed named as the collective authors of this work, addressed to the entire worldwide Christian community, but its contents do not correspond to the apostolic or pseudo-apostolic letters of the New Testament. The major part of the *Epistula* records a dialogue supposed to have taken place on Easter morning in which Jesus answers questions put to him by his disciples in preparation for their future mission. The dialogue occurs within a narrative frame that includes a collection of miracle stories from Jesus's childhood and ministry (chapters 4–5), a version of the empty tomb story together with an appearance to female and male disciples (chapters 9–12), and a concluding ascension narrative unrelated to the more familiar version in Acts (chapter 51). In many respects this text is more like a gospel than an epistle.

The *Epistula* has Jesus announcing the date of his return (17.1–4), after 120 years (Coptic) or 150 years (Ethiopic). Either way, this passage supports an origin in the mid-second century, and other indications suggest an Asian provenance and a date of ca. 170. The *Epistula* features an incarnational theology in which Jesus is at some points virtually identified with the Father (3.1–12) and in which he becomes flesh by means of a miraculous conception (3.13–14, a passage showing affinities to the Gospels of both Luke and John). Although there are signs of a rudimentary Logos theology (18.1), Jesus appears to Mary at the annunciation disguised as the angel Gabriel (13.1–14.8). Most of the points in Jesus's heavenly or earthly career that feature in later creeds are already present at one point or another in this text: creation, incarnation/virginal conception, crucifixion, descent into Hades, resurrection, ascension, parousia, and judgment. In spite of the repeated references to the heretics Simon and Cerinthus (1.2, 7.1–3), there are few further traces of a polemical agenda.

The *Epistula* is preserved in one badly damaged Coptic manuscript from the fourth century, only about half of which has survived, and in numerous Ethiopic manuscripts dating from no earlier than the fourteenth century. The later Ethiopic text may therefore be used to fill the gaps in the Coptic, and major transitions between the two are noted in the translation here. The translation is based on C. Schmidt's edition of the Coptic text in *Gespräche Jesu mit seinen Jüngern nach der Auferstehung: Ein katholisch-apostolisches Sendschreiben des 2. Jahrhunderts* (Leipzig: J. C. Hinrichs, 1919); L. Guerrier's edition based on four Ethiopic manuscripts in *Le Testament en Galilée de Notre-Seigneur Jésus-Christ*, PO 43 (9.3) (Paris: Firmin-Didot, 1912; repr. Turnhout: Brepols, 2003); and Francis Watson's *An Apostolic Gospel: The Epistula Apostolorum in Literary Context*, Society for New Testament Studies Monograph Series (Cambridge: Cambridge University Press, 2020), where the present translation is supported by an extensive textual apparatus citing previously unedited Ethiopic manuscripts and by additional notes.

The following sigla are used in the translation below to indicate transitions between source texts:

<COP> Translation of Coptic text, from the manuscript IFAO Copte inv. 413–433, Bibliothèque nationale, Paris, ed. Schmidt, checked against digitized images.

<ETH> Translation of Ethiopic (Gəʿəz) text in major sections where Coptic is lacking.[1]

TRANSLATION

Introduction[2]

1, 1. **<ETH>** What Jesus Christ revealed to his disciples and to all: 2. on account of Simon and Cerinthus the false apostles this has been written, so that no one should associate with them, for there is in them a venom by which they kill people; 3. so that you may be strong and not waver or be

1 Major passages missing from the Coptic manuscript are 1.1–6.3 (MS pp. 1–8), 18.5b–19.8 (MS pp. 19–20), 21.3b–22.3b (MS pp. 25–26, except for fragments), 31.1–38.3a (MS pp. 37–50, except for fragments), 49.1–51.5 (MS pp. 65–68?). Thus 30 out of (probably) 68 pages are entirely or almost entirely missing. All extant pages have suffered more or less significant damage.

2 The section headings are insertions of the translator – Ed.

disturbed or depart from what you have heard, the word of the gospel. 4.
What we have heard and remembered and written for the whole world we
entrust to you, our sons and daughters, in joy. 5. In the name of God, ruler
of the whole world, and of Jesus Christ, grace be multiplied to you.

2, 1. John and Thomas and Peter and Andrew and James and Philip
and Bartholomew and Matthew and Nathanael and Judas the Zealot and
Cephas 2. to the churches of the east and the west, to those in the north and
the south: 3. proclaiming and declaring to you our Lord Jesus Christ, as we
heard so have we written; and we touched him after he rose from the dead,
when he revealed to us what is great and wonderful and true.

Confession of Faith

3, 1. This we declare, that our Lord and Saviour Jesus Christ is God, the Son of God,

2. who was sent from God, ruler of the whole world, maker of every name that is named;

3. who is above all authorities, Lord of lords and King of kings, Power of the heavenly powers;

4. who sits above the Cherubim at the right hand of the throne of the Father;

5. who by his word commanded the heavens and founded the earth and what is in it, and established the sea so that it did not cross its boundary, and depths and springs to gush forth and flow into the earth day and night;

6. who established the sun and moon and stars in heaven;

7. who separated light and darkness;

8. who summoned Gehenna, and summons rain in the twinkling of an eye for the winter time, and mist and frost and hail, and the days each in its time;

9. who shakes and makes firm;

10. who made humankind in his image and likeness;

11. who spoke with the forefathers and prophets in parables and in truth;

12. whom the apostles preached and the disciples touched.

13. And God the Son of God do we confess, the Word who became flesh
of Mary, carried in her womb through the Holy Spirit. 14. And not by
the desire of the flesh but by the will of God was he born; 15. and he
was swaddled in Bethlehem and manifested and nourished and grew
up, as we saw.

The Miracle Cycle

4, 1. This is what our Lord Jesus Christ did when he was taken by Joseph and Mary his mother to where he was to be taught letters. 2. And the teacher said to him as he taught him, "Say, Alpha." 3. He answered and said to him, "You tell me first what Beta is, and then I will trust you and say Alpha!"

5, 1. And then there was a wedding in Cana of Galilee, and they invited him with his mother and his brothers, and water he made wine; 2. and the dead he raised, and paralytics he made to walk, and the man whose hand was withered he restored.

3. And a woman who suffered her periods twelve years touched the hem of his garment and was immediately well. 4. And as we considered and wondered at the glorious things he had done, he said to us, "Who touched me?" 5. And we said to him, "Lord, the press of the crowd touched you!" 6. And he answered and said to us, "I felt that power came forth upon me." 7. Immediately that woman came before him and answered him and said to him, "Lord, I touched you." 8. And he answered and said to her, "Go, your faith has made you well." 9. And then the deaf he made to hear and the blind to see and those with demons he exorcized and those with leprosy he cleansed.

10. And the demon Legion, who dwelt in a man, met Jesus and cried out and said, "Before the day of our destruction have you come to drive us out?" 11. And Jesus rebuked him and said to him, "Go out of this man and do nothing to him!" 12. And he went into the pigs and plunged them into the sea and they were drowned.

13. And then he walked on the sea, and the winds blew and he rebuked them, and the waves of the sea he stilled.

14. And when we his disciples had no denarii, we said to him, "Teacher, what shall we do about the tax-collector?" 14. And he answered and said to us, "Let one of you cast a hook into the deep and draw out a fish, and he will find denarii in it. 16. Give them to the tax-collector for myself and for you."

17. Then when we had no food except five loaves and two fishes, he commanded the men to recline. 18. And their number was found to be five thousand besides women and children, and to these we brought pieces of bread. 19. And they were satisfied and there was some left over, and we removed twelve basketfuls of pieces. 20. If we ask and say, "What do these five loaves mean?" they are an image of our faith as true Christians; 21. that

is, in the Father, ruler of the whole world, and in Jesus Christ and in the Holy Spirit and in the holy church and in the forgiveness of sins.

6, 1. And these things our Lord and Savior revealed to us and showed us, as we likewise do to you, 2. so that you may be partakers in the grace of the Lord and in our ministry and our praise, as you think of eternal life. 3. Be strong and do not waver in the knowledge and certainty of our Lord Jesus Christ, and he will be merciful and gracious and save constantly, to the end of the age.

Recapitulation: Reasons for Writing

7, 1. **<COP>** Cerinthus and Simon have gone out, they go around the world, 2. but they are enemies of our Lord Jesus Christ, for they pervert the words and the work, that is, Jesus Christ. 3. So beware of them, for in them there is death and a great defilement of corruption. 4. Their end will be judgment and eternal perdition.

8, 1. For this reason we have not delayed to write to you about the testimony of our Savior the Christ, 2. the things he did as we watched him and that are still in our thoughts and deeds.

The Dawn of Easter Faith

9, 1. This we confess, that the Lord was crucified by Pontius Pilate and Archelaus between the two thieves, and he was buried in a place called "The Skull." 2. There came to that place three women, Mary and Martha and Mary Magdalene. 3. They took ointment to pour over his body, weeping and grieving over what had happened. 4. But when they reached the tomb and looked inside they did not find the body.

10, 1. And as they were grieving and weeping the Lord appeared to them and said to them, "For whom do you weep? Weep no longer! I am the one you seek. 2. But let one of you go to your brothers and say, 'Come, the Teacher has risen from the dead!'"

3. Martha came and told us. 4. We said to her, "What do you want with us, O woman? One who died and is buried, can he live?" 5. We did not believe her that the Savior had risen from the dead. 6. Then she returned to the Lord and said to him, "None of them believed me that you are alive."

7. He said, "Let another of you go to them to tell them again." 8. Mary came, she told us again, and we disbelieved her. 9. She returned to the Lord, and she too told him.

11, 1. Then the Lord said to Mary and her sisters, "Let us go to them." 2. And he came and found us within. 3. He called us forth, but we thought it was a phantasm and we did not believe that it was the Lord. 4. Then he said to us, "Come, fear not, I am your teacher whom you, Peter, denied three times, and now do you deny again?" 5. And we came to him doubting in our hearts whether it was he. 6. Then he said to us, "Why do you still doubt, you disbelieving ones? I am he who spoke to you about my flesh and my death and my resurrection. 7. That you may know that it is I, Peter, put your fingers into the nail-marks of my hands; and you, Thomas, put your fingers into the spear wounds in my side; and you, Andrew, look at my feet and see if they are not in contact with the ground. 8. For it is written in the prophet, 'As for an appearance of a demon, its foot is not in contact with the ground.'"[3]

12, 1. And we touched him, that we might know that he had truly risen in flesh. 2. And we fell on our faces, confessing our sins, because we had been unbelieving.

3. Then the Lord our Savior said to us, "Rise and I will reveal to you what is above the heavens and what is in the heavens and your rest in the kingdom of the heavens. 5. For my Father gave me authority to take you up and those who believe in me."

The Descent through the Heavens

13, 1. And what he revealed are these things that he said to us: "It came to pass that when I came from the Father of all and passed through the heavens, I put on the wisdom of the Father and clothed myself in the power of his might. 2. I was in the heavens, and archangels and angels I passed in their likeness as though I were one of them. 3. Among the powers and rulers and authorities I passed, having the wisdom of the one who sent me. 4. And the commander of the angels is Michael, with Gabriel and Uriel and Raphael, and they followed me down to the fifth firmament, for they were thinking in their hearts that I was one of them – such was the power given me by the Father. 5. And on that day I prepared the archangels, in a voice

3 It is likely that the author invented this citation.

of wonder, so that they might go in to the altar of the Father and serve and fulfill the ministry until I returned to him. 6. This is what I did in the wisdom of the likeness, for I became all in all so that I might fulfill the will of the Father of glory who sent me and return to him.

14, 1. "For you know that the angel Gabriel brought the good news to Mary?"

2. We answered, "Yes, Lord."

3. Then he answered and said to us, "Do you not remember that I told you a moment ago that I became an angel among angels and all in everything?"

4. We said to him, "Yes, Lord."

5. Then he answered and said to us, "When I took the form of the angel Gabriel, I appeared to Mary and I spoke with her. 6. Her heart received me, she believed, she molded me, I entered into her, I became flesh. 7. For I became my own servant in the appearance of the likeness of an angel. 8. I will do likewise after I have returned to the Father.

Pascha and Parousia

15, 1. "And as for you, celebrate the memorial of my death when the Feast of the Pascha comes. 2. Then one of you will be thrown into prison for the sake of my name. 3. And he will be grieved and distressed that you celebrate Pascha while he is in prison and away from you, for he will be grieved that he does not celebrate Pascha with you. 4. And I will send my power in the form of the angel Gabriel, 5. and the doors of the prison will open, and he will go out and come to you, 6. he will keep vigil with you and stay with you until the cock crows. 7. And when you have completed my Memorial and my Agape, he will again be thrown into prison as a testimony, until he comes out from there and preaches what I have given you."

8. And we said to him, "Lord, is it again necessary for us to take the cup and drink?"

9. He said to us, "Yes, it is necessary until the day when I come with those who were put to death for my sake."

16, 1. And we said to him, "Lord, great indeed are the things you have now revealed to us! 2. But in what power or likeness will you come?"

3. And he answered and said to us, "Truly I say to you, I shall surely come like the rising sun, shining seven times more than it in my glory. 4. On the

wings of clouds I shall be borne in glory, the sign of the cross before me. 5. And I will come down to the earth and judge the living and the dead."

17, 1. And we said to him, "Lord, after how many years will these things be?"

2. He said to us, "When the hundred and twentieth/fiftieth[4] year is completed, between Pentecost and the Feast of Unleavened Bread, the coming of my Father will take place."

3. And we said to him, "Just now did you not say to us, 'I will come'? So how can you say to us, 'The one who sent me will come'?"

4. Then he said to us, "I am wholly in my Father and my Father is in me."

The Interim

5. Then we said to him, "Will you really leave us until your coming? Where will we find a teacher?"

6. And he answered and said to us, "Do you not know that I am already both here and there, with the one who sent me?"

7. And we said to him, "Lord, is it possible that you should be both here and there?"

8. And he said to us, "I am wholly in the Father and the Father is in me, by likeness of form and power and fullness and light and the full measure and the voice.

18, 1. "I am the Word, I became a reality to him – that is, I am the thought fulfilled in the type, 2. I came into being on the eighth day, which is the Lord's Day. 3. And the fulfillment of all fulfillment you will see through the redemption which has come to pass in me. 4. And you will see me go to heaven to my Father who is in heaven. 5. But behold, I give you a new commandment: love one another, and **<ETH>** that there may be continual peace among you. 6. Love your enemies, and what you do not wish them to do to you, do not do to another, or that one to you.

19, 1. "Preach and teach those who believe in me, and preach about the kingdom of my Father. 2. And as he has given me authority, I have given it to you so that you may bring his children near to my heavenly Father. 3. Preach and they will believe, you who are to bring the children to the kingdom of heaven."

4 The Coptic reads "twentieth" and the Ethiopic "fiftieth."

4. And we said, "Lord, it is possible for you to do what you have told us, but how is it possible for us?"

5. And he said to us, "Truly I say to you, preach and proclaim, as I will be with you. For I am pleased to be with you; you will be heirs of the heavenly kingdom of the one who sent me. 6. Truly I say to you, you will be brothers and companions, for my Father is pleased with you and with those who believe in me through you. 7. Truly I say to you, such and so great a joy has my Father prepared, which angels and authorities longed to behold, and it will not be permitted them."

8. And we said to him, "Lord, what is this that you are saying?"

9. And **<COP>** he said to us, "You will surely see a light from shining light, the perfect perfected in the perfect. 11.[5] I am wholly the right hand of the Father, in the one who is the fullness."

12. And we said to him, "Lord, in everything you have become to us salvation and life, proclaiming such a hope to us!"

13. And he said to us, "Have confidence and be content! 14. Truly I say to you, such will be your rest, where there is no eating or drinking and no anxiety or grief and no corruption for those who are above. 15. For you will participate not in the lower creation but in that which is incorruptible, that of my Father; you yourselves will be incorruptible. 16. As I am always in him, so are you in me."

The Resurrection of the Flesh

17. And again we said to him, "In what form? That of angels or flesh?"

18. And he answered and said to us, "Behold, I have put on your flesh, in which I was born and in which I was crucified and raised by my heavenly Father, 19. that the prophecy of David the prophet might be fulfilled, concerning what was proclaimed about me and my death and my resurrection, saying:

> 20. 'Lord, many are those who afflict me, and many have risen against me!
>
> 21. 'Many there are who say of my soul, "There is no salvation for you with God."

5 *Epistula Apostolorum* 19.10 occurs in the Ethiopic only, and the text is corrupt: "And the Son will be perfected by the Father, the light – for the Father who perfects is perfect … death and resurrection, and the perfection will surpass perfection."

22. 'But you, Lord, are my support, my glory and the lifter of my head.
23. 'With my voice I cried to the Lord, and he heard me.
24. 'I lay down and slept, I was raised, for you, Lord, are my support.
25. 'I will not be afraid of tens of thousands of people who oppose me round about.
26. 'Rise, Lord, save me, my God, for you have struck all those who are my enemies without cause, the teeth of sinners you have broken.

27. 'Salvation is the Lord's, and his love is upon his people.'[6]
28. And if all the words spoken by the prophets are fulfilled in me – for I
was in them – then how much more what I say to you! 29. Truly what I say
to you will come to pass, so that the one who sent me will be glorified by you and by those who believe in me!"

20, 1. And when he had said these things to us, we said to him, "Lord, in everything you have been merciful to us and you have saved us and you
have revealed everything to us. 2. Once again we wish to inquire of you, if you permit us."

3. He answered and said to us, "I know indeed that you will bear it and
that your heart is pleased to hear me. 4. So ask about what you wish, and I will gladly speak with you.

21, 1. "Truly I say to you, as my Father raised me from the dead, so you too will rise and they will take you up above the heavens to the place of which I spoke to you in the beginning, to the place prepared for you by the
one who sent me. 2. And thus will I fulfill every dispensation, being unborn
yet born among humans, without flesh yet I have borne flesh. 3. For this is
why I came, so that you **<ETH>** who were born in flesh might be raised in your flesh as in a second birth, a garment that will not perish, with all who hope and believe in the one who sent me. 4. For so it has pleased my
Father, that to you and to those whom I will I should give life, the hope of the kingdom."

5. And then we said to him, "Great is the hope you give, of which you speak!"

6. He answered and said to us, "Do you believe that everything I say to you will come to pass?"

7. And we answered him and said to him, "Yes, Lord!"

8. And he said to us, "Truly I say to you that I have received all authority from my Father so that those in darkness I may turn to light and those in

6 Ps 3:1–8.

corruption to incorruption and those in error to truth and those in death to life, and that those in prison should be released. 9. For what is impossible for humans is possible for the Father. 10. I am the hope of the despairing, and the helper of those who have no helper, the wealth of the needy, the physician of the sick, the resurrection of the dead."

22, 1. And when he said this to us, we said to him, "Lord, is the flesh really to be judged with the soul and the spirit? 2. And will some find rest in the kingdom of heaven and others be condemned for ever while living?"

3. And he said **<COP>** to us, "How long will you question and seek?"

23, 1. Again we said to him, "Lord, it is necessary for us to question you, for you command us to preach; 2. so that we ourselves may know with certainty through you and be useful preachers, and that those who will teach through us may believe in you. 3. That is why we question you so much!"

24, 1. He answered us, saying, "Truly I say to you that the resurrection of the flesh will occur with the soul and spirit within it."

2. And we said to him, "Lord, is it possible for what is dissolved and destroyed to be saved? 3. Not that as unbelieving do we ask you, or as if it were impossible for you, but we truly believe that what you say will come to pass."

4. And he was angry with us, saying to us, "O you of little faith, how long will you question? But what you wish, say to me, and I will tell you unreservedly. 5. Only keep my commandments and do what I tell you, and do not turn your face from anyone so that I would turn my face from you. 6. But without delay or shame or partiality, serve in the way that is straight and narrow and difficult. 7. This is the way of my Father himself, and he will rejoice over you."

25, 1. Again we said to him, "Lord, we are now ashamed that we are questioning you so much and are wearying you."

2. Then he answered and said to us, "I indeed know that in faith and with your whole heart you ask of me – therefore I rejoice over you! 3. Truly I say to you, I am glad, and my Father who is in me, that you ask me, for your shamelessness brings me joy and gives you life."

4. And when he said this to us, we were glad that we were questioning him. 5. And we said to him again, "Lord, in everything you grant us life and show us mercy. For you will tell us what we ask!"

6. Then he said to us, "Which is it that perishes, the flesh or the spirit?"

7. We said to him, "It is the flesh that perishes!"

8. Then he said to us, "Indeed, what has fallen will rise and what is lost will be found and what is weak will recover so that in this the glory of my Father may be revealed. 9. As he has done to me, so I will do to all of you who believe.

26, 1. "Truly I say to you that the flesh will rise with the soul alive, so that they may be judged on that day for what they have done, whether good or evil, 2. so that there may be a selection of believers who have performed the commandments of my Father who sent me. 3. Thus the judgment will take place in severity. 4. For my Father said to me, 'My Son, on the day of judgement you shall neither be ashamed before the rich nor pity the poor, but according to the sin of each you shall deliver them to eternal punishment.' 5. But to my beloved, who have performed the commandments of my Father who sent me, I will give rest of life in the kingdom of my Father in heaven. 6. And they will see what he has granted me: he has given me authority to do as I will, and to give what I promised and what I willed to give them and grant them.

The Descent into Hell

27, 1. "For this is why I descended to the place of Lazarus and preached to your fathers and the prophets that they would go forth from the rest below and ascend to that which is in heaven. 2. And with my right hand I poured over them the baptism of life and forgiveness and deliverance from all evil, as I have done for you and for those who believe in me. 3. But if anyone believes in me and does not do my commandments, after confessing my name, he receives no benefit at all and has run his course in vain. 4. For such people will incur loss and punishment, because they have transgressed my commandments.

28, 1. "But I have granted you to be children of life, I have delivered you from all evil and from the power of the rulers, with everyone who believes in me through you. 2. For what I have promised you I shall also give them, so that they may come forth from the prison and chains of the rulers and the terrible fire."

3. We answered and said to him, "Lord, you have surely given us rest of life and you have given us joy with signs to confirm faith. Will you now preach to us what you preached to our fathers and the prophets?"

4. Then he said to us, "Truly I say to you, everyone who believes in me and who believes in the one who sent me I will lead up to heaven, the place

which my Father prepared for the elect. 5. And I will give you the kingdom that is chosen in rest and eternal life.

Other Teachings

29, 1. "But those who transgress my commandments and teach teachings other than what is written, and who add to them and establish their own glory, teaching with different words those who believe in me rightly – if they fall away through such people, they will receive an eternal punishment."

2. And we said to him, "Lord, will there come teachings other than what you have told us?"

3. He said to us, "It is indeed necessary for them to come, so that those who do evil and those who do good may be revealed. 4. And in this way the judgment will reveal those who do these works, and according to their works they will be judged and delivered to death."

Mission

5. Again we said to him, "Lord, blessed are we that we see you and hear you as you say such things, for our eyes have seen these great signs that you have done."

6. He answered and said to us, "Blessed rather are those who have not seen and yet believed, for such will be called sons of the kingdom, and they will be perfect in the perfect one, and I will be life to them in the kingdom of my Father."

7. Again we said to him, "Lord, how will they believe, when you are to go and leave us behind? For you say to us, 'There comes a day and an hour when I shall ascend to my Father.'"

30, 1. And he said to us, "Go and preach to the twelve tribes and preach also to the Gentiles and to the whole land of Israel from east to west and from south to north, and many will believe in the Son of God."

2. We said to him, "Lord, who will believe us, or who will listen to us or who will then teach the mighty works and signs you have done, and the wonders?"

3. Then he answered and said to us, "Go and preach the mercy of my Father, and what he has done through me I will do through you, since I will be in you. 4. And I will give you my peace and by my Spirit I will give you

power, and you will prophesy to them their eternal life. 5. And to others also I will give my power, and they will teach the rest of the Gentiles.

Paul the Persecutor and Confessor

31, 1. **<ETH>** "And behold, you will meet a man whose name is Saul (which being interpreted is Paul), who is a Jew, circumcised by the commandment of the law, and he will hear my voice from heaven with astonishment and fear and trembling. 2. And he will be blinded, and by your hand shall his eyes be sealed with saliva. 3. And do everything for him that I have done for you, and convert him for others. 4. And immediately this man's eyes shall be opened and he will praise God, my heavenly Father. 5. And he will be strong among the people, and he will preach and teach many, and they will be glad to hear him, and many will be saved. 6. And then they will hate him and deliver him into the hand of his enemy, and he will confess before transitory kings. 7. And the fulfillment of his confessing me will come upon him, so that instead of persecuting me and hating me he confesses me. 8. And he will preach and teach, and he will be with my elect an elect vessel and a wall that shall not fall. 9. The last of the last shall be a preacher to the Gentiles, perfected by the will of my Father. 10. As you have learnt from the scriptures that the prophets spoke about me and in me it is truly fulfilled, so you must provide guidance in them. 11. And every word that I have spoken to you and that you write about me, that I am the Word of the Father and the Father is in me, you also must pass on to that man, as is fitting for you. 12. Teach him and remind him what is said in the scriptures about me and is now fulfilled, and then he will be the salvation of the Gentiles."

32, 1. And we said to him, "O Master, do we have one hope of inheritance with them?"

2. He answered and said to us, "Are the fingers of the hand alike, or the ears of corn in the field? Or do fruit-bearing trees give the same fruit? Do they not bear fruit each according to its kind?"

3. And we said to him, "Lord, you are again speaking with us in parables!"

4. And he said to us, "Do not be troubled! Truly I say to you, you are my brothers, participants in my Father's kingdom, for so it pleased him. 5. Truly I say to you, to those whom you teach and they believe in me, I will give that hope."

33, 1. And we said to him again, "Lord, when shall we meet that man? And when will you go to your Father and ours, our God and our Lord?"

2. And he answered and said to us, "That man will go out from the land of Cilicia to Damascus in Syria in order to tear apart the church that you are to found. 3. It is I who will speak through you, and it will happen soon. 4. In this faith he will be strong, so that what the prophetic voice said might be fulfilled: 5. 'Behold, from the land of Syria I will begin to call a new Jerusalem, and Zion I will subdue to myself and it will be captured.'[7] 6. And the barren one who has no children will have a child; and she will be called the daughter of my Father, and to me she will be my bride – for so it has pleased the one who sent me. 7. And that man I will turn aside so that he may not come and fulfill his evil intention, and his shall be the glory of my Father. 8. For when I have gone and am with my Father, I will speak with him from heaven. 9. And all that I have predicted to you about him will take place."

The Time of Trial

34, 1. And we said to him again, "Lord, what great things you have spoken to us and announced to us and revealed to us, things never yet spoken, and in everything you have comforted us and been gracious to us! 2. For after your resurrection you revealed all this to us, so that we might truly be saved. 3. But you have told us only that there will be signs and wonders in heaven and on earth before the end of the world comes – so teach us, that we may know."

4. And he said to us, "I will teach you, and it is not only to you that this will happen but also those whom you teach and who believe, and those who hear this man and believe in me. 5. In those years and in those days it will happen."

6. And we again said to him, "Lord, what is it that will happen?"

7. And he said to us, "At that time believers and unbelievers will perceive the sound of a trumpet from heaven and the sight of great stars that appear during the day, 8. and a sign from heaven that reaches the earth, and stars falling like fire, and great hailstones like raging fire, 9. and sun and moon fighting together, and constant terror of thunder and lightning and thunderbolt and an earthquake following, 10. and cities shall fall and people shall die in their ruins, and there will be constant drought from lack of rain, and a great plague and widespread death and many trials, so that funerals will cease for one who dies. 11. And the passing of child and parent will

7 It is likely that the author invented this citation.

be on a single bed, and the parent will not turn to the child nor the child to the parent, and one person will not turn to another. 12. And those who are bereaved will rise up and see those who had departed from them being carried out. 13. For there will be a plague everywhere, hatred and suffering and jealousy, and they will take from one and give to another. 14. And what follows will be worse than this.

35, 1. "And then my Father will be angry because of human evil, for many are their transgressions and the abomination of their uncleanness is greatly against them in the corruption of their life."

The Fate of the Elect

2. And we said to him, "Lord, what then of those who hope in you?"

3. And he answered and said to us, "How long are you still slow of heart? 4. Truly I say to you, as the prophet David spoke about me and about those who are mine, so likewise God wills for those who believe in me. 5. And there will be in the world deceivers and enemies of righteousness, and there shall come to pass David's prophecy about them which says:

> 6. 'Swift are their feet to shed blood, and their tongue weaves deceit, and the venom of snakes is under their lips.
> 7. 'And I see you as you go about with a thief, and with an adulterer is your portion.
> 8. 'And while you sit you slander your brother and set a stumbling-block for your mother's son. What do you think, that I am like you?'[8]

9. And behold, see how the prophet spoke about everything, so that everything may be fulfilled that was said before."

36, 1. And we said to him again, "Lord, will the Gentiles not say, 'Where is their God?'"

2. And he answered and said to us, "By this the elect will be made known, that they depart after enduring such torment."

3. And we said to him, "Will their departure from the world be through the plague that torments them?"

4. And he said to us, "No, but when they are tormented such an affliction will be to test them. 5. If there is faith within them and if they remember

8 Ps 49(50):19, 18, 20–21.

these words of mine and obey my commandments, they will be raised. 6. And their situation will be for a few days, so that the one who sent me may be glorified and I with him, for he sent me to you. 7. This I tell you, and you must tell it to Israel and to the Gentiles, that they may hear and be saved and believe in me and depart out of the affliction of the plague. 8. And whoever survives the affliction of death will be taken and kept in prison, punished like a thief."

9. And we said to him, "Lord, will they be like those who do not believe? And will you punish those who survive the plague in the same way?"

10. And he said to us, "If they believe in my name but acted as sinners, they have behaved like unbelievers."

11. And we said to him again, "Lord, so this is the fate of those who survive, that they fail to attain life?"

12. And he answered and said to us, "Whoever glorifies my Father will dwell with my Father."

37, 1. And we said to him, "Lord, teach us what will happen after this."

2. And he said to us, "In those years and days there will be war upon war, and the four corners of the world will be shaken and will war on one another. 3. And then, a tumult of clouds, darkness, drought and persecution of those who believe in me and of the elect! 4. And then, dissension, strife, and evil conduct among them, and there are some of those who believe in my name but follow evil and teach vain teaching. 5. And people will follow them and obey their wealth, their wickedness, their drunkenness, and their bribery; and there will be partiality among them.

38, 1. "And those who desire to see the face of God, and who do not show partiality to rich sinners, and who are not ashamed before the men who go astray but rebuke them, these will be crowned in the presence of the Father. 2. So too those who rebuke their neighbor will be saved. This is a son of wisdom and faith. 3. But if he is not a son of wisdom he will hate and persecute and not turn to **<COP>** his neighbor but will despise and reject him. 4. Those who conduct themselves in truth and in the knowledge of faith having love for me endured abuse; and they will be despised as they walk in poverty and endure those who hate them, who mock them and torment them; 5. destitute, since men were arrogant against them as they walk in hunger and thirst. 6. Yet because they have endured for the blessedness of heaven, they will be with me for ever. 7. But woe to those who walk in arrogance and boasting! For their end is perdition."

Divine Justice

39, 1. And we said to him, "Lord, it is in your power not to allow these things to befall them!"

2. He answered and said to us, "How will the judgment take place for either the righteous or the unrighteous?"

3. And we said to him, "Lord, in that day they will say to you, 'You did not separate righteousness and unrighteousness, light and darkness, evil and good!'"

4. Then he said, "I will answer them, saying: 'Adam was given the power to choose one of the two. 5. And he chose the light and stretched out his hand for it, but the darkness he rejected and cast it from him. 6. So all people have the power to believe in the light, which is the life of the Father who sent me.' 7. Everyone who believes and does the works of light will live through them. 8. But if there is someone who confesses that he belongs to the light while doing the works of darkness, such a person has no defense, nor will he lift his face to look at the Son of God, which is I myself. 9. For I shall say to him, 'As you sought you have found, and as you asked you have received! 10. Why did you condemn me, O man? Why did you proclaim me and deny me? And why did you confess me and deny me?' 11. Therefore every person has the power to live or to die, and so the one who keeps my commandments will become a son of light, that is, of the Father who is within me. 12. And because of those who corrupt my words I have come down from heaven, I the Word who became flesh and suffered, 13. teaching that these who are called will be saved and that those who are lost will be lost eternally and tormented alive and punished in their flesh and their soul."

40, 1. And we said to him, "Lord, truly we are concerned for them!"

2. And he said to us, "You do well, for the righteous are concerned for sinners and pray for them, interceding with my Father."

3. Again we said to him, "Lord, so does no one intercede with you yourself?"

4. And he said to us, "Yes, and I will hear the prayer the righteous make for them."

Ministry

5. And when he had said this to us we said to him, "Lord, in everything you have taught us and pitied us and saved us so that we may preach to those who are worthy of salvation – and do we gain a reward with you?"

41, 1. And he answered and said to us, "Go, preach, and you will be good workers and servants."

2. And we said to him, "It is you who will preach through us."

3. Then he answered us, saying, "Will you not all be fathers? Will you not all be teachers?"

4. We said to him, "Lord, you said to us, 'Do not call anyone your father on earth, for there is one who is your Father who is in heaven, and your teacher.' 5. Why do you now say to us, 'You will be fathers of many children, and servants and teachers'?"

6. And he answered and said to us, "It is as you have said. 7. For truly I say to you, whoever hears you and believes in me will receive from you the light of the seal through me. You will be fathers and servants and teachers."

42, 1. And we said to him, "Lord, how can each of us be these three?"

2. And he said to us, "Truly I say to you that you will indeed be called fathers, because with a willing heart and love you have revealed to them the things of the kingdom of heaven. 3. And you will be called servants because they will receive the baptism of life and the forgiveness of their sins by my hand through you. 4. And you will be called teachers because you have given them the word without envy. 5. You admonished them, and when you rebuked them they separated themselves. 6. You were unafraid of their wealth and their person, but you kept the commandments of my Father and did them. 7. There will be a great reward for you with my Father who is in heaven, and for them there will be forgiveness of sins and eternal life, and they will share in the kingdom of heaven."

8. And we said to him, "Lord, if each of us had ten thousand tongues for his speech, we would not be able to give thanks to you that you promise us such things!"

9. Then he answered, saying to us, "Just do what I tell you, the things I myself have done.

Parable of the Virgins

43, 1. "And you will be like the wise virgins who watched and did not sleep but went out to meet the Lord and entered with him into the wedding-chamber. 2. But the foolish ones were unable to watch but slept."

3. And we said to him, "Lord, who are the wise and who are the foolish?"

4. He said to us, "There are five wise. Of them the prophet said, 'They are children of God.'[9] Hear their names!"

5. But we were weeping and distressed at heart about those who slept.

6. He said to us, "The five wise are Faith and Love and Grace, Peace and Hope. 7. Those who possess these among those who believe will be guides to those who believe in me and in the one who sent me. 8. For I am the Lord and I am the bridegroom whom they received, and they entered the bridegroom's house and reclined with me in my wedding-chamber and rejoiced. 9. But as for the five foolish ones who had slept, they awoke and came to the door of the wedding-chamber and knocked, for it had been shut against them. 10. Then they wept and grieved that they did not open to them."

11. And we said to him, "Lord, those wise sisters of theirs who were in the bridegroom's house, did they fail to open to them? And did they not grieve for them or did they not plead with the bridegroom on their behalf to open to them?"

12. He answered, saying to us, "They were not yet able to find grace on their behalf."

13. We said to him, "Lord, when will they enter for their sisters' sake?"

14. Then he said to us, "Whoever is shut out is shut out."

15. And we said to him, "Lord, is this matter decided? Who then are the foolish?"

16. He said to us, "Hear their names: Knowledge, and Wisdom, Obedience, Patience, and Mercy. 17. For it is these that slept among those who believe and confess me.

44, 1. "Since those who slept did not fulfill my commandments, they will remain outside the kingdom and the fold of the shepherd and his flock. 2. And whoever remains outside the sheepfold the wolves will eat, and he will hear them; he will die in great pain, and distress and endurance shall come upon him. 3. And he will be terribly tortured and lacerated and torn apart with a great punishment and he will be in agony."

45, 1. And we said to him, "Lord, you have revealed all things to us well."

2. Then he answered, saying to us, "Do you not understand these words?"

3. And we said to him, "Yes, Lord, through the five they will enter your kingdom. 4. Yet those who watched and were with you, the Lord and bridegroom, surely they do not rejoice over those who slept?"

9 It is likely that the author invented this citation.

5. And he said to us, "They indeed rejoice that they entered with the bridegroom, the Lord, and they grieved over those who slept, for they are their sisters. 6. For the ten are daughters of God the Father."

7. And we said to him, "Lord, it is in your power to be gracious to their sisters!"

8. He said to us, "That is not your affair but his who sent me, and I myself agree with him."

Discipline

46, 1. "But as for you, preach and teach uprightly and well, showing partiality to no one and fearing no one, especially the rich, for they do not do my commandments but delight in their wealth."

2. And we said to him, "Lord, do you speak to us only of the rich?"

3. He answered, saying, "If one who is not rich, having a little property, gives to the poor and needy, people will call him a benefactor.

47, 1. "But if one should fall, bearing a burden because of the sins he has committed, let his neighbor reprove him for what he did to his neighbor. 2. And when his neighbor has reproved him and he returns, he will be saved and the one who reproved him will be awarded eternal life. 3. But if a man who is in need sees his benefactor sinning and does not reprove him, he will be judged with an evil judgment. 4. And if a blind man leads a blind man, both will fall into a pit. 5. And whoever shows partiality and whoever receives partiality will both be judged with a single judgment. 6. As the prophet said, 'Woe to those who show partiality, who justify the sinner for a bribe, whose stomach is their god.'[10] 7. Consider how it is with the judgment! 8. For truly I say to you, in that day I will neither fear the rich nor have pity on the poor.

48, 1. "If you see a sinner, reprove him between yourself and him. 2. But if he does not listen to you take up to three others with you and teach your brother. 3. If he again does not listen to you, set him before you as a Gentile and a tax-collector.

49, 1. **<ETH>** "If you hear of a matter, do not believe anything against your brother and do not slander and do not love the word of slander. 2. For as it is written, 'Let your ear not listen to anything against your brother.'[11] 3. But only if you have seen, reprove him, instruct him, and convert him."

10 It is likely that the author invented this citation.
11 It is likely that the author invented this citation.

4. And we said to him, "Lord, you have taught us and warned us in every way. 5. But, Lord, among the believers, those among them who truly believe the preaching of your name, will there really be division and strife and jealousy and quarreling and hatred and slander among them? 6. For you have said, 'They will reprove one another, and they shall show no partiality to those who sin and who hate the one who reproves them.'"

7. And he answered and said to us, "Why then will the judgment take place? 8. So that the wheat may be put into its barns and its chaff put onto the fire!"

50, 1. "So they hate the one who loves me and who reproves those who do not keep my commandments, and they will be hated and persecuted and despised and mocked. 2. And they will speak what is untrue, taking counsel and conspiring together against those who love me. 3. And these will reprove them so that they may be saved, but those who reprove them and instruct them and warn them they will hate and ostracize and scorn, and those who wish to do good to them will be prevented. 4. But those who endure will be witnesses before the Father, for they were zealous for righteousness, and it was not with a zeal for corruption that they were zealous."

5. And we said to him, "So will this happen among us?"

6. And he said to us, "Do not fear what will not happen to many but to a few."

7. And we said to him, "Tell us how!"

8. And he said to us, "There will be strange teaching and strife, and they will desire their own glory, putting forward unprofitable teaching, and there will be a deadly stumbling-block within it. 9. And they will teach and turn those who believed in me from my commandments and deprive them of eternal life. 10. But woe to those who falsify this my word and my commandments, and also to those who listen to them and who are far from the life of the teaching! 11. With them they will be eternally punished."

Ascension

51, 1. And when he had said this and finished speaking with us, he said to us again, "Behold, on the third day, at the third hour, the one who sent me will come so that I may go with him." 2. And as he spoke there was thunder and lightning and an earthquake, and the heavens were torn asunder, and a bright cloud came and took him. 3. And we heard the voice of many angels as they rejoiced and blessed and said, "Gather us, O priest, into the light of glory!" 4. And when he drew near to the firmament of heaven, we heard him saying, "Go in peace!"

5. In the name of our Lord Jesus Christ.

4

The First Letter of Clement (Selections)

Introduction and Translation by Mark DelCogliano

INTRODUCTION

The First Letter of Clement is an epistle addressed by the church in Rome to its counterpart in Corinth in response to an outbreak of factionalism there. In ancient sources it is ascribed to Clement, a leading figure of the church in Rome toward the end of the first century, but this attribution is now doubted. A late first-century date seems likely nonetheless, with most scholars placing the letter between 80 and 100 CE, and some more precisely in the mid-90s. *The First Letter of Clement* is thus one of the earliest extant Christian writings, as old as some of the documents that were later incorporated into the New Testament. It was greatly esteemed and extensively read in early Christianity; as late as the fourth century it was even regarded by some as part of the New Testament canon. Since the seventeenth century it has been included in the collection of early Christian writings known as the Apostolic Fathers.

In the course of its admonition to the Corinthians the letter bears witness to early Christian reflection on Christ. In particular, the letter spells out the ethical implications and obligations of Christ's advent, suffering, death, and resurrection for the Christian community in its quest for peace and harmony. In the excerpts translated below, Christ's suffering and death are viewed as an offer of salvation through repentance (7–8) and an act of divine love (49–50). Christ himself is seen as a model of humility (16). The significance of the resurrection for Christians is elaborated and proofs for its possibility are offered (24–26). Jesus is presented as the means to salvation by conformity to the divine will through unity and mutual service (35–38). The letter also provides several examples of early Christian use of *testimonia*, passages from the Septuagint that are applied to Christ in an effort to interpret and understand more deeply his life, death, and resurrection.

The translations here are based upon the edition of Michael W. Holmes, *The Apostolic Fathers*, 3rd ed. (Grand Rapids: Baker Academic, 2007), in consultation with the edition of Bart D. Ehrman, *The Apostolic Fathers I*, Loeb Classical Library 24 (Cambridge, MA: Harvard University Press, 2003).

TRANSLATION

7, 1. We write these things, beloved ones, not only to admonish you, but also to remind ourselves. For we are in the same arena and the same contest lies before us. 2. Therefore, let us forsake empty and futile thoughts, and come to the renowned and revered rule of our tradition. 3. Let us also realize what is good, what is pleasing, and what is acceptable in the sight of the one who made us. 4. Let us fix our gaze on the blood of Christ, and understand how precious it is to his Father, because having been poured out for our salvation it offered the grace of repentance to the whole world. 5. Let us review all the generations and learn that in every generation the Master gave an opportunity for repentance to those who desire to return to him. 6. Noah proclaimed repentance, and those who heeded were saved.[1] 7. Jonah proclaimed a catastrophe to the Ninevites, and those who repented of their sins appeased God by their supplications and received salvation, even though they had been strangers to God.[2]

8, 1. The ministers of God's grace spoke about repentance through the Holy Spirit, 2. and indeed the Master of all things himself spoke about repentance with an oath, "As I myself live, says the Lord, I do not desire the death of the sinner but rather his repentance."[3] And to this he added good advice:

3. Repent, house of Israel, from your lawlessness.
Say to the children of my people:
"Even if your sins stretch from the earth to heaven
and even if they are redder than scarlet
and blacker than sackcloth,
but you return to me with your whole heart and say, 'Father,'
I will listen to you as a holy people."[4]

1 See Gen 6–9. 2 Jon 3:4–9. 3 See Ezek 33:11.
4 Quoted from an unknown source, possibly an apocryphal work attributed to Ezekiel.

4. And in another place he speaks in this way:

> Wash yourselves and become clean;
> remove the evils from your souls before my eyes;
> cease from your evil deeds;
> learn to do good;
> seek out judgment;
> rescue the wronged;
> defend the orphan;
> and grant justice to the widow.
> And come, and let us discuss it, says the Lord:
> even if your sins are like crimson,
> I will make them white like snow,
> and even if they are like scarlet,
> I will make them white like wool.
> And if you are willing and listen to me,
> you shall eat the good things of the land,
> but if you are not willing and do not listen to me,
> the dagger shall devour you.
> For the mouth of the Lord has spoken these things.[5]

5. So then, desiring all his beloved ones to have a share of repentance, he established it by his almighty will.

* * *

16, 1. For Christ belongs to those who are humble, not to those who exalt themselves over his flock. 2. The scepter of God's majesty, our Lord Jesus Christ, did not come in a bustle of arrogance and pride (though he could have), but in humility, just as the Holy Spirit spoke about him. 3. For it says:

> Lord, who believed our report?
> And to whom was the arm of the Lord revealed?
> We made our announcement before him:
> he was like a child, like a root in thirsty land.
> He has no form or glory,
> and we saw him, and he had no form or beauty.
> Instead his form was without honor,

5 Isa 1:16–20.

eclipsed by the form of others.
He was a person familiar with blows and toil,
and knew how to bear affliction.
For his face is turned away;
he was dishonored and held to be of no account.

4. This one bears our sins and suffers pain for us,
and we accounted him to be familiar with toil, blows, and
ill-treatment.

5. He was wounded because of our sins
and afflicted because of our transgressions.
The punishment that brings our peace was upon him;
by his bruise we were healed.

6. We all went astray like sheep;
each one went astray on his own path.

7. And the Lord delivered him up for our sins.
And he did not open his mouth throughout his ill-treatment;
like a sheep he was led to the slaughter,
and like a lamb is silent before its shearer,
so he does not open his mouth.
In his humiliation his judgment was taken away.

8. Who shall describe his generation?
For his life was taken away from the earth.

9. Because of the transgressions of my people he came to death.

10. And I will exchange the wicked for his burial
and the rich for his death,
for he committed no transgression,
nor was deceit found in his mouth.
And the Lord desires to cleanse him of his blows.

11. If you give an offering for sin,
your soul will see a long-lived offspring.

12. And the Lord wants to take away the toil of his soul,
to show him light and form him with understanding,
to justify one who is just who serves many well,
and he himself shall bear their sins.

13. Therefore, he will inherit many,
and he shall divide the spoils of the strong,
because his soul was delivered to death
and he was accounted among the transgressors.

14. And he bore the sins of many
and he was handed over because of their sins.[6]

15. And again he says:

But as for me, I am a worm and not a human being,
the butt of humanity and the laughingstock of the people.

16. All who saw me mocked me;
they spoke with their lips and wagged their head:
"He hoped in the Lord; let him rescue him,
and let him save him, because he delights in him."[7]

17. Do you see, beloved men, the model that he has given to us? For if the Lord was so humble, what should we ourselves do, seeing that through him we have come under the yoke of his grace?

* * *

24, 1. Let us consider, beloved ones, how the Master continually shows us that there will be a future resurrection, of which he made the Lord Jesus the first fruit by resurrecting him from the dead.[8] 2. Let us contemplate, beloved ones, the resurrection that happens routinely. 3. Day and night reveal a resurrection to us: the night falls asleep and the day is resurrected; the day departs and night returns. 4. Let us ponder the crops: how and in what way does the sowing take place? 5. The sower goes out and throws each of the seeds into the earth. Since they are dry and bare they decay when they fall to the earth. But then the majesty of the Master's providence raises them up out of their decay, and from the one seed many grow and bear fruit.

25, 1. Let us reflect on the incredible sign that occurs in the eastern regions, that is, in the vicinity of Arabia. 2. There is a bird called a phoenix, a one-of-a-kind bird who lives five hundred years. When it has reached the point of dissolution by death it builds a nestlike tomb for itself out of

6 Isa 53:1–12. 7 Ps 21(22):7–9. 8 See 1 Cor 15:20.

frankincense, myrrh, and all the other spices. When its days have come to an end, it enters into the nestlike tomb and dies. 3. As its flesh decays, a worm is born, which by feeding on the ooze of the dead animal sprouts wings. Then upon reaching maturity it takes possession of the nestlike tomb that has the bones of its precursor, and picking them up travels from Arabia to Egypt, to the city called Heliopolis. 4. During the day, with all watching, it flies to the altar of the sun, places the bones there, and starts its return. 5. Then the priests scrutinize the chronological records and discover that it has come after five hundred years have passed.

26, 1. So then, do we think it is a great and wonderful thing if the Creator of all things brings about the resurrection of those who have served him in a holy way with the confidence born of good faith, when he shows us the magnificence of his promise even through a bird? 2. For he says somewhere, "And you will raise me up and I will praise you,"[9] and, "I lay down and slept; I arose, because you are with me."[10] 3. And again Job says, "And you will resurrect this flesh of mine, which has endured all these things."[11]

* * *

35, 1. How blessed and wonderful are the gifts of God, beloved ones! 2. Life in immortality, splendor in righteousness, truth in boldness, faith in confidence, self-control in holiness! And all these things fall within the scope of our mind. 3. So then, what things are being prepared for those who persevere? The Creator and Father of the ages, the All-Holy One himself, knows their quantity and their beauty. 4. So then, let us strive to be found in the number of those who persevere,[12] so that we may share in the gifts he has promised. 5. How will this happen, beloved ones? If our mind is fixed on God through faith, if we seek out what is pleasing and acceptable to him, if we accomplish what reflects his blameless will and follow the path of truth, jettisoning from ourselves all wrongdoing and transgression, greed, strife, malice and deceit, gossip and slander, hatred of God, pride and arrogance, vainglory and inhospitality. 6. For those who do these things are hateful to God – and not only those who do them, but also those who approve of them. 7. For the scripture says,

9 See Ps 27(28):7. 10 Ps 3:6. 11 Job 19:26.
12 Here we omit *auton* with Ehrman.

God said to the sinner:
"Why do you recite my statutes
and take my covenant on your lips,

8. you who despised instruction
and cast my words behind you?
If you saw a thief, you joined him,
and with adulterers you threw in your lot.
Your mouth multiplied evil,
and your tongue slipped in deceitfulness.
You sat and slandered your brother,
and you placed a stumbling-block
in the way of your own mother's son.

9. These things you did, and I kept silent;
you assumed, transgressor, that I would be like you.

10. I will convict you and bring you face-to-face with yourself.

11. Mark this, you who forget God,
lest he seize you like a lion,
and there be no one to rescue you.

12. A sacrifice of praise will glorify me,
and by this path I will show him God's salvation."[13]

36, 1. This is the path, beloved ones, on which we find our salvation, Jesus Christ, the high priest of our offerings,[14] the champion and helper of our weakness. 2. Through him we gaze into the heights of the heavens; through him we behold as in a mirror his blameless and supreme countenance;[15] through him the eyes of our heart have been opened; through him our clueless and clouded mind revives into the light; through him the Master has willed us to taste immortal knowledge. As radiance of his majesty he is greater than the angels by as much as the name he has inherited is more excellent.[16] 3. For thus it is written, "He who makes his angels spirits and his ministers tongues of fire."[17] 4. And the Master said the following in reference to the Son, "You are my Son; today I have begotten you. Ask from me, and I will bequeath you the nations as your inheritance, and the ends

13 Ps 49(50):16–23. 14 See Heb 4:14. 15 See 2 Cor 3:18.
16 See Heb 1:3–4. 17 Ps 103(104):4; 1 Cor 15:25; Heb 1:7.

of the earth as your possession."[18] 5. And again he says to him, "Sit on my right, until I make your enemies a footstool under your feet."[19] 6. So then, who are his enemies? Those who are wicked and oppose his will.

37, 1. So then – men, brothers – let us serve as soldiers with all diligence for his blameless regulations. 2. Let us consider those who serve our leaders as soldiers, how orderly, how promptly, how submissively they execute orders. 3. Not all are generals,[20] nor lieutenants,[21] nor centurions,[22] nor squadron commanders,[23] and so on, but each in his own rank[24] executes the orders given by the king and the leaders. 4. The high in rank cannot exist without the low, nor the low without the high. All of them combine together, as it were, and there is a connection between them. 5. Ponder our body: the head is nothing without the feet; so too are the feet nothing without the head. Our body's lowest members are indispensable and beneficial for the whole body, but all of them breathe together and subject themselves to a single member so that the whole body can be preserved.[25]

38, 1. So then, let our whole body be preserved in Christ Jesus, and let each subject himself to his neighbor, in accordance with how he has been established in his spiritual gift. 2. The strong must not ignore the weak, and the weak must respect the strong. The rich must provide for the poor, and the poor must give thanks to God because he has given him someone through whom his needs can be satisfied. The wise must show his wisdom not in words but in good deeds. The humble must not vouch for himself, but allow another to vouch for him. The pure must remain so in the flesh and not brag, knowing that it is another who provides him with self-control. 3. So then, brothers, let us figure out from what sort of material we came into existence, who and what sort of people we were upon our entry into the world, from what sort of tomb and darkness our Fashioner and Creator brought us into his world, after preparing his benefaction in advance before we were born. 4. So then, with all these things from him in our possession we ought in every way to give thanks to him, to whom be the glory for ever and ever. Amen.

* * *

18 Ps 2:7–8; Heb 1:5. 19 Ps 109(110):1; Heb 1:13.

20 In Greek, *eparchoi*, or "eparches," a term often used for Roman prefects.

21 In Greek, *chiliarchoi*, or "chiliarchs," a term often used for Roman military tribunes who commanded a thousand soldiers.

22 In Greek, *hekatontarchoi*, who commanded one hundred soldiers.

23 In Greek, *pentēkontarchoi*, who commanded fifty soldiers.

24 See 1 Cor 15:23. 25 See 1 Cor 12:14–26.

49, 1. Anyone in possession of love in Christ should do what Christ commands. 2. Who can describe the bond of God's love? 3. Who has what it takes to declare the magnificence of its beauty? 4. The height to which love elevates is beyond description. 5. Love binds us to God; love covers a multitude of sins;[26] love bears all things and endures all things.[27] There is nothing crude in love, nothing arrogant. Love has no faction; love sows no discord; love does everything in harmony. In love all God's elect were perfected. Without love nothing is pleasing to God. 6. In love the Master gained us. Because of the love that he had for us, Jesus Christ, our Lord by God's will, gave his blood for us, his flesh for our flesh, and his life for our lives.

50, 1. Do you see, beloved ones, how love is a great and wonderful thing? How there is no describing its perfection? 2. Who is fit to be found in it, except those whom God deems worthy? So then, let us beg and beseech from his mercy, that we may be found blameless in love free of any human partiality. 3. All the generations from Adam until today are gone, but those perfected in love by God's grace have a place with the pious: they will be revealed at the visitation of Christ's kingdom. 4. For it is written, "Enter into the chambers ... for just a little while until my anger and wrath have passed,"[28] and I will remember a good day and "raise you from your graves."[29] 5. Blessed are we, beloved ones, if we follow God's commandments in the harmony of love, so that our sins may be forgiven through love. 6. For it is written, "Blessed are those whose transgressions were forgiven and whose sins were covered. Blessed is the man whose sin the Lord does not count, and in whose mouth is no deceit."[30] 7. This blessedness has come to those chosen by God through Jesus Christ our Lord, to whom be the glory for ever and ever. Amen.

26 See 1 Pet 4:8. 27 See 1 Cor 13:7. 28 Isa 26:20. 29 Ezek 37:12. 30 Ps 31(32):1–2.

5

Ignatius of Antioch, *Letters* (Selections)

Introduction and Translation by Mark DelCogliano

INTRODUCTION

Ignatius, bishop of Antioch in Syria, penned seven letters while being escorted under guard to Rome for execution during the reign of Trajan (98–117 CE). No explicit evidence confirms that he reached the imperial capital, but there is no reason to doubt the tradition that he was martyred there. These letters illuminate numerous aspects of early Christian life and thought, providing as well insight into their author's concerns. Since the seventeenth century these letters have been included in the collection of early Christian writings known as the Apostolic Fathers. Three matters above all repeatedly surface in these letters: (1) Ignatius's struggle against those whose teaching differed from his own; (2) his pleas for the unity of the church by communion with and obedience to the bishop; and (3) his own suffering and impending death and their meaning, which he interprets in Christological categories.

For Ignatius, the greatest threat to the church is false teachers within it rather than hostile pagans outside of it, teachers whose interpretation of the Christian message he deems distorted because it is divisive. Scholars debate the precise identity of the group or groups censured by Ignatius; perhaps he is railing against certain tendencies rather than clearly demarcated sects. In any event, he rebukes those who profess to be disciples of Jesus while living according to Jewish law and those who deny the reality of Jesus's humanity, claiming that he only appeared to be so – figures whom later tradition would polemically label "Judaizers" and "docetists," respectively.

The excerpts translated below contain some of the key Christological passages in Ignatius's letters, thereby providing a valuable sample of early Christian reflection on Christ. In them he hints at the meaning and significance of

Jesus's birth, baptism, anointing, suffering, death, and resurrection, as well as his flesh, the cross, salvation, and eternal life, without ever examining them in any detail. One of the striking features of Ignatius's letters is his lack of hesitation in confessing Jesus Christ as God (see *Ephesians* 7.2, 18.2; *Trallians* 7.1; and *Smyrnaeans* 1.1). There are several explicitly anti-docetic passages in which Ignatius affirms the reality of Jesus's flesh and blood, his human descent from David, his birth from Mary (and her virginity), as well as the historical and fleshly reality of his suffering, death, and resurrection, and their unfolding in the time of Pontius Pilate, including the embodied existence of Jesus after the resurrection (see, e.g., *Magnesians* 11; *Trallians* 10; and *Smyrnaeans* 2–3). On numerous occasions he offers anti-docetic statements of Christological belief that are creed-like and hymnic (see *Ephesians* 7.2 and 18.2; *Trallians* 9.1; *Smyrnaeans* 1.1–2; and *Polycarp* 3.2). In these selections, Ignatius also provides a glimpse into his struggles with his suffering and impending death, as he attempts to divine their meaning by analyzing them in Christological terms as an imitation of the suffering of Jesus so as to become his true disciple; he holds that a docetic view of Christ would render his own suffering and death meaningless (see *Smyrnaeans* 4.2).

The translations here are based upon the edition of Michael W. Holmes, *The Apostolic Fathers*, 3rd ed. (Grand Rapids: Baker Academic, 2007), in consultation with the edition of Bart D. Ehrman, *The Apostolic Fathers I*, Loeb Classical Library 24 (Cambridge, MA: Harvard University Press, 2003). The numbering of the sections follows Holmes.

TRANSLATION

Letter to the Ephesians 7–9 and 16–19

7, 1. For some are in the habit of bearing around the name with evil cunning, doing other things unworthy of God. You must shun them as wild beasts. For they are rabid dogs who bite without warning. You must guard against them since they are hard to heal. 2. There is one physician, fleshly and spiritual, begotten and unbegotten, God come in flesh,[1] true life in death, both from Mary and from God, first subject to suffering and then incapable of suffering, Jesus Christ our Lord.

1 See John 1:14. Here Ehrman is followed, *en sarki genomenos theos*. On the basis of other ancient witnesses Holmes has *en anthrōpōi theos*, "God in a human being."

8, 1. So then, let no one deceive you, just as you are not deceived, since you belong wholly to God. For when no strife that can torment you is established among you, then you are living in accord with God. I am your humble servant, and I dedicate myself on behalf of you Ephesians, a church renowned for the ages. 2. The fleshly cannot do spiritual things nor the spiritual fleshly things,[2] just as faith cannot do what belongs to faithlessness nor faithlessness what belongs to faith. But even what you do according to the flesh is spiritual. For you do everything in Jesus Christ.

9, 1. I have learned that some people with evil teaching have passed through there.[3] You did not allow them to sow it among you, having blocked your ears to avoid receiving what is sown by them. For you are stones of a temple, prepared beforehand for the edifice of God the Father, borne up to the heights by the crane of Jesus Christ, which is the cross, using the Holy Spirit as a cable. And your faith is your hoist, and your love is the path that bears you up to God. 2. So then, you are all fellow travelers, God-bearers and temple-bearers, Christ-bearers, bearers of holy things, adorned in every way with the commandments of Jesus Christ. I too celebrate with you, because I have been deemed worthy, through this letter I am writing, to converse and rejoice together with you, because you love nothing in human life except God alone.

* * *

16, 1. Do not be led astray, my brothers! Those who corrupt households will not inherit the kingdom of God![4] 2. So then, if those who do these things in the flesh die, how much more [will someone die], if someone by evil teaching corrupts faith in God, on behalf of which Jesus Christ was crucified? Such a person, having become defiled, will depart into the inextinguishable fire; so too will anyone who listens to him.

17, 1. The reason the Lord received ointment upon his head[5] was so that he might breathe incorruptibility upon the church. Do not be anointed with the stench of the teaching of the ruler of this age, lest he sequester you away from the life set before you. 2. Why do we all not become wise by reception of the knowledge of God, which is Jesus Christ? Why do we foolishly perish by ignorance of the gift which the Lord has in fact sent?

2 See Rom 8:5 and 8:8. 3 That is, Ephesus. 4 See 1 Cor 6:9–10.
5 See Matt 26:7; Mark 14:3.

18, 1. My spirit is a humble servant of the cross, which is a stumbling-block for unbelievers[6] but salvation and eternal life to us. Where is the wise man? Where is the disputer?[7] Where is the boasting of those called clever? 2. For our God Jesus the Christ was conceived by Mary according to the plan[8] of God, from the seed of David and the Holy Spirit. He was born and baptized that he might cleanse the water by his suffering. **19,** 1. And the virginity of Mary and her childbearing escaped the notice of the ruler of this age; so too did the Lord's death – three mysteries to be cried aloud[9] that were accomplished in the stillness of God. 2. So then, how was he revealed to the ages?[10] A star shone in heaven that surpassed all the stars, and its light was indescribable, and its newness caused astonishment. All the other stars, together with the sun and the moon, formed a chorus around the star. It was overpowering; its light surpassed all of them. And there was a perplexity over the source of this newness that was unlike them. 3. Accordingly, all magic and every spell began to perish, ignorance caused by evil began to fade, and the ancient kingdom began to be razed [and] destroyed, when God appeared in a human way for the newness of eternal life. And what had been prepared by God received its beginning. From then on all things began to be set in commotion because the dissolution of death was being pursued.

*
* *

Letter to the Magnesians 8–11

8, 1. Do not be led astray by different beliefs[11] or by the ancient fables that are useless. For if we have been living until now according to Judaism, we are acknowledging that we have not received grace. 2. After all, the most divine prophets lived according to Christ Jesus. This is why they were persecuted, being inspired by his grace to make the disobedient fully convinced that there is one God who manifested himself through Jesus Christ his Son, who is his Word that came forth from the silence, who has in every way pleased the one who sent him.

6 See 1 Cor 1:23. 7 See 1 Cor 1:20.

8 In Greek, *oikonomian*, often translated "economy." The sense of the term in Ignatius is Pauline, signaling the divine plan of salvation (see Eph 1:10, 3:9) and the mystery of the redemptive incarnation.

9 Literally, "of a cry." 10 Or, "to the aeons." 11 In Greek, *heterodoxiais*.

9, 1. So then, if those who followed the ancient practices came to the newness of hope, no longer keeping the Sabbath, but living in accordance with the Lord's day, on which our life arose through him, and his death, which some deny, the mystery through which we have received faith – and the reason we endure is so that we may be found to be disciples of Jesus Christ, our only teacher – 2. how then will we be able to live apart from him when even the prophets, who were his disciples in the Spirit, expected him as a teacher? And this is why the one whom they righteously awaited raised them from the dead when he arrived.

10, 1. So then, we should not be insensible to his kindness. After all, if he were to imitate us in our actions, we would no longer exist! For this reason, having become his disciples, we should learn to live according to Christianity.[12] For anyone called by another name besides this one is not God's. 2. So then, lay aside the bad yeast, which has become old and sour, and turn to the new yeast, which is Jesus Christ. Be salted with him, so that no one among you becomes spoiled, for what you are will be exposed by your odor. 3. It is absurd to profess Jesus Christ and to practice Judaism. For Christianity did not believe in Judaism, but Judaism in Christianity, by which every believing tongue has been gathered to God.[13]

11 Now [I write] these things, my beloved ones, not because I have learned that any of you are like this. Rather, as someone who is less than you, I want to warn you in advance not to get caught on the fishhooks of pointless opinion but to be fully convinced of the birth and the suffering and the resurrection that took place in the time of Pontius Pilate's governorship – these things have really and certainly been done by Jesus Christ, our hope, from which may none of you be turned away!

*
* *

Letter to the Trallians 6–11

6, 1. I exhort you, then – not I, but the love of Jesus Christ: nourish yourselves on Christian food alone, and abstain from the strange plant, which

12 In Greek, *christianismon*. This is the first appearance of the term "Christianity" in extant Christian literature, coined in opposition to "Judaism" (*ioudaismos*). See also Ignatius, *Romans* 3.1, *Philadelphians* 6.1, and *Magnesians* 10.3.

13 See Isa 66:18.

is factionalism.[14] 2. In a show of trustworthiness these people mingle Jesus Christ with themselves, like those who offer deadly poison mixed with honeyed wine, which the unsuspecting person gladly[15] takes with pernicious pleasure then dies. **7,** 1. So then, guard against such people. You can do this if you are not proud and remain inseparable from [our] God Jesus Christ,[16] the bishop, and the commands of the apostles. 2. Whoever is within the sanctuary is pure but whoever is outside the sanctuary is not pure; that is, whoever does anything apart from the bishop, the presbytery, and the deacons is not pure in his conscience.

8, 1. It is not that I have learned of any such thing among you, but I am forewarning you who are my beloved ones and I foresee the snares of the devil. So then, you should take up meekness and renew yourselves both in faith, which is the flesh of the Lord, and in love, which is the blood of Jesus Christ. 2. None of you should bear a grudge against a neighbor. Give the Gentiles no opportunities, lest the majority of the godly congregation be blasphemed because of a few fools. For woe to the one through whose foolishness "my name is blasphemed" before them![17]

9, 1. So then, be deaf whenever anyone speaks to you apart from Jesus Christ, who was from the stock of David, who was from Mary, who was really born, who both ate and drank, who was really persecuted in the time of Pontius Pilate, who was really crucified and died with those in heaven and on earth and under the earth watching.[18] 2. He also was really raised from the dead when his Father raised him, just as,[19] in accord with this pattern, his Father will also raise us in Christ Jesus in the same way, we who believe in him. Apart from him we do not possess true life.

10 And if it is true, as some who are godless[20] (that is, unbelievers) say, that he only appeared to have suffered[21] – it is they themselves who only appear! – then why am I in chains? Why too do I pray to fight with

14 In Greek, *hairesis*. Ignatius does not use this term in the sense of "false teaching" or "heresy" opposed to orthodox teaching, as it would later connote, but to describe those whose teaching causes disunity and division into factions.

15 In Greek, *ēdeōs*. Here the ancient manuscripts and Ehrman are followed. Holmes's edition employs an emendation, *adeōs*, "without fear."

16 Here Ehrman is followed rather than Holmes, who omits "God" (*theou*).

17 See Isa 52:5.

18 See Phil 2:10.

19 Here we read *hōs* instead of *hos* with some ancient manuscripts.

20 In Greek, *atheoi*, or "atheists."

21 In Greek, *to dokein peponthenai auton*. The expression *to dokein*, "to appear," is the source of the label "docetism."

wild beasts? I am dying in vain then! Even more, I am in error about the Lord!

11, 1. So then, flee the evil offshoots that produce deadly fruit. If anyone were to taste it, he dies immediately. For these people are not the Father's planting. 2. If they were, they would show themselves to be branches of the cross and their fruit would be immortal, the same cross through which by his suffering he summons you who are his members. So then, a head cannot come to exist apart from its members, since God promises unity, which he himself is.

*

* *

Letter to the Smyrnaeans 1–8

Ignatius, also called God-bearer, sends abundant greetings in the blameless spirit and the word of God to the church of God the Father and his beloved Jesus Christ at Smyrna in Asia, which by his mercy is endowed with every charism, filled with faith and love, not lacking any charism, most fit for God, and a bearer of holy things.

1, 1. I glorify Jesus Christ, the God who has made you so wise. For I understand that you have been confirmed in an unshakeable faith, as if nailed to the cross of the Lord Jesus Christ in both flesh and spirit, and that you have been established in love by the blood of Christ, totally convinced regarding our Lord, who was really of the stock of David according to the flesh,[22] Son of God according to the will and power [of God], who was really born of a virgin, who was baptized by John so that all righteousness might be fulfilled by him,[23] 2. who under Pontius Pilate and Herod the Tetrarch was really nailed in the flesh for us (from its fruit we come to be, that is, from his divinely blessed suffering) so that he could raise a signal[24] for the ages through his resurrection for his holy and faithful ones, whether among Jews or among Gentiles, in the one body of his church. **2** For he suffered all these things for us, so that we might be saved. And he really suffered just as he also really raised himself. It is not as certain unbelievers say, that he only appeared to have suffered – it is they themselves who only appear! Indeed, it will turn out for them just as they think, and be bodiless and daemonic.

22 See Rom 1:3. 23 See Matt 3:15.

24 See Isa 5:26. The "signal" is the cross. Here Ignatius is following an earlier exegetical tradition which sees the cross as uniting Jews and Gentiles. See also Eph 2:16, which is based on the same tradition.

3, 1. For my part, I know and believe that he was in the flesh even after the resurrection. 2. And when he came to those with Peter, he said to them, "Lay your hands upon me, feel me, and see that I am not a bodiless daemon."[25] And immediately they touched him and believed, having been merged with his flesh and blood. This is why they came to despise death, and indeed were found to be beyond death.[26] 3. And after the resurrection he ate and drank with them just as a fleshly person would,[27] even though he was spiritually united to the Father.

4, 1. Now I am recommending these things to you, beloved ones, even though I am well aware that you are of the same mind. I am guarding you in advance from the wild beasts in human form. Not only must you refrain from receiving them but, if possible, you must not even meet them. Only pray for them, that they may somehow repent – a difficult thing indeed! But Jesus Christ, our true life, has the power to do this. 2. For if it only appears that these things were done by our Lord, then it only appears that I am bound in chains! Why then have I delivered myself to death, to fire, to sword, to wild beasts? But to be near the sword is to be near God. To be with the wild beasts is to be with God. Only in the name of Jesus Christ! It is to suffer with him that I endure all things, since he himself, who is the perfect human being, empowers me.

5, 1. Some people deny him out of ignorance, or rather, they have been denied by him, since they are advocates of death rather than of truth. Neither the prophecies nor the law of Moses has persuaded them; then again, until now neither has the gospel nor our individual sufferings. 2. Indeed they think the same about us. For how does it benefit me if someone praises me but blasphemes my Lord by not confessing that he was a flesh-bearer? Whoever does not admit this denies him completely and is a corpse-bearer.[28] 3. Their disbelieving names didn't seem to me worth recording. In fact, I don't even want to remember them until they repent of their view of the suffering, which is our resurrection. **6,** 1. Let no one be led astray. Judgment is passed even upon the heavenly beings, and the glory of the angels, and the rulers, both visible and invisible, if they do not believe in the blood of Christ. Let the one who can accept this accept it. No leadership position

25 See Luke 24:39. 26 That is, they were willing to submit to martyrdom.

27 See Luke 24:41–43; John 21:5, 21:13.

28 In Greek, *sarkophoron* … *nekrophoron*, "flesh-bearer … corpse-bearer." Anyone who denies the reality of Christ's flesh will be deprived of the resurrection and thus be a "corpse-bearer" rather than experience eternal life.

should make anyone proud. For all that matters is faith and love, to which nothing is to be preferred.

2. Be aware of those with different beliefs[29] about the grace of Jesus Christ that has come to us, how they are opposed to the purpose of God. Love is no concern of theirs, nor are the widowed, nor the orphaned, nor the oppressed, nor the imprisoned or the released, nor the hungry or thirsty. They avoid the Eucharist and the [common] prayer because they do not confess that the Eucharist is the flesh of our Savior Jesus Christ,[30] which suffered for our sins,[31] which the Father by his kindness raised. **7,** 1. So then, those who dispute the gift of God perish as they squabble. Now it would be best for them to love, so that they may also be resurrected. 2. It is fitting, then, to avoid such people and not to speak about them either privately or publicly, and instead to focus on the prophets and especially the gospel, in which the suffering is disclosed to us and the resurrection perfected.

8, 1. Flee divisions as the source of evils. All should follow the bishop just as Jesus Christ followed the Father, and all should follow the presbytery as if they were the apostles. Respect the deacons as the commandment of God. No one should do anything that concerns the church apart from the bishop. That Eucharist should be considered valid which is under the bishop or his trustee. 2. The congregation should be in that place wherever the bishop appears, just as the catholic church is in that place wherever Jesus Christ is.[32] Neither baptizing nor holding the love feast is permitted apart from the bishop. But whatever he approves is also pleasing to God, so that everything you do may be sound and valid.

*

* *

Letter to Polycarp 3

3, 1. Do not allow those who appear trustworthy but teach differently[33] to bedazzle you. Remain steadfast like an anvil being struck. A great athlete

29 See Ignatius, *Magnesians* 8.1. 30 See 1 John 4:2–3. 31 See 1 Cor 15:3.

32 In Greek, *katholikē*. This is the first time in extant Christian literature that the adjective "catholic" is applied to the church. Ignatius uses the term in the sense of "universal" or "whole" to indicate that the church should not be divided, not in the later sense of "orthodox" in opposition to heresy.

33 See Ignatius, *Magnesians* 8.1 and *Smyrnaeans* 6.2.

gets thrashed but triumphs. But it is especially for God that we must endure everything so that he may also endure us. 2. Be more eager than you are. Note the times. Await the one who is beyond time, who is timeless, who is invisible, who for our sakes became visible, who cannot be touched, who is incapable of suffering, who for our sakes became subject to suffering, who in every way endured for our sakes.

6

Epistle to Diognetus 1 and 7–12

Introduction and Translation by Mark DelCogliano

INTRODUCTION

This anonymous letter to the otherwise unknown Diognetus is an early Christian apology in epistolary form. Since the seventeenth century it has been included in the collection of early Christian writings known as the Apostolic Fathers. Most scholars suggest a date between 150 and 200 for its composition – that is, at least for sections 1–10. The original text breaks off before its conclusion, and sections 11–12 were apparently appended at a later date from some other work. Sections 1–10 are addressed to an inquirer who wants to learn more about Christianity, whereas sections 11–12 appeal to Gentile converts to Christianity. The apologetic intent of the epistle is evident from its first part where the author mocks paganism and Judaism, emphasizing instead the distinctiveness and superiority of Christianity in terms of way of life (sections 2–6). In addition to section 1, translated below are sections 7–12. In sections 7–10 the author explicates the role of Christ in God's plan of salvation. Particular stress is placed on the necessity of acquiring the knowledge of God revealed by Christ and the moral obligation that it entails, which is described as imitating God. Sections 11–12 cover much the same ground but in a different manner and register, and they include a figurative interpretation of the trees of knowledge and life from the account of the garden of Eden in Genesis 2–3. In the course of its account of the divine plan of salvation this apology provides us with a valuable witness to early Christian reflection on the person and work of Christ.

The translation here is based upon the edition of Michael W. Holmes, *The Apostolic Fathers*, 3rd ed. (Grand Rapids: Baker Academic, 2007), in consultation with the edition of Bart D. Ehrman, *The Apostolic Fathers II*, Loeb Classical Library 25 (Cambridge, MA: Harvard University Press, 2003).

TRANSLATION

1 Since I see, most excellent Diognetus, that you are very eager to learn the Christians' piety toward God and are asking quite articulate and thoughtful questions about them – what God they believe in and how they worship him, whereby all of them spurn the world and scorn death, neither accepting those deemed gods by the Greeks nor observing the superstition of the Jews; what affection they have for one another; and precisely why this new race or way of life has come into the world now and not earlier – I applaud you for your enthusiasm, and I beg of God, who empowers us both to speak and to listen, that it be granted to me to speak in such a way that you become the best you can be after listening to me and that it be granted to you to listen in such a way that I won't be disheartened after speaking to you.

* * *

7, 2. ... [T]he truly all-powerful, all-creating, and invisible God himself established among human beings the truth and the holy and incomprehensible Word from the heavens and implanted it in their hearts, by having sent to human beings not, as one might imagine, some servant or an angel or a ruler or a manager of earthly affairs or someone entrusted with the administration of things in heaven, but rather the very Artificer and Creator of the universe, by whom he created the heavens, by whom he enclosed the sea within its proper boundaries, whose mysteries all the elements faithfully observe, from whom the sun has received the distances of the courses it is to follow each day, whom the moon obeys when he commands it to shine at night, whom the stars obey as they follow the moon's course, by whom all things have been organized and set in order and assigned their place, the heavens and the things in the heavens, the earth and the things in the earth, the seas and the things in the sea, fire, air, the abyss, the things in the heights, the things in the depths, the things in between – this is the one whom he sent to them. 3. And yet, did he send him, as one might conjecture, to tyrannize, frighten, and terrify? 4. Absolutely not! It was rather in gentleness and meekness. He sent him as a king sends his son who is a king. He sent him as God. He sent him to human beings as a human being. He sent him to save human beings by persuading them, not by compelling them, for compulsion is not an attribute of God. 5. He sent him to call human beings, not to prosecute them. He sent him to love human beings, not to judge them. 6. For he will send him to judge them, and who will endure his arrival? <...>[1] 7. Do you not see how they are thrown to the wild beasts to get them to deny the Lord, and yet they are not conquered? 8. Do you not see that as more of them are punished, the more others swell their ranks? 9. These things do not appear to be human works; these things are the power of God; these things are signs of his arrival.

8, 1. Now has there ever been any human being who knew what God is before he came? 2. Or do you accept the vacuous and silly claims of the ever-so-trustworthy philosophers? Some of them say that God is fire (they call "God" the very thing they themselves will go to!), others water, and others another one of the elements created by God. 3. And yet, if any of these claims merits acceptance, then one could similarly declare every one of the remaining created things to be God. 4. But all this is the portentous nonsense and trickery of enchanters. 5. No human being has either seen or known him, but he is the one who revealed himself. 6. And he revealed himself through faith, the only way in which it is permitted to see God. 7. For God, the Master and Creator of the universe, who made all things and arranged them by rank, was not only benevolent but also patient. 8. Or rather, he has always been and is and will be like this: kind, good, unwrathful, and true; indeed, he alone is good. 9. And after conceiving a great and inexpressible thought, he shared it with his child alone. 10. So then, as long as he kept it hidden and guarded his wise plan, he seemed to have neither care nor concern for us. 11. But when he disclosed it through his beloved child and made known the things prepared from the beginning, he communicated everything to us at once, so that we might share in, see, and understand his good works. Who among us would ever have expected these things?

9, 1. So then, having already arranged all things by himself together with his child, as long as it was still the previous time, he allowed us, as we wished, to be carried away by our disordered impulses, led astray by our pleasures and desires. By no means did he revel in our sins, but he put up with them. Nor did he approve that former season of unrighteousness, but created the present age of righteousness, so that after we were convicted in the previous time by our own deeds as unworthy of life we might now come to be considered worthy by the goodness of God, and after we made it apparent that we are unable to enter into God's kingdom on our own

1 There is a lacuna in the text here, of unknown length.

he wanted us to become capable of doing so by the power of God. 2. And when our unrighteousness had reached the maximum and it had become perfectly clear that the reward it could expect was punishment and death, then came the season appointed by God to manifest at last his goodness and power – Oh, the surpassing benevolence and love of God! He neither hated, nor rejected, nor resented us. Instead he showed us patience and forbearance; in mercy he took our sins upon himself; he himself gave up his own Son as a ransom for us, the holy one for the lawless, the innocent one for the wicked, the just one for the unjust,[2] the incorruptible one for the corrupt, the immortal one for the mortal. 3. For what else could have covered our sins except his righteousness? 4. In whom could we who were lawless and impious be made righteous except in the Son of God alone? 5. Oh, the sweet exchange! Oh, the unfathomable creation! Oh, the unexpected kindnesses! To think that the lawlessness of many should be hidden by a single righteous person and the righteousness of a single person should make many lawless persons righteous! 6. So then, having proven that in the former time our nature was unable to achieve life, and having now shown that the Savior is able to save what lacks that capability, for both reasons he wanted us to believe in his goodness, to consider him our nurse, father, teacher, counselor, physician, mind, light, honor, glory, strength, and life, and not to worry about clothing and food.[3]

10, 1. If you too yearn for this faith, acquire first knowledge of the Father. 2. For he loved human beings, on account of whom he made the world, to whom he subjected all things on earth, to whom he gave reason, to whom he gave mind, whom alone he allowed to gaze up to heaven,[4] whom he fashioned out of his own image,[5] to whom he sent his only-begotten Son, to whom he promised the kingdom in heaven and will give it to those who love him. 3. And once you have acquired this knowledge, with what joy do you think you will be filled? Or how will you love the one who so loved you first? 4. Upon loving him you will become an imitator of his goodness. And do not be astonished if a human being can become an imitator of God. It is possible if God is willing. 5. For human flourishing is not a question of oppressing your neighbors, nor desiring to have more than those weaker than you, nor being wealthy and abusing those needier than you. In none of these ways can anyone imitate God, but these things are excluded from

2 See 1 Pet 3:18. 3 See Matt 6:25, 28, and 31.

4 Here Ehrman has "him" (*auton*) instead of "heaven" (*ouranon*). 5 See Gen 1:26–27.

his magnificence. 6. But whoever takes his neighbor's burden upon himself, who in his good fortune wants to benefit another who has suffered a loss, who provides what he has received from God to those in need, becoming a god for those who receive them – this one is an imitator of God. 7. Then even though you happen to be upon earth you will behold that God lives in the heavens; then you will begin to speak the mysteries of God; then you will both love and admire those being punished for not wanting to deny God; then you will denounce the world's deceit and error, when you comprehend the true life in heaven, when you despise what seems to be death here, when you fear the true death, which is reserved for those condemned to the eternal fire that will punish those consigned to it until the end; 8. then you will admire and bless those who endure the temporary fire for the sake of righteousness, when you understand that other fire …[6]

11, 1. The subject of my discussion is not strange, nor does my investigation proceed irrationally, but already a disciple of the apostles I am now becoming a teacher of the Gentiles. I worthily administer the traditions to those who are becoming disciples of truth. 2. For who has been rightly taught and acquired affection for the Word without seeking to learn in a clear manner the things openly divulged by the Word to his disciples? The Word disclosed these things to them when he appeared, speaking candidly. By unbelievers he was not understood, but he explained these things to his disciples, who being considered faithful by him came to know the mysteries of the Father. 3. For this reason he sent the Word, so that he might appear to the world. Though dishonored by the [chosen] people, he was preached by the apostles and believed in by the Gentiles. 4. This is the one who is from the beginning, who appeared to be recent but was found to be ancient and is always young when born in the hearts of the saints.[7] 5. This is the one who always exists, who today is considered Son, through whom the church is enriched and grace is spread out and multiplied among the saints. This grace bestows understanding, discloses mysteries, proclaims seasons, rejoices in believers, and is given to seekers, among whom the pledges of faith are not broken and the boundaries of the fathers not overstepped.[8] 6. Then the fear of the law is hymned, the grace of the prophets acknowledged, the faith of the gospels established, the tradition of the apostles

6 The original text breaks off here. What follows in sections 11–12 is a later addition.
7 There is a possible faint echo here of Plato, *Symposium* 195b–c and 178a–c.
8 See Prov 22:28.

guarded, and the grace[9] of the church leaps for joy. 7. If you do not grieve this grace,[10] you will understand what the Word is saying, through whomever he decides, whenever he wants. 8. For having been stirred by the will of the commanding Word to declare such things with much labor, out of love we are becoming sharers with you in what has been revealed to us.

12, 1. Once you have read these things and listened to them earnestly, you will know what God confers upon those who love him rightly, who have become a paradise of delight by making a blossoming tree bearing fruits of every kind spring up within themselves and being decorated with sundry fruits. 2. For in this place a tree of knowledge and a tree of life have been planted. But it is not the tree of knowledge that kills; rather, it is disobedience that kills. 3. For not without significance has it been written that from the beginning God planted a tree of knowledge and a tree of life in the midst of paradise,[11] indicating that life comes through knowledge. After those there from the beginning used this knowledge in an impure manner, they were stripped naked by the deceit of the serpent.[12] 4. For there is neither life apart from knowledge nor reliable knowledge apart from true life; this is why each tree has been planted near the other. 5. Having understood this meaning, the Apostle criticizes the knowledge practiced apart from the truth of the commandment that leads to life, saying, "Knowledge puffs up, but love builds up."[13] 6. For whoever claims to know something apart from the true knowledge confirmed by life knows nothing; he is deceived by the serpent, having not loved life. But whoever has come to know with fear and seeks life plants in hope, anticipating fruit. 7. Let your heart be knowledge, and your life be the true word that is accepted. 8. If you bear this tree [within yourself] and pluck its fruit, you will always reap the things desired in God's presence, things which the serpent cannot touch and deceit cannot defile. Nor is Eve corrupted, but a virgin is trusted. 9. And salvation is made known, apostles are given understanding, the Lord's passover proceeds, the seasons are gathered together and arranged with good order,[14] and as he teaches the saints, the Word rejoices, through whom the Father is glorified. To him be the glory for ever and ever. Amen.

9 Here we follow Ehrman in reading *charis* ("grace") instead of Holmes's *chara* ("joy").
10 See Eph 4:30. 11 See Gen 2:17, 3:24. 12 See Gen 3:7. 13 1 Cor 8:1.
14 Here we follow Ehrman in reading *kairoi* ("seasons") instead of Holmes's *klēroi* ("congregations"), as well as in omitting the *panta* ("all things") which Holmes inserts before *meta kosmou harmozetai* ("arranged with good order").

7

Justin Martyr, *First Apology* 23, 30–32, 46, 63 and *Second Apology* 10, 13

Introduction and Translation by Andrew Radde-Gallwitz

INTRODUCTION

Justin hailed from the city of Flavia Neapolis, the modern West Bank city of Nablus, in the Roman province of Syria Palestina. According to his own account in the *Dialogue with Trypho the Jew*, Justin became a professional philosopher of the Platonist school before adopting Christianity as the true philosophy. From his pen, we have a few surviving works: the *First* and *Second Apologies*, which some scholars believe to have been originally a single treatise, probably written in the first half of the 150s, and the *Dialogue with Trypho the Jew*, written perhaps around 160. He also wrote a refutation of Marcion, which has not survived. Since antiquity, the philosopher Justin who authored these texts has been identified with the Justin who was martyred in Rome, as described in the *Acts of Justin*. According to that text, Justin was a Christian philosopher who taught in the city of Rome for many years prior to his execution, perhaps in the middle of the 160s.

Translated here are Christologically significant passages from the *First Apology* and *Second Apology*. Justin addresses the *First Apology* to the emperor Antoninus Pius (r. 138–161) and his adopted sons Lucius and Verissimus, the latter a nickname for his successor, the Stoic philosopher Marcus Aurelius. In his *Meditations*, Marcus Aurelius praises Antoninus's philosophic disposition as a model he himself emulates (6.30). Justin presumes his addressees hold a moral commitment to philosophy. The goal of Justin's work is to defend Christianity against the charges brought against it, especially that of atheism. He notes that the same accusation had been laid at the feet of Socrates and other philosophers before Christ. For Justin, this is no mere coincidence. Drawing on what we know as the Gospel of John – Justin does not cite what we call New Testament texts by name – Justin identifies Jesus

Christ with the Logos, the divine Word or Reason, as Logos is translated here. And what are philosophers but devotees of reason? Justin assumes that there can only be one Reason, and it is that which humans, as rational animals, partake in. Hence, Justin maintains, all "those who have lived with reason are Christians," even though many have been dubbed "atheists" (46). He lists here both Greeks (Socrates and Heraclitus) and Jewish prophets. He maintains that philosophers, poets, and scholars prior to Christ were able to glimpse Reason partially and indistinctly. Arrayed against such persons there have always been those who lived without reason, and they have been spurred on in their hostility by the wicked demons, which Justin identifies with the Greek gods.

In addition to appealing to the emperor's dedication to philosophy, Justin appeals also to the idea of prophecy, which was of importance for Stoicism as well as for emerging Christianity. Justin spends a great deal of time in all his extant writings developing his argument for Christianity from prophecy. One can see why it matters for the task of the *Apologies*. For Justin, Reason is Son of the true God, which is present in humanity as the spermatic or seed-like reason, an originally Stoic doctrine. Suppose Antoninus and his sons accepted Justin's account of Reason (in fact, we have no idea whether they ever read or even received Justin's work). It remains to ask how one knows that Reason is to be identified with Jesus of Nazareth. For Justin, the grounds are supplied by prophecy. His task in much of his writings is to demonstrate that the events that occurred in connection with Jesus's life, death, and resurrection, as well as the history of the church after him, were foretold by the Jewish prophets. For Justin, the match between ancient prophecy and recent events demonstrates that Jesus is the Son of God, and this, we have seen, is what Reason is. The argument leaves Justin with another point he needs to explain. His account implies that the Jewish people, the very ones who preserved these prophetic books, misunderstand their own prophecies. In fact, according to Justin, Reason's advent not only was prophesied by Old Testament prophets; he actually appeared in various forms prior to his incarnation, including the appearance to Moses in the burning bush. For Justin, the inability to see Jesus as the one foretold was itself prefigured by Isaiah, who referred to Israel as an uncomprehending people, a text that the gospels present Jesus himself taking up. Thus, although the following passages represent only a portion of Justin's writings, they convey the heart of his account of Christ's significance as the incarnate divine Reason.

This translation is made from the critical edition by Denis Minns and Paul Parvis, *Justin, Philosopher and Martyr: Apologies*, Oxford Early Christian Texts (Oxford: Oxford University Press, 2009). I have not included their versification. Justin's work survives in only a single independent manuscript, which is the basis of the text edited by Prudentius Maran that appears in PG 6. In a few cases, noted below, the translation follows the PG rather than adopting the conjectures of Minns–Parvis.

TRANSLATION

First Apology

23. Now in order that this point[1] might now become apparent to you, we say that everything we have learned from Christ and the prophets who preceded him is alone true and older than all the writers who have ever been. And it is not because we say them that we think them worthy of being accepted by you; rather, because they are true, we say them. And Jesus Christ alone has been uniquely begotten by God as Son, existing as his Reason and firstborn and power; and when by his will he became a human being, he taught us these things for the transformation and restoration of the human race.[2]

* * *

30. Now there might be someone who objects to us: "What prevents it being true as well[3] that the one called 'Christ' by us, since he is a human being from human beings, performed the miracles that we claim by the magical art and seems for this reason to be a son of God?" To avoid this objection, we will now make a demonstration, not trusting those who make claims[4] but being of necessity persuaded by those who prophesy before events happen, because even with our own eyes we see events that have happened and

1 Justin gestures to the preceding paragraph, in which he has asserted that Jesus's birth as Son and Reason is unique and that, even in his human suffering, he is superior to the sons of Zeus. He says there that, although Jesus's deeds have already made the point intrinsically apparent, he will need to demonstrate it for his audience.

2 At this point, the remainder of chapter 23 and chapters 24–29 are omitted from the translation.

3 The objection refers back to Justin's account of Simon, Helen, and Menander in *First Apology* 26. According to Justin, they used magic to deceive people and asserted that they were gods. The imagined objector here asks why the same cannot be said of Christ.

4 That is, claim to be gods, as did Simon and Menander, according to *First Apology* 26.

are happening as prophesied, which we believe will appear to you as well as the greatest and truest demonstration.

31. So then, among the Jews there were certain people through whom the prophetic spirit announced in advance future events before they occurred. And when kings among the Jews succeeded to the throne, they spoke of these prophecies, which they had preserved just as they had been spoken when they were prophesied in their own Hebrew language, in books put together by the prophets themselves. But when Ptolemy, the king of the Egyptians, was constructing a library and trying to gather the writings of all peoples, he inquired about these prophecies too and sent to the one who then was ruling the Jews to request that the books of the prophecies be delivered by him, written in their Hebrew language, as mentioned above.[5] But since their written contents were not recognizable to the Egyptians, he again sent a request that people be dispatched to translate them into the Greek language. And when this happened, the books remained to the present day in their Egyptian location and are found everywhere with the Jews, who despite reading them do not understand what is said, but regard us as enemies and combatants, like you killing and punishing us whenever they can, as you yourselves can believe. In fact, during the recent Jewish war, Bar Kochba, the leader of the rebellion of Jews, ordered Christians, and them alone, to be carried off to horrendous punishments.

Now in the books of the prophets we have found that what has come to pass had been foretold: one born from a virgin who became a man and healed every disease and infirmity and raised the dead and was envied and unrecognized and crucified, Jesus our Christ, who died and rose again and ascended into heaven and is Son of God and is called thus and that there were some who were sent by him to the whole human race to proclaim these things and that it is people from the nations instead who would believe in him. But these things were prophesied before he appeared, first five thousand years prior, then three thousand years before, then two thousand, and again one thousand, and yet again eight hundred years before – for in generational succession new prophets succeeded older ones.

32. Moses, then, who was the first of the prophets, said the following verbatim: "A ruler will not fail from Judah nor a governor from his loins until

5 Caveat lector: Minns and Parvis have done a fair amount of conjectural reconstruction here. I accept their reading, for the reasons they give in their notes, but one should note that it departs significantly from the MS text, which includes an anachronistic reference to "Herod" as the king of the Jews in the third century BCE.

there comes the one for whom it is reserved, and he will be the one awaited by the nations, binding his colt to the vine, washing his robe in the blood of the grapes."[6] It falls to you, then, to examine accurately and to learn at what point there ceased being a ruler and king among the Jews of their own. It was at the point of the appearance of Jesus Christ, our teacher and expositor of the unrecognized prophets, as was foretold by the divine, holy, prophetic Spirit through Moses, "a ruler shall not fail from the Jews until there comes the one for whom the kingship is reserved." For Judah is forefather of the Jews, from whom they are called "Jews." And you, after [Christ's] appearance, have ruled over the Jews and have held sway over their entire land. Now the phrase, "He will be the one awaited by the nations," revealed that people from all the nations will await him who is coming again, which it is possible for you to see with your own eyes and to believe based on the facts, for from all races of humanity people await the one crucified in Judea, immediately after which the captive land of the Jews was handed over to you. And the phrase "binding his colt to the vine," and "washing his robe in the blood of the grape" was a sign indicative of the things that would happen to Christ and those done by him. For a donkey's colt stood tied to a vine along the entry to a village, and he commanded that his companions bring it to him. And when it was brought and he had mounted it, he sat upon it and entered into Jerusalem, where the greatest temple of the Jews was, which was later destroyed by you.[7] And after this he was crucified to fulfill the remainder of the prophecy. For "washing his robe in the blood of the grape" was a pre-announcement of the suffering which he was going to undergo, when through blood he would cleanse those who believe in him. Now what was called a "robe" by the divine Spirit through the prophet are those people who believe in him, among whom the seed from God dwells, which is Reason. The saying "blood of the grape" signified that the one who would appear will have blood, though not from human seed but rather from divine power. And after the Father of all and lord God, the first power and Son is Reason, who was made flesh and became a human being in some manner we will speak of in what follows. For just as it is not a human being but God that makes the blood of the grape, so too this blood was revealed as coming not from human seed but from the power of God, as we said above. And Isaiah, another prophet, prophesying the same things through different words, said as follows: "A star will rise from Jacob,"[8] "and a flower will shoot up from the

6 Gen 49:10–11. 7 See Matt 21:1–7; Luke 19:29–35. 8 Num 24:17.

root of Jesse,"[9] and "in his arm nations will place their hope."[10] And a luminous star has risen and a flower has shot up from the root of Jesse. This is Christ, for through a virgin who was from the seed of Jacob, who was father of Judah, who has been shown to be father of the Jews, he was born by the power of God. And in keeping with the oracle, Jesse, who was son of Jacob and of Judah by generational succession, became his forefather.[11]

* * *

46. Now lest some, in their senseless attempt[12] to overturn what is taught by us, say that, according to us, Christ was born 150 years ago, under Quirinius, and taught the things we say he taught at a later time under Pontius Pilate, and bring the accusation that all human beings who were born previously are not accountable, we shall preemptively resolve the difficulty. We have been taught, as we mentioned previously, that Christ is firstborn of God, being the Reason in which the whole race of human beings participates. And those who have lived with reason are Christians, even if they have been dubbed "atheists," for instance, among the Greeks, Socrates, Heraclitus, and those like them, and, among the barbarians, Abraham, Ananias, Azarias, Misael, Elijah, and many others, whose deeds or names we will leave off listing, since we know it would be tedious. Consequently too, those who came before and lived without Reason were useless[13] and enemies to Christ and murderers of those who lived with Reason, but those who have lived or do live with Reason are Christians and are fearless and undisturbed. But as to the reason why, through the power of Reason in accordance with the will of the Father of all and the lord God, he was born and given the name Jesus, and when he was crucified and died, he rose again and ascended into heaven, the intelligent person will be able to grasp from what has been said at such length.[14]

* * *

63. All Jews even now teach that the unnameable God spoke to Moses. This is why when the prophetic Spirit through Isaiah, the aforementioned

9 Isa 11:1. 10 Isa 51:5.
11 At this point, chapters 33–45 are omitted from the translation.
12 In Greek, *alogistainontes*, a hapax legomenon.
13 In Greek, *achrēstoi*, a word that approximates "Christless" (*achristoi*).
14 At this point the remainder of paragraph 46 and paragraphs 47–62 are omitted from the translation.

prophet, chided them, as we have already written, it said, "An ox knew its owner, and an ass the manger of its master. But Israel did not know me and the people did not heed me."[15] And when Jesus, the Christ, similarly chided them because the Jews did not know what the Father is and what the Son is, he too said, "No one has known the Father except the Son, nor [has anyone known] the Son except the Father and those to whom the Son reveals."[16] Now the Reason of God is his Son, as we have said. And he is called "angel" and "apostle," for he proclaims all that must be known and is sent to reveal all that is proclaimed, as the Lord himself also said, "Who hears me hears the one who sent me."[17] And this point will be made apparent also from the writings of Moses. It is said in them as follows: "And an angel of God spoke to Moses in a flame of fire from the bush. And it said, 'I am the one who is, God of Abraham, God of Isaac, God of Jacob, the God of your fathers. Go down into Egypt, and bring out my people.'"[18] If you wish, you can learn what follows after these, for it is impossible to record them all herein. But these statements came about as proof that Jesus the Christ is Son of God and apostle, being Reason formerly and appearing at that time in the form of fire, and in the other time in an incorporeal image, but now, when through the will of God on behalf of the human race he became a human being, he submitted even to suffer all that the demons wrought in his handling by the senseless Jews. These people, who have it said expressly in the writings of Moses – "And an angel of God spoke to Moses in a flame of fire in a bush and said, 'I am the one who is, the God of Abraham and the God of Isaac and the God of Jacob'[19] – say it is the Father and Maker of the universe[20] who said these things. This is why when the prophetic Spirit chided them, it said, "Israel did not know me and the people did not heed me."[21] And again, as we have shown, Jesus, when he was with them, said, "No one has known the Father except the Son, nor [has anyone known] the Son except the Father and those to whom the Son reveals."[22] So then, the Jews, because they think it is in every case the Father of the universe who spoke to Moses, although the one who spoke to him is the Son of God, who is called "angel" and "apostle," they are justly chided both through the prophetic Spirit and through Christ himself since they have not known the Father or the Son. For those who say that the Son

15 Isa 1:3. 16 See Matt 11:27; Luke 10:22. 17 See Luke 10:16.
18 Exod 3:2, 6, 10. 19 Exod 3:2, 6. 20 See Plato, *Timaeus* 28c3–4.
21 See Isa 1:3. 22 See Matt 11:27; Luke 10:22.

is Father are chided for not knowing the Father and not realizing that he is Son of the Father of the universe, who being firstborn Reason of God, also *is* God. And previously he appeared through the form of fire and an incorporeal image to Moses and the other prophets, but now in the time of your reign,[23] as we said earlier, through a virgin he has become a human being in accordance with the will of the Father for the salvation of those who believe in him, and he submitted to be reviled and to suffer, in order that by dying and rising he might defeat death. Now that which was said from the bush to Moses, "I am the one who is, the God of Abraham and the God of Isaac and the God of Jacob and the God of your fathers,"[24] is indicative of the fact that even though those human beings died, they remain and belong to Christ himself. For they were the first of all human beings to pursue inquiry about God – Abraham being father of Isaac, Isaac of Jacob, as Moses also recorded.

*

* *

Second Apology

10. Our teachings appear to be loftier than any human teaching because the whole rational principle[25] became Christ, who was made manifest for our sake, body and reason and soul. For all [the things] that the philosophers or lawgivers have spoken well and have discovered have been worked by them as partial discovery and contemplation of Reason.[26] But since they did not recognize all that pertains to the Reason who is Christ, they also often contradicted themselves. And those born before Christ who tried through human reason to perceive reality and bring it to light were brought to court for being impious and meddlesome. The one who was more vigorous than all others at this – Socrates – was accused of the same things as we are. For they said that he introduced "new spirits" and "did not believe in those

23 A reference to the Roman Empire governed by Antoninus Pius and his sons, the work's addressees.

24 Exod 3:2, 6.

25 In Greek, *to logikon to holon*.

26 This sentence translates the manuscript text, as printed in PG 6: 460c, rather than the conjectural reconstruction of Minns–Parvis. The relevant section from the PG, corresponding to the end of our English sentence, reads *kata Logou meros heureseōs kai theōrias*. Minns and Parvis conjecture *kata logou heuresin kai theōrian* (p. 308). Compare *Second Apology* 7.3: *kata spermatikou logou meros*.

whom the city regarded as gods."[27] And he taught people to disregard the wicked demons and those who did what the poets said, casting out Homer and the other poets from the republic.[28] But as for the god who was unknown to them, he exhorted them to knowledge through the principle[29] of inquiry, saying, "The father and maker of all is not easy to find, nor, once found, is it safe to declare him to all"[30] – which our Christ did through his own power. For no one was persuaded by Socrates to deny on behalf of this doctrine. But by Christ, who was known in part by Socrates – because [Christ] was and is Reason, who is in all and foretold future events both through the prophets and through himself, when he had come to be similarly affected as we are[31] and taught these things – not only philosophers and scholars have been persuaded, but even artisans and entirely unskilled persons, and they despise glory and fear and death, since he is the power of the ineffable father[32] and not a construct of human reason.[33]

* * *

13. Indeed, I too, when I learned of the wicked garb placed on the Christians' divine teachings by the wicked demons in order to deter other people, I laughed at those who had fabricated these things and at the garb itself and at popular acclaim. For though I pray and am fighting tooth and nail to be found a Christian, I do confess that Plato's teachings are not foreign to those of Christ, nor that they are completely similar, just as neither is true of the teachings of others – those of Stoics and poets and prose writers. For upon seeing in part of the spermatic divine Reason what is connate with it,[34] each of them spoke well, but on their principal teachings they contradicted themselves since they apparently lacked firm understanding and irrefutable

27 Justin's quotations combine Plato, *Apology* 24b9–c1 and 26b4–5, with the verb *hōgeisthai* ("believe in") from 27d1–28a2.

28 See Plato, *Republic* III, 387b1–395d3; X, 595a1–607e2.

29 In Greek, *logou*.

30 See Plato, *Timaeus* 28c3–5, but Justin's version of the saying is closer to Alcinous, *Didaskalikos* 27.1.

31 In Greek, *homoiopathous genomenou*.

32 See 1 Cor 1:24.

33 In Greek, *anthrōpeiou logou kataskeuō*. At this point paragraphs 11–12 are omitted from the translation.

34 In Greek, *apo merous tou spermatikou theiou logou to suggenes horōn*. Justin appears torn between saying that each of these people saw *part* of the spermatic divine Reason and that each saw its *like*, and so he affirms both. Then again, the sentence is famously difficult, so any account of its meaning is essentially a best guess.

knowledge. So then, everything that has been well said by anyone belongs to us who are Christians, for after God we worship and adore the Reason from the unbegotten and ineffable God, since it became a human being for our sakes so that upon becoming a sharer in our afflictions it might bring healing. Indeed, by the inherent seed of innate reason, all the prose writers have been able to see reality indistinctly. For something's seed and likeness, which are bestowed according to capacity, are different from that of which the participation and imitation occur by the gift which comes from him.

8

Tatian, *Address to the Greeks* 4–7

Introduction and Translation by Bradley K. Storin

INTRODUCTION

Born to a pagan family in second-century Syria, and well educated in rhetoric and philosophy, Tatian embraced the "barbarian philosophy" of Christianity and wrote numerous works after his conversion. He traveled extensively throughout the Mediterranean, making it as far west as Rome, where, according to his slightly later contemporary Irenaeus of Lyons (*Against Heresies* 1.28.1), he came into contact with the various teachings of Justin Martyr,[1] Marcion of Sinope, Saturninus,[2] and Valentinus. He would later return to eastern Syria and set up a school that would influence Christianity in the region for the next several centuries. He initially crafted the *Diatessaron* (a harmony of the gospels) for students in his school, but it became the standard "version" of the gospels in Syriac liturgy well into the fifth century. He also wrote a series of treatises on the ascetic life, reflecting a regional emphasis on sexual and dietary renunciation that would endure throughout late antiquity.

The sections translated here come from the only work of Tatian's that survives in its original form, the *Address to the Greeks*. The text is important from a rhetorical perspective because it offers an example of the florid and bombastic style of composition prevalent within the eastern Mediterranean sophistic circles, but it also shows the ways that Christians appropriated classical literary tools while criticizing the culture that produced them. The *Address* pits Christian beliefs, practices, and scriptures against Greek religion, myth, philosophy, and law in spite of the fact that Tatian takes full advantage of Greek intellectual and rhetorical constructs. In other words,

1 On Justin Martyr, see the introduction to the selections from his writings translated in this volume on pp. 69–78.

2 Saturninus (also called Satornilus) was a second-century Gnostic teacher.

Tatian provides modern readers with a window into the complicated relationship between Christianity and Greek culture.

The portions of the text translated here, however, focus not on Greek culture, but provide a brief sketch of Tatian's vision regarding God and creation. In doing so, Tatian asserts monotheism and rejects material divinities, since all matter came into existence for the sake of humanity; why, he asks his reader, should he venerate what serves him? Like other contemporary Christians who were influenced by Middle Platonist metaphysics, Tatian understood God to exist outside time, to have no beginning, and to remain completely beyond sensory perception. From God, though, a cascade of production flows. First, from the divine nature the Word "sprang forth" (to use Tatian's phrase), and from the Word all of creation, including inanimate matter, as well as free creatures: angels, humanity (which is alone endowed with the image of immortality), demons, and Satan (the "first created" who "rose up against God's law"). Without directly discussing the incarnation, Tatian here provides in a classic expression of Logos theology an account of the production of the Word and the Word's role in the administration (*oikonomia*) of the universe.

The critical edition from which this translation has been made is Edgar J. Goodspeed, *Die ältesten Apologeten. Texte mit kurzen Einleitungen* (Göttingen: Vandenhoeck & Ruprecht, 1914; repr. 1984), 271–274.

TRANSLATION

4, 1. Why, Greek gentlemen, do you want to bring the powers of government down hard against us, as if we are in a fight? Even if I do not want to take advantage of the customs of certain people, why have I been reviled as the most abominable? Should the emperor order me to pay tributes, I stand ready to offer them. Should the master order me into slavery and servitude, I would recognize the sentence of slavery. For we must honor the human being in a human way, but we must fear God alone, he who is not visible to human eyes and not comprehensible by [any human] skill. I will not obey when I am commanded to deny him alone, and I would rather die than be proven to be a liar and an ingrate. God has no existence in time as we do, being the only one without a beginning and being the beginning of the universe. God is spirit,[3] not that which extends 2. through matter;

3 John 4:24.

rather, he is the maker of material spirits and the forms therein; he is invisible and impalpable, himself being the father of perceptible and visible things. We know him through his creation, and we grasp the invisibility of his power in the deeds.[4] I refuse to worship the handiwork that he brought to existence for our sake. The sun and the moon came to be on account of us; why, then, would I worship my servants? Why would I declare wood and stones to be God? For a spirit that extends throughout matter is still inferior to the divine spirit, and although it is comparable to soul, we ought not give it the same honor as we do the perfect God. Rather, one cannot win over with gifts the nameless God. For the one who is not deficient at all 3. ought not be slandered by us as if he were deficient. I will set forth my ideas more openly.

5, 1. In the beginning was God, and we have learned that the beginning is the power of the Word. For the Master of the universe, himself being the foundation of all,[5] was alone in that creation had not yet come to exist. Yet inasmuch as he was the foundation of things seen and unseen, every power was with him; he and the Word that was in him gave subsistence, through a rational power, to all things with him. By the will of his simplicity, the Word sprang forth; not proceeding purposelessly, though, the Word became the Father's firstborn work.[6] We know it to be the beginning of the world, but it came to be for distribution, not for division.[7] For what has been cut off has been separated from the first [object], whereas, when [the Word] assumed a share of the economy, 2. the distribution did not render the one from whom it was taken deficient. For just as, from one torch, many fires can be kindled without the light of the first torch fading due to the kindling of the many torches, so too the Word, coming forth from the Father's power, has not turned the begetter into something devoid of the Word.[8] Indeed, I am talking and you are listening; and doubtless I do not, through the transfer of speech, lose my speech while I converse [with you], but, while sending forth my own voice, I propose to give order to the disordered matter within you; just as the Word, begotten in the beginning, begot, by itself, in turn creation for us by fashioning matter, so too do I, 3. being born again[9] in imitation of the Word and having attained the apprehension of the truth, remodel the mixture of matter with which I was born. Indeed, matter is not beginningless as God is; nor is it, on account of being

4 Rom 1:20. 5 In Greek, *tou pantos hē hypostasis*. 6 See Col 1:15.
7 In Greek, *kata merismon, ou kata apokopēn*. 8 In Greek, *alogon*. 9 See John 3:3.

beginningless, equal in power to God.[10] Rather, it was made to exist, and nothing else brought it into existence since it was produced exclusively by the creator of all things.

6, 1. And that is why we believe that there will be a resurrection of bodies after the consummation of all things, not as the Stoics teach [happens] according to certain courses of cycles, with the same things always coming and going to no useful end,[11] but according to us, once our ages have reached their limit, there will be a one-time-only restoration among human beings alone for the sake of a judgment. Neither Minos nor Rhadamanthus[12] are to judge us – no souls have been sentenced before the end, as the myths tell! – but the creator God is himself the examiner. You might think that we are really bumblers and babblers,[13] but we do not care since we believe in this doctrine. I did not know what I was before I came to be 2. – since I did not exist and only existed in this subsistence of fleshly matter – I have come to believe that, having formerly not existed, I came to exist in birth. In the same way, when what has come to be no longer exists and in death is no longer seen anymore, I will again be not in the way that I had formerly come to exist and then been born. Even if fire were to consume my fleshiness, the world would contain my evaporated matter. Even if I were drowned in rivers, even if in the sea, even if I were torn apart by beasts, I am stored up in the treasuries of the rich Master. Neither one who is poor nor one who is godless knows what has been stored up, but God the ruler, whenever he wants, will restore the substance, visible only to him, back to its original state.

7, 1. For the heavenly Word – which became a spirit from the Spirit[14] and Word from the rational power, in imitation of the Father who begot it – made the human being as an image of immortality so that, just as incorruption comes from God, in the same way a human being, sharing in God's

10 The concession of matter being beginningless in the second half of this sentence is strange, given that Tatian has just rejected the possibility that matter is beginningless in the first half of the sentence.

11 Indeed, the Stoics taught that all of existence is characterized by a life cycle, so to speak. Currently we live in a period of condensation, when matter congeals into the form that we know. Later, however, all matter will heat up to such a degree that a universal conflagration breaks out that begins the full instantiation of divine providence. As the fire subsides, all matter begins to cool and to reconstitute itself as it was before, thereby beginning a new stage of condensation. The process is infinitely recurring.

12 Two mythological judges of the dead in Hades.

13 See Acts 17:18.

14 Other manuscripts read, "from the Father."

portion, may also have the immortal. And so, while the Word became the creator of angels before the construction of human beings, both kinds of creation were endowed with free will, since neither had the nature of the good, which exists only in God, but is perfected in the freedom of choice [made] by human beings, so that the wicked person who was bad on his own account would be justly punished and the just person, due to acts of virtue, 2. and not transgressing the will of God, is deservedly praised according to the endowment of free will. That is the way of things with respect to angels and human beings, but the Word's power – which within itself has foreknowledge of future occurrences, not as something fated to happen but as the freely willed decision of those who made the choice – foretold the results of things to come, and it also became a hinderer of wickedness through prohibitions and a praiser of those who remained good. And after human beings and angels closely followed a certain being, cleverer than the rest on account of its being the first created, and proclaimed it to be a god in spite of the fact that it rose up against God's law, then the Word's power 3. cast out the originator of the insanity and his followers from his abode. The one who was in the image of God became mortal, since the more powerful spirit was separated from him. But because of the transgression and the ignorance, the first-created was appointed as a demon and his imitators, his apparitions, turned into a legion of demons. Because of the endowment of free will, they were handed over to their own depravity.

9

Odes of Solomon 7, 19, 41, and 42

Introduction and Translation by Aaron Michael Butts

INTRODUCTION

The *Odes of Solomon* consist of forty-two short poems. Their provenance, date, and original language are all disputed. At least some of the *Odes* must have been written before the third century since *Ode* 11 is found in Greek in Papyrus Bodmer XI, which is datable to the third century, and since Lactantius (ca. 240–ca. 320) includes a quotation of *Ode* 19 in Latin translation in his *Divinarum Institutionum* (IV.xii.3). Parts of five odes (1.1–5, 5.1–11, 6.8–18, 22.1–12, and 25.1–12) are also found in Coptic translation in the *Pistis Sophia*, which is preserved in a single Coptic manuscript, probably from the fourth or fifth century, though scholars think the *Pistis Sophia* itself goes back to the third or fourth century. The Syriac tradition preserves the most complete witness to the *Odes of Solomon*, albeit in later manuscripts: *Odes* 17–42 are extant in a Syriac manuscript datable to the tenth century, and *Odes* 3–42 in a Syriac manuscript datable to the fifteenth to seventeenth century. Previous scholars have debated whether the original language of the *Odes of Solomon* was Syriac or Greek, with some even suggesting a "bilingual" origin, but it seems better to think of an "open text" without a single point of origin that grew over time. Though the *Odes of Solomon* are undoubtedly pseudonymous, the association with Solomon led to their inclusion in the Old Testament *antilegomena* (texts of disputed value/authenticity), which also include works such as the Wisdom of Solomon, the Wisdom of Ben Sirah, Esther, Judith, Tobit, Susannah, and books associated with the Maccabees, in the *Synopsis* of Pseudo-Athanasius (ca. sixth–seventh centuries) and in the *Stichometria* of Nicephorus (mid-ninth century).

The *Odes of Solomon* are a rich yet enigmatic text. Some scholars have argued that at least some of the *Odes* may have originated among Jews, often drawing parallels with literature from Qumran, including especially the Thanksgiving Scroll (*Hodayot*) and the Psalms Scroll. Others have stressed connections with Gnostic texts, even reading the *Odes* themselves as "Gnostic."[1] While parallels between Gnostic texts on the one hand and poetry from Qumran on the other hand are undeniable, it is much less clear what conclusions are to be drawn from these parallels. What is, however, certain is that the *Odes of Solomon* provide an interesting witness to one form of early Christianity. Especially to be noted for this volume is the Trinitarianism of *Ode* 19, as well as the accompanying feminine imagery, which includes the milking of the breasts of the Father. In addition to *Ode* 19, several other *Odes* (7, 41, and 42) are translated here due to their Christological themes.

The following translation is based on the edition of the Syriac text in M. Lattke, *Oden Salomos. Text, Übersetzung, Kommentar*, 3 vols., Novum Testamentum et orbis antiquus 41.1–3 (Göttingen: Vandenhoeck & Ruprecht, 1999–2005), with verse numbers sometimes reflecting J. H. Charlesworth, *The Odes of Solomon* (Oxford: Clarendon Press, 1973). Reference was also made to the facsimile edition of the two Syriac manuscripts in J. H. Charlesworth, *Papyri and Leather Manuscripts of the Odes of Solomon* (Durham, NC: Duke University Press, 1981).

TRANSLATION

Ode 7

1. Just like the course of anger over iniquity,
so also is the course of joy over the beloved.
He brings from the fruit of joy without hindrance.

2. My joy is the Lord, and my course is toward him;
this path of mine is beautiful.

3. I have the Lord as a helper,
and he has made himself known to me without envy in his simplicity,
for his kindness has diminished his majesty.

1 On such attempts to label a wide range of early Christian texts as "Gnostic," see the important methodological corrective in David Brakke, *The Gnostics: Myth, Ritual, and Diversity in Early Christianity* (Cambridge, MA: Harvard University Press, 2010).

4. He became like me that I might receive him;
in image he seemed like me so that I might put him on.

5. I did not tremble when I saw him;
because he is, he had compassion on me.

6. He became like my nature so that I might comprehend him,
and like my form so that I not turn away from him.

7. The father of knowledge
is the speech of knowledge.

8. The one who created wisdom
is wiser than his works.

9. The one who created me before I came to be
knew what I would do when I came to be.

10. Therefore, he had compassion on me in his great compassion,
and he let me beseech him and to receive from his sacrifice.

11. Because he is, he is indestructible –
the fullness of the ages and their father.

12. He let him appear to those who are his,
so that they might recognize the one who had made them,
and so that they not suppose that they had come about from
themselves.

13. For he set his path to knowledge;
he widened and extended it and brought it to[2] the entire fullness.

14. He set upon it[3] the footsteps of his light,
and it proceeded from the beginning until the end.

15. By him he was served,[4]
and he was pleased with the Son.

16. Because of his salvation, let him hold everything,
and let the Most High be made known by[5] his holy ones,

2 Or "over." 3 That is, the path.

4 The parallelism with the next line suggests the interpretation: "By the Son the Father was served."

5 Or "among."

17. to announce to those who have the psalms of the coming of the Lord,
so that they might go out to meet him and to sing to him,
with joy and with the harp of many tones.

18. Let the seers go before him,
and let them be seen before him.

19. Let them praise the Lord in his love,
because he is near and sees.

20. Let hate be raised from the earth,
and with jealousy be drowned.

21. For ignorance has been destroyed,
because the knowledge of the Lord has come.

22. Let those who sing sing the grace of the Lord, the Most High,
and let them offer their psalms.

23. Let their hearts be like the day,
and their voices like the majesty of the beauty of the Lord.

24. Let nothing with a soul
either be without knowledge or without speech.

25. For he gave a mouth to his creation,
to open the sound of the mouth toward him
and to praise him.

26. Confess his power,
and demonstrate his grace.
Hallelujah.

*
* *

Ode 19

1. A cup of milk was offered to me,
and I drank it in the sweetness of the kindness of the Lord.

2. The Son is the cup,
the one who was milked is the Father,
and the one who milked him is the Holy Spirit.

3. Because his breasts were full,
and because it was not desired that his milk be poured out in vain,

4. the Holy Spirit opened her bosom,
and she mixed the milk of the two breasts of the Father,

5. and she gave the mixture to the world when they did not know,
and those who receive are in the fullness of the right hand.

6. The womb of the virgin trapped it,
and conceived and gave birth.

7. The virgin became a mother through great mercy,
and she labored and gave birth to a son, and it did not pain her,

8. because it did not happen in vain.

9. She did not require a midwife,
because he[6] gave life to her like a man.[7]

10. She gave birth willingly;[8]
she gave birth in demonstration;
she took possession in great power;

11. she loved in salvation;
she guarded in kindness;
she demonstrated in majesty.
Hallelujah.

*
* *

Ode 41

1. Let all the offspring of the Lord praise him,
and let them receive the truth of his faith.

2. Let his children be known to him.
Therefore, let us sing in his love.

6 That is, presumably, God.
7 Reading against the punctuation of the manuscripts, which take "like a man" with the next line.
8 Literally, "in will," paralleling the prepositional phrases that conclude each of the remaining lines of the ode.

3. We are alive in the Lord through his grace,
and we receive life through his Messiah.

4. For he has made a great day shine upon us,[9]
and amazing is the one who has given to us from his praises.

5. Let us all therefore be united together in the name of the Lord,
and let us honor him in his goodness.

6. Let our faces shine in his light,
and let our hearts meditate on his love,
night and day.

7. Let us exult out of the exultation of the Lord.

8. Let everyone who sees me be astounded,
because I am of another race.

9. For the Father of truth remembered me –
the one who has possessed me from the beginning.

10. For his riches gave birth to me,
and the thought of his heart.

11. His word is with us on our entire path –
the savior who gives life and does not reject our souls,

12. the man who humbled himself
and was exalted through his own righteousness.

13. The Son of the Most High has appeared
in the fullness of his Father.

14. The light has dawned from the word,
which was in him[10] from the beginning.

15. The Messiah is, in truth, one,
and he has been known since before the foundation of the world,
so that he might give life to souls forever through the truth of his name.

16. A new praise to the Lord from those who love him.
Hallelujah.

9 Alternatively, "a great day has shone upon us."

10 That is, the Father.

*

* *

Ode 42

1. I extended my hands and drew near to my Lord,
because the stretching out of my hands is his sign.

2. My extension is the simple[11] wood,[12]
which was hung on the path of the upright one.

3. I have become useless to those who knew me,
because I hide myself from those who have not held me.

4. Let me be with those
who love me.

5. All of my persecutors have died,
and those who proclaimed me sought me because I am alive.

6. I have arisen,[13] and I am with them,
and I shall speak through their mouths.

7. For they rejected those who were persecuting them,
and I have set upon them the yoke of my love.

8. Just like the arm of the bridegroom on the bride,
so also is my yoke on those who know me.

9. Just as the bridal chamber that is set up in the house of the bridal pair,
so also is my love on those who believe in me.

10. I was not rejected even if I seemed to have been,
and I did not perish even if they thought so of me.

11. Sheol saw me and was weakened,
and death vomited me up – and many with me.

11 Or "straight." Note the play on "stretching out" (*pšiṭutā*) and "simple, straight" (*pšiṭā*).

12 That is, the cross.

13 This could be a reference to resurrection; or, it could mean more generally "I have stood up."

12. I became vinegar and bitterness to it,[14]
and I descended with it as far as it had depth.

13. It forsook feet and head,[15]
because it was unable to endure my face.

14. I made a congregation of the living among his[16] dead ones,
and I spoke to them with living lips,
so that my speech would not be futile.

15. Those who were dead ran toward me,
and they cried out and said, "Have compassion on us, Son of God!

16. Deal with us according to your kindness,
and bring us out of the bounds of darkness!

17. Open for us the door,
so that through it we might go out toward you!
For we see that our death will not approach you.

18. Let us also be saved with you,
because it is you who is our savior."

19. I heard their voice,
and I set in my heart their faith,

20. and I set on their head my name,
because they are free people, and they are mine.
Hallelujah.

14 That is, to death. 15 Presumably a merismus for the entire body.
16 Again, that is, death.

10

Treatise on Resurrection

(Nag Hammadi Codex I, Work 4)

Introduction and Translation by Melissa Harl Sellew

INTRODUCTION

Sometime in the late second century a Christian theologian wrote this brief exposition of the true meaning of resurrection. Adopting the form of the didactic epistle, the unknown author addresses his remarks to an individual named Rheginos, who himself is also otherwise unknown. From the contents of the treatise we may infer that the author has been asked to supply a defense for the "advanced" position that resurrection for believers in Christ takes the form of a spiritual transformation, experienced by the intellects of those predestined to be saved, perhaps even in this lifetime. Neither the fleshly body nor its animating soul survives physical death, whereas the spirit-mind of the believer departs this material plane of existence for return to the heavenly realm called "the Fullness" (*plērōma*).

The Christology of the treatise is interesting in its use of conventional titles (calling Jesus our Lord and Savior, the Christ, Son of God, and Son of Man), while also offering vivid pictures or symbols of his role in salvation. Christ took on flesh when entering this material world, and is said to have "swallowed up death," to have "dissolved" death, and by his own resurrection enabled that of his faithful. He is called the preexistent "seed of Truth," referring to his work of sharing knowledge of divine mysteries. He revealed to humanity "the path to immortality." He holds his believers safe in his grasp, as the sun grips its rays of light. Indeed, Christ effects their resurrection by drawing the spirit-minds of the elect up from this place of corruption and death, like the sun and its rays, into the realm of the Divine Fullness. Belief in the reality of Christ's resurrection is required for one's own salvation to be effective, says our author, while scholarly argument and debate are denigrated.

It is possible to place the author within the complexities of second-century Christian thought with some precision. He participates in the popular dualistic Platonism common to most intellectuals of his day, such as in the distinction between true, spiritual existence and perishable, material being. He appeals to both "the Apostle" and "the Gospel" for authoritative support for his interpretations of the process and meaning of resurrection; but he makes no allusion to or criticism of the Jewish scriptures. His views remind one of the "heretical" positions opposed by Irenaeus (*Against Heresies* 2.31.2) and Tertullian (*On the Resurrection of the Flesh* 19). Several terms of special import to Valentinian theologians appear, such as the Fullness, the Entirety, the Realm, Repose, or the Deficiency to be restored by Return of the Elect, but there is bare allusion to the classic "Gnostic" mythology known from such writings as the *Apocryphon of John* or the *Tripartite Tractate*. This silence is likely a deliberate choice in an "exoteric" work that presumes a basic knowledge of a fundamental mythic narrative, yet hesitates to reveal too much of the more advanced understanding of the group; a similar strategy is operative in Ptolemy's *Letter to Flora*.

The work was composed in Greek, though it survives only in translation into Coptic (the Lycopolitan dialect), and in a single manuscript. This book, which contains five treatises of a Valentinian flavor, was buried in a jar in the Nile valley toward the end of the fourth century, along with eleven other codices, as part of the so-called Nag Hammadi Library. This larger collection consists of Coptic translations of various philosophical, moral, and theological treatises, many of a "Gnostic" bent, apparently copied and read by late ancient Egyptian monastics. The process of conveying the author's thoughts in an unrelated language resulted in a number of unclarities of expression, but the general force of the argument is clear enough. (Numbered sections have been provided to aid the reader.) As mentioned, the format is of the didactic letter, in a conversational style involving direct address, use of rhetorical questions, acknowledgment of difficulty, repetition, and some mild rebukes for the implied audience, called "children." The title of the work is supplied at the end (as was common): *The Treatise on Resurrection*.

This translation follows the edition of Malcolm Peel in *Nag Hammadi Codex I (The Jung Codex)*, edited by Harold W. Attridge (Leiden: Brill,

1985), 1: 123–157, along with the translation and commentary of Bentley Layton, *The Gnostic Treatise on Resurrection from Nag Hammadi*, Harvard Dissertations in Religion (Missoula: Scholars Press, 1979).

TRANSLATION

1. There are some people, my child Rheginos, who want to become very learned – that's their goal when they lay hold of problems that lack solutions. And if they meet that goal, then they typically think highly of themselves. But I don't think that they've actually set themselves within the Word[1] of Truth; instead, it's repose[2] for themselves that they seek. We have received this rest from our Savior, our Lord Christ[3] – we received it once we came to know the Truth and came to rest upon it.

However, I'm writing to you since you have asked so pleasantly after what really matters with regard to resurrection – it is a fundamental topic, something that many people fail to believe, and only a few understand. Therefore, let our discourse tackle this subject.

2. How did the Lord arrange[4] matters when he was in the flesh, after he had revealed that he was God's Son?[5] He walked in this place where you also walk, discussing nature's law – by which I mean death. The Son of God, Rheginos, was a Son of Man,[6] and he exercised dominion in two regards. He had both humanity and divinity, so that he might indeed conquer death through his being Son of God, and that through the Son of Man, the return to Divine Fullness[7] might occur. From the very beginning he existed as a seed of Truth from above, before this world[8] ever came into being, with lordships and deities being so very numerous.

1 *Logos*, which can also mean "story," "discourse," "treatise," "argument," or "reason." In this writing, the "Word of Truth" refers to a set of fundamental beliefs, perhaps found through spiritual interpretation of religious texts.
2 Rest or "repose" is a technical term for salvation.
3 The manuscript consistently reads *chrēstos*, a common phonetic spelling of the title Christ in Greek and Coptic, with a punning allusion to a word meaning "good" or "kind."
4 More literally, "exercised strength, conquered, controlled" things.
5 That is to say, "was divine." The word "god" is used in this text only as part of this phrase, "Son of God."
6 That is to say, "a human being," used in this text with a titular meaning.
7 The *plērōma* (Divine Fullness) refers to the spiritual realm that is eternal, invisible, imperishable, and immaterial; the goal is "return" to and thus "restoration" of that Fullness through faith in the resurrection of Jesus Christ.
8 The *kosmos* for this author is the visible, corruptible, and material world in which embodied spirit-minds dwell.

I'm aware that I'm explaining some difficult matters – but there is actually nothing difficult in the Word of Truth. It was indeed to explain things that he came into our midst, that nothing be left a mystery, but instead that he could reveal with utter simplicity all that concerns coming into being – the doing away with the lesser part and the manifestation of the better.[9] This is the upshot[10] of Truth and Spirit, and Grace belongs to Truth.

3. The Savior swallowed up death[11] – you should know this – for he set aside the perishable world and exchanged it for an imperishable, eternal realm.[12] He rose up when he swallowed up the visible by means of the invisible and granted us the path to our immortality. And thus, just as the Apostle said, we have suffered with him, and risen with him, and ascended with him.[13]

Since we manifestly exist in this world, we bear it [like a garment].[14] We are the Savior's rays, and are held fast by him until our sunset – that is, until our death in this lifetime. We are drawn up by him just as rays are by the sun, with nothing holding them back. This is the spiritual resurrection, swallowing up that of the soul and likewise the fleshly resurrection.

4. If someone does not believe, that person cannot be persuaded. For it is a matter of faith, my child, not a matter of persuasion, that the dead will rise. Assuming there is a believer among the philosophers here, even such a person can rise! Philosophers in this place must not believe that they can turn about[15] all by themselves – (instead) it is due to our faith. For we have come to know the Son of Man, and we believe that he rose from the dead. He is the one of whom we proclaim, "He became the dissolution of death." Those who believe are as great as that[16] by which they believe, and so their power

9 The fleshly body is "the lesser," as contrasted with the spirit-mind; and so "the greater" part could also refer to the Elect, those who are saved.

10 The term *probolē* likely refers to the notion of "emanation" of a divine explanatory principle from the Fullness.

11 Seemingly an allusion to Paul's metaphor for Christ overcoming death, as in 1 Cor 15:54 and 2 Cor 5:4.

12 The "eternal *aiōn*" is apparently where Christ went when he set aside this perishable world.

13 These Paulinist phrases remind one of Rom 8:17 and Eph 2:5–6, with echoes from Rom 6:5, 8; Col 2:12–13.

14 A clothing metaphor: "we bear the [material] world as a garment" = "we are clothed with fleshly bodies."

15 That is, unbelieving scholars living in the material world cannot be saved by their own intellectual efforts.

16 The antecedent is unclear: perhaps the reference is to divine grace or truth, or perhaps even the Savior himself.

of thinking will not perish, nor will the intellect of those who have come to know him ever perish. For this reason, we are the ones chosen for salvation and redemption, since we have been destined from the beginning not to fall into the foolishness of the ignorant, but instead to enter into the wisdom of those who know the Truth.

Indeed, the Truth that is kept safe cannot be set aside, nor has it ever been lost. The structure of the Divine Fullness is mighty, whereas the part that broke off and became the world is insignificant. But the Entirety,[17] that which is held fast, did not come into being, but instead it exists [eternally].

5. And so, my child Rheginos, do not have doubts about the resurrection! For if you had not (previously) existed in the flesh, then you took on flesh when you came into this world; so why would you not take the flesh with you when you ascend to the divine realm?[18] What gives life to the flesh is better[19] than it; so, doesn't what comes into being for your sake belong to you? Doesn't that which belongs to you exist along with you? Rather, while you are here (in the world), what is it that you lack? – that is exactly what you are so eager to learn about.

The afterbirth of the body is old age, and so if you exist as corruption, then absence is your gain. For you will not give up the better part when you depart.[20] The lesser part experiences a loss, but there is grace for it. There is nothing that redeems us from here, but instead it is us, as the Entirety, who are saved. We have received salvation from beginning to end. Let's think of it this way; let's understand it this way.

6. But some people wish to know, as they inquire after the things they investigate, whether the people who are saved will be saved immediately when they leave their bodies behind. No one should have any doubt about this. And yet, how could the visible parts of the body, which are dead, not be capable of being saved, seeing as the living parts within them would arise?

Now then, what is the resurrection? It is always the disclosure of those who have arisen. For if you recall reading in the Gospel that Elijah and

17 The Entirety (or: the All) is made up of all the spirit-minds of the Elect, ultimately part of the Divine Fullness.

18 Another use of the term *aiōn*. This paragraph consists of rhetorical questions meant to lead to clarity.

19 The soul as the animating force of the fleshly body is probably meant as "what gives life."

20 There may be a reminiscence here of Paul's language of death and departure as "gain" in Phil 1:21–23.

Moses appeared with him,[21] do not imagine that the resurrection is a mere illusion – it is not an illusion, but rather Truth. It would be better to call the world an illusion, than the resurrection, this which came to pass through our Lord, the Savior Jesus Christ. So, what am I trying to explain to you? Those now alive will die, since they are living in an illusory way. The rich have become poor, the rulers have been overthrown. Everything changes, the world is an illusion.

Lest I should rant on too long – the resurrection is not of this illusory sort, for it is Truth.

It is what stands firm, and the disclosure of what really is. It is the transformation of things, and the change into newness. For incorruption [flows down] upon corruption, and the light flows down upon the darkness, swallowing it up; the Divine Fullness is filling up its deficiency.[22] These are symbols and likenesses of resurrection, and this is what makes the Good.

7. Therefore, Rheginos, do not think only partially, nor live in accordance with the flesh. Rather, for the sake of Oneness, abandon divisions and bondage, and then, you "already have the resurrection"![23] If the mortal part "knows itself,"[24] that it is going to die, that it is being brought to death, even if it lasts for many years in this lifetime, why don't you realize that you yourself have already risen? Indeed, you are brought to this end, if you have the resurrection. Instead, you persist as though you will die, even though that part "knows" that it has already died. Why do I forgive this misunderstanding, except for your lack of experience? Everyone must train[25] oneself in many ways, that they might be set free from this Element,[26] lest they wander off the path; instead, they will obtain their own original state of existence. That which I have received through the generosity of my Lord Jesus Christ I have taught to you and your siblings, my children, having

21 The account of Jesus's transfiguration, as known from Matt 17:1–8; Mark 9:2–8; or Luke 9:28–36.

22 The spirit-minds of the Elect have somehow been separated from their existence in the Divine Fullness, creating a "deficiency," but through faith in Christ's resurrection the resulting lack in the *plērōma* can be restored.

23 Cf. the complaint by ps.-Paul in 2 Tim 2:18 about "profane chatter" that the resurrection has already occurred.

24 The proverbial Greek call to self-scrutiny and self-awareness. Once one realizes through faith in Christ's resurrection that one's mortal parts have already died, then the spirit-minds already have their resurrection.

25 The verb *askein* has implications of athletic, military, or "ascetical" training of mind and body.

26 The stultifying effects of the material, perishable world.

omitted nothing that is necessary to strengthen you.[27] If, however, anything written in my explanation of the Word is too profound, I will explain it to you, if you ask. Now, please share this with anyone who is worthy, since it should be of benefit. Many people are looking into this topic that I have written you about; to these I pronounce peace and grace. I send you greetings, with those who love you all with familial love.

The Treatise on Resurrection

27 This and the next sentence use the plural form of "you."

11

A Ptolemaic Theology as Recounted by Irenaeus of Lyons in *Against Heresies* 1.8.5

Introduction and Translation by Anthony Briggman

INTRODUCTION

The first eight chapters of Irenaeus's *Against Heresies* (1.1–8) contain the oldest surviving account of Valentinian Gnosticism.[1] No account has influenced ancient and modern understandings of Valentinian Gnosticism more than this one. Irenaeus, however, does not here relate Valentinus's own thought. He provides, rather, a theological account circulating amongst Valentinians near the Rhône who considered themselves followers of the influential Valentinian named Ptolemaeus (Ptolemy).[2] Irenaeus states (*Against Heresies* 1.pref.2) that his account draws upon conversations held with these Ptolemaic Valentinians as well as written sources obtained from them. But the particular author of these written sources and the relative importance of these writings to this group of Valentinians remains unknown.

Irenaeus introduces the text of *Against Heresies* 1.8.5 as a verbatim quotation from a Valentinian document. The theological account that appears there belongs to the Ptolemaic school of Valentinianism insofar as it regards the Aeons as having a separate existence outside of the Father.[3] That being said, the account Irenaeus presents in *Against Heresies* 1.1–8 differs in substantial ways from the only account we have from Ptolemaeus's pen, his *Letter to Flora*. Therefore, it seems best to understand Irenaeus's

1 Justin Martyr's *Dialogue with Trypho* 35.6 mentions Valentinus but does not offer a substantial account of his thought or that of his followers. On Irenaeus himself, see the introduction to the selections from *Against Heresies* below, on pp. 103–105.

2 *Against Heresies* 1.pref.2. From what we can tell Ptolemaeus occupied an important place in the development of western Valentinian thought. Tertullian (*Against the Valentinians* 4.2), for instance, suggests he was the originator of the theological system that identified the Fullness (*plērōma*) as constituted by thirty Aeons.

3 See Tertullian, *Against the Valentinians* 4.2.

account as representing a later, modified form of Ptolemaeus's system then circulating amongst Ptolemaic Valentinians. Moreover, the account given in *Against Heresies* 1.8.5 differs in certain ways from the main Ptolemaic account Irenaeus presents in *Against Heresies* 1.1–8.4, which suggests the account in *Against Heresies* 1.8.5 drew upon a different, more primitive source than the main account.

The Ptolemaic account that appears in *Against Heresies* 1.8.5 reads the prologue of the Gospel of John as providing a basis for Ptolemaic theology and protology. That is to say, the Johannine prologue is interpreted as revealing the generation of the Ogdoad, the first eight Aeons, of this Ptolemaic system. The eight Aeons of the Ogdoad exist in a series of four conjugal couples: Father and Grace, Only-Begotten and Truth, Word and Life, and Human Being and Church.[4] Each couple in the series engenders the couple that follows. In addition to providing insight into Ptolemaic theology and protology, this text provides an example of the scriptural interpretation that sustained Ptolemaic thought. As such it illustrates that much of the debate between various so-called Gnostics and those representing the "Great Church," as did Irenaeus, centered upon the proper reading of scriptural texts and, by extension, the proper practices governing the reading of those texts.

The following translation is based upon the critical edition established by Adelin Rousseau and Louis Doutreleau, *Irénée de Lyon, Contre les hérésies*, SChr 263 and 264 (Paris: Éditions du Cerf, 1979), 128–137.

TRANSLATION

1.8.5. Furthermore, they teach that John, the disciple of the Lord, indicated the first Ogdoad, saying in these very words: John, the disciple of the Lord, wishing to relate the genesis of all things – according to which the Father emitted all things[5] – postulates a certain First-Principle,[6] which was the first

4 The Greek word for the first member of each conjugal couple is grammatically masculine, while the word for the second member is grammatically feminine. This pattern corresponds to the Ptolemaic understanding of Aeons as gendered beings that procreate sexually.

5 The first "all things" in this sentence translates the Greek *tōn holōn*, whereas the second translates *ta panta*: both refer to the Aeons of the Fullness (in Greek, *plērōma*).

6 In Greek, *archē*. This term entails the idea of "beginning" and could just as easily be rendered "Beginning" as English translations usually render its use in John 1:1–2. But the translation "First-Principle" better captures the Ptolemaic interpretation of the term.

begotten by God. What is more, he calls this one Son and only-begotten God,[7] in whom Father emitted all things in a seminal manner. By this one, he says, Word[8] was emitted and in him the whole substance of the Aeons [was emitted], which Word himself afterwards formed.

Since then [John] speaks about the first genesis, he rightly commences his teaching from First-Principle, that is, Son, and from Word. Thus, he says: "In the First-Principle was the Word, and the Word was with God and the Word was God; he was in the First-Principle with God."[9] Having first distinguished [these] three – God and First-Principle and Word – he in turn unites them so that he may explain both the emission of each of them – of Son as well as Word – and at the same time [their] unity with one another and with Father. For First-Principle is in Father and of Father, and Word is in First-Principle and of First-Principle.

[John], then, rightly said: "In the First-Principle was the Word," for [Word] was in Son. "And the Word was with God," for also [was] First-Principle. "And," consequently, "the Word was God" – for that which was begotten of God is God. "He was in the First-Principle with God," explained the order of the emission. "All things were made through him, and apart from him not one thing was made"[10] – for Word was made the cause of the formation and genesis for all the Aeons after him. But "what was made in him," [John] says, "is Life."[11] Here he also indicated the conjugal couple.[12] For, he said, all things were made through him, but Life [was made] in him. She,[13] who was made in him, is then more closely related [to him] than what has been made through him, for she is joined with[14] him and bears fruit through him. Again, when he adds, "And the Life was the Light of Human Beings,"[15] he, while here speaking of Human Beings, also indicated Church by means of the same name, so that by means of the one name he might disclose the union of the conjugal couple. For Human Being and Church come from Word and Life. Moreover, he called Light the Life of Human Beings because they have been illuminated by her, meaning of course that they were formed and manifested [by her]. This is also what Paul says, "For anything that is manifested is Light."[16] Since, therefore, Life manifested and begot both Human Being and Church, she is called their Light.

7 John 1:18. 8 In Greek, *logon*. 9 John 1:1–2. 10 John 1:3.
11 John 1:3–4. 12 In Greek, *suzugian*. 13 That is, Life.
14 In Greek, *sunesti*, a verb which also bears the meaning "to have intercourse with" – a sense well suited to the Ptolemaic hypothesis.
15 John 1:4. 16 Eph 5:13.

Clearly, then, by these words John has revealed among other things the second Tetrad: Word and Life, Human Being and Church. Yet, truly, he also indicated the first Tetrad. For by giving a detailed account of Savior and stating that all things outside the Fullness were formed by him, he says that [Savior] is the fruit of the entire Fullness.[17] For [John] called him the Light which shines in the darkness and which was not comprehended by it,[18] because while harmonizing everything that comes into being from passion, he was not known by those things. And he also calls him Son and Truth and Life and Word which was made flesh. We have seen his glory, [John] says, and his glory was like that of the Only-Begotten – that which was given to him by the Father – full of Grace and Truth. As [John] says in these words: "And the Word was made flesh and dwelt among us, and we have seen his glory, the glory like that of the Only-Begotten from the Father, full of Grace and Truth."[19] [John], therefore, in a precise manner indicated the first Tetrad, when he referred to Father and Grace, and Only-Begotten and Truth. Thus, John spoke of the first Ogdoad, the mother of all the Aeons. For he spoke of Father and Grace, Only-Begotten and Truth, Word and Life, and Human Being and Church. – So much then for Ptolemaeus.

17 According to the Ptolemaic hypothesis, Savior is the common product of every member of the Fullness (see *Against Heresies* 1.2.6).

18 See John 1:5.

19 John 1:14. Some debate surrounds the proper reading of this quotation and the sentence that precedes it. It is best to understand these sentences, with Rousseau, as both belonging to the Ptolemaic hypothesis. The first sentence conveys the Ptolemaic interpretation of John 1:14, in which the use of *hoia* ("like that of") indicates their interpretation of *hōs* ("as") in the text of John 1:14. The translation of John 1:14 above renders *hōs* in a way that accords with the Ptolemaic reading, "like that of."

12

Irenaeus of Lyons, *Against Heresies* (Selections)

Introduction and Translation by Anthony Briggman

INTRODUCTION

We first learn of Irenaeus in a letter he carried to Eleutherius, bishop of Rome, from the churches of Vienne and Lyons which were seeking a peaceful resolution to the Montanist controversy.[1] The letter introduced Irenaeus as an esteemed presbyter in their community. By the time Irenaeus returned from his embassy a severe persecution (ca. 177 CE) of the churches in Vienne and Lyons had claimed the lives of many, including that of Pothinus, the aged bishop of Lyons. Irenaeus was installed as his successor.

We know little about the new bishop of Lyons. We do know he was not a native of Roman Gaul, where Vienne and Lyons were located, but rather from Asia Minor. Irenaeus tells of seeing and hearing in his early youth Polycarp, the bishop of Smyrna (d. ca. 155 CE), a disciple of the apostle John. At some point he left Asia Minor for points west, likely spending time in Rome before arriving in the vicinity of Vienne and Lyons. Irenaeus's death is usually dated to the first few years of the third century. He is commemorated as a martyr, but evidence for his martyrdom is late, the earliest possible testimony coming from the pen of Jerome nearly two hundred years later.

Eusebius of Caesarea's *Ecclesiastical History* credits Irenaeus with various treatises, but only two have come down to us: a short work entitled *Proof of the Apostolic Preaching*, long thought to be lost until an Armenian translation was discovered in 1904, and the work for which he is best known, *A Refutation and Overthrow of Knowledge Falsely So Called*, which is more commonly

1 Eusebius, *Ecclesiastical History* 5.4.2.

referred to as *Against Heresies*. The original Greek version of the five books that constitute *Against Heresies* was available to Armenian translators in the sixth century and was read by Photius in Baghdad in the ninth century but has since disappeared. Of the original Greek all that remains are extracts, some lengthy, preserved in the works of other writers, and a few fragments in papyri. About thirty fragments from a Syriac version are extant, and the fourth and fifth books of *Against Heresies* are preserved in Armenian in the same manuscript that holds his *Proof*. Fortunately, a Latin translation was made of the original Greek during the third or fourth century. Versions of this translation have come down to us in nine Latin manuscripts, copied between the ninth and sixteenth centuries. Taken together, the Armenian and Latin translations preserve the work in its entirety.

The following selections come from the first, third, and fifth books of *Against Heresies* (*AH*). They show Irenaeus to be not just a polemicist bent on defeating his Valentinian and Marcionite opponents, though he certainly was that, but a theologian intent on preserving the tradition of the faith by promulgating his own theological account. What follows is a peek into one of the most important and influential accounts of the person and work of Jesus Christ authored in the first hundred years after the New Testament writings. Irenaeus argues that Jesus Christ is one and the same Word-Son of God now incarnate, and that Jesus is both as human as we are human, excepting sin, and as divine as the Father is divine.

The selections begin with texts from *Against Heresies* 1 which present a brief critique of a hypothesis advanced by Ptolemaic Valentianians,[2] as well as Irenaeus's articulation of his own hypothesis of scripture. These are followed by lengthier selections from *Against Heresies* 3 and 5. His arguments are often polemical in tone, since Irenaeus desired to challenge theologies that assert, amongst other points, that Jesus was less than fully human, was less than fully divine, or was not one being. Nevertheless Irenaeus's own thought emerges through and throughout the polemic. Indeed, his polemical and constructive arguments often go hand in hand. The principal themes found in these pages include the unity of Jesus Christ as the incarnate Word-Son of God; the divine and human generations of Jesus; the recapitulation of all things, including humanity, by the incarnate Word-Son; the union of God and humanity accomplished in the Christological

2 See the account of Ptolemaic theology above, pp. 99–102.

union; the identification of Jesus as the second Adam; the epistemic value of the incarnation for learning the things of God; and the redemptive work of Jesus's death on behalf of human beings.

The following translations are based upon the critical edition of A. Rousseau et al., *Irénée de Lyon: Contre les hérésies*, SChr 152, 153, 210, 211, 263, and 264 (Paris: Éditions du Cerf, 1965–1982).

TRANSLATION

Against Heresies 1.9.1–3 and 1.10.1

9, 1. You see then, my friend, how they deceive themselves by using this method,[3] how they abuse the scriptures by attempting to establish their fiction[4] from them. On account of this I have reported their very words,[5] so that you might learn from them the treachery of their methods and the wickedness of their deviation.[6] First of all, if John had intended to disclose the Ogdoad on high, he would have preserved the order of its emission. He would have placed the first Tetrad – being the most venerable, as they say – among the first names, and he would have added the second in the same way, so that the order of the Ogdoad would be manifested by the order of the names. And he would not, after so long an interval [in the text], as if it had been completely forgotten and then remembered, have mentioned the first Tetrad in the last place. Second, if he had intended to indicate the conjugal couples,[7] he would not have omitted the name Church,[8] or else, in the case of the rest of the conjugal couples, he would have been content with mentioning the masculine Aeons,[9] since the female Aeons[10] would be implied, so as to preserve

3 In *AH* 1.8.1 Irenaeus identifies two methodological concerns: his opponents mishandle scriptural texts by adapting them to their fantasy and by abstracting them from their original contexts and rearranging them. He elaborates upon these methodological concerns in *AH* 1.9.4.

4 In Greek, *plasma*. Irenaeus makes use of several terms from ancient literary and rhetorical theory in his polemic. He uses the term *plasma*, "fiction," several times (he also uses *mythos*, "myth") between *AH* 1.8.1 and 1.9.4 in order to characterize the hypothesis of his opponents as fictional rather than factual.

5 That is, the Ptolemaic account in *AH* 1.8.5, translated above on pp. 99–102.

6 The deviation of which Irenaeus speaks is from the true hypothesis, Irenaeus's version of which may be found in *AH* 1.10.1.

7 In Greek, *suzugia*.

8 In Greek, *ekklēsia*; referring to the Aeon of that name: see *AH* 1.1.2.

9 In Greek, *arrēn*.

10 In Greek, *dunamenōn kakeinōn* (literally, "those other powers").

uniformity across all of them. Or, if he had enumerated the conjugal partners[11] of the rest [of the Aeons], he also would have disclosed the conjugal partner of Human Being[12] and would not have left it to us to find out her name by divination.

2. Therefore, the fabricated nature of their exegesis is obvious. For when John proclaims one God Almighty and one only-begotten Christ Jesus through whom all things were made,[13] he says that the latter is the Word of God,[14] the Only-Begotten,[15] the Maker of all things, the true Light who enlightens every human being,[16] the Maker of the world,[17] the one who came to his own,[18] the one who became flesh and dwelt among us.[19] These people, [however], distort [these statements] by a specious exegesis. They maintain that one is Only-Begotten[20] by emission, whom they also call Beginning,[21] but another they maintain became Savior,[22] another is Word,[23] the son of the Only-Begotten, and another is Christ, who was emitted for the restoration of the Fullness.[24] By wresting each one of these terms from the truth and by misusing the names, they have transferred them to their own hypothesis.[25] As a result, according to them, John makes no mention of the Lord Jesus Christ in all of these passages. For when he was speaking of Father, Grace, Only-Begotten, Truth, Word, Life, Human Being, and Church, according to their hypothesis he was speaking about the first Ogdoad,[26] in which there was as of yet neither Jesus, nor Christ, the teacher of John. But the Apostle has made it clear that he was not speaking about their conjugal couples but about our Lord Jesus Christ, whom he knew to be the Word of God. For recapitulating the word he

11 In Greek, *suzugia*. 12 In Greek, *anthrōpos*. 13 John 1:3. 14 John 1:1.
15 See John 1:18. 16 John 1:9. 17 John 1:10. 18 John 1:11. 19 John 1:14.
20 In Greek, *monogenēs*. 21 In Greek, *archē*. 22 In Greek, *sōtēr*.
23 In Greek, *logos*.
24 The Greek term *plērōma*, "fullness," refers to the totality of Aeons as found in the hypothesis of Ptolemaeus recounted by Irenaeus in *AH* 1.1–8.
25 In Greek, *hypothesis*. As with the term *plasma*, Irenaeus appropriates the term *hypothesis* from ancient literary and rhetorical theory. In Irenaeus *hypothesis* is a technical term referring to the plot or argument of a literary narrative or rhetorical discourse (as is most easily seen in *AH* 1.9.4). He uses the term to speak of the theological systems affirmed by his opponents as well as the church catholic. Over the course of these sections Irenaeus is contending that his opponents abstract verses, names, and expressions from scripture and rearrange them such that they support a *hypothesis* (a plot, narrative, or subject matter) different from that articulated by scripture. Which is to say, he is arguing that the Ptolemaic account is a fictional *hypothesis*.
26 The first eight Aeons.

said earlier about what was in the beginning,[27] he adds: "And the Word became flesh and dwelt among us."[28] But according to their hypothesis it is not Word who became flesh, since he in fact never even went outside of the Fullness, but rather it is Savior, who was made out of all of them[29] and was born later than Word.

3. Learn then, you fools, that Jesus who suffered for us and dwelt among us is himself the Word of God. For if another one of the Aeons became flesh for our very own salvation, it would be reasonable for the Apostle to have spoken about another. But if the one who descended and ascended is the Word of the Father, the only-begotten Son of the only God, who was made flesh for human beings according to the good pleasure of the Father, it is neither about another one nor about the Ogdoad that John wrote this account, but about the Lord Jesus Christ. For according to them Word did not become flesh directly.[30] In fact, they say Savior put on a soulish body,[31] which had been furnished from Economy by an ineffable providence, so that he could become visible and tangible.[32] The flesh, however, is that ancient handiwork made by God from the dust on account of Adam, and it is that which John declares the Word of God has truly become. And [thus] their primary and fundamental Ogdoad has been dismantled. For, since it has been proven that the Word, Only-Begotten, Life, Light, Savior, Christ, and Son of God are one and the same, and it is this very one who became flesh for us, [then] the framework[33] of their Ogdoad has been dismantled. And with this dismantled, their whole hypothesis has crumbled into pieces; it is by falsely ejaculating this hypothesis that they ravage the scriptures.

* * *

27 Irenaeus structures the clause *anakephalaioumenos gar peri tou eirēmenou autō anō en archē logou* ("For recapitulating the word he said earlier about what was in the beginning") in a way that brings together the words *en archē logou*, a construction which suggests the opening words of the Gospel of John, *en archē ēn o logos* ("in the beginning was the Word"). This is a clever play on words for the word (*logos*) John said earlier about what was the beginning is that the Word (*logos*) was in the beginning.

28 John 1:14.

29 According to the Ptolemaic account, the Aeon Savior is derived from all the other Aeons (see *AH* 1.3.4 and 1.7.1).

30 In Greek, *proēgoumenōs*. The idea behind this statement seems to be that rather than taking flesh himself (which is to say, "directly"), Word took on a body indirectly insofar as Savior (who is derived from all the other Aeons, including Word) took on a soulish body.

31 In Greek, *sōma psychikon*.

32 For further details, see *AH* 1.6.1.

33 In Greek, *skēnopēgia*. Irenaeus's use of this term in this context would surely bring to mind the use of *skēnoō* in John 1:14, thus suggesting that the Ptolemaic conception of the incarnation has also been dismantled.

10, 1. Now although the church is dispersed throughout the whole world, even to the ends of the earth, it has received from the apostles and their disciples the faith in one God, Father Almighty, "who made the heaven and the earth and the sea and all that are in them,"[34] and in one Christ Jesus, the Son of God, who became flesh for our salvation, and in [the] Holy Spirit, who has proclaimed the economies through the prophets: the coming, the birth from the virgin, the passion, the resurrection from the dead, and the bodily ascension into the heavens of the beloved Christ Jesus, our Lord, and his coming from the heavens in the glory of the Father "to recapitulate all things,"[35] and to raise up all flesh of the whole human race, so that "every knee should bow, in heaven and on the earth and under the earth," to Christ Jesus our Lord, and God, and Savior, and King, according to the good pleasure of the invisible Father, "and every tongue confess"[36] him, and so that he should render a just judgment toward all, on the one hand sending to the eternal fire the "spiritual forces of evil,"[37] the angels who transgressed and became apostates, and the impious, unjust, lawless, and blasphemous among human beings, but on the other hand graciously conferring life incorruptible and laying eternal glory upon the righteous, and holy, and those who have kept his commandments and have persevered in his love, both those who did so from the beginning and those who did so after repentance.

*

* *

Against Heresies 3.16.1–9

16, 1. There are some who say that Jesus was the receptacle of Christ, and it was upon him that Christ descended from above as a dove, that once [Christ] had disclosed the unnamable Father he entered into the Fullness in an incomprehensible and invisible manner (for not only was he not perceived by human beings, but also not by those Authorities and Powers who are in heaven), and that Jesus is a son, Christ is a father, and God is the father of Christ.[38] Others say that he suffered only in appearance, being impassible by nature. The followers of Valentinus say that Jesus of the economy is the very one

34 Exod 20:11 LXX; Ps 145(146):6; Acts 4:24, 14:15. 35 Eph 1:10.
36 Phil 2:10–11. 37 Eph 6:12. 38 See *AH* 1.12.4.

that passed through Mary and the one on whom Savior descended from on high, who is also called Christ[39] because he possessed the names of all those who emitted him. And [they say] that [Savior] shared his own power and his own name with [Jesus] of the economy, so that death might be abolished through him, and that Father might be known through that Savior, who descended from on high, whom they also say is himself the receptacle of Christ and of the entire Fullness. Though they confess one Christ Jesus at least with words, in truth their thinking divides him. For this is their hypothesis, as we have said before: they say that one was Christ who was emitted beforehand by Only-Begotten for the restoration of the Fullness, that another is Savior who was emitted for the glorification of Father, and that another is [Jesus] of the economy, whom they say suffered when Savior returned to the Fullness carrying Christ. On account of this, we think it necessary to summon the entire teaching of the apostles about our Lord Jesus Christ, and to show that they not only thought nothing like this about him, but even more that by the Holy Spirit they indicated that there would be some who would undertake to teach such things, sent under the auspices of Satan to overthrow the faith of some and drag them away from life.

2. That John knew one and the same Word of God, and that this one was the Only-Begotten, and that this one became incarnate for our salvation, Jesus Christ our Lord, we have sufficiently demonstrated from the words of John himself.

Moreover, Matthew also knew one and the same Christ Jesus. When [Matthew] set forth his human generation from the virgin (seeing that God promised David to raise up an eternal king "from the fruit of his loins"[40] after having much earlier made the same promise to Abraham), he said: "The book of the generation of Jesus Christ, the son of David, the son of Abraham."[41] Then, in order to free our minds from suspicion about Joseph, he said: "Now the generation of Christ took place in this way: when his mother had been betrothed to Joseph, before they came together, she was found with child from the Holy Spirit."[42] Then when Joseph had it in mind to send Mary away because she was pregnant, an angel of God appeared before him, saying: "Do not be afraid to take Mary as your wife; for that

39 The Latin has *Christum* but W. W. Harvey, *Sancti Irenaei episcopi Lugdunensis Libros quinque adversus haereses*, 2 vols. (Cambridge: Cambridge University Press, 1857), vol. 2, p. 82) has suggested *Totum* ("All"), which better fits the logic of the sentence and better conforms to other passages of Irenaeus (e.g. *AH* 1.2.6).

40 Ps 131(132):11. 41 Matt 1:1. 42 Matt 1:18.

which she has in her womb is from the Holy Spirit. She will bear a son, and you will call his name Jesus: for he will save his people from their sins. Now all this took place so that what the Lord had spoken by the prophet might be fulfilled: 'Behold! A virgin will conceive and will bring forth a son, and they will call his name Emmanuel, which means, God with us.'"[43] Thus, he clearly indicates that the promise made to the fathers has been fulfilled, that the Son of God was born of the virgin, and that this very one is the Savior, Christ whom the prophets foretold. It is not as they themselves[44] say, that Jesus himself is the one who was born of Mary but it is Christ who descended from above. Besides, Matthew could have said, "Now the generation of *Jesus* took place in this way," but the Holy Spirit, foreseeing these distorters [of scripture] and guarding against their fraud, said through Matthew, "Now the generation of *Christ* took place in this way," and that this one is Emmanuel, so that we would not think him to be only a human being (for not by the will of the flesh, nor by the will of man, but by the will of God was the Word made flesh),[45] nor suppose that Jesus was one and Christ another, but so that we would know that they are one and the same.

3. This is precisely what Paul explains when writing to the Romans: "Paul, an apostle of Christ Jesus, appointed for the gospel of God, which he promised beforehand through his prophets in the holy scriptures, [the gospel] concerning his Son, who was from the seed of David according to the flesh and was appointed the Son of God in power according to the Spirit of holiness by the resurrection from the dead, Jesus Christ our Lord."[46] And again when writing to the Romans he says about Israel: "To them belong the patriarchs[47] and from them, according to the flesh, is the Christ, who is God over all and blessed forever."[48] Once more in the letter to the Galatians he says: "When the fullness of time had come, God sent his Son, made of a woman, made under the law, to redeem those under the law, so that we might receive adoption."[49] [These texts] plainly indicate one God, who through the prophets made the promise of his Son, and one Jesus Christ our Lord, who was from the seed of David according to his generation from Mary, and that this Jesus Christ was appointed Son of God in power according to the Spirit of holiness by the resurrection from the

43 Matt 1:20–23, quoting Isa 7:14. 44 Speaking of his Valentinian opponents.
45 See John 1:13–14. 46 Rom 1:1–4. 47 In Latin, *patres* (literally, "fathers").
48 Rom 9:5. 49 Gal 4:4–5.

dead, that he might be the firstborn of the dead,[50] just as he is firstborn of all creation.[51] The Son of God was made the Son of Man, so that by him we might receive adoption, humankind bearing, taking hold of, and embracing the Son of God.

For this reason also Mark says, "The beginning of the gospel of Jesus Christ, the Son of God, as it is written in the prophets."[52] He knows one and the same Son of God, Jesus Christ, who was announced by the prophets, who was from the fruit of David's loins,[53] Emmanuel,[54] the "Messenger of Great Counsel"[55] of the Father.

This is the one by whom and in whom[56] God made the dawn[57] and the just one[58] to rise in the house of David[59] and erected in it a horn of salvation,[60] and, as David says when discussing the reasons for his birth, "established a testimony in Jacob and he put into place a law in Israel ... so that the next generation, the children who will be born from them, would know it, and they themselves will arise and tell it to their children, so that they place their hope in God and seek after his commandments."[61] Again, the angel, proclaiming the good news to Mary, said, "He will be great, and will be called the Son of the Most High, and the Lord shall give to him the throne of his father David,"[62] thereby declaring that he who is the Son of the Most High is the very same one as the son of David. And David too, knowing through the Spirit the economy of his coming, [that economy] by which he rules over all the living and the dead,[63] confessed that he is the Lord who is sitting at the right hand of the Most High Father.

4. And Simeon too, who "received a revelation from the Holy Spirit that he would not see death until he had first seen the Christ,"[64] "when he took" Jesus, the first-begotten of the virgin, "into his hands, he blessed God and said, 'Now, O Lord, you are letting your servant depart in peace, according to your word, because my eyes have seen your salvation, which you have prepared in the presence of all peoples, a light for revelation to the

50 See Col 1:18. 51 See Col 1:15. 52 Mark 1:1–2.
53 See Ps 131(132):11. 54 See Isa 7:14. 55 Isa 9:5 LXX.
56 In Latin, *per quem*. The sense of this phrase is that the Word is both the agent of the activity and the product of that activity. See Rousseau, SChr 210, pp. 316–317; see also *AH* 3.10.2, "for all things had entered upon a new phase the Word arranging in a new manner, the coming of the flesh."
57 Luke 1:78. 58 See Jer 23:5.
59 Luke 1:69. This reference and that to the rising sun indicate that Irenaeus has shifted his discussion to the Gospel of Luke.
60 Luke 1:69. 61 Ps 77(78):5–7, with omissions. 62 Luke 1:32.
63 See *AH* 3.16.6. 64 Luke 2:26.

Gentiles and the glory of your people Israel.'"[65] [In saying this] he confessed that the infant he was holding in his hands, Jesus born of Mary, was himself Christ, the Son of God, the light of the human race and the glory of Israel itself, and the peace and consolation of those who have fallen asleep. For [Jesus] was already despoiling human beings by removing their ignorance, giving them knowledge of himself, and making plunder of those who came to know him, as Isaiah says, "Call his name: Swiftly Spoil, Speedily Plunder."[66] Now these are the works of Christ.

Therefore, it was Christ himself whom Simeon was holding when he blessed the Most High; whom the shepherds saw when they glorified God;[67] whom John recognized as Lord and greeted with leaping when he was still in his mother's womb and [Christ] in Mary's womb;[68] whom the magi saw and adored and to whom they brought the aforementioned gifts when they prostrated themselves before the eternal king, before departing by another way,[69] returning no longer by the way of the Assyrians – "for before the child knows how to call father or mother, he will receive the power of Damascus and the spoils of Samaria before the king of Assyria,"[70] thereby making known in a mysterious but powerful manner that the Lord would overcome Amalech with a hidden hand.[71] For this reason too he snatched away those boys in the hometown of David who had the happy lot to be born at that time, that he might send them ahead into his kingdom.[72] Though a child himself, he prepared children of human parents as witnesses: they were killed, according to the scriptures, on behalf of Christ who was born "in Bethlehem of Judaea,"[73] "in the city of David."[74]

5. For this reason too the Lord said to his disciples after his resurrection, "O how foolish and slow of heart you are to believe all that the prophets have spoken! Was it not necessary for the Christ to suffer these things and so to enter into his glory?"[75] And again he said to them, "These are the words that I spoke to you while I was still with you: that everything written about me in the law of Moses, the prophets, and the psalms had to be fulfilled. Then he opened their minds so that they could understand the scriptures, and he said to them, 'Thus it is written, that the Christ is to suffer and to rise again from the dead, and that remission of sins is to be

65 Luke 2:28–32. 66 Isa 8:3 LXX. 67 See Luke 2:20.
68 See Luke 1:41. 69 See Matt 2:11–12. 70 Isa 8:4 LXX.
71 See Exod 17:16. Also Justin Martyr, *Dialogue with Trypho* 49.8 and 77–78.
72 See Matt 2:16. 73 Matt 2:5. 74 Luke 2:11. 75 Luke 24:25–26.

proclaimed to all people in his name.'"[76] Now it is this one who was born of Mary, for he said, "It is necessary for the Son of Man to suffer many things, to be rejected, to be crucified, and on the third day to rise again."[77] Therefore, the gospel does not know any other Son of Man except the one who was from Mary and who also suffered, and it does not know another Christ who flew away from Jesus before his passion,[78] but it knows this one who was born as Jesus Christ, the Son of God, and that this same one suffered and then was resurrected.

This is what John, the disciple of the Lord, confirmed when he said, "These things have been written so that you may believe that Jesus is the Christ, the Son of God, and so that by believing you may have eternal life in his name."[79] [He said this] because he foresaw these blasphemous hypotheses[80] that divide the Lord (insofar as they can) by saying that he was made from two different substances.[81] For this reason he has also given us this testimony in his epistle: "Little children, it is the last hour! And as you have heard that antichrist is coming, now many antichrists have appeared. From this we know that it is the last hour. They went out from us, but they were not of us; for if they had been of us, they would certainly have remained with us. And so, they have made it clear that they are not of us."[82] "Know, therefore, that every lie is from without and is not from the truth. Who is the liar, except the one who denies that Jesus is the Christ? This is the antichrist."[83]

6. Now even though all those we have previously mentioned certainly confess one Jesus Christ with their tongue, they make fools of themselves by thinking one thing but saying another. For their various hypotheses,[84] as we have shown, proclaim one who suffered and was born, namely, Jesus,

76 See Luke 24:44–47.

77 Luke 9:22; Matt 16:21; Mark 8:31. Irenaeus, as does Justin (*Dialogue with Trypho* 76.7), has "crucified" where the New Testament texts have "killed."

78 The Latin here is: *Non ergo alterum Filium hominis novit Euangelium nisi hunc qui ex Maria, qui et passus est, sed neque Christum avolantem ante passionem ab Iesu.* Rousseau's Greek retroversion suggests that the underlying Greek was *allon* for *alter*, *alla* for *nisi*, and *oude* for *sed*. However, this sentence seems to make the best sense if underneath *nisi* was *ei mē*, and under *sed* a second *allon* (which the Latin translator mistook for *alla* and, therefore, translated as *sed* instead of using another *alterum*, as would have been proper).

79 John 20:31. 80 In Latin, *regula*.

81 In Latin, *ex altera et altera substantia dicentes eum factum*. By "substances" Irenaeus means individual entities. His argument is that Jesus Christ is not constituted by the joining of the human Jesus and the aeonic Christ, two distinct entities, but rather that the one Jesus Christ, the Son of God, was born of Mary.

82 1 John 2:18–19. 83 1 John 2:21–22. 84 In Latin, *argumentum*.

and another who descended on him and ascended again, namely, Christ. The first of these, they say, is the one who belongs to the Creator, either [Jesus] of the economy or the one who is from Joseph, and they argue that this one is passible. The second, they say, has descended from the invisible and ineffable [sphere], and they declare this one to be invisible, incomprehensible, and impassible. Accordingly, they stray from the truth because their thinking forsakes the one who is truly God. For they are ignorant of the fact that his only-begotten Word, who is always present with the human race, was united to and interspersed in his own formation, according to the pleasure of the Father, and was made flesh: he himself is Jesus Christ our Lord, who suffered for us and rose on account of us and will come again in the glory of the Father to resurrect all flesh and to manifest salvation and to extend the rule of just judgment to all who were made by him.[85] Therefore, there is one God the Father, as we have shown, and one Christ Jesus our Lord, who came through the whole economy[86] and recapitulated all things in himself. Now, included in "all things" is also humanity, the handiwork of God; therefore, humanity also was recapitulated in him, the invisible made visible, the incomprehensible made comprehensible, the impassible passible, the Word human. He recapitulated all things in himself so that, just as the Word of God is preeminent among supercelestial, spiritual, and invisible beings, so too he might have preeminence among visible and corporeal beings and might, by taking primacy to himself and appointing himself head of the church, draw all things to himself at the proper time.

7. For with [the Word] there is nothing disorderly or untimely, just as there is nothing disharmonious with the Father. For all things are foreknown by the Father, but they are accomplished by the Son in a harmonious and orderly manner at the proper time. For this reason when Mary was pushing for the wonderful miracle of the wine – wanting to partake of the cup of blessing[87] ahead of time – the Lord rebuffed her untimely haste, saying, "Woman, what is this to me and to you? My hour has not yet come,"[88] as he was awaiting the very hour foreknown by the Father. For this reason [too] when people were frequently trying to arrest him, it says, "No one laid

85 In Latin, *regulam iusti iudicii extendere omnibus qui sub ipso facti sunt*. This phrase could also be translated: "to extend … to all who were made subject to him." With this translation the phrase would refer to the judgment of the guilty that also follows upon Christ's return.

86 In Latin, *per universam dispositionem*.

87 In Latin, *compendii poculo*: see 1 Cor 10:16–17 (*potērion eulogias*).

88 John 2:4.

a hand on him because the hour" of his arrest "had not yet come."[89] Nor had the time of his passion [come], which was foreknown by the Father, as also the prophet Habakkuk says, "When the years will draw near, you will be recognized; when the time comes, you will be revealed; when my soul is disturbed by anger, you will be reminded of your mercy."[90] And Paul too says, "When the fullness of time had come, God sent his Son."[91]

This makes it clear that our Lord accomplished all the things foreknown by the Father according to the order, time, and hour that was foreknown and proper. He is one and the same, as well as rich and great. For he serves the rich and great will of the Father since he is himself the Savior of those who are saved, the Lord of those who are under dominion, God of those who have been created, the Only-Begotten of the Father, the Christ who was announced beforehand, the Word of God who was incarnated, when the fullness of time had come at which it was proper for the Son of God to become the Son of Man.

8. All, therefore, are outside the economy who consider, under the pretext of knowledge, Jesus to be one, Christ another, the Only-Begotten another again, the Word still another, and yet another the Savior, whom the disciples of error say is an emission of those which were made Aeons in a diminishing manner.[92] Such people appear to be sheep, for they have a veneer of language which makes them appear similar to us insofar as they say the same thing as we do, but in reality they are wolves.[93] For their doctrine is homicidal, as they concoct numerous gods and invent many Fathers while breaking up and dividing the Son of God in many [ways].

The Lord warned us in advance to avoid such people, and his disciple John, in the previously cited letter, instructed us to flee from them, saying, "Many deceivers have gone out into this world who do not confess that Jesus Christ has come in flesh. Such a person is the deceiver and the antichrist. Be on your guard against them, so that you do not lose that for which you have worked."[94] And again in this letter he said, "Many false prophets have gone out from the world. By this you know the Spirit of God: every spirit which confesses that Jesus Christ has come in the flesh is of God, and every spirit which divides Jesus is not of God but is of the antichrist."[95] And these statements resemble what was said in his gospel,

89 John 7:30. 90 Hab 3:2 LXX. 91 Gal 4:4. 92 In Latin, *in deminoratione*.
93 In Latin, *a foris oues* ("outwardly sheep"); *intrinsecus lupi* ("inwardly wolves"). See Matt 7:15.
94 2 John 7–8. 95 1 John 4:1–3.

that "the Word was made flesh and dwelt among us."[96] For the same reason again he proclaims in his letter, "Everyone who believes that Jesus is the Christ has been born of God,"[97] as he knows one and the same Jesus Christ, for whom the gates of heaven have been opened because of his bodily ascension, and who will come in the same flesh in which he suffered, revealing the glory of the Father.

9. Moreover, Paul agrees with these statements, and so when addressing the Romans he said, "How much more will those who receive the abundance of grace and righteousness reign in life through the one Jesus Christ."[98] Therefore, he does not know the Christ who flew away from Jesus, nor does he know the Savior who is on high, whom they say is impassible. For if one has suffered but another remained impassible, and one was born but another has descended on him who was born and then abandoned him, not one but two are manifested. Since, however, the Apostle knew [only] one who was born and suffered, Christ Jesus, he says again in the same letter, "Do you not know that all of us who have been baptized into Christ Jesus have been baptized into his death, so that, just as Christ was resurrected from the dead, so too we might walk in newness of life?"[99] Again [Paul] indicates that Christ suffered and is himself the Son of God who died for us and redeemed us by his blood at the appointed time, when he says, "For why did Christ, when we were still infirm, at the right time die for the ungodly? ... But God shows his love to us, in that, while we were still sinners, Christ died for us. How much more, now that we have been justified by his blood, will we be saved through him from wrath. For if while we were enemies we were reconciled to God through the death of his Son, how much more, now that we have been reconciled, will we be saved by his life."[100] In saying this he announces in the clearest possible way that the Christ, the Son of God, is the same one who was arrested and suffered and shed his blood for us, the one who also rose and was assumed into the heavens. As he himself says in the same place, "Christ has died, or rather rose, who is at the right hand of God."[101] And again, "Knowing that Christ, rising from the dead, will never die."[102] Seeing in advance through the Spirit the subdivisions of evil teachers and wanting to deprive them of every one of their opportunities

96 John 1:14. 97 1 John 5:1. 98 Rom 5:17, with omissions.
99 Rom 6:3–4, with omissions. 100 Rom 5:6, 8–10. 101 Rom 8:34.
102 Rom 6:9.

for dissension, he said all that has just been cited. [And once more:] "But if the Spirit of him who raised Jesus from the dead dwells in you, he who raised Christ from the dead will give life to your mortal bodies."[103] He all but cries out to those who wish to listen: Do not err! There is one and the same Jesus Christ, the Son of God, who reconciled us to God through his suffering and rose from the dead, who is at the right hand of the Father, and perfect in all things,[104] "who when he was beaten did not strike back, who when he suffered did not threaten,"[105] and when he endured tyranny he beseeched his Father to forgive those who crucified him. For he is the one who has truly saved, he is the Word of God, he the Only-Begotten of the Father, Christ Jesus our Lord.

*

* *

Against Heresies 3.18.1–3 and 3.18.5–7

18, 1. It has been clearly shown that the Word, who was with God in the beginning, by whom all things were made,[106] and who is always present with the human race, in the last days, at the time predetermined by the Father, was united to his own handiwork and made a human being capable of suffering: these points exclude, therefore, every objection of those who say, "If therefore he was born at that time, then the Christ did not exist beforehand." For we have shown that the Son of God did not begin to exist at that time, since he has always existed with the Father. But when he was incarnated and became a human being, he recapitulated in himself the lengthy narrative of humankind, granting salvation to us by way of summary,[107] so that we might receive in Christ Jesus what we had lost in Adam, namely, being according to the image and likeness of God. 2. Indeed, because man himself,[108] who had once been conquered

103 Rom 8:11. 104 See Matt 5:48; Col 1:28; Heb 2:10. 105 See 1 Pet 2:23.

106 See John 1:1–3.

107 Irenaeus is here using three terms with literary definitions – "recapitulated" (*recapitulavit*), "narrative" (*expositionem*), and "summary" (*compendio*) – to express his Christology and soteriology.

108 In Latin, *eum hominem*. This term may be an allusion to Adam, but, if so, Irenaeus's federalistic thinking (see, e.g., *AH* 5.16.3) on this matter would include the human race descended from Adam.

and expelled[109] through disobedience, could not refashion himself[110] and obtain the prize of victory, and again because the one who had fallen under sin could not obtain salvation, the Son, who is the Word of God, accomplished both of these things by descending from the Father, becoming incarnate, descending all the way to death, and completing the economy of our salvation.

Encouraging us to believe in him without misgivings, [Paul] says, "Do not say in your heart, 'Who ascends into heaven?' (that is, to bring Christ down), or 'Who descends into the abyss?' (that is, to free Christ from among the dead)."[111] Then he continues, "For if you confess with your mouth that Jesus is Lord and believe in your heart that God raised him from the dead, you will be saved."[112] And he gave the reason why the Word of God did these things, saying, "For to this end Christ lived and died and rose again, so that he might be Lord of the dead and the living."[113] And again, when writing to the Corinthians, he says, "But we preach Christ Jesus crucified,"[114] and he continues, "The cup of blessing which we bless, is it not a sharing[115] in the blood of Christ?"[116] 3. Now who is it that shared food with us? Would it be the Christ from on high invented by these people, who extended himself beyond Limit[117] and formed their Mother? Or would it be Emmanuel from the virgin, who ate butter and honey, and about whom the prophet said, "He is also a human being, and who will know him?"[118]

This is the same one who was proclaimed by Paul: "For I passed on to you, as of first importance," he said, "that Christ died for our sins in accordance with the scriptures, and that he was buried and rose again on the third day in accordance with the scriptures."[119] Therefore, it is clear that Paul knew no other Christ except only that one who suffered and was

109 In Latin, *elisus*. This term could be translated as "had been destroyed" or "had been shattered," making an abstract allusion to the Fall.

110 In Latin, *replasmari*. Rousseau suggests a perfect passive (*anaplasthēnai*) underlies the Latin perfect passive, but, given the context, *replasmari* more likely renders a perfect middle.

111 Rom 10:6–7; Rousseau follows the New Testament (future), but there is a strong Latin tradition of Rom 10:6–7 that corresponds closely to Irenaeus's use of *ascendit* and *descendit* (present/perfect) – cf. *vetus latina* in Cod. g. We have translated in present but perfect is possible.

112 Rom 10:9. 113 1 Cor 15:3–4. 114 1 Cor 1:23.

115 In Latin, *communicatio*. For the use of *communicatio* to render *koinōnia*, see, perhaps, Cicero, *de Or.* 3.53.204 and Quintilian 9.1.30, 9.2.20, 23, where *communicatio* is a figure of speech equivalent to *anakoinōsis*.

116 1 Cor 10:16. 117 In Latin, *Horos*: see *AH* 1.2.2, 4; 1.3.5. 118 Jer 17:9.

119 1 Cor 15:3–4.

buried and rose again, who was born, and whom he called a human being. For after he said, "Now if it is proclaimed that Christ has risen from the dead," he added the following to give the reason for his incarnation: "For as death came through a human being, so also through a human being came the resurrection from the dead."[120] And whenever it is a question of the passion of our Lord, his humanity, and his death, [Paul] makes use of the name "Christ," as in this [passage]: "Do not let what you eat ruin the one for whom Christ died."[121] And again, "But now in Christ you who were once far off have been made near by the blood of Christ."[122] And again, "Christ redeemed us from the curse of the law by becoming a curse for us, for it is written, 'Cursed is everyone who hangs on a tree.'"[123] And again, "And by your knowledge the weak person will die, the brother for whom Christ died."[124] [In these passages] he indicates that an impassible Christ did not descend on Jesus, but rather that Jesus himself is the Christ, who suffered for us, who died[125] and rose again, who descended and ascended, who is the Son of God made Son of Man, as the name itself indicates. For in the name of Christ is implied the one who has anointed, the one who has been anointed, and the unction itself with which he has been anointed. And indeed it is the Father who has anointed, the Son who has been anointed with the Spirit, who is the unction. As the Word said through Isaiah, "The Spirit of God is upon me, because he has anointed me,"[126] thereby indicating the Father who anoints, the Son who is anointed, and the unction who is the Spirit.

* * *

18, 5. … Now granting for the sake of argument that there are two who exist,[127] if anyone should pass judgment on them, the one who will be found much better, more patient, and truly good is that one who is beneficent in the midst of his own wounds, stripes, and the rest of the things done to him[128] and who does not remember the evil things done to him,[129] rather than that one who flew away and suffered no injury at all nor insult.

6. Now this same [reasoning] also counters those who claim that he suffered only in appearance. For if he did not actually suffer, he does not

120 1 Cor 15:21. 121 Rom 14:15. 122 Eph 2:13. 123 Gal 3:13.
124 1 Cor 8:11. 125 In Latin, *decubo* ("to lie down, sleep").
126 Isa 61:1; Luke 4:18.
127 Referring to the distinction his Valentinian opponents draw between Jesus and Christ.
128 See Isa 53:5, 7. 129 See Lev 19:18; Isa 43:25; Jer 31:34; Heb 8:12, 10:17.

deserve any thanks since there was not any suffering; and when we will begin to actually suffer, he will seem like a deceiver when he exhorts us to be beaten and to offer the other cheek,[130] seeing that he himself did not first suffer this in actuality; and just as he deceived them in seeming to them to be what he was not, so too he deceives us by exhorting us to endure that which he himself did not endure; and we will surpass the master by suffering and enduring what the master neither suffered nor endured.[131] But since our Lord alone is truly the master, and the Son of God is truly good, and the Word of God the Father is patient, he became the Son of Man. For he fought and conquered: he was a human being who contended on behalf of his fathers and paid the debt of disobedience through obedience, and he bound the strong one,[132] freed the weak ones, and gave salvation to his handiwork by destroying sin. For the Lord is most kind and merciful and he loves humankind.[133]

7. Therefore, he joined and united, as we said before, humanity to God. For if it were not a human being who defeated the enemy of humanity, the enemy would not have been defeated justly. Then again, unless God had given salvation, we would not possess it securely. And unless a human being had been united with God, human beings would not have been able to become partakers of incorruptibility. For it was necessary for the mediator between God and human beings to lead both back to friendship and concord by virtue of his relationship to both, and to do so in such a way that God takes up humanity and human beings give themselves to God. For in what way could we have shared in adoption as sons of God, if we had not, through the Son, received from God fellowship with God himself, and if his Word had not entered into fellowship with us when he was made flesh? This too is why he passed through every stage of life, restoring to everyone fellowship with God.

Therefore, those who claim that he was manifested in appearance only, having been neither born in the flesh nor made truly human, are still under the ancient condemnation. [In making this claim] they give patronage to sin, insofar as they think that death has not been overcome, though it "reigned from Adam to Moses, even in those who did not commit sins like Adam's transgression."[134] But when the law given by Moses came and testified about sin, that it is sinful,[135] it indeed took away [death's][136] kingdom by

130 Luke 6:29; Matt 5:39. 131 John 15:20. 132 Mark 3:27; Matt 12:29.
133 See Ps 102(103):8. 134 Rom 5:14.
135 Reading the Latin *peccator est* as a rendering of the substantive *hamartōlos*: see Rom 7:13.
136 In Latin, *eius*.

exposing [death][137] as a robber not a king and showing it to be a murderer. But the law was burdensome to human beings, who had sin in themselves, thereby showing them to be liable to death.[138] For even though the law was spiritual, it merely made sin known but did not destroy it – for sin did not have dominion over the Spirit, but over human beings. Therefore, it was necessary that the one who undertook to destroy sin and to redeem humankind from liability to death to himself become exactly what he[139] was, namely a human being, who had been dragged by sin into bondage and was held by death, so that sin might be destroyed by a human being and humankind might escape from death. For just as through the disobedience of the one human being,[140] the first formed of the virgin earth, many were made sinners and lost life, so also it was necessary that through the obedience of the one human being,[141] the first born of the virgin, many are justified and receive salvation.[142] So it was, then, that the Word of God was made human, just as Moses said, "God, his works are true."[143] Now if he were to appear to be flesh without having been made flesh, his work would not be true. But he was exactly what he appeared to be: God who recapitulated in himself the ancient formation of the human being,[144] so that he might destroy sin, eviscerate death, and give life to humankind. And for this reason his works are true.

*

* *

Against Heresies 3.19.1–3

19, 1. But, again, those who claim that the one begotten from Joseph is just a mere human being are stuck in the bondage of the ancient disobedience and are dying, as they have not yet been blended with the Word of God the Father, nor have they received liberty through the Son, as he himself said, "If the Son makes you free, you will be free indeed."[145] After all, since they do not know that the one [born] of the virgin is Emmanuel,

137 In Latin, *eum*, with the masculine indicating the underlying Greek *thanatos*.
138 In Latin, *reum mortis*. 139 Namely, Adam. 140 Namely, Adam.
141 Namely, Jesus. 142 See Rom 5:19. 143 Deut 32:4.
144 Here Irenaeus is referring to Adam and indirectly to the human race he began.
145 John 8:36.

they are deprived of his gift, which is eternal life. Moreover, since they have not accepted the Word of incorruption, they persist in mortal flesh and are debtors to death, because they have not received the antidote of life. It is to them that the Word speaks about his gift of grace, saying, "I have said, 'You are all gods and sons of the Most High, but you will die like human beings.'"[146] Without a doubt he says [these words] to those who refuse to receive the gift of adoption, but rather disdain the incarnation of the pure generation of the Word of God, defraud humankind of its ascent to God, and are ungrateful to the Word of God who became incarnate for them. For this is why the Word of God [was made] human, and the Son of God was made the Son of Man, that the human being, having been blended with the Word of God, and receiving adoption, might become Son of God. For by no other way could we have received incorruptibility and immortality, except by having been united to incorruptibility and immortality. But how could we be united to incorruptibility and immortality, unless incorruptibility and immortality had first become exactly what we are, so that the corruptible might be absorbed by incorruptibility, and the mortal by immortality, "that we might receive adoption as sons"?[147]

2. On account of this, "Who shall declare his generation?"[148] For "he is a human being, and who shall recognize him?"[149] Now the one who knows him is the one to whom the Father who is in heaven has revealed him[150] so that he may understand that the Son of Man, who "was born not of the will of flesh nor of the will of man,"[151] is "the Christ, the Son of the living God."[152] For we have demonstrated from the scriptures that not a single one of the sons of Adam is called "God" or named "Lord" with respect to their being.[153] And it is easy for all who may attain to even a modicum of the truth to see that [Christ] is proclaimed, in the proper sense of the terms and in a way unlike all who were human beings at that time, "God" and "Lord" and "eternal King" and "Only-Begotten" and "incarnate Word" by all the prophets and apostles and by the Spirit himself. Now the scriptures would not have given this testimony about him if he had been a mere human being like all the others. In fact, the divine scriptures give a double testimony about him, that he possessed in himself, in a way unlike all others, that noble generation[154] which is from the Most High Father, and that he

146 Ps 81(82):6–7. 147 Gal 4:5. 148 Isa 53:8. 149 Jer 17:9 LXX.
150 See Matt 16:17. 151 John 1:13. 152 Matt 16:16.
153 In Latin, *secundum eum*. 154 In Latin, *genituram*.

experienced that noble birth[155] which is from the virgin, and furthermore that he was a man lacking beauty[156] and capable of suffering, sat upon the foal of an ass,[157] was given vinegar and gall to drink,[158] was despised by the people,[159] and descended even into death,[160] and that he is the holy Lord,[161] wonderful Counselor,[162] the Beautiful in appearance,[163] mighty God,[164] and will come on the clouds as the judge of all:[165] the scriptures made all these prophecies about him.

3. For just as he was a human being so that he might be tempted, so also was he the Word so that he might be glorified: the Word remains quiescent[166] when he is tempted, dishonored, crucified, and put to death, whereas the human is absorbed when he conquers, endures [suffering], performs acts of kindness, rises again, and is taken up [into heaven]. It is this one, then, the Son of God, our Lord, who is the Word of the Father, that is also the Son of Man, because he is from Mary, who was descended from human beings and who was herself a human being, that has received a generation in the manner of human being and thereby was made the Son of Man.

It is because of this too that the Lord himself gave us a sign in the depths below and in the heights above, a sign for which a human being did not ask,[167] because [Ahaz] never expected that a virgin could become pregnant while still a virgin and give birth to a son, nor that this child would be "God with us,"[168] nor that he would descend into the lower parts of the earth[169] to seek the sheep which had been lost[170] (that which was his very own handiwork) and ascend to the heights above[171] to offer and commend to the Father

155 In Latin, *generatione*. Irenaeus here speaks of the two generations (births) of the Word-Son, the first divine and the second human. Rousseau (SChr 210, pp. 285 and 343) argues that the different Latin terms used of each generation, *genitura* and *generatio*, correspond to the Greek terms Irenaeus consistently uses to speak of his divine and human generation, *genea* and *gennēsis* (as seen, e.g., in *AH* 3.11.8), which in turn correspond to Isa 53:8 LXX and Matt 1:18 (as seen here and in *AH* 3.11.8).

156 See Isa 53:2. 157 Zech 9:9. 158 See Ps 68(69):22.

159 See Isa 53:3; Ps 21(22):7. 160 See Ps 21(22):16.

161 Possibly a reference to Isa 6:3. 162 Isa 9:6.

163 See Ps 44(45):3; possibly Ps 26(27):4. 164 Isa 9:6. 165 Dan 7:13, 26.

166 In Latin, *requiescente*; in Greek, *hēsuchazontos*.

167 Irenaeus is here glossing Isa 7:11–12, 14. In *AH* 3.20.1 Irenaeus discusses Jonah as foreshadowing the work of salvation, thus suggesting that Irenaeus means for Jonah to be understood as the sign from the depths below and Emmanuel as the sign from the heights above.

168 Isa 7:14. 169 See Eph 4:9. 170 See Luke 15:4–6.

171 See Eph 4:10.

the very humanity which had been found,[172] and thereby constitute in himself the first fruits of the resurrection of humanity. Accordingly, just as the head has risen again from the dead, so too the rest of the body, that is, every human being who is found in life, will rise when the time of its condemnation for disobedience has been fulfilled. [At that time the body], having been strengthened by the increase of God, will be knit together by its joints and ligaments,[173] each of the members having its proper and fitting place in the body. For there are many rooms in the Father's house,[174] since there are many parts in the body.

*

* *

Against Heresies 3.22.1 and 3.22.3

22, 1. They err, therefore, who say that he received nothing from the virgin, [saying this] to reject the inheritance of the flesh and to reject also the likeness. For if the one[175] received his formation and substance from the earth and by the hand and craftsmanship of God, but the other[176] did not [receive his] by the hand and craftsmanship of God, then the Craftsman has not preserved the likeness of the human being who was made according to his image and likeness,[177] and he will seem inconsistent and without anything on which to display his wisdom. Saying this also means that he merely appeared as a human being when he was not a human being, and that he was made a human being while receiving nothing from a human being. For if he did not receive the substance of his flesh from a human being, he was made neither a human being nor the Son of Man. And if he was not made exactly what we are, then he did nothing great when he suffered and endured. Moreover, everyone will profess that we are a body taken from the earth and a soul that receives the Spirit from God. And so, this is what the Word of God became, recapitulating his own handiwork in himself, and because of this he professes himself the Son of Man and blesses "the

172 See Luke 15:24, 32. It is not clear whether this clause is speaking of the human race or Jesus's human nature. The former is suggested by what comes before, the latter by what comes after.
173 See Col 2:19. 174 See John 14:2. 175 That is, Adam.
176 That is, Christ. 177 A periphrastic conflation of Gen 1:26–27.

meek, for they shall inherit the earth."[178] And, moreover, the apostle Paul in his letter to the Galatians plainly says, "God sent his Son, made from a woman."[179] And again, in the letter to the Romans, he says, "concerning his Son, who was made from the seed of David according to the flesh, who was constituted the Son of God in power according to the Spirit of holiness by his resurrection from the dead, Jesus Christ our Lord."[180]

* * *

22, 3. For this reason Luke shows that the genealogy that goes from the generation of our Lord to Adam contains seventy-two generations, and thereby he joins the end to the beginning and indicates that it is [our Lord] who has recapitulated in himself all the nations dispersed from the time of Adam, and all the languages and generations of human beings, including Adam himself. For this reason too Paul called Adam himself "a type of the one who is to come,"[181] because the Word, the Artisan of all things, prefigured in [Adam][182] the future economy of the Son of God for the human race,[183] in that God constituted the soulish human being first,[184] clearly so that he could be saved by the spiritual [human being].[185] After all, since the one who saves existed beforehand, it was necessary for the one who would be saved to come into existence, so that the one who saves would not exist in vain.

*
* *

Against Heresies 5.1.1–5.2.3

1, 1. For in no other way could we have learned the things of God, except if our teacher, who is the Word, was made a human being. After all, no one else could have revealed to us the things of the Father, except his own

178 Matt 5:5. 179 Gal 4:4. 180 Rom 1:3–4. 181 Rom 5:14.
182 Here Rousseau's emendation of *in semetipsum* with *in eo* is adopted.
183 In Latin, *Filium Dei humani generis*. This construction could also refer to the Son of God's human birth or humanity, as Rousseau understands it (SChr 210, p. 371), but see D. J. Unger's argument for the above meaning in Irenaeus: M. C. Steenberg and D. J. Unger, *St. Irenaeus of Lyons: Against the Heresies (Book 3)*, Ancient Christian Writers 64 (New York and Mahwah: Newman Press, 2012), pp. 195–196.
184 Namely, Adam. 185 Namely, Jesus. See 1 Cor 15:46.

proper Word. "For who" else "has known the mind of the Lord? Or who" else "has been his counselor?"[186] Again, in no other way could we have learned [the things of God] except by seeing our teacher and perceiving his voice with our ears, thus enabling us to become imitators of his works and doers of his words and thereby to have communion with him. As a result, we who have been made only recently receive increase from the one who is perfect before all creation and are made in his likeness by the one who alone is beautiful and good and in possession of the gift of incorruptibility. Indeed, according to the foreknowledge of the Father we are predestined to be what we were not yet, having been made at times known in advance according to the ministry of the Word,[187] who is perfect in every way since he is mighty Word and true human being. It is he who redeemed us by his blood in accordance with reason when he "gave himself as a ransom"[188] for those who had been led into captivity. And because apostasy was ruling over us without justice and had alienated us from our nature by making us its own disciples (even though by nature we belonged to the omnipotent God), the Word of God, who is mighty in every way and not lacking in his own justice, has turned with justice against that apostasy itself. From it he has redeemed those who are his own, not with violence as that [apostasy] used when it began to rule over us in the beginning by insatiably dragging off those who were not its own, but by means of persuasion, as suits a God who obtains what he desires by persuasion and not by inflicting violence, so that what is just may not be subverted and the ancient handiwork of God may not perish. The Lord, therefore, redeemed us by his own blood, giving his soul for our souls and his flesh for our flesh,[189] and he poured out the Spirit of the Father to bring about the union and communion of God and human beings: bringing God down to human beings by the Spirit, lifting the human being up to God by his own incarnation, and at his coming giving us incorruptibility in a stable and true manner by communion with him. For these reasons all the teachings of the heretics have come to ruin.

2. How vain are those who claim that he only seemed to appear! For these things did not happen only in appearance but in reality and truth.[190]

186 Rom 11:34.

187 Here we follow Rousseau in omitting the Latin *initium facturae accepimus* which is not found in the Armenian (SChr 152, pp. 198–199).

188 1 Tim 2:6.

189 See *The First Letter of Clement* 49.6, translated in this volume on p. 52.

190 In Greek, *en hupostasei*.

Moreover, if he appeared to be a human being when he was not a human being, then he did not remain what he was in truth, namely, Spirit of God, since the Spirit is invisible, and there was no truth in him, for he was not what he appeared to be. Moreover, we already said that Abraham and the rest of the prophets saw him prophetically, prophesying through their visions what would come to pass. So then, if someone appeared right now who was not what he appeared to be, then some kind of prophetic vision has come to human beings, and it is necessary to wait for him to come on another occasion when he will be what he is now perceived to be prophetically. In addition, we have already demonstrated that saying that he only seems to have appeared is the same as saying that he received nothing from Mary. For he would not have truly had flesh and blood, by which he redeemed us, unless he had recapitulated in himself the ancient formation of Adam. How vain, then, are the disciples of Valentinus who teach this doctrine, in order that they might exclude life from the flesh and disdain the handiwork of God.

3. How vain too are the Ebionites! For they do not receive into their souls, by faith, the union of God and the human being, but persist in the old leaven[191] of their birth. Nor do they want to understand that the Holy Spirit came upon Mary and the power of the Most High overshadowed her,[192] and that because of this what was generated is holy and the Son of the Most High God, the Father of all. It is he who brought about the incarnation of his Son and made known a new birth, so that, just as we have inherited death through the first birth, so too we may inherit life through this birth. And so, these people disdain the commixture of the heavenly wine and wish to be only water of this world,[193] not accepting the commixture of God with them, but persisting in that Adam who was conquered and expelled from paradise. They do not take into consideration that, just as at the beginning of our formation in Adam when the breath of life from God was united to what had been formed it animated the human being and showed him to be soulish and endowed with reason, so too in the last days when the Word of the Father and the Spirit of God, having been united to the ancient substance of the formation of Adam, rendered the human being living and perfect, capable of grasping the perfect

191 See 1 Cor 5:7. 192 See Luke 1:35.

193 Epiphanius reports that the Ebionites used only water in their celebration of the Eucharist (*Panarion* 30.16.1).

Father, that just as in the soulish [human being][194] we all die, so too in the spiritual [human being][195] we may all be made alive. For at no time did Adam escape the Hands of God, to whom the Father was speaking when he said, "Let us make the human being after our image and likeness."[196] And on account of this, in the last days it is "not by the will of the flesh nor by the will of man,"[197] but by the good pleasure of the Father that his Hands have rendered the human being living, so that Adam might be made after the image and likeness of God.

2, 1. How vain too are those who claim that the Lord has come to that which belonged to another![198] They make it seem like he covets another's belongings, so that he might offer the human being made by another to that God who neither made nor formed but who from the beginning was deprived of his own formation of humanity. Therefore, his coming to that which, according to them, belonged to another, was not just. Nor has he truly redeemed us by his blood, if he was not truly made a human being. For when he restores to his own handiwork that which was said [of it] in the beginning, that the human being was made according to the image and likeness of God,[199] he is not fraudulently pillaging another's belongings but justly and benevolently recovering what belongs to him: justly with respect to the apostasy from which he redeems us by his blood and benevolently with respect to us who have been redeemed. For we gave nothing to him beforehand, and he does not desire anything from us as if he is in need; rather, it is we who are in need of him, that is, of communion with him. And for this reason he benevolently poured out himself[200] so that he might gather us to the bosom of his Father.

2. Vain, moreover, in every way are those who despise the whole economy of God, deny the salvation of the flesh, and scorn its regeneration, saying that it is not capable of receiving incorruption. But if this [flesh] is not saved, clearly the Lord has not redeemed us by his blood,[201] nor is the cup of the Eucharist a sharing in his blood, nor is the bread which

194 Namely, Adam. 195 Namely, Christ. 196 Gen 1:26. 197 See John 1:13.

198 In Latin, *in aliena*, which also yields the sense of the Lord coming to a strange domain, a realm not his own. Marcionite theology maintained that the God revealed in the Old Testament differs from the God revealed in the New Testament. This being the case, Jesus would have come to redeem human beings created by another God, "that which belonged to another."

199 See Gen 1:26. 200 See Isa 53:12. 201 See Col 1:14.

we break a sharing in his body.[202] For it is not blood unless it comes from veins, flesh, and the rest of the human substance – that which[203] the Word of God truly became.[204] He redeems us by his blood, just as the Apostle says of him, "In whom we have redemption by his blood, the remission of sins."[205] And since we are his members and are nourished by means of his creation (the creation that he himself presents to us when he causes his sun to rise and sends the rain according to his will),[206] he acknowledged the cup taken from creation as his own blood, by which he fortifies our blood, and affirmed the bread taken from creation as his own body, by which he fortifies our bodies.

3. So then, when the cup that has been mixed and the bread that has been prepared receive the word of God[207] and become the Eucharist, [that is] the blood and body of Christ,[208] by which the substance of our flesh is increased and fortified, how can they claim the flesh is incapable of receiving the gift of God, which is eternal life, when it is nourished by the blood and body of the Lord[209] and is a member of it? It is just as the blessed Apostle says in the epistle to the Ephesians that "we are members of his body, of his flesh, and of his bones."[210] [Here] he is not speaking about some spiritual and invisible human being, "for a spirit has neither bones nor flesh,"[211] but about a fully human organism[212] composed of flesh and nerves and bones that is nourished by the cup, which is his blood, and is fortified by the bread, which is his body. For the tree of the vine, having been placed[213] in the earth, bears fruit at the proper time, and "the grain of wheat falls into the earth,"[214] decomposes, and rises abundantly by the Spirit of God who holds together all things, and then by wisdom from God [the grain] comes

202 See 1 Cor 10:16.
203 Here the textual evidence supporting *quam* rather than *quae* is preferred.
204 These sentences make the most sense if we place a full stop here.
205 Col 1:14.
206 See Matt 5:45.
207 Following Rousseau's argument that *ton logon tou Theou* refers to the epiclesis offered at the celebration of the Eucharist (SChr 152, pp. 212–213). See *AH* 4.18.5.
208 Following Rousseau's proposed restitution (SChr 152, p. 213).
209 In Greek, *tou Kuriou* (fragment 4); Latin: *Christi*. Following the Greek as the *lectio difficilior*.
210 Eph 5:30.
211 Luke 24:39.
212 In Greek, *peri tēs kata ton alēthinon anthrōpon oikonomias*.
213 In Greek, *klithen*. The term here conveys the idea of being planted or sown; the same term is used in the next sentence to refer to the burial of the human body which will also rise to life after being placed in the earth.
214 John 12:24.

to be used by human beings,[215] receives the word of God, and so becomes the Eucharist, which is the body and blood of Christ. In the same way too, our bodies are nourished by [the Eucharist], are placed in the earth, and undergo decomposition in it, and they shall rise at the proper time, when the Word of God grants resurrection to them, "to the glory of God the Father,"[216] who procures immortality for that which is mortal and freely grants incorruptibility to that which is corruptible, for the power of God is made perfect in weakness.[217] [Now things happen in this way] so that we do not, as if we have life from ourselves, become puffed up and exalted against God by adopting ungrateful thoughts. Rather, [things happen in this way] so that, learning by experience that it is by means of his preeminence and not because of our nature that we endure forever, we may never have an incorrect opinion concerning God as he is, nor fail to understand our own nature, but we may know what God is able [to do] and what benefits humanity, and never be led astray from the true comprehension of things as they are, that is to say, of God and humanity. And could it not be the case, as we said before, that God allowed our dissolution into the earth precisely for this reason, so that we may be instructed in every way and thereby in the future be accurate in every respect, failing to understand neither God nor ourselves?

*

* *

Against Heresies 5.7.1–2

7, 1. Therefore, the manner in which Christ rose in the substance of the flesh and showed to the disciples the marks of the nails and the opening in his side (now these are proofs that his flesh rose from the dead) is the same as the manner in which, as [the Apostle] says, "he also will raise us up by his

215 In Greek, *dia tēs sophias Theou eis chrēsin elthonta anthrōpōn*. Rousseau argues against the originality of *Theou*, which has no equivalent in the Latin and Armenian texts (SChr 152, pp. 213–215). The strength of his argument lies in his demonstration that this clause speaks of human agency, which leads him to conclude that "wisdom" must refer to human ingenuity or skill and, in turn, to the belief that a reference to the "wisdom of God" is out of place. As the above translation shows, however, it is not necessary to emend the Greek text in order to convey human agency. Moreover, the phrase *eis chrēsin* makes better sense when *Theou* is preserved.

216 Phil 2:11. 217 See 2 Cor 12:9.

power."[218] And again, he says to the Romans, "But if the Spirit of him who raised Jesus from the dead dwells in you, he who raised Christ from the dead will also give life to your mortal bodies."[219] What, then, are "mortal bodies"? Could they be souls? On the contrary, souls are incorporeal when compared to mortal bodies: for God "breathed into the face" of the human being "the breath of life, and the human being was made into a living soul."[220] Now the breath of life is incorporeal. So they certainly cannot call it[221] mortal, since it is the breath of life. And accordingly David says, "My soul also shall live for him,"[222] as its substance is immortal. Neither, though, can they say that the mortal body is the Spirit. What, then, is there left to call "the mortal body," except that which was formed – that is, the flesh, about which it is said that God "will give life" to it? For it is this which dies and is decomposed, but not the soul nor the Spirit. For to die is to lose the capacity to live, and then to become breathless, and inanimate, and devoid of motion, and to dissolve into those [elements] from which one has the beginning of [one's] substance. But this happens neither to the soul, for it is the breath of life, nor to the Spirit, for the Spirit, which cannot be decomposed and is itself the life of those who receive it, is uncompounded and simple. As it stands, then, death is shown to be a matter of the flesh, which, after the soul has departed, is made breathless and inanimate, and is decomposed little by little into the earth from which it had been taken. This, then, is [what is] mortal. Moreover, it is this of which [the Apostle] says, "He will give life to your mortal bodies."[223]

And accordingly he says about [the flesh] in the first [epistle] to the Corinthians, "So is it also with the resurrection of the dead: it is sown in corruption, it rises in incorruption."[224] For he says, "what you sow cannot be given life unless it first dies."[225] 2. Now what is that which is sown as a grain of wheat and will rot in the earth, except bodies which are placed into the earth, into which seeds are also thrown? And on account of this he said, "It is sown in dishonor, it rises in glory," for what is more dishonorable than dead flesh? Or in turn, what is more glorious than that which rises and receives incorruptibility? "It is sown in weakness, it rises in power" – indeed in a "weakness" that is its own because it is earth and it goes into earth, but

218 1 Cor 6:14. 219 Rom 8:11. 220 Gen 2:7.
221 In Latin, *ipsum*, with Rousseau who understands the referent as the "soul" (SChr 152, pp. 236–237).
222 Ps 21(22):30. 223 Rom 8:11. 224 1 Cor 15:42. 225 1 Cor 15:36.

in a "power" that belongs to God, who resuscitates it from the dead. "It is sown a soulish body, it rises a spiritual body."[226] Beyond any doubt [the Apostle] taught that what he said concerns neither the soul nor the spirit, but bodies which have been made dead. For these are soulish bodies, that is, [bodies] which partake of a soul. When they have lost their soul, they are made dead; and then, rising by means of the Spirit, they become spiritual bodies, so that by the Spirit they have life which endures forever.

"For now," [the Apostle] says, "we know in part and we prophesy in part ... but then, face to face."[227] And this is what was said by Peter, "Although you have not seen him, you love him; and even though you do not see him now, you believe in him; and by believing you will rejoice with inexpressible joy."[228] For our face will see the face of God, and it will rejoice with inexpressible joy, namely, when it sees that which is its own joy.

*

* *

Against Heresies 5.17.1–3

17, 1. Now the Creator is the one who is Father according to his love, Lord according to his power, and our Maker and Former according to his wisdom.[229] It was by transgressing his command that we became his enemies. And for this reason in recent times the Lord restored us to friendship by means of his own incarnation when he became "the mediator between God and human beings,"[230] not only making the Father, against whom we sinned, favorably disposed toward us and assuaging our disobedience by his own obedience, but also bestowing upon us [the gift of] conversion and submission to our Maker. For this reason also he taught us to say in the prayer, "And forgive us our debts,"[231] since the one to whom we were indebted is certainly our Father because we transgressed his command. Now who is this? Is he someone unknown, a Father who never at any time gives a command? Or rather is he the God who is proclaimed by the scriptures, to whom we were indebted because we transgressed his command? Now the command was given to the human being by the Word. For it is said,

226 All quotations in this section come from 1 Cor 15:43–44.

227 1 Cor 13:9, 12. 228 1 Pet 1:8.

229 In Greek, *plastēs*. The title evokes the formation of Adam from the dust (Gen 2:7).

230 1 Tim 2:5. 231 Matt 6:12.

"Adam heard the Voice[232] of the Lord God."[233] Rightly, then, does his Word say to the human being, "your sins are forgiven you"[234] – [for] the one against whom we had sinned in the beginning is the same as the one who gives remission of sins in the end. Or else, if we transgressed the command of one but it was another who said, "your sins are forgiven you,"[235] then the latter would be neither good, nor true, nor just. For how is one good if he gives from what does not belong to him? Or how is one just if he appropriates what belongs to another? And how have sins been truly forgiven unless he himself against whom we have sinned has granted forgiveness "by the tender mercy of our God in which he has visited us"[236] through his Son?

2. And for this reason, [the evangelist] says that when the paralytic had been healed, "upon seeing him the people glorified God, who gave such power to human beings."[237] Which God, then, did the people gathered there glorify? Could it really have been the unknown Father invented by the heretics? And how would they glorify him when he was completely unknown by them? It is clear, therefore, that the Israelites glorified the one who has been proclaimed God by the law and prophets, who also is the Father of our Lord. And for this reason he taught human beings truly, by the signs which he was doing, to give glory to God. But if he himself came from one Father, while the human beings who saw his powerful works glorified another Father,[238] then he has made them ungrateful to that Father who had sent the healing. But since it is from him who is God that the only-begotten Son had come for the salvation of human beings, he provoked the unbelievers, by the very miracles which he accomplished, to give glory to the Father. And to the Pharisees who did not accept the coming of his Son and for this reason did not believe in the forgiveness that came from him, he said, "So that you may know that the Son of Man has the power to forgive sins,"[239] and after he had said this, he commanded the paralytic to pick up the pallet on which he was lying and to go to his home.

232 In Latin, *vocem*. Irenaeus also uses *vox* as a name for the Word of God in *AH* 5.16.1 and 5.17.2.
233 Gen 3:8. 234 Matt 9:2; Luke 5:20. 235 Matt 9:2; Luke 5:20.
236 Luke 1:78. 237 Matt 9:8.
238 The Latin here is *patrem* but the Armenian testimony has the equivalent to *deum*, "God." The Latin is probably correct because the next part of the sentence has *eum patrem* as if two Fathers had been discussed before and only one of them is being specified there. If so, *patrem* is the *lectio difficilior*, which was changed in the Armenian version.
239 Matt 9:6.

By accomplishing this miracle, he confounded the unbelievers and signified that he himself is the Voice of God through whom, on the earth,[240] the human being received the commands: it was because he transgressed these that he became a sinner and the paralysis came as a consequence of the sins.

3. Therefore, when he forgave the sins he not only healed the human being but also clearly showed himself to be who he was. For if no one is able to forgive sins except God alone, and the Lord forgave them and healed the human being,[241] it is clear that he himself was the Word of God who was made the Son of Man, receiving from the Father the power of the forgiveness of sins because he was both human and God. In consequence of this, just as he would suffer for us as a human being, so too as God he would have compassion on us and forgive us our debts, which we owe to God our Creator.[242] And on account of this David said beforehand, "Blessed are they whose iniquities have been forgiven and whose sins have been covered! Blessed is the human being to whom the Lord will not impute[243] sin!"[244] [In saying this] he points out in advance the very forgiveness which comes by means of his coming, by which "he nullified the record" of our debt and "nailed it to the cross."[245] For[246] just as by a tree we became debtors to God, by a tree we receive the forgiveness of our debt.

240 The Armenian has the phrase "on the earth," but the Latin does not have the comparable phrase (*super terram*). Rousseau acknowledges the difficulty but leans toward the Armenian (SChr 152, pp. 280–283). While his argument is not wholly convincing, the inclusion of the phrase constitutes the *lectio difficilior*, so it appears in the translation.

241 Here the Armenian testimony (equivalent to *hominem*) is preferred to the Latin *homines*.

242 Here the Armenian testimony (equivalent to *tamquam* and *compatiatur*) is preferred to the Latin *quomodo* and *compassus est*.

243 Here the Armenian testimony (equivalent to *imputabit*) is preferred to the Latin *imputavit* because of its correspondence to Ps 31(32):1–2 and Rom 4:7–8.

244 Ps 31(32):1–2; Rom 4:7–8.

245 Col 2:14.

246 Here the Armenian testimony (equivalent to *enim*) is preferred to the Latin *uti*.

PART II

Developing Christological Traditions

13

Tertullian, *Apology* 21

Introduction and Translation by Jared Secord

INTRODUCTION

Little is known with certainty about the life of Tertullian, who authored some of the very earliest Christian literature written in Latin. He was from the city of Carthage in Roman North Africa, and his literary career in this city spanned from roughly 196 to 212; he was perhaps born around 170. From the few scattered comments he made about his own life, we learn that he was raised as a pagan, and became a Christian under unknown circumstances. Most scholars now doubt other details about Tertullian's life which come from later sources, such as Jerome's belief that his father was a Roman centurion, and Eusebius's suggestion that he was a lawyer in his pre-Christian career. One further point from Jerome about Tertullian's life likewise requires cautious treatment. This is the claim that Tertullian in middle age "lapsed" away from the catholic church into Montanism, a revivalist movement of Christianity established in the second century and eventually branded as heretical.[1] Though Tertullian's later works do show increasing signs of Montanism, it is impossible to divide up his career neatly into catholic and Montanist phases, as previous generations of scholars tended to do.

Questions of Montanism aside, Tertullian's *Apology* is one of his earliest works. This defense of Christianity was written in 197, soon after Septimius Severus (r. 193–211) had become the sole ruler of the Roman Empire, adding a Latin voice to an existing tradition of Christian apologetic literature written in Greek. His goals were to challenge popular rumors about Christian behavior and to offer a rational demonstration of Christianity's truth. In the process, Tertullian offered an explanation for the complicated

1 For more on Montanism, see the introduction to Tertullian's *Against Praxeas* in this volume on pp. 173–174.

relationship that Christianity had with Judaism, and presented many attacks of his own against what he believed to be the absurdities and hypocrisies of pagan belief.

The present selection displays Tertullian's characteristic erudition and argumentative spirit, offering a range of proofs to support the Christian belief that Christ was both human and God. What Christians believed about Christ, Tertullian claimed, was no less plausible than what some pagans believed about their gods. Christ's coming and his special status, moreover, were prophesied in the ancient writings of the Jews, and even recognized by none other than Pontius Pilate himself. According to Tertullian, there was no shortage of proof to justify Christian belief in Christ, and no reason for any rational person to doubt it.

There are two different manuscript traditions for the *Apology*. The translation offered here favors the tradition preserved in the Fulda manuscript, and is based on the Latin text as printed in Tobias Georges, *Tertullian. Apologeticum. Verteidigung des christlichen Glaubens*, Fontes Christiani 62 (Freiburg: Herder, 2015).

TRANSLATION

21, 1. But now that we have shown this sect[2] to have been inspired by the very ancient documents of the Jews, even though most people know, and we ourselves admit, that it is somewhat recent, as it is from the time of Tiberius,[3] perhaps there should be some reexamination of its status, seeing that as if under the cover of a very famous religion that is certainly lawful, it conceals something of its own thought. 2. After all, apart from the issue of antiquity, in matters of dietary restrictions, feast days, the very seal of the body,[4] and a common name, we do nothing in common with the Jews, which would certainly be fitting if we were subject to the same God. 3. Moreover, even the masses now understand Christ to be some human being, and such is what the Jews judged him to be: so it is quite easy for anyone to consider us worshipers of a human being. In truth we are not ashamed about Christ, as it pleases us to be identified and punished under his name, and neither do we think any differently about God. It is therefore necessary to say a little about Christ as God.

2 That is, Christianity.

3 The Roman emperor Tiberius (r. 14–37 CE).

4 That is, circumcision.

4. In every respect the Jews found favor with God, by reason of their remarkable justice and the faith of their original founders. Because of this they flourished by the greatness of their people and the loftiness of their kingdom, and so great was their prosperity in regard to the words of God, by which they were taught to be deserving of God and forewarned not to displease him. 5. But how greatly they failed! For they had become so puffed up that they fell through overconfidence in their fathers and turned aside from their teaching into a profane way of life. Although they themselves do not admit it, the present outcome would prove it. Scattered, wandering, exiled from their land and sky, they roam through the world without man or God as their king; they are not allowed to visit – or even to take a footstep – in their ancestral land, having the status of foreigners.[5] 6. Those holy voices warned them in advance of these things and at the same time all of these voices were always making known that in the very last course of time from every race and people and place God would gather to himself worshipers much more faithful than they, upon whom he would bestow more favor, on account of their capacity for greater teaching.

7. So he came, the one who was proclaimed in advance by God as destined to come for the restoration and illumination of the teaching, Christ the Son of God. As the overseer and instructor of this grace and teaching, as the illuminator and guide for the human race, the Son of God was prophesied, but he was not indeed born in such a way to be ashamed at the name of son or the seed of his father. 8. Born neither from incest with a sister nor from illicit sex with a daughter or another man's wife, he did not endure a god for a father who had scales or horns or feathers, a lover of Danaë turned into gold. These are the human acts of your Jupiter. 9. Moreover, the Son of God has a mother without any sexual impurity; the one he seems to have was not even married. But first let me tell about his substance, and so the character of his birth will be understood.

10. We have already said that God formed the entirety of this world by his Word and Reason and Power.[6] Even the wise among you agreed that the *Logos*, that is, Speech and Reason, seems to be the artificer of the universe. For Zeno defines this *Logos* as the maker that shaped all things in order; the same thing is also called fate and god and the mind of Jupiter

5 Jews received this punishment from Rome in the aftermath of the Bar Kokhba revolt (132–136 CE).

6 Chapter 17 of the work, not included in this selection.

and universal necessity. All these things Cleanthes brings together into Spirit, which he asserts pervades the universe.[7] 11. To Word, Reason, and likewise Power, through which we said that God formed all things, we too also attribute Spirit as its proper substance: when Spirit makes a proclamation, Word is in it; when Spirit puts things in order, Reason is present in it; and when Spirit brings things to completion, Power presides. We say that this [Word] was uttered from God and generated through utterance, and therefore is called "Son of God" and "God" on account of unity of substance: for God is also Spirit. 12. Even when a ray is put forth from the sun, it is a part of the whole; but the sun will be in the ray, because the ray is the sun's, nor is its substance divided, but extended, like a lamp lit from another lamp. The source of the material remains complete and undivided, although you may borrow many offshoots of its kind from it. 13. Thus what proceeded from God is God and the Son of God, and both are one. Thus it is Spirit from Spirit and God from God, a second in measure; it came to hold this position in terms of relative position, not in terms of permanent station,[8] and it did not cut itself off from its source, but went out from it. 14. So this ray of God, as was continually foretold in past times,[9] having descended into a certain virgin and having in her womb been shaped into flesh, is born, a human being mixed with God. Flesh built by Spirit is nourished, reaches adulthood, speaks, teaches, works, and is Christ. Accept this "story"[10] (which is like yours) for now, while we show how Christ is proved and who those beings are that provided you with rival stories of this sort for the destruction of the truth.

15. The Jews, too, knew that Christ would come, as it was of course to them that the prophets spoke. Even now they await his coming, and there is no greater source of contention between us and them than that they do not believe that he has already come. Two comings of his were specified: the first, which has already been fulfilled, when he came in the lowliness of the human condition; the second, which is imminent for the world when it reaches its end, when he will come in the loftiness of the power he received from his Father and the divinity he displays. The

7 Zeno of Citium founded the Stoic school of philosophy around 300 BCE. Cleanthes was his pupil, and his successor as head of the school.

8 In Latin, *numerum gradu non statu fecit*. See the similar language in *Against Praxeas* 2.4, translated in this volume on p. 177.

9 See Isa 7:14.

10 In Latin, *fabulam*.

first they failed to understand and the second, which was more clearly foretold and the object of their hope, they judged to be the only one. 16. The first coming they would have believed, if they had understood it, and if they had believed it, they would have obtained salvation: their failure to understand it was the desert of their sins. They themselves read what is written: they have been punished with the loss of their wisdom and understanding, the fruits of their eyes and ears.[11] 17. Based on his lowliness, then, they presumed that he was only a human being; it followed that based on his power they judged him to be a magician. For with a word he cast demons out of people, gave sight back to the blind, cleansed lepers, made the paralyzed walk again, and, finally, with a word he restored the dead to life; he made the very elements his slaves, restraining storms and walking on seas, showing that he was that Son who was both foretold earlier by God and born for the salvation of everyone, that primordial Word of God, firstborn, accompanied by Power and Reason and supported by Spirit.

18. But the Jews became so enraged at his teaching, by which their teachers and elites were refuted, particularly because huge crowds were flocking to him, that at last they brought him before Pontius Pilate, who was at that time the Roman procurator of Syria, and by the vehemence of their demands extorted from Pilate that Jesus be given to them for crucifixion. He himself had foretold that they would do this; this would not be enough, if the prophets also had not foretold the same in times past. 19. And yet when fixed to the cross he gave many indications of the special character of his death. For with a word he released his spirit of his own accord, anticipating the duty of the executioner. At the same moment, though the sun indicated it was midday, the day was withdrawn. Of course they judged it to be an eclipse, as they did not know that this too was foretold about Christ.[12] Not understanding why it happened, they denied it, and yet you have this worldwide catastrophe recorded in your archives. 20. Then his body was taken down and placed in a tomb; with great care the Jews surrounded it with a military guard. For he had foretold that he would be resurrected from death on the third day, and they wanted to prevent his disciples from furtively removing the body and deceiving those who were suspicious of them. 21. But on the third day suddenly the earth shook, the structure that had blocked the grave was knocked

11 See Isa 6:9–10. 12 See Amos 8:9.

down, and the guard was driven away in fear. Though none of his disciples appeared, nothing was found in the grave besides the burial cloths. 22. Nevertheless, the Jewish elite, in whose interest it was to spread news of a crime and to reclaim from the faith a people who would pay tribute and be subject to themselves, let it be known that the body had been stolen by his disciples. For he did not show himself to the crowds, lest the impious be freed from their error, and also so that faith, which is not destined for a mediocre reward, would remain a difficult thing. 23. With some of his disciples, however, he spent fifty days in Galilee, in a region of Judea, teaching them what they should teach. Then, after he had appointed them to the duty of preaching throughout the world, he was taken up into heaven enveloped by a cloud, far more convincingly than what the Proculi among you are accustomed to claim about Romulus.[13] 24. All these things about Christ were reported to Tiberius, at that time the emperor, by Pilate – who was himself already a Christian in the secret of his heart. Now even emperors would have believed these things about Christ, if emperors had not been necessary for the world, or if emperors could also be Christians. 25. Truly, in obedience to the precept of God their teacher the disciples spread themselves out through the world. They certainly suffered much when the Jews persecuted them but did so gladly because of their confidence in the truth; finally at Rome through the savagery of Nero Christian blood was sowed.[14]

26. But we shall show you that the very beings whom you worship are suitable witnesses of Christ.[15] It will be a great thing if I can employ these beings, because of whom you do not believe the Christians, in order to get you to believe Christians! 27. In the meantime, here you have an ordered exposition of our founding; here we have given an account of the origin of our community and our name, together with its founder. Let no one now hurl slanders upon me, let no one judge things to be different from what I have said, because it is not right for anyone to speak falsely about his religion. For when anyone claims to worship something different from what he worships, he denies what he worships, and transfers worship and honor to something else, and by this transference no longer worships what he

13 "Proculi" is the plural form of the Roman name Proculus. According to Roman tradition, a man of this name told a story about the encounter he had with Romulus, the legendary founder of Rome, after his death.

14 Nero (r. 54–68 CE) was responsible for the first major imperial persecution of Christians.

15 This looks ahead to the remainder of the *Apology*, not included in the present selection, where Tertullian cites pagan testimonies to Christ.

has denied. 28. We say it, we say it openly, and even when we are tormented and bleeding from your whips, we cry out: "We worship God through Christ!" Him you judge to be a human being, but through him God wished to be known and worshiped. 29. In response to the Jews I can say that they themselves learned to worship God though Moses; in answer to the Greeks I can say that Orpheus in Pieria, Musaeus at Athens, Melampus at Argos, and Trophonius in Boeotia bound men with their initiatory rites;[16] and in retort to you as well, rulers of the nations, I can say that Pompilius Numa was a human being who burdened the Romans with the most laborious superstitions.[17] 30. Christ may also be permitted to prepare divinity for himself, not in the way that Numa took rustic and still savage people and formed them into civilized human beings by terrifying them with a great multitude of many divinities that had to be favored, but as someone who should open the eyes of those who are already highly refined but misled by their very urbanity, so that they may recognize the truth. 31. Ask, therefore, if this divinity of Christ is true. If it is, what follows from this is the realization that falsehoods must be renounced, especially when the entire rationale is confirmed, which, hiding beneath the names and images of dead men, produces by certain signs and miracles and oracles confidence in his divinity.

16 All four figures were associated with initiatory mystery cults in the regions listed.

17 Pompilius Numa (r. 715–673 BCE) was Romulus's successor as king of Rome, and traditionally regarded as the founder of many of the city's religious rituals and institutions.

14

Tertullian, *On the Flesh of Christ* 1–16 and 24–25

Introduction and Translation by Jared Secord

INTRODUCTION

Tertullian's *On the Flesh of Christ* offers a defense of the reality of Christ's human body and the sufferings that he experienced during his time on earth. The work, written around 206, roughly in the middle of Tertullian's literary career, was directed against alternative views prevailing among some Christian groups concerning the body of Christ. The Christians who held these views are now called docetists. They believed that Christ only seemed to have a human body, and that his sufferings and death were consequently not real. Tertullian's attack on the docetic perspective targets three influential figures of the second century who had questioned the reality of Christ's body in different ways. The first of these is Marcion, treated in chapters 2–5, who denied the reality of Christ's birth and flesh. Second is Marcion's disciple Apelles, treated in chapters 6–9, who believed that Christ did have flesh during his time on earth, but that he had not really been born. Finally, in chapters 11–16, Tertullian addresses the views of Valentinus and his followers, who granted the reality of Christ's birth and body, but suggested that his flesh was not human.

Throughout the work, Tertullian takes much for granted about the lives and doctrines of Marcion, Apelles, and Valentinus, assuming that his readers were already familiar with them. The attack on Marcion, for example, expects that readers will know about the edited version of the New Testament that he had produced, which contained only an abridged version of Luke's gospel, plus ten of the letters attributed to Paul by early Christians (1 and 2 Timothy and Hebrews were omitted). Tertullian likewise makes much of the fact that Marcion and Apelles rejected the authority of the Hebrew Bible over Christians, and that they believed the God of Moses to be different from the God of Jesus. There is also innuendo about what Tertullian implies to be Marcion's personal hatred of the human body, as well as about a sexual lapse that apparently led Apelles to turn away from the more rigorous asceticism of his teacher. Less is said, meanwhile, about Valentinus and his disciples, though Tertullian does make it clear that he regards them as little more than pagans with an excessively philosophical conception of Christ.

Alongside the frequent personal attacks against his opponents, Tertullian still makes clear the significance that Christ's possession of a real human body had for his views about the salvation of the human race. The reality of Christ's body meant that he had undergone the basic experiences of all humanity, including the real pain of death. Even more, the resurrection of Christ's human body provided hope and proof for Christians of their own salvation. In Tertullian's view, the docetism of Marcion, Apelles, and Valentinus called into question this basic element of the Christian message.

The translation is based on the edition of Jean-Pierre Mahé, *Tertullien. Le chair du Christ*, 2 vols., SChr 216 and 217 (Paris: Éditions du Cerf, 1975).

TRANSLATION

1, 1. Some people are eager to disturb our faith in the resurrection – a faith which remained without controversy before these relatives of the Sadducees arose.[1] They do this to deny that hope extends even to the flesh. With good reason, then, do they tear apart the flesh of Christ with their doubts: they think that it didn't exist at all or was in some way other than human. For they fear that if it were established that it was human, a foregone conclusion would be presented against them that the flesh must by all means rise up again since it rose up again in Christ. So then, it is at the very place where they destroy the longings of the flesh that we must build up our defense. 2. Let us examine the bodily substance of the Lord; for there is no dispute over his spiritual substance. It is his flesh that is in question; its reality and quality are under examination: whether it existed, where it came from, and of what type it was. A verdict about it will furnish a norm for our own resurrection.

1 See Acts 23:8. Tertullian connects his opponents with the Sadducees, who denied the resurrection of the body.

In order to deny the flesh of Christ, Marcion also denied his birth. Or rather, in order to deny his birth, he also denied the flesh. He did this, of course, so that the birth and the flesh couldn't vouch for each other, because there's no birth without the flesh and no flesh without the birth. 3. It's as if he couldn't avail himself of that same heretical license as did Apelles, his disciple who later deserted him, and deny the birth while admitting the flesh, or as did his fellow pupil and fellow deserter Valentinus,[2] and confess both the flesh and the birth but explain them differently. 4. And moreover he who suggested that the flesh of Christ was imaginary was equally able to fabricate a phantom birth too, so that the virgin's conception, pregnancy, childbearing, and subsequently the infant's course of life, would have to be regarded as only appearing to be real,[3] deceiving the same eyes and same senses which the belief in flesh eluded.

2, 1. The birth is obviously announced by Gabriel.[4] Why does Marcion want nothing to do with the Creator's angel? And the conception is introduced as being in the womb of a virgin. Why does Marcion want nothing to do with the Creator's Isaiah?[5] Hating delays, he brought Christ down from the heavens unexpectedly.[6] "Away," he says, "with the ever-irritating censuses of Caesar, the cramped inns,[7] the dirty rags, and the comfortless mangers! Let the angelic multitude focus on honoring its God at night.[8] Let the shepherds watch over their flocks instead.[9] Let the magi not tire themselves out by coming from so far away;[10] their own gold is my gift to them.[11] 2. Let Herod be a better man, lest Jeremiah boast.[12] But don't let the infant be circumcised, lest he feel pain; don't let him be brought to the temple, lest he burden his parents with the cost of an offering; don't let him be placed in the hands of Simeon, lest he sadden this old man on

2 There is no evidence to support the implication here of any personal connection between Marcion and Valentinus.

3 Tertullian here uses *tō dokein*, a form of the Greek verb "to seem or appear," from which derives the adjective "docetic."

4 See Luke 1:26–30. 5 See Isa 7:14; Luke 1:31.

6 See Luke 4:31. By "unexpectedly" here Tertullian is suggesting that Marcion's excisions of prophecies about the birth of Jesus from his gospel results in its being completely unannounced.

7 See Luke 2:1–14.

8 That is, the angelic multitude should focus on God in heaven rather than the newborn Jesus.

9 See Luke 2:1–20. That is, watch over their own flocks instead of the newborn Jesus.

10 See Matt 2:1. 11 See Matt 2:11. 12 See Matt 2:16–18; Jer 31:15.

the verge of death. And let that old woman be silent, lest she cast a spell on the boy."[13]

By such decisions, I suppose, you dared to blot out so many original records about Christ, lest his flesh be proved real. 3. On what authority, I ask you? Reveal it! If you're a prophet, foretell something. If you're an apostle, preach in public. If you're apostolic, agree with the apostles. If you are only a Christian, believe what has been passed down.[14] If you are none of these things (which I can claim with good reason), die! 4. For you are already dead, insofar as you are not a Christian because you do not believe that which makes people Christians when it is believed. And you are all the more dead to the extent that you are not a Christian because, when you were one, you fell away by retracting your previous belief, just as you yourself confess in a certain letter; your people do not deny it, and our people have proven it.[15] 5. Therefore, when you retracted your belief, you retracted it as one no longer believing it. But it was wrong to make a retraction just because you ceased to believe it. Indeed, by retracting your belief you prove that before your retraction you held a different belief [than you do now]. This different belief was what was passed down. In turn, what was passed down was true, as it was passed down by those whose duty it was to do so. Therefore, by retracting what was passed down, you retracted what was true. You had no right to do this! 6. But in another place we have already made fuller use of such prescriptions against all heresies.[16] With this superabundance of material in place we can now move forward in our present discussion, given our desire to know the reason why you think that Christ was not born.

3, 1. However much you think it is within your competence to pass judgment on this matter, it is unavoidable that you deem the birth to be either impossible or unfitting for God. But nothing is impossible for God, save that which is not his will. Therefore, let us consider whether it was his will to be born, because if it was his will, he both could be and was born. I will have recourse to a shortcut: If it was, for whatever reason, not God's

13 Here and elsewhere in the text, Tertullian engages in an imaginary back and forth with his opponents. The use of quotation marks in the translation marks out these exchanges, but it must be emphasized that Tertullian is not actually quoting the real words of his opponents. At best, he is trying to imagine the sorts of objections that they might have raised against the arguments he makes.

14 In Latin, *quod traditum est*, "what has been passed down," refers to the apostolic "tradition" or teachings about the Christian faith that the apostles transmitted to subsequent generations.

15 Tertullian also refers to this letter at *Against Marcion* 1.1 and 4.4.

16 A reference to Tertullian's extant *On the Prescription against Heretics*.

will to be born, the better option for him would have been not to seem to be a human being. For who upon seeing him as a human being would deny that he had been born? Thus, whatever it was not his will to be, in every way it was also not his will to seem to be. 2. In the case of a displeasing thing, every conjecture about it is also rejected, because it does not matter at all whether it is or is not, if when it is not it is presumed to be. Clearly what does matter is that God does not give a pretense of experiencing what he is not.

"But," you say, "his own self-understanding was enough for him. It was the fault of human beings if they judged him to have been born simply because they saw him as a human being." 3. With how much more dignity, then, with how much more steadfastness, would he have put up with this human conjecture if he had truly been born, when even on the supposition that he had not been born he was subject to the same conjecture along with the damage done to his self-understanding! How confident are you in supposing that even though he was not born he, contrary to his own self-understanding, put up with the conjecture that he was born? Explain to me why it was so important for Christ, when he knew what he was, to show himself as something that he was not? 4. You cannot say: "To avoid ceasing to be God, if he had been born and had truly clothed himself as a human being, losing what he was while becoming something that he was not." For God is in no danger of losing his permanent station.

"But that's the reason why," you say, "I deny that God was truly changed into a human being, resulting in his both being born and being embodied in flesh, because he who is without end must of necessity also be unchangeable. For being changed into something else is the cessation of the original thing. 5. Change, therefore, cannot be attributed to someone to whom an end cannot be attributed." It is clear that the nature of changeable things is to be subject to that law whereby they do not remain in that state which is being changed in them, and so they perish by not remaining, given that they lose what they were by changing. But nothing is equal to God. His nature is different from all other things in terms of condition. So then, if those things which differ from God and from which God differs lose what they were when they are changed, how will there be any difference between divinity and all the rest of things, unless the opposite is true, namely, that God can be changed into anything but remain the sort of thing that he is? 6. Otherwise he will be equal to those things which lose what they were when changed, things to which God is certainly not equal in any way, certainly not in being the result of change.

You have read, and you believed it, that the angels of the Creator were once changed into human form and had such an embodied reality that Abraham washed their feet[17] and by their hands Lot was rescued from the men of Sodom,[18] and furthermore an angel, having wrestled with a man with the whole weight of his body, asked to be let go when he was so tightly held.[19] 7. So then, when it was permitted to angels of the inferior God to be changed into human embodiment while nevertheless remaining angels, are you taking this away from the more powerful God, as though his Christ when clothed as a human being was unable to remain God? Or is it the case that those angels also appeared as phantoms of flesh? But this you will not dare to say. For if it is your opinion that the Creator's angels are just like his Christ, then Christ will belong to that God whose angels are such as Christ is.

8. If you had not deliberately rejected some and corrupted other passages of the scriptures that are opposed to your views, the Gospel of John would have confounded you in this matter, when it stated that the Spirit in the body of a dove came down and sat on the Lord.[20] Even though it was the Spirit, it was truly as much a dove as the Spirit, and yet it did not obliterate its own proper substance when it assumed a substance that was not its own. 9. "But," you ask, "where was the body of the dove when the Spirit was taken back in heaven?" In the same way as [the bodies of] the angels, it was removed in the same manner as it had been produced. If you had seen it when it emerged from nothing, you also would have known when it was withdrawn into nothing. If its beginning was not visible, neither was its end. Nevertheless, its body had three dimensions, at whatever moment the body was seen. It is impossible for what is written not to have happened.

4, 1. Therefore, if you do not reject embodiment as either impossible or dangerous to God, the only option left for you is to scorn and reproach it as unworthy. Beginning with birth itself, which you find so offensive, come now, deliver a speech on the filthiness of genital elements in the womb, the foul curdling of moisture and blood, and of the flesh nourished from that same filth for nine months. Describe the womb, growing larger day by day, heavy, troublesome, not without danger even during sleep, capricious in its whims of loathing and craving. Attack now even the very decency of the pregnant woman, which should either be honored because of the danger

17 See Gen 18:4. 18 See Gen 19:10. 19 See Gen 32:27.
20 See John 1:32–34.

involved or held to be sacred by nature. 2. And surely you are horrified by the infant when it is poured out with its own equipment and baggage.[21] Surely you also loathe the infant after it has been washed, arranged in swaddling-cloths, beautified with ointments, and made to laugh with fawning. This natural object of veneration, Marcion, you abhor. But how were you born? You hate the person being born. But how do you love anyone? It is plain that you do not even love yourself, since you have withdrawn from the church and faith in Christ. But who cares if you dislike yourself or if you were born in another way!

3. Christ certainly loved that human being[22] who was curdled in filthiness in the womb, who was brought forth by means of shameful parts, and who was nourished by means of ridiculed parts. On account of this one he descended, on account of this one he preached, on account of this one he abased himself in every humiliation even to the point of death, and death on the cross.[23] Certainly he loved this human being whom he redeemed at so great a cost.[24] If Christ belongs to the Creator, with good reason he loved his own. If he is from another god, he showed even more love since he redeemed one that was not his own. So then, along with this human being he also loved his birth, and his flesh too. Nothing can be loved apart from that by which it is what it is. 4. If not, take away the birth and show the human being; do away with the flesh and present the one whom God redeemed. If these are what constitute the human being whom God redeemed, do you make them shameful for him when he redeemed them, and unworthy of him when he would not have redeemed them unless he loved them? Birth he refashions from death by heavenly regeneration; flesh he restores from every distress; the leprous he cleanses; the blind he makes see again; the paralyzed he makes whole again; the demon-possessed he purifies; the dead he revives – and he is ashamed to be born in flesh!

5. In fact, if he had wished to come forth from a wolf, a pig, or a cow, and he had preached the kingdom of the heavens while clothed in the body of a wild or domestic animal, I imagine your rebuke of him would go something like this: "This is disgraceful for God, unworthy of the Son of God, and accordingly foolish for anyone to believe!" It surely would be foolish

21 In Latin, *cum suis impedimentis*. Using a military metaphor, here Tertullian refers to the afterbirth as the equipment and baggage that traveled with an army.
22 Here Tertullian is speaking of the whole of humanity as a single human being.
23 See Phil 2:8. 24 See 1 Cor 6:20, 7:23.

if we were to judge God according to our own lights! But consider this, Marcion, if only you have not blotted it out: "God chose the foolish things of the world, so that he might confound those that are wise."[25] 6. What are these foolish things? The conversion of people to the worship of the true God, the rejection of error, instruction in justice, chastity, mercy, patience, and all innocence? These are not foolish things. So then, seek what he was talking about. And if you think that you have found them, will any of them be as foolish as believing in a God who was born, and in fact from a virgin, and what is more that he is fleshy, and that he wallowed through these outrages of nature? 7. Let someone claim that these things are not foolish, and that there are other things which God has chosen in rivalry to worldly wisdom. Nevertheless, it is easier for the wise of this world to believe that Jupiter became a bull or a swan than for Marcion to believe that Christ truly became a human being!

5, 1. There are clearly also other things just as foolish, those which have to do with the outrages and sufferings experienced by God. If not, then let them call God's being crucified "prudence"! Excise this too, Marcion, or rather excise this instead. For what is more unworthy of God? What is more shameful? To be born or to die? To carry a body or a cross? To be circumcised or to be crucified? To be breastfed or to be buried? To be laid down in a manger or to be laid away in a tomb? You will be wiser if you believe none of these things. But you will not be wise unless you become a fool in the present world by believing the foolish things of God. 2. Or is it the case that you did not remove the sufferings of Christ because as a phantom he was devoid of the ability to feel them? Earlier we stated that it would have been equally possible for him to be subject to the empty mockeries of an imaginary birth and infancy.[26]

But right here, right now, answer this question, you murderer of truth: Wasn't God truly crucified? Wasn't he truly dead just as he was truly crucified? Wasn't he truly raised just as he was truly dead? 3. Was it falsely that Paul decided to know nothing among us except Jesus crucified?[27] Falsely that he placed him in a grave?[28] Falsely that he insisted that he rose again?[29] In this case, then, our faith is false, and everything that we hope for from Christ will be a phantom. O you most wicked of men, you who absolve the murderers of God! For Christ suffered nothing from them, if he truly suffered nothing.

25 1 Cor 1:27. 26 See 1.4 above. 27 See 1 Cor 2:2. 28 See 1 Cor 15:4.
29 See 1 Cor 15:17.

Spare the one and only hope of the whole world! Why do you destroy the shame that is necessary for our faith? Whatever is unworthy of God is of benefit to me. I am saved if I am not ashamed of my Lord. For he said: "Whoever is ashamed of me, of him I shall also be ashamed."[30] 4. I find no other causes of shame that will prove that through a contempt of shame I am nobly shameless and happily foolish. The Son of God was crucified; I am not ashamed because it is necessarily shameful. And the Son of God died; it is believable because it is absurd. And after being buried he was resurrected; it is certain because it is impossible.

5. But how will these things be really true in his case, if he was himself not real, if he did not really have in himself that which could be nailed [to the cross], that which could die, that which could be buried and raised again, namely, this flesh of ours, filled with blood, built of bones, interlaced with nerves, and entwined with veins? This flesh which knew how to be born and to die, which was undoubtedly human, since it was born from a human being, and thus mortal: it is this flesh which in Christ must be a human being and Son of Man. 6. If not, then why is Christ a human being and Son of Man, when he has nothing that belongs to a human being and nothing derived from a human being? This could only be true if either a human being is something other than flesh, or the flesh of a human being is derived from another source than from a human being, or Mary is something other than a human being, or Marcion's God is a human being. In no other way could Christ be called a human being without flesh, nor Son of Man without some human parent, just as [he could not be called] God without the Spirit of God nor Son of God without God the Father. 7. And so, the inheritances of both substances have shown him to be a human being and God: because of the one [substance], he was born, because of the other [substance], he was not born; because of the one, he is fleshy, because of the other, spiritual; because of the one, weak, because of the other, exceedingly strong; because of the one, dying, because of the other, living. The distinguishing characteristics of these conditions, the divine and the human, are surely verified by the equal reality of each nature, since there are identical grounds for believing in both Spirit and flesh. The mighty deeds of God's Spirit proved him to be God, whereas the sufferings proved him to be the flesh of a human being. 8. If his mighty deeds did not happen without

30 Matt 10:33; Mark 8:38; Luke 9:26.

Spirit, likewise his sufferings did not happen without flesh. If his flesh was fictitious along with its sufferings, so too, then, was his Spirit false along with its mighty deeds.

Why do you, with a lie, make Christ half of what he is? He was truly real in every respect. 9. He preferred, believe me, to be born rather than to tell partial lies – and indeed lies against himself! – such as that he had flesh hard without bones, three-dimensional without muscles, blooded without blood, clothed without a tunic [of skin], hungry without hunger, [flesh] that could eat without teeth and speak without a tongue, resulting in his word having been a phantom conveyed to ears through ventriloquism. Thus he would also be a phantom after the resurrection when he offered his hands and feet to his disciples for inspection, saying: "See that it is I myself, because a spirit does not have bones as you see that I have."[31] 10. Undoubtedly, what has hands and feet and bones is not a spirit but flesh. How do you interpret this statement, Marcion, seeing that you bring Jesus in only from a God who is simple, good, and supreme? See how he deceives and cheats and tricks the eyes of everyone, the sense-perceptions of everyone, the approaches of everyone, and the touches of everyone! So then, you should not have brought Christ down from heaven, but taken him from some throng of hustlers, not as God plus a human being but as a human magician, not as the high priest of salvation[32] but as the mastermind of a show, not as one who raises the dead but as one who distracts the living – except that, even if he was a magician, he was born!

6, 1. But there are at present certain disciples of this man of Pontus,[33] who, in a quest to be wiser than their teacher, concede the true reality of Christ's flesh yet without the foregone conclusion that he was also born – which they think should be denied. "He would seem," they say, "to have had flesh, except that in no way was it born." We have gone, then, "from the kiln into the furnace," as the saying goes,[34] from Marcion to Apelles. After falling away from the teaching of Marcion through a carnal encounter with a woman and then being overthrown spiritually when he encountered the virgin Philumena,[35] he was inspired by her to preach that Christ's body was

31 Luke 24:39. 32 See Heb 9:11. 33 That is, Marcion.
34 The equivalent English proverb would be "out of the frying pan into the fire."
35 This Philumena was a prophetess, and Tertullian has many negative things to say in other works about the nature of her relationship with Apelles, in keeping with the suggestion here about sexual misconduct.

three-dimensional but not born. 2. And indeed, the Apostle will respond to that angel of Philumena using the same statement which he used long ago to predict the very man himself,[36] saying: "Even if an angel from the heavens should preach to you a gospel that is different from the gospel we are preaching to you, let him be anathema."[37] But it shall be our task to oppose any additional arguments of theirs.

3. They confess that Christ truly had a body. What was the source of its material if not that sort of thing in which it was seen? What was the source of the flesh if the body was not flesh? What was the source of the flesh if it was not born? For that which would become something that is born had to be born! "It is from the stars," they say, "and from the substances of the higher world that he borrowed his flesh." And surely they propose that a body that was not born is nothing to marvel at, since it was granted even to angels to present themselves among us in flesh without the exertions of a womb.[38] 4. We certainly acknowledge that this is what is reported [in scripture]. But how is it that a faith that belongs to another rule should borrow evidence for its own arguments from the faith that it is attacking? What has it to do with Moses, since it rejects the God of Moses? If its God is different, then everything about its God must be different. But let all the heretics use the scriptures of the God whose world they also use – and this too will be for them a testimony of judgment, that they construct their blasphemies from examples furnished by him. It is easy for the truth to prevail, even when it puts forth no such objection against them.

5. So then, I would want those who explain the flesh of Christ by reference to the example of angels, claiming that, though flesh, it was not born, to compare the reasons why Christ and the angels presented themselves in flesh. No angel ever descended with the express purpose of being crucified, experiencing death, and being raised from death. If there was never such a reason as these for the angels becoming embodied, you have the reason why they took on flesh but were not born: they had not come to die and for this reason they were not born. 6. But, in contrast, Christ was sent to die and so of necessity also had to be born, precisely in order to die. For normally nothing dies except what is born. Birth and death are mutually indebted: the law which dictates death is the reason for birth. 7. If Christ died for that which dies, and if what dies is that which is born, the necessary consequence – or rather, the antecedent necessity – must be that he

36 That is, Apelles. 37 Gal 1:8. 38 See Gen 19:1.

was equally born for that which is born, because he had to die for the very thing that dies precisely because it is born. It wasn't fitting for him not to be born on behalf of that for which it was fitting for him to die. Now at that time the Lord himself also appeared to Abraham among those angels,[39] and though not born he had flesh, obviously for the same difference in reasons. 8. But you do not accept this, you do not accept that [the Lord who appeared to Abraham] was Christ, who at that time was already learning to converse with, to liberate, and to judge the human race[40] while clothed in a flesh that had yet to be born because it had yet to be destined to die, unless his birth and death had already been announced.

So then, let them prove that those angels received flesh from the stars. 9. If they cannot prove this because nothing like this is written in scripture, then neither will the stars be the source of the flesh of Christ, which they explain by appeal to the example of the angels. It is agreed that the angels had flesh that was not their own, inasmuch as by nature they have a spiritual substance – even if they have some sort of body, it is nevertheless of its own kind. And [it is also agreed] that they can be transformed into human flesh temporarily, so that it is possible for human beings to see and meet with them. 10. Therefore, since the source from which they took flesh is not reported, the only option left for our understanding is to entertain no doubts that it is a special feature of angelic power to take a body to itself from a non-material source. "All the more reason, then," you say, "[that they must take it] from something!" Certainly. But there is no agreement on this subject, because scripture does not speak of it.

11. So why is it that those, who can make themselves that which by nature they are not, can't make themselves this from that which is not a substance? If they become that which they are not, why can't they become this from that which does not exist? Now when that which does not exist comes into existence, it is from nothing. Accordingly, [in scripture] there are neither questions about nor proofs of what afterwards became of their bodies. What was from nothing became nothing. Those who could turn themselves into flesh can turn nothing itself into flesh. It is a greater feat to change one's nature than to make material. 12. But even if it were necessary for the angels to take flesh from a material source, it would certainly be easier to believe that it was from earthly material rather than from any kind of the heavenly substances, since [their flesh] was to such an extent of an

39 See Gen 18:1. 40 See, e.g., Gen 18:5.

earthly quality that it was nourished on earthly sustenance.[41] Now it may well be the case too that in the same way that heavenly flesh was nourished on earthly sustenance when not itself earthly, so too was earthly flesh nourished on heavenly sustenance when not itself heavenly – for we read that at that time manna was food for the people: "Humanity," it says, "ate the bread of angels."[42] Even still, the condition of the Lord's flesh, having once and for all been set apart, is not diminished by a reason that belongs to a different dispensation. 13. Since he was destined to be a human being truly even unto death, it was right for him to clothe himself in that flesh to which death also belongs. And in turn, that flesh to which death also belongs is preceded by a birth.

7, 1. Now whenever a debate about the birth arises, all who reject it on the grounds that it makes a foregone conclusion about the reality of Christ's flesh propose that the Lord himself denied having been born, insofar as he said: "Who is my mother and who are my brothers?"[43] So then, let Apelles listen to what we have already said in response to Marcion in the book where we challenged his gospel,[44] namely, that the basis of this remark must be considered. 2. In the first place, no one would have ever announced to him that his mother and brothers were standing outside[45] without being certain that he had a mother and brothers and that it was precisely these persons whom he was announcing at that time, having either become acquainted with them previously or met them then and there – and this in spite of the fact that heresies have removed from the gospel the statements that those who marveled at his teaching[46] said, namely, that his reputed father Joseph the carpenter,[47] his mother Mary, and his brothers and sisters were very well known to them. 3. "But," [they say], "it was for the sake of tempting him that they announced to him the mother and brothers that he didn't [really] have." This is certainly not what scripture says! And yet elsewhere it does not maintain silence when something was done to him for the sake of temptation. "Behold," it says, "a teacher of the law rose up to tempt him."[48] And in another place: "And the Pharisees approached him to tempt him."[49] The fact is that no one prevented it being indicated here too [in the passage we are discussing]

41 See Gen 18:8, 19:3. 42 Ps 77(78):25. 43 Matt 12:48; Mark 3:33; Luke 8:21.
44 See Tertullian, *Against Marcion* 4.19. 45 See Matt 12:47; Mark 3:32; Luke 8:21.
46 See Matt 13:55–56; Mark 6:2–4. 47 See Luke 3:23. 48 Luke 10:25.
49 Matt 19:3.

that it was done for the sake of tempting him, and so I refuse to accept an inference made according to your own lights that goes beyond scripture.

4. Next, there must be an underlying basis for the temptation. What did they consider it necessary to tempt in him? Certainly, whether he was born or not. For if this is what his answer has denied, then this is what the announcement of the tempter had aimed at catching. But no temptation that strives to ascertain what has been made the subject of temptation by calling it into doubt comes up so suddenly that it is not preceded by a disputed point that raises doubts and so prompts the temptation. 5. Accordingly, if the birth of Christ never became a topic of conversation, why do you argue that they intended by means of a temptation to inquire into a subject that they had never brought into controversy? To this we add: even if it were necessary to tempt him in regard to his birth, he would certainly not be tempted in this way, by the announcement of those persons who might possibly not have existed, even if Christ was born. All of us are born and yet not all of us have either brothers or a mother. 6. It is more possible still that he has a father rather than a mother and maternal uncles rather than brothers. Thus, the temptation about his birth is ill-suited, since it could have been made without mentioning both a mother and brothers. It is obvious that it is easier [to think] that, being certain of his having both a mother and brothers, they were testing his divinity rather than his birth, checking whether while busy inside he knew what was outside, by targeting him with false news about the presence of people who were not [actually] present. But even this trick to tempt him would have utterly failed. 7. For it could have happened that those whom they announced to him as being outside he himself knew to be absent, whether by the demands of illness, business, or travel that were already known to him. No one devises a temptation in such a way that he would entertain the possibility of the embarrassment of the temptation falling back on himself! 8. So then, since there is no suitable basis for the temptation, the sincerity of the announcement is confirmed: his mother and brothers truly had arrived!

But the reason for [Christ's] response in which for the moment he denied his mother and brothers should be learned by Apelles too. 9. The brothers of the Lord had not believed in him,[50] as is preserved in the gospel published before Marcion. His mother likewise is not shown to have adhered to him, although Martha and the other Marys are often in his

50 See John 7:5.

company.[51] In this passage at last their disbelief becomes evident. When Jesus was teaching the way of life, when he was preaching the kingdom of God, when he was busy healing infirmities and diseases, even though non-family members were riveted on him, his own closest relatives were absent. 10. At last they arrive and stay outside: neither do they go in, evidently having no interest in what was going on inside, nor can they even be bothered to wait, as if they were bringing something more pressing than what he was engaged with so intently, and even more egregiously they interrupt him and want to call him away from such a great work. I ask you, Apelles, or you, Marcion, if by chance you were playing a board-game or placing bets on actors or charioteers, and you were called away by such an announcement, would you not say: "Who is my mother, and who are my brothers?" 11. When Christ was preaching God and giving proof of him, fulfilling the law and the prophets, and scattering the darkness of so long a past age, was it without justification that he used this saying to castigate the disbelief of those standing outside or to repulse their lack of consideration for calling him away from his work? Besides, if he were planning on denying his birth, he would have chosen another place and time, and different words, not those which could also be said by one who had both a mother and brothers: when one denies relatives out of indignation, it is not a question of denying them but reproving them. 12. Finally, he gave a preference to others,[52] and when he reveals why they deserved this preference, namely their hearing of the word, he demonstrates on what basis he denied his mother and brothers. For as he adopted to himself those others who adhered to him, so too he rejected those who stood apart from him. It is the custom of Christ also to put into practice what he teaches others.

13. How was it, then, that when he was teaching not to value mother, father, or brothers as much as the word of God, he himself would abandon the word of God when his mother and brothers were announced? And so, he denied his relatives just as he taught they should be denied: for the work of God. But there is another meaning too: in his mother who is set apart there is a figure of the synagogue and in his brothers who do not believe a figure of the Jews. In these persons Israel was outside, whereas the new disciples, listening and believing inside, by keeping close to Christ represented the

51 See Luke 8:2–3, 10:38–41; John 11:5, 19:25; Matt 27:58; Mark 16:1.

52 See Matt 12:50; Mark 3:34–35; Luke 8:21.

church, which he designated, in repudiation of fleshly kinship, the mother that was preferable and the band of brothers that was worthier. It was in the same sense, then, that he also responded to that exclamation [of a woman]: he was not denying his mother's womb and breasts, but pointing out that those who hear the word of God are more blessed.[53]

8, 1. These isolated passages, on which Marcion and Apelles seem to have especially based their opinion, but which we have now interpreted according to the truth of the unmutilated and uncorrupted gospel, ought to have sufficed to prove the human flesh in Christ by a defense of his birth. 2. But since these followers of Apelles strongly emphasize the disgraceful character of the flesh, which they maintain to have been formed for souls seduced by that fiery prince of evil and thus to have been unworthy of Christ, and for this reason a substance drawn from the stars was suitable for him, I am obliged to fend them off on the ground they have prepared. A certain angel they call "Illustrious," who established this world and once it was established mixed repentance with it.[54] 3. This too we have discussed in its own place – for we ourselves penned a small book against them[55] – asking whether [this angel] who seems to have possessed the spirit, will, and power of Christ in the doing of these works could have done something worthy of repentance. This angel they even interpret by the figure of the lost sheep.[56] So then, on the evidence of the repentance of its establisher, the world must be a mistake, since all repentance is a confession of sin, inasmuch as there is no place for it except in cases of sin.

4. If the world is a mistake, then, by analogy with a body and its members,[57] heaven must likewise be a mistake and the heavenly beings [must be mistakes too] along with heaven. If the heavenly beings [are mistakes], then whatever was conceived and brought forth from them [must be mistakes]: an evil tree necessarily produces evil fruits.[58] So then, the flesh of Christ, if it has been formed from heavenly beings,[59] is made up of the elements of sin and is sinful by reason of its sinful origin, and must then be equal to that substance in which they deem it unworthy to clothe Christ on the grounds that it is sinful – namely, ours! 5. And so, if the disgraceful character [of our flesh] doesn't make any difference at all, either let them dream up some

53 See Luke 11:27–28. 54 That is, the angel repented of making the world.
55 Whatever this book may have been, it is no longer extant among Tertullian's works.
56 See Matt 18:12; Luke 15:4–7. 57 See 1 Cor 12:12.
58 See Matt 7:18, 12:33; Luke 6:43.
59 The assumption here is that the stars are heavenly beings.

other material for Christ that is purer in character, being so dissatisfied with ours as they are, or else let them recognize that it[60] is something than which not even the heavenly [material] could be better. Sure, we read: "The first human being is from the mud of the earth, the second human being is from heaven."[61] 6. But the point [of this verse] is not the difference of material, but only to contrast the earlier earthly substance of the flesh of the first human being, that is, Adam, with the heavenly Spirit-derived substance of the second human being, that is, Christ. And so closely does it relate the heavenly human being to Spirit rather than to flesh, that those whom it likens to him surely become heavenly in this earthly flesh – which is done of course by the Spirit. 7. But if Christ were also heavenly according to the flesh, those who are not heavenly according to the flesh would not be likened to him. So then, if those persons who are becoming heavenly like Christ have an earthly substance of flesh, then this provides further confirmation that Christ himself too was heavenly in earthly flesh, just as are those persons who are put on the same level as him.[62]

9, 1. An additional point that we emphasize is that nothing derived from something else, such that it is different from that which it was derived, is so entirely different that it does not suggest the source from which it was derived. No material lacks evidence of its origin, even if it changes into a new proper character. 2. Certainly, this very body of ours, which was formed from clay, as truth has transmitted even to the mythologies of the Gentiles, acknowledges both elements of its origin: earth by its flesh and water by its blood. For although its quality has taken on a different appearance – this is because it became one thing from another – yet what is blood besides red liquid? What is flesh besides earth transformed into shapes of its own? 3. Consider its qualities one at a time: the muscles are like clods, the bones like rocks, and even around the nipples there are pebbles of sorts. Look at the tightly bound conglomerations of sinews, they are like a root system, the branching courses of the veins like the meandering channels of streams, the downy hair [on our bodies] like moss, the hair [on our heads] like grass, and the very treasures of marrow in its hidden place like quarries for flesh.

4. All these signs of an earthly origin were also in Christ, and these are what concealed that he was the Son of God, as he was thought to be only a human being for no other reason than that he manifested himself in the

60 That is, our flesh. 61 1 Cor 15:47. 62 See 1 Cor 15:49.

human substance of a body. If not, point out something heavenly in him begged from the Great Bear or the Pleiades or the Hyades! For what we have enumerated is evidence that his flesh was as earthly as ours is. I detect nothing new, nothing strange. 5. Indeed, it was because of his words and deeds only, because of his teaching and power alone, that people were astonished at Christ. And furthermore, a new kind of flesh in him would have been noted and considered remarkable. But it was precisely the unremarkable condition of his earthly flesh that made all the other things about him remarkable, seeing that they said: "From where did this man get this teaching and these signs?"[63] 6. This was the utterance even of those who despised his appearance, to such a degree did his body lack human attractiveness,[64] to say nothing of heavenly glory. And even though among you the prophets are silent about his contemptible appearance,[65] the sufferings and the abuses speak for themselves: the sufferings [proved] that his flesh was human whereas the abuses that it was unattractive. 7. Would anyone have dared to nick a new kind of body with the tip of his fingernail, or to defile his face with spittle unless it was deserving?[66] Why do you say that his flesh is heavenly when you have no basis for understanding it as heavenly? Why do you deny that it was earthly when you have a basis for recognizing it as earthly? He was hungry with the devil,[67] thirsted with the Samaritan woman,[68] wept over Lazarus,[69] trembles at the prospect of death[70] – for "the flesh," he said, "is weak"[71] – and at last he sheds his blood.[72] 8. These are, I suppose, heavenly signs! But how, I say,[73] could he be contemned and suffer as he said he would,[74] if from that flesh there had shone some of its heavenly excellence? On the basis of this fact, then, we have convincingly demonstrated that nothing in that [flesh] was from the heavens precisely so that it could be contemned and suffer.

10, 1. I turn [now] to others who also claim to be wise,[75] those who contend that Christ's flesh was soul-derived on the grounds that soul was made into flesh. His soul was flesh, then, and just as his flesh was soul-derived,

63 Matt 13:54. 64 See Isa 53:3. 65 See Isa 53:3.
66 See Matt 27:30; Mark 15:19; Luke 22:64. 67 See Matt 4:2–4.
68 See John 4:7. 69 See John 11:35. 70 See Mark 14:33.
71 Matt 26:41; Mark 14:38.
72 See John 19:34. Tertullian points to the same scriptural passages about Christ in *Against Praxeas* 27.11, translated in this volume on p. 181.
73 Here the reading *inquam* is preferred to *inquitis*, though both have manuscript support.
74 See Matt 16:21; Mark 8:31; Luke 9:22. 75 See Rom 11:25, 12:16; Prov 3:7.

so too was his soul fleshly. In this case too I want to know the reasons. If it was in order to save soul that Christ took up soul within himself because it could not be saved except through him by being in him, I do not see why he would have made soul into flesh and clothed himself in soul-derived flesh,[76] as if he could not have saved soul in any other way except by it being made fleshy.[77] 2. After all, given the fact that he offers salvation to our souls when they are not only not fleshy but even separate from the flesh, how much more was he able to bring salvation to that soul which he himself took up even without it being fleshy! Again, when they assume that Christ came forth for the purpose of delivering not our flesh but only our soul, in the first place how absurd is it that when intending to deliver only soul he should have made it into that kind of body which he had no intention of delivering! 3. Secondly, if he had taken it upon himself to deliver our souls by means of that soul which he bore, that soul which he bore too ought to have been ours, that is, the same as ours in form – whatever the form of our soul is in secret it is nevertheless not fleshy! And furthermore, it was not our soul that he delivered if he had a fleshy soul, for ours is not fleshy. 4. In turn, if he did not deliver our soul because he freed one that was fleshy, it does nothing for us, because he did not deliver ours. Then again, as fleshy, of course, it did not even need to be delivered since it was not ours. For it was not in danger if it was not ours, that is, not fleshy. But it is agreed that it was delivered. Therefore, it was not a fleshly soul, but it was ours, since it was one that needed to be delivered precisely because it was in danger. Now, therefore, if in Christ soul was not fleshly, neither could his flesh have been soul-derived.

11, 1. But we come upon another argument of theirs when we demand why Christ is supposed to have come into possession of fleshly soul and to have submitted to soul-derived flesh. "Because it was God's desire," they say, "to manifest soul visibly to human beings by making it into a body: for previously it had been invisible, and by nature it saw nothing, not even itself, because of the impediment of this flesh, so that it was even debated whether soul was born or not, whether it was mortal or not. And so, soul was made into a body in Christ so that we might see it both being born

76 This passage is also legitimately rendered: "I do not see why he made his soul into soul-derived flesh when clothing himself in flesh."

77 Throughout this translation, the Latin *carnalis* is rendered with "fleshly," and *carneus* with "fleshy."

and dying, and, even more importantly, rising up again." 2. But how could it be that by means of flesh soul is demonstrated to itself or to us when it was precisely by means of flesh that it couldn't be known, and so comes to be manifested by becoming that thing by means of which it was hidden, namely flesh? Apparently it took on darkness so that it could shine!

At this point, then, let us consider first whether it was necessary for soul to be manifested in this way, since they allege that previously it was totally invisible, whether because it was, as it were, incorporeal or in possession of some kind of body of its own. 3. However, when they claim that it was invisible, they affirm that it was bodily because it is in possession of something that is invisible. For if it is in possession of nothing invisible, how can it be called invisible? But indeed it cannot even exist if it is in possession of nothing by which it can exist. But since it does exist, it must be in possession of something by which it can exist. 4. If it is in possession of something by which it exists, this must be its body. Everything that exists is a body of its own kind; nothing is incorporeal, except that which does not exist. So then, assuming that soul is in possession of an invisible body, he who took it upon himself to make it visible would have surely acted more appropriately if what he had made visible was that thing deemed invisible which belonged to it. For in this case neither falsehood nor weakness can be attributed to God: falsehood, if he demonstrated soul to be something other than what it was; weakness, if he was not capable of demonstrating that which it was. 5. No one who intends to bring a person into view puts a helmet or a mask on him! But this is precisely what has been done to the soul, on the supposition that it was changed into flesh and clothed itself in a shell that belonged to something else. But even if the soul were to be regarded as incorporeal, so that by some mysterious force of reason the soul indeed exists and yet is not a body regardless of what the soul actually is, then indeed it would not have been impossible for God – and it would have been more appropriately suitable for his purposes – to manifest soul in some new kind of body rather than in what is common to everyone and is already known to be different, so as to avoid groundlessly desiring to make invisible soul visible and exposing it to justified doubts through a defense of the human flesh in it. 6. "But Christ could not have been seen among human beings unless he were a human being!" Then give Christ back his trustworthiness! If you do, then the one whose will it was to walk as a human being also manifested soul in a human condition without making it fleshy but by clothing it in flesh.

12, 1. Now it might be the case that soul was manifested by means of flesh, if it could be established that it needed to be manifested in some way or another, that is, because it was unknown to itself and to us. But the distinction being made here is worthless, as it assumes that we exist apart from soul, when all that we are is soul. In fact, without soul we are nothing, a [mere] name, not even of a human being but of a corpse. So then, if we are ignorant of soul, it is soul that is ignorant of itself. 2. So all that's left to do is to investigate whether soul was ignorant of itself such that it [needed to] become known in some way or another. In my opinion, it is soul's nature to be able to perceive. Accordingly, nothing animated by soul lacks perception and nothing that can perceive lacks soul. To say it more precisely, perception is the soul of soul. 3. So then, since soul enables all to perceive and soul itself perceives even the perceptions of all, to say nothing of their properties, does it seem likely to anyone that it has not had perception of itself from the beginning? Where did it get the ability to know what it periodically needs for itself because of the requirements of the features it has by nature, if it did not know the sort of thing it was and what it needs? This indeed is something that can be recognized in all soul, I mean self-knowledge; without this self-knowledge no soul would be able to make itself function.

4. But the human being, the only soul-animated being who is rational, even more so, I think, has received soul that possesses the ability to make him a rational soul-animated being, as soul itself is primarily rational. But how can that which makes a human being a rational soul-animated being be rational, if through its self-ignorance it has no knowledge of its own rationality? Rather, so far is it from being ignorant of itself that it knows its author and judge and its own status. 5. Even if it has still learned nothing about God, it mentions God's name; even if it has still acknowledged nothing about his judgment, it says that it commends itself to God; even if it hears nothing besides that there is no hope after death, it calls down blessings or curses upon any who are dead. These ideas are pursued at greater length in a book we have written called *On the Testimony of the Soul.*[78] 6. In any case, if soul were ignorant of itself from the beginning, there is nothing that it would have needed to learn from Christ besides what sort of thing it was. As it happens, however, it was not its qualities that it learned from

78 This short work is extant.

Christ, but its salvation. The Son of God descended and submitted to soul for this reason, so that soul could recognize, not itself in Christ, but Christ in itself. For it was not ignorance of itself that put its salvation at risk, but rather ignorance of the Word of God. 7. "Life," he said, "was made visible,"[79] not the soul. And, "I came," he said, "to save soul."[80] He did not say "to manifest soul." Did we really not know that soul, even if invisible, is born and dies in a non-incorporeal manner, and so had to be shown to us being born and dying in a corporeal manner? We clearly did not know that it will rise again along with the flesh. This will be what Christ revealed: but even this no differently in himself than in such a person as Lazarus[81] whose flesh was not soul-derived just as his soul was not fleshly. So then, what additional information was communicated to us about the condition of that soul which was previously unknown? What was its invisible feature that needed to be made visible by means of flesh?

13, 1. "Soul was made flesh so that soul could be manifested." So then, was flesh likewise made into soul so that flesh could be revealed? If soul is flesh, it's definitely not soul but flesh; if flesh is soul, it's definitely not flesh but soul. So then, where is flesh and where is soul, if each has been made into the other, or rather, if each is neither, given that each has been made into the other? It is indeed utterly perverse that in using the word "flesh" we understand "soul" and in talking of "soul" we mean "flesh." 2. All things will be at risk of being taken for something different from what they are and of losing what they are when taken for something else, if the names given them are different from what they are. Reliability in the naming of things safeguards their distinctive properties. Indeed, when their qualities are changed, they acquire [new] names. For example, when clay is baked it receives the name "earthenware," and it has nothing in common with the name of the kind of thing it was originally, because it [has nothing in common] with that kind of thing. 3. Hence, if Christ's soul is made flesh, it cannot be anything other than what it was made into and cannot be what it was, since it has indeed been made into something else. And because we have just employed an example, we shall make further use of it. Now earthenware [made] from clay is certainly a single corporeal entity and indeed there is a single word for this single corporeal entity. 4. Earthenware cannot also be called "clay," because it is not what it was and [the name] is not valid

79 See John 1:4; 2 Cor 4:10. 80 See Luke 9:56. 81 John 11:23–25.

for what it isn't. So then, when soul is made flesh and becomes uniformly three-dimensional, it is both a stable entity and an indivisible substance.

But in Christ we find soul and flesh designated with simple and transparent words – that is, soul as soul and flesh as flesh, never soul as flesh or flesh as soul, since they would have had to be named in this way if that's what they were. And moreover each substance in itself is mentioned by him separately, in line, surely, with the distinction between their two qualities, soul apart by itself and flesh apart by itself. 5. What? "My soul," he said, "is troubled even unto death,"[82] and, "The bread which I shall give for the salvation of the world is my flesh."[83] But if his flesh had been soul, there would be one thing in Christ: fleshy soul or soul-derived flesh. But since he distinguishes the kinds, flesh and soul, he reveals that they are two things. 6. If they are two things, they are definitely not one thing; if they are not one thing, his soul is definitely not fleshly nor is his flesh soul-derived. For the "one thing" would have to be soul as flesh or flesh as soul – unless he also had another soul apart by itself in addition to the one that was flesh and he were carrying around another flesh in addition to the one that was soul. But if there is one flesh and one soul, the one is "troubled even unto death" and the other is "bread for the salvation of the world," the plurality of two substances, each distinct according to its own type, is preserved, removing [the possibility] of a single type of a fleshy soul.

14, 1. "But," they say, "Christ also wore an angel." For what purpose? For that which [he wore] a human being too? So then, the reason would have to be the same [in both cases]. The reason for Christ to wear a human being was the salvation of the human being, namely, to restore what had perished.[84] The human being had perished; the human being needed to be restored. There is no such reason for Christ to wear an angel. 2. For though perdition is imputed to angels "in the fire prepared for the devil and his angels,"[85] restoration however has never been promised to them. Christ received from the Father no commandment about the salvation of angels.[86] Christ cannot do what the Father has neither promised nor commanded. For what reason, then, did he wear an angel, except perhaps as an accomplice with whom he might bring about the salvation of the human being? 3. Indeed, was the Son of God not qualified to act on his own to free the human being who had been overthrown by a single serpent acting

82 Matt 26:38; Mark 14:34. 83 John 6:51. 84 See Luke 19:10.
85 Matt 25:41. 86 See John 10:18.

on his own? In this case, there would no longer be a single Lord or a single Savior, but two authors of salvation, with one of them certainly needing the other. Or was it that he freed the human being through an angel? In this case, why did he himself descend for a task that he was going to effect through an angel? If through an angel, why also himself? If through himself, why also an angel? Certainly, he is called "Angel of great counsel,"[87] that is, a messenger, a term for his function, not his nature. For he was destined to announce to the world the great counsel of the Father regarding the restoration of the human being. Yet he should not for this reason be understood as an angel, like some sort of Gabriel or Michael. 4. For the son, too, is sent by the lord of the vineyard to the laborers, just as his servants were, to seek out its fruits.[88] But the son is not going to be regarded for this reason as one of the servants, insofar as he performed a function of servants. So then, perhaps it will be easier for me to say that the Son himself was an angel, that is, the messenger of the Father, rather than that there was an angel in the Son. But given the fact that "you have made him a little less than the angels"[89] was said about him, how can it appear that he was an angel when he was lowered beneath the angels in this manner, by being a human being in terms of flesh and soul and Son of Man? 5. Now insofar as he is Spirit of God and Power of the Most High,[90] he cannot be regarded as below the angels, being as he is God and Son of God. So then, he is made less than the angels by wearing a human being just as much as he is not by wearing an angel. This opinion could have suited Ebion,[91] who presents Jesus as a mere human being and only from the seed of David, that is, not also Son of God (even if it is clear that he is more glorious than the prophets to some extent), so as to declare that in Jesus there was an angel just as there was in Zechariah. 6. Except that the words, "And the angel who spoke in me said to me,"[92] were never said by Christ, and neither was that usual phrase of all the prophets: "Thus says the Lord."[93] For he was himself the Lord who spoke in his own person and from his own authority: "But I myself say to you."[94] And what besides this [is needed], when Isaiah cries out: "Neither an angel nor an envoy saved them, but the Lord himself"?[95]

15, 1. In addition, it was permitted to Valentinus, in virtue of his heretical privilege, to feign that the flesh of Christ was spiritual. Anyone who has

87 Isa 9:5 LXX. 88 See Matt 21:33–43. 89 Ps 8:6. 90 Luke 1:35.
91 On Ebion, see the Introduction, p. xlii. 92 Zech 1:14.
93 See, e.g., Isa 1:2. 94 Matt 5:34, 39. 95 Isa 63:9 LXX.

refused to believe that it was human can make it into anything whatsoever, since – and let this be said to everyone – if it was not human and not from a human being, I do not understand on the basis of which substance Christ himself proclaimed that he was both a human being and Son of Man: "But now you wish to kill a human being who has spoken the truth to you,"[96] and: "The Son of Man is lord of the Sabbath."[97] In fact, it is about him that Isaiah [says]: "A human being in calamity and knowing how to bear sickness."[98] And Jeremiah: "And he is a human being, and who can understand him?"[99] And Daniel: "And behold, above the clouds [there comes one] like a Son of Man."[100] Paul the apostle too: "Mediator between God and human beings, the human being Christ Jesus."[101] Likewise Peter in the Acts of the Apostles: "Jesus of Nazareth, a man sent to you by God,"[102] surely [implying] a human being. 2. These passages alone ought to have sufficed by way of prescription[103] as evidence that his flesh was human and taken from a human being, and that it was not spiritual, just as it was neither soul-derived, nor made of stars, nor imaginary, if heresies were capable of existing without contentious zeal and cunning. 3. For, as I have read in the works of one of the clique of Valentinus, they do not think that an earthly and human substance was formed for Christ, primarily to avoid having the Lord be regarded as lower than the angels, who are not made of earthly flesh, and secondly because it would have been necessary, if his flesh was like ours, for it to have been born in a similar way, neither of Spirit nor of God, but of the will of man.[104] "And why is it said, 'not from corruption, but from incorruption?'[105] And why is it that, just as his [flesh] rose up and was taken back into heaven, ours is not immediately received in the same manner when it is equal to his? Or why is it that his is not similarly dissolved into the earth when it is equal to ours?" 4. Such did the pagans once muse! "So then, the Son of God was emptied to such a great degree of lowliness!" And: "If he rose up as an example for our hope, why has no such thing been approved for us?" Such things are fitting for pagans, but they are also fitting for heretics! After all, is there any difference between them, except that pagans believe by not believing but heretics do not believe by believing? 5. For at

96 John 8:40. 97 Matt 12:8. 98 Isa 53:3. 99 Jer 17:9 LXX.
100 Dan 7:13. 101 1 Tim 2:5. 102 Acts 2:22.
103 Elsewhere in his writings Tertullian defends his position through "prescription," the idea that legal right to something is established by its longstanding and unchallenged possession.
104 See John 1:13. 105 1 Pet 1:23.

last they read, "You have made him a little less than the angels,"[106] and they deny that the substance of Christ is inferior, even though he declares that he is not a human being but a worm,[107] even though he "had neither form nor beauty, but his form was not notable, forsaken more than all human beings, a human being in calamity and knowing how to bear sickness."[108] 6. They acknowledge that he was a human being mixed with God but they deny the human being. They believe that he died but they insist that what died was born from incorruption, as if corruption were something other than death. "But our flesh too ought immediately to rise again!" Expect it to happen! Christ has not yet put down his enemies,[109] so as to triumph with his friends over his enemies.

16, 1. And moreover, by lust for arguing the infamous Alexander[110] has made a mark for himself, in line with the heretical way of thinking, by suggesting that we ourselves affirm that Christ clothed himself in flesh of earthly origin so that he could destroy in himself the flesh of sin.[111] But even if we were to say this, we could defend our position by any reasoning whatsoever, all the while avoiding that utter madness by which he supposes that we consider the very flesh of Christ, as if sinful, to have been destroyed in him. For we call to mind that it presides in the heavens at the right hand of the Father[112] and declare that it will come from there on the throne of the Father's glory.[113] 2. Accordingly, just as we cannot say that it was destroyed, so too cannot we say that it was sinful, because that was not destroyed in which there was no deceit.[114] We maintain, moreover, that it was not the flesh of sin which was destroyed in Christ but the sin of the flesh, not the material but the condition,[115] not the substance but the guilt, according to the Apostle's authority when he says: "He destroyed sin in the flesh."[116] 3. For even if in another place he says that Christ was "in the likeness of the flesh of sin,"[117] it is not that he received "the likeness of flesh" as if it merely resembled a body and was not the real thing; rather, he wants "the likeness of sinful flesh" to be understood in the sense that the

106 Ps 8:6. 107 See Ps 21(22):7. 108 Isa 53:2–3.
109 See Ps 8:8; 1 Cor 15:27–28.
110 Little is known about this Alexander, besides that he was a follower of Valentinus. In a passage of *On the Flesh of Christ* omitted from this selection, Tertullian makes clear that Alexander applied syllogistic logic in his treatment of the nature of Christ. This implies that Alexander had some training in philosophy.
111 See Rom 6:6. 112 See Mark 16:19. 113 See Matt 16:27.
114 See 1 Pet 2:22; Isa 53:9. 115 In Latin, *natura*. 116 Rom 8:3.
117 Rom 8:3.

flesh of Christ himself, which was itself not sinful, was equal to that flesh to which sin did belong and is to be equated with Adam's in terms of kind, not in terms of fault. 4. On the basis of this passage too we confirm that the flesh in Christ was the same as that whose condition[118] in the human being is sinful; accordingly, it was in this flesh that sin was destroyed: in Christ it exists without sin while in the human being it does not exist without sin. And furthermore it would not contribute to Christ's purpose of destroying the sin of the flesh, not to destroy it in that flesh in which there was the condition[119] of sin, nor would it contribute to his glory. For would he really have accomplished something great if it was in a better flesh and in one of a different nature – that is, of a non-sinful nature – that he wiped out the birthmark of sin? "So then," you reply, "if it is our flesh with which he clothed himself, the flesh of Christ was sinful." 5. Don't limit the sense when it can provide an explanation! For in clothing himself with our flesh he made it his own, and in making it his own he did not make it sinful. And moreover let this be said to everyone who does not think that the flesh in Christ was ours because he was not from the seed of a man:[120] remember that Adam himself was made into this flesh not from the seed of a man. Just as the earth was transformed into this flesh without the seed of a man,[121] so too the Word of God was able to cross over into the material of this same flesh without the curdling [of moisture and blood in the womb].[122]

* * *

24, 1. For when in other places too [the Holy Spirit] launches attacks to injure the heretics, especially, "Woe to those who make sweetness bitter and darkness light,"[123] he is of course referring to those who do not keep words themselves in the clarity of their proper meanings, resulting in the soul being no different from whatever bears this name, and the flesh no different from whatever has this appearance, and God no different from whatever is preached. 2. Accordingly, with Marcion in his sights, he said: "I am God, and there is no other besides me."[124] And when he says the same in a different way, "Before me there was no god,"[125] I have no idea which of those Valentinian genealogies[126] of Aeons he attacks. And, "He

118 In Latin, *natura*. 119 In Latin, *natura*. 120 See John 1:13.
121 See Gen 2:7. 122 See 4.1 above. 123 Isa 5:20. 124 Isa 45:5–6.
125 Isa 43:10. 126 See 1 Tim 1:4.

was born not of blood nor of the will of flesh or the will of man, but of God,"[127] was his response to Ebion. Similarly, "Even if an angel from the heavens should preach to you a gospel that is different from the one we preached, let him be anathema,"[128] is aimed at the activity of Apelles's virgin Philumena. 3. Certainly, "Whoever denies that Christ has come in the flesh is the antichrist,"[129] in virtue of the fact that it speaks of "flesh" without adornment, without qualification, and by using the simple word for its proper nature, strikes a blow against all who debate it. Similarly, when he defines that Christ himself is one,[130] he shakes the proponents of a multiform Christ, who make Christ one thing and Jesus another: one who escaped from the midst of the crowd[131] and another who was detained,[132] one who in retreat on the mountain was glorious in the midst of a cloud in front of three witnesses[133] and another who being quite ordinary was accessible to all the rest,[134] one who was courageous and another who was truly anxious,[135] and lastly one who suffered and another who was resurrected (because of which they assert a resurrection of their own too, but one into other flesh). 4. But it's a good thing that the one who suffered is the same as the one who will come from the heaven, and the one who was resurrected is the same as the one who will appear to everyone![136] "And they who pierced him will see and recognize him,"[137] meaning, to be sure, the same flesh against which they unleashed their savagery, without which he could neither exist nor be recognized. Accordingly, they must blush with shame who assert that his flesh sits in the heavens devoid of sensation, like a sheath from which Christ has been withdrawn, or who assert that his flesh and soul are the same, or who assert that there is only soul but no longer flesh.

25, 1. But so much for this subject. For I think sufficient proof has now been assembled that the flesh in Christ both was born from a virgin and was human. Even though a detailed investigation of the matter alone could have sufficed, without engaging with the individual opinions from various quarters, we have challenged these opinions far more extensively than

127 John 1:13. 128 Gal 1:8. 129 1 John 4:2–3. 130 See 1 Cor 8:6.
131 See Luke 4:30. 132 See Matt 26:57; Luke 22:54; John 18:12.
133 See Matt 17:1–9; Mark 9:14–29; Luke 9:37–42.
134 See Matt 26:55; Mark 14:49; Luke 22:53; John 18:20.
135 See Mark 14:33, 38. 136 See Acts 1:11. 137 John 19:37.

necessary, along with the arguments and the passages of scriptures that they employ, so that, by having demonstrated what Christ's flesh was and where it came from, we could present against them all a foregone conclusion about what his flesh was not. 2. Now, to make the end of the treatise bring to mind the beginning, the resurrection of our flesh (which will have to be defended in another book)[138] will here have a foundation laid, since it is now clear what sort of thing it was that was resurrected in Christ.

138 A reference to Tertullian's extant work *On the Resurrection of the Flesh*.

15

Tertullian, *Against Praxeas* 1–4 and 27–30

Introduction and Translation by Jared Secord

INTRODUCTION

Tertullian wrote *Against Praxeas* in the early 210s. It is thus a product of the latest part of his career, when he had become a vocal supporter of what he called the New Prophecy. This was a controversial, revivalist movement, termed Montanism by its opponents, which owed its origins to the region of Phrygia in Asia Minor. There, in the late 150s, a new convert to Christianity named Montanus began making prophecies about the coming end of days, and the consequent need for Christians to follow a more rigorous code of behavior. Other prophets followed him, including two women named Prisca and Maximilla. As *Against Praxeas* makes clear, the followers of Montanus placed great significance on the Paraclete ("Advocate" or "Helper" in Greek), who is identified with the Holy Spirit in the Gospel of John (see especially 14:26). Tertullian says that the Paraclete had provided him with new insight into the relation between God and Christ, thus suggesting that his account of the Father and Son was closely linked with the New Prophecy of Montanism, which was subsequently dismissed as heretical.

At the same time, Tertullian's work helps to make clear the influence that Praxeas's understanding of the relation between God and Christ, which was subsequently regarded as heretical, had among ostensibly orthodox Christians of their time, including several bishops of Rome. As Tertullian claims, Praxeas enjoyed a close connection to an unnamed bishop of Rome, who must be either Victor (r. 189–198/199) or Zephyrinus (r. 198/199–217). From other sources, we know that both bishops, along with their successor Callistus (r. 218–222/223), sympathized with Praxeas, whose views are commonly termed "monarchianism": there was a single, unified God, conceived of as having a single rule and power (or "monarchy"), that existed in three distinct modes of being, as Father, Son, and Holy Spirit. Though this account offered a strong defense of the unity of God against possible allegations of polytheism, it also implied that God the Father suffered together with Christ the Son on the cross (a view called patripassianism), as Tertullian emphasizes in the present selection. The monarchianism of Praxeas eventually lost its influence, but, for a time, it held sway among large groups of Christians in Rome and Carthage, despite the objections of Tertullian and other followers of the New Prophecy.

One final note about Praxeas is important. Apart from *Against Praxeas*, he is attested in only one other source, and quite briefly, at that; all subsequent references to him derive from Tertullian's account. It has therefore been suggested that Praxeas was an unflattering nickname – it means something like "busybody" in Greek – applied by Tertullian to a better-attested and more significant monarchian, such as the future bishop Callistus of Rome. This suggestion, however, is impossible to prove, though Tertullian's attack of Praxeas clearly was meant to target more prominent monarchianists, including Callistus. *Against Praxeas* should therefore be regarded not as a simple attack on a figure of little significance, but rather as a contribution to an ongoing controversy of major importance.

The translation is based on the edition of A. Kroymann and E. Evans in *Quinti Septimi Florentis Tertulliani Opera, pars 2. Opera Montanistica*, CCSL 2 (Turnhout: Brepols, 1954), 1157–1205.

TRANSLATION

1, 1. In various ways has the devil shown hostility to the truth. Sometimes he has tried to rattle it by defending it. He affirms a single Lord, the Almighty, the Creator of the world, so that he may make a heresy out of this singularity. He says that the Father himself has descended into the virgin, that he himself was born from her, that he himself suffered, and finally that he himself was Jesus Christ. The serpent refutes himself because, when he was tempting Jesus Christ after the baptism by John, he attacked him as the Son of God, sure that God had a son precisely on the basis of the very scriptures from which he was then devising a temptation: 2. "If you are the Son of God, speak so that these stones be made bread."[1] Likewise: "If you are the Son of God, cast yourself down from here. For it is written that he" – without doubt, the Father – "commanded his angels concerning you,

1 Matt 4:3.

that they might bear you up in their hands lest you ever strike your foot against a stone."[2] 3. Or can it be that he will accuse the gospels of falsehood, saying: "Let Matthew and Luke take note: in contrast [to what they claim] I approached God himself, I tempted the Almighty himself in close combat; that's why I approached him, that's why I tempted him. Otherwise, if he had been [only] the Son of God, perhaps I would have never bothered with him." But indeed he is a liar from the beginning,[3] as is any person he has ever marked as his own, like Praxeas.

4. For this man was the first from Asia to import this type of perverse opinion onto Roman soil. He was a man unsettled in other ways too and furthermore was puffed up from boasting that he had borne witness [to Christ] on account of a single, unremarkable, and brief experience of discomfort in prison. When and if he had handed over his body to be burned, he would have accomplished nothing, because he did not have love of God,[4] whose spiritual gifts he drove out. 5. For at that time the bishop of Rome[5] was on the point of recognizing the prophecies of Montanus, Prisca, and Maximilla, and because of this [imminent] recognition was offering peace to the churches of Asia and Phrygia. But Praxeas, by declaring false things about these prophets and their churches and by defending the authoritative judgments of the bishop's predecessors, compelled him to recall the letters of peace that were already sent out and to abandon his plan of receiving the spiritual gifts. Thus Praxeas accomplished two items of the devil's business at Rome: he drove out prophecy and brought in heresy; he chased away the Paraclete and crucified the Father.

6. The weeds of Praxeas were also sown here[6] and sprouted, while many people were sleeping in simplicity of doctrine;[7] later they were detected by the person God wanted[8] and seemed even to have been rooted out. In the end, the teacher[9] corrected himself and pledged his former opinion, and his written guarantee remains among the carnal people,[10] among whom this was done at that time. 7. Then there was silence. And indeed afterwards our recognition and defense of the Paraclete separated us from the carnal

2 Matt 4:6; Luke 4:10, quoting Ps 90(91):11–12. 3 See John 8:44.
4 See 1 Cor 13:3.
5 Either Victor (189–198/199) or Zephyrinus (198/199–217); see the introduction.
6 That is, in Tertullian's own Carthage. 7 See Matt 13:25.
8 A likely reference to Tertullian himself. 9 That is, Praxeas.
10 "Carnal people" (*psychici*) is Tertullian's preferred terminology for rival Christians who did not follow the New Prophecy of Montanus. See 1 Cor 2:14, 15:41–46; Jas 3:15; Jude 19.

people. But those weeds at that time had spread out their seed everywhere, so for a considerable time through a pretense it lay hidden, being deceptive about its vitality, and now it has once more burst forth. But it will once more also be rooted out, if God wishes, in this present time, and if not, on his day,[11] when all the false fruits will be collected and burned along with all the other stumbling-blocks in an inextinguishable fire.

2, 1. And so, since that time, the Father is proclaimed to have been born, the Father to have suffered, and the Lord God, the Almighty himself, to be Jesus Christ. But both always in the past and all the more so now, as we are better instructed by the Paraclete, who guides into all truth, we believe in a single God.[12] And yet under this dispensation, which we call the economy,[13] we believe that the single God has a Son, his Word who proceeded from him, through whom all things are made and without whom nothing is made.[14] This same one was sent by the Father into the virgin and born from her, human being and God, Son of Man and Son of God and called Jesus Christ. This same one suffered, this same one died and was buried according to the scriptures,[15] and was raised up by the Father and was taken back into heaven to sit at the right hand of the Father,[16] and will come to judge the living and the dead.[17] Then, according to his promise,[18] from the Father he sent the Holy Spirit, the Paraclete, sanctifier of the faith of those who believe in the Father and the Son and the Holy Spirit. 2. That this rule has come down from the beginning of the gospel, even before those earlier heretics, and even more so before yesterday's Praxeas, will be demonstrated by the very lateness of all heretics as much as by the very novelty of yesterday's Praxeas. For this reason, against all heresies without exception let it from now on be a foregone conclusion that whatever is earlier is true and whatever is later is false. 3. But even while preserving this rule, there must nevertheless always be an opportunity for reviewing [the statements of heretics] for the instruction and protection of certain people, lest it seem that every perverse opinion is condemned by a previous judgment without being examined, especially this perverse opinion which deems itself to possess the unadulterated truth, thinking that there is no other way to believe in the single God except by saying that the Father,

11 That is, the eschatological day of the Lord. 12 See John 16:13.
13 Tertullian here uses the Greek word *oikonomia*, transliterated into Latin.
14 John 1:1–3. 15 1 Cor 15:3–4. 16 Mark 16:19.
17 Acts 10:42. 18 John 16:7.

Son, and Spirit are one and the same. 4. It is as if the one [God] cannot also be all these things in the following manner, by all these things being from the one, namely, through unity of substance. And yet the mystery of that economy is preserved which arranges the unity into a trinity, setting in order Father, Son, and Spirit as three, but three not in terms of permanent station but of relative position, not in terms of substance but of form, not in terms of power but of manifestation, and yet they are of one substance, of one permanent station, and of one power, because it is one God from whom these relative positions and forms and manifestations are considered in the name of the Father and the Son and the Holy Spirit.[19] The following discussions will demonstrate how they admit of plurality without division.

3, 1. Now simple people (I don't want to call them ignorant and uneducated) always constitute the greater part of the faithful, and because the rule of faith itself conveys us from the many gods of this world to the single and true God, they do not understand that they must believe in the single [God] but only together with his economy. Thus they become frightened of his economy. The plurality and arrangement of the trinity they presume to be a division of its unity, even though a unity which derives a trinity from itself is not destroyed but rather is administered by it. And so they toss around [the charge] that two or three [gods] are preached by us, while they presume themselves truly to be worshipers of a single God, as if unity irrationally gathered together does not make a heresy and trinity rationally established does not establish truth. 2. "We hold," one of them said, "to the monarchy," and even the Latins utter this very term so loudly, and in such a masterly way, that you would think they understand monarchy as well as they enunciate it. Though the Latins are eager to say "monarchy," even the Greeks are not inclined to understand the economy. But as for me, if I have grasped anything of the two languages, I know that monarchy signifies nothing other than solitary and single rule, and yet monarchy, because it belongs to a single person, does not for that reason demand that the one to whom it belongs cannot have a son or must have made himself his own son or cannot administer his monarchy through whichever

19 In Latin, ... *et nihilominus custodiatur oikonomiae sacramentum, quae unitatem in trinitatem disponit, tres dirigens Patrem et Filium et Spiritum, tres autem non statu sed gradu, nec substantia sed forma, nec potestate sed specie, unius autem substantiae et unius status et unius potestatis quia unus Deus ex quo et gradus isti et formae et species in nomine Patris et Filii et Spiritus sancti deputantur*. See the similar language of *status* and *gradus* in *Apology* 21.13.

persons he may choose. In fact, I say that no dominion belongs to a single person in such a way, is singular in such a way, and is a monarchy in such a way that it may not also be administered through other closely related persons whom it has provided for itself as officials. 3. If indeed the one to whom a monarchy belongs also has a son, it is not at once divided and the monarchy does not cease to exist, if his son also is taken on as his partner. Instead, the monarchy principally belongs to the one who shared it with his son, and as long as it belongs to him, it is then a monarchy which is jointly held by two who are so closely united. 4. Therefore, even if the divine monarchy is administered through so many legions and armies of angels as it is written, "Ten thousand times ten thousand were attending him, and a thousand thousands were serving him,"[20] it has not for that reason ceased to belong to a single one, such that it ceases to be a monarchy, because it is governed through so many thousands of celestial powers. 5. Why would it be the case that God should seem to suffer division and dispersion in the Son and the Holy Spirit, who are assigned to second and third place and share so greatly in the Father's substance, when he does not suffer these things in the great number of angels who are indeed so greatly foreign to the Father's substance? Do you regard provinces and family relations and governing apparatuses and the very force and the entire system of a monarchy to be its destruction? You're wrong if you do! 6. I would prefer you to occupy yourself with the meaning of the thing itself rather than the sound of the word. For you should understand that the destruction of a monarchy happens when another power is introduced in addition to it, a power that is a rival because it shares the monarch's condition and permanent station, such as when another god is brought in against the creator, as in the case of Marcion, or when many gods are brought in, according to the Valentinians and the Prodicans.[21] Then there is destruction of the monarchy, when there is destruction of the creator.

4, 1. In contrast to this, since I derive the Son from no other source but from the substance of the Father – the Son who does nothing without the will of the Father and who has obtained all power from the Father – how, then, with regard to the faith, could I demolish the monarchy when

20 Dan 7:10.

21 Three rival groups of Christians in the second century all deemed heretical by Tertullian. Much less is known about Prodicus and his followers than is the case for Marcion, Valentinus, and their followers.

I preserve it in the Son just as it was passed down by the Father to the Son? Let me say the same thing also in the case of the third relative position, because I judge that the Spirit is from no other source than from the Father through the Son. 2. Therefore, make sure that it is not you instead who are demolishing the monarchy when you destroy its arrangement and dispensation, which has been constituted in as many names as God wished. To such a degree, however, does it remain in its own permanent station, although a trinity has been brought in, that it must also be restored to the Father by the Son, inasmuch as the Apostle writes concerning the final end: " ... when he hands over the kingdom to the God and Father. For he must reign until God puts his enemies under his feet."[22] (Now this of course is in line with the psalm, "Sit on my right, until I put your enemies as a stool for your feet.")[23] "When all things are subject to him, except for the one who subjected all things to him, then he himself also will be subjected to the one who subjected all things under him, so that God may be all in all."[24] 3. We see, therefore, that the Son causes no harm to the monarchy, although today it is in the Son's hands, because it is held in the Son's hands in its permanent station and it will be restored to the Father by the Son in its permanent station. Thus no one on this account will destroy it by admitting the Son, since it is agreed that it has been passed down to him by the Father and that it will be restored by him to the Father at some point. 4. With this one passage of the apostolic letter we have already been able to show that the Father and Son are two: not only on the basis of the names of Father and Son, but also on the basis of the fact that there is one who handed over the kingdom and one to whom he handed it, and likewise one who subjected it and one to whom he subjected it, they are by necessity two.

* * *

27, 1. And why shall I linger over things that are so obvious, when I should be engaging those [arguments] with which they seek to obscure these obvious things? For having been refuted on every side by the distinctness of the Father and the Son – which we arrange in such a way that their conjunction remains, like that of the sun and a ray of light, and that of a spring and a river, and yet we do this by means of an indivisible plurality of twos and threes – they try to interpret this distinctness differently but

22 1 Cor 15:24–25. 23 Ps 109(110):1. 24 1 Cor 15:27–28.

in a way that agrees nonetheless with their opinion. In the same way, then, they distinguish both Father and Son in one person, saying that the Son is flesh, that is, a human being, that is, Jesus, while the Father is Spirit, that is, God, that is, Christ. 2. And those who contend that Father and Son are one and the same now begin to divide them rather than to unite them. For if Jesus is one and Christ another, the Son will be one and the Father another, because Jesus is the Son and Christ is the Father. Such a monarchy, which makes Jesus and Christ two, they perhaps learned from Valentinus. 3. But this suggestion of theirs too has already been blunted by our previous discussion, because the one they make the Father is said to be the Word of God or the Spirit of God and the Power of the Most High. For he is not those things that are said to belong to him, but they are from him and belong to him.[25]

4. And they will be disproven in another way from their own text. "Behold," they say, "it was foretold by an angel: 'Therefore, what shall be born shall be called holy, the Son of God.'[26] And so, it was flesh that was born, and so it is flesh that must be the Son of God." On the contrary, this was said of the Spirit of God. 5. For without doubt it was of the Holy Spirit that the virgin conceived and what she conceived she brought to birth. So then, that had to be born, which was conceived and brought to birth, that is, the Spirit, whose "name will be called Emmanuel, which means: God with us."[27] But flesh is not God, such that it can be said about it, "It shall be called holy, the Son of God," but that one who was born in it is God, about whom also the psalm says: Because God "as a human being was born in her and he built her up" by the will of the Father.[28] 6. Which God was born in her? The Word, and the Spirit who along with the Word was born from the will of the Father. Therefore, the Word is in flesh.

Next, we must investigate this: how the Word was made flesh, whether he was transformed into flesh or clothed himself in flesh. By all means he clothed himself! And yet it is necessary to believe that God is immutable and untransformable, as he is eternal. 7. But transformation means the destruction of the original [form]: for everything that is transformed into something else ceases to be what it was and begins to be what it was not. God, however,

25 In Latin, *non enim ipse sunt, cuius dicuntur, sed ex ipso et ipsius*. In other words, the Father is not to be identified with those things (Word, Spirit, Power) that are said to belong to him (Word *of God*, Spirit *of God*, Power *of the Most High*).

26 Luke 1:35. 27 Matt 1:23. 28 Ps 87(88):5.

neither ceases to be nor can be something else. And the Word is God, and "the Word of God abides forever,"[29] namely by continuing in its own form. If he is not capable of being transformed, it follows that he should be understood to have been made flesh in this way, that he comes to be in flesh, and that he appears and is seen and is handled by means of flesh,[30] because everything else requires acceptance of this as well. 8. For if the Word was made flesh by means of a transformation and change of his substance, Jesus will then be one substance from two [substances], from flesh and Spirit, a mixture of sorts, like electrum from gold and silver, and he begins to be neither gold, that is, Spirit, nor silver, that is, flesh, since that one thing is changed by another and a *tertium quid* comes about. 9. Therefore, Jesus will not be God; for he ceases to be the Word when he has been made flesh, nor will the human being be flesh; for it is not properly flesh, because it was the Word. Thus from both things there is neither; there is a *tertium quid*, far different from either.

10. But in fact we have found that he is expressly set out as both God and human being, as this very psalm suggests: Because God was born "as a human being in her, and he built her up" by the will of the Father.[31] In every conceivable way, to be sure, he is Son of God and Son of Man, since he is God and a human being without doubt according to each substance that differs in its proper characteristics. For the Word is nothing other than God and the flesh nothing other than a human being. 11. This is what the Apostle teaches about both his substances: " … who was made," he says, "from the seed of David" (here he will be a human being and the Son of Man), " … who has been designated the Son of God according to the Spirit" (here he will be God and the Word of God).[32] We see [here] a double station, not confused but conjoined in a single person, God and the human being Jesus. (I am postponing, however, [discussion] of Christ.) And to such a degree is the proper character of each substance preserved, that the Spirit performed his own acts in him, that is, mighty deeds and works and signs, and the flesh was occupied with its passions: being hungry with the devil,[33] thirsting with the Samaritan woman,[34] weeping for Lazarus,[35] troubled even to death,[36] and finally dying. 12. But if there had been a *tertium quid*, a confusion of both, like electrum, there would not be such definite proofs for both substances, but instead the Spirit would have done

29 Isa 40:8. 30 See 1 John 1:1–2. 31 Ps 87(88):5. 32 Rom 1:3–4.
33 See Matt 4:2. 34 See John 4:7. 35 See John 11:35. 36 See Matt 26:38.

things of the flesh, and the flesh would have done things of the Spirit because of a transference, or else neither things of the flesh nor of the Spirit, but of some third type because of the confusion. 13. On the contrary, either the Word would have died or the flesh would not have died, if the Word had been turned into flesh; for either the flesh would have been immortal or the Word mortal. But because both substances were active separately in their own permanent stations, therefore to these both their own works and their own departures accrued. 14. Learn, therefore, along with Nicodemus that "that which is born in flesh is flesh and that which [is born] of Spirit is spirit."[37] Neither does flesh become Spirit nor Spirit flesh. They can clearly exist in one [individual]. From these Jesus is composed: from flesh, a human being, from Spirit, God. At that time the angel pronounced him to be the Son of God on the basis of that part of him which was Spirit,[38] reserving for the flesh to be called the Son of Man. 15. So too did the Apostle, by calling him also the mediator between God and human beings,[39] confirm that he was of both substances. At long last, then, you who understand the Son of God to be the flesh, show us who the Son of Man is. Or will he be Spirit? But you wish Spirit to be considered the Father himself because God is Spirit, as if he were not also the Spirit of God, just as the Word is God and he is also the Word of God.

28, 1. You most foolish man! You make "Christ" to be the Father since you do not examine the actual meaning of this name – assuming that "Christ" is a name[40] and not rather a title.[41] For it means "anointed." And yet "anointed" is no more a name than "clothed" or "shod,"[42] since it is a quality that belongs to a name. Now if Jesus were also called "Clothed" on the basis of some argument, just as [he is called] "Christ" from the mystery of anointing, would you in like manner claim that Jesus is the Son of God and believe that "Clothed" is the Father? 2. Now then, concerning "Christ." If the Father is Christ, the Father was anointed – without a doubt by someone else. If he anointed himself, prove it! But this is not what the Acts of the Apostles teaches in that cry of the church to God: "For everyone gathered in that city against your holy Son whom you anointed, both Herod and Pilate with the Gentiles."[43] 3. In this way they testified both that Jesus is the Son of God and that the Son was anointed by the Father. Therefore, Christ will be the same as Jesus who was anointed by the Father, not [the same as] the Father

37 John 3:6. 38 Luke 1:35. 39 See 1 Tim 2:5. 40 In Latin, *nomen*.
41 In Latin, *appellatio*. 42 That is, wearing shoes. 43 Acts 4:27.

who anointed the Son. 4. So too Peter: "Therefore, let all the house of Israel know most assuredly that God made him both Lord and Christ" – that is, anointed – "this Jesus, whom you crucified."[44]

5. Furthermore, John reprimands the one who has denied that Jesus is Christ as a "liar,"[45] but in contrast [says] that everyone who believes Jesus to be Christ is born of God.[46] For this reason he also exhorts us "to believe in the name of his Son, Jesus Christ," namely so that "we may have fellowship with the Father and his Son, Jesus Christ."[47] 6. In the same way too Paul everywhere specifies "God the Father and our Lord Jesus Christ." When he writes to the Romans, he gives thanks to God through our Lord Jesus Christ.[48] When [he writes] to the Galatians, he presents himself as an apostle, not from human beings nor through a human being, but through Jesus Christ and God the Father.[49] 7. And you have in all his documents [passages] which make statements in this same way and speak of two, God the Father and our Lord Jesus Christ, Son of the Father, and [say] that Jesus himself is Christ, and, using another name too, the Son of God. 8. Accordingly, then, by that rule whereby both names belong to one, that is, the Son of God, one [name] even without the other belongs to the same one. And if only "Jesus" is specified, "Christ" is also to be understood because it was Jesus who was anointed; or if "Christ" alone [is specified], the same is also Jesus because it was Jesus who was anointed. One of these names is a proper name insofar as it was bestowed by an angel, whereas the other is indicative of an attribute insofar as it came about from the anointing – as long as Christ is the Son, not the Father!

9. Finally, how blind is he who fails to understand that in the name of Christ another God is implied if he ascribes the name of Christ to the Father? For if Christ the Father is the God who says, "I am ascending to my Father and your Father and to my God and your God,"[50] he surely reveals above himself another Father and God. And likewise, if Christ is the Father, there is another "who gives strength to the thunder and creates Spirit and announces to human beings his Christ."[51] 10. And if "the kings of the earth stood up and the rulers gathered together against the Lord and against his Christ,"[52] there will be another Lord against whose Christ the kings and rulers gathered. 11. And if "the Lord speaks thus to

44 Acts 2:36. 45 See 1 John 2:22. 46 See 1 John 5:1. 47 1 John 1:3.
48 See Rom 1:8. 49 See Gal 1:1. 50 John 20:17.
51 Amos 4:13. 52 Ps 2:2.

Christ my Lord,"[53] there will be another Lord who speaks to Christ the Father. 12. And when the Apostle writes, " … that the God of our Lord Jesus Christ may give you a spirit of wisdom and knowledge,"[54] there will be another God of Jesus Christ, the giver of spiritual gifts. 13. Certainly – and not wanting to get sidetracked by going through every passage – "he who raised Christ and will also raise our mortal bodies"[55] will be, as it were, another one who raises in addition to the Father who died and the Father who was raised, if Christ who died is the Father.

29, 1. Let this blasphemy fall silent, let it fall silent! Let it be enough that Christ, the Son of God, is said to have died, and that this is so because it is so written. For even the Apostle, when declaring not without difficulty that Christ died, adds "according to the scriptures,"[56] so that by the authority of the scriptures he might soften the harshness of this declaration and remove a stumbling-block for the listener. 2. Even though it is held that there are two substances in Christ Jesus, a divine and a human, and moreover it is agreed that the divine is immortal since that which is human is mortal, it is nonetheless clear in which sense he said that he died,[57] namely, *qua* flesh and human being and Son of Man, not *qua* Spirit and Word and Son of God. In saying, then, "Christ died," that is, the anointed, he shows that it was what was anointed that died, namely, flesh. 3. "So then," you say, "since by the same reasoning as you we say that the Son [died], we do not blaspheme against the Lord God. For we say that he died not in respect of his divine substance, but of his human." But even still you blaspheme, not only because you say that the Father died, but also because [you say that he was] crucified. For by converting Christ into the Father you blaspheme against the Father, insofar as the curse laid upon the crucified one[58] is, by law, owed to the Son, since it was "Christ who was made a curse for us,"[59] not the Father.

4. But as for us, in saying that Christ was crucified, we do not curse him but [merely] call to mind the curse of the law, for when the Apostle said this he did not blaspheme either. Now, just as one speaks without blasphemy when something valid is said about someone, so too if something invalid is said it is blasphemy. 5. Therefore, by no means did the Father co-suffer with the Son. For being afraid of a direct blasphemy against the

53 Isa 45:1. 54 Eph 1:17. 55 Rom 8:11. 56 1 Cor 15:3.
57 That is, in which sense the Apostle said that Christ died.
58 See Deut 21:23. 59 Gal 3:13.

Father they hope for their blasphemy to be minimized in this way: already conceding that the Father and the Son are two, [they say that] if indeed the Son suffers, then the Father co-suffers. But in doing this too they are fools. For what is it "to co-suffer" besides "to suffer along with another"? Furthermore, if the Father is incapable of suffering, he is certainly incapable of co-suffering. Or if he is capable of co-suffering, he is certainly capable of suffering. You do nothing for him with this fear of yours. 6. You are afraid of saying that he is capable of suffering even though you say that he is capable of co-suffering. Now the Father is incapable of co-suffering to the same extent that the Son is incapable of suffering by reason of that status by which he is God. But how did the Son suffer, if the Father did not also co-suffer? He is separated from the Son but not from God. For even if a river is polluted by some muddying, although one substance flows down from its source and it is not separated from the source, yet the harm to the river will not reach to the source. And though the water that suffers in the river belongs to the source, as long as it suffers in the river and not at the source, it is not the source that suffers but the river which is from the source.

7. So then, how could the Spirit of God suffer in the Son? Because [the Spirit] did not suffer in the Father but in the Son, does it seem that the Father did not suffer? But it is enough that the Spirit of God suffer nothing on its own account, because, if it did suffer anything in the Son, it would indeed be true that the Father suffered with the Son in the flesh. But this has already been discussed, nor will anyone deny it, since not even we can suffer for God unless the Spirit of God is in us. On our account it speaks what pertains to our confession, and yet does not itself suffer but grants the ability to suffer.

30, 1. But if you press on with further [questions], I will be able to give you an answer even harder to resist and put you in conflict with a statement of the Lord himself; if you do I will say: "Why are you asking about this? You have him crying out at his passion: 'My God, my God, why have you abandoned me?'"[60] Therefore, either the Son abandoned by the Father was suffering and the Father who abandoned the Son did not suffer, or else, if it was the Father who was suffering, to which God was he crying out? 2. But this voice of flesh and soul, that is, of a human being, not of Word or Spirit, that is, not of God, was sent out with the express purpose of revealing that

60 Matt 27:46.

the God, who abandoned the Son in this way when he handed over his humanity to death, was incapable of suffering. 3. The Apostle perceived the same thing, writing: "If the Father did not spare the Son."[61] Earlier Isaiah foretold the same thing: "And the Lord handed him over for our failings."[62] And so, he abandons by not sparing; he abandons by handing over. 4. And yet, the Father did not abandon the Son, inasmuch as it was into the Father's hands that the Son placed his own Spirit. When at long last he placed it [there] immediately he died, for with the Spirit remaining in the flesh the flesh is totally unable to die. And so, the abandonment by the Father was death for the Son.

Therefore, the Son both dies and is raised up again by the Father according to the scriptures.[63] The Son ascended to the higher places of the heavens having also descended into the lower parts of the earth.[64] 5. He sits at the right hand of the Father;[65] the Father does not sit at his. When Stephen was being stoned, he saw him still standing at the right hand of God,[66] in such a way that from that point onward he will sit until the Father places all his enemies under his feet.[67] He will also come again upon the clouds of heaven, in the same way as he ascended.[68] And in the meantime he poured forth a gift that he received from the Father, the Holy Spirit, the third name of divinity and the third position of majesty, the preacher of one monarchy, as well as the interpreter of the economy for anyone who has accepted the words of its new prophecy[69] and the one who guides into all the truth[70] which is in the Father and the Son and the Holy Spirit according to the Christian mystery.

61 Rom 8:32. 62 Isa 53:6. 63 See 1 Cor 15:3. 64 See Eph 4:9.
65 See Mark 16:19. 66 See Acts 7:55. 67 See Ps 109(110):1.
68 See Acts 1:11; Luke 21:27.
69 That is, Montanism. See the introduction for details. 70 See John 16:13.

16

Origen, *On First Principles* 2.6

Introduction and Translation by Bradley K. Storin

INTRODUCTION

Origen of Alexandria (ca. 185–254) was a brilliant theologian who led an instructional program under the authority of Bishop Demetrius. His reputation for learning and teaching was strong throughout the eastern Mediterranean, and he frequently embarked upon philosophical speaking tours. On one such tour Origen was ordained a priest by two Palestinian bishops, a move that, when coupled with his controversial teaching about the interrelatedness of creation and the eventual apocalyptic reunification of all rational existence (God, the angels, human souls, demons, and even the devil), spurred Bishop Demetrius to publicly censure him. Rather than subject himself to Demetrius's episcopal rebukes, Origen relocated to Caesarea Maritima in Palestine where he would continue to teach and preach in his capacity as priest. There he would remain until his death in 253 or 254, caused by injuries he sustained under torture during the Decian persecution of 251.

Among Origen's most important works must be counted *On First Principles*, which provides one of the most extensive treatments of Christian thought from late antiquity. Due to controversies that emerged involving later readers of Origen's work, it survives in full only in the early fifth-century Latin translation of Rufinus (some specific sections have survived in the Greek original). Topics in the work include, among many others, the divine nature, rational nature, diversity within creation, moral and spiritual movement, the freedom of individual will, and the multiple layers of scriptural meaning. In the preface to this work Origen outlines the "ecclesiastical proclamation," something like a statement of faith regarding all the theological topics that Origen understands as universally accepted throughout Christian communities everywhere. In the section on Christ, Origen says:

> Next, Christ Jesus, he who came, was born of the Father before all creation. After having served the Father in the foundation of all things – for all things were made through him[1] – in recent times he emptied himself, was made human, and became incarnate even though he was God. Made human, he remained what he was, God. He assumed a body like our body, differing only in his being born of a Virgin and the Holy Spirit. Since this Jesus Christ was born and suffered in truth and not through a mere semblance,[2] he truly died this common death. Furthermore, he truly resurrected from the dead and, having spent time with his disciples after his resurrection,[3] he was taken up.[4]

Even in this brief summary we see the basic elements of Origen's Christology: the preexistence of Christ, his becoming human while remaining divine, and an anti-docetic insistence upon the true humanity of Christ and the reality of his human experiences, especially his suffering and death.

But Origen also explored these Christological issues in greater depth. The selection presented here contains Origen's treatment of Christ as the "God-human being" (*deus-homo*, in Latin), in which he enunciates views about the Christological union of divine and human natures, while providing notable examples of his exegetical method of tracking the appearance of specific words throughout the scriptures in order to develop a sense for the spiritual meaning of the word (see, for example, his discussion of the word "shadow" in section 7). Here Origen explains how the Word of God first became ensouled (joined in a union with a human soul) before becoming incarnate (joined in a union with human flesh). In the beginning God through his Word created a fixed number of minds or souls whose purpose was to contemplate God. Being creatures subject to instability, all but one of these preexistent souls fell away from contemplating God into various degrees of embodiment. The one that did not – the future soul of

1 John 1:3.

2 This assertion opposes docetist Christological trends prevalent in the second and third centuries, which posited Christ's suffering and death as phantasmal and not real.

3 See Matt 26:16–20; Luke 24:36–49; John 20:1–21:23.

4 *On First Principles* 1.Pref.4; translation by Bradley K. Storin in CEECW 1 on p. 74.

Jesus – was rewarded with union with the Wisdom of God on account of its unceasing, unshakeable devotion to God. Later, the Word who was in union with this particular soul became incarnate in Jesus Christ to accommodate those who had fallen so far from the prelapsarian state that they could no longer contemplate unmediated divinity. Thus, Origen conceives of the incarnation as the Word of God taking on flesh through the intermediary of the soul of Christ, which enables a *communicatio idiomatum*.

The edition from which this translation was made is Henri Crouzel and Manlio Simonetti, *Origène. Traité des principes. Tome I (Livres I et II)*, SChr 252 (Paris: Éditions du Cerf, 1978), 308–324.

TRANSLATION

1. Now that we have run through the previous topics, it is time for us to return to the incarnation of our Lord and Savior, how he became a human being and lived among human beings.[5] To recap: as far as our deficient abilities allowed, we contemplated the divine nature through a survey of his works rather than from the viewpoint of our perceptions, and we gazed upon his visible creatures no less than we also contemplated his invisible creatures with faith, since human frailty can neither see everything with its eyes nor comprehend everything with reason, on account of the fact that we human beings are living things that are weaker and frailer than all rational beings – after all, those who dwell in heaven or above the heavens are more excellent [than us]. And so, it remains for us to seek out the intermediary between all these creatures and God, that is, "the mediator"[6] whom the apostle Paul calls "the firstborn of all creation."[7] For when we see what the sacred scriptures record about his majesty, and when we consider that he is called the "image of the invisible God" and "firstborn of all creation," and that "in him all things visible and invisible were created, whether thrones or dominions or principalities or powers, all things were created through him and in him, and he exists before all things, and all things remain in him,"[8] who is the head of all things, having for his own head only God the Father, as it is written, "But the head of Christ is God,"[9] and when we also perceive that it is written, "No one knows the Father except the Son, and no one knows the Son except the Father"[10] – for who

5 See John 1:14. 6 1 Tim 2:5. 7 Col 1:15. 8 Col 1:15–16.
9 1 Cor 11:3. 10 Matt 11:27.

can know what Wisdom is except the one that begot it? Or who has certain knowledge of what truth is except the Father of truth?[11] Who can indeed investigate the complete nature of his Word and that God who is from God, except for God alone with whom the Word was?[12] – when we do all of that, we ought to possess certainty that none else but the Father alone knows this Word (or maybe we should call him Reason), this Wisdom, this Truth, about whom it is written, "I suppose that the world itself could not even contain the books that might be written"[13] – written, that is, about the glory and majesty of the Son of God. Yes, it is impossible to commit to writing what pertains to the glory of the Savior.

Therefore, now that we have surveyed so many of these substantive points about the nature of God's Son, with utter amazement we stand dumbstruck at the fact that that nature, preeminent over all things, would empty itself of its majestic station[14] and become a human being and live among human beings,[15] as the grace poured upon his lips testifies,[16] and as the heavenly Father bore witness to him,[17] and as is confirmed by the signs, portents, and various acts of power performed by him. And before he exhibited his very presence in the body, he dispatched the prophets as precursors and messengers of his coming, but after his ascension into heaven, he caused the holy apostles – inexperienced and untrained persons drawn from the ranks of tax-collectors or fishermen, but filled with the power of his divinity – to canvass the whole world in order to gather together from every tribe and from all nations a people made up of pious individuals who believe in him.[18]

2. However, of all the marvelous and magnificent things about him, what completely overwhelms the human mind's capacity for astonishment, and what our weak mortal understanding fails to find a way to perceive or understand, is how this great power of divine majesty – the very Word of the Father and the very Wisdom of God, in which all things visible and invisible were created[19] – can be believed to have been confined to that human being[20] who appeared in Judea; that the Wisdom of God entered into a woman's womb, was born as a little child, and cried out in the way that little children wail; that he is reported to have been anxious at the prospect of death, as he himself admitted by saying, "My soul is sorrowful, even to

11 See John 18:38. 12 See John 1:1. 13 John 21:25. 14 See Phil 2:5–11.
15 See John 1:14. 16 See Ps 44(45):3. 17 See Matt 3:17; Mark 1:11; Luke 3:22.
18 See Rev 7:9. 19 See Col 1:16.
20 In Latin, *intra circumscriptionem eius hominis*.

death";[21] and that, at the end, he was led to that death which people regard as the most reprehensible, even though he did rise the third day after. Accordingly, when we see in him certain things so human that they appear no different from the common fragility of mortals, and certain things so divine, which are appropriate to nothing else except that primal and ineffable nature of the divinity, the narrow straits of the human intellect are paralyzed and, struck with the stupor of such astonishment, it has no idea where it should go, what it should grasp, or which way it should turn. If it supposes him to be God, it sees a mortal; if it supposes him to be a human being, it sees him returning from the dead with his spoils in the wake of death's tyranny being vanquished. For this reason we should contemplate [these matters] with all dread and respect in order to demonstrate that the actual reality of each nature exists in one and the same individual, so as to prevent anyone from supposing that something unworthy and unbecoming exists in that divine and ineffable substance, and contrariwise, to prevent anyone from thinking that his deeds were the illusions of a deceptive imagination. Certainly, to profess these things to human ears and to explain them with words far exceeds the powers of our worth, cleverness, or discourse. Moreover, I believe that it may even surpass the capacity of the holy apostles. Yes indeed, it may even be that an explanation of this mystery is too lofty for the whole creation of heavenly powers. On this subject, not in some flight of fancy but because the sequence of argumentation[22] requires it, we shall profess, in the fewest possible words, what our faith holds rather than what an assertion stemming from a human mode of thinking is accustomed to claim, openly professing our suppositions rather than any clear statements of fact.

3. So then, the only-begotten Son of God, through whom all things visible and invisible were made,[23] as I taught in the discussion above, both made all things and loves what he made according to the teaching of scripture.[24] For since he is the invisible "image of the invisible God,"[25] he invisibly offered participation in himself to all rational creatures in such a way that each obtained from him a measure of participation proportionate to how much it clung to him with the affection of love. But when, by reason of the faculty of free will, variety and diversity had come to possess every single soul, resulting in one being fixed on its author with a more blazing

21 Mark 14:34; Matt 26:38. 22 In Latin, *ordo loci*. 23 See Col 1:16.
24 See Wis 11:24. 25 Col 1:15.

love and another with a fainter and weaker love, one particular soul – that about which Jesus said, "No one takes my soul from me,"[26] and which from the beginning of creation and ever after clung inseparably and indivisibly to him, as to the Wisdom and the Word of God and the Truth and the true Light, and received the entirety of him entirely and was changed into his light and splendor – became one spirit with him to the highest degree, just as the Apostle also promises to those who should imitate this soul, "He who is joined to the Lord is one spirit."[27] With this substance of the soul, then, serving as intermediary between God and flesh (for it was impossible that God's nature be mingled with a body without a mediator), the "God-human being" was born, as we have said, with this substance being the intermediary since it was certainly not contrary to its nature to assume a body. But neither was it contrary to nature for that soul, inasmuch as it was a rational substance, to receive God, into which, as we have said above, it had already entirely changed as Word, Wisdom, and Truth. Therefore, either because it was entirely in the Son of God or because it received the entirety of the Son of God into itself, this soul, along with that flesh that it assumed, is deservedly called the Son of God, the Power of God, and the Wisdom of God;[28] and in turn, the Son of God, through whom all things were created, is deservedly named Jesus Christ and Son of Man. For just as the Son of God is said to have died doubtless because of that nature which could certainly undergo death, so too the Son of Man is said to be the one about whom it is foretold that he would come in the glory of God the Father with the holy angels.[29] And for this reason throughout the whole of scripture, the divine nature is designated with human appellations just as much as the human nature is adorned with the honors of divine titles. Indeed, the following scripture could be said to be more about this than about anything else: "Both will be in one flesh, and they are no longer two, but one flesh."[30] Yes, one should think of the Word of God being in one flesh with that soul more than a man is with his wife. But also, to what is being one spirit with God more suitable than to this

26 John 19:18. Jerome, *Ep.* 124.6.2, offers another Latin version of Origen's Greek: "No other soul, which came down into a human body, has represented in itself a pure and genuine likeness of its previous image except that about which the Savior said, 'No one takes [in Latin, *tollit*, in contradistinction to the *aufert* quoted in Rufinus's translation] my soul from me, but I will lay it down by myself.'"

27 1 Cor 6:17. 28 See 1 Cor 1:24. 29 See Matt 16:27; Mark 8:38; Luke 9:26.

30 Gen 2:24; see Matt 19:5–6.

soul, which joined itself to God through love so much that it is deservedly said to be one spirit with him?

4. Now it was the perfection of love and the purity of authentic desire that produced for that particular soul this inseparable unity with God. Accordingly, the assumption of that soul [by God] was neither accidental nor an expression of preference for the individual,[31] but rather was granted to that soul as a reward for its virtues. That this is so, listen to what the prophet says to it: "You have loved righteousness and hated iniquity; therefore, God, your God, has anointed you with the oil of gladness above your partakers."[32] It is anointed, then, with the oil of gladness as a reward for its love – that is, the soul with the Word of God is made Christ. For to be anointed with the oil of gladness should not be understood in any other way except to be filled with the Holy Spirit. However, when [the Psalmist] said, "above your partakers," he means that the grace of the Spirit was not given as it was to the prophets, but that the essential[33] fullness of God's Word itself was in that soul, just as the Apostle also says, "In him the whole fullness of the divinity dwells bodily."[34] Finally, this is why he did not just say, "You have loved righteousness," but he added, "and hated iniquity." For to have "hated iniquity" amounts to the same thing as what scripture says about him: "He committed no sin, nor was any deceit found in his mouth."[35] This too: he was "tempted in every respect as we are, yet without sin."[36] But the Lord himself also says, "Who among you accuses me of sin?"[37] And again, he says about himself, "Behold! The ruler of this world is coming, and he finds nothing in me."[38] All this indicates that no inclination toward sin[39] existed in him. To more clearly demonstrate that no inclination toward iniquity ever entered him, the prophet says, "Before the child knew to call out for father and mother, he turned himself away from iniquity."[40]

5. But if what we have shown above, that there is a rational soul in Christ, should seem too difficult for anyone because we have often showed in all our discussions that the nature of souls is undoubtedly capable of receiving good and evil, the difficulty of this issue will be resolved in the following way. Indeed, there can be no doubt that this nature of his soul

31 In Latin, *cum personae acceptione*. 32 Ps 44(45):8. 33 In Latin, *substantialis*.
34 Col 2:9. 35 Isa 53:9. 36 Heb 4:15. 37 John 8:46.
38 John 14:30. 39 In Latin, *peccati sensum*.
40 A combination of Isa 8:4 and perhaps Isa 7:16.

is that which belongs to all souls; otherwise, it couldn't be called a soul were it not actually a soul. But since the faculty of choosing good and evil is the province of all [souls], the particular soul that belongs to Christ has chosen to love righteousness to such a degree that, in accordance with the immensity of its love, it clings to it without change or separation, to such a degree that the firmness of its resolution, the immensity of its desire, and the inextinguishable glow of its love have destroyed every inclination toward deviation and change. Consequently, what resided in its will has now been transformed into nature by a condition of long-lasting habit. We must believe, then, that a human and rational soul indeed existed in Christ, and we should think that it had no inclination toward, or possibility of, sin.

6. To explain the issue more fully, however, it would not seem absurd if we were even to use an analogy, conceding that there is not an abundance of suitable examples to use with an issue so hard and difficult. Here is an analogy that doesn't obscure the point: the metal iron is capable of receiving both cold and heat. If, then, a piece of iron is permanently placed in fire, receiving the fire into itself through all its openings and all its veins so that the whole thing becomes fire, and if the fire is never withdrawn from the mass and the mass is never pulled out of the fire, would we ever say that what is indeed a mass of iron by nature could receive coldness into itself after having been placed in the fire and burning continuously? Of course not! Instead we say (because it is more correct) that, just as we often see it happen with our own eyes in furnaces, the whole thing becomes fire because nothing is discernible in it except the fire. And even if someone were to try to touch or handle it, they would feel the fire's energy, not the iron's. In this way, then, that particular soul, which like the iron in the fire was placed permanently in the Word, permanently in Wisdom, permanently in God, is God with respect to all that it does, all that it perceives, and all that it understands. And on that account it cannot be said to be changeable or mutable, since by being continuously fiery it has come to possess unchangeability from its unity with the Word of God.

Furthermore, even though we should think that some degree of the heat from the Word of God has reached all the saints, in that soul we should believe that the divine fire itself has come to repose in a substantial way, and from this fire some degree of the heat has come to others. And moreover, the fact that it says, "God, your God, has anointed you with the oil of gladness above your partakers,"[41] shows that this particular soul is anointed in one way, with the oil of gladness, that is, with the Word of God and his Wisdom, and his partakers, that is, the holy prophets and apostles, in another way. For the latter are said "to have run in the fragrance of his perfumes,"[42] but that particular soul was the jar containing the perfume itself, of whose good odor all the prophets and apostles became worthy partakers. Just as, then, the perfume's fragrance is one thing and the perfume's substance is another thing, so too is Christ one thing and his partakers another. And just as the jar itself, which contains the perfume's substance, can in no way receive any stench into it, while it is possible for those who partake of its fragrance, were they to remove themselves a little bit further away from its good odor, to receive into themselves any stench that happens upon them, so too it was impossible for Christ, who is like the very jar in which the perfume's substance resided, to receive into himself a contrary fragrance, while his partakers will be partakers and recipients of his fragrance in proportion to how near the jar they were.

7. I certainly believe too that it was because the prophet Jeremiah understood what was the nature of God's wisdom in Christ, and what was that which he assumed for the salvation of the world, that he said, "The breath of our face is the Lord Christ,[43] about whom we said, 'In his shadow we shall live among the nations.'"[44] For just as our body's shadow is inseparable from the body and impeccably adopts and performs the body's movements and gestures, so too I think that it was because [Jeremiah] wanted to make known the work and motion of Christ's soul, which inseparably clung to him and performed everything in accordance with his movement and will, that he called it the "shadow" of Christ the Lord, in which shadow we shall live among the nations. For the nations live in the mystery of his assumption when they by imitating this soul through faith attain salvation. And it seems to me that David makes known something similar when he says, "Be mindful of my reproach, Lord, with which they have reproached me in exchange for your Christ."[45] And what else does Paul mean when he says, "Our life has been hidden with Christ in God"?[46]

41 Ps 44(45):8. 42 See Song 1:3–4.

43 In Latin, *Christus dominus*. The prophetic text, of course, would not have been referring to the Christian Savior, Jesus Christ, but Origen and other Christian interpreters read it that way.

44 Lam 4:20. 45 Ps 88(89):51–52. 46 Col 3:3.

And also in another place he says, "Or are you seeking a proof of him who speaks in me – Christ?"[47] And now he says that Christ is hidden in God. Unless the meaning of this passage is something like what we said above was indicated by the prophet with "the shadow of Christ," it may very well exceed the comprehension of the human mind. Furthermore, we see how there are many other passages contained in the divine scriptures that are important for understanding "shadow." For instance, there is that occasion in the Gospel according to Luke when Gabriel says to Mary, "The Spirit of the Lord will come upon you, and the power of the Most High will overshadow you."[48] And the Apostle says with respect to the law that those who have a fleshly circumcision "serve a copy and a shadow of heavenly things."[49] And elsewhere it says, "Isn't our life on earth but a shadow?"[50] So then, if both the law that is on earth is a shadow and our whole life that is on earth is a shadow, and we are to live among the nations in the shadow of Christ, then we must ponder whether or not the true reality behind all these shadows will become known in that revelation when all the saints will deserve to contemplate the glory of God and the causes and true reality of things, no longer "through a mirror and in a mystery, but face to face."[51] Since a pledge of this true reality has already been received through the Holy Spirit,[52] the Apostle said, "Even if we once knew Christ according to the flesh, now we no longer know him so."[53]

For the time being, this is what occurs to us at present when discoursing on such difficult topics, that is, on the incarnation and deity of Christ. If anyone can discover something better and confirm what he asserts with clearer proofs from the holy scriptures, let those be accepted in the place of mine.

47 2 Cor 13:3. 48 Luke 1:35. 49 Heb 8:5. 50 Job 8:9.
51 1 Cor 13:12. 52 See 2 Cor 5:5. 53 2 Cor 5:16.

17

Paul of Samosata, *Selected Fragments*

Introduction and Translation of Syriac Fragments by Emanuel Fiano
Translation of Armenian Fragments by Michael Papazian
Translation of Greek and Latin Fragments by Mark DelCogliano

INTRODUCTION

In the 260s the recently elected Antiochene bishop Paul of Samosata faced an offensive from fellow Syrian church leaders, ostensibly on account of his theological persuasions. In his *Ecclesiastical History* Eusebius of Caesarea reports that as soon as it became clear that Paul "held low and base views about Christ, contrary to ecclesiastical teaching, that he was in nature an ordinary human being (*koinou tēn phusin anthrōpou genomenou*),"[1] a first synod was summoned (ca. 264), to which clergymen from across the empire hastened. Shortly after this synod, and probably after a few more, Hymenaeus of Jerusalem and five colleagues composed a letter full of *ad hominem* attacks against Paul and containing a creed that insisted on the eternity of the Son. Finally, at a synod that gathered in 268/269, Paul was cornered by Malchion, an Antiochene priest of great rhetorical skill, and was deposed.

Since Paul never recorded his doctrine, all of our information about it comes from three sources: (1) the six bishops' letter cited above; (2) the synodal letter of the council of 268/269 and the stenographic report of the discussion between Malchion and Paul contained in its synodal acts, both of which are only extant in fewer than fifty Greek, Syriac, Armenian, and Latin fragments of problematic textual transmission; and (3) Eusebius's narrative, which includes four excerpts of the synodal letter, contained

1 *Ecclesiastical History* 7.27.2.

in *Ecclesiastical History* 7.27–30. The first source tells us virtually nothing about Paul's own theology. The third source for the most part informs us about the process against Paul, and the fragments from the synodal letter preserved by Eusebius focus on Paul's character and conduct. Accordingly, the fragments from the synodal letter and from the stenographic report provide the best insight into Paul's own theology, and these are what is translated below.

Although Paul's monarchianism was a far cry from the Logos Christology of his Origenist opponents, its positing of a preexistent Word also deviated sharply from psilanthropic or adoptionist theologies. Paul spoke to a large degree interchangeably of the Word and Wisdom, the latter of which appears to acquire at times the semblances of the Holy Spirit. Word/Wisdom, though not a hypostatically subsistent entity, is supremely honored, incorporeal, and most likely divine. The dignity of the Word for Paul was such that it was not susceptible of mixture. Influenced by imperial Aristotelianism, he saw the incarnation not as a substantial union between the immaterial Word and a body, but rather as an instance of the Word's inhabitation of what his Antiochene predecessors Ignatius and Theophilus had already taken pains to describe as a full human being. Although, for Paul, the Word's inhabitation of Jesus was qualitatively akin to its presence in all righteous human beings, the permanence and completeness he envisioned for its indwelling in the Savior were such as to make it resemble the natural union typical of Christological models conventionally deemed higher (barring Paul's failure to postulate an ontological foundation for such union).

The deposition of a bishop-monarch, who is tendentiously portrayed as autocratic, by the local clergy may testify to the resistance met by an onrush of episcopal centralization in the Syrian church, to which clues are found in contemporary documents tied to Syria (*Pseudoclementines* and Aphrahat's *Demonstrations*). Paul's adversaries sought the involvement of global ecclesiastical leaders, and particularly of the bishops of Rome and Alexandria. At a time when the patriarchate of Antioch was rising to prominence within the triarchy (Rome, Alexandria, and Antioch), the Syrian leadership resolved to make a local doctrinal disagreement global. In the formation of trans-regional alliances surrounding Paul's prosecution and eventual deposition, later church writers recognized a precursor to the functioning of global ecclesiastical power which they saw at work in later times. This helped crystalize the affair of Paul of Samosata as a foundational episode for late ancient Christian identity. As a result, Paul's memory was kept alive in the West and the East alike until the sixth century, his name integrated into heretical genealogies including the likes of Artemon, Ebion, Sabellius, Photinus, and Nestorius.

Later authors' ideological investment in the story of Paul might explain part of its ambiguous or inaccurate memorialization. For example, ancient sources report on Paul's association with the Palmyrene queen Zenobia, grounded in the Judaizing they allegedly shared. Skepticism now prevails about the historicity of this connection. The stringing together of Paul's xenophilia, Judeophilia, and heresy is the ideological product of a post-Constantinian orthodox Christianity that has severed its ties with Judaism and has constituted itself into an imperial religion. Similarly, historians hesitate to read Aurelian's order (recorded by Eusebius) to drive Paul out of his church as the earliest intervention of the secular Roman power in an ecclesiastical matter. It is likely, however, that Eusebius and his readers attributed precisely this meaning to that event.

The translation of the fragments below has been made with reference to the texts re-edited by Patricio de Navascués in his milestone work *Pablo de Samosata y sus adversarios. Estudio histórico-teológico del cristianismo antioqueno en el s. III* (Rome: Institutum Patristicum Augustinianum, 2004). The enumeration of the fragments translated here is our own; there is an appendix to the translation with a table that correlates our fragment numbers to those of de Navascués. In a number of cases (Fragments 2–5, 22, and 24–25) parts of the same text have been preserved several times. This has necessitated a special presentation, in which multiple independently preserved fragments are printed side by side, with other related independently preserved fragments arranged accordingly in an overall approximation of the original sequence of the text. In these cases, the number within the curved braces indicates number assigned to the fragment by de Navascués. Fragments 3–5 are a special case: the fragments independently preserved are clearly related to each other, though it is difficult to determine precisely how.

TRANSLATION

Fragments from the Stenographic Report of the Discussion between Malchion and Paul: Remarks of Paul of Samosata

Fragment 1

(Translated from Greek)

The Word came together with the one begotten from David, who is Jesus Christ, begotten from the Holy Spirit. The Virgin bore the latter through the Holy Spirit, but God begot the former without the Virgin and without anyone and no one was involved except God, and that's how the Word came into existence.

Fragment 2

(Translated from Greek)

Greek	**Greek**
{26} A human being is anointed; the Word is not anointed. The Nazarene is anointed our Lord. For indeed the Word was greater than Christ.[2] For Christ became great through Wisdom.	{38} The Word was greater than Christ. Christ became great through Wisdom. Let us not degrade the dignity of the Wisdom.
For the Word is from above; Jesus Christ, a human being, is from here.	
Mary did not give birth to the Word. For Mary was not before the ages. Mary is not older than the Word, but she gave birth to a human being that is equal to us, in fact better in every way, because he is from the Holy Spirit.	{1} Mary did not give birth to the Word. {2} For she was not before the ages. {3} Mary received the Word and she is not older than the Word. {4} Mary gave birth to a human being that is equal to us, {5} in fact better in every way, because he is from the Holy Spirit and the grace upon him is from the promises and from the scriptures.

2 The Greek here is *Christos*, which means "Anointed."

Fragment 3

(Translated from Greek)

Greek	**Greek**
{6} So that the anointed one from David would neither be alien to the Wisdom nor would the Wisdom dwell in any other in this way. For it was also in the prophets, but even more so in Moses and in many lords, and even more so in Christ as in a temple. {7} For Jesus Christ is one and the Word another.	{27} So that the anointed one from David would neither be alien to the Wisdom nor would the Wisdom dwell in any other in this way. {39} For [Wisdom] was also in the prophets, but even more so in Moses and in many lords, and even more so in Christ as in a temple. For Jesus Christ is one and the Word another.

Fragment 4

(Translated from Armenian)

Armenian	**Armenian**
{9} In this one Lord properly [Wisdom dwells], for [Wisdom] was also in the prophets and in Moses and in many lords, but even more so in Christ as in the temple of God.	{41} [Wisdom] dwells in the one Lord properly, for [Wisdom] was also in the prophets but even more so in Christ as in the temple of God.

Fragment 5

(Translated from Greek and Armenian)

Greek	**Armenian**	**Armenian**
{8} So that Wisdom benefits the human being in the way that it benefits one who can no longer be harmed. And it dwelt in this human being by filling him in every way,		
and it dwelt in him as it never did in anyone else, in the manner in which the incorporeal is able to dwell in a body, that is in	{40} The Wisdom dwelt in the human being as the incorporeal is able to dwell in a body. It was in this way that it dwelt [in	

Greek	Armenian	Armenian
the whole person. It was in this way that it dwelt [in him], so that the anointed one from David would not be alien to the Wisdom and that the Wisdom would not dwell in this way in any other.	him], so that the anointed one from David would not be alien to the Wisdom and that the Wisdom would not dwell in any other in this way.	{42} So that the one begotten of David would not be alien to the Wisdom, and that the Wisdom would not dwell in any other in this way, for he who appeared was not Wisdom because it could not be known in form.
{28} He who appeared was not Wisdom because it could not be found in a particular form, nor in the appearance of a man. For Wisdom is greater than visible things.	{12} He who appeared was not Wisdom, for it could not be known in the form or appearance of a human being. For it is greater than visible things.	

Fragment 6

(Translated from Armenian)

The Word was not begotten of the Holy Spirit. The Word was not a human being [but] dwelt in a human being, in Abraham and David. The Word was not begotten but all these proceeded from [him] [in] succession, because through their birth salvation was prepared in the Virgin Mary.

Fragment 7

(Translated from Armenian)

The Virgin is said to bear; the Virgin gave birth; and the one born of the Virgin is Jesus Christ. And Jesus Christ really suffered, and in suffering he restored us to life. The wise one was beaten to bear our sinfulness[3] and he took upon himself from us the burial of humankind, and he had compassion, as a sheep to the sacrifice he suffered like the lamb led to slaughter, like the lamb mute before his shearer.[4] The things written cannot turn us away from our faith.

3 Here we read the Armenian *meghanchakanut'iwn* instead of *meghkut'iwn*.

4 See Isa 53:7; Acts 8:32.

Fragment 8

(Translated from Armenian)

We know one unbegotten God [and] one begotten Christ, [who] became his Son. It is not that the Son of God is circumscribed by the seed of David according to the flesh, in whom, through the Spirit of holiness, the Word, the first chosen, became incarnate; rather, the Word [is the] Son, the Word [is] God begotten.

Fragment 9

(Translated from Syriac)

Jesus Christ, who is from Mary, was conjoined to Wisdom and became one with it and through it: Son and Christ. For ([Paul of Samosata] said that) he who suffered, he who endured slapping and blows, he who was buried and descended into Sheol, he who rose from the dead is Jesus Christ, the Son of God. It is not fitting in fact to distinguish him who is from before the ages from this one who was begotten at the end of days. Indeed, I am terrified to speak of two sons; I am terrified to speak of two Christs.[5]

Fragment 10

(Translated from Armenian)

Jesus Christ suffered tortures and in suffering restored us to life; sin and burial of humankind was undone; and he was tortured like the sheep led to sacrifice.[6]

5 The context of the miaphysite tractate where the fragment is reported (PO 13.2: 185–186 Nau) makes it clear that the entirety of the contents of this fragment are attributed to Paul. As such, the parenthetical phrase "he said that" (in Syriac, *'emar ger d-*), which is rendered in our text as "([Paul of Samosata] said that)," is probably to be understood as an insertion of the reporter who recorded the fragment. See de Navascués, *Pablo de Samosata y sus adversarios*, 105 n. 10 (with further references) and 345–350.

6 See Isa 53:7; Acts 8:32.

Fragments from the Stenographic Report of the Discussion between Malchion and Paul: Remarks of Malchion

Fragment 11

(Translated from Syriac)

About the hypostasis of our Savior, it is necessary to understand this: That the Word by himself, while not incarnate, did not need the Holy Spirit – for the Spirit receives from him[7] – nor was he "under the law."[8] But by being united substantially to his human body, [it was] as if the things that happened to it, he himself endured [too], on account of his composition and substantial union with the body.

Fragment 12

(Translated from Latin)

A composite thing unquestionably comes into existence from its basic elements, as is the case with Jesus Christ. For he became one individual from God the Word and a human body (which is from the seed of David), existing no longer with any division but in unity. In contrast, you seem to me to be unwilling to confess the composite reality [of Christ] in this sense, and as result [you say] that the Son of God is not in him[9] by substance but that Wisdom is [in him] by virtue of participation. Now you have said this because Wisdom would suffer a loss and therefore would not be able to be composite. And you do not think that the divine Wisdom remained undiminished as it was before it would have emptied itself; and so, even in this emptying that was done out of mercy,[10] Wisdom is undiminished and unchanged. And you also say this, that Wisdom dwelled in him. We too dwell in houses as one thing in another, but neither are we part of the houses nor is the house a part of us.

Fragment 13

(Translated from Greek)

I did not say this just now because you do not concede that the only-begotten Son, who existed eternally before all creation, exists substantially in the whole Savior.

7 See John 16:15. 8 Gal 4:4. 9 Namely, in Jesus Christ. 10 See Phil 2:5–11.

Fragments from the Stenographic Report of the Discussion between Malchion and Paul: Dialogue between Paul and Malchion

Fragment 14

(Translated from Syriac)

PAUL says: It is impossible that the Word be composite, lest he lose his honor.

MALCHION: Were the Word and his body not composed?

PAUL: God forbid he should have been composed or mixed!

MALCHION: Here is why you do not want to confess the composition: in order not to say that the Son of God existed in essence in his body.

Fragment 15

(Translated from Greek)

MALCHION: Unquestionably, this Word having independent subsistence himself came to be in that body, as you also conceded with the statement "from Mary," insofar as the scriptures say that he has shared in what is ours in the same way that we ourselves participate in it, and so, "since the children," it says, "have shared in flesh and blood,"[11] for this reason the Son of God did too. So then, I ask: in whatever way we human beings, this composite living thing, have an assemblage of flesh and some being in the flesh, was then the Word itself, the Wisdom itself, in that body in the same way as [in the body] of the life in us here? Just as in our case it[12] is accomplished from the composition, so too in his case it is accomplished from the concurrence in himself of God the Word and that which is from the Virgin.

PAUL: I think you've also responded in our favor too, as you supposed.

MALCHION: I asked you a question. Since you speak of Wisdom and Word, and say that one human being participates in Word [and] Wisdom and another one lacks [them], do you say [in the case of Christ] that it is in virtue of participation in these, or because the Word itself and the Wisdom descended upon him? For substance and participation are not alike. For that which is by substance is like a part of the whole

11 Heb 2:14. 12 The referent is unclear.

individual, who became our Lord through the combination of God and human being, whereas that which is by participation is not like a part of the one in which it exists.

PAUL: Everyone here says what I am saying. Now you tell me – I am asking first [this time]! Your argument has attempted to propose as an illustration something that is in no way analogous. For the human condition has a constitution that is different. We are talking about Word and Wisdom. And all ...[13]

Fragments of the Synodal Letter of 267/268

Fragment 16

(Translated from Greek)

Paul is not willing to confess along with us that the Son of God has come down from heaven.

Fragment 17

(Translated from Greek)

[Paul says that] Jesus Christ is from below.

Fragment 18

(Translated from Greek)

Well then, Paul says in his memoranda that he is preserving the dignity of the Wisdom.

Fragment 19

(Translated from Greek)

If the Wisdom was conjoined in terms of constitution and generation, then this is what happened to the human being.

13 Here the fragment breaks off.

Fragment 20

(Translated from Greek)

For we believe that the Wisdom was generated together with the human being, not substantially, but qualitatively.

Fragment 21

(Translated from Greek)

But what does it mean too [when Paul] says that the constitution of Jesus Christ was different from ours? Our opinion is that his constitution differed in a single but utterly important way: that God the Word in him was precisely what "the inner man"[14] is in us.

Fragment 22

(Translated from Greek and Syriac)

Greek	**Syriac**
{31} Or [what does it mean when Paul] says that the Wisdom indwells in Jesus as in no other? For this indicates that the manner of indwelling is the same as but exceeds [that of others] in measure and extent, as if Jesus gained knowledge from the Wisdom twice as much as others – or however much more or less than twice as much. But the catholic and ecclesiastical canons do not consider this appropriate. Rather, human beings have participated in Wisdom, which inspires them from without and is distinct from them; the Wisdom itself, however, of its own accord has resided substantially in the body that was from Mary.	{16} But the catholic and ecclesiastical canons do not allow this. Rather, [human beings] have participated in Wisdom, which impels [them] from without and is distinct from them; that Wisdom, however, of its own accord came substantially to that body that was from Mary.

Fragment 23

(Translated from Syriac)

But why does [Paul of Samosata] add that the Wisdom was in Jesus Christ like in a temple unless because [he thinks that] Jesus Christ contained

14 See Rom 7:22; 2 Cor 4:16; Eph 3:16.

Wisdom and was not united to it in substance? [Why does Paul add this], unless on account of what is written as a statement of God: "They shall be for me a temple and I shall be for them God,"[15] [namely] because he will be like one in another? Just as a dress girds a human, being other to and not the same as the human nor a part thereof, so too would the Word be girded by Jesus Christ as another outside of the Word and not as one united substantially in such a way that God and body, though being two, became one.

Fragment 24

(Translated from Greek and Syriac)

Greek

{32} Yet [Paul] says that he does not conceive of two sons. But if Jesus Christ is a son of God and also the Wisdom is a son, and the Wisdom is one thing and Jesus Christ is another, two sons exist.

Syriac

{17} But if Jesus Christ is a son of God, and also the Wisdom is a son, and the Wisdom is one thing and Jesus Christ is another, two sons exist. It is then right to consider that perhaps, by hypocritically acknowledging these words, it is as if he wants to deceive.

Fragment 25

(Translated from Greek and Syriac)

Greek

{33} He understands the conjunction with the Wisdom in a different way, by learning and participation, not by a substance existing substantially in a body.

Syriac

{14a} But he understands the conjunction with Wisdom in a different way, by learning and participation but not by substance.

Syriac

{24} But he understands the conjunction with Wisdom in a different way: by participation and not by substance.

Fragment 26

(Translated from Greek)

Neither was God, who bore and put on humanity, without a share in the principally human passions, nor was humanity, in which he was and

15 The Greek behind this Syriac citation of Jer 7:23 ostensibly misread the Greek *laon* for *naon*.

through which he did the principally divine works, without a share in these. He was constructed principally as a human being in the womb, and in a secondary sense was God in the womb, existing substantially together with the humanity.

Fragment 27

(Translated from Syriac)

This Word, then, is he whose going forth is from the days of eternity, he about whom it was prophesied that he would go forth from Bethlehem.[16] According to the opponents, the master of heresies says again: "Jesus Christ was born from Mary, but the Word from God. And look, it is written (so that here, too, we might avail ourselves of one witnessing statement): 'The Father of Jesus Christ is God.'[17] For through the fact that he is the Father of the Word, he has become the Father of the whole of Jesus Christ, who was constituted from the Word and from the body that was from Mary."

Fragment 28

(Translated from Syriac)

He was worshiped and received offerings from the magi at his birth firstly as God, but secondly also [as] a human body, the one that carries God.

Fragment 29

(Translated from Syriac)

At this point we should make this thing clear: [Paul of Samosata] also distinguishes between the Word and Jesus Christ [and considers them] as two: the one who nods[18] and [the one] who became weary,[19] fell asleep,[20] and became hungry,[21] even though more commonly he says that he in his entirety underwent these things, for previously he stated [concerning] the Word that he came into being in the entire human being.

16 See Mic 5:1–2. 17 See 2 Cor 1:3.
18 This verb can signify the beckoning associated with dominion. 19 John 4:6.
20 Matt 8:24. 21 Matt 4:2.

Fragment 30

(Translated from Syriac)

John witnessed that [Christ] came after him as a human being,[22] but he exists before him as God.[23] He became weary,[24] hungry,[25] and thirsty,[26] he fell asleep[27] and was crucified as a result of our weakness, primarily as a human being because of the body, and secondarily [as] God suffering on account of the union with a human body, which he took on, and which received the suffering.

APPENDIX

CEECW	**de Navascués**
1	37 (Greek)
2	1–5, 26, and 38 (Greek)
3	6, 7, 27, and 39 (Greek)
4	9 and 41 (Armenian)
5	8, 12, 40, 42 (Armenian) + 28 (Greek)
6	10 (Armenian)
7	11 (Armenian)
8	13 (Armenian)
9	21 (Syriac)
10	43 (Armenian)
11	23 (Syriac)
12	25 (Latin)
13	35 (Greek)
14	22 (Syriac)
15	36 (Greek)
16	30.11 (Greek)
17	30.11 (Greek)
18	29a (Greek)
19	29b (Greek)

22 See John 1:15. 23 See John 1:1–2. 24 John 4:6. 25 Matt 4:2.
26 See John 19:28. 27 Matt 8:24.

CEECW	de Navascués
20	29c (Greek)
21	30 (Greek)
22	31 (Greek) + 16 (Syriac)
23	14 (Syriac)
24	32 (Greek) + 17 (Syriac)
25	33 (Greek) + 14a and 24 (Syriac)
26	34 (Greek)
27	18 (Syriac)
28	15 (Syriac)
29	19 (Syriac)
30	20 (Syriac)

18

Aphrahat, *Demonstration* 17: *On the Son*

Introduction and Translation by Ellen Muehlberger

INTRODUCTION

One of the two most important fourth-century Syriac writers,[1] Aphrahat is known only through the *Demonstrations* attributed to him, twenty-two short pieces that address various topics. Nothing about his biography is known.[2] The style of the *Demonstrations* is instructive but often also polemical; Aphrahat poses a problem or describes someone else's erroneous understanding of a theological point, and then offers a response supported by abundant biblical citation. In many of the *Demonstrations*, Aphrahat takes issue with positions he attributes to Jews, and this *Demonstration* is no different. Though it is not explicitly titled *Against the Jews*, as other pieces attributed to him are, this *Demonstration* is written as advice to an imagined Christian friend who seeks to answer several objections supposedly raised by Jews about how Christians speak of Jesus. Whether those objections were voiced in reality or were imagined by Aphrahat, the fact that he frames his work as a response to Jewish claims about scripture suggests that he sees as much intellectual and cultural continuity between Christianity and Judaism as he sees difference.

Aphrahat's work is also important for the perspective it gives us about the theological assumptions of a writer outside the Greek and Latin worlds, which are habitually seen as the center of Christological argumentation in late antiquity. This *Demonstration* shows that Aphrahat's concerns and his methods of proof are not peculiar; rather, they correspond quite closely to the concerns and methods of other Christian writers. For example, like

1 The other is Ephrem the Syrian, some of whose *Hymns on Faith* are translated in this volume, on pp. 235–269.

2 Indeed, recent scholarship has called into question whether these twenty-two *Demonstrations* belong to the unified author of "Aphrahat." I refer to the author of *Demonstration* 17 as Aphrahat with this caveat in mind.

his counterparts elsewhere, Aphrahat is interested in the names given to Christ because he sees them as indications of Christ's nature. Like other theologians, Aphrahat's arguments rest on the vocabulary used in Christian scripture. Many of his arguments, and even specific phrases he adopts, are given voice in other theological treatises of the fourth century. Though Syriac writings are often used by historians as comparisons that point out the special nature of Greek (or less frequently Latin) texts, Aphrahat's work more clearly shows the commonalities between the arguments forwarded in Syriac and those made in other languages.

This translation is based on the Syriac in D. Iohannes Parisot, *Aphraatis Sapientis Persae Demonstrationes*, vol. 1, Patrologia Syriaca 1 (Paris: Firmin-Didot, 1894), 785–816. The section numbers are traditional and appear in all modern editions of the Syriac text. For the ease of readers, I have provided references to the scriptural passages Aphrahat uses as they will be found in English Bibles; Aphrahat was citing from the Syriac Bible, so at times what he quotes in this text will differ slightly from what a reader will find when she compares a passage in scripture.

TRANSLATION

A Demonstration about Christ, the Son of God

1. This is a reasoned response against the Jews who revile the people of the Gentiles when they say, "You worship and serve a man who was born, a human being who was crucified. You call a human being 'God,' and while God has no son, you say, 'This crucified Jesus is the Son of God!'" They base their argument on God saying, "I am God, and there is no other beyond me,"[3] and again, him saying, "You shall not worship another god."[4] Consequently, they say, "You are opposing God when you call a human being 'God.'"

2. As much as I am able, as much as my deficiency can attain, I will convince you, my dear, about these things: while we grant that he is a human being, we still revere him and call him God and Lord; it is not unusual that we apply these terms to him. Nor do we grant him an inappropriate name, of the sort that they themselves would not respect. Rather, we

3 Deut 32:39. 4 Exod 34:14.

trust that our Lord Jesus is God, Son of God; and king, son of a king;[5] and light from light;[6] and creator;[7] and counselor;[8] and guide;[9] and the way;[10] and the savior;[11] and the shepherd;[12] and the gatherer;[13] and the door;[14] and the pearl;[15] and the lamp.[16] He is called by many names. Leaving all the rest of these names aside, we will show you that he is the Son of God, and also God from God.

3. For the honored name of the divinity is granted even to righteous human beings, when they are worthy of being called by it. Those human beings whom God wills, he calls "children" and "friends." But when he chose Moses, his friend and his beloved, and made him the head, teacher, and priest for his people, he called him "god." For he said to him, "I have appointed you god for Pharaoh."[17] And he gave him his priest as a prophet, saying, "Aaron your brother will speak with Pharaoh for you. You will be a god to him and he will be an interpreter for you."[18] It was not solely for Pharaoh the wicked that he made Moses a god, but also for Aaron, the holy priest, did God make Moses a god.

4. So now, listen to why we call Christ "Son of God." They say, "Though there is no Son of God, you turned this crucified Jesus into God's son and firstborn." It was Israel, though, that he called "my son" and "my firstborn" when he sent word to Pharaoh through Moses, saying to him, "My son and my firstborn, Israel. I said to you, 'Let my son go so that he might serve me,' yet you did not want to release him. Now I will kill your son and your firstborn."[19] He also testified to this through the prophet, reproaching the people as he said to them, "Out of Egypt I have called my son. As often as I called them, they went and worshiped Baal; they offered incense to graven images."[20] Isaiah said about them, "I reared children and exalted them, and they rebelled against me."[21] It is also written, "You are children of the Lord your God."[22] And regarding Solomon it says, "He will be my son, and I will be his father."[23] And ourselves too, we call this one – Christ – the Son of God, through whom we know God, just as he called Israel "my son, my firstborn," and as he said of Solomon, "He will be my son." We call him God, then, just as he named Moses with his own name.[24] Even David spoke

5 See John 18:37. 6 See John 8:12. 7 See John 1:1–3. 8 See John 14:16. 9 See Heb 12:2. 10 See John 14:6. 11 See John 4:42. 12 See John 10:11. 13 See Matt 23:37. 14 See John 10:7. 15 See Matt 7:6. 16 See Rev 21:23. 17 Exod 7:1. 18 Exod 7:1–2. 19 Exod 4:22–23. 20 Hos 11:1–2. 21 Isa 1:2. 22 Deut 14:1. 23 2 Sam 7:14. 24 By calling Moses "god."

about them: "I have said, 'You are gods, and all of you are children of the Most High.'"[25] And when they did not prosper, then he said about them, "As human beings, you will die; as any prince, you will fall."[26]

5. The name of the divinity was granted for great honor in the world. To whom he wishes, God appoints it. The names of God, though, are many. They are also venerable, as I know from his names for Moses. He says to him, "I am the God of your ancestors, the God of Abraham, the God of Isaac, the God of Jacob ... This is my name forever, and my remembrance for the generations."[27] He spoke his name, "*Ahiyeh ashar Ahiyeh, Elshaday, Adonai Sabaoth.*"[28] God was called by these names. And though the name of divinity is great and honorable, he did not withhold even it from his righteous ones.

While he is the great king, without any reservation he also granted the great and honored name of kingship to human beings, his creation. 6. Nebuchadnezzar, the wicked king, God called "the king of kings" by the mouth of his prophet. For Jeremiah said, "To every nation and kingdom that does not bring his neck under the yoke of Nebuchadnezzar, king of kings and my servant, I will visit upon that nation famine and desolation and plague."[29] Though God is the great king, he did not withhold the name of kingship from human beings. Though he is the great God, he did not withhold the name of divinity from children of flesh. Though fatherhood is entirely his, he still called human beings "fathers," for he said to the synagogue, "In the place of your fathers will be your sons."[30] Though sovereignty was his alone, he gave sovereignty to human beings, one over another. Though worship and honor are his, he granted that one person could honor another in this world.

Even if a human being should worship the iniquitous and the wicked, those who deny God's lovingkindness, he is accused by God. For he commanded his people regarding worship, that they should not worship the sun or moon or all the heavenly powers, nor should they lust to worship all the creatures of the earth. Observe our good Maker's goodness and compassion in his not withholding the name of divinity or the name of worship, the name of kingship or the name of sovereignty from human beings. For it is he who is the father of the creatures on the face of the earth.

25 Ps 81(82):6. 26 Ps 81(82):7. 27 Exod 3:6, 15.

28 Exod 3:14; Jer 32:18. This phrase in Hebrew, which reads "I am who I am: God Almighty, Lord of hosts," was simply transliterated into Syriac by Aphrahat.

29 Jer 17:8. 30 Ps 44(45):17, a psalm which is taken as addressing a synagogue.

Among all that he created, he honored and elevated and glorified human beings, since he formed them by his holy hands, inspired them with his spirit, and from the beginning was a dwelling place for them. In them, he found rest and in them he moves. As he said through the prophet, "I will dwell in them and move among them."[31] Jeremiah the prophet also said, "You are a temple of the Lord, when you make your ways and your actions pleasing."[32] Before that, David had said, "Lord, you have been our dwelling place for generations – before the mountains had been conceived, before you gave birth to the world, and before you settled the earth. From everlasting to everlasting, you are God."[33]

7. And how should you understand the fact that one prophet said, "Lord, you have been our dwelling place," while another said, "I will dwell in them and move among them"? First, he was our dwelling place, and afterward he dwelled and moved in us. Both are true and plain to wise people. For David said, "Lord, you have been our dwelling place for generations – before the mountains had been conceived, before you gave birth to the world, and before you settled the earth."

My dear, I know that all creatures, above and below, were created first, and human beings were created after all of them. For when God thought to create the world and all its ornaments, he first conceived and depicted Adam in his mind. And after Adam had been conceived in his thought, he then conceived the creatures, as he said, "Before the mountains had been conceived, and you gave birth to the earth," the begotten. For the human being, with respect to creation, is elder to and earlier than the creatures. In the order in which they were brought forth, though, the creatures are elder to and earlier than Adam. Adam was conceived and dwelled in the thought of God, and while he remained a conception in [God's] mind, [God] created all the creatures by the word of his mouth. It was when God had perfected and embellished the world, so that in it nothing was lacking, that he brought Adam forth from his thought.

He fashioned human beings with his own hands, and Adam watched the world as he constructed it. And God made him sovereign over all he had created, like a man who has a son and wishes him to be wed: he promises him a wife, builds him a house, and prepares and arranges everything his son might need. Only then does he put on the wedding and make his son sovereign over his house. Thus, it is after the conception of Adam that he brings him forth and makes him sovereign over all his creation. About this,

31 Lev 26:12; 2 Cor 6:16. 32 Jer 7:4–5. 33 Ps 89(90):1–2.

the prophet said, "Lord, you have been our dwelling place for generations, before the mountains had been conceived, before you gave birth to the world, and before you settled the earth. From everlasting to everlasting, you are Lord."[34] So that no one would think there to be another God, whether before or after, he said, "From everlasting to everlasting." Isaiah said the same: "I am first and I am last."[35]

After God brought forth Adam from his thought, he formed him and inspired him with his own breath, giving him knowledge of how to discern good from evil, so that he might know that God made him. And when the human being knows his maker, then God is depicted and conceived inside his thought, and it becomes for him a temple to God his maker, as it is written, "You are the temple of God,"[36] and as he said, "I will dwell in them and move among them."[37] But as for the children of Adam, who did not know their maker, God was not depicted among them, nor did he dwell among them, nor was he conceived in their thought. Rather, they are reckoned as sheep before him, like the rest of the creatures.

8. In such passages, difficult things are prefigured, so what we call Christ – namely, the "Son of God" – is not inappropriate. Look, he conceived all human beings and brought them forth from his thought. They needed to be corrected; the name of divinity was his, though he appointed the name of God even for his righteous ones.

But while we worship Jesus, through whom we know God, they should be ashamed that they bow and worship and honor even the wicked ones who hold sovereignty among the impure nations. And yet there is no kind of censure [for them]. And God has given this particular honor of worship to the children of Adam, so they might honor one another, especially those who are great and honorable among them. For if they worship and honor the wicked ones in the name of worship, even those who in their wickedness deny the name of God, as long as they do not worship them as their maker or as their only [gods], they do not sin. For us, then, how much more fitting is it that we worship and honor Jesus, who turned hardened minds from all our worship of empty error and taught us to worship and serve and minister for the one God, our father and our maker?

And they will know that the kings of the world call themselves gods, in the name of God the great, though they are infidels and apostates. They fall down and worship before them, working for and honoring them, as if they

34 Ps 89(90):1–2. 35 Isa 48:12. 36 2 Cor 6:16. 37 Lev 26:12; 2 Cor 6:16.

are graven images and idols, and the law never faulted them – there is no sin. Even as Daniel worshiped Nebuchadnezzar, the infidel and apostate, there was no censure. And Joseph worshiped Pharaoh, but it was not written that he sinned. So, we are certain that Jesus is God, the Son of God, and in him we know his Father; in this way we are held back from other kinds of worship. For there is no way for us to repay the one who bore these things on our behalf, except in worship, by which we repay him honor for his difficulty [undertaken] on our behalf.

9. Now it is right for us to show that this Jesus was first promised beforehand by the prophets and was called "Son of God." David said, "You are my son. Today, I have begotten you."[38] Elsewhere, he said, "In holy splendor from the womb, from the first, I will bring forth a son for you."[39] And Isaiah said, "A child has been born for us; a son has been given to us. His sovereignty rests on his shoulders. His name will be called 'wonderful' and 'counselor,' 'mighty God of the ages,' and 'prince of peace'; his authority will increase and his peace will be infinite."[40] So tell me, O wise teacher of Israel, who is it who is born and whose name is called "child" and "son" and "wonderful" and "counselor," "mighty God of the ages," and "prince of peace," whose "authority will increase" and whose peace, it says, "will be infinite"? If David teaches us to call Christ the Son of God, then we understand from Isaiah to call him God. He says, "Sovereignty was placed on his shoulders," which happened when he bore his cross and went out of Jerusalem. Isaiah said elsewhere about the child born, "Behold! A virgin will conceive and will bear. His name will be called 'Emmanuel,' which means 'our God is with us.'"[41]

10. And if you say that Christ has not yet come, I will attribute this, too, to your contrary nature. For it is written that whenever he comes, the nations will expect him.[42] Behold, I have heard from the nations that Christ has come; before he came, I already had faith in him. Through him I worship the God of Israel. Why would he, once he has come, rebuke me for having had faith in him before he came? How silly!

The prophets do not allow you to say that Christ has not yet come. Daniel, for one, chastises you when he says, "After sixty-two weeks, Christ will come and will be killed. With his arrival, the city of holiness will be corrupted, and its end will be in a flood. Until the completion of the

38 Ps 2:7. 39 Ps 109(110):3. 40 Isa 9:6–7. 41 Isa 7:14.
42 See Ps 21(22):28; Zeph 2:11.

judgments, it will remain in desolation."[43] You, though, wait and hope for the arrival of Christ in which Israel will be gathered together from all places; and in which Jerusalem will be rebuilt and inhabited. But Daniel testifies that when Christ came and was killed, Jerusalem was desolate and remains forever in desolation until the completion of its judgments.

About the suffering of Christ, David said, "They pierced my hands and my feet. All my bones wail. They beheld and looked upon me; they divided my garments amongst themselves and cast lots for my clothes."[44] Isaiah said, "Behold, my servant will become famous – he will be revealed and exalted, so that many will be speechless before him. For his appearance will be transformed beyond that of a man, and his face beyond that of human beings";[45] and he said, "He will purify many nations, and kings will be speechless before him."[46] And he said in the same passage, "He arose like a babe before me, like a shoot from the dry ground."[47] And he said at the end of the passage, "He was killed because of our sins; he was brought low because of our iniquity. The instruction that led to our wholeness is upon him and by his wounds we are healed."[48]

So, by which wounds are human beings healed? David was not killed, since he died at a ripe old age and was buried in Bethlehem. And if they say it about Saul, Saul died on Mount Gilboa during a battle with the Philistines. If they say, "They pierced his hands and feet," and the following is about when they fastened his body to the wall in Beth-Shan, the piercing [that the passage speaks of] was not actually done to Saul. For Saul's limbs were pierced, but his bones did not suffer any pain, since he was dead – it was after Saul's death that they suspended his body and those of his sons on the wall of Beth-Shan.[49]

And when David said, "They have pierced my hands and my feet; all my bones wail," he said in the next sentence, "God, come to my aid, deliver my soul from the sword."[50] It was Christ who was delivered from the sword and ascended from Sheol, lived, and rose again after three days, for God had come to his aid. But when Saul called the Lord, the Lord did not answer him. He asked the prophets but was not given a word; he hid himself, asked necromancers [about his fate], learned it, and then was condemned before the Philistines. He killed himself with a blade when he saw that the battle was too much for him.

43 Dan 9:26–27. 44 Ps 21(22):16–18. 45 Isa 52:13–14.
46 Isa 52:15. 47 Isa 52:2. 48 Isa 53:5. 49 See 1 Sam 31:10.
50 Ps 21(22):19–20.

And David said, in the same passage, "I will make your name known to my brothers; and in the midst of the congregation I will glorify you."[51] How could these things be fulfilled by Saul? David also said, "You did not permit your holy one to see corruption."[52] Now, all these things were fulfilled by Christ: when he came to them and "they did not receive him,"[53] and when they judged him by injustice and false testimony, and when he was hung on the wood by their hands. They pierced his hands and his feet with nails and fastened them, and all his bones wailed.

On that day a great wonder happened: the light grew dark in the middle of the day, just as Zechariah prophesied when he said, "The day will be known to the Lord, in which there will be no day and no night, and in the evening there will be light."[54] Now, what day was it that was distinguished for its wonder, with no day and no night, when in evening there was light, if not that day when they crucified him, when there was darkness in the middle of the day and light in the evening? Zechariah also said, "That day, there will be frost and ice," which accords with what I know: the day they crucified him was chilly. For when Simon came and stood near them, they had made themselves a fire to keep warm.

Again, Zechariah said, "O spear, oppose the shepherd and oppose my friends the sheep; strike the shepherd and the lambs of his flock will be scattered. And I will turn my hand against my shepherds."[55] And David said elsewhere about his passion: "They gave me bitter herbs as food, and gave me vinegar to drink for my thirst."[56] He also said in the same passage, "They pursued the one you struck, and they added to the pain of the one who was killed."[57] They added many things to that pain, things that were not written about him: curses and abuses such as even scripture could not reveal, as their abuses were so odious. The Lord, though, "was willing to humiliate and afflict him,"[58] and "he was killed for our iniquity and he was humiliated for our sins,"[59] and he was even "made to be sin."[60]

11. We worship these mercies and kneel before the greatness of his Father, who turned our worship to him. We call him "God" like Moses; "firstborn" and "son" like Israel; and "Jesus," like Joshua, son of Nun; "priest" like Aaron; "king" like David; "great prophet" like all the prophets; "shepherd" like the shepherds who steer and guide Israel. He calls us

51 Ps 21(22):22. 52 Ps 15(16):10. 53 John 1:11. 54 Zech 14:7. 55 Zech 13:7. 56 Ps 68(69):21. 57 Ps 68(69):26. 58 Isa 53:10. 59 Isa 53:5. 60 2 Cor 5:21.

"children," as he said, "Foreign children will listen to me."[61] And he makes us his brothers, as he said, "I will make your name known to my brothers."[62] We also have become his friends, as he said to his disciples, "I have called you my friends,"[63] and just as his Father called Abraham his friend.[64] He said to us, "I am the good shepherd, the door, the way, the vineyard, the seed, the bridegroom, the pearl, the lamp, the light, the king, God, life-giver, and Savior." He is designated by many names.

12. I have written you this short explanation, my friend, so you can go out with the Spirit against the Jews, when they say that God has no son, or when they take exception to us calling him God, the Son of God, and King, and first-born of all the creatures.

Here ends the demonstration about Christ, the Son of God.

61 Ps 17(18):45. 62 Ps 21(22):22. 63 John 15:15. 64 Isa 41:8.

19

Hilary of Poitiers, *On the Trinity* 9.1–14

Introduction and Translation by Mark DelCogliano

INTRODUCTION

Hilary of Poitiers was one of the premier theologians of the Latin West in the fourth century, along with Ambrose of Milan and Augustine of Hippo. In 356 he was banished at a synod at Béziers for his support of Athanasius and the Alexandrian bishop's "anti-Arian" program, and exiled to Asia Minor for four years. Here Hilary became far more knowledgeable about the theological debates rocking the church, and his own theology was decisively shaped by the encounter. He was particularly influenced by the Homoiousian theology of Basil of Ancyra. Hilary attended the Council of Seleucia in 359, which promulgated a broadly Homoian creed that was given official approval, under the auspices of Emperor Constantius, at Constantinople in January 360. During his exile in the East he penned a number of theological works, including *On the Trinity*, against Homoian theology. Shortly after the synod in Constantinople he returned to his homeland, where he worked against those who supported Homoian theology. He died in 367 or 368.

The excerpt below is from the ninth book of *On the Trinity*. In this selection Hilary refutes the idea that the Son is by nature inferior to the Father simply because of the incarnation. Rather, he understands the Father and Son to share a natural unity in virtue of the Son's birth from the Father. Hilary lists several passages of scripture used by his theological opponents (whom he elsewhere calls "Arians") to claim that Father and Son are united only in will, but he attributes their misinterpretation of these passages to an improper understanding of the divine economy, particularly the incarnation of the Word of God. This prompts Hilary to articulate his own understanding of these matters. He affirms that Christ is both God and a human being, lacking nothing of either nature. In the incarnation, God lowers himself to the human condition without ceasing to be fully God, for the purpose of divinizing human beings. In the gospels Christ reveals himself as both God and a human being, and thus any of Christ's expressions of weakness (such as his ignorance or death) must be attributed to his human nature, not taken as proof of his lesser divinity. Everything that Christ says and does must, in fact, be situated within the three stages of the economy of salvation: (1) the Word before the incarnation, when he was "God only" (*Deus tantum*), (2) the incarnate Word up to the point of his resurrection, when he was "God and a human being" (*Deus et homo*), and (3) the incarnate Word resurrected and glorified, when he becomes "whole human being and whole God" (*totus homo totus Deus*). Hilary explains in some detail how it is God who raises Christ from the dead and yet Christ the God was raised from the dead, arguing that the resurrection of Christ is the work of both the Father and the Son. Hilary also expounds upon the mysteries of the economy by giving an extended exegesis of Colossians 2:8–15 (see in particular sections 8–10). The selection ends with an interpretation of Philippians 2:6–8 where there seems to be an endorsement of what is now call kenoticism, that the Son of God had to abandon the form of God in order to adopt the form of a slave.[1]

This translation is based on the critical edition of P. Smulders, *Sancti Hilarii Pictaviensis Episcopi De Trinitate libri duodecim*, 2 vols., CCSL 62 and 62a (Turnhout: Brepols, 1979–1980), vol. 2, 370–386. The same edition (with slight emendations) was reprinted as *Hilaire de Poitiers: La Trinité*, critical text by P. Smulders, introduction and translation by M. Figura, J. Doignon, G. M. De Durand, C. Morel, and G. Pelland, SChr 443, 448, and 462 (Paris: Éditions du Cerf, 1999–2001).

TRANSLATION

Book 9

1. In the preceding book we discussed how the nature of God the Father is indistinguishable[2] from that of God the Son. We showed that the statement "I and the Father are one"[3] does not contribute to the idea of a solitary

1 Hilary denies this, however, in *On the Trinity* 10.22.
2 In Latin, *indifferenti*. 3 John 10:30.

God,[4] but a divinity whose unity is not divided by generation.[5] For God has been born from no other source than from God, and the one who is God from God cannot be anything other than that which God is. Even though we did not examine all the evidence from the divine and apostolic sayings in which the inseparable nature and power of the Father and Son was taught, we nonetheless went through a sufficient number of them to achieve understanding of the issue. And then we came to this passage which expresses the apostolic faith, where it says, "See to it that no one leads you astray by philosophy and empty deceit according to human tradition, according to the elements of the world, and not according to Christ. For in him the whole fullness of the divinity dwells bodily."[6] Because of "the fullness of the divinity dwelling bodily in him," we taught that in him is manifested the true and perfect God who is of his Father's nature. Thus, "the fullness dwelling in him" is not to be understood as signifying either a different God or a monadic God. For the "bodily dwelling" of the incorporeal God teaches that the unique feature of natural unity exists in the God who subsists from God. And God dwelling in Christ proves the birth of the subsistent Christ, insofar as God dwells in him.[7]

By all this I think a sufficient and more than sufficient response has been given to the impiety of those who claim that certain sayings of the Lord make reference only to unity and harmony of will: "He who sees me sees the Father,"[8] "The Father in me and I in the Father,"[9] "I and the Father are one,"[10] and "All that the Father has is mine."[11] Although our confidence in [the truth of] these sayings remains, their reverence for God has been falsified by deceitful doctrine to corrupt their meaning. And since they could not deny that an agreement of wills exists in those whose natural unity is proclaimed, nonetheless, to destroy that unity in virtue of the birth,[12] they believed only in an association of harmony.

But when the blessed Apostle, after many unambiguous proclamations of the reality of the nature, taught "the fullness of the divinity dwelling bodily in Christ," he preempted every assertion of impious rashness, since the bodily dwelling of the incorporeal divinity brings about a natural unity.

4 If there is a "solitary God" (*solitarius Deus*), the Son is not God. Hilary associates this idea with the Sabellians.
5 That is, the Father's generation of the Son. 6 Col 2:8–9.
7 The stress on the Son subsisting is anti-Sabellian. 8 John 14:9.
9 John 14:10. 10 John 10:30. 11 John 16:15.
12 That is, the Son's birth from the Father.

So it is not a matter of mere words but of the real truth that the Son is not alone but the Father abides in him, and not only abides in him but also works and speaks in him, and not only works and speaks in him but also is seen in him. For through the mystery of the birth,[13] he is strength with Strength in himself, power with Power in himself, and nature with Nature in himself. Through birth it[14] keeps what belongs to it, and as the image[15] it repeats on its own what it contains, inasmuch as it is the image and truth of its originator.[16] For a perfect birth produces a perfect image, and the fullness of the divinity dwelling bodily in him indicates the nature in its true reality.

2. And indeed these things are ever so much as they are because there cannot be one who is by nature God from God unless through his birth he is in that nature by which he is God, and the unvarying unity of the living nature is not divided from itself when there is the birth of a living nature. Yet the heretics feign a salutary confession of the gospel faith to destroy the truth: they remove the Son from the natural unity by forcing things said in one way and for one purpose to be understood in a different way and for a different purpose. And so, to deny that he is the Son of God, they draw upon the authority of his own words: "Why do you call me good? No one is good except the one God."[17] Because his words proclaim that God is one, it follows that anything else which has the name of God no longer remains in the nature of God, because God is one. And they attempt to confirm that he is called God as a mere title not as the real truth on the basis of these words, "But this is eternal life, that they may know you, the only true God."[18] And to banish him from the proper nature of the true God, they add this: "The Son cannot do anything on his own, but only that which he sees the Father doing."[19] They also use this, "The Father is greater than I."[20] Finally, when they cite, "But of that day or hour no one knows, not even the angels in heaven nor the Son, but only the Father,"[21] they boast, as if these words irrefutably denied his divinity, that they have now overthrown the faith of the church. For it does not seem that a nature is equal by birth when it is necessarily different because of its ignorance. And the Father in virtue of his knowing and the Son in virtue of his ignorance makes it clear that they are dissimilar in divinity, because God ought not to be ignorant of anything, and the one who is ignorant should not be connected with the one who knows.

13 That is, the Son's birth from the Father. 14 Strength, power, or nature.
15 See Col 1:15. 16 That is, the Father. 17 Mark 10:18.
18 John 17:3. 19 John 5:19. 20 John 14:28. 21 Mark 13:32; Matt 24:36.

With regard to all these passages, however, since they neither understand them by reason nor distinguish among them according to the stages[22] at which they were said nor comprehend them according to the mysteries of the gospel nor grasp their meaning according to the force of the words, they speak against the nature of the divinity in a foolish and unlearned rage. They bring up only these out-of-context passages to fill the ears of the ignorant, passing over in silence either the explanations given to them or motives which prompted them, for the meaning of these statements must be sought from those passages which either precede or follow them.

3. Even though we plan to discuss these passages we have just mentioned on the basis of the very statements in the gospels or the apostles, we think all need to be reminded about our common faith, that the confession which brings eternal life is the same as the one which brings knowledge of eternal reality.[23] He does not know anything about his own life, he does not know it at all, if he does not know Christ Jesus as true God and true human being. And it is equally dangerous to deny that Christ Jesus is God the Spirit[24] or flesh of our body. "So everyone who will confess me before human beings, I will confess before my Father who is in heaven. But whoever will deny me before human beings, I will deny before my Father who is in heaven."[25] This was said by the Word made flesh[26] and taught by the human being Jesus Christ, the Lord of majesty,[27] who in himself was made mediator for the salvation of the church. And by the very mystery of his being the mediator between God and human beings,[28] he exists as one of both. Because of the natures united in the same one, he is one and the same reality in both natures, but in such a way that he lacks nothing in either. So he neither ceases to be God by being born as a human being nor fails to be a human being by remaining God. And so, this is the true faith which brings human blessedness: to preach that he is God and a human being, to confess that he is Word and flesh, neither overlooking that he is God who is also human nor ignoring that he is flesh which is also the Word.

4. Though it is contrary to the nature of our thinking that he should be born a human being while remaining God, it is not contrary to the nature of our hope that he remains God while being born a human being. For the higher nature being born into the lower gives us confidence that the lower

22 That is, at the stages of the economy of salvation. See p. 223 above.
23 See John 17:3. 24 See John 4:24. 25 Matt 10:32–33. 26 See John 1:14.
27 See 1 Cor 2:8. 28 See 1 Tim 2:5.

nature can be born into the higher. And indeed, according to the law and custom of the world, the realization of our hope is easier than the realization of the divine mystery. For in those things which are born, the world has the power to increase, but it does not have the power to decrease. Look at the trees, the crops, the cattle! Gaze also upon the human being, who shares in reason! He always advances by growth, he never shrinks by decrease; nor is he ever deprived of the self into which he has grown. Though he may indeed waste away with age or be destroyed by death, this happens by undergoing change through a lapse of time or by reaching the end allotted to his life. Yet it is not within his power to cease to be what he is, as if he could make a new self by a decrease from his old self, that is, become a child again from an old man. So our nature necessarily by the law of the world always proceeds to an increase, and this leads us to expect without any shame its advancement into a higher nature, since its increase is according to nature and its decrease is contrary to nature.

And so, it was proper that God become something other than what he continued to be and yet not fail to be what he continued to be, to be born as God in a human being and yet not cease to be God, to diminish himself even to the point of being conceived, lying in the cradle, and being an infant, and yet not depart from the power of God. This is a mystery, not for him, but for us. Assuming us was not an advancement for God, but his willingness to debase himself is our promotion. For he did not lose that which God is, and he enabled human beings to become God.

5. So then, the only-begotten God, who was born as a human being from the virgin and who in the fullness of time[29] would in himself raise the human being to God, kept to the following method in every gospel teaching: he taught us to believe in him as the Son of God, and exhorted us to proclaim him as the Son of Man. As a human being, he said and did everything that belongs to God, and then as God he said and did everything that belongs to the human being – and yet this was such that despite speaking in this twofold manner, he never spoke without indicating that he was both a human being and God; and yet, he always revealed the one God the Father and declared that he was in possession of the nature of the one God through the true reality of his birth; and yet, in his dignity as Son and in his condition as a human being he did not fail to subject himself to God the

29 See Gal 4:4.

Father. For everything that is born must refer itself back to its originator, and all flesh must confess itself weak in relation to God.

And so, here is an opportunity for the heretics to deceive the simple and ignorant. They falsely claim that the words said by him according to the human being were said according to the weakness of [his] divine nature, and because it is one and the same speaker who said all these things, they contend that he said everything about himself.

6. Of course, we do not deny that all his extant sayings belong to his nature. But if Jesus Christ is both a human being and God, and if he does not become God for the first time when he becomes a human being, and if he does not cease to be God anymore when he becomes a human being, and if, after his having become a human being in God, the whole God is the whole human being, then it is necessarily true that the mystery of his words is one and the same with the mystery of his kind. And so, when you make a distinction between the human being and God at a certain stage [in the divine economy], you need also to make a distinction between the speech of God and the speech of the human being at the same stage. And when you confess him to be God and a human being at one particular stage, you also need to distinguish at the same stage between what was said by God and what was said by the human being.

Then again, after he has become a human being and God, when you come to a stage at which you recognize that the whole God is already the whole human being, if anything was said that might indicate that stage, apply what was said to that same stage. Accordingly, since it is one thing to be God before he became a human being, and another thing to be a human being and God, and still another thing, after having been the human being and God, to be the whole human being and whole God, do not confuse the stages and the kinds in the mystery of the divine plan. For according to the attributes of his different kinds and natures, he must speak, in relation to the mystery of his humanity, in one way before he was born, in another while he was still going to die, and in another as already eternal.[30]

7. Jesus Christ, therefore, who for our sake tarried in all these states and was born as a human being in our body, spoke in accordance with the custom of our nature, yet without forgetting that it is his own nature to be God.

30 On Hilary's understanding of the three stages in the divine plan of salvation, see p. 223 above.

For even though in his birth and passion and death he went through the realities of our nature, nonetheless he did all of these things by the power of his own nature, insofar as he was himself the cause of his being born, insofar as he willed to suffer what he was not permitted to suffer, insofar as he who lives died. And yet even though God did all these things through the human being – for he was born as a result of his own doing, he suffered by his own doing, and he died as a result of his own doing – he did not do all this as if he were not a human being when he was born and suffered and died.

But these mysteries of the heavenly secrets were already established before the foundation of the world:[31] that the only-begotten God would will to be born as a human being and the human being would abide in God eternally;[32] that God would will to suffer, in order to prevent the savage devil from using the passions of human weakness to retain the law of sin in us,[33] when God had assumed our weakness; that God would will to die, in order to prevent any arrogant power from either rising up against God or being able to arrogate the nature of the power created in him when the immortal God had put himself under the law of death. Thus, God was born to bring about our adoption, but suffered to win our innocence, and finally died to avenge us, seeing that our humanity abides in God, and the passions of our infirmities are allied with God, and the spiritual powers of iniquity and wickedness[34] are subdued by the triumph of the flesh, when God dies through the flesh.

8. The Apostle, then, was aware of this mystery and received the knowledge of the faith from the Lord himself, and since he knew quite well that the world, and human beings, and philosophy were incapable of grasping it, he writes, "See to it that no one leads you astray by philosophy and empty deceit according to human traditions, according to the elements of the world, and not according to Christ. For in him the whole fullness of the divinity dwells bodily, and you have come to fullness in him, because he is the head of every principality and power."[35] So, after explaining the fullness of the divinity dwelling in him bodily, he immediately added the mystery of our adoption, saying, "You have come to fullness in him." For just as the fullness of the divinity is in him, so too we have come to fullness in him. Indeed, the Apostle does not say, "You have come to fullness," but, "You

31 See 1 Pet 1:20; Eph 1:4; John 17:24.
32 That is, the glorious humanity of Christ resides in heaven for eternity.
33 See Rom 7:23. 34 See Eph 6:12. 35 Col 2:8–10.

have come to fullness in him," because all those who are or shall be reborn through the hope of faith into eternal life even now abide in fullness in the body of Christ, and afterwards they shall no longer come to fullness in him, but in themselves, at the time about which the Apostle says, "Who shall transform the body of our humility to make it like the body of his glory?"[36] Now, therefore, we have come to fullness in him, that is, by his assumption of flesh, in which the fullness of the divinity dwells bodily. And there's no mean power in this hope of ours. For our coming to fullness in him means that he is the head and beginning of every power, according to this: "So that at his name every knee should bend, of those in heaven, and of those on earth, and of those below, and every tongue should confess that Jesus is Lord, in the glory of God the Father."[37] So this will be the confession: Jesus is in the glory of God the Father and was born in a human being, yet now no longer abides in the infirmity of our body but in the glory of God. And every tongue shall confess this. And since those in heaven and on earth bend the knee, it means that he is the head of every principality and power in such a way that the universe by bending the knee is subject to him, in whom we have come to fullness and who, in virtue of the fullness of the divinity dwelling in him bodily, should be confessed in the glory of God the Father.

9. Now after the mystery of his nature and our adoption had been made known (for the fullness of the divinity abides in him and we come to fullness in him by his being born as a human being), the Apostle continues with the remaining plan of human salvation, saying, "In him also you were circumcised with a circumcision not performed by hand, by stripping off the body of flesh, but by the circumcision of Christ; you were buried with him in baptism, in which you were also resurrected with him through faith in the working of God, who raised him from the dead."[38] So we are not circumcised with a fleshly circumcision, but with the circumcision of Christ, that is, we are born again into a new human being. For since we are buried with him in his baptism, we must die to the old human being[39] because the regeneration of baptism is the power of the resurrection.[40] And this circumcision of Christ does not mean the stripping off of the flesh of the foreskin but to die entirely with him, and by that death to live afterwards entirely with him. For we rise again in him through faith in his God, who

36 Phil 3:21. 37 Phil 2:10–11. 38 Col 2:11–12. 39 See Rom 6:4–6.
40 See Phil 3:10.

raised him from the dead. We must, therefore, believe in God, by whose activity Christ was raised from the dead, because that faith rises again together with Christ.

10. Then the whole mystery of the assumed human being is completed in this manner: "And you, when you were dead because of your sins and the uncircumcision of your flesh, he brought you to life together with him, having forgiven you all your sins, canceling what stood against us, namely, that statement of our debts with its legal demands, which was not in our favor; this he set aside completely, nailing it to the cross when he stripped off the flesh, and he exposed the powers to mockery, triumphing over them in himself."[41] A worldly person does not grasp the apostolic faith, nor do any other words except his own explain his meaning.[42] God raised Christ from the dead[43] – the Christ in whom the fullness of the divinity dwells bodily.[44] But he brought us to life together with him, forgiving us our sins and canceling the statement of our debts incurred from the law of sin, which, through the previous legal demands, was not in our favor, taking this completely away and nailing it to the cross, stripping himself of the flesh by the law of death, holding up the powers to mockery, triumphing over them in himself. Now his triumph over the powers in himself and his holding them up to mockery, as well as his canceling of the statement of our debts and his bringing us to life, these topics we have already discussed above.[45]

But who can comprehend or articulate this mystery? The activity of God raises Christ from the dead, and this same activity of God brings us to life together with Christ, and this same activity forgives our sins, cancels the statement of our debts, nails it to the cross, strips Christ of his flesh, holds up the powers to mockery, and triumphs over them in his person. You have an activity of God who raises Christ from the dead and yet at the same time you also have Christ who does in himself the very things which God is doing. For it was Christ who died, stripping himself of his flesh. So then, hold fast to Christ the human being, who was raised from the dead by God! Hold fast to Christ the God, who worked the works of our salvation when he was about to die! So, when God works these things in Christ, although it is God who works, yet it is Christ who strips himself of the flesh when he is about to die. And when Christ died, although he worked as God before

41 Col 2:13–15.
42 That is, Paul is best interpreted by cross-reference to other Pauline texts.
43 See Col 2:12. 44 See Col 2:9. 45 See *On the Trinity* 1.13.

his death, yet it is the activity of God that raised the dead Christ. For the one who worked as Christ before his death is the very same one who raises Christ from the dead, and the same stripped himself of the flesh when he was about to die.

11. Do you already understand the mysteries of the apostolic faith? Do you already comprehend Christ? Then I ask you: who strips himself of the flesh, and what is that flesh which is stripped off? The Apostle, I maintain, means two distinct things: the flesh that is stripped off and the one who strips it off. And in the midst of all this I hear that Christ was raised from the dead by the activity of God. And so, when God is the one who raises Christ from the dead and Christ is raised from the dead, I ask: who is the one who strips himself of the flesh, and who is the one who raises Christ from the dead and brings us to life together with Christ? For if the dead Christ is not the same as the flesh that has been stripped off, then give me the name of the flesh that has been stripped off, and explain to me the nature of the one who strips himself of the flesh. For I find that Christ the God, who was raised from the dead, is the same as the one who stripped himself of the flesh, and furthermore that the flesh which has been stripped off is the Christ who was raised from the dead. And then I find him holding up the principalities and powers to mockery and triumphing in himself.

Don't you understand this one who triumphs over the powers in himself? Don't you perceive that the flesh which is stripped off and the one who strips himself of it are not different from one another? For he triumphs in himself, that is, in that by which he stripped himself of the flesh. Don't you realize that he is proclaimed to be God and a human being in such a way that death is attributed to the human being and the raising of the flesh to God, but yet not in such a way that the one who died and the one through whom the dead one rises again are different from each other? For the flesh that is stripped off is the dead Christ, and furthermore the one who raises Christ from the dead is the same Christ who stripped himself of the flesh. In the power of the resurrection, recognize the nature of God! In the death, perceive the divine plan for the human being! And even though each event belongs to its own nature, yet remember that it is the one Christ Jesus who is of both of them.

12. Even though the Apostle, as I remember, frequently attributes Christ's being raised from the dead to God the Father,[46] the Apostle does

46 See Rom 4:24.

not contradict his own statements[47] by going outside the gospel faith, especially since the Lord says, "For this reason the Father loves me, because I lay down my life, so that I may take it again. No one takes it from me, but I lay it down by myself. I have power to lay it down, and I have power to take it again. This command I have received from the Father."[48] And when he was asked to show a sign about himself in order to elicit faith in him, he says about the temple of his body,[49] "Destroy this temple, and in three days I will raise it up."[50] For both by the power of taking up his life again and by the power of raising the temple up, he teaches that he himself is for himself the God of his own resurrection, and yet he attributes everything to the authority of his Father's command. The Apostle is understood not to be teaching anything contrary to this when he proclaims that Christ, the power of God and the wisdom of God,[51] has attributed all the magnificence of his own work to the glory of the Father. For whatever Christ does, the power and the wisdom of God does, and whatever the power and the wisdom of God does, without a doubt God does, whose power and wisdom Christ is. So then, Christ was raised from the dead by the activity of God because he himself did the works of God the Father with a nature indistinguishable from God's. And faith in the resurrection is directed to that God who raised Christ from the dead.

13. The blessed Apostle, then, stuck to this twofold way of signifying Christ in his preaching, so that he might teach that there is in him both the weakness of the human being and the power and nature of God. This accords with what he said to the Corinthians, "For though he was crucified through weakness, still he lives through the power of God,"[52] showing that his death is to be attributed to the weakness but his life to the power of God. And it also accords with what he said to the Romans, "For in that he died, he died to sin once for all; but in that he lives, he lives to God. But you too should consider yourselves dead to sin, but alive to God in Christ Jesus,"[53] ascribing death to sin, that is, to our body, but life to God, who is by nature alive. Because of this, we too ought to die to our body, so that we may be alive to God in Christ Jesus, who having assumed the body of our sin now is alive wholly to God, thanks to the fellowship that united him with our nature in a communion with divine immortality.

47 Perhaps a reference to Col 2:11–12. 48 John 10:17–18. 49 See John 2:21.
50 John 2:19. 51 See 1 Cor 1:24. 52 1 Cor 13:4. 53 Rom 6:10–11.

14. Therefore, I had to deal with these passages in brief, so that we would remember that in the case of our Lord Jesus Christ it is a question of a person of both natures.[54] For he who was abiding in the form of God took the form of a slave in which he was obedient even unto death.[55] Now the obedience unto death is not in the form of God, just as the form of God is not included in the form of a slave. Because of the mystery of the gospel's divine plan, however, the one who is in the form of a slave is not different from the one who is in the form of God. And yet it is not the same thing to take the form of a slave and to be abiding in the form of God; nor could the one who was abiding in the form of God take the form of a slave without emptying himself, since the concurrence of both forms would be incongruous. But the one who emptied himself is not different and distinct from the one who took the form of a slave. For the taking cannot be attributed to someone who does not exist, since the taking can be attributed only to someone who already exists.

The emptying of the form, then, is not the destruction of the nature, for he who emptied himself does not lose his very self and he who takes the new form remains what he was. And since it is he himself who empties and takes, there is indeed a mystery in this, in that he emptied himself and took the form of a slave, and yet there is no destruction; he neither ceases to exist when he empties himself nor ceases to exist when he takes the form of the slave. So the emptying has this effect: it brings about the form of the slave, but not in such a way that Christ, who was in the form of God, ceases to continue to be Christ. For no one else but Christ took the form of a slave. When he, abiding as Christ the Spirit,[56] emptied himself to become the same Christ the human being in the body, the changing of his outer appearance and the assumption of our nature did not destroy the nature of his abiding divinity. For it is the one and the same Christ who both changed his outward appearance and assumed our nature.

54 In Latin, *utriusque naturae personam*. 55 See Phil 2:6–8. 56 See John 4:24.

20

Ephrem the Syrian, *Hymns on Faith* 4, 10, 24, 31, 36, 51, 54, 77, 78, and 79

Introduction by Mark DelCogliano
Translation by Paul S. Russell

INTRODUCTION

Ephrem the Syrian is one of the two most important fourth-century Syriac writers.[1] He was born ca. 307–309 in the Roman city of Nisibis (modern-day Nusaybin in Turkey) and was likely raised as a Christian, having close relationships with the city's bishops from his youth. He was a member of the *îḥîdāyê* ("single ones"), a group within the larger Christian community whose members devoted themselves to asceticism and celibacy without forming a distinct monastic community. This was a pattern of Christian living that was peculiar to Syriac-speaking regions. Ephrem also served his community as a teacher and perhaps also as a deacon. Above all, Ephrem was a writer: he wrote in multiple genres, including biblical commentaries and metrical homilies (*memre*), but he is especially known for his hymns (*madrāse*), about 400 of which are extant. In 363 Ephrem relocated to Edessa (modern-day Urfa in Turkey) when Nisibis, on the border between the Roman and Persian Empires, was ceded by the Romans to the Persians, prompting Christians to emigrate. In Edessa he continued to serve the Christian community as a "single one," deacon, teacher, and writer, but also encountered greater religious and Christian diversity than in Nisibis, leading him to enter into contemporary theological debates in his writings. Ephrem died in Edessa in 373.

His participation in contemporary theological debates is especially evident in his *Hymns on Faith*, the longest of his collections of hymns,

1 The other is Aphrahat, whose *Demonstration* 17: *On the Son* is translated above on pp. 212–221.

containing eighty-seven in total. Generally speaking, the hymns in this collection address the issue of the limits of human knowledge when it comes to divine topics such as Christ's divinity and his begetting from the Father. His approach is more poetic, symbolic, and biblical than technical and dogmatic. His theological stance seems generally to reflect the anti-Heteroousian polemics of the 360s, but at the same time he seems to be wary of fully embracing the Nicene position. Thus his theology bears a resemblance to some trajectories within the Homoian and Homoiousian movements of his era. At any rate, he is not unambiguously pro-Nicene, as later generations would make him out to be.

The theme of the incarnation and the issue of the limits of human knowledge in regard to the incarnation are found in all the hymns translated here. These come to the fore in Hymns 4, 51, and 54 especially, where Ephrem gives hints of his own understanding of the incarnation while at the same time affirming its ultimate ineffability. In Hymn 10 Ephrem connects the incarnation and the Eucharist. Hymn 24 stresses the soteriological purpose of the incarnation (though this topic is found in the other hymns as well). Hymn 31 is a reflection on biblical language and the incarnation, how they are acts of divine condescension for the purposes of revelation and instruction, enabling human beings to be led back to God. Hymn 36 is a retelling of the passion of Christ. Hymns 77, 78, and 79 go together; they deal with the extent of Christ's knowledge, taking Matthew 24:36 (=Mark 13:32) as the starting point of the reflections. This verse suggests that Christ's knowledge was inferior to the Father's, and pro-Nicenes considered it the key biblical proof used by their opponents to argue for Christ's ontological subordination to the Father. Ephrem adopts the position of the pro-Nicenes, refuting the subordinationist reading of the biblical verse.

The edition used for the translations here is Edmund Beck, *Des heiligen Ephraem des Syrers Hymnen de fide*, CSCO 154–155 (Louvain: Secrétariat du CSCO, 1955).

TRANSLATION

Hymn 4

1. A thousand thousands are standing,
ten thousand ten thousands are running;
thousands and ten thousands

are not able to inquire into One.
For they all are standing in silence to serve.
He has no counselor
but the offspring who is from him.
The search for him is [carried on] in the midst of silence.
When the angels went to inquire,
they took up silence and restrained themselves.

Refrain: Glory to your Father who sent you!

2. The Firstborn entered into the womb,
but the purity did not suffer.
He entered and came out with birth-pangs,
and the beautiful one[2] perceived him.
Glorious and hidden was his coming,
despised and open was his exit,
because he was God in his coming
and human in his exit.
[It is] a wonder and beautiful to hear:
fire[3] entered the womb, put on flesh, and came out.

3. Gabriel called him who was king of the angels "my Lord."
He called him "my Lord" so that we would learn
that he is the Lord and not his fellow [servant].
Michael is Gabriel's fellow;
the Son is Lord of the servants.
His nature is as great as his name:
a servant is not able to inquire into it.
For how could that which is made grow great enough
to be greater than its Maker?

4. Its sight took in a wonder of the mind
so that it might open slightly to gaze on your brightness.
Your little brightness came out.
Scattering, it poured itself out to everyone.
Who will look at the Begotten,
whose rays are fearful?

2 Or "fitting one." The form is feminine singular and refers, presumably, to Mary.
3 Fire is a common symbol of the Holy Spirit, though here used of the Son.

They are all packed into all of him.
He is the sun about which the prophets proclaimed:
"Healing is in his wings,"[4]
and [there is] pain in seeking him.

5. But will one grope for you with [his] hands,
while a keen mind is not even able to feel and seek you out,
although you are a great mountain,
to whom one can give heed with the ears?
Although you are more frightening than thunder,
you are stillness which cannot be sensed
and silence which cannot be heard.
Will a person see you with the eye?
Although you are shining light,
sight of you is hidden from all.

6. Sight of you was not only too great for,
but searching for you [was also] hidden from,
the weak senses of the body,
because they are very much
in need of other senses
which reside in thought.
But they do not comprehend even the little things
in the midst of the search.
Let us ask the angels
who are near your gate.

7. Although the angels stand before you with hymns,
they do not know
on which side they will see you.
They sought you on high,
they saw you below in the depth.
They inquired into you in heaven,
they saw you in the abyss.
They beheld you with that which is worshiped;
they found you in creation.
They came down with you and praised.

4 Mal 4:2.

8. When they began to seek
the sight of you in the midst of creation,
they did not come to the point of understanding the search for you
by running.
Because they saw you in the depth,
they saw you above on high.
Because they saw you in the grave,
they saw you in a heavenly resting place.
Because they saw you dead,
they found you raising the dead.
They wondered, they marveled, and they were speechless.

9. Everywhere, my Lord, are signs of you,
but you are hidden from everywhere.
Although a sign of you is on high,
it does not perceive that you exist.
Although a sign of you is in the depth,
it does not understand what you are.
Although a sign of you is in the sea,
you are hidden from the sea.
Although a sign of you is on the dry land,
it does not know that you exist.
Blessed is the hidden shining thing!

10. Also, a little sign of you
is a fountain of signs.
Who can fail to expound
signs without end?
For a person who takes on your likeness
it would be a spring pouring forth all likenesses
by which we will be able to see
your image in our hearts.
In one revered icon
are ten thousand close-packed beauties.

11. You are a complete marvel
in every direction that we seek you.
You are near and far and who reaches you?
Searching, [even when] it has extended itself,

cannot attain to you.
When it stretched out to reach you
it was cut off and fell away.
It was too short for your size.
Faith does reach [you], though,
and love, with prayer.

12. Thought is easier for us than the spoken word.
It is thought which is able
to stretch out to every place.
But yet when it comes to walk
on your path to search for you,
its path disappears before it:
it is confused and leaves off.
If thought was overcome,
how much the more will speech [be overcome],
whose path is in the midst of confusion?

13. This is suitable for the mouth:
that it might praise and be still and,
if it should be asked to run on,
it would entirely resist, in silence.
Then it will be able to comprehend,
unless it runs on[5] in order to comprehend.
Stillness is able to comprehend
more than the insolent [person] who runs on.
[It is] the weak who will inquire into [this].
Behold, the sick will toil to measure the dreadful sea.

14. Behold, my Lord, if the mouth were to cease from inquiring
into you
it will not have done a good thing,
because it was able to inquire and to turn away.
Its weakness forbade it [to inquire]
but its insolence took it captive.
It would have been a good thing for him

5 "Running on," either in speaking too much or trying to proceed too far, is a way to lose what progress can be legitimately expected.

if he directed [his tongue] to be still
because silence would be a harbor for him
so that he might not perish in your sea
and in your overwhelming deluge.

15. If there is a way to inquire [into him],
come, let us inquire into the Hidden One.
Come, let us be distracted,
let us feel him, if he is one who can be comprehended.
You are revealed to children, my Lord,
but hidden from the shrewd.
You are present to one who believes,
but for one who inquires you are concealed.
Blessed is the one who is sincere in searching for you
but shrewd in regard to [making any] declaration about you.

16. Searching, O my Lord, is too small
because it shuts you up inside it.
[Only] the strength that extends to every place
is sufficient to inquire into you
because it can represent you on high
and touch you in the depths.
If it did not reach every place
it could not inquire into you.
Blessed is he who realizes that the whole search for you
rests in the bosom of your begetter.

17. The seraph who flies and floats on high
is too weak to inquire into you.
His wing is [too] weak to reach to your greatness.
In your bosom lie the ages.
As much as one is bound inside it
will one go astray.
The seraph whose voice is pronouncing praises
will honor inquiry into you with silence.
Woe to the one who presumes, for, behold,
the seraph before you conceals his face with his wings![6]

6 Isa 6:2.

18. The cherubim bear the power that bears all.
[The cherub] sinks beneath his gaze
because it [is] in awe.
It hides [itself] beneath your chariot,
fearing to gaze within it.
They bear [it]
but they cannot inquire into it.
When they are near they withdraw.
Blessed is he who has learned your value from them,
he praises and keeps silence, in reverence.

*

* *

Hymn 10

1. You, my Lord, caused to be written: "Open your mouth and I will fill it."[7]
Behold, the mouth and mind of your servant are open to you.
Fill it with your gift, my Lord, so that I may sing your glory according to your will.

Refrain: Make me worthy of approaching your gift in awe.

2. There are ranks of all statures for each person [according to how well they] speak of you.
Should I be insolent, I would draw near to the lowest rank.
Your generation is sealed in silence. What mouth would dare meditate upon it?

3. Although your nature is one, explanations of it are many.
There are lofty and middling and lowly tellings [of it].
Draw me up to the lowly level as to a bread crumb so that I can gather the crusts of your wisdom.[8]

4. Your lofty genealogy is hidden with your Begetter.
Indeed, the angels are stupefied by a modicum of your riches.
My Lord, a small trickle of your persuasion [makes for] a deluge of interpretations among the lowly.

7 Ps 80(81):11. 8 See Matt 15:21–28.

5. If the great John proclaimed,
"I am not worthy, my Lord, to undo the straps of your sandals,"[9]
then like the sinful woman I will take refuge in the shadow of your robe so that I can begin from that.[10]

6. Heal my fright as [you did with] her, she who was frightened and was encouraged to be cured.
I will be encouraged by you from [my] fear and be handed over from your robe to your body
so that I can tell of it, as far as my strength [allows].

7. Your robe, my Lord, is a source of medicines.
In your visible clothing dwells your hidden power.[11]
A great wonder of light dwells even in the mud made into a little spittle from your mouth.[12]

8. In your bread is a hidden spirit which is not eaten.
In your wine dwells fire which is not drunk.
The spirit in your bread and the fire in your wine – a distinct marvel which our lips receive.

9. By the Lord coming down to earth among mortals
he made them a new creation, like angels,
mixing fire and spirit in them so that they could be fire and spirit secretly.

10. The seraph did not put the fiery coal near to Isaiah's mouth with his fingers,[13] [and], indeed, it only came very near [to him].
[Isaiah] did not lay hold of it or eat it.
But, behold, our Lord gave both these things to us!

11. Abraham offered the food of bodily beings to spiritual angels[14]
and they ate it, [which was] a new miracle,
but our great Lord makes the bodily ones eat and drink fire and spirit.

9 Mark 1:7 and parallels. 10 See Luke 7:37.
11 This stanza and the one preceding refer to the healing of the woman with the issue of blood in the story from Luke 8:43–48.
12 See John 9:1–7. 13 See Isa 6:7. 14 See Gen 18:8–9.

12. Fire came down on sinners and devoured them in wrath.[15]
Merciful fire came down into the bread and dwelt there.
Instead of that fire which devoured the human being, you eat the fire in the bread and live.

13. Fire came down and devoured Elijah's sacrifice.[16]
The fire of love has become the sacrifice of life for us.
The fire devoured the offering. We eat your fire, our Lord, in your offering.

14. "Who has taken hold of the Spirit in his hands?"[17]
Come and see, O Solomon, what your father's Lord did:
He mixed fire and spirit against their nature and poured [them] in the hands of his disciples.

15. "Who bound the waters in a garment?"[18] he asked.
Behold, in a garment, the skirt of Mary, was a spring.
From the cup of life [came] the drop of life. We received your handmaids in a garment.

16. Behold, power is hidden in the garment of the temple,
power which the mind has never comprehended.
He inclined his love and came down and hovered over the veil of the altar of reconciliation.

17. Behold, the fire and spirit were in the bosom of her who birthed you.
Behold, fire and spirit were in the river where you were baptized.[19]
Fire and spirit were at our baptism; in the bread and cup were fire and the Holy Spirit.

18. Your bread killed the greedy one who made us his bread.
Your cup destroyed the death which swallowed us up.
We ate you and drank you, my Lord, not so that we might consume you but so that we might live through you.

19. The strap of your sandal is a terror to those who are insightful;
the hem of your cloak is fearsome among the knowing.

15 Possibly a reference to 2 Kgs 1:10 or Gen 19:24. 16 See 1 Kgs 18:21–40.

17 Prov 30:4. The reader must keep in mind the Semitic use of the same word for wind, breath, and spirit.

18 Prov 30:4. 19 See, e.g., Matt 3:13–17.

Our generation is foolish in its investigation of you; behold, it is intoxicated, drunken with your new wine.

20. There is wonder in your footsteps which went upon the water.
You subdued the great sea under your feet.[20]
The little river was also subdued when he bent down and was baptized in it.

21. The river was like John who baptized in it:
the two were with each other in [their] smallness.
To the little river and the weak servant did the Lord of both subject himself.

22. My Lord, fill my bosom with the crumbs of your crusts[21]
because there is no more room in my lap.
Although I am worshiping you, withhold your grace and keep it like a deposit in your treasury so that you can turn it back to us again.

*
* *

Hymn 24

1. Our Lord conquered in the armor of a condemned athlete.
He put on a body from Adam and David[22]
so that with that body, which the Evil One condemned, he might be brought low to repair its dishonor.

Refrain: Lord, glory to you from the nations[23] which believe in you.

2. Even your littleness is too great for words,
for who can open his mouth about the sustainer of all
who was nurtured at the poor table of Joseph and Mary?

3. From a great womb, rich and making everything rich,
you were nurtured in Mary's poor womb.
On earth, you had a mortal father although you are living and one who keeps all alive.

20 See Matt 14:22–33 and parallels. 21 See Matt 15:21–28.
22 See Matt 1:1. 23 That is, the Gentiles (not the nation of Israel).

4. He rode a despised colt, hidden in his lowly triumph.[24]
Riders of horses and chariots succumbed, although victorious.
For David conquered the valiant ranks and [his] weak rib[25] was subject to his firmness.[26]

5. The ass spoke and knew that it was an ass
and also, in the same way, knew that her master was her master,
who, as he traveled, was not able to distinguish a made creature from the Creator.[27]

6. Even if Nabal was struck for [only] sticking out his tongue,
[he was] still outrageous, because he opened his mouth fiercely,
for he belittled the great king David and named him among the servants.[28]

7. Who, indeed, would be foolish enough to imitate Nabal?
Flee his tongue[29] as you do his death, my brothers,
for it is not the son of Jesse that his mouth treats shamefully, but rather the Son of David.

8. The cross is the seal and form of creatures:
everything, both in length and breadth, is imprinted with its type.
The cross [is imprinted] on every bird which is borne on two wings by the power of the establisher of all.

9. The Lord bent down and descended and became a servant for [the sake of his] servant.
He became as a companion; he became as a colleague and washed [their] feet.[30]
O my beloved, let us inquire into these things if we are capable [of it] in the face of goodness.

10. The Lord of heaven came down to earth and sojourned.
He became a sojourner and inhabitant and wayfarer

24 A reference to the entrance to Jerusalem on Palm Sunday: see Luke 19:28–40.
25 That is, wife. See *Hymns against Heresies* 6.3 and 7.2.
26 For example, 2 Sam 8:1 and 2 Sam 12:24.
27 Balaam and his ass: Num 22:21–35. Balaam mistakes the reluctance of his ass for stubbornness instead of recognizing in it the results of an intervention by God through his angel.
28 See 1 Sam 25:10–38. 29 That is, speech. 30 See John 13:1–17.

so that he might raise us up and cause us to dwell in his kingdom in an everlasting dwelling place.

11. Let us praise with every mouth the Lord of all tongues!
How long will we wander and how long will we praise the Son of the Living One,
whom, because he bore a body because of his love, the crucifiers assault and against whom the inquirers rage?

*
* *

Hymn 31

1. Let us praise him who put on the names of limbs:
who called himself "ears" so that we could learn that he hears us;
who called himself "eyes" so that we could know that he sees us.
He alone put on the names of desires.
Although anger and remorse of spirit do not exist in his essence,
he put on their names because of our weakness.

Refrain: Blessed is he who appeared to our humanity in every [kind of] likeness.

2. We should know that, unless he had put on the names of the desires,
he would not have been able to speak with our humanity.
By means of our [names], he came near to us
and put on our names so that he might put his own on us through discipline.
He asked [about] our form and put [it] on.
He spoke to our childishness as a father speaks to [his] babies.

3. For he put on this likeness of ours and did not put it on.
He cast it off and did not cast it off. Although it was put on, it was [also] cast off.
He put it on for a benefit and cast it off by a change.
For, when he cast off and put on every likeness,
he taught that this particular likeness was not that of his essence.
Because his essence is hidden, he depicts it through revealed things.

4. He was in a place as an old man and "Ancient of Days."[31]
He was also like a mighty, strong warrior.[32]
He was an old man as a judge[33] and a mighty [man] in a wrestling match.[34]
In [one] place he was running as if he were slow,[35]
in [one] place he was tired,[36] in [one] place he was sleeping,[37]
in [one] place he was needy.[38] In every way he worked hard to win us over.

5. This Good One, although he was able to adorn us by force without effort,
toiled in every way to adorn us according to our will,
so that we might depict our beauty
[by] collecting together the pigments of our freedom.
When he adorns us, we resemble the image of others
he is adorning and painting for himself with his own pigments.

6. He is also teaching a bird how to speak.
In the shelter of the mirror is he hiding and teaching it.
This [bird], when it turns to him as he speaks,
finds its own image before its eyes
but the idea[s] of its companion who is talking with it.
He sets his image before it so that it can learn his speech through it.

7. This bird is akin to a human being,
though the relationship is like that of strangers.
He cajoles it with this [relationship] and teaches him to speak with it.
The Being which is entirely above everything
bowed down its loftiness because of his love, took on our customs from us,
and toiled in every way so that everything might turn to it.

8. For his likeness is that of an old man[39] or that of a mighty [man].[40]
For it was written that he slept[41] or that he did not slumber.[42]

31 Dan 7:9. 32 See Exod 15:3. 33 See Ps 74(75):8.
34 See Gen 32:24–32. 35 It is uncertain what Ephrem has in mind here.
36 See John 4:6. 37 See Mark 4:38. 38 See Matt 21:3.
39 See Dan 7:9. 40 See Ps 77(78):65. 41 See Mark 4:38–40.
42 See Ps 120(121):4 and Ps 77(78):65.

It was written that he was weary or that he was not weary.[43]
In that he bound, he unburdened [us and] helped us to learn.
The sapphire tile was collected together and he stood on it.[44]
He spread and filled the heavens[45] but they were all in the palm of his hand.[46]

9. He showed himself in a place and he showed [himself] in every place.
We thought, "Behold, he is in a place," but everything was filled with him.
He was small so that he might be suitable for us; he grew so that he might be a gain for us.
He was small and he was also great so that we might grow great.
If he had been small but not great he would have been small and despicable to us
so that he would have been thought weak. For that reason he was both small and great.

10. Let us marvel that, while he was small, he increased our littleness.
If he had not changed and been great he would have shrunk our opinion [of him],
so that, thinking that he was weak, it[47] would have been small while [we] thought so.
We are not capable [of attaining to] the essence of his greatness.
He was [so] great [that] we [could] not even wander distracted toward his littleness;
he was [so] small [that] we abased ourselves in everything he did with us.

11. He wants us to learn two things: that he was and that he was not.
Because of his love he made a face for himself so that his servants might see him.
But, so that we might not be damaged and think that he [really] was like that,
he changed from likeness to likeness so we might learn that he had no likeness.

43 See Isa 1:14, 40:28. 44 See Exod 24:10. 45 See Job 9:8; Jer 23:23–24.
46 See Isa 40:12. 47 That is, our opinion.

Although he did not leave the form of humanity,
he did leave it through his alterations.

*

* *

Hymn 36

1. The Son came down to visit the servants
because their sicknesses continued to drag on and pressed
hard [upon them]
and doctors[48] had come and toiled and grown weary.
They healed a little and they left much.

Refrain: Blessed is he who sent you!

2. Because they were not able to see him,
he took clothing for himself from among the sheep.
The flock approached him and did not treat him as something vile
because the scent of sheep exuded from his clothes.

3. But wolves who were crafty
feared him because he had changed.
They rent his clothes, revealed his glory, and,
although they did not intend to, they made his brightness shine out
from under his covering.

4. [Some of] today's pastors, who see
that he is greatly despised for the sake of his sheep,
think, as if they were drunk with the taste of wine,
that he is the head pastor and shepherd.

5. The husbandmen who crucified him realized
that he was the heir and lord of the vineyard.[49]
The shepherds thought he was a colleague of the sheep
because he became the Passover Lamb on account of his love.

6. Let the tears in [our] eyes break through.
Those who were made slandered with their names

48 This seems to be a reference to the biblical judges and prophets.

49 See Matt 21:33–41.

the Son of the Maker through whom we were made;[50]
they gave him [this] reward because he had magnified them with his own names.

7. Oh, for the lump of clay which changed
its potter in name but not in nature![51]
The color of the wool is also changed
so that you would not call the Son by the name of the creatures.

8. He separated you from the animals.
You must not reckon him along with the creatures.
There is freedom in your own slavery;
you must not place your yoke on the lordship of the one who sets all free.

9. Tell us why you are accused
because perhaps [his grief] resembles yours.
Who can define how many or of what kind
these things were that he bore for your sake?

10. What have you borne for his sake?
If you do not honor [him], at least do not despise him.
In what fire have you burned in his place,
so that the smoke of your contention has risen up to him?

11. Behold, you are on fire with the zeal for Being.
But One cannot be divided into Three.
Leave aside his name and show his nature,
because that nature is what makes [one] acquire eyes for the searching.

12. Rock is divisible by nature,
as are its other companion natures.
The nature of light is not divisible.
The proof of their nature for us is [in] the eyes.

13. They are akin in their names,
though far apart in their natures.

50 See John 1:3. 51 See Isa 45:9.

Indeed, you cannot show us a name shared in common
under which there are alike things that are divisible and indivisible.

14. Behold, everything is named individually.
Every body, every object:
each one along with everything that can be numbered.

15. If, because you called something [a name,
you think that] it is not divisible, you have gone far astray.
The nature of water is one and it is also divisible
and it is changed in fruit and seeds.

16. There is no way that we can rise up to him
without putting his nature to the test.
For, the fact that he is One does not allow us
to investigate [and] find an explanation of his generation which is hidden from all.

17. There are two separate furnaces:
faith and testing.
Either a person believes in the truth
or a test can teach him what it is.

18. The faith of the children of Truth
is not in need of investigating.
For us, the way [that] goes toward seeking
every test and trial [comes] from the rash.

19. Take [him] and throw him into the waves
so that he will entirely cease from questions.
You must seek proof of the Existent:
what it is and where it is and whence it is.

20. If the birth is plainer than [any] thing
or [if] creatures [are plainer] than nothing,
plow and replow the thorny earth
and, behold, it gives you the word of Truth, although it is not pleased [about it].

*

* *

Hymn 51

1. Who could repay [you for the fact] that you bent down your greatness to utter littleness,
and your stateliness came down to the end of humiliation,
and that you brought your life to the level of mortality,
and your wealth came down and dwelt in utter poverty,
and that you subjected your lordship to the banner of servitude?
Praises to your goodness!

2. Who could gaze on your hiddenness, our Lord, which came to revelation,
and your secrecy came to brightness and manifestation,
and your invisibility appeared publicly without end,
and your awesomeness came to the hand of [your] seizers?
These things happened to you, my Lord, because you became human.
Praises to your sender!

3. Who would not be afraid because,
although your manifestation and human birth were revealed,
your birth[52] is incomprehensible, which has led the disputers astray.
For, behold, there is one who preaches that you bore a body alone,[53]
and there is also one who teaches that [you bore] a body and a soul.[54]
Others go astray and think that [your] body was heavenly.[55]
Praises to your Begetter!

4. Our Lord, seal our mouth, because,
if your revelation has led astray the wise because they were not capable of
comprehending your birth from Mary,

52 This seems to refer to his human birth, since the difficulties described relate to the human nature of Christ.

53 Most probably a reference to Apollinarius of Laodicea, though it misunderstands his ideas.

54 Apparently a reference to the viewpoint that Christ lacked a human spirit, which Ephrem might associate with Apollinarius.

55 Epiphanius of Salamis mentions this belief as current among some of the followers of Apollinarius at *Panarion* 7.2, 1–2, 4.

the learned divided your birth by [their] controversies.
If human beings do not comprehend your humanity,
who could be capable of comprehending your divine birth?
Praises to your begetter!

5. My Lord, let us sing what is right with our lyre,
[but] let us not sing with it something that is not lawful, my Lord,
because it is a frail lyre.
Its sounds are not capable of investigating your birth.
Your birth cannot be comprehended even by the princes and the spiritual among the angels on high with [their] lyres.
Praises to your hiddenness!

6. Our Lord, let my tongue be a pen for your praise,
and may the finger of your goodness set down and write with it a helpful discourse.
My Lord, a pen cannot write unless someone holds it in his finger[s];
let my tongue not fall into fault by speaking apart from you something which is not helpful.
Praises to your teacher!

7. It is insolence to call you by a name that is foreign
to the one by which your Father called you,
for he simply called you "my Son"
by the Jordan River where you were baptized.
The threefold mysteries baptized your humanity:
the Father through his voice, the Son through his power, and the Spirit through his descent.
Praises to your descent!

8. Who could deny that the descent of the threefold names served [its purpose] previously by the Jordan?
It is true that your body was baptized by the names,
by which, behold, bodies are [still] being baptized.
Although the names of the Lord of All are many,
we baptize distinctly in [the name of] "the Father and the Son and the Spirit."
Praises to your greatness!

9. Who would not wonder at a painter
if he painted a mere horse [and],
although he was able to add the head and the limbs, he was afraid to add them?[56]
Oh, you are too smart for your own good! You have made the Begotten,
who is not small, small with [your] questions and,
although he is like the One, you have likened him to the many!
Praise to the Son of our King!

10. Who saw in the thin air a way like to that way, the way of a bird?
If a person were walking as on the back of the wind,
the storm would stretch out and make a path for the walker,
and the prudent would not go entirely out of it
because death [lies] outside of it.
Praises to your warning!

11. Our Lord, agree with me that I should go in that fear
and be afraid lest I cross the depth of my faith.
Your truth is clear and direct: to believers it is clear and to the perverse it is difficult.
The simple proceed and go forth,
the learned turn aside and fall into the deep of investigation
so that our Lord has to draw them out.
Praises to him who finds [them] all!

12. The power of interpretation shone and came out to us from the names.
Their names of "servant" and "Son of the Lord" bear witness,
for the name "servant" also teaches that he was not Son
and the name "Son" also proclaims that he was not one of the companions.
Their names proclaim about them without controversy.
Praises to your greatness!

56 That is, if you're afraid to paint a horse (apparently thought to be hard to depict), but you're not afraid to "paint" (that is, describe) the divine, how foolish are you?

13. Therefore let us rebuke and speak to the insolent one who teaches a new thing.
My faith is complete, my pearl is perfect:[57] your polishing is not acceptable.
It will not become beautiful in your furnace because beauty [comes] from the soul,[58]
and if it were carved it would be rejected for the crown of the heavenly King.
Praises to your kingship!

*
* *

Hymn 54

1. The heavenly King, when his Son came down to earth,
knew from the things they said [that] the people[59] did not know [him].
For the Father witnessed to the Son and the Son called out to the Father.[60]
Even in his humiliation it was understood that he was Lord
because he was honored by everything,
for the sea was his mount and the air his chariot.

Refrain: Praises to the one who sent you!

2. Learn from the service he received whose son he was,
for, although he was in a humble state,
angels came down and served the glorious Son of their Lord.[61]
He commanded as his maidservants the creatures,
and he commanded the [whole] world with a gesture as would a servant,[62]
in the manner of his Begetter, whose silence commands everything.

3. Because he is Lord he exalted those of his household,
but fools despised themselves and fell and wallowed around.

57 A trope in Syriac literature. Matt 13:45–46 is likely a source of this image.
58 Or "from [the faith] itself."
59 That is, Israel.
60 See, e.g., Matt 3:7 and Luke 23:46.
61 See, e.g., Matt 4:11.
62 See, e.g., Matt 8:23–27.

So he came down and rescued them from the wallowing.
Error erred, because it saw our spattering on his garments.
Knowledge alone knew that he had come near to the wallowing to bring cleansing.

4. From [the fact that] he bore his burden it was understood that he was the King's Son,
because he took care of his Father's house like a good heir.
He saw a servant who was laid [out]: He raised him up in health.[63]
He saw a handmaid who was laid [out sick]: He rebuked her fever.[64]
He saw that bread was lacking and he satisfied those of his household
and they praised the one who sent him.[65]

5. Who would not love the one who loves the children of humanity?
It happened that he was mixed and mingled with his handmaid and his servant.
They invited him and he was not loath [to go].
He went to the feast, made it merry with his greatness, and gave a gift, too:
wine in bowls, because the treasure of his kingdom went along with him.[66]

6. Who would not be pious and purify his body?
When he entered his Father's house, the great temple,
he chastised them with cords.[67]
Because they had cut off their hope, [because] they had despised the temple,
he gave Jerusalem a writ of divorce.
He took the vineyard away from the husbandmen.[68]

7. Who would not be pious and who would not love
because he praised his merchants who increased the talents they received
and punished the wicked and vicious servant?[69]
Who[70] [was it who] harmed members of his household and corrupted his companion?[71]

63 See Matt 9:2–7. 64 A reference to Peter's mother-in-law: see Matt 8:14–15.
65 See John 6:1–14. 66 See John 2:1–11. 67 See John 2:13–17.
68 See Matt 21:33–46. 69 See Matt 25:14–30.
70 Satan is meant. 71 That is, Judas Iscariot.

He was an infidel who, when he was struck, howled with the mouth of his demons:
"What is there between us and you, Jesus?"[72]

8. It is written [that] the good Lord "repented"[73] and "was weary"[74]
because he put on our weakness.
He also turned us back and put on [us] the names of his greatness.
Fools saw what belonged to us and thought that what was from us was his.
They were rebuked, but they did not therefore perceive
that we should also consider as ours what belonged to him.

9. When those who listened to the True One surrounded him with love,
they did not judge his words.
The doubtful were deceitfully lying in wait for his sayings,
because, indeed, the adversary of his uprightness is their hateful controversy
which labors to overthrow fitness with a [mere] story.

10. [When] our Lord was speaking, the pure were merry, but the fearful were gloomy.
The simple heard and trusted, the cunning heard and disputed:
"How is this one able to give us his body?"[75]
Their disputation deprives them of the medicine of life.[76]
Let not our disputation deprive us also because we do not trust!

11. The words of God should not be in the furnace to be tested.
Look at the disciples and look also at the infidels;
while the innocent stand firm, the disputers are raving;
they thought that the Begotten, whose measure could never be comprehended,
was not yet fifty years old![77]

12. Therefore, let us say briefly that all investigation is of the left hand,
for even the robber who was crucified on the left hand [side of Christ]
was investigating to learn by his questioning the impudence of the inquirers!

72 See, e.g., Mark 1:21–27. 73 See Gen 6:5–6. 74 See John 4:3–6.
75 John 6:52. 76 A reference to the Eucharist and to Christ himself.
77 See John 8:56–59.

Woe to you who, cut off from hope,
investigated his Lord, even while he was fixed [on the cross] and being crucified!

13. Who would not also wonder at the robber who was crucified on the right
[who], while he was hanging there,
looked and believed that he was the Son of God?
We believe that he went up in glory and is seated on the right hand [of God the Father].
The crucified one persuaded him,
but not even the cherubim who bore him can persuade us.[78]

*

* *

Hymn 77

1. The simple weigh [the verse], "He does not know that hour,"[79]
against the Son
as if it were greater![80]

Refrain: Blessed is your knowledge!

2. For if the Firstborn knows the Father,
what is there that is greater than the Father
so that he[81] does not know it?

3. "No one knows that hour"
except the Firstborn,
because he alone knows the Father.

4. If, as they think, he does not know it because he is a creature,
behold, they are making him [a creature]
by their investigations!

78 See Luke 23:39–43 for these two stanzas.

79 Mark 13:32, a favorite verse of the Heteroousians, used in their argument against the Son's divinity being equal with that of the Father. This entire hymn argues against their reading of this verse, while *Hymns* 78 and 79 continue the discussion.

80 Namely, as if the verse, Mark 13:32, were greater than the Son himself.

81 That is, the Son.

5. Come, wonder whether our Lord,
on account of his being a creature,
"Did not know that hour."

6. These people, who were created by his hand,
dare to inquire into the Lord of Hours
instead of that "hour"!

7. Let them, indeed, support their statement
so that everything which is a creature may keep silence
before the Creator.

8. By the same knowledge by which he knows the Father
is "that hour" also contained for him
in his knowledge.

9. If [the Father] should grant to [the Son] to know his glory
and hide from him an hour of time,
[the hour] would be greater than he[82] is!

10. Set the hour he does not know beside the Father which he does know
and weigh [them]
and see which is greater.

11. "It is the Son alone who knows the Father."[83]
He knows him entirely;
he lacks none of him.

12. Because the root is true,
the fruit that it produced
knows it truly.

13. What fruit knows [only] a little of its root?
It is entirely mingled together
with all of it!

82 That is, the Father.

83 Matt 11:27. Note the use of another scriptural passage to rebut the "Arian" interpretation. As so often among the pro-Nicene writers, Ephrem argues implicitly that only the full Nicene position can make sense of all of scripture together.

14. If it should fall short of its tree with regard to knowledge of it,
it would also fall short [of it] with regard to its name
because it would not be its fruit.

15. If the fruit corresponds to the root in its name,
it would also correspond to it
in knowledge.

16. The sweetness in them both is one;
the knowledge in them both is one,
because they are mingled together.

17. The fruit is mingled in the midst of its tree
and its root is also in the midst of the fruit.
Who can separate [them]?

18. They cannot be divided with regard to that sweetness.
They also cannot be divided with regard to knowledge
of the whole truth.

19. The love of the fruit is in the midst of its root
and in the midst of the fruit is also [the love] of its tree.
Who can divide [them]?

20. The names "Father," "Son," and "Spirit" agree and are in concord
because of [their] descent
at baptism.

21. The names are in concord.
The series [of them] is in concord because [they have] one will,
just as they bear one yoke and go [forward together];

22. just as when they agree about the descent at baptism,
so do they agree also
in [their] concord.

23. The fruit bent down and put on a body
and put on with it the weak names
of the children of its race.

24. But, when he put on our human nature,
he also, on account of us,
put on our [level of] knowledge.

25. He who knows all became unknowing.
He asked questions and listened [to the answers] just like a human being
on account of human being[s].

26. If the feeble inquired into Being,
would he who is the Son not also be capable
of comprehending "the hour"?

27. Indeed, either let them be still [about] whether he knows [the hour],
but if they do inquire, let them confess
that the Son knows everything.

28. But if they do inquire,
([that is], although this insolence is not permitted, or, if it is permitted,
[it is] as a grace):

29. He who grants to the dust to investigate [him],
how would he forbid his Son
to know an hour of time?

30. "He does not know that hour."
The cause of this lack of knowledge
is the body he put on.

*

* *

Hymn 78

1. You would never want to say
that "the Son does not know that hour"[84]
because he knows it.

Refrain: Blessed is he who knows everything!

2. He knows that hour which is [decided] by reckoning,
because all numbers
were devised by him.

84 Mark 13:32.

3. If it is [an hour] of a year, he would know it,
because the months of the year were devised by him
like limbs.

4. If it is [an hour] of a month, he would know it,
because the days of the months were devised by him
like nerves.[85]

5. If it is [an hour] of days, he would not mistake it,
because the hours and Sabbaths were also divided by him
like weeks.

6. If it is [an hour] of the sun, he would know it,
because he is the one who treads out the paths of winter
and the steps of summer.

7. If it is [an hour] of the moon, he would also know it,
because he is the one who made the times of the full moons
along with the new moon.

8. On high and in the depths,
if something exists, it is in the palm [of] his [hand].
All creatures hang[86] on his finger.

9. Compare the hour which he does not know
to that Holy Spirit which he does know:
which is greater?

10. Come, explain to us the cause:
how and why did it[87] conceal from him
the hour of its procession?

11. If it concealed [it] from him for this:
so that he[88] would be smaller than he[89] [was],
lest he slip away [and] become like himself.

85 Or "veins." 86 Or "depend."
87 The Syriac refers to the Holy Spirit in this passage as "he," but in order to more closely approximate common English idiom, and to avoid confusion, I have referred to the Holy Spirit as "it."
88 That is, the Son incarnate. 89 That is, the Son as he is in the divinity.

12. That scheme is very weak.
See how it would be:
It could end it with one word.[90]

13. For when that hour was revealed
and the horn blew and the procession occurred,
it was finished.

14. Therefore, he was on the same level with him[self]
and discord became concord
according to their word.

15. One of [these] two [possibilities must be the solution]:
if he is small in that he does not know it, [then] he would be on the same level
when he does perceive it.

16. And if, when he does perceive it, he is great – behold,
for he knows it
but he is still small!

17. For Satan is also able to know that hour,
but when [it] is revealed
he will be consumed by it.

18. Therefore, great [is] the hour
which he concealed from his Beloved
that even Satan could know!

19. Come, hear the cause of his glory,
because he is the Lord of all who is greater than all
and everything depends on him.

20. For the cause of the glory of God
[is] this which is with us:
his goodness which is everlasting;

90 Ephrem holds that the ignorance of the incarnate Son about the Spirit's procession must be one that is falsely assumed. If the Son were truly ignorant, and the Spirit were to speak a word to the incarnate Son out of turn, the incarnate Son would become "like himself" and again enjoy the fullness of divine knowledge, obviating to some degree the incarnation. Ephrem objects here to any scheme that would falsify the experience of the incarnation, making it one of appearance rather than of reality.

21. and the cause of his glory which is with his offspring
[is] his Fatherhood which also
is always and everlasting.

22. O [you] holy causes,
which never finish with the creatures
and the Firstborn!

23. But [creation] is an hour of time, and the cause of time,
and the fullness of time, and, along with time,
its time passes.[91]

24. [It is] the great necessity of making
that a made thing can never be
as great as its Maker.

25. [It is] the great necessity of Fatherhood
that his offspring can never become
like the Begetter.

26. Indeed, [there is] another argument regarding that hour.
Let us go and seek it out,
since that earlier one has been explained.

27. Confess and reveal what has been deduced:
that our Redeemer did also
know that hour,

28. since he whispered to us as by a symbol:
"Strife put together [and] spoke it
so that it might prevail through it."

29. Strife is guilty and truth has won.
Disputation has passed away
and the crown has come to the victor.

*
* *

91 This stanza is awkward in this position. It seems to stress the transitory nature of creation and created things in contrast to the changeless eternity of the divine. That contrast sits well before stanzas 24 and 25, which proclaim the gulf between God and the world and God the Father and all else, but its manner of expression is jarring.

Hymn 79

1. My Son, which is [more] glorious in comparison
and which also is preeminent in weight:
that he does not know the hour
or that he knows that Father who is great beyond comparison?
Show that he does not know.
Show that he does not try to inquire into the hour
in order to restrain [us] by the hour
so that the hour might also rebuke you,
lest you inquire into the Lord of all hours.

Refrain: Glory be to you, Christ-Son, who knows all!

2. Know in yourself that he knows.
Behold, he anticipated and bound your knowledge
because your freedom [of will] is a defiled handmaid
who plunders her Lord's treasures for the sake of her wine.
He prepared chains and got bonds ready for her.
Behold, the hedges bound it and, behold, bulwarks encompassed it.
And if they did not keep it,
its frenzy would be known because of them.

3. He knew that races and tongues
and the Greeks who contemplate hidden things,
were prepared to come for his instruction,
for this is the net which gathered all races.[92]
His leaven[93] led and brought the wild asses to his teaching and,
so that they would not be upset in their paths by the one yoke of truth,
he would teach one path of concord.

4. He did not give a place to the swift
for him to run separately on his own.
He did not give a place to the inquirer
for him to be freed from the yoke of faith.
The learned and the commoners, the subtle and the innocent:
on all of them [lies] one equal yoke.
May the chariot's yoke persuade the divided to gain concord by it![94]

92 See Matt 13:47–48. 93 See Matt 13:33.
94 That is, by submitting themselves to be hitched to it together.

5. That we should eat and drink and sleep and rise:
this power dwells in freedom [of the will].
But horses also possess this freedom
concerning what they want and how much they want.
Taskmasters, therefore, are not under the yoke
which Love put on for them, [which] Truth girded on for them.
They did not turn aside nor turn [others] aside
because they are obedient to the will of the driver.

6. If, where there is no freedom, in the race of animals,
(and, behold – there is [a kind of freedom there]!),
how, then, will it be found in its own house –
the human being, a vessel [with] impulses in its soul?[95]
Bound by Truth but freed in manner of life,
he transgresses against the good things
through variations from [his] true state.
If he slips to error, he will be dragged down.

7. For he keeps watch and sleeps, and when he sleeps
the wage for his watching is [still] kept for him.
He also fasts and eats in his time
but the fast does not really vanish for him in the eating.
For tasting and fasting are both pure and seemly.
Truth is solitary and its neighbor is error,
and if you creep away from it [as] a little ray [of light]
that "little" will be like a gulf.

8. There are diverse desires in one gathering
but they will never be blamed for being divided.
But they are blameworthy for one thing by which they are divided:
because they rebel against the yoke of faith.
Since horses [can] agree together in one yoke,
David wrote about his own [nature] that
"Human beings are likened to animals."[96]
Oh, may they be likened to a marvel which is not also like them!

95 If animals can go astray without even enjoying real freedom of will, what will be the fate of humans who fully enjoy this power to err or go straight?

96 Ps 48(49):21.

9. Behold, the courses are confused in the midst of the gatherings
and the desires are wounded by the inhabitants [of the gatherings].
Questions are divided in the churches
and minds are sick in the congregations.
Therefore, whose is the woe,
which [makes] a raging in the midst of the sea and turmoil on the dry land?
They inquired into the Creator by whose hand they were established.
Behold, his creatures are upset by [their] inquiry into him.

10. Therefore, behold, the house of the Lord is nailed up
as an example for the instruction of his servants.
His creation and its number are arguing
that it cannot be concealed from the Creator.
When they came to inquire into him
they saw him in that hour when it depicted his humiliation,
so that they were quickly ashamed
and were restrained by the type of his lowliness
from [inquiring into] his powerful generation.

11. Look at these things with the eye of consideration –
at all creatures, at everything,
because they are put together like a body
by the one who establishes all,
and cannot be hidden from their Creator.
My brothers, how could its parts[97] conceal an image
from its Artificer when it is being depicted?
That hour cannot be hidden from the knowledge of its Creator!

12. My brothers, look at "number"
which is composed like a body by the one who knows all.
His computations are in the type of its limbs
and the seasons and times are like its constructions.
The hours are like its features, the years are like its forms.
That hidden hour is a type of his thought

97 Or "limbs."

and similarly [with] the rest of its limbs –
behold, its months, also, its Sabbaths and its days!

13. Who, indeed, would go astray or be changed
and destroy his thoughts and become like drunkards
who destroy their own minds
to the point that the fool would now think
that the image, which was embellished by the true Father
through the finger of his beloved, should [provide]
a means for that glorious hour to conceal itself
from the finger of the one who fashions all?

14. Therefore, if it should be impossible
for his foreknowledge to err,
and he also prepared a place in which it might be established,
at which time it might come from being hidden to being manifest;
although it was not possible, it was possible for its Lord.[98]
Now, behold, [his foreknowledge] is kept in the treasury of his knowledge.
[Even] if its root is hidden,
the fruit which is in its bosom is not hidden.

98 God, as Lord of all, was able to give up or make quiescent his foreknowledge. Ephrem wishes to emphasize that God's lordship, or power of control, has the strength to overrule his usual relation to the created order.

PART III

Traditions of Pro-Nicene Christology

21

Tome to the Antiochenes 7

Introduction and Translation by Mark DelCogliano

INTRODUCTION

The so-called *Tome to the Antiochenes* was penned by Athanasius of Alexandria and others in connection with the Council of Alexandria in 362. It was sent to the Christians of Antioch to help reconcile two factions there with longstanding differences and rival bishops. The first group was the "Meletians," supporters of Meletius, who was consecrated bishop of Antioch in 361 with the support of Eudoxius, bishop of Constantinople. Meletius had had some association with the imperially backed Homoianism of the late 350s, but by 361 was seen as Homoiousian-leaning – the public expression of which views got him exiled soon after his consecration.[1] The other group was the "Eustathians," Nicene supporters of the long-dead Eustathius, who had been deposed as bishop of Antioch in 327. The leader of the Eustathians in the 360s was Paulinus, who was consecrated as bishop of Antioch by Lucifer of Cagliari in 361. Paulinus was supported by the bishop of Rome – and Athanasius himself – as the rightful bishop. Accordingly, the *Tome* was addressed to the Meletians, whom Athanasius viewed as once tainted by Arianism but, as Homoians leaning toward Homoiousianism, potential allies for the Nicene cause.

While the bulk of the *Tome* is spent making a case for reconciliation between the factions, particularly in regard to the terminology used to speak about the Trinity, in section 7 it notes the harmony of the two parties with regard to Christological issues and then proceeds to summarize those agreements while at the same time mentioning several rejected viewpoints. This section of the *Tome*, therefore, offers a precious snapshot of the Christological issues under debate in 362; it is an extremely useful

1 This incident is mentioned in Fragments 16 and 17 of Theodore of Mopsuestia's *On the Incarnation*, translated in this volume on pp. 433–436.

point of comparison and contrast with Athanasius's Christological letters.[2] Like those letters, it affirms that the Word did not indwell Christ in the same manner that he dwelt in the prophets, but really became a human being, taking flesh from Mary, for the redemption and salvation of humanity, emphasizing that that salvation is of the whole human being, body and soul. Furthermore, it stresses the personal unity of the incarnate Word against any division of Christ's humanity and divinity into separately acting and experiencing agents. The *Tome* also confirms that the humanity assumed by the Word consists of body, soul, sense, and mind, a point not explicitly made in Athanasius's Christological letters but something which later became a routine anti-Apollinarian assertion.

The translation of this excerpt from the *Tome to the Antiochenes* is based on the edition of Hanns Christof Brennecke, Annette von Stockhausen, Christian Müller, Uta Heil, and Angelika Wintjes, *Athanasius Werke. Band III/Teil 1: Dokumente zur Geschichte des arianischen Streites. Lieferung 4: Bis zur Synode von Alexandrien 362* (Berlin: De Gruyter, 2014), 600–602.

TRANSLATION

7. But also, since some of them appeared to be in conflict with one another over the Savior's economy in the flesh, we questioned both parties, and what the one confessed, the other agreed to as well, namely, that it was not in the same manner by which "the Word came to the prophets"[3] that he also dwelled in a holy human being "at the end of the ages,"[4] but that "the Word himself became flesh,"[5] and though "in the form of God" the Son assumed "the form of a slave,"[6] and from Mary that which is according to the flesh was begotten as a human being for our sake, and thus the human race, being completely and wholly liberated from sin[7] in him and given life from the dead,[8] is brought into the kingdom of heaven. For they also confessed that the Savior had a body that was neither without a soul, nor without sense, nor without a mind.[9] For it would be impossible, after the Lord became a human being for our sake, for his body to be without

2 Translated in this volume on pp. 276–300. 3 See Jer 1:4, etc.
4 Heb 9:26. 5 John 1:14. 6 Phil 2:6. 7 See Rom 6:18.
8 See 1 Cor 15:22.
9 In Greek, *ou sōma apsychon oude anaisthēton oude anoēton*. The last two adjectives typically mean "imperceptible" and "unintelligible," but here they are used to deny that the body assumed by the Savior is unable to perceive and know.

a mind.[10] Nor was the salvation effected in the Word himself only of the body, but it was also of the soul. And truly being Son of God, he became also Son of Man, and being the only-begotten Son of God, the same also became "firstborn among many brothers."[11] Therefore, there is not one who was Son of God before Abraham and another who was that after Abraham.[12] Nor was there one who raised up Lazarus and another who asked about him, but it was the same one who humanly asks where Lazarus is laid and who divinely raised him up.[13] And it was the same one who bodily as a human being spat and who divinely as Son of God opened the eyes of the man blind from birth.[14] And [it was the same one] who suffered in the flesh, as Peter said,[15] and divinely opened the tombs and raised the dead.[16] For all these reasons, then, understanding everything in the gospel in this manner, they affirmed that they held the same opinion about the incarnation and humanification of the Word.

10 In Greek, *anoēton*. See the previous note. 11 Rom 8:29.
12 See John 8:58. 13 See John 11:34 and 11:43. 14 See John 9:1–11.
15 See 1 Pet 4:1. 16 See Matt 27:52–54.

22

Athanasius of Alexandria, *Christological Letters to Epictetus, Adelphius, and Maximus*

Introduction and Translation by Mark DelCogliano

INTRODUCTION

Athanasius was bishop of Alexandria on and off for nearly fifty years, from his contested election in 328 until his death in 373. He is perhaps best known for the unflinching promotion of a theology which he claimed represented the traditional Christian viewpoints articulated at the Council of Nicaea, against Trinitarian heterodoxies he connected with Arius and those supposedly influenced by him. Various emperors irked by his ecclesio-political efforts deposed Athanasius from his see no fewer than five times, causing him to spend many years in exile. Though Athanasius is most famous for his defense of the Nicene doctrine of the Trinity, Christological concerns were never far from his mind and some works of his, or at least sections thereof, are even specifically Christological in focus. For example, *On the Incarnation* (composed ca. 328–335) is a meditation on the person of Christ and soteriology, arguing that the salvation of humanity could only be achieved through the fully divine Word becoming incarnate, whereas his *Oration against the Arians* 3.26–58 (early 340s) defends the reality of the incarnation of the Word against "Arian" scriptural arguments against it. Another document of Athanasius with a Christological focus is section 7 of the so-called *Tome to the Antiochenes* issued by the Council of Alexandria in 362 under the presidency of Athanasius.[1] The Christological teachings endorsed and rejected in this section of the *Tome* have some parallels with those endorsed and rejected by Athanasius in the three Christological letters translated here.

The three Christological letters to Epictetus, Adelphius, and Maximus (traditionally numbered 59, 60, and 61 in Athanasius's epistolary corpus)

1 Translated in this volume on pp. 273–275.

are his responses to their reports of Christological aberration. We know very little about his correspondents. Epictetus the bishop of Corinth is known only through this letter. Some have identified Maximus the philosopher with the Cynic Maximus of Alexandria, but this is quite uncertain. Adelphius, the bishop of Onuphis in the Nile Delta, was exiled during the episcopacy of George of Cappadocia in Alexandria (356–361), and was also a signatory of the *Tome to the Antiochenes* in 362.

In these three letters Athanasius confronts a range of Christological views. In *Letter to Epictetus* 2 he lists eleven teachings about the incarnation reported to him that he takes to be mistaken, most of which he refutes in the remainder of the letter:

1. The Word's body is same-in-substance with the Word.
2. The Word abandoned his own nature and transformed himself into flesh.
3. The Word only appeared to have a human body.
4. The Word himself and not his body was the subject of Christ's sufferings.
5. The Word's passible body comes from his own substance, not from Mary.
6. If Christ's body were from Mary and not same-in-substance with the Word, then the Trinity becomes a Quaternity.
7. The Lord's body is co-eternal with the Word, having its origin in the substance of Wisdom.
8. The Lord is not both Son of God by nature and human flesh.
9. The Christ who suffered and died is not to be identified with the Son of God.
10. The Word came to Jesus as he came upon one of the prophets.
11. The Son is one and the Word is another.

As some of these positions are inconsistent with others, it seems likely that Athanasius is dealing with a hodgepodge of Christological views rather than a cohesive Christological system. In the other two letters Athanasius does not provide such a list of specific positions to be refuted, but rebuts teachings such as that Christ was a mere human being or that the Word only appeared to become a human being.

It is difficult to connect the reported views with clearly identifiable groups. In his Trinitarian writings, Athanasius generally called all his opponents "Arians" and "Ariomaniacs," regardless of their differences, as if they were all somehow indebted to Arius, whose teachings had been anathematized by the Council of Nicaea in 325. The three Christological letters contain a similar anti-Arian rhetoric, and it is quite possible that some of the Christological ideas that Athanasius refutes in these letters reflect currents in "Arian" theology. Some of these views later became associated with Apollinarianism, such as the idea that Christ's body was eternal. Engaging in a well-worn polemical tactic, Athanasius connects some of the Christological views reported to him with "classic" heretics: Valentinus, Marcion, Manichaeus, and Paul of Samosata, thought to be espousers of such views as docetism and the division of Christ's humanity and divinity into separately acting and experiencing agents.

In response to these Christological aberrations, Athanasius affirms that at the end of the ages the divine Word became incarnate without any change to his divine properties. He repeatedly emphasizes the single subjectivity of the incarnate Word (though he lacks precise technical language for this), insisting that the humanity, its properties, and its experiences *belong to* the Word, making them his own. The Word acts and experiences in a twofold manner, divinely and humanly, and yet he remains a single individual. In the end, the incarnation for Athanasius is God's coming in the flesh for the purposes of redemption, salvation, and deification.

These three letters are usually thought to have been written in close proximity and are traditionally dated to 370–371, often on the presumption that they are responding to Apollinarianism; connecting the synods mentioned in the letter to Epictetus (1.2) with synods held in this timeframe, as some scholars have done, supports that dating. The editors of the new edition of these letters, on which this translation is based, continue this line of reasoning and date all three letters to 372. But if Apollinarianism is not the target in these letters – and it is possible that it is not – then the question of dating is thrown wide open. For example, long ago a case was made for dating the letters to 360–361.[2] Yet it is perhaps best not to be so precise when there is hardly any internal or external evidence that would make any such narrow dating conclusive. Since Gaius is connected with Ursacius and Valens starting only in the very late 350s, as he is in the letter to Epictetus (1.2), all we can say with confidence is that these letters were composed by Athanasius between ca. 360 and his death in 374. Even without such

2 Charles E. Raven, *Apollinarianism: An Essay on the Christology of the Early Church* (Cambridge: Cambridge University Press, 1923), 103–108.

precise dates as have often been proposed, these letters remain the product of Athanasius's mature Christological thinking.

Of these three letters, the *Letter to Epictetus*, the longest, enjoyed a storied reception as an authoritative Christological statement. Only a few decisive examples need be mentioned here. Apollinarius himself, no doubt soon after the letter was written, mentions it approvingly in a letter to Serapion.[3] But in 377 it was quoted in full by Epiphanius of Salamis in his refutation of Apollinarianism (*Panarion* 77.3–13), launching its anti-Apollinarian use. The letter was also viewed as anti-Nestorian. Two extracts from it were included in the anti-Nestorian florilegium read out at the Council of Ephesus.[4] A translation of the letter was also included in the Latin acts of this council.[5] Cyril of Alexandria appealed to the letter numerous times for the same reason, and he reports that the Nestorians falsified the text to gain it for their side.[6] At the same time, Cyril's opponents also thought the letter supported their cause, presumably because they suspected Cyril of being an Apollinarian.[7] The Council of Chalcedon also pointed to the *Letter to Epictetus* as a confirmation of its own faith, alongside other Christological monuments such as Gregory of Nazianzus's *Letter* 101 *to Cledonius*.[8]

The edition on which the translations of the three letters are based is Kyriakos Savvidis and Dietmar Wyrwa, *Athanasius Werke. Band I/Teil 1: Die Dogmatischen Schriften. Lieferung 5: Epistulae Dogmaticae Minores* (Berlin: De Gruyter, 2016).

TRANSLATION

Epistle of Athanasius to Epictetus, Bishop of Corinth

1, 1. I myself thought that all foolish talk of all heretics, however many there may be, had been brought to a halt by the synod held at Nicaea. For the faith confessed there by the fathers in accordance with the divine scriptures is sufficient in itself for the overthrow of all impiety and for

3 Fragment 159, translated in this volume on p. 317.

4 ACO 1.1.2: 40, 15–31 Schwartz.

5 ACO 1.5.2: 321–334 Schwartz.

6 See *Letters* 39.8 (the *Letter of Reunion to John of Antioch*, translated in this volume on pp. 718–725), 40.25, 44.8, and 45.14 (the *First Letter to Succensus*, translated in this volume on pp. 731–739).

7 *Letter of John of Antioch and the Easterners to Cyril* (ACO 1.1.7: 146 Schwartz).

8 See the *Address to Marcian* (ACO 2.1.3: 472 Schwartz), translated in CEECW 4 on pp. 97–103.

the establishment of the pious faith in Christ. 2. For this reason, then, quite recently at the various synods held both in Gaul and Spain, and in Great Rome,[9] all those assembled, as if moved by one spirit, unanimously anathematized those who still harbor and entertain the opinions of Arius – namely, Auxentius in Milan,[10] and Ursacius, Valens, and Gaius from Pannonia.[11] And they wrote everywhere that, because men like these were thinking up names of synods to cite on their behalf, no synod is to be cited as an authority in the catholic church except only that one held in Nicaea, being as it is a monument to victory over every heresy and especially over the Arian one. For it was especially because of this heresy that that synod assembled long ago. 3. After so much time, then, how can some still be attempting to raise doubts and questions? If they are from among the Arians, it is no wonder if they criticize what[12] was written against them, just as the Greeks, when they hear, "The idols of the nations are silver and gold, the works of human hands,"[13] think that the teaching about the divine cross is foolishness.[14] But if these people who want to destroy everything by raising questions are from among those who seem to believe rightly and love what has been set forth by the fathers, they are doing nothing other than, as scripture puts it, "giving their neighbor turbid confusion to drink,"[15] and engaging in argumentativeness to no useful end but only to the ruin of the simple.

2, 1. I'm writing this letter after reading the memorandum drawn up by Your Godliness. It ought not to have been written at all, so that no record at all of such things would remain for posterity. For who has ever yet heard such things? Who has taught or learned them? "For out of Zion shall go forth a law of God and a word of the Lord from Jerusalem,"[16] but where do these ideas come from? 2. What infernal pit has spewed forth the claim

9 It is not clear precisely to which synods Athanasius refers.

10 Anti-Nicene bishop of Milan from 355 to 374.

11 Ursacius, bishop of Singidunum (modern-day Belgrade in Serbia), and Valens, bishop of Mursa (modern-day Osijek in Croatia), were active in the controversies of the era, starting with their opposition to Athanasius at the Council of Tyre in 335. While both supported Athanasius briefly in the late 340s, afterward they supported Emperor Constantius's anti-Nicene and anti-Athanasian efforts in the West. Gaius, of an unknown see in Illyria and about whom nothing more is known, was frequently, as here, linked with Ursacius and Valens from the late 350s onward.

12 Reading *ta* instead of *to*. 13 Ps 113:12(115:4). 14 See 1 Cor 1:23.

15 See Hab 2:15. 16 Isa 2:3.

that[17] (T1) "the body from Mary is same-in-substance with the divinity of the Word"? Or that (T2) "the Word has been changed into flesh, bones, hair, and the whole body, and that he was altered from his own proper nature"? Who has heard in church or from Christians in general that (T3) "the Lord wore his body putatively and not by nature?"[18] Or who has been so impious that he at the same time voices and entertains the opinion that (T4) "the divinity itself, which is same-in-substance with the Father, was circumcised and went from being perfect to imperfect, and that what was nailed on the wood was not the body but its Fashioner, the very substance of Wisdom?"[19] 3. And who, hearing that (T5) "the Word transformed for himself a passible body, not from Mary, but of his own substance," would say that anyone who speaks like that is a Christian? Who cooked up this abhorrent impiety so that it enters into his imagination even to claim that (T6) "whoever says the Lord's body is from Mary no longer holds that there is a Trinity in the divinity but a Quaternity"? Consequently, then, those with this frame of mind claim that "the flesh, which the Savior put on from Mary, is of the substance of the Trinity." 4. And again, on what basis do certain individuals spew forth an impiety on par with those already mentioned, so that they claim that (T7) "the body is not more recent than the divinity of the Word, but has always been co-eternal with it, since it has its origin in the substance of Wisdom"? How did these so-called Christians dare even to raise doubts over whether (T8) "the Lord who came forth from Mary is not only Son of God by substance and nature, but also 'from the seed of David according to the flesh,'[20] and of the flesh of the holy Mary"? Who then has become so daring that they claim that (T9) "the Christ who suffered and was crucified in the flesh is not the Lord, Savior, God, and Son of the Father"? Or how do they wish to be called

17 In this section it is possible that Athanasius is quoting the words of his opponents, at least as reported by Epictetus, and so quotation marks are used (see also section 3.2 below). But this is not certain and he may simply be summarizing the Christological teachings Epictetus had told him about. The editors identify eleven distinct Christological "theses" described by Athanasius in this section, and these are indicated in the translation by a parenthetical "T" (to avoid confusion with section and subsection numbering) followed by the thesis number. This enumeration of the theses is an editorial insertion and is not found in the original text. The same identifiers are used in the translation below when Athanasius discusses one of these theses.

18 On wearing the body "putatively," see section 7.1 below.

19 In Greek, *autē ē dēmiourgos ousia tēs sophias*.

20 Rom 1:3.

Christians when they claim that (T10) "the Word has come into a holy human being as upon one of the prophets, and that in taking the body from Mary he himself did not become a human being, but that Christ is one and the Word of God is another, who was the Son of the Father before Mary and before the ages"? Or how can they be Christians when they claim that (T11) "the Son is one and the Word of God is another"?

3, 1. Such were the contents of your memorandum: though expressed in different ways, the sense and meaning of these statements is one and the same and tends toward impiety. Over such matters those who boast in the confession of the fathers at Nicaea were arguing and fighting with each other. But I marveled at how Your Godliness tolerated all this, and that you neither stopped them from saying such things nor set the pious faith before them, which would have led them to keep quiet, if they heeded it, or unmasked them as heretics, if they rejected it. For none of the previously mentioned things has ever been said or heard by Christians; rather, in every way such things are foreign to the apostolic teaching. 2. At any rate, for this reason, as I said, I have included what they said in my letter without any dissembling, so that anyone who merely hears such things may perceive their inherent disgracefulness and impiety. And even though it would be appropriate to denounce and fully expose the stupidity of those who think such things, nevertheless it would be a good idea to stop this letter here and to write nothing further. 3. For it is not appropriate to examine and waste time further investigating what has so clearly been shown to be detestable, since we don't want these matters to be considered unsettled by those who love to quarrel. Or it is enough only to answer this in reply to these things and say: such ideas do not belong to the catholic church, nor did the fathers hold such opinions. But lest these "inventors of evil"[21] take from our complete silence a shameless pretext for their agenda, it is a good idea to bring up a few points from the divine scriptures, in case they may in this way pay them some respect and cease from these disgusting ideas.

4, 1. From where did it occur to you, gentlemen, to claim that (T5) the body is same-in-substance with the divinity of the Word? It's a good idea indeed to start with this point, so that, once this claim has been shown to be unsound, all the rest too can be shown to be the same. So then, we get nothing like this from the divine scriptures, for they say that God came in a *human* body. But also the fathers who assembled at Nicaea stated that

21 Rom 1:30.

the Son himself, not the body, is "same-in-substance with the Father," and while he is "from the substance of the Father," they also confessed in accordance with the scriptures that the body is from Mary.[22] 2. So, either deny the synod at Nicaea and smuggle in your ideas like heretics, or, if you wish to be children of the fathers, do not entertain opinions that are contrary to what they themselves wrote. And in fact, you can perceive the absurdity that results from your claim: If the Word is same-in-substance with the body whose nature is from earth,[23] yet the Word is same-in-substance with the Father according to the confession of the fathers, then the Father himself too will be same-in-substance with the body from earth. 3. And why would you still criticize the Arians for calling the Son a creature, when you yourselves say that even the Father is same-in-substance with creatures, and then, switching to another form of impiety, you assert that (T2) the Word has been changed into flesh, bones, hair, sinews, and the whole body, and that he was altered from his own proper nature? It's really time for you to declare openly that he has come into being out of earth! For the nature of the bones and the whole body is from earth. 4. What then is this great madness of yours, that you fight even with one another? For in saying that the Word is same-in-substance with the body, you are indicating one thing in relation to another, yet at the same time you are envisioning a change happening to the Word himself by his being transformed into flesh. And who will tolerate you after this even for merely uttering such things? For you have sunk further into impiety than every heresy. For if the Word is same-in-substance with the body, the mention of Mary and the need for her would be superfluous, since the body could have existed before Mary eternally, just as the Word himself also exists – if, that is, he is, as you say, same-in-substance with the body. 5. And what need would there have been even for the visitation of the Word, so that he could put on what was same-in-substance with himself or change from his own nature and become a body? For the divinity does not take hold of itself, so that it could put on what is same-in-substance with itself, any more than sins are committed by the Word, who redeemed the sins of all, so that, after changing himself into a body, he could offer sacrifice on his own behalf and redeem himself.

22 The Nicene Creed of 325 does not explicitly state that the incarnate Son's body is from Mary.

23 See Gen 2:7.

5, 1. But it is not so – absolutely not! For as the Apostle said, "he takes hold of the seed of Abraham, and for this reason he had to become like his brothers in every way"[24] and to take a body like ours. Accordingly, then, Mary is truly necessary,[25] so that he could take the body from her and offer it on our behalf as his own. And Isaiah pointed to her when he prophesied, saying, "Behold, the virgin!"[26] And also Gabriel is sent to her, not simply to a virgin, but "to a virgin betrothed to a man,"[27] so that he might show by Mary having a fiancé that she is truly a human being. And the scripture recounts that she "gave birth"[28] and says that she "wrapped him in swaddling clothes,"[29] and the breasts he suckled were called blessed.[30] And a sacrifice was offered because he who was born had "opened the womb."[31] 2. Now all these things were indications that a virgin gave birth, and Gabriel proclaimed this in no uncertain terms, saying to her not merely "that which is begotten" is *in you* (lest anyone think that a body entered into her from the outside), but rather saying that it is "*from you*," so that "that which is begotten" would be believed to be from her naturally.[32] For nature clearly shows that it is impossible for a virgin to produce milk unless she has given birth, and it is impossible for a body to be nursed on milk and wrapped in swaddling clothes unless it has already been born naturally. 3. This is what was circumcised when it was eight days old.[33] This is what Symeon "took up into his arms."[34] This is what became a boy, grew into a twelve-year-old,[35] and reached his thirtieth year.[36] For it is not, as some suppose, the very substance of the Word that was changed and circumcised, since it is inalterable and unchangeable. For the Savior himself said, "See me, that I am and I do not change,"[37] and Paul also writes, "Jesus Christ is the same yesterday and today and forever."[38] But in the body that was circumcised and carried, that ate and grew tired, that was nailed on the wood and suffered, there was the impassible and incorporeal Word of God. This is what was placed in the tomb, when he "went to preach to the spirits in prison," as Peter said.[39]

24 Heb 2:16–17. 25 In Greek, *upokeitai*, literally, "presupposed."
26 Isa 7:14. 27 Luke 1:27. 28 Luke 2:7. 29 Luke 2:7.
30 See Luke 11:27. 31 Luke 2:23.
32 See Luke 1:35. The phrase "from her" (in Greek, *ek sou*) is found only in some ancient manuscripts and is generally not considered original in modern critical editions of the Gospel of Luke.
33 See Luke 2:21. 34 Luke 2:28. 35 See Luke 2:42. 36 See Luke 3:23.
37 Mal 3:6. 38 Heb 13:8. 39 1 Pet 3:19.

6, 1. This in particular shows the stupidity of those who claim (T2) that the Word has been changed into bones and flesh. For if this had happened, there wouldn't have been any need for a tomb, since the body would have gone on its own to preach to the spirits in hell. But what really happened was that he himself went to preach, while "Joseph wrapped the body in a linen shroud and buried it" at Golgotha.[40] And it is shown to all that the body was not the Word, but that the body belonged to the Word. 2. And this is what Thomas handled when it had risen from the dead and he saw in it "the prints of the nails,"[41] which the Word himself endured, seeing them being nailed into his own body and though able to prevent it, he did not prevent it. Instead, as the body was his own, the incorporeal Word also appropriated the body's properties. When the body was struck by the servant, it was unquestionably he himself who said as he suffered, "Why do you strike *me*?"[42] 3. And though by nature unable to be touched, nonetheless he said, "I have given *my* back to scourges, and I did not turn away *my* face from spittings."[43] For whatever the human [body] of the Word suffered, the Word with the body attributed this to himself so that we ourselves might be enabled to partake in the divinity of the Word. And it was extraordinary that he himself both suffered and did not suffer: he suffered insofar as the body proper to him suffered and he was in it when it suffered, yet he did not suffer insofar as the Word, being God by nature, is impassible. And while he himself, the incorporeal, was in the body that suffered, the body had in itself the impassible Word doing away with the frailties of his body. 4. But he did this, and it happened thus, so that by taking what is ours and offering it in sacrifice, he might do away with it, and then by enveloping us with what is his, he might cause the Apostle to say, "This perishable nature must put on imperishability and this mortal nature must put on immortality."[44]

7, 1. Now this did not happen putatively,[45] as some again have supposed – absolutely not! But through the Savior having in reality and in truth become a human being, the salvation of the whole human being occurred. For if it is as they say, (T3) that the Word was in the body putatively, and anything said to be putatively is an illusion, then what is said to be the salvation and the resurrection of human beings will turn out to be only apparent, in the manner of the most impious Manichaeus. But without a doubt our salvation

40 Mark 15:46. 41 John 20:25. 42 John 18:23. 43 Isa 50:6.
44 1 Cor 15:53. 45 In Greek, *thesei*.

is not an illusion, nor is it of the body alone, but the salvation of the whole human being, soul and body, truly occurs in the Word himself. 2. What came from Mary according to the divine scriptures, then, was human by nature, and the body of the Savior was genuine. But it was genuine because it was identical with ours. For Mary is our sister inasmuch as we are all from Adam. And no one can doubt this if he remembers what Luke wrote. After his resurrection from the dead, when some thought that they were not seeing the Lord in the body from Mary but instead were beholding a ghost,[46] he said, "Look at my hands and my feet," and the prints of the nails, "that it is I myself. Handle me and see, for a ghost does not have flesh and bones as you see that I have. And when he had said this, he showed them his hands and his feet."[47] By these words those who have dared to claim that the Lord was changed into flesh and bones can once again be refuted. 3. For he did not say, "as you see that I *am* flesh and bones," but "that I *have* flesh and bones," so that it might not be thought that the Word himself was changed into these, but that he himself might be believed to possess them as much before his death as after his resurrection.

8, 1. Such being the case, it is superfluous to undertake any further demonstration of the other points and to delve into anything else about them because the body, in which the Word was, is not same-in-substance with the divinity but was truly born from Mary, and the Word himself was not changed into bones and flesh but came in the flesh. 2. For this is the meaning of what was said by John, "The Word became flesh,"[48] as can be discovered from a similar passage. For it is written by Paul, "Christ became a curse for us."[49] And just as he himself did not become a curse, but it is said that he became a curse insofar as he took on the curse for our sake, 3. so too he became flesh, not by being changed into flesh, but insofar as he assumed flesh for our sake and became a human being. And in fact saying, "The Word became flesh," is equivalent to saying, "The Word became a human being," in keeping with what is said in Joel, "I will pour out of my spirit on all flesh."[50] For this promise did not extend to irrational beings, but it is limited to human beings, for whose sake the Lord indeed became a human being. 4. With this text having this meaning, it makes sense that all will find themselves self-condemned for supposing that the flesh from Mary existed prior to her and that prior to her the Word had a human soul

46 In Greek, *pneuma*, or "spirit." 47 Luke 24:39–40. 48 John 1:14.
49 Gal 3:13. 50 Joel 2:28.

and that he existed in it always before his visitation. And moreover they will be stopped when they claim that the flesh is not receptive of death but is of an immortal nature. For if he did not die, how could Paul deliver to the Corinthians that which he had received, namely, "that Christ died for our sins in accordance with the scriptures"?[51] And how could he have been raised up at all, unless he first died? But they will blush greatly for even imagining at all that it is possible for there to be a Quaternity instead of a Trinity, if it should be said that the body is from Mary. For they claim (T6) that if we should say that the body is same-in-substance with the Word, the Trinity remains a Trinity, for in this case the Word adds nothing foreign to it, whereas if we should say that the body from Mary is human, it necessarily follows, since the body is foreign in substance and the Word is in it, that there is a Quaternity instead of a Trinity on account of the addition of the body.

9, 1. When they make such claims, they do not realize that they are contradicting themselves. For even though they claim (T5) that the body is not from Mary, but rather is same-in-substance with the Word, it can be proved by the logic of their own concepts that they endorse nothing less than the very thing they pretend to reject in hope that they won't be credited with their true opinion – namely, a Quaternity. 2. For just as the Son, who according to the fathers is same-in-substance with the Father, is not the Father himself, but the Son is called same-in-substance in relation to the Father, so too the body, which [they claim] is same-in-substance with the Word, is not the Word himself, but another in relation to the Word. But if it is another, then by their own lights their Trinity will be a Quaternity. For the true, really perfect, and indivisible Trinity is not receptive of addition, though this is what is imagined by them. 3. And how are they still Christians when they dream up another alongside the God that there is? Once again also in that other sophism of theirs it is possible to see their stupidity. If they suppose, because it is contained and stated in the scriptures that the body of the Savior is from Mary and human, that a Quaternity is posited instead of a Trinity, as if the body constitutes an addition, they are quite mistaken, as they put something made on par with its Maker and conjecture that the divinity can be receptive of an addition. And they fail to understand that the Word became flesh, not because of an addition

51 1 Cor 15:3.

to the divinity, but so that the flesh may rise again. Nor was it so that the Word might be improved that he came forth from Mary, but so that the human race might be redeemed. So then, how can they think that the body that was redeemed and given life[52] by the Word constitutes an addition to the divinity for the Word that had given it life? 4. On the contrary a magnificent addition came to the human body itself from the Word's communion and union with it. For from being mortal it became immortal,[53] and what was soulish became spiritual,[54] and though being from earth it passed through the heavenly gates. And yet the Trinity, even though the Word takes a body from Mary, remains a Trinity, since it is receptive of neither addition nor subtraction, but it is always perfect, and in the Trinity one divinity is recognized, and so in the church one God is proclaimed, the Father of the Word.

10, 1. For the same reason, then, those who once said (T8) that he who came forth from Mary is not himself Christ and Lord and God will keep silence from now on. For if he were not God in the body, how could he immediately after coming forth from Mary be called "Emmanuel, which means God with us"?[55] 2. And if he were not the Word in the flesh, why did Paul write to the Romans, "from whom according to the flesh comes the Christ, who is God over all blessed forever, Amen."[56] Therefore, let them confess that they were mistaken when in the past (T9) they denied that the Crucified was God, and let them be persuaded by the divine scriptures and especially by Thomas, who after seeing in him the prints of the nails cried out, "My Lord and my God!"[57] 3. For the Son, being God and "Lord of glory,"[58] was in the body that was disgracefully pierced by nails and dishonored. But while the body suffered by being pierced on the wood and there flowed from his side blood and water,[59] yet also, as it was the temple of the Word, it was full of the divinity. It must be for this reason, then, that the sun, seeing its own Fashioner[60] enduring in that mistreated body, retracted its rays and darkened the earth.[61] 4. But though the body itself had a mortal nature, surpassing its own nature it rose again on account of the Word in it, and ceased from its natural corruption, and, having put on the Word that surpasses any human being, it has become incorruptible.

52 See 1 Cor 15:22. 53 See 1 Cor 15:53–54. 54 See 1 Cor 15:44.
55 Matt 1:23. 56 Rom 9:5. 57 John 20:28. 58 1 Cor 2:8.
59 See John 19:34. 60 In Greek, *dēmiourgos*. 61 See Luke 23:44–45.

11, 1. But in regard to the delusion of some who claim (T10) that, just as he came upon each of the prophets, so too the Word came upon one particular human being from Mary, it is superfluous to delve into this, since their stupidity faces a clear condemnation. For if he came in this manner, why is he from a virgin? Why didn't he just come from a man and woman? 2. In fact, that's how each of the saints was born. Or if the Word came in this manner, why isn't the death of each prophet said to have occurred on our behalf, but only his death is? And if the Word visited each of the prophets individually, why is it said only in the case of the one from Mary that he visited "once for all at the end of the age"?[62] 3. Or if he came just as he came in the saints of the past, why did all the others die without as yet rising again, whereas only the one from Mary rose again after three days? Or if the Word came in a manner similar to the others, why is only the one from Mary called Emmanuel, as though the body born from her were full of divinity? For "Emmanuel" means "God with us."[63] 4. Or if he came in this manner, why, when each of the saints ate, drank, grew tired, and died, is it not said [in their case] that the Word himself ate, grew tired, and died, but this is said only in the case of the one from Mary? For the very things that this body suffered are said to belong to the Word who suffered them. And of all the others it is said only that they were born and begotten, but only in the case of the one from Mary it is said, "And the Word became flesh."[64]

12, 1. All this shows that, while the Word came to all the others for the purpose of prophesying, the Word himself took flesh to himself from Mary and came forth a human being. Though he is Word of God by nature and substance, he "descended from David according to the flesh"[65] and became a human being of the flesh of Mary, as Paul said. The Father made him known when he said both at the Jordan and on the mountain, "This is my beloved Son, in whom I am well pleased."[66] 2. While the Arians denied him, we ourselves acknowledge and worship him without dividing the Son and the Word but being fully aware that the Son is the Word himself, through whom all things came to be[67] and we ourselves have been redeemed. Therefore, we were quite shocked by how squabbling arose at all among you over these issues that are so clear. But thanks be to the Lord that however much it pained us to read your memorandum, the cessation of these matters has

62 Heb 9:26. 63 Matt 1:23. 64 John 1:14. 65 Rom 1:3.
66 Matt 3:17 and 17:5. 67 See John 1:3.

brought us as much joy. For they have departed with concord and made peace by the confession of the pious and orthodox faith.[68] 3. It was this, then, that persuaded me, after reflecting on the matter considerably, to write these few things, taking into account that my silence would bring pain instead of joy to those who have given us an occasion for rejoicing over this concord. So I ask Your Reverence above all and secondarily those who listen with good conscience to approve this letter, and if anything pertinent to piety is missing, set that right and let me know. 4. But if it is written neither worthily nor perfectly as if from one unskilled in speech, all should excuse our incompetence in speaking. Greet all the brothers with you; all with us greet you. Farewell in the Lord, my beloved whom I pine for most of all!

*

* *

Epistle of Athanasius to Adelphius, Bishop and Confessor, against Arians

1, 1. When we read the letter written by Your Godliness we truly approved your piety toward Christ. And we gave glory above all to God who has given you such great grace that not only do you have correct judgments, but also, as much as is possible, you are not ignorant of "the wiles of the devil."[69] But we were shocked by the wicked teaching of the heretics, seeing how they have fallen so deeply into a pit of impiety that they no longer keep their senses but have their thinking corrupted in every possible way. 2. But this attempt is not only a plot of the devil, but also an imitation of the disobedient Jews. For just as the Jews, when they were refuted on all sides, kept coming up with self-detrimental pretexts aimed only at denying the Lord and bringing what was prophesied upon themselves, in the same way too these people, seeing themselves held up to public scorn on all sides and realizing that their heresy had become repugnant to everybody, became "inventors of evil,"[70] so that, never ceasing to fight against the truth, they might truly remain "Christomachians" – fighters against Christ. 3. From where did this evil well up in them? How the heck have they dared to

68 It is unclear under what circumstances the letter carriers came over to the orthodox confession.

69 Eph 6:11. 70 Rom 1:30.

utter this novel blasphemy against the Savior? But whoever is impious, as it seems, is a wicked thing and in fact reprobate in regard to the faith.[71] For when they formerly denied the divinity of the only-begotten Son of God, they at least pretended to acknowledge his coming in the flesh. 4. But now, gradually descending lower and lower, they have fallen away even from this pretense and become atheists in every possible way, so that they neither acknowledge him as God nor believe that he became a human being. For if they believed this, they would not have uttered such things as Your Godliness has reported against them.

2, 1. As for you, then, my beloved for whom I pine most of all, you have done the appropriate thing with respect to the ecclesiastical tradition and piety toward the Lord by refuting, exhorting, and censuring such people. But since, provoked by their father the devil,[72] they "neither know nor understand," as scripture puts it, but "wander in darkness,"[73] let them learn from Your Reverence that their wicked teaching is such as belongs to Valentinus, Marcion, and Manichaeus. Some of these men introduced appearance in place of reality,[74] whereas others denied the fact that "the Word became flesh and dwelt among us"[75] by dividing what is indivisible. 2. Since they entertain the same opinions as these men, why haven't they also inherited their names? For it would make sense for them to have the names of those whose wicked beliefs they hold, so that from this point onward they should be called Valentinians, Marcionites, and Manichaeans. Perhaps thus they will be so ashamed by the stench of these names that they will be able to comprehend how deeply they have fallen into impiety. 3. And it would be right to respond to them no longer, in accordance with the Apostle's exhortation that says, "after a first and a second admonition, have nothing more to do with a heretic, knowing that such a person is perverted and sinful; he is self-condemned,"[76] and especially because of what the prophet says about such people: "The fool will speak folly, and his heart will devise vain things."[77] 4. But since like their leader they themselves also prowl around like lions seeking to devour someone innocent,[78] we feel compelled for this reason to write in reply to Your Reverence so that the brothers may

71 See 2 Tim 3:8. 72 See John 8:44. 73 Ps 81(82):5.

74 That is, introduced docetism. Valentinians, Marcionites, and Manichaeans were routinely considered by their opponents to have taught a docetic Christology; see Tertullian's *On the Flesh of Christ*, translated in this volume on pp. 144–172.

75 John 1:14. 76 Titus 3:10–11. 77 Isa 32:6. 78 See 1 Pet 5:8.

be once again tutored by Your Intelligence and comprehend even more the nonsense of these people.

3, 1. We do not worship a creature – absolutely not! For such an error belongs to the pagans and Arians, but we worship the Word of God, the Lord of creation, made incarnate. For even if this flesh on its own is part of the created world, nonetheless it has become God's body. And we neither divide the body as such from the Word and worship it by itself, nor when we wish to worship the Word do we set him at a great distance from the flesh, but knowing full well, as we said before, that "the Word became flesh,"[79] we acknowledge him as God come in flesh. 2. Who then is so clueless that he would say to the Lord, "Remove yourself from the body, that I may worship you"? Or who is so impious that on account of the body he would say along with the clueless Jews, "Why do you, a human being, make yourself God?"?[80] By no means was the leper such a person! For he worshiped the God who was in the body and recognized that he was God, saying, "Lord, if you will, you can make me clean."[81] 3. The flesh did not lead him to suppose that the Word of God was a creature, and the fact that the Word was the Fashioner of all creation did not prompt him to despise the flesh that [the Word] had put on, but he worshiped the Creator of the universe as in a created temple and was made clean. In the same way too the woman with the flow of blood believed and, having only touched the fringe [of his garment], was healed.[82] And the sea foaming with waves heard the incarnate Word and ended its storm,[83] whereas the man blind from birth was healed by the Word with the spittle of the flesh.[84] 4. And what is even greater and more extraordinary (for perhaps this even scandalized those most impious people), even when the Lord was hanging upon the cross itself (for it was his body and the Word was in it), the sun grew dark, the earth shook, rocks were split, the curtains of the temple were torn, and many bodies of those who had already fallen asleep rose again.[85]

4, 1. Now these things came to pass, and no one questioned, as the Arians dare to do now, whether one should believe in the *incarnate* Word, but even when they beheld the human being they acknowledged that he was their Fashioner. And when they heard the human voice, its humanness did not lead them to claim that the Word was a creature, but on the contrary they trembled and realized nothing less than that he was

79 John 1:14. 80 John 10:33. 81 Matt 8:2. 82 See Matt 9:20–22.
83 See Matt 8:26. 84 See John 9:1–12. 85 See Matt 27:51–52; Luke 23:45.

speaking from a holy temple. 2. So then, why aren't the impious afraid that, "since they did not see fit to acknowledge God, they have been given up to a base mind and to improper conduct"?[86] For creation does not worship a creature, nor again does it refuse on account of his flesh to worship its Lord but in his body it beheld its Fashioner. And "at the name of Jesus Christ every knee" bended and "will bend in heaven and on earth and under the earth, and every tongue will confess" – even if it doesn't seem right to the Arians – "that Jesus Christ is Lord, to the glory of God the Father."[87] 3. For the flesh did not transmit its ingloriousness to the Word – absolutely not! But rather the flesh was given glory from him. And though the Son was in the form of God when he assumed the form of a slave, he did not experience any diminishment of his divinity.[88] On the contrary, he himself became the liberator of all flesh and of all creation. 4. And if "God sent forth his Son born of a woman,"[89] this fact brings us no dishonor but instead good glory and great grace. For he became a human being, so that he might deify us in himself. And he came "of a woman"[90] and was born of a virgin, so that he might transfer to himself our sinful birth and we might become from that point forward "a holy race" and "sharers in the divine nature," as the blessed Peter wrote.[91] 5. "For God has done what the law, weakened by the flesh, could not do: by sending his own Son in the likeness of sinful flesh and to deal with sin, he condemned sin in the flesh."[92]

5, 1. Well then, in view of the flesh being assumed by the Word to liberate all human beings, resurrect all from the dead, and redeem all from sin, how can they not appear ungrateful and deserving of all hatred, when they despise the flesh or when on account of the flesh they accuse the Son of God of being something made or a creature? 2. For they practically cry out to God, saying, "Don't send your only-begotten Son in the flesh! Don't cause him to take flesh from the Virgin, lest he redeem us from death and sin! We don't want him to be in a body, lest he accept death on our behalf! We don't desire the Word to become flesh, lest in this flesh he becomes our mediator of access to you and we inhabit a heavenly dwelling-place! Let the gates of heaven be shut, lest your Word inaugurate a new way into heaven for us through the veil of his flesh!" 3. These are their declarations uttered with diabolical effrontery through the wicked teaching they

86 Rom 1:28. 87 Phil 2:10–11. 88 See Phil 2:6–7. 89 Gal 4:4.
90 Gal 4:4. 91 1 Pet 2:9; 2 Pet 1:4. 92 Rom 8:3.

have concocted. For those who do not want to worship the Word when he became flesh are ungrateful for his humanification, and those who divide the Word from the flesh do not think that the one redemption of sin has taken place, nor the one destruction of death. 4. Where the heck will these impious people find the flesh taken by the Savior to be alone by itself, so that they will dare to claim, "We ourselves do not worship the Lord with the flesh but we divide the Lord from the body and give reverence to him alone"? In fact, blessed Stephen saw the Lord standing at the right hand [of God] even in heaven,[93] and the angels said to the disciples, "he will come in the same way as you saw him go into heaven."[94] 5. And the Lord himself spoke in address to the Father, "I desire that, wherever I am, they also may always be with me."[95] And in sum, if the flesh is indivisible from the Word, isn't it necessary that [our opponents] either lay aside their error and from this point onward worship the Father in the name of our Lord Jesus Christ, or, if they neither worship nor adore the Word become flesh, be totally expelled [from the church] and be counted no longer as Christians but either as pagans or in league with the Jews?

6, 1. So then, such as we have described is the madness and audacity of these individuals. But our faith is correct: its starting point is the apostolic teaching and the tradition of the fathers, and it is confirmed by the New and Old Testaments. For the prophets say, "Send forth your Word and your Truth,"[96] and "'Behold, a virgin shall conceive and bear a son, and his name shall be called 'Emmanuel,' which means, God with us,"[97] What does this mean but that God has come in flesh? 2. And the apostolic tradition gives instruction not only when blessed Peter says, "Therefore, Christ suffered in the flesh on our behalf,"[98] but also when Paul writes, " … awaiting our blessed hope, the appearing of the glory of our great God and Savior Jesus Christ, who gave himself on our behalf to redeem us from every sin and to purify for himself a people of his own who are zealous for good deeds."[99] 3. How then has he given himself on our behalf unless it was by wearing flesh? For by offering his flesh he has given himself on our behalf, so that he might undertake death in this flesh and "destroy him who has the power of death, that is, the devil."[100] Therefore, we also always give thanks in the name of Jesus Christ, and we do not reject the grace that comes

93 See Acts 7:55. 94 Acts 1:11. 95 John 17:24, altered.
96 Ps 42(43):3, altered. 97 Matt 1:23, quoting Isa 7:14. 98 1 Pet 4:1.
99 Titus 2:13–14. 100 Heb 2:14.

to us through him. 4. For the Savior's coming in the flesh has become redemption from death and salvation of all creation. And so, my beloved for whom I pine most of all, if any love the Lord, let them ponder these remarks, but if any have imitated the manner of Judas and abandoned the Lord to join themselves with Caiaphas, let them be better educated by these remarks, assuming they want to, and assuming they are ashamed. And let them know that when we worship the Lord in flesh we do not worship a creature but rather, as we said before, the Creator who has put on the created body.

7, 1. What we wished Your Reverence to learn from them is this: when Israel was commanded to go up to Jerusalem to worship in the temple of the Lord, the place where the ark was and "above this the cherubim of glory overshadowing the mercy seat,"[101] did they act rightly or not? Well then, if they acted wrongly, how did those who had been neglectful of this law become liable to the penalty? For it is written, "If any despise [this law] and do not go up, he shall be exterminated from his people."[102] 2. But if they acted rightly, and thereby became acceptable to God, how are the repulsive Arians, who are the most disgraceful of any heresy, not deserving of destruction many times over? For even though they approve that ancient people for the honor they show to the temple, they choose not to worship the Lord who was in the flesh as in a temple. 3. And yet that ancient temple was built of stones and gold as a shadow,[103] but when the reality came, the type thereafter ceased and there remained, according to the Lord's utterance, not one stone upon another that was not thrown down.[104] And they did not, when they saw the temple made of stones, suppose that the Lord who spoke in the temple was a creature, nor did they despise the temple and go far away to worship; rather, entering the temple in accordance with the law, they adored the God who made pronouncements from the temple. 4. This being the case, how could the Lord's body not be worshiped, being as it is truly all-holy and all-sacred, and proclaimed by the archangel Gabriel, formed by the Holy Spirit, and made the garment of the Word? At any rate, the Word raised the woman sick with fever[105] by stretching out his bodily hand and he raised Lazarus from the dead by uttering a human voice.[106] 5. And again, by stretching

101 Heb 9:5. 102 See Lev 17:9; Num 9:13. 103 See Heb 8:5.
104 See Matt 24:2. 105 See Matt 8:14–15. 106 John 11:43.

out his hands upon the cross he cast down "the prince of the power of the air that is now at work in the sons of disobedience,"[107] and cleared our path into the heavens.

8, 1. Therefore, whoever dishonors the temple dishonors the Lord in the temple. And whoever divides the Word from the body rejects the grace given to us in it. And let those most impious Ariomaniacs not suppose that, because the body is created, the Word is also a creature, nor let them, because the Word is not a creature, revile his body. 2. Their wicked teaching is truly shocking in that they at the same time confuse and muddle everything and come up with pretexts aimed only at classifying the Creator with the creatures. But let them listen: if the Word were a creature, he would not have assumed the created body in order to give it life.[108] For what help would come to creatures from a creature that itself also needs salvation? 3. But being Creator, the Word himself became Fashioner of the creatures. For this reason, also at the end of the ages[109] he himself put on something created so that he himself as Creator might once again renew it and be able to recover it. Now a creature could never be saved by a creature, just as the creatures were not created by a creature – that is, if the Word were not Creator. 4. Accordingly, let [our opponents] not make false claims against the divine scriptures nor scandalize the simple brothers. But if they wish, let them repent and themselves no longer "worship the creation rather than God the Creator of all."[110] 5. However, if they should wish to stick to their impieties, let them gorge only themselves on them and let them gnash their teeth[111] like their father the devil,[112] because the faith of the catholic church knows that the Word of God is Creator and Fashioner of all things. 6. And we know that while "in the beginning was the Word and the Word was with God,"[113] yet also, now that he himself has become a human being "for our salvation,"[114] we worship him, not as if he had come to the body as equal to equal, but as Master assuming "the form of a slave,"[115] and as Fashioner and Creator coming in a creature, so that, liberating all things in it, he might bring the cosmos to the Father and reconcile all things, both those in heaven and those upon earth.[116] For in this way we recognize his paternal divinity and worship his presence in the flesh, even

107 Eph 2:2. 108 Perhaps an allusion to Rom 8:11 or 1 Cor 15:22.
109 See Heb 9:26. 110 Rom 1:25, altered. 111 See Mark 9:18.
112 See John 8:44. 113 John 1:1. 114 Nicene Creed. 115 Phil 2:7.
116 See Col 1:20.

if the Ariomaniacs burst themselves asunder.[117] 7. Greet all those who love our Lord Jesus Christ. We pray that you are doing well and remembering us to the Lord, my beloved whom I pine for most of all. If necessary, read this letter to Hieracas the presbyter.[118]

*

* *

Epistle of Athanasius to Maximus the Philosopher

1, 1. Athanasius sends greetings in the Lord to Maximus the philosopher, his beloved son for whom he truly pines most of all. Upon reading your recent letter I approved Your Reverence, but being utterly shocked by the recklessness of those who "understand neither what they are saying nor the things about which they make assertions,"[119] I had actually resolved to stay silent. In matters that are so clear and shine more brightly than light, replying does nothing other than to supply those who commit such outrages with pretexts for shamelessness. 2. And this we have learned from the Savior. For when Pilate had washed his hands[120] and acceded to the false accusations of the Jews of that time,[121] the Lord replied to him no more,[122] but instead he got Pilate's wife involved,[123] so that the one being judged might be believed to be God "not in word but in power."[124] Nor did the Lord reply to Caiaphas in response to his nonsense, and he himself brought everyone over to knowledge by [quoting] the promise.[125] 3. Accordingly, having delayed for a long time I have reluctantly honored your zeal for the truth, seeing the argumentativeness of these shameless people. And I have dictated nothing beyond the letter you wrote so that our adversary may finally be convinced on those matters he has disputed and stop his "tongue from evil and his lips from speaking deceit."[126] 4. And

117 Here Athanasius alludes to the purported manner of the death of Arius himself, first recounted in his *Letter to Serapion* 3, where the comparison of Arius's death to that of Judas related in Acts 1:18 is made clear.

118 Like Adelphius, Hieracas was also banished during the episcopacy of George of Cappadocia in Alexandria (356–361).

119 1 Tim 1:7. 120 See Matt 27:24. 121 See Matt 27:18.

122 See Matt 27:14.

123 See Matt 27:19. Athanasius interprets the dream Pilate's wife had as having been sent by the Lord.

124 1 Cor 4:20. 125 See Matt 26:63–64. 126 Ps 33(34):14.

these people must no longer join with the Jews of long ago who passed by[127] as they upbraided the one who hung upon the wood. But in case they are still not overcome with shame, you yourself must be mindful of the Apostle's precept, "after a first and a second admonition, have nothing more to do with a heretic, knowing that such a person is perverted and sinful; he is self-condemned."[128] 5. For if those who dare to say such things are Greeks or from among today's imitators of the Jews, let them, like Jews, think the cross of Christ a scandal or, like Greeks, think it foolishness.[129] But if they pretend to be Christians, let them learn that the crucified Christ is himself not only "Lord of glory"[130] but also "God's power and God's wisdom."[131]

2, 1. If they doubt that he is even God, let them defer to Thomas, who handled the Crucified and proclaimed that he was Lord and God.[132] Let them also fear the Lord himself, who said after he washed the feet of his disciples, "You call me Lord and Teacher; and you speak rightly, for so I am."[133] Now in the very same body in which he was when he washed their feet he also "bore our sins on the wood."[134] 2. Furthermore, he was witnessed to as Master of creation when he retracted the rays of the sun,[135] and the earth shook and rocks were split,[136] and the executioners recognized that the Crucified was truly Son of God.[137] For the body they saw was not that of some human being but of God; while in this body he raised the dead even when he was being crucified.[138] 3. Therefore, it's no good gamble on their part to claim (T10) that the Word of God came into a certain holy human being, since precisely the same thing happened in each of the prophets and the other saints, and any suggestion that he was begotten and died over and over again in each of them should be avoided. 4. But it is not so – absolutely not! Instead, it is the same "the Word" who "became flesh"[139] "once for all at the end of the age to put away sin,"[140] and came forth from the Virgin Mary as a human being in our likeness, who also said to the Jews, "Why are you seeking to kill me, a human being who has told you the truth?"[141] We are deified not by partaking of the body of some human being, but by receiving the body of the Word himself.

3, 1. By this too I am quite shocked: how the heck have they dared even to imagine that the Word became a human being in a way consistent with

127 See Matt 27:39. 128 Titus 3:10–11. 129 See 1 Cor 1:23.
130 1 Cor 2:8. 131 1 Cor 1:24. 132 See John 20:28. 133 John 13:13.
134 1 Pet 2:24. 135 See Luke 23:45. 136 See Matt 27:51.
137 See Matt 27:54. 138 See Matt 27:52–54. 139 John 1:14.
140 Heb 9:26. 141 John 8:40.

nature? For if that were so, the mention of Mary would be superfluous. For nature knows nothing of a virgin giving birth without a man. Therefore, by the good pleasure of the Father, he who is "true God"[142] and the Word and Wisdom of the Father by nature became a human being "bodily"[143] "for our salvation,"[144] so that, having something to offer on our behalf, he might save us all, "who through fear of death were subject to lifelong bondage."[145] 2. For it was not just some human being who gave himself on our behalf, since every human being is liable to death, according to what was said to all in Adam, "you are earth and to earth you will depart."[146] Neither was it any other of the creatures, since all creation is prone to change. Rather, it was the Word himself who offered his own body on our behalf, that our faith and hope might not be in a human being,[147] but that we might have our faith be in God the Word himself. 3. Now that he has become a human being, we indeed contemplate "his glory, glory as of the only-begotten from the Father, full of grace and truth."[148] For what he endured by means of the body he exalted as God: though in the flesh he was hungry,[149] he also fed the hungry divinely.[150] And if anyone is scandalized by reason of his bodily experiences, let him believe by reason of what he did as God. 4. For humanly he asks where Lazarus is laid but divinely he raises him.[151] Therefore, let none laugh, calling him a "child"[152] and citing his "stature,"[153] growing, eating, drinking, and suffering, lest while denying what is proper to his body he will completely deny too his visitation for our sake. And just as he did not become a human being in a way consistent with nature, so too it was consistent that when he took the body he showed what was proper to it, lest the delusion of the godless Manichaeus prevail. Again, it was consistent that when he went about bodily he did not hide what was proper to the divinity, lest the Samosatene[154] find an excuse to call him a human being, as if another alongside God the Word.

4, 1. Well then, now that the unbeliever comprehends these matters, let him learn that while he was a babe in a manger,[155] he also subjected the magi and was worshiped by them.[156] And while he went down into Egypt

142 Nicene Creed. 143 Col 2:9. 144 Nicene Creed. 145 Heb 2:15.
146 Gen 3:19. 147 See Jer 17:5; Ps 117(118):8. 148 John 1:14, altered.
149 See Matt 21:18; Luke 4:2. 150 See Matt 14:20, 15:37.
151 See John 11:34 and 11:43. 152 Luke 2:40. 153 Luke 2:52.
154 Paul of Samosata, bishop of Antioch 260–268, was deposed for Christological heresy; see his *Selected Fragments*, translated in this volume on pp. 197–211.
155 See Luke 2:16. 156 See Matt 2:11.

as a child,[157] he also incapacitated the handmade objects of the idolatry there.[158] And while crucified in the flesh, he raised the dead long moldering.[159] 2. It has been demonstrated to everyone that he endured all these things not for his own sake, but for ours, so that we ourselves might put on impassibility and incorruptibility through his sufferings[160] and persevere unto everlasting life.

5, 1. So then, I have dictated these remarks to you concisely, following, as I said above, the lines of your own letter, without elaborating any further point but only mentioning what relates to the divine cross, so that these despisers may become better educated in the matters by which they were scandalized and worship the Crucified. 2. But as for you, persuade the unbelievers with all sincerity. Perhaps somehow they may come from ignorance to knowledge and believe rightly. And even if the letter you wrote is sufficient, nonetheless it is good to have added these remarks for these contentious individuals by way of reminder, not so much to refute them and make them feel ashamed of their brazen statements as to remind them so that they don't forget the truth. 3. Let what was confessed by the fathers at Nicaea reign supreme. For it is correct and sufficient to overthrow every most impious heresy, and especially that of the Arians, which blasphemed against the Word of God and consequently spoke impiously against his Holy Spirit. Greet all who entertain correct opinions. All with us greet you.

157 See Matt 2:14. 158 Perhaps a reference to Isa 19:1.
159 See Matt 27:52–53. 160 See 1 Cor 15:53.

23

Apollinarius of Laodicea, *Recapitulation*

Introduction and Translation by Mark DelCogliano

INTRODUCTION

Apollinarius was born ca. 310–315 at Laodicea in Syria. He was the son of an Alexandrian native, also named Apollinarius, who was a grammarian by profession. The elder Apollinarius came to Laodicea to serve the church as a presbyter, and eventually the younger Apollinarius served the same church as a reader. At some point between 328 and 335 both father and son were excommunicated by their bishop, Theodotus of Laodicea, who was a member of the Eusebian alliance and a supporter of Arius, for listening against Christian custom to the recitation of a pagan hymn. Both were soon, however, readmitted to communion after the appropriate penance. In 346 Apollinarius was again excommunicated, this time by the new Laodicean bishop, George, another member of the Eusebian alliance (and later a guiding spirit of the Homoiousian movement), for meeting with Athanasius of Alexandria. It is unclear, however, whether the sentence could be or ever was put into effect. It was probably at this point that Apollinarius and the Alexandrian bishop began a lifelong friendship and sharing of theological sympathies. At some point Apollinarius embarked upon a career as a teacher of rhetoric, but in 362 he was forced to discontinue this profession as a result of anti-Christian legislation by the emperor Julian. Around 360, shortly after the death of George of Laodicea, in unclear circumstances Apollinarius was elected bishop of the pro-Nicene community in Laodicea, alongside a rival, Pelagius, who led the Homoians. This thrust Apollinarius into greater prominence, and if Basil of Caesarea's correspondence with Apollinarius is genuine, in which the young Cappadocian regards the Laodicean as an expert in pro-Nicene theology, it would date to around this time. Eventually Apollinarius shifted his sphere of activity to Antioch, where by the 370s he had established himself as a Christian teacher, and one of his students for a time was Jerome. As a testament to his early involvement in the affairs of the Antiochene church, in 362 Apollinarius sent representatives to the Council of Alexandria that produced the *Tome to the Antiochenes.*[1] From the early 360s onward Apollinarius was recognized as a key pro-Nicene thinker, allied not only with Athanasius but also with Damasus of Rome and Basil of Caesarea.

A prolific writer, Apollinarius authored numerous works, including epistles, theological treatises, biblical commentaries, and apologetic works against the Neoplatonist Porphyry and Emperor Julian, and polemical works against Marcellus of Ancyra, Eunomius of Cyzicus, and the Manichaeans. In time, however, in spite of his pro-Nicene bona fides, some begin to suspect Apollinarius of unorthodox Christology. Around 377 at Rome, at a synod presided over by Damasus of Rome, Apollinarius's Christological teachings – albeit as taught by his disciples – were explicitly censured, a censure that was repeated and affirmed at Antioch in 379, at Constantinople in 381, and at Rome and Constantinople in 382. In the same period Apollinarius and his disciples started to set up schismatic Apollinarist hierarchies rival to those of the Nicene communities. In the early 380s Gregory of Nazianzus wrote his celebrated *Letter* 101 *to Cledonius* against Apollinarius,[2] and Gregory of Nyssa wrote a short letter against the Apollinarians to Theophilus of Alexandria as well as the *Antirrheticus*, a lengthy point-by-point refutation of Apollinarius's *Apodeixis* or *Demonstration of the Divine Enfleshment according to the Likeness of a Human Being.*[3] Furthermore, an intervention of Gregory of Nazianzus eventually led the imperial administration to issue anti-Apollinarist decrees in 387. Apollinarius died ca. 392, and the Apollinarist hierarchy he had worked to establish lingered on for a few decades before disappearing. Because of his condemnation, only a handful of Apollinarius's works have survived intact, often pseudepigraphically under such names as Gregory Thaumaturgus, Julius of Rome, and Athanasius himself. Numerous fragments are also extant, preserved in later polemical tracts.

Later generations regarded Apollinarian Christology as an extreme heresy to be avoided, and its threat, seemingly ever-present, cast a shadow

1 Translated in this volume on pp. 273–275.
2 Translated in this volume on pp. 388–398.
3 Both these writings of Gregory of Nyssa are translated in Robin Orton, *St. Gregory of Nyssa: Anti-Apollinarian Writings*, FOTC 131 (Washington, DC: Catholic University of America Press, 2015).

over all subsequent Christological debate. Apollinarius himself, however, had worked out his Christology within a pro-Nicene framework. He stressed the absolute unity of divinity and humanity in Christ, whom he called one person (*prosōpon*), one hypostasis, and "one incarnate nature of God the Word." The last expression was for a time favored by Cyril of Alexandria, mistakenly believing that Athanasius was its source, and thus Apollinarius came to be viewed as a precursor of the miaphysite Christology supported by later anti-Chalcedonians. Intending to avoid any dualistic subjectivity in Christ, he conceptualized the incarnation as the Word assuming human flesh or a human body through an integrative union and thus eliminated the humanity's rational soul from the Christological compound, with the Word effectively taking the place of Christ's human power of self-determination. His opponents seized on this precise point as the chief defect of his teaching. Because Apollinarius so emphasized the identity of the Word and Jesus, he formulated a robust doctrine of *communicatio idiomatum* that permitted him, for example, to speak of Christ's flesh as "heavenly" and same-in-substance with God precisely on account of the union. But this led his opponents to accuse Apollinarius of teaching that the flesh of Jesus had descended from heaven, even though Apollinarius himself denied it. The translations presented in this volume allow us to hear Apollinarius speaking in his own voice, his views for the most part set within their own argumentative context and not subjected to the polemical conjectures and distortions of his opponents.

A good overview of Apollinarius's Christological thinking is found in the work commonly called the *Recapitulation*, whose title in Greek, *Anakephalaiōsis*, can also mean "summary." This work is a series of syllogisms that collectively sketch out the contours of his Christology. The syllogisms frequently take as their starting points scriptural affirmations about Christ. It is not a systematic presentation but rather an almost dialectical attempt to synthesize the two main ways in which Apollinarius conceived of Christ – as a composite or mixture of divine and human, and as the divine assumption of human flesh. Yet in each case the result is a single entity. The first fourteen syllogisms demonstrate that "Christ is not a human being," and the remaining syllogisms prove that the one and the same individual is both God and human being. The text itself provides no clues about its literary, polemical, or historical context, so Apollinarius could have produced it at any point during his career. That he wrote a "summary" of his Christological views probably indicates that the text originated in a context where Apollinarius felt his views were misunderstood or maligned, and this might point to a period of composition between the mid-370s and early 380s, but any attempt to secure a more precise dating based on this would be ultimately too speculative. And so, in spite of its unclear date and context, the *Recapitulation* provides an excellent introduction to some of the main themes of Apollinarius's Christology.

This translation is based on the critical edition established by Hans Lietzmann, *Apollinaris von Laodicea und seine Schule: Texte und Untersuchungen* (Tübingen: Mohr, 1904), 242–246.

TRANSLATION

1. When God worked in a human being, the result was a prophet or an apostle, not "the Savior of the world." However, Christ is "the Savior of the world."[4] Therefore, when God worked in a human being, the result was not Christ.

2. Every human being is part of the world, and no part of the world "takes away the sin of the world"[5] to which it is subject. However, Christ takes it away. Therefore, Christ is not a human being.

3. Every human being is subject to death, and no one who is subject to death destroys death. However, Christ destroys it.[6] Therefore, Christ is not a human being.

4. Every human being is of earth. However, Christ is not of earth but of heaven.[7] Therefore, Christ is not a human being, unless the term "human being" is being used homonymously.[8]

5. He who gives "the power to become children of God"[9] did not also himself become [one]. However, Christ gives it. Therefore, he did not become Son but is so by nature.

6. No human being exists before his elders. However, Christ exists before his elders in the flesh.[10] Therefore, he is not a human being, except according to the flesh.

7. No human being has glory before the ages. However, Christ has it.[11] Therefore, Christ is not a human being.

8. If God is in Jesus, it is not the case that all things exist through him; rather, they exist because of the one in him. However, all things are through

4 John 4:42. 5 John 1:29. 6 See 1 Cor 15:26. 7 See 1 Cor 15:47–49.
8 That is, unless the term "human being" means one thing when applied to Christ and something else when applied to human beings.
9 John 1:12. 10 See John 8:58. 11 See John 17:5.

him.[12] Therefore, it is not the case that God is in Jesus but that he himself is God.

9. He who saves from sin is above sin and it is Christ who saves from it.[13] However, no human being is above sin. Therefore, Christ is not a human being.

10. Every human being has discord between flesh and mind.[14] However, Christ does not have it. Therefore, Christ is not a human being.

11. Every human being mortifies the flesh in order to be perfected in virtue.[15] However, Christ does not. Therefore, Christ is not a human being.

12. No human being's flesh has been said to be from heaven. However, Christ's flesh is said to be from heaven.[16] Therefore, Christ is not a human being, according to the divinity which assumed the flesh. In this way, then, he is also said to be from heaven because he was united with the one from heaven.

13. No human being gives life, for none is Christ. However, Christ gives life.[17] Therefore, Christ is not a human being.

14. "The name which is above every name"[18] and "the glory of the only God"[19] are not applicable to any human being. However, they are applicable to Christ. Therefore, Christ is not a human being.

15. If God dwelled in a human being, he was not emptied. However, he who was in the form of God was emptied when he took the form of the slave.[20] Therefore, he did not dwell in a human being.

16. God dwelling in a human being is not a human being. Rather, a human being is spirit united to flesh. Christ is a human being, as has been said, homonymously. Therefore, he is divine spirit united to flesh.

17. It belongs to a human being to be raised from the dead, whereas it belongs to God to do the raising. However, Christ did both. Therefore, the same one is God and a human being.

18. If Christ were only a human being or if he were only God, he would not be the mediator between God and human beings.[21]

19. If Christ were only a human being, he would not have saved the world, and if he were only God, he would not have saved it through suffering. However, Christ did both. Therefore, he is both God and a human being.

20. If Christ were only a human being, he would not have given life to the dead, and if he were only God, he would not have given life to some of

12 See 1 Cor 8:6. 13 See Matt 1:21. 14 See Rom 8:23. 15 See Col 3:5. 16 See John 3:13. 17 See 1 Tim 6:13. 18 Phil 2:9. 19 John 5:44. 20 See Phil 2:7. 21 See 1 Tim 2:5.

the dead of his own accord alongside the Father. However, Christ did both. Therefore, the same one is God and a human being.

21. A human being in whom God works is not God, whereas a body conjoined to God is God. However, Christ is God. Therefore, he is not a human being in whom God works but a body conjoined to God.

22. If a temple of God was begotten from Mary, the novelty of the begetting from a virgin would have been superfluous. For human beings are temples of God even without this.[22]

23. If Christ's nature were the same as ours, he would be "the old human being,"[23] "a living soul and not a life-giving spirit,"[24] that kind [of nature] which does not give life. However, Christ does give life[25] and is a life-giving spirit.[26] Therefore, he is not of our nature.

24. Does Christ live on account of his own nature or on account of God's grace? If on account of his own nature, then he is God, but if on account of God's grace, then he is neither above us nor will he give us life.

25. If he became virtuous because of an ability to make a free choice, how could that be? For the human ability to make a free choice does not successfully produce genuine righteousness. But if he was righteous because of [his] nature, then he is God. However, if he became righteous because of an activity that comes from God while he himself remained inactive, then [both of them] would be enactors of the virtues.

26. If in Christ there is a human being intertwined with God, does he prescribe laws of himself or not? If it is of himself, then he is God, but if it is not of himself, why didn't he say, "Thus says the Lord," instead of, "I say to you"?[27] And why wasn't the one who didn't speak[28] distinguished from the one who spoke?[29]

27. Moreover, did he perform miracles or not? If he did perform them, then he was not a human being. However, if not, then how could he claim to have performed them? Or how could he be the same[30] as the one who performed them?

22 See 1 Cor 3:16–17, 6:19; 2 Cor 6:16. 23 Rom 6:6; Eph 4:22; Col 3:9.

24 1 Cor 15:45. 25 See 1 Cor 15:22.

26 See 1 Cor 15:45. In this chapter Apollinarius exploits the Pauline distinction between two Adams, the one a living being and the other (Christ) a life-giving spirit.

27 The former is the typical formula used to announce prophetic utterances in the Old Testament, e.g., Isa 45:1. The latter comes from the Sermon on the Mount in Matt 5:22, etc.

28 That is, God. 29 That is, Christ. 30 In Greek, *ho autos*.

28. Is the human being worshiped by angels or not?[31] If he is not worshiped, then why has he been united [to God] and why does the Son of Man send his angels?[32] If he is worshiped because divine power indwells in him, then why is he worshiped by those who always have divine power indwelling in them?[33] And shall we ourselves worship the human being or not? If we do not worship [the human being], why should we consider him united [to God] and why are we baptized into his death?[34] However, if we should worship the human being just as we do God, we would commit impiety by setting a creature in a position of equality with the Creator. And if we expect the human being to be a judge who, along with the Father, illuminates "the hidden things of darkness,"[35] then we would be assigning God's judgment to a human being. But if we don't [expect this], how is it that the Father gave "him authority to execute judgment, because he is the Son of Man,"[36] and how is it that he has been united with the judge?

29. A human being, with the vital motions of reasoning and suffering, yoked to God is another alongside God. And when he suffers, he suffers as another,[37] and when he is worshiped, he is worshiped as another. However, the flesh of the living God is an instrument suited to the sufferings with a view to the divine plans, and neither words nor deeds are proper to the flesh, and being subject to the sufferings in a way appropriate for flesh, it prevails against the sufferings because it is God's flesh, in such a way that it is the beginning of impassibility for bodies which, though not like it, nonetheless share the same life as it. And it is worshiped as God's flesh, since the one thus worshiped is God, and it gives us a connection with him whose body it is, and it is not worshiped as a creature, because no creature is a part of God. Therefore, those who have believed that God took flesh both receive benefits and are not transformed into another thing.[38] Those who say a human being was yoked to God hold the opposite position.

30. If flesh is distinguished from the mind (since according to the Apostle the flesh wars against the mind),[39] the God who took the flesh has from it the motions that war against the mind; however, they are not subject to him as if to a rival mind. If this were the case, he would not be the one suffering, insofar as he is God.

31 See Heb 1:6. 32 See Matt 24:31.

33 Those who always have divine power indwelling in them are angels.

34 See Rom 6:3. 35 1 Cor 4:5. 36 John 5:27. 37 In Greek, *hōs heteros*.

38 That is, a human being in addition to God. 39 See Rom 7:23.

24

Apollinarius of Laodicea, *Selected Letters*

Introduction by Mark DelCogliano and Bradley K. Storin
Translation of Letter to Emperor Jovian
and First Letter to Dionysius by Bradley K. Storin
Translation of Letter to the Bishops in Diocaesarea, Synodical Tome,
and Fragments of Letters to Dionysius, Serapion, Terentius,
and Julian by Mark DelCogliano

INTRODUCTION

All that survives of the epistolary corpus of Apollinarius of Laodicea (ca. 315–392) are four intact letters and fragments of four others.[1] What is probably the earliest Christological statement we have from Apollinarius is found in his *Letter to Emperor Jovian*, also called *The Profession of Faith to Emperor Jovian*, a letter to the new (pro-Nicene) emperor Jovian, who ascended to the throne in June 363 and ruled until his death in February 364. This letter might simply be an introductory statement of faith to a new emperor, which other bishops generally saw as unavoidable formalities to be completed without making waves. Indeed, Athanasius's letter to Jovian (*Ep.* 56) simply repeated the Nicene Creed with little interpolation or interpretation. However, the fact that Apollinarius took the exercise as an opportunity to submit his Christological thought for imperial consideration might suggest a different context, perhaps that he was offering the new emperor a way forward in the efforts to reconcile the Christian factions in Antioch (Eustathians, Meletians, "Arians" of various stripes) by highlighting his own position. Whatever the historical context, in this letter Apollinarius affirms that, in the incarnate Christ, there is but a single divine nature, God the Word enfleshed, which is the single object of Christian worship.

1 For a fuller introduction to Apollinarius, see his *Recapitulation*, translated in this volume on pp. 301–307.

He articulates his own position as an alternative to any sort of dualistic Christology, rejecting any understanding of Christ as composed of two sons. Moreover, he issues a brief series of anathemas, indicating some of the polemical parameters that informed Christological conflicts in this era.

Two of Apollinarius's *Letters to Dionysius* survive, the first wholly intact but only a single fragment of the second. The addressee in both cases is probably an Apollinarian presbyter, but the contexts and dates of these two letters are difficult to determine. They tend to be placed by scholars in the late 360s or 370s, but the letters could have been written at any point in Apollinarius's career. In the first letter Apollinarius offers Dionysius advice about dealing with Christological dissent in his community. Here Apollinarius engages in loaded polemic against "those who say two natures." He identifies them as devotees of Paul of Samosata, the third-century Christian bishop who advocated for a kind of adoptionist Christology and whom fourth-century writers often identified as the source of their contemporary opponents' wrong Christology.[2] This letter argues in favor of a basic unity in Christ as one nature, but also against any conceptual separation of Christ's humanity from his divinity. Christ is one person who inseparably exists as uncreated divinity in a created body. As for the second letter, the sources that preserve the fragment note that it comes from the very beginning of the letter. Here Apollinarius affirms his friendship with Dionysius based on their shared piety but dissociates himself from other supporters of his who have abandoned his understanding of Christ's flesh. He repeats his own position that Christ's flesh is God insofar as it is united to the divinity in a single person.

Three fragments of Apollinarius's *Letter to Serapion* are extant. All deal with the same subject: a rejection of the idea that Christ's flesh is same-in-substance with God and an affirmation that it is same-in-substance with human flesh by nature, even though it can be said to be divine through its union with the Word. The addressee is likely bishop Serapion of Thmuis, a close theological-political ally of Athanasius from the late 330s and himself the addressee of Athanasius's three letters on the Holy Spirit written between 359 and 361. Since Apollinarius mentions Athanasius's *Letter to Epictetus* in the first fragment (159) and seems to be in some

2 A selection of fragments from Paul of Samosata are translated in this volume on pp. 197–211.

sense responding to it, the *Letter to Serapion* must have been written after the *Letter to Epictetus*, traditionally dated to 370–371.[3]

Two fragments of Apollinarius's *Letter to Terentius* are preserved. The addressee is probably Terentius, the *comes orientis* (Count of the East), to whom Basil of Caesarea also wrote letters, two of which are extant (*Epp.* 99 and 214). A possible scenario is that Terentius had visited Antioch or was at least concerned with Christian factionalism there, and Apollinarius might have written to him to demonstrate his own Christological orthodoxy and its potential usefulness for resolving the factionalism. If so, this letter probably dates to ca. 375–376. Whatever the context and date of this letter, the first fragment denies that the Word and Christ's body are same-in-substance, and the second anathematizes this view and two others, namely, that the Son is two persons and that Christ's flesh descended from heaven. Thus it seems that in this letter Apollinarius marked out his own Christological position by distinguishing it from approaches he considered incorrect.

Three fragments of Apollinarius's *Letter to Julian* are extant, all affirming Christ's single nature, will, activity, and mind against dualistic claims to the contrary. Julian was a disciple of Apollinarius, and the same source that preserves the fragments of the *Letter to Julian* also preserves fragments of an epistolary exchange between Julian and his fellow disciple Polemon.[4] The letters of Julian and Polemon, which were most likely written in the mid- to late 370s because Polemon mentions Basil and Gregory (probably of Nazianzus), affirm Apollinarius's doctrine of Christ as one composite nature against dyophysite claims. And so it appears likely that Julian himself is the ultimate source of the fragments of the letter written to him, having quoted them in his letter to Polemon in support of his own position. While the *Letter to Julian* could date to the same period as the epistolary exchange between Julian and Polemon, it might also have been written earlier.

Apollinarius's *Letter to the Bishops in Diocaesarea* is addressed to eleven pro-Nicene bishops from Egypt who had been forced into exile after the death of Athanasius in 373 during the episcopate of the "Arian" bishop Lucius of Alexandria (373–378). The extant letter is apparently Apollinarius's second letter to them, his first having gone unanswered. Apollinarius's

3 On the dating of Athanasius's *Letter to Epictetus*, see the introduction to the translation in this volume on pp. 278–279.

4 See Fragments 176, 177, and 180.

purpose in both letters seems to have been to establish communion with these bishops, and in order to convince them to be in communion with him he provided an account of his theology. In the extant letter he emphasizes his connections with Athanasius and quotes from the Christological section of the *Tome to the Antiochenes* to demonstrate his agreement with Athanasian orthodoxy. The letter dates to around 376.

The *Synodical Tome* is a confessional statement issued by an unknown Apollinarian synod, though some scholars have connected it with the Apollinarian synod at Antioch in 379. It contains a brief summary of Apollinarian Christology and soteriology, and seems designed to mute its more controversial aspects yet without dissembling. It explains in what sense Christ is heavenly and how in Christ humanity acquires a likeness to the heavenly one. The statement concludes with Christological anathemas.

All the translations here are based on the critical edition of Hans Lietzmann, *Apollinaris von Laodicea und seine Schule: Texte und Untersuchungen* (Tübingen: Mohr, 1904), 247–262. The numbering of fragments is that of Lietzmann. In cases where Leontius of Byzantium's *Adversus Fraudes Apollinaristarum* is the source of the fragment, reference has been made to the Greek text in Brian Daley, *Leontius of Byzantium: Complete Works* (Oxford: Oxford University Press, 2017).

TRANSLATION

Letter to Emperor Jovian: The Profession of Faith to Emperor Jovian

1. We confess that the Son of God, eternally begotten before the ages, has been begotten of Mary in flesh in these last times for our salvation, as the divine Apostle teaches by saying, "When the fullness of time had come, God sent out his Son, born of a woman."[5] [We] also [confess that] the same one is Son of God and God in spirit but Son of Man in flesh, that the one Son is not two natures, one worshiped and one not worshiped, but one incarnate nature of God the Word[6] who is worshiped with his flesh in a single act of worship. [We also confess that] there are not two sons, one true and

5 Gal 4:4.
6 This phrase – in Greek, *mia physis tou logou sesarkōmenē* – later became central to the miaphysite movement because Cyril used it, mistakenly believing its source was Athanasius.

worshiped Son of God, and another, a human being from Mary, not worshiped, who became a Son of God by grace, even as other human beings do, but there is one Son of God from God, as I said; it was the same one, and not another, who in these last days was begotten of Mary in flesh. Accordingly, in response to Mary the Theotokos, who had asked, "How will this be, since I have known no man?"[7] the angel said, "The Holy Spirit will come upon you, and the power of Most High will overshadow you. That is why your holy offspring[8] will be called Son of God."[9]

2. He who is begotten of the Virgin Mary is accordingly Son of God and true God by nature, not by grace or participation, a human being only in flesh from Mary, but the same Son of God and God in spirit who experienced our [human] sufferings in the flesh, as it was written, "Christ suffered in the flesh"[10] for us, and again, "He did not spare his own Son, but gave him up on behalf of us all."[11] In the divinity he remains impassible and unchangeable in accordance with what was spoken by the prophet, "I am God and I have not changed."[12] In his flesh he died our death for our sins so that he might destroy death through his death on our behalf, in accordance with the Apostle's saying, "Death has been swallowed up in victory. Where is your victory, O Death? Where is your sting, O Hades?"[13] and again, "Christ died for our sins in accordance with the scriptures."[14] But as the Father's impassible power, he remains immortal and unconquered by death because of the divinity, in accordance with Peter's saying, "For he was not," he says, "able to be conquered by death."[15] As to the Word's flesh, it ascended to heaven and is seated on the right side of the Father, exalted from earth into heaven in accordance with what was said by David, "The Lord said to my Lord, 'Sit on my right side,'"[16] and confirmed by the Lord himself and by the apostles.[17] But as to the divinity, it is uncircumscribed and eternally encompasses every place along with the Father as the ineffable paternal power in accordance with Paul's teaching, "Christ is God's power and God's wisdom."[18] The same Son of God and God, as was proclaimed, comes to judge the living and the dead, just as the Apostle says, "judging the hidden things of the darkness, making plain the hidden things of the heart, and bringing praise and blame to each as they deserve."[19]

7 Literally, "since I know no man." 8 In Greek, *gennōmenon*. 9 Luke 1:34–35.
10 1 Pet 4:1. 11 Rom 8:32. 12 Mal 3:6. 13 1 Cor 15:55.
14 1 Cor 15:3. 15 Acts 2:24. 16 Ps 109(110):1. 17 See Matt 22:44.
18 1 Cor 1:24. 19 1 Cor 4:5.

3. If anyone teaches contrary to these points from the divine scriptures, saying that one is Son of God and another is a human being from Mary who, like us, is made a son by grace – as if there were two sons, one Son of God by nature (the one from God) and one by grace (the human being from Mary) – or if anyone says our Lord's flesh is from above and not from the Virgin Mary, or turns the divinity into flesh, either commingled or subjected to change, or [says that] the Son's divinity is subject to suffering, or [that] the flesh of our Lord is not to be worshiped since it belongs to a human being, and [that] it is not to be worshiped as the flesh of the Lord and God, the catholic church anathematizes him, being convinced by the divine Apostle who says, "If anyone proclaims something to you contrary to what you have received, let him be anathema."[20]

*

* *

First Letter to Dionysius

1. I am amazed to learn about certain people who confess the Lord God incarnate but who fall into the division wickedly introduced by the Paulinizers.[21] Indeed, those slaves to Paul the Samosatene say that one [part] is from heaven, acknowledging it to be God, and the other from earth, a human being. They say that one is uncreated, the other created; one eternal, the other recent;[22] the one master, the other slave. They would commit impiety if they were to worship what they claim is a slave and created, or if they were to fail to worship the one who redeemed us with his own blood! 2. By confessing that God from heaven has been made flesh from the Virgin and is one with the flesh, they stir up folly and are carried away in the words of their impiety. Indeed, as I'm hearing, they even claim that there are two natures, even though John plainly indicates the Lord to be one by saying, "The Word became flesh,"[23] and Paul does too by saying, "One Lord Jesus Christ, through whom everything exists."[24] For if the one born of the holy Virgin is designated "one," and he is the same as the one "through whom all things come to be," then there is one nature, since one person[25] cannot

20 Gal 1:9. 21 In Greek, *tōn paulianizontōn*.
22 In Greek, *ton de chthesinon*; literally, "of yesterday."
23 John 1:14. 24 1 Cor 8:6. 25 In Greek, *prosōpon*.

maintain a division into two; for in the incarnation the body is not its proper nature and the divinity is not its proper nature. Rather, just as a human being is one nature, so too did Christ "come to exist in a likeness to human beings."[26] 3. But if they do not recognize oneness in cases of union, they can also partition a single [human being] into many things and claim that there are several natures, since there is one nature to the body and yet it consists of many parts – bones, tendons, veins, flesh, skin, fingernails, hair, blood, and spirit, all of which are quite different from each other. Consequently, the truth of the divinity is that it is one with the body and not distributed among two natures. 4. For it would not be possible for the whole to be called Son of Man, descended from heaven, and Son of God, begotten of a woman, if it admitted a division into two natures. Rather, the one who descended from heaven would be called Son of God and not Son of Man, while the one begotten of the woman would be called Son of Man and not Son of God. This too is in line with the division of Paul [of Samosata]. 5. The divine scriptures, though, teach us how to understand the one Lord in his descent from heaven and in his being begotten of a woman on earth. Accordingly, let those who understand it like this not veer into agreement with those who understand everything contrary, lest they speak sacrilegiously[27] in their words even though they remain reverent[28] in their thought. 6. For those who say "two natures" would need to worship one and not worship the other, and to be baptized into the divine one and to not be baptized into the human one. But if we are baptized into the Lord's death,[29] we confess one nature of the impassible divinity and the passible flesh so that our baptism into God and into the Lord's death may be accomplished like this. 7. For we are unafraid of slanderers who divide the Lord into two persons, even if, since we give privilege to the evangelical and apostolic unity, they vilify us for saying that the flesh is from heaven when we read the divine scriptures saying the Son of Man is from heaven. When we say that the Son of God is born of a woman,[30] we cannot be vilified as if we were claiming the Word is from earth and not from heaven. Rather, we say both: the whole is from heaven on account of the divinity and the whole is from a woman on account of the flesh, acknowledging no division of the one person and severing neither the earthly from the heavenly nor the heavenly from the earthly. Such severing is impious. 8. Let those who say "two natures," then,

26 Phil 2:7. 27 In Greek, *dusphēmōsin*. 28 In Greek, *euphēmountes*.
29 See Rom 6:3. 30 Gal 4:4.

give no pretense to those who sever, for in the case of the one Christ the body is not a nature in and of itself,[31] since it is not a life-giver in and of itself and it cannot be severed from[32] the life-giving Word. Neither is the Word in and of himself cordoned off in his proper nature, which he keeps in its fleshless condition – since the Lord dwelled in the world in the flesh and not fleshlessly – nor does the created body live apart from the uncreated divinity so that someone could separate the created nature, nor did the uncreated Word dwell [in the world] without the body so that someone could cordon off the nature of the uncreated. 9. But if each one exists in accordance with the union as well as the conjunction[33] and composite in human form, then one name should be adapted to the composite: the uncreated from the divinity and the created from the body; the impassibility from the divinity and the passibility from the body. And just as, when we hear from Paul that Christ is passible, we do not hear "with respect to one part"[34] but we still do not consider the divinity passible, so too when he says "created" and "slave" he did not say "with respect to one part" and yet does not make the divinity a "creation" or a "slave." Inversely, by saying "uncreated" he does not make the flesh "uncreated" nor does he say "with respect to one part" about the divinity alone. Let those who think these things thus keep quiet because they contort their over-the-top questions, and let us not divide the basic principles[35] because of words.

10. It has been agreed, and agreeably confessed, that the body is from the Virgin, the divinity from heaven; that the body was formed in the womb, the divinity is uncreated, eternal; and that, in the composite, the body remains a body and the divinity divinity so that, once the Word is united to the body, the divinity remains indivisible. But if scripture is accustomed to speak both of the whole as God and of the whole as human, it is we who should follow the divine words and not split what is unsplit, neither dividing the divinity from the body out of reverence, such as when the body is said to be formed in the womb, nor splitting the body from the divinity because of our confession of the presence, such as when the uncreated divinity is glorified. For in one life, the one participates in the name with the other; neither does the bodiless change into body nor the body into the bodiless. 11. How, then, is it not distressing that those who thus confess or think these things in the right way (as they also received) have broken

31 In Greek, *kath' heauto.* 32 In Greek, *aneu.* 33 In Greek, *synodon.*
34 In Greek, *merikōs.* 35 In Greek, *ta dogmata.*

into factions against each other because of words? Sometimes the [scriptures] apply a term proper to the body for the Word, as John does when he speaks of the Word becoming flesh,[36] while other times they accept a term proper to the divinity for the whole slave, as Paul does when he says, "The last Adam gives life in the Spirit."[37] 12. Christ confesses that he worships the Father according to the flesh by saying, "We worship what we see,"[38] and the divinity is not separated. The body is worshiped in correspondence with the divinity and is not split [from the divinity] in the worship of the divinity. Neither do we avoid the body when we worship, nor would it be possible […][39] the divinity is not even separated from the body's suffering. For they are united. Indeed death needed to be conquered by God – and it has been.

13. Exhort those who, in these matters, differ pointlessly, and may the confession corresponding to our teaching be preserved without division over words. For in the latter case, it is impious for those who disagree with our teachings to pretend to agree with us in words, while in the former, it is stupid and foolish for those who agree with our teachings to differ from us with their words. Let those who possess this agreement, that Christ is God incarnate, both from heaven and earth, the same one being slave in form and God in power, remain in concord with us; let them not differ vainly; let them not fall into a war of words with the heretics, but instead strive for the simplicity of the church. Live well, good sir.

*

* *

Fragment from Another *Letter to Dionysius*
Fragment 164

To me piety is a foundation of friendship and there can be no pretense of hostility with those who preserve piety. Let no one seek anything new from me now nor demand that I keep silent about the truth, as if he were making peace [with me]. That no one can charge us with statements uttered against certain people is clear from what we have always written. For we say neither that the flesh of the Savior is from heaven, nor that the flesh is

36 See John 1:14. 37 1 Cor 15:45. 38 John 4:22.
39 The text is defective here.

same-in-substance with God insofar as it is flesh and not God, but it is God insofar as it has been united to the divinity in one person.

*

* *

Three Fragments from the *Letter to Serapion*

Fragment 159

I received the letter of Your Charity, my lord, and we helped the letter-carrier as best we could with the request made by him. And we very much appreciated the epistle of my lord that was sent to Corinth, and we condemn the utter insanity of those who said that the flesh is same-in-substance with God.[40]

Fragment 160

For the flesh is divine by its union with the Word, not by nature. Accordingly, in the union it remains so,[41] as he himself says, "The spirit gives life" to the flesh.[42] For indeed it is impossible for the bodiless to become a body, as others stupidly claim.

Fragment 161

So then, you are quite right to say, "We and Christ are not equal." But to say that his flesh is not same-in-substance with us since it is God's flesh requires a little more precision. For it is better to say that he assumed flesh that was same-in-substance with us by nature but showed that it was divine by the union. Now you yourself are saying the same thing, that in this respect it is not same-in-substance with us since it is God's flesh. But one could say it with much more precision in this way: the flesh is same-in-substance with us by nature but it is divine by the union and it retains the difference through the union.

*

* *

40 Apollinarius refers to Athanasius's *Letter to Epictetus of Corinth*, translated in this volume on pp. 279–290. The claim that Christ's flesh was same-in-substance with God was among the teachings refuted by Athanasius in this letter.

41 That is, remains divine; in Greek, *to diamenein*.

42 John 6:63.

Two Fragments from the *Letter to Terentius*

Fragment 162

And John censures the one who destroys Jesus, but these people destroy him outright when they confess the conjunction [of the Word] with the body. For the body is not conjoined to itself, nor is something same-in-substance conjoined to something else same-in-substance with it, as these people do not hesitate to say. For that would be neither a composition nor a conjunction because nothing is conjoined to itself but one thing is conjoined to another thing. But if the Word were same-in-substance with the body and the body same-in-substance with the Word, surely both would be invisible in accordance with [the passage], "No one has ever seen or can see God."[43] If this, then, were the case, he neither appeared nor was he touched, being invisible, nor was John truthful when he said, "We have seen him and our hands have touched him."[44]

Fragment 163

If anyone claims either that the Son is two persons, or that [the flesh] is same-in-substance with God and not so with our flesh, or that the flesh descended from heaven and was not assumed by the one from heaven, saying that the divinity is passible, let him be anathematized.

*

* *

Three Fragments from the *Letter to Julian*

Fragment 150

Those who profess the dogma of two minds in Christ, I mean a divine and a human one, are engraving a stone with a finger. For if every mind is autonomous, moving itself by its own will according to [its] nature, then it is impossible for two [minds] to coexist in one and the same subject, as they could will the opposite to each other, with each one doing what it wants according to its own self-moving impulse.

43 1 Tim 6:16; see John 1:18. 44 1 John 1:1.

Fragment 151

Nor were they able to perceive this, even though it is obvious to all, that while the divine mind is self-moving and moves without variation[45] – for it is unchangeable – the human mind, though self-moving, does not move without variation – for it is changeable. And [they were not able to perceive] that a changeable mind is not mixed with an unchangeable mind in the formation[46] of one subject. For in that case discord would arise because of the opposite wills and the one subject would be torn apart by them. For this reason we ourselves confess that Christ is one, and since he is one, we worship one nature and one will and one activity, which saves by miracles as much as by sufferings.

Fragment 152

For those who say that Christ is one but allege that he has two intellectual natures complete in themselves[47] do not know that the Word himself became flesh[48] and remained within his natural oneness,[49] as they present him as divided into unlike natures and activities.

*
* *

Letter to the Bishops in Diocaesarea

To my most honorable lords, the bishops in Diocaesarea: greetings in the Lord.

1. We expected, having sent you a letter of respect, to be sent a similar letter in return from Your Charity, most honorable lords, such as we always received from the blessed bishop Athanasius, who knew that we were both in agreement with him in his teachings and obedient in all matters. But since you did not write back to us, we therefore concluded that perhaps the length of our epistle did not make our position clear to you. So then, we

45 In Greek, *autokinētos esti kai tautokinētos.*
46 In Greek, *systasin.* The term suggests the bringing together of elements into a single composite reality.
47 In Greek, *dyo physeis autou noeras autoteleis.* The implication is that each nature possesses a mind.
48 See John 1:14.
49 In Greek, *meinanta tēs physikēs autou monados entos.*

now write what clearly accords with our common teacher, yours and mine. I am saying these things about the divine incarnation, since a great uproar has arisen over this matter, incited not by us but by others, about whom I will keep silent.

2. We confess that the Word of God did not dwell in a holy human being as happened in the prophets, but that the Word himself became flesh, not assuming a human mind (a mind which changes and is captive to filthy thoughts), but a mind that is divine, unchanging, and heavenly. Therefore, "the Savior had a body that was neither without a soul, nor without sense, nor without a mind. For it would be impossible, after the Lord became a human being for our sake, for his body to be without a mind. And truly being Son of God, he became also Son of Man, and being the only-begotten Son of God, the same also became 'firstborn among many brothers.'[50] Therefore, there is not one, who was Son of God before Abraham, and another, who was that after Abraham,"[51] but there is one perfect Only-Begotten of God, perfect with respect to divine perfection and not human perfection. We confess that we are in communion with those who hold such opinions, but we are not in communion with those who hold and write the opposite.

*

* *

Synodical Tome

I, Apollinarius, and my supporters hold the following opinions about the divine incarnation.

The living Word of God assumed from Mary flesh that is same-in-substance with our flesh, in union with his divinity from the first moment of his conception in the Virgin, and thus became a human being. For a human being is flesh and spirit, according to the Apostle, and the Word becoming flesh means his being united to flesh like the human spirit. For even a human being of our sort is called flesh, but the Lord is a human being

50 Rom 8:29.

51 See John 8:58. The quoted material is from *Tome to the Antiochenes* 7 (Hanns Christof Brennecke, Annette von Stockhausen, Christian Müller, Uta Heil, and Angelika Wintjes, *Athanasius Werke. Band III/Teil 1: Dokumente zur Geschichte des arianischen Streites. Lieferung 4: Bis zur Synode von Alexandrien 362* [Berlin: De Gruyter, 2014], 600, 25–602, 9), translated in this volume on pp. 273–275.

superior to us. Therefore, he is also heavenly on account of his own spirit, which is heavenly, to which "the thoughts of the flesh"[52] were not opposed. And so, in Christ sin is destroyed and the death that comes from sin is nullified. And we ourselves, by sharing in this accomplishment by faith, are saved and, though we come from an earthly father, we are becoming a likeness of the heavenly one.[53] So then, whoever denies that the flesh is from Mary and says that it is of an uncreated nature and same-in-substance with God is anathema, as is whoever says that the divinity is passible and that the sufferings of the soul come from it.

52 Rom 8:6–7. 53 See 1 Cor 15:44–49.

25

Apollinarius of Laodicea, *On the Faith and the Incarnation*

Introduction and Translation by Bradley K. Storin

INTRODUCTION

The date of this text written by Apollinarius of Laodicea (ca. 315–392) is difficult to determine with specificity.[1] It should simply be placed in the late 360s or 370s. Here Apollinarius demonstrates the union between divinity and flesh in Christ. He employs the Greek term *hypostasis* to express the basic union between Christ's flesh and divinity. Perhaps more radically than he does in *On the Body's Union with the Divinity in Christ*,[2] Apollinarius now applies "same-in-substance" (*homoousios*) to Christ's flesh. This text, once attributed falsely to Julian of Rome, does not fully survive in Greek. Only sections 3–7 do, and the critical edition from which the translation of those sections is made is Hans Lietzmann, *Apollinaris von Laodicea und seine Schule: Texte und Untersuchungen* (Tübingen: Mohr, 1904), 194–199. The other four sections – 1–2 and 8–9 – survive in a Syriac translation, for which the critical edition from which this translation has been made is Johannes Fleming and Hans Lietzmann, "Apollinaristische Schriften syrisch. Mit den griechischen Texten und einem syrisch-griechischen Wortregister," in *Abhandlungen der Königlichen Gesellschaft der Wissenschaften zu Göttingen*, Philologisch-Historische Klasse, Neue Folge, Band 7 (Berlin: Weidmannsche Buchhandlung, 1904), 24, 30–32. This translation followed the eleventh-century manuscript Vatic. Syr. 135.

1 For a fuller introduction to Apollinarius, see his *Recapitulation*, translated in this volume on pp. 301–307.
2 Translated in this volume on pp. 327–332.

TRANSLATION

1. Our Lord Jesus Christ, only Son of God, has made us worthy of great mysteries, great things, the likes of which no one knows how to relate, mysteries that only faith is able to comprehend. They were so great that we were unworthy of them; yet, it was fitting for him to impart [them to us]. For if one were to discern the poverty of faith, then we would not only be unworthy of the gift of the glorious mysteries, but also condemned to a special[3] blindness and anguish. Because he is good and son of goodness, however, he not only saved us from special blindness but also gave us eternal life, which is far more glorious and excellent than this first one. He has enabled us to enter into a new world and he has created us as a new creation. 2. "So whoever is in Christ is a new creation."[4] What kind of new creation could it be if it did not raise us up to heaven? But among the initial ones we were not found to be believers and he put into our hands still greater things. We could not guard ourselves against just one tree but, behold! he gave us eternal gladness. In paradise we did not exercise restraint, and yet he opened heaven to us and he gave us the kingdom of heaven. What's greater than all this is that he came to us, God to human beings, Lord to servants, rich one to the poor, living and life-giver to the house of the dead, they who were enslaved to the slavery of death throughout their entire lives. Not only this, but he also gave us his body and his blood.

3. Let no one disparage the lordly and saving flesh of our Lord Jesus Christ under the pretense of "same-in-substance." For neither we, nor our assembly, nor anyone who thinks like a normal human being,[5] says or thinks that a body of its own accord is "same-in-substance." We do not say that the flesh of our Lord Jesus Christ is from heaven, but we confess that God the Word has become incarnate from the holy Virgin Mary. We do not divide him from his flesh, but [we confess that] there is one person,[6] one hypostasis – wholly human being, wholly God. 4. And so if we are to believe that, from the same virginal conception according to which the Virgin has been proclaimed Theotokos, our Lord Jesus Christ "came in a likeness to human beings"[7] (and this – the Word of God becoming incarnate – is the mystery of our salvation), then he must be inseparable and indivisible from his own flesh and, in the union with God the Word,[8] his flesh – whose

3 In Syriac, *brysh'*. 4 2 Cor 5:17. 5 In Greek, *tis tōn anthrōpinon logismon echontōn*.
6 In Greek, *hen prosōpon*. 7 Phil 2:7.
8 "In the union with God the Word" is lacking in some manuscripts.

flesh it indeed is – must share in the name of "same-in-substance," which the Word has with the Father by nature, if we really confess that the Word of God became flesh. But if it does not share [in the name of "same-in-substance"], it must be detached altogether, [and in that case] salvation resulting from the incarnation would not accrue to the faithful given that the divine Trinity would exist outside it. 5. Indeed, nothing is worthy of worship or offers salvation outside the divine Trinity. Instead, the incarnation would be proclaimed as something superfluous and ill-suited for the faithful and the passages of the divine scriptures found pertaining to them would be a lie, passages like, "The Word became flesh"[9] and, "Today in the city of David, the Lord Savior Christ has been born for us."[10] These too will be a lie: "the mighty God," the "child," and all phrases like these.[11] The Virgin will no longer be believed to be Theotokos, which is unlawful, tremendously impious, and foreign to every pious soul. Yes indeed, Christians' every hope would be upended for the faithful and Christianity itself reckoned for nothing. For the great and precious gift that belongs to Christians – the washing that brings someone into Christ's death – will be reckoned not as something divine but human if the incarnation of our Lord Jesus Christ is not tallied to the divine Trinity.

6. We must confess that Jesus Christ, our Lord, Savior, and Redeemer, whom the Virgin begot, is God's Son, genuine [Son] before the ages, same-in-substance with the Father. To him we deservedly offer worship, and his flesh is not excluded from the worship. For the objects of worship cannot be distinguished without the divine life being distinguished. Anyone who does not worship his flesh does not worship him. Moreover, in the union of the Word with his ensouled and rational flesh, we also offer one worship as though to one son,[12] since the evangelist evangelizes one life of the Word and the flesh: "The Word," he says, "became flesh."[13] Moreover, if the Word became flesh, anyone who worships the Word will also worship the flesh, and anyone worshiping the flesh will also worship the divinity, and the apostles who worshiped Christ Jesus worshiped God the Word when they worshiped him in the body. When the angels approached his body, they also served him as if he were their own Lord; at the very moment

9 John 1:14. 10 See Luke 2:11. Apollinarius has slightly altered the original.
11 See Isa 9:6, which Christians interpreted as a prophecy of Christ's birth.
12 The first part of this sentence is lacking in some manuscripts.
13 John 1:14.

when the Virgin gave birth to the flesh she gave birth to the Word and was Theotokos; when the Jews crucified his body, they crucified God – there is no division of the Word from his flesh offered in the divine scriptures. Instead, there is one nature, one hypostasis, one power,[14] one person,[15] the same being wholly God, wholly human being.

7. For according to the invisible, his substance[16] is the divinity, but according to the visible, his substance is the flesh. The incarnation of our Lord Jesus Christ, then, is neither estranged nor divided from the divine Trinity. For in the numbering of the Trinity, he declares that baptism was given for the forgiveness of sins and resurrection of the flesh, which is a task suited to divinity, not to created nature. One and the same are the body and God, whose body it is, since the flesh is not changed into something incorporeal, but retains its own special character[17] from us according to its being begotten of the Virgin, and for us according to its mixture or union with God the Word.

8. And so, my beloved, let us believe and not doubt in the advent of God the Word; let us not be led astray by heresies. For the one who confesses God's advent with his mouth, but understands that he is a human being like us, that he came from a woman and yet says that the Son of God was not born from a woman[18] – that person is against the believers and is counted among unbelievers. For our part, though, we ought to guard over the divinity in line with the tradition of the holy fathers. We pay no mind to human disputes, for it is not because of disputes that we became believers, but by the divine words that came to us in the witness [given] through the blessed apostles, those who saw our Lord's glory – more sublime than human nature – and by the witness that they heard from heaven[19] and proclaimed to the world: the incarnate God, the Word that became flesh, and the life-giving Spirit, our Lord Jesus Christ, who was fatherless in his birth here on earth because he was God come down from heaven and not a human being sprouted from a human seed. He was still called Son of Man; however, as God, he showed his divine authority. In the blood of his hypostasis he redeemed the whole creation; he exercises authority over things heavenly and earthly; he has a throne over heaven; he is worshiped by the angels and praised by the Holy Spirit. 9. But if anyone should err by thinking or teaching beyond what the prophets, apostles, and our holy fathers

14 In Greek, *mia energeia*. 15 In Greek, *hen prosōpon*. 16 In Greek, *ousia*.
17 In Greek, *to idion*. 18 Gal 4:4. 19 See 1 Pet 1:16–18.

taught – those who were gathered from all over the world in the city of Nicaea – he runs a great risk. For [Jesus] said, "Blessed is the one who is not offended by me."[20] But such a one is offended because of the body, and because of the suffering he changed our Savior and understands him to be a human being instead of God. For anyone who calls the one who came from Mary a human being, and the one who was crucified a human being, changes him from God into a human being instead. It is not possible to find within a human being that life which was given by God. For he who was born from a woman gives life, and in his birth he gave life to the woman because she had given the world the fruits of death.[21] By virtue of the fact that he was a human being, he drew humanity to communion with life; in his death he rescinded the authority of death and summoned us to life in his resurrection from the abode of the dead. Well, if life and salvation are from God, liberating the world is not from anyone else. But if he who was born and crucified gives life and offers salvation, it was not a human being to whom Mary gave birth and it was not a human being whom the Jews crucified; rather, it was he who, for the salvation of humanity, became embodied and became a human being. Praise, thanks, and dignity be upon his Father, him, and the Holy Spirit now and in every time for ever and ever. Amen. The end.

20 Matt 11:6. 21 See 1 Tim 2:14–15.

26

Apollinarius of Laodicea, *On the Body's Union with the Divinity in Christ*

Introduction and Translation by Bradley K. Storin

INTRODUCTION

The date of this text written by Apollinarius of Laodicea (ca. 315–392) is difficult to determine with specificity.[1] It should simply be placed in the late 360s or 370s. Here Apollinarius lays out his understanding of the *communicatio idiomatum*, a Latin phrase that refers to the transference of traits in the incarnate Christ. As Apollinarius presents it here, the *communicatio idiomatum* permits a theologian to observe and speak of both the divinity sharing in the body's characteristics and the body sharing in the divinity's characteristics with respect to the incarnate Christ. Apollinarius notes that the conjunction of the two natures in Christ (see 4 below) results in a single, fundamental, undivided, and indivisible union between what is "same-in-substance" with God and what is "same-in-substance" with humanity. This "double consubstantiality," as it is called – that is, Christ is *homoousios* with God and *homoousios* with humanity – is the Christological mechanism, so to speak, that allows for each nature to share in the qualities of the other without the philosophical or theological implications of sharing. The critical edition from which this translation is made is Hans Lietzmann, *Apollinaris von Laodicea und seine Schule: Texte und Untersuchungen* (Tübingen: Mohr, 1904), 185–193.

TRANSLATION

1. The Lord is rightly confessed to be, from the beginning, a holy offspring even in the body, and in this respect he is different from every [other] body. For actually,[2] he was not conceived in his mother apart from

1 For a fuller introduction to Apollinarius, see his *Recapitulation*, translated in this volume on pp. 301–307.
2 In Greek, *holōs*.

the divinity; rather, he was united to it, as the angel says, "The Holy Spirit will come upon you and the power of the Most High will overshadow you. That is why your holy offspring[3] will be called Son of God,"[4] and there was a descent from heaven, not just the birth from a woman. For not only is it said, "born from a woman, born under the law,"[5] but also, "No one has ascended to heaven except the one who descended from heaven, the Son of Man."[6] 2. One cannot even speak of the body separately as a creature, since it is something utterly inseparable from the one whose body it is; rather, he partook of the Uncreated's title and God's appellation because he is joined to God in a union, just as it is said, "The Word became flesh,"[7] and by the Apostle, "The last Adam gives life in the spirit."[8] 3. Just as, on account of the divine conception[9] and the union with God, we attribute glorious traits to the body, so too must we not deny him the inglorious traits that come from the body, which is being "born of a woman" according to the Apostle, and being "formed as a slave of God in the womb" according to the prophet.[10] He is wholly named a human being and Son of Man, and numbered among the many generations of Abraham, after which he became a human being. 4. To be sure, we ought to speak and listen in a human way, as when he is called a whole human being (lest anyone, because of the term, deny that the divine substance[11] is made known with the body), and when he is named a slave in the body (lest anyone, because of the term slavery, deny that the superior nature[12] is made known with the body), and finally, when the one who descended from heaven is proclaimed a heavenly human being (lest anyone deny that there is an interlacing of an earthly body with divinity). Just because there is a conjunction[13] with the form of a slave[14] and with a body that is formed, [the divinity] is not dissevered in reality or in name when the Lord is called a slave and when the Uncreated is dubbed a formation.[15] 5. In him, though, it is confessed that the created exists in a union with the Uncreated, while the Uncreated exists in a mixture with the created – one nature composed out of each part, with the Word having contributed a special power[16] to the whole with [its] divine perfection. In the case of the average human being, the whole entity comes from two imperfect parts,

3 In Greek, *gennōmenon*. 4 Luke 1:35. 5 Gal 4:4. 6 John 3:13.
7 John 1:14. 8 1 Cor 15:45. 9 In Greek, *syllēpseōs*. 10 Gal 4:4; Isa 49:5.
11 In Greek, *theian ousian*. 12 In Greek, *kyrieutikēn physin*.
13 In Greek, *tēi synapheiai*. 14 See Phil 2:7. 15 See Gen 1:26.
16 In Greek, *merikēn energeian*.

filling one nature and made known in a single name, since the whole thing is called flesh (even though the soul is not omitted in this name), and the whole thing is designated as soul (even though the body is not omitted, even if it is something else alongside the soul). 6. He was neither diminished nor increased – he who is God made human; he who is the Lord, surpassing begottenness[17] even if he was begotten from a woman; he who is Lord even if he assumed the form of slaves; he who is spirit even if flesh is what was seen because of his union with the flesh;[18] he who, according to the Apostle, is not a human being even if the same [Apostle] proclaims him to be a human being; he who is (speaking with reference to the whole) the invisible God who assumed the form of a visible body; he who is uncreated God made manifest in a created garment; he who emptied himself in the form of a slave[19] but [remained] unemptied, unchangeable, and undiminished in divine substance (for there is no change in the divine nature). 7. And when he says, "Glorify me," the voice comes from the body and the glorification pertains to the body since he is speaking about the whole, [and] therefore the whole is one. And he continues further: "[Glorify me] with the glory that I had in your presence before the existence of the world."[20] With that he indicates that his divinity is always glorious; even if his statement is particularly fitting for the divinity, it indeed applies universally to the whole. 8. Thus in the invisible spirit he is same-in-substance with God, with the term also implying the flesh because it was united to what is same-in-substance with God and, in turn, to the one who is same-in-substance with human beings; and with the body implying the divinity because it was united to what is same-in-substance with us; and with the body's nature not undergoing change in the union with what is same-in-substance with God and in the association with the term "same-in-substance," just as the divinity's nature underwent no change in the association with the human body, nor did it undergo change in the flesh's designation of being same-in-substance with us.

9. Paul stated that the Son of God submitted to this begottenness when he said, "born of the seed of David according the flesh";[21] he did not say, "The flesh came from the seed of David," which would denote the flesh as something separate. And when he says, "Have this mind among yourselves, which was also in Christ Jesus, who was in the form of God but did not

17 In Greek, *tēs gennēseōs*. 18 In Greek, *ei kai sarx kata hēn henōsin tēs sarkos apodedeiktai*.
19 See Phil 2:7. 20 John 17:5. 21 Rom 1:3.

regard being equal with God as something to be prized,"[22] he does not impose a separation by saying, "whose divinity was in the form of God"; [rather,] he says, "[he] did not regard being equal with God as something to be prized." Furthermore, the divinity was not named Jesus before being begotten of a virgin, nor did it have an anointing in the Holy Spirit because the Word of God is the dispenser of the Spirit, not the one who is sanctified in the Spirit. 10. And he says, "On their behalf do I sanctify myself, that they may be sanctified in truth,"[23] not imposing a separation by also saying, "I sanctify the flesh," but instead joining [the whole] by saying, "I sanctify myself." Furthermore, he who considers the matter with precision will note that it is not possible for him to be sanctified by himself. For if a whole [individual] sanctifies, what is it that is sanctified? If the complete entity is sanctified, what is the sanctifier? But still, while maintaining the one person[24] and the undivided presentation of a single life, he has imposed sanctifying and being sanctified throughout the whole so that it would be precise and clear to us that, in a way neither prophetic nor apostolic, one individual sanctifies another, like the Spirit does the prophets and apostles, as Paul says about the entire church, "To those who are called saints and who have been sanctified in Christ Jesus,"[25] and the Savior himself says about the apostles, "Sanctify them in truth."[26] 11. The whole human nature exists in being sanctified and not in sanctifying. The angelic order too, like all creation, has been sanctified and illuminated, but the Spirit is the sanctifier and illuminator. In that the Word sanctifies and illuminates through the Spirit, yet is in no way sanctified, he is indeed Creator, not creation. With respect to human nature[27] there is being sanctified, and with respect to the Word[28] there is being embodied; while the acts may be divided, they are unified according to the union of the flesh with the divinity, lest the sanctifier be differentiated from the sanctified and the very act of incarnation be an act of sanctification. 12. For to those who say, "Even though you are a human being, you fancy yourself God," the Savior responds with a statement about his own humanity, saying, "To him whom the Father has sanctified and sent into the world, you say, 'You blaspheme!' because he says, 'I am the Son of

22 Phil 2:5–6. The Greek word *harpagmon* has customarily been translated "something to be grasped," but the context of Paul's doxographical hymn clearly shows that the word indicates something like a prize, wreath, or trophy. The idea is that Christ, in the form of God, did not rest on his laurels.

23 John 17:19. 24 In Greek, *to hen prosōpon*. 25 1 Cor 1:1–2.

26 John 7:17. 27 In Greek, *entautha*. 28 In Greek, *entha*.

God'?"[29] What sanctification does he mean here except that of the flesh by the divinity? For thus the body lives by the sanctification of the divinity, and not by the construction of a human soul, and the whole exists wholly in the conjunction. In that place he says, "He whom the Father has sanctified and sent," to mean that sanctifier and sanctified are both sanctified since sanctifier is conjoined to sanctified. 13. He also explains this sanctification in another place, that it was the act of being begotten from a virgin. "For I was begotten for this and for this I have come into the world, so that I may bear witness to the truth."[30] Indeed, from the will of flesh and the will of a man, an ordinary human being is animated and lives, since ejaculated spermatic material confers the life-giving power to the receptive womb. However, from the entrance of the Spirit and the overshadowing power the holy infant came to exist of the Virgin.[31] It was not spermatic material that fashioned the divine life; rather, it was a spiritual and divine power that permitted the divine conception in the Virgin and granted the divine childbirth.

14. In this very way, corresponding to the mode of union, Christ too is exalted and on him is bestowed the name that is above every name.[32] And yet, the exaltation particularly applies to the flesh that ascends from below. But because he does not ascend in a particular way, the exalted whole in general is therefore mentioned, and what has been bestowed to him is applied to the flesh that has been honored out of dishonor.[33] For glory is not added through grace to the Word, who has glory eternally; it existed and perdured, it existed in the form of God, and it was equal to God. 15. [In the Gospel] according to John, he affirms his equality with God even in the flesh by saying that God is his own Father and by regarding himself equal to God.[34] Now equality with God does not undergo any alteration, but the divinity remains unchangeable in his identity. It is impossible to receive what he possesses [by nature], even though the flesh receives what it does not have [by nature] – impassibility in the place of passions, a heavenly [way of life] in the place of an earthly way of life, royalty in the place of enslavement to human beings, being worshiped by all creation in the place of worshiping. His being bestowed with the name above every name is affirmed with respect to the whole.[35] 16. And if anyone dares to impose a separation

29 John 10:36. 30 John 18:37. 31 See Luke 1:35. 32 See Phil 2:9.
33 In Greek, *ex adoxias doxazomenēn*. 34 See John 5:18. 35 See Phil 2:9.

between the word of grace and the name above every name, neither will be stated properly. For had it been bestowed upon the Word as if he did not have it [by nature], then the name above every name would never have been given through grace. And if it has this not by gift but by nature (since he has it in accordance with its divinity), it would not be possible that it be given to him. 17. That's why, by necessity, what is said of the body applies to the whole and what is said of the divine applies to the whole, and what cannot be known in unified distinctions – [that is,] what is particular to each one – inharmoniously encounters an incompatibility, and he who knows the particular features and preserves the union neither falsifies the nature nor remains ignorant of the union.

27

Apollinarius of Laodicea, *Fragments of Other Writings*

Introduction and Translation by Mark DelCogliano

INTRODUCTION

The ecclesiastical condemnation of Apollinarius of Laodicea (ca. 315–392) resulted in few of his writings surviving intact, unless they had been transmitted under the names of church fathers of unimpeachable orthodoxy such as Gregory Thaumaturgus, Julius of Rome, and Athanasius of Alexandria.[1] However, fifth- and sixth-century writers such as Theodoret of Cyrrhus, Leontius of Byzantium, Emperor Justinian, and others still had access to more texts than we do today, and in works of Christological polemics they excerpted passages from the writings of Apollinarius to demonstrate his problematic views. Thus more than 150 fragments of Apollinarius are extant, preserved mainly in these polemical tracts. A selection of these fragments is translated here. Though they derive from various writings of Apollinarius about which little or nothing is known, these fragments have been selected because they bring out the most distinctive features of his Christology.[2] And yet, since these fragments were quoted by those who preserved them precisely because they were deemed to reveal the most controversial aspects of Apollinarius's Christology, they must be interpreted with care and caution (particularly 111 and 113). The translations here are based on the critical edition of Hans Lietzmann, *Apollinaris von Laodicea und seine Schule: Texte und Untersuchungen* (Tübingen: Mohr, 1904), 206–208, 232–235, and 247–249. The numbering of fragments is that of Lietzmann. In cases where Leontius of Byzantium's *Adversus Fraudes*

1 For a fuller introduction to Apollinarius, see his *Recapitulation*, translated in this volume on pp. 301–307.

2 Fragments of his letters and his writings against Diodore and Flavian are translated in this volume on pp. 339–347.

Apollinaristarum is the source of the fragment, reference has been made to the Greek text in Brian Daley, *Leontius of Byzantium: Complete Works* (Oxford: Oxford University Press, 2017).

TRANSLATION

Fragment 9

If the same one is entirely a human being and God, the pious mind that does not worship the human being but does worship God will be found to be both worshiping and not worshiping the same one – which is impossible. And while as a human being he would not consider himself an object of worship (for he would not be impious), as God he would know himself to be an object of worship. But it is impossible that the same one knows himself to be and not to be an object of worship. Therefore, it is impossible for the same one to be both God and entirely a human being. Rather, he exists in the singleness of a mixed divine-incarnate nature,[3] so that those who worship him behold God inseparable from the flesh; they do not behold one who is not to be worshiped and another who is to be worshiped. Nor is there in him one who refuses to be worshiped and one who accepts the worship [performed] by the worshipers for their salvation. But they are one in actuality as befits their one substance and by no means are they two individuals in persons who exist according to their own standards and their own ranks.

Fragment 10

O new creation and sacred mixture! God and flesh have constituted one and the same nature!

Fragment 11

He already sees that the body is greater on account of the one who is mixed with it – greater, I say, not only than his own body but also than the fiery bodies of angels. For God has been mixed with none of those, and none of those bodies gives life to the world. None of the angels is made equal to

3 In Greek, *en monotēti sugkratou phuseōs theikēs sesarkōmenēs*.

God in the way that he who has been mixed together from body and divinity makes himself equal to God when he says, "As the Father has life in himself, so he gave it also to the Son to have life in himself."[4]

Fragment 12

And even though you realize that the Spirit produces in itself a kind of separable activity, do you consider yourself divine, so that the robe removed from your skin can heal diseases? Do you suppose that his flesh is neither divine nor God, seeing that it was inseparably conjoined to God and has become identical to him on account of the substantial union? For it says, "The Word became flesh."[5]

Fragment 108

For Christ is one, moving himself by a single divine will, just as we know too that his activity is one, manifested in the various miracles and sufferings of his one nature. For he is, and is believed to be, God enfleshed.

Fragment 109

And the verse, "Father, if possible, let this cup pass from me, but let not my will but your will be done,"[6] does not indicate one and another will at variance with each other, but one and the same [will], which acts in a manner befitting divinity while begging to be excused from death in a manner befitting the economy, since the one who said this [sentence] was flesh-bearing God, who possesses no variance in the act of willing.

Fragment 110

But if he had come to the suffering and the cross as equipollent to and a sharer of the Father's substance, then why did he pray during his anguish for the cup to pass from him and that not his will but rather the Father's be done? And why was it necessary to draw attention to the will of the one praying unless it was dissonant with and contrary to God?

4 John 5:26. 5 John 1:14. 6 Matt 26:39; Luke 22:42.

Fragment 111

Christ is one human being as the Father is one God. Just as the latter is [so] by nature, so too is the former [so] by nature – a composite that is [somewhere] between God and human beings.

Fragment 112

If the Word is same-in-substance with the body, then it was not united to him. However, the Word was united to the body. Therefore, the Word is not same-in-substance with the body. If the body is same-in-substance with the Word, then the body was not seen and touched. For both would be invisible and untouchable if they are same-in-substance [with the Word]. But John says, "We have seen and touched him."[7] Therefore, the spirit of the Lord and the body are not same-in-substance. But the invisible and the untouchable was conjoined to the visible and touchable for the purpose of a union. As a result, in this [union] he became visible and touchable. Whoever says the body is same-in-substance with God blasphemes by holding that the incorporeal has a body, because the Son, who is same-in-substance with the Father, retains what is proper to him even when united to the flesh. And just because he is same-in-substance with God does not mean that he is not separated from his own body, lest the body be considered same-in-substance [with him].

Fragment 113

Intermediate states come into existence when different attributes come together into one entity, as the attributes of a donkey and a horse in a mule, and the attributes of white and black in the color gray, and the attributes of winter and summer in the air, effecting spring. No intermediate state has each of the extremes in its entirety but rather mixed together partially. Now the intermediate state of God and human beings is in Christ. Therefore, he is neither whole human being nor God but a mixture of God and human being.

Fragment 114

How is it not the true God who says, "Have I been with you so long, Philip, and you do not know me?"[8] With "so long" he indicates his time spent as a

7 1 John 1:1. 8 John 14:9.

human being with human beings and shows that the human being is God. Accordingly, we ought not be ashamed to say that such a human being is same-in-substance with God, recognized by the form of his Father's divinity as matter is by the body.

Fragment 116

His flesh gives us life on account of the divinity united to it in a substantial way. And what gives life is divine.[9] Therefore, the flesh is divine because it was conjoined to God. And it saves, while we are saved by sharing in it as if in nourishment. Now the nourishing agent is not[10] same-in-substance with that which is nourished and, being active in the thing being nourished, is not likewise nourished. And if it gives life, it is not given life like that which is given life, as it is not same-in-substance with that which is given life. Otherwise, then, it would be a "body of death"[11] like ours in need of being given life. Now Christ's body is not a body of death but of life. Therefore, the divine is not same-in-substance with the human.

Fragment 149

We say that the Lord is God by nature and a human being by nature, but in a single mixed nature, both fleshly and divine.

Fragment 153

The Lord Jesus Christ, then, is sinless as God and, along with the flesh, is same-in-substance with the only God and the fashioner before the ages. And the flesh, as God's flesh, is God, because it is same-in-substance with God, a part united to him that is same-in-substance with God and not separated. For it moves neither separately nor on its own, in the way that a human being does, being a self-directed animal. For by sharing in the flesh, God is the human being he would not be on his own, while, by sharing in God, the flesh is the God it would not be on its own. And God keeps all the things that accompany the flesh by reason of his unity with the flesh, while the flesh takes on God's characteristics by reason of its union with God.

9 See John 6:63; 2 Cor 3:6. 10 Here I add *ouk* with Daley. 11 Rom 7:24.

Fragment 154

Surely it is not the case that both together are from heaven; rather, it is the case that what is united to the heavenly and became one person with it is heavenly according to the union, and it is worshiped as heavenly by virtue of [our] worship of the heavenly God, and it saves as [something] heavenly does by virtue of the heavenly's power.

Fragment 155

The living Christ is a body inspired by God and a divine spirit in flesh, a heavenly mind of which we pray to partake according to [the verse], "But we have the mind of Christ,"[12] a holy flesh that is naturally united to the divinity and establishes the divinity in its partakers, the foundation of eternal life, the initiator of incorruption for human beings, the fashioner of everlasting creation, "the father of the age to come."[13]

12 1 Cor 2:16. 13 Isa 9:6.

28

Apollinarius of Laodicea, *Fragmentary Writings against Diodore and Flavian*

Introduction and Translation by Mark DelCogliano

INTRODUCTION

The motivations behind Apollinarius of Laodicea's Christology are debated by scholars, but it is safe to say that from the beginning he opposed any sort of dualist Christology.[1] In Antioch, in whose ecclesiastical affairs Apollinarius was involved since the early 360s, two presbyters connected with the pro-Nicene Meletian faction, Diodore and Flavian, espoused a dyophysite Christology.[2] Diodore became bishop of Tarsus in 378 and Flavian bishop of Antioch in 381. It seems that it was not until the late 370s that Apollinarius came into conflict with them, over issues that were as much ecclesio-political as Christological. Fragments of Apollinarius's writings against Diodore and Flavian are preserved in three later polemical treatises: Theodoret of Cyrrhus's *Eranistes*, Leontius of Byzantium's *Adversus Fraudes Apollinaristarum*, and the *Doctrina Patrum de Incarnatione Verbi*. These treatises mention a number of different Apollinarian sources for the fragments they preserve, but it is unclear if they refer to a single tract by Apollinarius or several. At least one of Apollinarius's writings against Diodore was addressed to a certain Herakleion who is otherwise unknown (Fragments 117–120). No more than titles are known about the others, however many there were. Fragments 121–146 are from tracts against Diodore, whereas Fragments 147–148 are drawn from a tract against Flavian. All the translations here are based on the critical edition of Hans Lietzmann, *Apollinaris von Laodicea und seine Schule: Texte und Untersuchungen*

1 For a fuller introduction to Apollinarius, see his *Recapitulation*, translated in this volume on pp. 301–307.

2 On Diodore, see his *Selected Fragments* in this volume on pp. 366–387.

(Tübingen: Mohr, 1904), 235–242 and 246–247. The numbering of fragments is that of Lietzmann. In cases where Theodoret of Cyrrhus's *Eranistes* is the source of the fragment, reference has been made to the Greek text in G. H. Ettlinger, *Theodoret of Cyrus: Eranistes* (Oxford: Clarendon Press, 1975). In cases where Leontius of Byzantium's *Adversus Fraudes Apollinaristarum* is the source of the fragment, reference has been made to the Greek text in Brian Daley, *Leontius of Byzantium: Complete Works* (Oxford: Oxford University Press, 2017).

TRANSLATION

Fragment 117

After God took up an instrument, he is both God insofar as he exerts agency and a human being insofar as he is the instrument. But since he remains God he has not been changed. The instrument and its mover naturally produce a single activity. But if there is a single activity, then there is also a single substance. Therefore, it has come to pass that there is one substance of the Word and the instrument.

Fragment 118

Any two beings that are united, whether in outward appearance or by agreement, remain two.

Fragment 119

It is unlawful for there to be one and the same worship of one and another substance, that is, of Maker and thing made, of God and human being. But there is a single worship of Christ. And in line with this, God and human being are understood in the one name [of "Christ"]. Therefore, God and human being are not one and another substance, but one [substance] according to the combination of God with a human body.

Fragment 120

Indeed, how is it not an impiety for one created and slavish substance to have one and the same worship as the Creator and Master?

Fragment 121

If one is not changed into what one assumes, and Christ assumed flesh, then he was not changed into flesh.

Fragment 122

For he gave himself to us in kinship through the body for the purpose of providing salvation. But that which saves is far nobler than that which is saved. Therefore, he is far nobler than us even in his embodiment. However, he would not be nobler if he had changed into flesh.

Fragment 123

The simple is one, but the composite cannot be one. So then, whoever proclaims that the one Word became flesh[3] admits that a change happened to him. But if the composite is one, in the same way as a human being [is one], whoever says, "The Word became flesh,"[4] because of the union with the flesh admits that there is oneness according to composition.

Fragment 124

Incarnation is emptying.[5] And the emptying revealed not a man, but the Son of Man,[6] who emptied himself in terms of the garment, not in terms of a transformation.

Fragment 125

Therefore, the characteristics of God and body are united. Fashioner to be worshiped, wisdom and power that is eternal – these things come from the divinity. Son of Mary, born at the last moment, a worshiper of God who advances in wisdom and is strengthened in power – these things come from the body. The suffering for sin and the curse passed away and changed into

3 See John 1:14. 4 John 1:14. 5 See Phil 2:7.
6 Literally, "not a human being but the Son of a human being."

impassibility and blessing, but the flesh did not pass away, nor will it pass away, nor will it be transformed into something incorporeal.[7]

Fragment 126

[Just as] human beings are same-in-substance with the irrational animals in that the body is irrational but are different-in-substance in that they are rational, so too God, though same-in-substance with human beings as far as the flesh is concerned, is different-in-substance in that he is Word and God.[8]

Fragment 127

The qualities of things mixed together are mixed and not destroyed, so that they are somehow[9] also distinct from the things mixed together, as wine is from water. There is neither a combination with a body, nor is the combination like that of bodies combining with bodies, but the combination also retains something that is unmixed, such that, on each occasion, according to need, the activity of the divinity is either independent or mixed together, as happened in the case of the Lord's fasting. When the divinity was mixed in, by the self-sufficiency of the divinity hunger was thwarted, but when the divinity no longer counterbalanced its need with self-sufficiency, hunger happened so as to destroy the devil. If the mixing of bodies made no alteration, how much more is this true of the mixing involving the divinity?

Fragment 128

If the mixture [of fire] with iron, which turns the iron into the fire itself so that it produces a fiery effect, does not change the iron's nature, neither does the union of God with the body constitute a change of the body, even though the body bestows divine powers upon those who can touch it.

7 For this sentence I follow the reading of Ettlinger p. 184, *kai hē katara parēlthen kai metepesen eis apatheian kai eulogian; hē de sarx ou parēlthen oude pareleusetai oude eis asōmaton metablēthēsetai*, instead of Lietzmann's *kai hē katara proēlthen oude pareleusetai oude eis asōmaton metablēthēsetai*. Lietzmann's text is defective in two ways: (1) it omits *kai metepesen eis apatheian kai eulogian; hē de sarx ou* due to homoioteleuton (*parēlthen … parēlthen*), and (2) it has *proēlthen* instead of *parēlthen*.

8 This fragment is nearly identical with Fragment 146.

9 Here I read *tropon tina* with Ettlinger instead of Lietzmann's *tina*.

Fragment 129

If a human being has both soul and body, and they remain as they are even in the union, how much more does Christ, who has divinity along with a body, have each of them, which persist and are not confused?

Fragment 130

For that which is human shares in the divine activity to the extent that it can, but it is as different as the least is from the greatest. And the human being is a slave of God, but God is not a slave of the human being nor of himself. And the one is something made by God, while the other is not something made by the human being or by himself.

Fragment 131

If someone takes [the passage], "Whatever he sees the Father [doing], he also does,"[10] as referring to Christ according to the divinity and not according to the flesh, according to which the one who became flesh differs from the Father who did not become flesh, he distinguishes between two divine activities. However, [the passage] makes no such distinction. Therefore, it does not speak in reference to the divinity.[11]

Fragment 132

Just as the human being is not irrational even though the rational is added to the irrational, so too the Savior is not a creature even though the creature is added to the uncreated God.

Fragment 133

The invisible, even when conjoined to a visible body and beheld through it, remains invisible. However, it also remains unconjoined insofar as it is not limited to the body. And the body, while remaining within its own limit, receives the union with God in accordance with the fact that it is given life, and that which is given life does not give life.

10 John 5:19, altered.
11 Here I read *eis theotēta* with Ettlinger instead of Lietzmann's *theotēta*.

Fragment 134

If the mixture of the soul with the body exists from the beginning in an organic union, and it neither makes the soul visible through the body nor transforms it into the other attributes of the body such that it can be both cut and diminished, then how much more is it true that God, since he is not organically united to a body by nature,[12] is united to the body immutably. And if the body of a human being remains in its own nature, even when endowed with soul, then in the case of Christ the mixture did not change the body such that it is no longer a body.

Fragment 135

Whoever confesses that scripture proves soul and body to be one contradicts himself when he claims that such a union of the Word with the body constitutes a change, for this change is not beheld in the case of the soul.

Fragment 136

If those who deny that the flesh of the Lord continues to exist are impious, so much more are those who do not confess that he has become incarnate in the first place!

Fragment 137

John said that the temple would be destroyed, that is, the body of the one who would raise it.[13] The body is entirely one with him and [the temple] is not another one alongside them. But if the body of the Lord has become one with the Lord, the properties of the body became his properties because of the body.

Fragment 138

For this is true, that the conjunction with the body does not involve a circumscription of the Word, in such a way that he has nothing more than

12 Here I read *phusei sōmati sumphuēs* with Ettlinger instead of Lietzmann's *sōmati sumphuēs*.
13 See John 2:19.

embodiment. Accordingly, even in death immortality remains with him. For if the Word transcends this composition, he also transcends the dissolution of it. And death is dissolution. For he was neither contained by the composition (in which case the [rest of the] world would have been emptied [of him]), nor did he have in the dissolution that deficiency which comes from dissolution, like the soul does.

Fragment 139

Just as the Savior says that the dead will go forth from their tombs,[14] even though their souls will not go forth from there, so too he says that he will be raised from the dead, even though it is the body that is raised.

Fragment 140

God's union with the flesh was remarkable and marvelous, and it happened only once and not a second time. Your soul[15] does not accept this in the least, nor do the souls of those who are leading you to this impiety and antichrist-like faithlessness. And you joke about the supreme union and say that the properties of God and the properties of the flesh no longer remain if there is a union, but that the supreme union is dissolved if we confess the supreme union in the flesh from David.

Fragment 141

So you[16] are irritated that we do not accept that what comes from the seed of David received immortality by God's grace. And if we are asked for the reason [that we don't accept it], we say: [he received immortality] because of the supreme union.

Fragment 142

And [Diodore] is not ashamed to say that the nature is the same but the birth is different, even though it is pointless and superfluous for the birth from the Virgin to be introduced if the one born were not deserving of this birth but rather was identical with those born of a man and a woman. He

14 See Matt 11:5. 15 That is, Diodore of Tarsus's soul.
16 That is, Diodore of Tarsus.

ridicules the supreme union as supreme impiety, even though the divine scriptures clearly introduce it, neither making what is human destructive of God nor negating what is human through what is divine.

Fragment 143

And since you exhort us to answer, "How is the seed of David from the divine substance?", listen: "It's so in accordance with the incarnation." "How is the created uncreated?" "Because it was united to the uncreated." "How is the fruit of David's loins the fashioner of creation?" "Because it was united to the fashioner." "How is what comes from Abraham before Abraham?" "Because it was united to what was before Abraham."

Fragment 144

But as he prattles on about these things, let him explain how what was conjoined with God in a union of person is not God along with him, how what was united to the uncreated in a living union is not uncreated along with him. For if there isn't a shared name, then what has been mixed together like this amounts to nothing. And it would be the most illogical thing of all if we were to apply names used for the body to the incorporeal when we say that the Word became flesh but not ascribe the name used for the incorporeal to the body, even if only because of its union with it. And if he wonders how the created is united in the name used for the uncreated, by how much more will someone else rightly wonder how the uncreated is united in the name used for the created flesh.

Fragment 145

If the Word was called flesh because of the union, it follows also that the flesh is called Word because of the union. Just as it is the Word, so also it is uncreated, not because it was not created but because the Word is shown forth from this union.

Fragment 146

Just as human beings are same-in-substance with the irrational animals in that the body is irrational but are different-in-substance in that they are rational, so too the Lord, though same-in-substance with human beings as far as the flesh is concerned, is different-in-substance insofar as he is Word and God.[17]

Fragment 147

And by how much more does that which characterizes each of the united natures remain in the case of the mixture of the incorporeal with a body? For indeed the body remains a body and the incorporeal remains incorporeal. And by a most perfect union God is said to be embodied and the body to be deified. And insofar as the embodied God is human being, he is both together, and insofar as the deified body is God, again, it is both together.

Fragment 148

The body is not[18] already far removed from being something fashioned and being in the form of a slave, but it has been glorified by its natural union with the uncreated, at the very moment of its birth from the Virgin. And in this it did not change from being something fashioned into being uncreated, but it was united to the uncreated. And being God according to its union with God, it is uncreated because it is God. And since it could not become the Father's body (for the Father is not embodied), for this reason the body can never be called "unbegotten." It is neither "unbegotten in its own nature" just as it is not "begotten of God," nor "unbegotten by union" just as it is "Son" and "offspring" by reason of its union with the begotten Son, a union that is both natural and from the beginning.[19]

17 This fragment is nearly identical with Fragment 126.
18 Here I add *ouk* with Daley.
19 It is possible that the phrases in quotation are from Flavian.

29

Basil of Caesarea, *Letters* 261 and 262

Introduction and Translation by Mark DelCogliano

INTRODUCTION

Basil of Caesarea (ca. 330–378) spent most of his ecclesiastical career combating what he took to be the triple threat of the Heteroousian theology of Eunomius, the Pneumatomachian theology of Eustathius of Sebasteia, and the modalist theology of Marcellus of Ancyra, in the course of which he played a seminal role in the development of the doctrine of the Trinity declared orthodox at the Council of Constantinople in 381. He has generally not been recognized for his Christological contributions. While it is true that the controversy over Apollinarius emerged in the last few years of his life, he did not leave behind a specifically anti-Apollinarian work as did his fellow Cappadocians Gregory of Nazianzus and Gregory of Nyssa. Nonetheless, Basil's Christology is important because it is a witness to the Christological concerns in the mid-fourth century *before* the controversy over Apollinarius came to dominate the Christological agenda in the East for the next generation or two. Unfortunately, his Christology has to be pieced together from various comments scattered throughout his corpus.

Letters 261 and 262 are extremely valuable for this task. In these letters, which can be dated no more precisely than to the mid- to late 370s, Basil refutes some contemporaries who maintain that Christ's body was "heavenly." It appears that this claim was motivated by a concern to preserve Christ's divinity from being somehow affected by the passions of his human body. The Son's impassible divinity is protected by keeping it away from any real contact with humanity, by positing that his body was heavenly. Basil thought his opponents' way of affirming the divine immutability was grossly deficient. Among several counterarguments that he offers, Basil assumes that the incarnation can be saving only if human nature is united to divinity; if God turns himself into his own kind of body, a heavenly body, then humanity is not saved. Furthermore, Basil affirms that Christ experienced all those human passions that are natural and necessary, but none of those which led to sin, in order to demonstrate that the incarnation is not an illusion but rather true – that is, it involves an assumption of real human nature. It appears that for Basil Christ's ability to come into close contact with human passions without being affected by them is essential for the soteriological effect of the incarnation. Basil sees the birth of Jesus from Mary as further confirmation of Christ's assumption of true humanity. He stresses that by being born from Mary, Christ was able to assume the "lump" (*phyrama*) of Adam, that is, the "clay," "matter," or physical "stuff" common to all human beings.[1] Basil was keen to affirm the soteriological effect of Christ's visitation in the flesh and accordingly stressed Christ's full humanity, like ours in all things and even subject to human passions, but sinless, while at the same time upholding the impassibility and immutability of Christ's divine nature.

This translation is based on Yves Courtonne, *Saint Basile. Correspondance. Tome III* (Paris: Société d'Édition "Les Belles Lettres," 2003), 115–120, in consultation with Roy J. Deferrari, *Basil: The Letters, Volume IV*, Loeb Classical Library 270 (Cambridge, MA: Harvard University Press, 1934), 72–88.

TRANSLATION

Letter 261

To those in Sozopolis

1. I have read the letter, most honored brothers, which you sent about your situation. And for your having invited us to share your worries in dealing with the things that are pressing for you and worthy of attention, we have given thanks to the Lord. But we have groaned upon hearing that, in addition to the turmoil brought by the Arians upon the churches and the confusion they have caused over the account of the faith, yet again another silly idea[2] has sprung up among you, which is throwing the brotherhood into great distress, as you have written to us: people are introducing things that are novel and unfamiliar to the ears of the faithful as if they were actually

1 Basil's language here is Pauline: see Rom 9:21, 11:16; 1 Cor 5:6–7; and Gal 5:9.
2 In Greek, *kenophōnia*. Other manuscripts read *kainophōnia*, "novelty."

from the teaching of the scriptures. For you have written that there are some among you who are destroying the saving economy of our Lord Jesus Christ, insofar as they can, and are nullifying the grace of the great mystery,[3] which was concealed in silence from the ages[4] but was manifested "at the proper time,"[5] when the Lord, having gone through all things pertaining to the care of the human race, after all these things graciously bestowed upon us his own visitation. For he helped what he himself had formed, first through the patriarchs whose lives were set forth as examples and rules for those who want to follow in the footsteps of the saints and with a zeal like theirs to arrive at the perfection of good works. Then he gave the law to help them, having ordained it through angels by the hand of Moses,[6] then prophets who announced beforehand the salvation that was going to come, and judges, kings, and righteous men and women who performed mighty deeds by a hidden hand. After all these things, "in the last days,"[7] he was himself "manifested in the flesh,"[8] "born of a woman, born under the law, in order to redeem those under the law, so that we might receive adoption as sons."[9]

2. So if the Lord's visitation in the flesh has not happened, the Redeemer has not paid the penalty to death on our behalf, nor has he shattered the reign of death by himself. For if that which was reigned over by death were one thing and that which was assumed by the Lord were another, then death would not have ceased from its own works, the sufferings of the God-bearing flesh would not have become our gain, he would not have killed sin in the flesh,[10] we who died in Adam would not have been made alive in Christ,[11] that which had fallen apart would not have been refashioned, that which had broken down would not have been set right again, and that which had been alienated through the serpent's deceit would not have been brought into intimacy with God. For all these things are denied by those who claim that the Lord arrived with a heavenly body. And what need was there of the holy Virgin, if the God-bearing[12] flesh had not been

3 See 1 Tim 3:16. 4 See Eph 3:9; Col 1:26. 5 Titus 1:3. 6 See Gal 3:19.
7 Heb 1:2. 8 1 Tim 3:16. 9 Gal 4:4–5. 10 See Rom 8:3–4.
11 See 1 Cor 15:22.
12 In Greek, *theophoros*. The same word appears a few lines above. Here we follow the edition of Deferrari; Courtonne has *christophoros*, "Christ-bearing." The manuscripts have both. Basil also calls Christ's flesh "God-bearing" in *On the Holy Spirit* 5.12, *Homily on Psalm 59* 4, and *Homily on the Holy Birth of Christ* 3, and some manuscripts of these texts also have *christophoros* instead of *theophoros*. The thesis that Christ was a "God-bearing" man was condemned as Nestorian in the fifth of the Twelve Anathemas which

destined to be assumed from the lump of Adam? But who is so brazen as now to renew once again, through sophistical words and evidence purportedly drawn from the scriptures, that doctrine of Valentinus which had long ago been silenced? For this impiety of docetism is not very recent but it took its origin long ago from the empty-headed Valentinus, who by having wrenched a few sayings of the Apostle from their context constructed for himself an impious fabrication, saying that he assumed "the form of a slave"[13] and not the slave himself, and saying that the Lord had been born "in likeness"[14] but the human being itself was not assumed by him. These people are accustomed to utter statements akin to these, and it is fitting to bemoan them for introducing these novel blasphemies to you.

3. Claiming that the passions of the human being pass over to the divinity itself is a mark of those who never preserve consistency in their thinking and do not understand that passions of the flesh are one thing, those of the flesh endowed with soul another, and those of the soul using a body still another. So then, it is a property of the flesh to be cut, made smaller, and dispersed, and again for the flesh endowed with soul to be weary, in pain, hungry, thirsty, and overcome by sleep, but for the soul using a body to have grief, anxiety, cares, and all such things. Some of these are natural and necessary for [every] living being, whereas others arise from a depraved will and are introduced through an undisciplined life and lack of training in virtue. Accordingly, it appears that the Lord took upon himself the natural passions in order to confirm that the humanification was true and not a mirage, but as for the passions stemming from vice, which sully the purity of our life, these he repelled as unworthy of his undefiled divinity. This is why he is said to have come "in the likeness of sinful flesh."[15] And so, he assumed our flesh with its natural passions but "he committed no sin."[16] But just as death, which was transmitted to us in the flesh through Adam, was swallowed up by the divinity,[17] so too sin was utterly destroyed by the

Cyril of Alexandria appended to his *Third Letter to Nestorius*, translated in this volume on pp. 623–637, a letter which became viewed as a standard expression of Christological orthodoxy, especially among those who tended to the miaphysite position. Accordingly, the reading *christophoros* is probably an intentional alteration made by scribes concerned to bring Basil into step with later Christological orthodoxy.

13 Phil 2:7. 14 Phil 2:7.

15 Rom 8:3. At this point some manuscripts include an additional sentence: "For it was not in the likeness of flesh, as it seems to these people, but 'in the likeness of sinful flesh.'"

16 1 Pet 2:22. 17 See 1 Cor 15:54.

righteousness that is in Christ Jesus, so that in the resurrection we might receive flesh that is neither subject to death nor liable to sin.[18]

These, my brothers, are the mysteries of the church; these are the traditions of the fathers. We warn every human being who fears the Lord and awaits God's judgment not to be led astray by diverse teachings. If someone teaches differently, if he does not have recourse to sound formulations of the faith but instead rejects the oracles of the Spirit and places more value on his own teaching than the teachings of the gospel, be on guard against such a person. And may the Lord grant that some day we meet one another in the same place, so that whatever has escaped our missive we may supply through conversation. For we have written you only a few things out of many, not wanting to exceed the proper bounds of an epistle and at the same time being convinced that for those who fear the Lord even a brief treatment suffices.

*

* *

Letter 262

To the Monk Urbicius

1. You have done well to send us a letter, for you have demonstrated the fruit of love to no small degree – so do this unceasingly. Yet do not think that you need to apologize whenever you send us a letter. For we understand ourselves and we know that every human being is by nature equal to all in terms of honor, and that preeminence among us is not based on family, nor on an abundance of riches, nor on the body's physique, but on the preeminence of fear with respect to God. So what prevents you, when you fear the Lord more, from being better than us in this regard? So then, send us letters unceasingly and inform us how the brothers in your circle [think][19] and which members of your church have sound views, that we may know to whom we need to write and on whom we can rely. Because I am hearing that there are some who are debasing the correct teaching about the humanification of the Lord by twisted suppositions, I exhort them

18 See Rom 5:12 and 17.

19 Here Basil could simply mean "how the brothers are doing," but since in what follows he wants Urbicius to provide names, his inquiry "how" may be more specific.

through Your Charity to drop that absurd idea which we are told some are holding, that God himself was turned into flesh and did not assume the lump of Adam through Mary but by means of his own divinity he himself was transformed into the material nature.

2. It is very easy to refute this absurdity. But since the blasphemy is immediately evident, I think a [brief] treatment alone suffices for the one who fears the Lord. For if he was "turned," he was also changed. But this is something that should remain both unsaid and unthought, because God said, "I am and I do not change."[20] Next, how does the benefit of the humanification pass over to us, unless our body having been conjoined to the divinity became mightier than the reign of death? For it was not by being "turned"[21] that he brought his own body into existence, as if it came to exist by his divine nature being thickened. And how can the unbounded divinity be circumscribed in the mass of a small body, even if the whole nature of the Only-Begotten was "turned"?

But I think no one with any sense and in possession of the fear of God suffers this debility. Since however the rumor came my way that some of those connected with Your Charity are in the grip of this mental illness, I have judged it essential for our letter not to provide a mere greeting but to contain something that is also able to edify the souls of those who fear the Lord. So then, we exhort that these things be subjected to ecclesiastical correction and that you avoid communion with the heretics, knowing that indifference in these matters deprives us of our freedom of expression in Christ.

20 Mal 3:6.

21 Here the translation follows the Greek text of Deferrari (*ou gar trapeis*) rather than Courtonne (*ho gar trapeis*), for which there is no manuscript support.

30

Basil of Caesarea, *Homily on the Holy Birth of Christ*

Introduction and Translation by Mark DelCogliano

INTRODUCTION

Among other things, Basil of Caesarea was renowned for his preaching.[1] Both as a presbyter and then a bishop, he preached on a regular basis on the various Sundays, feasts, and celebrations of the church's liturgical calendar, as well as at synods and other ecclesiastical gatherings. Only about fifty of his homilies are extant, one of which is his *Homily on the Holy Birth of Christ*. Some scholars claim it is one of the earliest witnesses to the celebration of Christmas on December 25, but if not, it was probably preached on January 6 in celebration of the feast of the Theophany (also known as Epiphany). The year cannot be determined with any precision, but Basil probably delivered it during his episcopacy, 370–378, which is roughly the same period in which *Letters* 261 and 262 were written.

After a preface in which Basil speaks about the incomprehensibility of Christ's eternal birth from the Father, he answers a series of questions about the incarnation, posed by an imaginary interlocutor. Throughout Basil stresses the redemptive purpose of the incarnation: God became a human being to deliver humanity from sin and death and to restore human beings to kinship with God. Basil conceives of the incarnation as God's presence in human flesh, in a human body that is just like ours, but in a unique way unlike his intermittent presence in the prophets. Basil affirms divine immutability even in the incarnation, explaining that the Word was not diminished or changed when he came to dwell among us. Nor does the human body impart its weakness to the Word; rather, human flesh comes

1 For a fuller introduction to Basil, see his *Letters* 261 and 262, translated in this volume on pp. 348–353.

to share in the divinity in order to be saved. This parallels a concern seen in *Letters* 261 and 262.

The final question posed by the imaginary interlocutor concerns the "workshop" of the divine economy, which Basil identifies as the body of the holy Virgin, citing Matthew 1:18.[2] The remainder of the sermon, except for the exhortatory conclusion, is devoted to providing a commentary on selected verses of the infancy narrative in Matthew 1:18–2:11. He discusses in detail why Mary was betrothed to Joseph, why Joseph was afraid to marry Mary and decided to divorce her quietly, whether Mary was a virgin when she conceived and remained so after the birth of Jesus, and who the magi were and what sort of star they followed to Bethlehem. In the exhortatory conclusion Basil once again affirms that in the incarnation the Word's divinity remained intact and undefiled even though it had come to be in a material nature.

This translation is based on the edition of Luigi Gambero, *L'omelia sulla generazione di Cristo di Basilo di Cesarea. Il posto della vergine Maria*, Marian Studies Library n.s. 13–14 (Dayton: University of Dayton, 1981–1982), 177–200. It was originally published in *St. Basil the Great: On Fasting and Feasts*, translations by Susan R. Holman and Mark DelCogliano, introduction by Susan R. Holman, Popular Patristics Series 50 (Yonkers: St. Vladimir's Seminary Press, 2013), 27–40. It appears here by permission of St. Vladimir's Seminary Press (www.svspress.com).

TRANSLATION

1. Revere in silence that birth of Christ which was first and fitting and proper to his divinity. We should keep our mind from searching into it or being inquisitive about it. For when no time nor age comes between them,[3] when there is no way to imagine things, no spectator present, no narrator, how can the intellect even form a thought? How can the tongue serve the mind? Indeed, the Father was and the Son was born. Do not say, "When?" That's a stupid question. Do not ask, "How?" An answer is impossible. For "when" has temporal overtones and "how" makes us slide toward corporeal

2 The image of Mary as the "workshop" is adopted later, for example, in Proclus's *Homily on the Holy Virgin Theotokos* 1, translated in this volume on pp. 577–584.

3 That is, between the Father and Son. The thought here is that since the Son's birth from the Father is non-temporal, the human mind, which can operate only in a temporal manner, is unsuited for understanding it.

ways of conceptualizing his birth. I can say only what scripture says: as radiance from glory and as an image from the archetype.[4] But since this rationale for responding to such questions does not put an end to your inquisitive thoughts, I take refuge in the ineffability of its glory. I acknowledge that the manner in which the divine birth took place is incomprehensible to human thoughts and impossible to express with human words. Do not say, "If he was born, he was not."[5] Do not wickedly seize upon the vulgar interpretation of these words,[6] corrupting the truth and defiling the divine teaching on the basis of examples here below. I said, "he was born," so that I could indicate his origin and cause, not so that I could expose the Only-Begotten as posterior to time. Do not allow your intellect to tumble into the pitfall of making the ages prior to the Son, seeing that they did not yet exist nor had yet to come into being. For how can things that have been made be prior to the one who made them?[7] But I see that unawares I have gotten into what I wanted to avoid in the course of this sermon. So then, let us put aside talk about that eternal and ineffable birth, realizing that our intellect is quite unequal to understanding such realities and our speech quite insufficient for expressing such thoughts.

2. So then, we must consider how far we fall when we move from the truth itself to speaking about the truth. Even though the intellect cannot ascend to the nature of incomprehensible realities, it is still impossible to find a mode of discourse that communicates whatever it does think. God is upon the earth. God is among human beings.[8] He does not establish the law by fire and trumpet and smoking mountain,[9] nor by thick darkness and a gloom and a storm that frightens the souls of those who hear it.[10] Instead, by means of a body he engages in gentle and pleasant conversation with those who are the same in kind. God is in flesh. He is not active at intervals as he was among the prophets. Instead he possesses a humanity[11] connatural and united to himself, and restores all humanity[12] to himself through flesh the same as ours in kind.

So then, one might say, "How did the splendor come to all by means of one?[13] How can divinity come to be in flesh?" As fire comes to be in iron: not

4 See Heb 1:3.
5 This of course is a version of what Arius is supposed to have claimed: it logically follows from the fact of the Son's birth that the Son did not exist before he was born. Pro-Nicene theologians such as Basil denied that the Son's birth implied a beginning to his existence.
6 That is, the words "he was born," not the sentence, "If he was born, he was not."
7 See Heb 1:2. 8 See Bar 3:38. 9 See Exod 20:18.
10 See Deut 4:11, 5:22; Heb 12:18–19. 11 In Greek, *to anthrōpon*.
12 In Greek, *tēn anthrōpotēta*. 13 Basil probably means "one body."

by a change of place, but by a sharing of itself. For the fire does not go out of itself and into the iron; rather, while remaining in its place, it shares its own power with the iron. It is in no way diminished when it shares itself, and the whole of it fills whatever shares in it. So it is in this way too that God the Word did not move out of himself when "he dwelt among us."[14] Nor did he undergo a change when "the Word became flesh."[15] Heaven was not deprived of what it contained, and earth received the heavenly one within its own embraces. Do not suppose that the divinity fell. For he did not move from one place to another as bodies do. Do not imagine that the divinity was altered when it was transferred into flesh. For the immortal is immutable.

So then, one might ask, "How was God the Word not filled with bodily weakness?" We reply: as the fire does not share in the distinguishing marks of the iron. Iron is black and cold, but nonetheless when turned in the fire it takes on the outward form of fire. The iron glows, yet the fire is not blackened. The iron is set ablaze, yet it does not cool the flame. So too it is with the human flesh of the Lord: it shares in the divinity, yet it does not impart its own weakness to the divinity. Can it be that you did not grant to the divinity an activity on par with that of this mortal fire? Did you imagine passibility in the impassible one on the basis of human weakness? Are you puzzled how the easily corruptible nature can have incorruptibility through its communion with God? Realize that it's a mystery. God is in flesh that he may kill the death that lurks therein. For as the harm caused by poisonous drugs can be overcome by antidotes when they are assimilated by the body, and as the darkness residing in a house is dissolved by the introduction of light, so too the death that dominates in human nature is obliterated by the presence of divinity. And as ice in water, for as long as it is night and dark, is stronger than the liquid that contains it, but the warming sun melts the ice by its ray, so too death rules until the advent of Christ, but when "the saving grace of God appears and the sun of righteousness rises, death is swallowed up in victory,"[16] unable to bear the visitation of true life.

O the depth of the goodness of God and his love for humanity! In response to his superabundant love for humanity we rebel against being his servants. We seek to know the reason why God is among human beings, though we should be adoring his goodness.

3. O human being, what should we do with you? When God remains in the heights, you do not seek him. When he comes down and converses with

14 John 1:14. 15 John 1:14.
16 A concatenation of Titus 2:11, Mal 4:2, and 1 Cor 15:54.

you through flesh, you do not receive him. But how will you be brought into affinity with God when you seek explanations? Realize that God is in flesh for this reason: because the flesh that was cursed needed to be sanctified, the flesh that was weakened needed to be strengthened, the flesh that was alienated from God needed to be brought into affinity with him, the flesh that had fallen in paradise needed to be led back into heaven.

And what is the workshop for this divine economy? The body of the holy Virgin. Who is responsible for the birth? The Holy Spirit and the Power of the Most High who overshadowed her.[17] [To answer these questions] even better, listen to what the gospel says: "When his mother Mary had been betrothed to Joseph, before they came together, she was found to be with child by the Holy Spirit."[18] Even though she was betrothed to a man, the Virgin was judged suitable for service in this economy, such that virginity would be honored and marriage not disparaged. While virginity was chosen as suitable for holiness, the initial phases of marriage were included through the betrothal. At the same time, so that Joseph could witness Mary's purity with his own eyes and she would not be subjected to ridicule as if she had defiled her virginity, she was given a betrothed who would defend her character. I must also mention another reason that is no less honorable than those already stated: the suitable time for the humanification of the Lord was predestined long ago and prearranged "before the foundation of the world."[19] It occurred when it was appropriate for the Holy Spirit and the Power of the Most High to form that God-bearing[20] flesh. Since the human race down to Mary did not have a purity that matched hers in honor, such that it could receive the Holy Spirit's activity, the blessed Virgin had been betrothed in anticipation of her being chosen for this, and the betrothal did not harm her virginity. But one of the ancients mentions another reason, that the betrothal to Joseph was intended to conceal Mary's virginity from "the ruler of this age."[21] The external form of the betrothal to the Virgin was

17 See Luke 1:35. 18 Matt 1:18. 19 1 Pet 1:20; see John 17:24.

20 In Greek, *theophoros*. The claim that Christ was a God-bearing human being was condemned in the fifth of Cyril's Twelve Anathemas appended to his *Third Letter to Nestorius*, translated in this volume on pp. 623–637. Some manuscripts of this homily of Basil read *christophoros* instead of *theophoros*, which is probably an intentional alteration made by a scribe concerned to bring Basil into step with a later Christological orthodoxy.

21 1 Cor 2:6, 8. This "one of the ancients" is Ignatius of Antioch, who wrote, "and the virginity of Mary and her childbearing escaped the notice of the ruler of this age" (*Epistle to the Ephesians* 19.1). Selections from Ignatius's letters are translated in this volume on pp. 53–62.

intended to be a kind of decoy for the wicked one. For he kept an eye on virgins for a long time, from the moment he heard the prophet say: "Behold, a virgin shall conceive and bear a son."[22] So then, he who hoped to ambush virginity was deceived by the betrothal. After all, he knew that his dominion would end when the Lord was manifested in the flesh.

4. "Before they came together, she was found to be with child of the Holy Spirit."[23] It was Joseph who discovered both of these things, that she had conceived and what caused her to conceive, that it was "of the Holy Spirit." And so, fearing to be called the husband of such a woman, "he resolved to divorce her quietly."[24] For he did not have the stomach to publicize what had happened to her. But "being a righteous man,"[25] he obtained a revelation of the mysteries. "For as he considered these things, an angel of the Lord appeared to him in a dream, saying: 'Do not fear to take Mary as your wife.'"[26] Do not think that he was trying to conceal some sin of hers in the face of absurd conjectures. For he was called a righteous man, and he who is righteous does not conceal transgressions through silence. "Do not fear to take Mary as your wife." This shows that neither was he vexed at her nor did he feel loathing for her; rather, it indicates that he feared to take her because she was filled with the Holy Spirit. "For that which has been born in her is of the Holy Spirit."[27] And here it is clear that the Lord's frame did not come into existence as the ordinary nature of the flesh does. For what she was pregnant with was immediately perfect in the flesh, not formed through incremental stages of construction, as is clear from the words themselves. For it did not say: "that which has been created," but "that which has been born." So then, since the flesh was formed from holiness, it was worthy of being united to the divinity of the Only-Begotten.

"And she will bear a son, and you shall call his name Jesus."[28] We have observed that names purposely imposed indicate the nature of those to whom they refer, as in the case of Abraham, Isaac, and Israel. For the designation given to each of these men does not intimate their bodily characteristic but rather the distinguishing mark of the virtuous deed accomplished by each of them. Therefore, in the present case he is designated "Jesus" – that is, salvation of the people.[29] It is at this point that the mystery appointed before the ages and announced long ago by the prophets had its fulfillment.[30] "Behold, a

22 Isa 7:14. 23 Matt 1:18. 24 Matt 1:19. 25 Matt 1:19.
26 Matt 1:20. 27 Matt 1:20. 28 Matt 1:21. 29 See Matt 1:21.
30 See Matt 1:22.

virgin shall conceive and bear a son, and they shall call his name 'Emmanuel,' which translated means 'God with us.'"[31] Long ago this very designation disclosed the whole mystery of God's being among human beings, when it says that "Emmanuel" is interpreted "God with us."

And no one should be misled by the captiousness of the Jews, who claim the prophet used the word "maiden" instead of "virgin," as in, "Behold, a maiden shall conceive." In the first place, it is a mark of the utmost irrationality to think that what the Lord gave as a sign could be something so ordinary and taken for granted by everyone. For what does the prophet say? "And again the Lord spoke to Ahaz, saying: 'Ask a sign from the Lord your God, in the depth or in the height.' And Ahaz said: 'I will not ask, and I will not put the Lord to the test!'"[32] Then a little bit after he said: "Therefore the Lord himself will give you a sign. Behold, the virgin shall conceive."[33] Seeing that Ahaz did not ask a sign in the depth or in the height,[34] so that you could learn that "he who descended to the lower parts of the earth is he who ascended above all the heavens,"[35] the Lord himself gave a sign. And this sign is something incredible and wonderful, and quite contrary to the ordinary nature of things. The same woman is both a virgin and a mother, remaining in the holy condition of her virginity while allotted the blessing of childbearing. But if some have rendered it "maiden" instead of "virgin" based on their interpretation of the Hebrew term, nothing is ruined by using this word. For we have found in the customary usage of scripture that "maiden" is often used instead of "virgin." For example, in Deuteronomy it says: "If a man meets a young virgin who is not betrothed, and seizes her and lies with her, and he is found, then the man who lay with her shall give to the father of the maiden fifty double-drachmas."[36]

5. "And when Joseph woke from sleep, he took her as his wife."[37] He undertook his marriage with the disposition that is incumbent upon spouses, having affection for his wife and caring for her in every way. But he abstained from marital relations. For it says: "He did not know her until she had given birth to her firstborn son."[38] Now this verse has given rise to the conjecture that, after rendering pure service in accomplishing the birth of the Lord through the Holy Spirit, Mary did not renounce the customary marital relations. But in our opinion, even if none of this harms the

31 See Matt 1:23. 32 Isa 7:10–12. 33 Isa 7:14. 34 See Isa 7:11.
35 Eph 4:9–10. 36 Deut 22:28–29. 37 Matt 1:24.
38 Matt 1:25. Modern critical editions excise the words "her firstborn" as a harmonization with Luke 2:7.

account of piety – for virginity was necessary for service in the economy, but inquiring into what happened next out of curiosity should be avoided by reason of its mystery – nonetheless, since lovers of Christ do not accept the opinion that the Theotokos ever ceased being a virgin, we think the following testimonies suffice. Let us return to: "He did not know her until she had given birth to her son." In many instances the word "until" seems to suggest a kind of temporal boundary, but in reality it indicates indefiniteness. What did the Lord mean when he said: "And behold, I am with you all days, until the close of the age"?[39] Indeed, not that the Lord was not going to be with the saints after this age! Rather, it means that the promise of the present age will not be rescinded in the age to come. So we say that in this case too the word "until" should be taken in the same way. Now when "firstborn" is said, by no means is he the firstborn in comparison to siblings who came after him. Rather, he is called the firstborn because he was the first one to open the womb of his mother.[40] It is also clear from the story about Zechariah that Mary was always a virgin. For there is an account, and it has been handed down to us from the tradition, that Zechariah entrusted Mary to the place for the virgins after conceiving the Lord. Then he was slaughtered by the Jews between the temple and the altar.[41] Charges had been brought against him by the people, on the grounds that by his actions he established that incredible and famous sign: a virgin gave birth and her virginity was not destroyed.

"Now when Jesus was born in Bethlehem of Judaea in the days of Herod the king, behold, magi from the East came to Jerusalem, saying: 'Where is he who has been born the king of the Jews?'"[42] The magi are a people of Persia. They are interested in divination, charms, and natural remedies, and devote themselves to the observation of the heavens. It appears that Balaam also practiced this sort of divination. When summoned by Balak to curse Israel using certain words, Balaam in his fourth oracle says the following about the Lord: "A man who sees, who hears the words of God, knows the knowledge of the Most High, and having seen a vision of God in sleep, his eyes were uncovered. I will point to him, but not now; I bless him, but he does not draw near. A star shall arise from Jacob, and a man shall spring out of Israel."[43] And so, as the magi searched for the place in Judaea mentioned in this ancient prophecy, they came to Jerusalem

39 Matt 28:20. 40 See Exod 13:2, 13:15, 34:19; Num 3:12. 41 See Matt 23:35.
42 Matt 2:1–2. 43 Num 24:15–17.

to learn where the king of the Jews had been born.[44] Perhaps when the Lord's epiphany weakened the power of the adversary at that time, they sensed their own actions becoming ineffectual and attributed great power to the one who had been born. Therefore, when they found the child they adored him with gifts. Even though they are a people alienated from God and a stranger to the covenants, the magi were the first deemed worthy to worship him, since the testimony of enemies is the most credible. Now if the Jews had been the first to worship him, it would have redounded to the glory of their people in the eyes of others. But as it is, they exhibited no interest in worshiping him as God. Hence foreigners worshiped the one whose own people condemned and crucified him.

Now since the magi were devoted to the motions of the heavens, they could not ignore it when they beheld something incredible among the heavenly spectacles: a new and unfamiliar star that had risen at the birth of the Lord. 6. No one should draw upon the arguments of astrology to explain the rising of this star. Those who suggest that birth is dependent upon the already existing stars maintain that what happens in each person's life is caused by a particular configuration of the stars. But no configuration of the stars signified the birth of a king in this case, nor was this star one of them. For those stars formed in the beginning along with the rest of creation are either totally motionless or possess unceasing motion. But when this star appeared it seems to have had both, in that it moves and is stationary. Now among the already existing stars, some are fixed and never move, whereas others wander and are never stationary. But since this star both moves and is stationary, it is clear that it belongs to neither category. For it moved from the East to Bethlehem, but it was stationary above that place where the child was. Therefore, when the magi set out from the East, they followed this star as their guide. Upon reaching Jerusalem, their arrival threw the whole city into a tumult, and the magi made the king afraid.[45]

So when the magi found what they had been seeking, they honored him with gifts: gold, frankincense, and myrrh.[46] Perhaps also in giving these gifts they are adhering to the prophecy of Balaam, who spoke of Christ as follows: "Lying down he rested like a lion and like a young lion. Who shall rouse him? Those who bless you are blessed, and those who curse you are cursed."[47] So then, since scripture uses the lion to indicate royalty, and ly-

44 See Matt 2:2. 45 See Matt 2:3. 46 See Matt 2:11. 47 Num 24:9.

ing down to indicate suffering, and the power to bless to indicate divinity, the magi are following the prophecy when they present gold as to a king, frankincense as to one who will die, and myrrh as to God.

Now those whose explanations of issues pertaining to this passage are based on futile investigations cannot claim that this star was similar to comets, which are observed in heaven at a fixed place especially when the successions of kings are revealed. Now on the whole comets are also motionless, since their combustion is confined to a circumscribed place. Comets, whether "beams" or "pits," vary in appearance and the designations given them are based on their appearance. But all of them come into existence in the same way. For when the air surrounding the earth overflows and is diffused into the aethereal region, as it rises there it produces something thick and turbid that is like fuel for a fire and thereby causes a star to appear. Yet when this star appeared in the East, it prompted the magi to seek for the one who had been born. But it did not appear again until it appeared for a second time to the puzzled magi in Judaea, so that they could learn whose star it was, whom it served, and why it had come into being. "For it came to rest over the place where the child was"; hence, "when they saw it they rejoiced with great joy."[48]

Therefore, let us also welcome this great joy into our hearts. The angels bring good news of this joy to the shepherds.[49] Let us adore with the magi.[50] Let us glorify with the shepherds.[51] Let us sing with the choirs of angels: "For to you is born today a Savior, who is Christ the Lord."[52] "The Lord is God, and he has shone upon us."[53] He did not shine upon us in the form of God[54] lest he frighten what is weak; rather, he shone upon us in the form of a slave[55] to free what is enslaved. Who is so sluggish of soul, who is so ungrateful, that he does not rejoice and exult and take delight in the present circumstances? It is the feast in which all creation shares. It bestows supercosmic realities upon the world. It sends archangels to Zechariah and to Mary. It forms choirs of angels who sing: "Glory to God in the highest, and on earth peace, good will among men."[56] The stars run from heaven. The magi move from the nations. The earth provides welcome in a cave. There is no one who has not received some profit, no one who is ungrateful. Let us too raise up the voice of exultation.[57] Let us

48 Matt 2:9–10. 49 See Luke 2:10. 50 See Matt 2:11. 51 See Luke 2:20.
52 Luke 2:11. 53 Ps 117(118):27. 54 See Phil 2:6. 55 See Phil 2:7.
56 Luke 2:14. 57 See Ps 40(41):5, 45(46):2, 117(118):15.

give our feast a name: the Theophany. Let us celebrate the salvation of the world, the birthday of humanity. Today the condemnation of Adam has been lifted. No longer "are you dust and to dust you shall return."[58] Rather, joined now to heaven, you shall be taken up into heaven. No longer "in pain shall you bring forth children."[59] For blessed is she who was in travail with Emmanuel, and blessed the breasts which reared him.[60] "For to us a child is born, to us a son is given, and on his shoulders shall be the government."[61] My heart is alive and well, and my mind is overflowing, but the tongue is deficient and words insufficient to proclaim such great joy.

Please think of the humanification of the Lord in a way appropriate to God: his divinity is undefiled even though it has come to be in a material nature. It corrects what is subject to passion, but it is not itself filled with passion. Don't you see that this sun has come to be in the mire but is not sullied, that it shines in the filth but does not acquire the stench? On the contrary, it dries up the putrefaction of those with whom it will associate forever.[62] So then, what is it about his passionless and inviolate nature that makes you fear its wiping away our stains? He was born that you might be cleansed by that which is of the same kind as you. He grew up that you might enter into affinity with him through good habits. O the depth of the goodness of God and his love for humanity! In response to his superabundant gifts we do not put our trust in our benefactor; in response to the Lord's great love for humanity we rebel against being his servants. O this absurd and wicked ingratitude! The magi adore him but Christians inquire how God can be in flesh, what sort of flesh he has, and whether the humanity he assumed was perfect or imperfect! In the church of God such superfluous matters should be passed over in silence. Hold in honor what we have long believed. Do not make what has been passed over in silence become the object of pointless speculation. Associate with those who welcome the Lord with joy when he comes from heaven. Think of the shepherds who display their wisdom, the priests who prophesy, the women who are delighted, Mary learning to rejoice from Gabriel, Elizabeth having John leap in her womb.[63] Anna announced good news.[64] Simeon took him in his arms, adoring the great God in a small infant: he did not

58 Gen 3:10. 59 Gen 3:16. 60 See Luke 11:27. 61 Isa 9:6.
62 Namely, the putrefaction of sin. 63 See Luke 1:41.
64 See Luke 2:36–38.

show contempt for what he saw, but glorified the majesty of his divinity.[65] For the divine power was manifested through the human body, as light through vitreous membranes, and shines upon those who have the eyes of their heart purified. May we also be found among them, "with unveiled face beholding the glory of the Lord," so that we too may "be transformed from glory to glory,"[66] by the grace of our Lord Jesus Christ and his love for humanity. To him be glory and might for ever and ever. Amen.

65 See Luke 2:28. 66 2 Cor 3:18.

31

Diodore of Tarsus, *Selected Fragments*

Introduction and Translation by Ellen Muehlberger

INTRODUCTION

Diodore of Tarsus was an influential Christian teacher and writer about whom we know very little. Born in Antioch at some point in the early fourth century, he was trained first in theology by Silvanus (later bishop of Tarsus) and then in traditional writing and interpretation techniques in Athens. Upon his return to Antioch, Diodore became an interpreter of scripture and a teacher of interpretation in the Christian community of his native city, and, along with his friend Flavian, he embraced the ascetical life. Both Diodore and Flavian were ordained presbyters in Antioch by Meletius in the early 360s, indicating their pro-Nicene sympathies in the fractured church of that city. In the years 362–363 Emperor Julian encountered Diodore in Antioch and ridiculed him in a letter (*Ep.* 55). Ancient historians also report that Diodore and another man, Carterius, headed an institution where other Christians studied; it has frequently been called a "monastery" by historians, but it is perhaps more descriptive to call it a school, as reading and learning seem to have been the primary activities. Among its students were both Theodore of Mopsuestia[1] and John Chrysostom, themselves influential thinkers in late ancient Christian culture. In 372 Diodore was driven from Antioch and joined Meletius in exile in Getasa, Armenia; here he met and impressed Basil of Caesarea (*Ep.* 99.3). Diodore was a prolific author of dogmatic and apologetic treatises, as well as scriptural commentaries. Aside from a commentary on Psalms 1–51, his writings are only extant in fragments preserved by later hostile authors. Despite later hostility, Diodore enjoyed a strong

1 On Theodore of Mopsuestia, see the introduction to his *On the Incarnation* on pp. 420–488.

reputation for theological rectitude during his own lifetime. In 378 he became the bishop of Tarsus, and in 381 he attended the Council of Constantinople. An edict of Emperor Theodosius issued in July 381 (*Episcopis tradi*) listed Diodore as one of the bishops with whom any bishop must be in communion to demonstrate their pro-Nicene bona fides. Around this same time Diodore was instrumental in getting his old friend Flavian ordained bishop of Antioch after Meletius died. Diodore himself probably died in the early 390s.

Diodore is not more well known to historians of early Christians because, though he was considered mainstream during his own lifetime, he was eventually condemned, long after his death. As a result, most of what he wrote and taught has been lost, as it was neglected or purposefully destroyed when Christians came to believe that he had held a fringe theological position. The change in how Christians thought of Diodore is, in fact, a strange artifact of the development of theological arguments over the course of the fourth and fifth centuries. In his own writings, selected fragments of which are translated here, Diodore was defending the theological position associated with the Council of Nicaea against other positions of the early and mid-fourth century that lent more weight either to the divinity or the humanity of Christ. In time, though, as Christians worried at the number of entities in Christ, Diodore's forceful arguments for the complete humanity and complete divinity of Christ began to seem as if they were espousing two different entities. At the point when he was condemned, in the middle of the fifth century, Diodore was described as a predecessor to Nestorius, whose own theological stance was caricatured as claiming two Christs. In this way, a writer who was orthodox in his own time came to be seen as the intellectual father of a theological position that was articulated long after his death.

So, what we have from Diodore is quite sparse. Because what follows are all fragments of his writing that have survived by being quoted by others, a reader must work carefully with them. First, and most basic, these are fragments taken from their original contexts, so reading them is often difficult – it is like hearing only a snippet of a wider conversation. They can seem cryptic, and a reader will have to work to reconstruct the questions or problems they are attempting to answer. Second, these fragments are only a selection of the whole of Diodore's writing, and most were selected and quoted in order to be refuted. Thus, we should be aware that these fragments are probably those most likely to confirm the idea that Diodore claimed two entities in Christ, and we should remain cautious about reading Diodore's words in the frame of his own lifetime, rather than in the frame of issues that gained traction after his death.

Overall, though, these fragments give a clear picture of Diodore's concerns. They demonstrate that he was comfortable voicing intellectual and theological positions as part of a conversation; rather than simply stating rules of faith or offering principles by which to arrive at a position, Diodore engaged in dialogue, giving questions and answers, testing out theories, and probing the weaknesses of opponents' arguments. This should point out to us the centrality of conversation and dialogue to the developing of Christian thinking about Christ – whether these conversations were real or hypothetical, a back-and-forth of ideas was the way that Diodore imagined to be the most convincing method to persuade his readers. We can also see in these fragments a preoccupation with specific biblical passages that Diodore revisits again and again in order to prove or disprove points about Christ. In general, he is providing a theory of the reproduction of the human being, what he calls "the seed of David" or "the one from Mary," concurrent with the incarnation of the entity without beginning, which he calls "God the Word."

As is probably obvious from their fragmentary nature, these texts survived in a haphazard way, so most of them survive in languages other than the original Greek. The translations below – only a selection of the fragments attributed to Diodore in various sources – are based on the Greek if it is available. Otherwise, they are based on the Syriac or Latin version. Whenever possible, however, reference has been made to the different language versions of the same fragment (including a few in Armenian) to gain insight from the ancient translators' interpretations. The sources that preserve Fragments 17, 22, 26, 40, and 41 indicate that these are taken from Book 1 of Diodore's *Against the Synousiasts*; in all other cases the original source of the fragment cannot be identified. All of the texts from which these translations were made are available in John Behr's edition in *The Case against Diodore and Theodore: Texts and their Contexts*, Oxford Early Christian Texts (Oxford: Oxford University Press, 2011). See the appendix below for a table correlating our fragment numbers to the codes that Behr assigned to each fragment on which our translation is primarily based; see Behr's volume for the different language versions of the same fragment.

TRANSLATION

Fragment 1

(Translated from Syriac)

And why do they maintain that he be understood as one and the same, as one from heaven and from earth (just as a single human being is immortal in soul but mortal in body), as from before the ages and from the seed of David, as from God but also in the manger and in every place, upon the cross and in heaven? As one and the same who suffered but who was not hung [upon the cross] and who did not receive nails? As before Abraham and after Abraham? As Creator of the earth and creature? As one who is dead and who raises [from the dead]? And then would some [of these things] belong to the flesh and the others to the divinity? One and the same, not one and another, but a single composite, as we previously said above, a single Son made perfect in two – the body and God the Word. It is not as if one is superior and the other inferior, not as if one is by nature and the other is by grace. For the divine scripture speaks of one Son and not two as if there were one from above and another from below, or as if the son who is from before the ages did not suffer while another who is recent did. Instead, one and the same is in the former and in the latter. This is the opinion of those "lovers of learning"[2] and they cannot claim to be misrepresented.

Fragment 2

(Translated from Syriac)

For this reason David called his own son "Lord,"[3] not because he came from Mary or even because it was in her that he was conceived and from her that he was born. Rather, it is because he saw the glory and the birth of the Only-Begotten who was from before the ages that he confesses him to be Lord. For Christ is the Lord of David even in this, namely in the flesh, just as is the case for the martyrs, who are so much greater than their parents that for the parents is reserved torment, while for the [martyrs] is reserved a kingdom. For our Lord is not superior to David as

2 This sarcastic phrase is meant as an insult against Diodore's opponents.
3 See Ps 109(110):1; Matt 22:41–45. David's "son" is his descendant Christ.

a ruler even though he is his son (I mean according to the flesh); instead, because he was the temple of God the Word and formed without intercourse (not by nature's law but by the handiwork of divine power), he is "Lord" of David.

Fragment 3

(Translated from Syriac)

So I have heard them say that he who was conceived in Mary and was born from her is also the Creator of all things. The one who was born was called "Jesus" because he saved the people from their sins.[4] The apostle Paul also preaches that "there is one God from whom are all things and one Lord, Jesus Christ, through whom are all things."[5] Therefore, the Creator of all things is a human being. But as for me, I know that whatever intelligence they have is weak and it takes little to find fault with it. And so let us not, by remaining silent, give a pretext to the simple-minded so that they find all of this to be convincing or true, when it is actually weak and alien to the truth. I will offer again this well-planned admonition: If he who is from Mary truly is a human being, how then could he exist before the heavens and the earth? For if he is from before these things, then he could not be a human being. If he is from Abraham, how could he exist before Abraham? If he is from the earth, how could he exist before the earth, and all the things that we previously said above? How could the son of David be the maker of David and the Creator of all things? Is it right to trust those whose lack of understanding has blinded the sight of their minds? Faith, though, belongs to things unseen and unshown;[6] things that are seen or proclaimed are not faith. [Their kind of faith shows] impudence and a lack of discernment beyond measure. And the divine scripture has not decreed that he who is the maker of all is from the seed of David, but it confesses God the Word to be the Creator of all.

Fragment 4

(Translated from Syriac)

How could it be that the Creator of all things came to exist very recently?

4 Matt 1:21. 5 1 Cor 8:6. 6 See Heb 11:1.

Fragment 5

(Translated from Syriac)

There are certain names for God the Word. You should not address God the Word with bodily names. Don't use "the body" to talk about God the Word, for he is without constraint. Don't use "son of David," either, for even our Lord himself, begotten from the Father before the ages, does not want to be called "the son of David."[7]

Fragment 6

(Translated from Syriac)

Before the ages, God the Word was born from the Father, the single one from the single one. The form of the slave,[8] the child of the holy Virgin in recent times, is a human being from the Holy Spirit.

Fragment 7

(Translated from Syriac)

But Paul does not mean that God the Word, when he became flesh and was formed, was the infant from Mary. In reference to the human being born from Mary he only says that he was sent for our salvation.[9] For God did not send his own Son to be born; instead, he sent the one who was born for salvation. Paul's words are about the one born from Mary.

Fragment 8

(Translated from Syriac)

But maybe someone wants to learn accurately whether this is truly proclaimed to us regarding the human being from Mary by the very Apostle himself, who in the following words teaches what that person wants [to learn]. So, what does he say? "When the fullness of time had come, God sent his own son; he came into being from a woman and he came into being under the law, so that he might redeem those under the law."[10] Who, then, was it who came to be "under the law"? Who was it who was also

7 See Matt 22:41–45. 8 See Phil 2:6–11. 9 See Gal 4:4–6. 10 Gal 4:4–5.

circumcised? And who was it who was raised as a Jew? Was it not the human being from Mary, or do those things apply to God the Word?

Fragment 9

(Translated from Syriac)

For "though he was in the form of God, he took the form of a slave"[11] does not mean the same thing as "he became a slave." Similarly, "he existed in the likeness of a human being"[12] does not mean "he came to be a human being" but rather "[he came to be] like a human being." He who is in the form of God is the one who assumed the form of the slave. For human nature is slavish, but that which is hidden because of the one who is manifest is like a human being.

Fragment 10

(Translated from Syriac)

When we read that "the Son of Man descended from heaven," from above, from where he had been, we, for our part, were not deceived by the outward appearance of the phrase into asserting that the seed of Abraham came from above.[13] Rather, we are persuaded that God the Word was designated a human being because of the fact that he dwelled in the Son of Man. In that same way, when the divine scripture says that "the Lord of glory" was crucified,[14] or that God "did not spare his own Son,"[15] we acknowledge the depth of meaning in scripture but the language does not lead us to believe that God the Word suffered; rather, [we believe] that what has been considered worthy of sonship is the human being from Mary, the temple of God the Word, which was destroyed by the Jews but raised by the one who dwelled in it.

Fragment 11

(Translated from Syriac)

Who is the one who, at the time of the crucifixion, promised that the robber would be with him in paradise?[16] Was it he who, once dead, was buried

11 Phil 2:6–7. 12 Phil 2:7. 13 See John 3:13. 14 See 1 Cor 2:8.
15 Rom 8:32. 16 See Luke 23:43.

and did not rise on that day or even on the next day? Is it not possible that he, dead, was buried, but living, brought the robber to paradise?

Fragment 12

(Translated from Syriac)

Paul, when he writes to Timothy, will come to testify that this is not just rhetoric but the truth: "Remember Jesus Christ, from the seed of David, who rose from the dead."[17] He makes clear that the suffering belonged to the human being. No person should engage in [such] worthless questions, nor should they give a simple answer. Let us refute the vanity of the opinion: if someone asks whether "the Lord of glory" were crucified, we should ask him who he thinks "the Lord of glory" is.[18] Does it apply to God the Word, who is before the ages, or to the one from the seed of David? If to the former, that doesn't even merit a response, as it is wickedness beyond measure and this person has already proclaimed something foul. (This much has already been made abundantly clear by the many things previously said above.) If to the latter, though, we agree with this and need no conflict.

They may claim, "If it were the flesh that was crucified, then why did the sun divert its light? Why did darkness take hold of the entire earth? Why were there earthquakes? Why were rocks split, and why did the dead rise?"[19] So, then, what do they have to say about the darkness that came over Egypt in the time of Moses, which lasted for three days not three hours?[20] What about the other wonders Moses performed, or those performed by Joshua son of Nun, the one who made the sun stand still, which also turned back contrary to nature in the days of King Hezekiah?[21] What of the bones of Elisha that raised a corpse?[22] If the events that happened at the time of the crucifixion showed that God the Word suffered, but they do not grant that they happened on account of a human being, then neither did those things that happened in the days of Moses on account of the nation of Abraham, nor those things that happened in the days of Joshua son of Nun or in the days of King Hezekiah. For if such things were wondrously performed for the people of the Jews, then how much more especially at the time of the crucifixion were they performed for the temple of God?

17 2 Tim 2:8. 18 See 1 Cor 2:8. 19 See Matt 27:45, 51–52.
20 Exod 10:21–23. 21 Josh 10:12–14; 2 Kgs 20:11. 22 2 Kgs 13:21.

Fragment 13

(Translated from Syriac)

The earth shook then and the sun turned back,[23] on account of the one from Mary – the temple of God the Word, the one through whom salvation came to humanity as well as the cancelation of the curse and the eradication of the Slanderer's dominion. All this happened to condemn the presumption of the Jews, as [the earth] would not put up with the reckoning, which they did not grow weary of making.

This phrase, "Eloi, Eloi, lama sabachthani," was not about God the Word nor, would I argue, even about the body, as if it had cried out because it had been abandoned.[24] Why would he appeal for help, as if he had been abandoned? Would he not have already seen his resurrection and his glory? Wasn't it from Peter that he heard, "The Son of Man will be handed over and they will crucify him"?[25] Peter was concerned about him, so he said what he was thinking, adding, "Far be it from you, my Lord."[26] He was forcefully rebuked and named "Satan."[27] It *was* Satan who, were he not to suffer, would still inviolably possess his own dominion – sin and death. Satan did not know that the human being was born from Mary, from virginity, precisely for this reason: to cleanse the human race with his very own blood.

Fragment 14

(Translated from Syriac)

Because the baby that was conceived by Mary and born from her was the seed of Abraham and David, and the flower of the root of Jesse,[28] it is obvious that the one who is born is from his parent. One and the same lineage extended to the holy Mary, who herself gave birth to the temple of God the Word. It was no stranger to her nature, but [was] in nature human, a holy formation and first fruit by which he killed sin and canceled death. This one, born from Mary, lived humanly: he got tired, he wore clothing, he hungered and thirsted, he was crucified – his side was pierced and out flowed blood and water; his crucifiers divided his garments. He died and was buried, and when he rose, he displayed himself to his disciples,

23 See Matt 27:45, 51. 24 Matt 27:46. 25 Matt 16:21. 26 Matt 16:22. 27 Matt 16:23. 28 See Isa 11:1.

[showing them] that he had a body and bones that no longer admitted suffering or death. For forty days he ate and drank with his disciples, and he was taken up to the clouds while visible to them; he is coming in the same way that he was taken up. We have already said this sufficiently and demonstrated [it] from the divine scriptures. God the Word, begotten by the Father from before the ages, does not admit change or suffering. Neither does he live as a body, nor was he crucified, nor did he die, nor did he eat, nor drink, nor did he tire. Instead, he remains incorporeal, beyond measure, without abandoning his likeness to the Father. This [too] we have clearly demonstrated by orthodox ideas and the divine scriptures.

Fragment 15

(Translated from Syriac)

The power of God descended upon Mary when it formed a temple for [the Word].[29] It did not mix with the body. Though in fact the Holy Spirit filled John the Baptist at the time he was being conceived, it was not from the Holy Spirit that he had his nature. For if the Son had undergone an irrational mixing, how could our Lord have said, "He who blasphemes against the Son of Man can be forgiven, but never the one who does so against the Holy Spirit," as was previously stated?[30] Because they are contesting this, it is only right that they be trapped in their own nets. If someone [argues that] God the Word's nature and the body mixed, how would the blasphemer against Christ gain forgiveness, but not the blasphemer against the Holy Spirit? Is the Son inferior to the Spirit? Tell me! What about the second to the third? Is the one who sends inferior to the one who is sent?[31] [Asserting that] God the Word mixed with the body is [apparently] the safe version of blasphemy, while blaspheming against the Holy Spirit is an inescapable wickedness, here or in the world to come. For while the one who blasphemes against the human being born of Mary gains some degree of forgiveness, the one who dishonors God the Word (who is dwelling in the temple of the body) and says that the holy power, the Holy Spirit, is an "impure spirit" or "Beelzebub" will have torment from which there is no relief.[32]

29 See Luke 1:35. 30 Luke 12:10. 31 See John 14:26, 15:26, 16:7.
32 Mark 3:30, 22.

Fragment 16

(Translated from Syriac)

Spiritual people do not go wrong if they affirm that the body from Mary is corruptible and passible – even up to the death by crucifixion – inasmuch as it is a created thing even after our Savior's ascension to heaven. [However,] those who do not accept the statements of the apostles dishonor the apostles' Lord. For even our Lord's disciples, the gospel writers, knew that he no longer wished to be called "the son of David" according to the flesh – and on this subject he expressed [himself directly] to the Jews with David's [own] words – and they both proclaimed that our Lord was not the son of David and of Abraham and taught others as much.[33] Instead, they were acutely aware that God the Word is the Lord of David and that he did not proclaim himself "son of David."

Fragment 17

(Translated from Latin and Greek)

Whenever[34] we are considering his ancestors according to nature, it is best for those who think rightly not to call God the Word "son of David" or "son of Abraham," but rather, "Creator." Also, they should not describe his body as "from the Father before the ages," but instead as "the seed of Abraham and David, born from Mary." And[35] when the discussion is about natural births, it should not be suspected that God the Word is son of Mary, since according to nature what is mortal gives birth to what is mortal and a body that is like hers.[36] God the Word did not undergo two births – one before the ages and one more recently – but[37] he was begotten from the Father by nature, while he formed for himself from Mary's womb the temple that was born from her.

Fragment 18

(Translated from Latin)

When the discussion moves to the saving economy, let God be called a human being (not because he was made a human being, but because he

33 See Matt 22:41–46. 34 The translation begins with the Latin version.

35 The translation switches to the Greek version here.

36 The Greek here is *homoousion*. The Latin versions of this fragment have *simile sibi* or *quod sibi simile est*, whereas the Syriac version has *ldma lh*, all of which translate as "like hers."

37 The translation returns to the Latin version here.

assumed a human being) and let the human being be called God (though not as if he became uncircumscribed or is ubiquitous). For his body was able to be touched even after the resurrection, and as such it was taken to heaven, and it will return in the same manner as it was taken.

Fragment 19

(Translated from Syriac)

Even if we hear that "the Son of Man descended from heaven,"[38] we should proclaim that this is the one from the Father, from before the ages, and not the one from the seed of David.

Fragment 20

(Translated from Syriac)

When it is said that "the Lord of glory" was crucified and died,[39] or that "the Son of Man descended from heaven,"[40] or that the one from Abraham is "before Abraham,"[41] not one of these things should be understood as they are.

Fragment 21

(Translated from Syriac)

There are people among them whom they especially honor, whom they think wiser than themselves and better trained in the divine scriptures. These people reject the idea of mixture; they think that others who *do* accept it are worthless. They proclaim that the body from Mary truly is the seed of David and of Abraham, recently formed in the Virgin's womb, and that it endured bodily existence,[42] and that God the Word, begotten from the Father before the ages, was exempt from all these things and remained unchanged, as he was in his nature.

They do not want it to be said that one is from above and the other from below, or that one is the son of David while the other is the Son of God. Instead, they want it to be said that they are one and the same, Son of God

38 John 3:13. 39 1 Cor 2:8. 40 John 3:13. 41 John 8:53.
42 In Syriac, *haleyn dpagra'*.

before the ages *and* recently son of David – Son of God according to the divinity, son of David according to the humanity. One and the same: impassible and passible – impassible according to the spirit, passible according to the flesh. One and the same: hungering and nourishing, suffering and not suffering – the first things according to the flesh, the second things according to the spirit. One and the same: he who died and he who gives life, buried and risen, being touched and not being touched. Moreover, do not divide him by saying that this one is the son of David and not the Son of God, while the other is the Son of God and not the son of David. Rather, the two of them are Son of God and son of David. Just as a person comprises soul and body (one invisible and immortal, the other visible and mortal), but is called [one] human being, so too the two of them brought to perfection one hypostasis and one complete Son. For the soul alone is not said to be the son of the begetter, nor is the body alone, but the two of them together. They stand far apart in nature, but in all other things they are joined.

Who has ever said that so-and-so's body is dead, or is sick, or wears clothes, or eats? Or, alternatively, who says that so-and-so's soul is furious or acts wickedly or blasphemes?[43] While the first things are proper to the soul and the others are proper to the body, we associate the natural properties of each of them with what is common to both. It is the same way with God the Word: he assumed the body that is from David and composed one Son and one hypostasis. God who is the Word is not rightly called the "Son of God," but neither is the body because the body is the seed of David and not God's son. But the two of them are one Son, whether of David or of God. We have already said these things.

You can find the argument of that innovator offered in a summary statement, here in his own words: "I proclaim that the Son of God became the Son of Man when he took flesh from Mary the Virgin and that he is one complete Son and not two (a Son of God and a Son of Man); one hypostasis, one person, and a single worship of the Word and the flesh. I anathematize those who speak of two, and who perform separate acts of worship (one [for] the divine and one [for] the human)."[44]

43 That is, as opposed to just saying "Ellen is furious" or "Mark wears clothes" or "Brad blasphemes" or "Andy eats."

44 Apollinarius, *Detailed Confession of Faith* 28 (*Apollinaris*: 177, 4–10 Lietzmann). The quotation is not exact.

All these people say these things when they argue in person, but when they write, they yield to the others with whom they wish to have peace.

Fragment 22

(Translated from Greek and Latin)

If[45] someone wants to use an improper name for the Son of God, that is, God the Word, and call him "the son of David" because the temple of God the Word is from David, let him call him that. Let him also designate the one from the seed of David as "Son of God" by grace and not by nature. For by doing this he neither ignores his natural parents, nor goes against the order of things, nor says that the incorporeal one is both before the ages from God and at the same time from David, that he both suffered and was incapable of suffering. A[46] body is not incorporeal; what is from below is not what is from above; what is before the ages is not from the seed of David; what suffered is not incapable of suffering. For all these things do not pertain to the same idea: what belongs to the body does not belong to God the Word; the body does not have what is proper to God the Word. Let us confess the natures and not deny the arrangements.

Fragment 23

(Translated from Syriac)

God the Word did not undergo two births, and neither did the body. They do not have two fathers. Instead, it was at a single moment that the Only-Begotten of God was born from the Father before the ages.

Fragment 24

(Translated from Syriac)

How would anyone know that God the Word is Son by nature? From the fact that he was born before the ages from the Father. However, are the body and the human being from Mary of God the Father's nature or do they say the second, [that they are] from the seed of David?

45 The translation begins with the Greek of LD4.
46 The translation switches to the Latin of C5D here.

Fragment 25

(Translated from Syriac)

Thus we do not say [there are] two [sons] of one Father, but instead we say that God the Word is one Son of God by nature, while the one from Mary is by nature son of David but Son of God by grace. We concede, though, that the two of them are one Son and repudiate impossible trains of thought.

Fragment 26

(Translated from Greek)

The human being from Mary is son by grace; God the Word is son by nature. That which is by grace is not by nature, while that which is by nature is not by grace. There are not two sons.[47] The sonship, glory, and immortality that come by grace will be enough for the body that comes from us, since it became the temple of God the Word. It should not be elevated above nature, and God the Word should not be insulted, especially when we owe him gratitude. What insult do I mean? Combining it with the body and thinking that it required the body for complete sonship. For God the Word does not want himself to be the son of David, but his Lord.[48] Not only did he not refuse that the body be called the son of David, but it was precisely for this reason that he came.

Fragment 27

(Translated from Syriac)

For our part, we do not say "two sons." We do say, though, that the one from Mary received sonship by grace. But those who say that he is son by nature and not by grace …

Fragment 28

(Translated from Syriac)

As that flesh was of Mary and not yet assumed, it was earthly.[49] So, it was no different in any way from other flesh. Just as Levi received tithes when

47 This sentence is not found in the Greek text preserved by Leontius, but is present in Latin, Syriac, and Armenian fragments preserved by others.

48 See Matt 22:41–45.

49 See Gen 2:7, 3:19.

he had still not been conceived[50] but assumed honor when he was born,[51] so too it was with the Lord. While in the Virgin's womb, he did not possess the honor of sonship from her substance, but once [that flesh] was fashioned, it became the temple of God the Word. Receiving the Only-Begotten, it assumed the honor of the name at the same time that it also assumed the one whose honor it is.

Fragment 29

(Translated from Syriac)

The one from the seed of David (who as he was being formed, was being formed solely for God the Word) belongs to God the Word. Our way of doing things is that a temple is first constructed and then the occupant enters it. But the one who dwelled in the Virgin's womb formed it and did not depart from the temple. He filled it with his glory and his wisdom. It was not like it was with the prophets, where there was no knowledge until the Spirit revealed it.

Fragment 30

(Translated from Latin and Syriac)

"Jesus[52] grew in both stature and wisdom."[53] Yet the same cannot be said about God the Word, for he is God, perfect begotten from perfect, wisdom from wisdom, power from power. Therefore, he did not grow, as he was not imperfect in such a way that he would need to grow step-by-step to perfection. Rather, the thing that grew in stature and wisdom was the flesh.[54] Also, when the flesh was formed or produced, the deity did not confer all of its wisdom upon it at once, but gave it to the body little by little.

50 Literally, when he was "in the loins."

51 See Heb 7:9–10.

52 The translation is from the Latin version except for one sentence, noted below.

53 Luke 2:52.

54 This sentence is lacking in the Latin version of the fragment and is only preserved in the Syriac version.

Fragment 31

(Translated from Syriac)

Is the substance of God that which is the seed of David? Is God the Word not from the substance of the Father, while what is from the seed of David is from the substance of David?

Fragment 32

(Translated from Syriac)

The complete form of God the Word [and] the complete form of the slave which it assumed …

Fragment 33

(Translated from Latin)

God the Word did not dwell in the one who is from the seed of David as he had in the prophets. For the latter by grace had the use of a specific and limited quantity of the Holy Spirit, but the former remained constantly in such a state as they only were at times and was filled with the glory and wisdom of the Word. Surely it should be understood that there is another beside him, who is properly and independently Son. That is because the Word did not fill himself with wisdom and glory but instead bestowed these things or signs upon another. We adore the purple on account of the one who wears it and the temple on account of the one who dwells in it; we adore the form of the slave on account of the form of God[55] and the lamb because of the high priest; we adore the one assumed because of the one who assumed and the one formed in the womb of the Virgin on account of the one who is Creator of all. Having acknowledged these things, offer a single veneration – a single adoration does no harm, as long as you have acknowledged these things beforehand. You speak of a single veneration, but with your "single veneration" you are introducing blasphemy, for your single adoration implies that there is also a single substance.

55 See Phil 2:6–7.

Fragment 34

(Translated from Syriac)

How do you offer a single adoration? Is it something like what happens with the soul and body of kings? [In their case,] the soul does not reign by itself, and the body does not reign by itself. But God the Word was king before the flesh. So, [the relationship between] God the Word and the flesh is not as it is with [a king's] soul and body.

Fragment 35

(Translated from Syriac)

"The Lord God will raise up for you a prophet like me from your siblings."[56] Why would it be someone less than the prophet Moses – was he not completely human? Likewise, the Nazarene, the one from the seed of David, is not less than a human being. Rather, he was complete God from complete God, taking on a complete human being.

Fragment 36

(Translated from Syriac)

But again, people say to me, "Well then, you're a divider! You say the flesh is one thing and God the Word is another." But I could be convinced if, when I make this distinction and say these things, [I get to] ask every person who contends against me to answer [these questions]. Let's say God the Word is the seed of David. Is anyone willing to say this? Is he the seed of Abraham? Is he a prophet like Moses? Is he the temple that was destroyed? Haven't you heard what has been read [aloud]? The Lord spoke like this: "Destroy this temple!"[57] Was he the very temple that was destroyed?

Fragment 37

(Translated from Syriac)

Is God the Word of recent times? Or is he who is the seed of David from before the ages? Is God the Word a mortal from mortals? Is the one from

56 Deut 18:15. 57 Mark 14:58.

the seed of David the substance of God? Could it be that God the Word is from the substance of David and thus he who is from the seed of David is also from the very substance of God? [Of course not!] It is that the one who is from the seed of David is from the substance of David.

Fragment 38

(Translated from Latin)

Say to them, "The Lord God will raise up for you a prophet like me from your siblings."[58] God the Word is not "from siblings." For a prophet is a person who receives the grace of the Spirit and prophesies the things which are to come, serving by the Spirit and announcing those things which will happen. To whom, then, did God the Word offer service? Or whose prophet was he revealed to be? So you see how precisely divine scripture speaks.

Fragment 39

(Translated from Latin)

Please, listen: they say to us, "Why do you distinguish [them]?" Well then, you who do not distinguish [them], respond to this: "Is God the Word really recent?" They say, "What? Do you really imagine that there are some who say this?" Of course not! But [some do say] that the one who was born recently is before the ages. But if that which is from the seed of David is before the ages, then he is much greater than David himself, from whose seed he is. And yet David is not before the ages, for he is attested by many people to have lived more recently than that, and that which is from the seed of David is twenty-eight generations *after* David![59] So, if what was formed in the womb is before the ages, it is not from the seed of David and thus the divine scriptures are false.

Fragment 40

(Translated from Greek and Latin)

We[60] urge you to take every precaution when it comes to the accuracy of the teachings. We labor on your behalf, so that we may not be accountable

58 Deut 18:15. 59 See Matt 1:17.

60 The translation is from the Greek version except for one sentence, noted below.

to the Lord for our silence.[61] The perfect Son who was before the ages assumed the perfect son of David, the Son of God [assuming] the son of David. You may say to me, "Aren't you proclaiming two sons?" I am not speaking of two sons of David – I didn't call God the Word son of David, did I? Nor am I speaking of two sons of God according to substance – I didn't say there were two from God's substance, did I? I am saying that God the Word who is before the ages indwelt in the one from the seed of David.

Fragment 41

(Translated from Greek)

The Son of God is not the Son of God through anyone – for he is Son by nature – while the flesh is Son through the Son. So why do I say "through the Son?" The flesh is for our sake. Don't judge this statement to be blasphemy, but seek out evidence. If human beings had not fallen, would the law have become necessary? "The law is not laid down for the just person."[62] If those subject to the law had not caused sin to increase, would grace have become necessary? No! When the law was not able to eradicate sin, didn't he take flesh for our sake so that both death and the sentence of death might be revoked by his crucifixion, death, and resurrection? If deception had not advanced against us, along with the sentence of death, would this economy of the Savior have become necessary? Why would the embodiment be necessary? Is it not for our sake that he took the flesh?

APPENDIX

BD = *The Blasphemies of Diodore, Theodore, and the Impious Nestorius*

C5 = *Acts of the Council of Constantinople* in 553, Fifth Session

LD = Leontius of Byzantium, *Unmasking and Triumph over the Nestorians*

SD = Severus of Antioch

PD = The Palantine Collection

61 This sentence does not appear in the Greek version of the fragment, but is found in the Latin version.

62 1 Tim 1:9.

CEECW	Behr
1.	BD2 (Syriac)
2.	BD3 (Syriac)
3.	BD4 (Syriac)
4.	BD5 (Syriac)
5.	BD6 (Syriac)
6.	BD11 (Syriac)
7.	BD12 (Syriac)
8.	BD13 (Syriac)
9.	BD14 (Syriac)
10.	BD15 (Syriac)
11.	BD16 (Syriac)
12.	BD17 (Syriac); cf. C4T28 (Latin) and C5D4 (Latin)
13.	BD18 (Syriac)
14.	BD19 (Syriac)
15.	BD20 (Syriac)
16.	BD21 (Syriac)
17.	C5D2a (Latin) + LD3 (Greek) + C5D2c (Latin); cf. BD22 (Syriac)
18.	C5D3 (Latin); cf. BD23 (Syriac)
19.	BD24 (Syriac)
20.	BD25 (Syriac)
21.	BD26 (Syriac)
22.	LD4 (Greek) + C5D1c (Latin); cf. BD27 (Syriac)
23.	BD28 (Syriac)
24.	BD29 (Syriac)
25.	BD30 (Syriac)
26.	LD2 (Greek); cf. BD31–32 (Syriac)
27.	BD33 (Syriac)
28.	SD1 (Syriac)
29.	SD4 (Syriac)
30.	PD1 (Latin); cf. SD5 (Syriac)
31.	SD6 (Syriac)
32.	SD7 (Syriac)
33.	PD6 (Latin); cf. SD8 (Syriac)
34.	SD9 (Syriac)
35.	SD10 (Syriac)

36.	SD12 (Syriac)
37.	SD13 (Syriac)
38.	PD2 (Latin)
39.	PD3 (Latin)
40.	LD1 (Greek) = PD5 (Latin)
41.	LD5 (Greek); cf. SD11 (Syriac)

32

Gregory of Nazianzus, *Letter* 101 *to Cledonius*

Introduction and Translation by Bradley K. Storin

INTRODUCTION

Gregory of Nazianzus (ca. 330–390) was one of the famous "Cappadocian Fathers" (along with Basil of Caesarea and Gregory of Nyssa). Gregory was not only an important ecclesiastical leader – indeed, he acted as bishop of several cities and briefly presided over the first Council of Constantinople in 381 – but also an innovative theologian. His understanding of the Trinity helped to articulate and publicize pro-Nicene theology in the 370s and 380s, and his Christological ideas had enduring effects on later Christian thought. Perhaps the most underappreciated aspect of Gregory was his literary genius. Highly trained in classical texts, he was an accomplished epistolographer (more than 240 of his letters survive) and poet (nearly 20,000 of his verses survive). The text presented below – *Letter* 101 to the presbyter Cledonius – was probably written in the spring of 382 or the spring of 383. Although quite long, it was indeed a genuine letter conforming to a new epistolographical type that developed among Christian leaders in the second, third, and fourth centuries, a type in which an author could explicate exegetical, moral, or doctrinal issues at (sometimes great) length. Gregory probably intended this letter to be read by its addressee in the presence of bishops attending the Council of Constantinople in 382 or the Council of Constantinople in 383. His argument lambastes the Christological mixture promulgated by Apollinarius of Laodicea.[1] *Letter* 101 shows Gregory taking on not only Apollinarian Christology, but also what Gregory considers to be its corollaries and consequences. The critical text from which this translation has been made is Paul Gallay, *Grégoire de Nazianze. Lettres théologiques*, SChr 207 (Paris: Cerf, 1974), 36–68.

1 Several writings of Apollinarius are translated in this volume on pp. 301–347.

TRANSLATION

1. To the most honorable and God-beloved brother, my fellow priest, Cledonius, Gregory sends greetings in the Lord.

2. Here is what we would like to learn: what innovation is pervading the church, that it permits everyone who so desires and everyone who passes through, as it is written,[2] to scatter the well-tended flock and wreak havoc on it with clandestine raids, or in this case, with bandit-like and unreasonable[3] teachings? 3. For if the current attackers really have something with which to condemn us regarding the faith, they wouldn't have needed, without warning us, to be so daring in such matters. 4. For one should want first to persuade or be persuaded (if there is any account of us as ones who fear God, toil for the Word, and render service to the church), and then, if even then, to make innovations; in that case, the insulters may perhaps have some defense. 5. But since our faith has been proclaimed in writing and orally, near and far, inside and outside of dangers, how is it that some undertake such attacks while others keep quiet about them?

6. And it wouldn't be too bad – still bad, though – if people used villainous acts to instill their wrong belief within guileless souls. However, they also spread lies about me – that I hold the same belief and mind as them – 7. putting the bait on the hook, wickedly using this cover to fulfill their own selfish desire, and turning my simplicity, because of which I used to see them as brothers and not strangers, into an opening for wickedness. 8. Not only this, but they also claim, as I'm learning, that they have been accepted by the western synod by which they had formerly been condemned,[4] as is well known to everyone. 9. Well, if the Apollinarian party was accepted either now or previously, let them show proof of it and I'll extend my affection. For then, if they had obtained this, it would be clear that they agreed with right doctrine[5] – there is no other way to admit them. 10. They must make their case entirely by means of a synodical decree or letters of fellowship. This indeed is the custom of our synods. 11. If the claim turns out to

2 See Ps 79(80):13.

3 In Greek, *paralogois*, literally, "contrary to reason" or "contrary to the Word."

4 In spite of later synodical rejections of Apollinarius and his followers, it does seem to be true that one of Apollinarius's followers, Vitalis, went to Rome and received a letter of approval from Bishop Damasus in 375. Later Damasus would withdraw support for Vitalis and warn others of his heterodoxy.

5 In Greek, *orthou logou*.

be a fiction and fabrication, invented for the sake of a good appearance and plausibility with the masses on account of the trustworthiness of the main characters,[6] instruct them to keep quiet and utterly refute them. I assume that this course suits your style of governance and orthodoxy.

12. Let the people neither deceive nor be deceived into accepting that the lordly human being, as they say, is a mindless human being, instead of our Lord and God. 13. For we do not separate the human being from the divinity, but we lay down as doctrine[7] one and the same, not a human being previously, but God and [God's] only Son before the ages, unmixed with a body and with whatever pertains to bodies, 14. who recently assumed a human being for our salvation – passible in flesh, impassible in divinity; circumscribed in body, uncircumscribed in spirit; 15. the same one is earthly and heavenly, seen [by the eyes] and contemplated [by the mind], contained and uncontained – so that a whole human being who has fallen under sin's sway may be refashioned by the whole human being, the same one who is also God.

16. If anyone supposes that the holy Mary is not Theotokos, he stands apart from the divinity. If anyone were to say that [Christ] ran through the Virgin as if through a conduit, and was not fashioned inside her in simultaneously divine and human ways as God and human at the same time (divinely, because it happened without a man; humanly, because it happened by the regular process of pregnancy), he is likewise godless. 17. If anyone were to say that he was fashioned as a human being, and then God slipped into him, he stands condemned. For this is not the birth of God, but a way of avoiding birth. 18. If anyone introduces two sons – one from God his Father, the other from his mother, but not one and the same[8] – he has also fallen away from the adoption promised to those who believe correctly.[9] 19. The natures are two, God and human being, since there is both soul and body. But there are neither two sons nor two gods. For in our case, there are not two humans, even if Paul talks about the inner and outer person like this.[10] 20. And if I must speak concisely, there is one thing and another out of which the Savior comes (unless the invisible is the same as the visible, or the atemporal as the temporal), not one and another.[11] Absolutely

6 In Greek, *tōn prosōpōn*. 7 In Greek, *dogmatizomen*.
8 Likely a jab directed at Gregory's contemporary opponent Diodore of Tarsus.
9 See John 1:12; Rom 8:15, 8:23; Gal 4:5; Eph 1:5.
10 See 2 Cor 4:16; Eph 3:16. 11 In Greek, *allo men kai allo … ouk allos de kai allos*.

not! 21. For the two things become one in the compound: God becomes human and the human being is made God, or whatever one might call it. But I say "one thing and another" differently than how it applies to the Trinity. In that case, it's "one and another" so that we do not confuse the hypostases,[12] and not "one thing and another" – for the three are one and the same with respect to their divinity.

22. If anyone were to say that [the divinity] acted in[13] him by grace as it does with a prophet, but that it neither was nor is linked to him essentially, he would be bereft of the superior activity[14] and even full of the contrary one. If someone does not worship the crucified, let him be anathema and ranked among the God-killers.[15] 23. If anyone were to say that he was deemed worthy of adoption once he had been perfected by his works, or after his baptism, or after his resurrection from the dead, like those whom the Greeks entered into their registries, let him be anathema. 24. For the one who has a beginning, makes progress, or becomes perfect is not God, even if he is spoken of like this because of his gradual manifestation. 25. If anyone were to say that his flesh has been stowed away for the time being and that his divinity exists now denuded of the body, but that it exists and will come without this garment, he will not see the glory of Christ's advent.[16] 26. For where is the body now if not with the one who assumed it? For certainly it is not stored away in the sun, as that Manichaean riff-raff supposes[17] – consequently, it would be honored through dishonor – 27. nor was it poured into the air and dissolved, like the nature of a sound, the waft of a scent, and the flash of a fleeting lightning bolt. 28. How would he have been touched after the resurrection,[18] or seen by his piercers way back then?[19] For, by itself, divinity is invisible. 29. But I argue that he will come with the body to the same degree that he was seen by or shown to his disciples on the mountain,[20] with the divinity wholly prevailing over the fleshiness. Just as I say these words to ward off suspicion, I also write them to set the innovation straight.

12 In Greek, *hypostaseis*. 13 In Greek, *enērgēkenai*. 14 In Greek, *energeias*.

15 A Christian epithet for Jews popular in late antiquity. 16 See 2 Thess 2:8.

17 This strange accusation may pertain to Manichaean understandings of the sun as a receiving station for light particles released from material bodies. Thus, Jesus, being pure light, was drawn up, refined, and absorbed into the sun.

18 See Luke 24:39; John 20:27. 19 See John 19:37.

20 See Matt 17:2; Mark 9:2–3; Luke 9:29.

30. If anyone were to say that the flesh came down from heaven, and that it is not from here and from us, let him be anathema.[21] For we ought to consider that the following verses (and any other such one) are spoken on account of his union with the heavenly: "The second human being is from heaven,"[22] "As the heavenly one, so too the heavenly ones,"[23] and, "No one has ascended to heaven except for the Son of Man, the one who descended from heaven."[24] 31. The same goes for, "Through Christ all things came to be,"[25] and, "Christ dwells within our hearts"[26] – not according to God's observable aspect, but according to God's intelligible aspect; just as the natures are mingled, so too are the names interchangeable with each other by virtue of the shared nature.[27]

32. If anyone has placed hope in a mindless human being, it is actually he who is mindless and wholly unworthy of being saved. For what is not assumed is not healed, but what is united to God is saved. 33. If half of Adam had fallen, then that's the half that would have been assumed and saved. But if the whole [Adam], then he was united as a whole to the Begotten and wholly saved. Well then, let them not begrudge us complete salvation and let them not attribute only bones and sinews – a sketch of a human being – to the Savior. 34. For if [they say that] the human being was soulless, the Arians said the same thing, resulting in the attribution of the passion to the divinity since the body's mover is also the sufferer! If, though, the human being was endowed with a soul but not with a mind, how would it even be human? For the human being is not a mindless animal. 35. [In this case] his form and tent[28] would necessarily be human, but his soul could be that of a horse, cow, or any other mindless being, and thus, this would be what was to be saved, and it would be me who had been deceived by the truth, since

21 Some fragments of Apollinarius's *Apodeixis* or *Demonstration of the Divine Enfleshment according to the Likeness of a Human Being*, which comes from a later stage in his career, suggest that he believed Christ's flesh preexisted in concert with the Word. He goes so far as to say in Fragment 34 that the "divine incarnation did not have its beginning from the Virgin; rather, it happened even before Abraham and the entire creation" (*Apollinaris*: 212, 10–13 Lietzmann). In Fragment 36 Apollinarius claims that the flesh "was co-existent (*synousiōmenē*) and congenital with the divinity" (*Apollinaris*: 212, 25–26 Lietzmann). Finally, in Fragment 50 he claims that "God was enfleshed before the ages" (*Apollinaris*: 216, 6 Lietzmann).

22 1 Cor 15:47. 23 1 Cor 15:48. 24 John 3:13.

25 John 1:3, although Gregory supplies "Christ" for the personal pronoun in John, which refers to "the Word."

26 Eph 3:17. 27 In Greek, *symphuias*. 28 See 2 Cor 5:1, 5:4.

one part of me would boast [of being saved] even though another part of me had the honor [of being saved].[29] But if the human being is endowed with a mind, and not mindless, let them stop being truly mindless.

36. But in the place of the mind, the divinity, [Apollinarius] says, suffices. What good does this do me? For a human being is neither divinity with flesh alone, nor with soul alone, nor with both [flesh and soul] but without mind, which is really what a human being is. So, keep the humanity whole and mix it with the divinity, so that you may benefit me completely. 37. But there is no room, he says, for two complete entities.[30] There's not, if you examine it corporeally; there's no room for two bushels of corn in a one-bushel vessel and one body doesn't have space for two or more bodies. 38. But if [you examine it] intellectually and incorporeally you would observe that even I myself have room for a soul, a rational faculty,[31] a mind, and the Holy Spirit, and before I existed, this universe (I mean, the whole complex of visible and invisible things)[32] had room for the Father, Son, and Holy Spirit. 39. That's the nature of intelligible entities: they incorporeally and indivisibly mix with each other and with bodies. Since there is room for several sounds in one act of hearing, and aspects of several things in the same field of vision, and [several] scents in [one act of] smelling, the senses aren't confined or oppressed by each other, nor are the things perceived lessened by the size of the apprehending faculty.[33]

40. How can a mind, human or even angelic, be perfect in comparison with the divinity so that the former is squeezed out by the presence of the superior? For the relation of a certain amount of light to the sun or a little bit of moisture to a river is not such that when we get rid of the smaller things beforehand – a house's light, the earth's moisture – there would thus be room for the greater and more perfect. 41. Let's investigate this issue, how there will be room for two complete entities, the house with respect to the light and the sun, and the earth with respect to the moisture and the river; indeed, the matter truly deserves a lot of attention. 42. Or do they not know that that which is perfect in relation to one thing may be imperfect in relation to something else? For instance, a hill relative to a mountain or a mustard seed to a bean or any larger seed, even if it is said to be larger than

29 The first part being the body, and the second being the mindless soul.
30 That is, two agents, both active and with independent volition – *Logos* and *nous*.
31 In Greek, *logos*.
32 See Col 1:16.
33 In Greek, *tōi plēthei tēs antilēpseōs*. The idea is that bigger ears do not hear more sounds.

those of the same kind? If you don't mind, what about an angel relative to God and a human being to an angel? 43. Our intellect is perfect, then, and it is the governing agent, but [only] of the soul and body; [it is] not perfect without qualification, since it is God's slave and subordinate, not God's partner in governing or honor. 44. For Moses was a god to Pharaoh,[34] but a servant to God, as it is recorded.[35] Stars, too, shine during the night but are obscured by the sun so that no one realizes that they exist during the day. 45. And when a measly torch joins with a great bonfire, it is not destroyed, it is not visible, it is not distinguished; rather, it is entirely bonfire, since the superior prevails.

46. But our mind, [Apollinarius] says, is condemned. What about the flesh? Isn't it condemned? Either abandon the latter for its sinfulness or add the former for its salvation. If the inferior was assumed so that it would be sanctified through the incarnation, won't the superior be assumed so that it would be sanctified through the humanification? If, O sages, the clay was leavened and a new dough[36] emerged, won't the image[37] be leavened and permeated with God, divinized by the divinity? 47. I'll also add this: if the mind was wholly spat upon as sinful and condemned, and for that reason the body was assumed but the mind left behind, those who lapse in the mind have an excuse. For God's testimony would plainly indicate the impossibility of healing. 48. May I mention a more important point? You dishonor my mind, good sir, as a "flesh-worshiper" (if I am a "human-worshiper") for this reason: you bind God to flesh despite the fact that God cannot be bound in any other respect, thereby taking away the partition.[38] 49. What then is my argument, unphilosophical and uneducated though I am? Because of their greater proximity and affinity, the mind is mixed with the mind and, through it, with flesh, since the mind acts as a mediator between divinity and materiality.[39]

50. Let's see what argument they have for the humanification, whether it is really an enfleshment as they say. If it's that God is contained, being otherwise uncontainable, and that he kept company with human beings[40] beneath a veil – the flesh – they would then have an exquisite mask and the

34 See Exod 7:1. 35 See Deut 34:5; Josh 1:2; Heb 3:5. 36 See 1 Cor 5:7.
37 See Gen 1:26–27, 9:6. 38 See Eph 2:14.
39 For Gregory, the mind is the instrument with which human beings can come to any knowledge and experience of God. This is why its inclusion in the Christological compound is so crucial for him.
40 See Bar 3:38.

drama of an outward show; let me not say that he could converse with us in another way, for instance, in a bush of fire[41] or in a human form even before that.[42] 51. But if it's that [God] would dissolve the condemnation of sin by sanctifying like with like, he would have needed flesh and soul due to the condemned flesh and soul, and in the same way [he would have needed] a mind because the mind not only fell in Adam, but also suffered an initial reaction, of which physicians speak in the case of illnesses. 52. For what received the commandment also failed to keep the commandment; what failed to keep it also dared a transgression; what transgressed stood in particular need of salvation; what needed salvation also was assumed. The mind was therefore assumed.

53. This has now been shown, even if they don't mean it to, by geometrical necessities and proofs, as even they admit. It is you[43] who act almost as if, when a person's eye fails and [consequently] the foot stumbles, you were treating the foot while letting the eye go untended; or when the painter fails to paint something well, you make a change to the painting while failing to set the painter straight. 54. If, constrained by the aforementioned suppositions, they appeal to God's ability to save humanity without a mind, I would bet that [God] could do it without the flesh, simply by his willing it, just like he does everything else, past and present, in an incorporeal way. Take away the flesh, then, along with the mind so that you put the finishing touch on your insanity! 55. They are deceived by the letter,[44] however, and therefore run to the flesh, ignorant of the custom of scripture. I'll educate them on this point too.

56. To those who know it, why do I need to say that, everywhere throughout scripture, he is called a human being and "Son of Man"? If they rely upon this verse – "The Word became flesh and dwelled among us"[45] – and for this reason scrape away the best part of the human being, as tanners do with the thicker parts of hides, in order to glue God to flesh, 57. it's time for them to admit that God would be a god of only the fleshly, but not of souls too, because of what is written: "As you gave him authority over all flesh,"[46] "To you all flesh will come,"[47] and, "Let all

41 See Exod 3:2.

42 See Genesis 18. Gregory reads the theophanies as appearances of the Son as the Word of God.

43 Gregory directly addresses Apollinarius.

44 See 2 Cor 3:6.

45 John 1:14.

46 John 17:2.

47 Ps 64(65):3.

flesh bless his holy name,"[48] that is, every human being. 58. Furthermore, [it's time for them to admit] that our forebears were incorporeal and invisible when they descended into Egypt and that it was only Joseph's soul that was bound by the Pharaoh,[49] because of what is written: "With seventy-five souls they descended into Egypt,"[50] and, "His soul went through iron"[51] – an object that cannot be bound. 59. Indeed those who say such things don't realize that they are named by way of synecdoche, where the whole of something is indicated by a part, as in this phrase, "Young ravens invoke God,"[52] so that the winged nature is indicated, and where the Pleiades, the Evening Star, and the Bear[53] are mentioned in the place of all stars and the administration of them.

60. And at the same time, God's love for us cannot be otherwise revealed except by mentioning the flesh and that he came down for us even to our inferior part. That the flesh is lowlier than the soul, everyone of sound mind would confess. 61. And so, I think that this verse – "the Word became flesh"[54] – means the same as the one that says that he became sin and a curse.[55] How could it not, since the Lord was transformed into them? No, by accepting them he took up our lawlessness and bore our ailments.[56] 62. These words, then, are sufficient for the present situation on account of their plainness and comprehensibility to the masses. For I write these things, not intending to draft a treatise but to keep their deceit in check, and I will offer up a longer, fuller account of these matters if it seems right.

63. This next point, more important than previous ones, must not be ignored. "Those who hassle you" – by introducing a second Judaism, a second circumcision, and a second sacrifice – "ought to castrate themselves."[57] 64. For if this were to happen, would anything prevent Christ from being born again for the annulment of those very things, and again being betrayed by Judas, crucified, buried, and raised, so that everything that occurred in its wake would be fulfilled like the Hellenic recurrence, when the stars' same motion brings the same events back around? 65. Isn't it just arbitrariness that one previous event [gets to] occur [again] while another

48 Ps 144(145):21. 49 See Gen 39:20. 50 Acts 7:14–15.
51 Ps 104(105):18. 52 Ps 146(147):9. 53 See Job 9:9, 38:31–32.
54 John 1:14. 55 See 2 Cor 5:21; Gal 3:13. 56 See Isa 53:4.
57 Gal 5:12.

is passed over?[58] Let the sages and fame-chasers[59] demonstrate this point with their multitude of books.

66. Since those who are puffed up[60] in their argument about the Trinity tell lies about me – that I am not sound in faith[61] – and since they lure the masses, one must be aware of the fact that Apollinarius, who gave the name of divinity to the Holy Spirit, does not safeguard the divinity's power. 67. For constituting the Trinity from great (the Spirit), greater (the Son), and greatest (the Father), as if from a sunbeam, brightness, and sun – which is plainly written in his own words – makes a ladder of divinity, not ascending to heaven[62] but descending from heaven. 68. As for me, I know God the Father, the Son, and the Holy Spirit; these are not mere names that divide the inequalities of their dignities or their powers, but just as there is one and the same designation, so too is there the same nature, substance, and power of divinity.[63]

69. If anyone supposes that these points are spoken correctly but still accuses me of communion with heretics, let anyone show this letter of mine, and we will either be persuasive or retire. Prior to a judgment, it is unsafe to make another innovation, only because the issue is serious and concerns important things. 70. Well, as for me, I have given and continue to give testimony on these matters before God and human beings. I wouldn't even write these words now, you know well, were I not watching the church being torn apart and divided by some tall tales and the current council of vanity.[64] 71. Given that I say these words and bear this witness, if anyone – because of any difficulty, human fear, absurd cowardice, longtime disregard for shepherds and leaders, or perverse pleasure in and readiness for innovations – 72. spits on me as worth no account, and runs to such people, and divides the noble body of the church,[65] it will be he who endures the

58 Gregory here links Apollinarius's notion of cosmic repetition with an idea common within multiple philosophical traditions. Context suggests that Gregory has Plato particularly in mind: see Plato, *Statesman*, 269c–270a; *Republic* 10.614b–621d. Against a cyclical cosmology, Gregory elsewhere posits a very linear one, in which three periods of time can be distinguished, corresponding to each member of the Trinity: the doctrine of the Father was made clear in Moses's time; the doctrine of the Son was made clear in Jesus's new covenant; the doctrine of the Spirit is being made clear contemporary to Gregory (*Oration* 31.26). This trinitarian temporal unfolding is threatened by Apollinarius's supposed cyclical worldview.

59 In Greek, *philotimoi*. 60 See 1 Cor 8:1. 61 See Titus 1:13, 2:2.

62 See Gen 28:12. 63 See *Oration* 29.17. 64 See Ps 25(26):4.

65 See Col 1:24.

judgment, whatever it may be,[66] and will provide an account to God on the day of judgment.[67] 73. But if long treatises, new psalteries that clash with David's, and the gracefulness of verses[68] are regarded as a third testament, I too will compose psalms, write many words, and give them meter, since I think that I too have God's Spirit,[69] if indeed this is the grace of the Spirit and not a human innovation. 74. I want you to bear these words as witness to the masses, so that I don't have to bear the weight of a wicked teaching gathering strength and spreading in the face of my own indifference, as I was overlooking so serious an evil.

66 See Gal 5:10. 67 See Matt 12:36.

68 Apollinarius was a prolific writer not only of dogmatic treatises but also poems and psalms. Gregory composed his own theological verses as a counter to Apollinarius's, some of which are presented in this volume on pp. 399–402.

69 See 1 Cor 7:40.

33

Gregory of Nazianzus, *Poems* 1.1.10–11

Introduction and Translation by Bradley K. Storin

INTRODUCTION

Here Gregory of Nazianzus fulfills his promise made at the end of his *Letter* 101 *to Cledonius* to "compose psalms, write many words, and give them meter."[1] Indeed, if Gregory's longest argument against Apollinarius's Christology comes in *Letter* 101, his most laconic one comes in these didactic verses, *Poems* 1.1.10–11. These texts, like *Letter* 101, reveal one of the most idiosyncratic features of his Christology, that Gregory takes heterodox Christologies as a personal affront; to deny that Christ had a mind, as he polemically frames Apollinarius's position, is to deny Gregory's mind access to salvation, and thus Gregory responded with aggressive polemic.[2] This gives Gregory's argumentation a special tenor relative to later, more technical discussions of Christology. Unfortunately, modern critical editions of *Poems* 1.1.10 and 1.1.11 do not exist; this translation is based on the Benedictine text contained in PG 37: 464–471.

TRANSLATION

Poem 1.1.10: *Against Apollinarius, on the Humanification*

We know that, to the nature of a human being whole, the Greatest Mind
[465] was fastened – [a nature] composed of three things,
soul, and mind, and material body –
the entire Adam of old except for the sinfulness.
Since, then, God indeed became a human being,

1 *Letter* 101 *to Cledonius* 73 (SChr 207: 68 Gallay).
2 Several writings of Apollinarius are translated in this volume on pp. 301–347.

God perfected the human being for my honor[3]
so that, by refashioning what he had given with the very things that he assumed,[4]
he would dismiss the judgment of sinfulness in its entirety
and slay the slayer by dying.
Simple on high, then composite[5] – God –
[466] then, posted[6] by God-killing hands.
This is God's Word, mixed with you.
He was God on high, since the Father is too.
He is God's Word and Creator of the universe –
superior to time, and passions, and body.
After Envy[7] struck with the tree of knowledge
and trampled over our entire nature
as easily imprisoned and condemned,
in order to dissolve Envy's elation
[467] and create anew a corrupted image,
[God] was born among us. For in a pure virgin
God is conceived, and [from her] emerges –
God and mortal wholly, the one who saves me wholly,
the Son, apprehended and seen!
A worshiper of the human being I am to you,[8] since I revere the whole
Word mysteriously integrated with me,
him, both saving God and mortal.
You are a worshiper of the flesh, introducing me as mindless,
to persuasively turn your clever phrase back around.[9]
Either accept it, dear friend, or leave me alone –
if, that is, you are still a fair judge of the Word,
if to you "God from God" implies an inferior entity[10]
(for flesh is far inferior to [what was made] according to the image);[11]

3 The Greek may also perhaps be translated: "The God-Human brought my honor to perfection."
4 The human soul, mind, and material body.
5 In Greek, *sympageis*.
6 In Greek, *pageis*.
7 Envy is a frequent epithet for the devil in Gregory's writings.
8 That is, Apollinarius.
9 Gregory's polemical retort to Apollinarius was that he taught a "mindless" Christ.
10 Gregory here quotes the Nicene Creed and tacitly accuses Apollinarius of interpreting the phrase with a subordinationist hermeneutic.
11 See Col 1:15.

to me God is something superior, for the mind is nearer to God.
[468] However, you risk turning yourself into a half-mortal:
what was not assumed is not saved.
What do you say, you, wisest defender of the Word,
angry with those who sever the divinity?
Isn't it you who severs the compound[12] from God
by attributing one of my features to him but not another,
by mixing in the flesh but removing the mind,
as though the prospect of being entirely integrated with him scares you?
Well how does the one have room for two complete entities?
Or are we scared of making the skin burst?
What insanity! One soul accepted
both Mind and Word! Where, then, do you think the Great
Mind is, with God being present? If the flesh is mindless,
I have been deceived. The skin is mine; whose soul is it?
What becomes of God's generation from the Virgin?
[469] How did a nature of separate [components] come into a single thing?
At the very least, it is indescribable; that's how it appears to me,
who, with a small reasoning faculty, measures things that are superior to reasoning.
The purifying Spirit came upon the Virgin,
but the Word was fastened within her as a mortal,
a complete change into a complete dying mortal.
But given that God is unmixed with flesh,
and the soul and mind occupy, so to speak, a middle ground,
the flesh is like a companion, an image, of God.
Mixed with its partner, God's nature
thereby has communion with the material.
Thus the deifier and the deified are one God.
What, then, did each experience? Here's what I think:
one was mingled with the material, while the other, being materiality,
[470] partook of what is mine except for the passions' sinfulness.
Shall I ask for whom God's blood was poured out?
If for the Wicked One … Ha! – Christ's blood for evil …
If for God, how so, since it was we who were held captive

12 In Greek, *syntheton*.

by another? But a ransom always goes to the captor.
Or is it true that he offered it to God,
so that he could personally snatch us from our captor,
and receive an exchange for the fallen –
Christ? The christener is not easy to understand.
That's my opinion, but we respect the general idea.
You have it right here: venerate the Trinity.

Poem 1.1.11: *On the Humanification*

Childish is anyone who does not revere God's royal eternally existing
Word as equally God with the supercelestial Father.
[471] Childish is anyone who does not revere the royal Word, which appeared
here as a mortal, as equally God with the heavenly Word.
To do so is to sever either the Word from the great Father or the mannish form
and our material from the Word.
He was God, but the Father's Word was fastened to our mortality,
that it may mix with God while being mixed with earthly things.
There is the one God in both regards, so mortal as to make me
God instead of mortal. Be gracious, you who are wounded up high![13]
This is possible for you. What do I think the mind and this inexpressible mixture is?
When it comes to God, you mortals, respect the limitations of your reasoning ability.
Indeed, it would be better for me to have persuaded you. But if you blacken
the page with many thousands of words,
come then, let me inscribe on your tablets these few lines of
letters with my stylus, which has no ink on it.

13 That is, wounded in the mind.

34

Gregory of Nyssa, *Oration on the Savior's Nativity*

Introduction and Translation by Andrew Radde-Gallwitz

INTRODUCTION

In the years following the death of Basil of Caesarea in 378, his younger brother Gregory of Nyssa (ca. 335–ca. 394) emerged as a leading Christian intellectual. Following his brother, Gregory wrote against Eunomius, the Pneumatomachians, and Apollinarius. He attended various synods, including the Council of Constantinople in 381. He was cited in a law of the emperor Theodosius dated July 30, 381, as one of the paragons of orthodoxy in the Eastern Roman Empire and was sent by the emperor on missions to supervise episcopal affairs as far as the province of Arabia. Dozens of his writings on various themes of Christian doctrine and practice have survived. As bishop, one of his roles was to preach at the annual feasts. The current sermon is one of the earliest pieces of evidence for a feast of the Nativity on December 25 separate from the Epiphany on January 6 – at the time this was a relatively recent distinction. We are uncertain as to which year Gregory delivered this Christmas homily, but a reasonable guess has been made that it was 386.[1] The sermon is closely connected to Gregory's *Catechetical Oration*, presenting some of the Christological arguments of that work in a more economical package tailored to the joy of the Nativity feast. In both works, Gregory addresses various "Greek" objections to the doctrine of the incarnation: If this intervention was providentially necessary, why was it delayed in human history? If evil and death were conquered by Christ, why are they still so powerful? Isn't the incarnation out of character for God, who is perfect and incorruptible?

1 Jean Daniélou, "La chronologie des sermons de Grégoire de Nysse," *Revue des sciences religieuses* 29 (1955): 346–72, at 365–66.

In addition to tackling these problems in his homily, Gregory addresses the role of Mary's virginity in the nativity story, providing evidence for the influence of the *Protevangelium of James* on Christian preaching. He also emphasizes the connection between Jesus's birth and the Paschal mystery. To this end, he elaborates, in a moving and dramatic passage, on Matthew's story of the massacre of the innocents, suggesting that the joy of Christian feasts is never a simple and unbothered joy, but something more like redeemed sorrow.

The text translated here is from the critical edition of Friedhelm Mann in Ernestus Rhein, Friedhelm Mann, Dörte Teske, and Hilda Polack, *Gregorii Nysseni Sermones, Pars III*, GNO 10.2 (Leiden: Brill, 1996), 235–269. Numbers in square brackets correspond to page numbers in this edition.

TRANSLATION

[235] "Blow the trumpet at the new moon," says David, "on the noble day of our feast."[2] Now the commands of the God-inspired teaching are surely law for those who hear them. So then, since the "noble day of our feast" is here, let us too fulfill the law and become trumpeters of this sacred time. The trumpet which the law requires, as the Apostle bids us to understand, is speech. For he says that the sound of the trumpet must not become indistinct, but must be clearly separated in distinct sounds so that what is said is **[236]** clear.[3] Accordingly, may we also resound, brothers, with a sound that is bright and no less worthy of being heard than the horn.[4]

Yes, and the same law that required the trumpets' resounding also sketched the truth with shadowy figures in the form of a tabernacle. And the theme of the feast today is the mystery of the true tabernacle.[5] For on this day, the human tent is made a tabernacle for the one who for our sakes put on the human being.[6] On this day, our tents, which had crumbled under death's power, are reconstructed by the one who originally built our house. Joining the Psalm-singing chorus alongside the mighty voice of

2 Ps 80(81):4. 3 See 1 Cor 14:8. 4 See Ps 97(98):6. 5 See Heb 8:2.

6 See John 1:14. Throughout, "human being" translates the Greek substantive *anthrōpos* and "humanity" translates *to anthrōpinon*. The reader should be aware that *ho anthrōpos* can be concrete (the human being), but often has an abstract sense in Gregory. Gregory also frequently uses the adjectival form of this term in such phrases as *anthrōpinē physis*, "human nature," and *anthrōpinē zōē*, "human life."

David, let us too say, "Blessed is he who comes in the name of the Lord."[7] How does he come? It was not by boat or carriage, but through virginal incorruptibility that he crossed over to human life. *This* is how our God, *this* is how the Lord "manifested himself to us" in order to "establish this feast among those who cover all the way up to the horns of the altar."[8]

[237] But surely we are not unaware, brothers, that in what has been said it is revealed that all creation is, as it were, one palace for the lord of creation. But when sin entered in, the mouths of those conquered by wickedness were closed, the sound of exultation was silenced, and the unison of those celebrating the festival was torn asunder, with human nature[9] no longer keeping the festival with the supercosmic nature. For this reason the trumpets of prophets and apostles came, which the law calls "horns" since they are fashioned from the true unicorn.[10] These trumpets make the word of truth resound with the Spirit's vigorous[11] power, so that when the hearing of those closed up by sin is opened there might be a single harmonious feast when, through the covering, the tabernacle of the creation below joins in chorus with the preeminent powers appointed around the altar above. For the horns of the intelligible altar, the preeminent and appointed **[238]** powers of the intellectual nature, are the "princes, authorities, thrones, and dominions"[12] to which human nature – covered in the renewal of bodies – is joined in the feast's communion through the tabernacling of the resurrection. After all, being covered is equivalent to being adorned or dressed, as those who know these matters explain.

Come, then, to the spiritual dance! Rousing our souls, let us make David the leader, guide, and conductor of our chorus and let us proclaim with him that sweet phrase, which we began to sing. Let us take it up once more: "This is the day that the Lord has made, let us rejoice and be glad in

7 Ps 117(118):26; Matt 23:39; Luke 13:35, 19:38. 8 Ps 117(118):27.

9 For sense, we are reading *physeōs* with six mss., instead of Mann's *ktiseōs*, which has the support of five mss.

10 In Greek, *monokerōs*. The reference is to Deut 33:17; see also Num 23:22, 24:8; Ps 21(22):22, 28(29):6, 91(92):11. The anonymous Christian text *Physiologus* (section 22) of perhaps the second or third century claims that in Luke 1:69 the Savior (called the "horn of salvation") is being likened to the legendary *monokerōs*. According to *Physiologus*, no such creature actually exists, although Aristotle identifies the Indian ass and a certain kind of gazelle as single-horned animals at *History of Animals* 499b18–20.

11 In Greek, *syntonon*, a term denoting modes of music that are intense or severe as opposed to relaxed; in ancient rhetorical and literary criticism, the same term denotes a seriousness, intensity, or formality of prose.

12 Col 1:16.

it"[13] – when the darkness begins to lessen and night's bounds are forced to recede before the daylight's growth. Brothers, it is no happenstance occurring willy-nilly, the kind of economy celebrated in this feast: that the divine life appears *now* in human life. Rather, through observable things creation declares, to those who are more perceptive, a mystery, all but giving voice and teaching the one able to hear what **[239]** it means that the day lengthens and the night shortens at the Lord's coming. Truly, I myself think I hear creation relating things like this: "O human being, as you look at these things, understand that what is hidden in the observable things is made plain to you. Do you see how the night, after it has proceeded to its greatest length, has ceased its forward motion, starts coming back? Understand that when the wicked night of sin had grown to the greatest possible extent and had passed through every conceivable kind of evil to the greatest depth of wickedness, on this day it broke off from spreading further and from this point was compelled to recede and vanish. Do you see how the ray of light is brighter and the sun higher than usual? Understand the coming of the true light who illumines the whole world with the rays of the gospel."

Perhaps too, someone might reasonably suppose that the reason why the Lord did not appear at the beginning but gave the manifestation of his deity to human life at the end of time is this: that the one who is going **[240]** to be mingled with human life in order to cleanse its wickedness must wait for every wickedness planted by the enemy to shoot up before bringing, as the gospel says, the ax to the root.[14] In fact, physicians who are devoted to the craft,[15] while a fever is still smoldering a body from within and being enkindled little by little by the noxious causes, will yield to the infirmity and bring the weak person no nutritional aid until the sickness has reached its apex. And when the evil stabilizes, they then apply their craft after the illness has completely come to light. In the same way too the one who heals those whose souls are in a bad condition waited for the illness of wickedness, by which the nature of human beings was dominated, to be completely revealed, lest there be something hidden that remained untreated, since a physician treats only what has appeared. For this reason he neither brought healing through his own appearance in the times of Noah when all flesh was destroyed for its unrighteousness, since the shoot of the Sodomite wickedness had not yet sprung up, nor did the Lord appear in

13 Ps 117(118):24. 14 See Matt 13:24–30 and 3:10.
15 That is, professional healers who know and follow the medical art (in Greek, *technē*).

the time of Sodom's demise, since many **[241]** other evils were still hidden in human nature. For where was God-fighting Pharaoh? Where the Egyptians' incorrigible wickedness? In fact, not even then – I refer to the Egyptians' evils – was it the proper time for the corrector of the whole to be mingled with [human] life. Rather, it was necessary for the transgression of the Israelites as well to appear. And it was necessary that the kingdom of the Assyrians and for Nebuchadnezzar's arrogance, still smoldering below the surface, to become manifest in life. It was necessary that bloodthirstiness against the holy ones spring up like a kind of wicked and thorny shoot from the devil's evil root. It was necessary that the Jews' fury against God's saints become manifest when they killed the prophets and stoned those sent by God and finally brought pollution in the case of Zechariah between the sanctuary and the altar.[16] Added to the list of wicked shoots is Herod's infanticide. And so, when the whole power of wickedness had shot up from its evil root and expanded in various forms, it grew to a thick forest with the **[242]** choices of those in each generation who were famous for wickedness. Then, as Paul says to the Athenians, "Although God looks past the times of ignorance,"[17] the last days came, when "there was no one who understood and sought God, when all had turned aside and were made worthless,"[18] when all things were imprisoned in sin,[19] when lawlessness had expanded, when the gloom of wickedness had grown to its greatest extent – then grace appeared,[20] then the true light's ray rose again, then the "sun of justice"[21] appeared to those seated in the darkness and shadow of death,[22] then he crushed the dragon's many heads,[23] placing his foot upon them through his human flesh, pressing them to the ground, and trampling them.

Now, no one who sees the evils currently in life should deem false the reasoning according to which we said that in the very last times the Lord shone upon in life. For **[243]** an opponent will likely say that the one who waited through the ages for the manifestation of wickedness so that once it had grown he might pull it out by its roots, ought to remove it entirely, so as to leave none of it behind in life. But as things are, murders, thefts, adulteries, and all the wickedest deeds are ventured. But one who approaches this matter with a familiar example can resolve the difficulty

16 See Matt 23:35–37; Luke 11:51. 17 Acts 17:30.
18 See Ps 13(14):2–3; Rom 3:11–12. 19 See Gal 3:22. 20 Titus 2:11.
21 Mal 3:20. 22 Luke 1:79; see Ps 106(107):10; Isa 9:1.
23 See Ps 73(74):13, 14; Rev 12:3.

regarding these issues. For just as when snakes are killed one can observe that the posterior coil does not immediately die along with the head. Rather, the head dies, but the tail is still animated with its own drive and is not deprived of its vital motion. In the same way the dragon-slayer too, when the beast had become great with augmentations of all the particular generations of human beings, when he slayed the head, that is, the capacity for discovering evils that contains many heads in itself, made no fuss about the posterior coil, turning the motion left in the dead beast into an impetus for exercise to those who come after. **[244]** Well then, what is the crushed head? The head that introduced death with wicked advice and hurled the death-dealing arrow at the human being through the bite. Therefore, he who destroyed death's reign also crushed the power in the snake's head, as the prophet says.[24] But the rest of the beast's coil, which is sown in human life so long as humanity remains in vicious movements, constantly makes life miserable with the scaly skin of sin. It is already virtually dead since the head has been made useless. But when the time comes and the motions cease at the hoped-for completion of this life, then the enemy's tail and his very end will be rendered idle. And this is death. And in the same way, the total vanishing of wickedness will occur when all are called again to life through the resurrection – the just immediately resettled in the dwelling-place above, but those **[245]** caught up in sins purified in Gehenna's fire.

But let's return to today's joy, which the angels proclaimed to the shepherds,[25] which the heavens declared to the magi,[26] which the Spirit of prophecy announced through many and diverse heralds,[27] as the magi too became heralds of the grace. For the one who causes the sun to rise on the just and the unjust, who makes it rain on the wicked and the good,[28] brings the ray of knowledge and the gift of the Spirit even to the mouths of foreigners, so that through testimony from opponents the truth might be all the more confirmed in us. Do you hear Balaam the augur prophesying to foreigners with a greater inspiration, "He causes a star to rise out of Jacob"?[29] Do you see the magi, whose race descended from Balaam, watching in accordance with what their forefather predicted for the rising of the new star, which alone – contrary to the nature of all other stars – **[246]** partakes of both

24 See Ps 73(74):14. 25 See Luke 2:8–14.
26 See Ps 18(19):2; Matt 2:1–12. 27 Rev 19:10; Heb 1:1; see 1 Cor 12:10.
28 Matt 5:45. 29 Num 24:17.

motion and stasis, participating in both of these for its purpose? In fact, although of all the other stars, there are some that are once and for all set in the fixed sphere and have an immobile stasis and others that never cease their motion, this one both moves to guide the magi and stops to disclose the location.[30] Do you hear Isaiah crying out, "A child has been born to us, and a son given to us"?[31] Learn from the prophet himself how the child has been born, how a son has been given. Well then, was it in accord with the law of nature? No, says the prophet, the master of nature is no servant to the laws of nature. But tell us how the child was born. "Behold," he says, "the virgin will conceive in her womb and will bear a son and will call his name 'Emmanuel,' which translated is 'God with us.'"[32]

What a marvel: the virgin becomes a mother and remains a virgin! Do you see the innovation of the nature? For other women, so long as she is a virgin, she is not a mother. And when she becomes a mother, she no longer has her virginity. But here the two descriptions go together simultaneously, **[247]** for the same woman is both mother and virgin. The virginity did not prevent the birth and the birth did not destroy the virginity. After all, it was fitting that the one who came into human life to take away the corruption of the whole should take his start from his own servant in a birth of incorruption. For human convention is acquainted with calling a woman with no sexual experience "incorrupt." To me, that great man Moses seems to have already observed this in the theophany that came to him through the light, when fire was kindled in the bush and the bush was not consumed. For it says, "After passing through, I will see this great sight."[33] I think by the "passing through" it indicates not locomotion but passing through as in traversing a period of time. For after an intervening period passed, that which had been prefigured in the flame and the bush was disclosed in the mystery of the virgin. For just as in the former case the shrub both kindles the fire and is not consumed, so too in the latter case the virgin both bears the light and is not corrupted. But if the bush prefigures the virgin's

30 In ancient astronomy, the fixed stars – or, as here, those fixed in the fixed sphere (in Greek, *tē aplanei sphaira*) – were what we call simply the stars, though the category did not include the sun. Although the fixed stars appear in different parts of the sky at different times, they do not change relative position (whence the stability of constellations). The moving stars are what we call the planets, and indeed the name planets comes from their motion as "wandering stars" (in Greek, *planēta astra*). See Plato, *Timaeus* 38c; Aristotle, *Metaphysics* 1073b19–25; *Meteorology* 342b–346a; Pseudo-Aristotle, *On the Cosmos* 392a; Ptolemy, *Mathematical Syntaxis* I, VII–VIII.

31 Isa 9:5. 32 Isa 7:14; Matt 1:23. 33 See Exod 3:3.

God-bearing body,[34] do not blush at the symbolism. For all **[248]** flesh, because of the transmission of sin, is in the same state – that it is simply flesh, it is sin. But sin is described by scripture under the label "thorn."[35]

But, at the risk of drifting far off topic, perhaps it is not untimely that Zechariah who was murdered between the sanctuary and the altar also be cited as testimony to the incorrupt mother.[36] This man Zechariah was a priest, yet not only a priest but also endowed with the gift of prophecy.[37] But the unremarked power of prophecy is proclaimed in the book of the gospel.[38] When the divine grace was preparing the way so that birth from a virgin not be considered unbelievable by human beings, it used as a preliminary exercise **[249]** the assent of unbelievers to lesser marvels: a child is born to a barren and elderly woman.[39] This became a prologue for the marvel concerning virginity. For just as it was not by a power of nature that Elizabeth became an infertile mother late in life, but rather the child's birth is ascribed to the divine will, in the same way too the incredibility of virginal birth-pangs gains credibility by reference to the divine. Therefore, since the one born from a barren woman preceded the one born from a virgin, leaping in his mother's womb at the voice of her who was pregnant with the Lord before he came forth into the light, as soon as the Word's precursor had come to birth, Zechariah's silence is broken through prophetic inspiration. And everything Zechariah relates is a prophecy of what is to come. Therefore, since this man was acting as a guide in the prophetic spirit to the knowledge of hidden things, understanding the mystery of virginity at the incorrupt birth, he did not set apart the unmarried mother in the sanctuary of the place set apart for virgins according to the law.[40] He was teaching the Jews that **[250]** the maker of beings and the

34 In Greek, *to theotokon sōma tēs parthenou*. The title *theotokos*, sometimes rendered "Mother of God," would become a point of controversy in the fifth century. Gregory uses it in two other works, *On Virginity* 19 and *Letter* 3.24. In the latter, he distinguishes the term *theotokos*, which he uses, from the title *anthrōpotokos*, "human-bearer," which he does not use. The Nestorian controversy would deal with the appropriateness of these two titles for the Virgin.

35 Gregory's reference is uncertain. See Gen 3:18; 2 Sam 23:6; Ps 31(32):4; Matt 7:16, 13:7–22; 2 Cor 12:7; Heb 6:8.

36 Matt 23:35–37; Luke 11:51.

37 See *Protevangelium of James* 23–24, with Matt 23:35–37 and Luke 11:51.

38 See Luke 1:67. Note that Gregory's phrase distinguishes "the book of the gospel" from the report in the *Protevangelium of James*, which he later at page 411 refers to as "a certain apocryphal history."

39 See Luke 1:36.

40 See *Protevangelium of James* 8–11.

king of all creation has, along with all things, his own human nature that is subservient to his own will, and he directs it as he sees fit. He is not ruled by it, since it is in his power to make a new birth that does not remove virginity from the one who becomes a mother. For this reason, Zechariah did not set her apart in the sanctuary of the virgins' chorus. This place was the intervening space between the sanctuary and the altar. And so when they heard that the king of creation had come forth to human birth in his economy, fearing that people might become servants to the king, they slaughtered the one who testified to these things about the birth, sacrificing the priest at the altar itself!

But we've wandered far off topic and must return in our speech to Bethlehem in the gospel. For if we truly are shepherds, keeping watch over our own sheep, then surely it is to us that the angels' voice declares the good news of this great joy.[41] Therefore, **[251]** let us gaze upward at the heavenly host; let us see the angels' choral dance; let us hear their divine hymnody. What is the response of those celebrating the feast? "Glory to God in the highest," they cry out![42] Why does the angels' voice give glory to the deity observed in the highest? Because, it says, "And on earth peace."[43] The angels became overjoyed at the appearance: "on earth peace." The earth that was formerly cursed, that produced thorns and thistles, the place of war, the exile for the condemned – she received peace. What a marvel: "truth sprouted from the earth and justice looked down from heaven."[44] The land of human beings gave as its fruit one of this kind and these things occurred on behalf of "good will among human beings."[45] God mixes with human nature so that humanity might be raised up to the loftiness of God. Having heard these things, let us make our journey to Bethlehem.[46] Let us see the new marvel: how the virgin glories in the birth; how the woman without sexual experience nurses the infant. First, let us hear from those who related the narratives about her who she is and whence she comes.

[252] So then, I've heard a certain apocryphal history laying out these stories about her.[47] The virgin's father was someone distinguished for a rigorous way of life in accordance with the law and was known for the most beautiful [deeds], but he grew old without a child since his wife was not suited for childbearing. Now based on the law there was a certain honor for

41 See Luke 2:8, 10. 42 Luke 2:14. 43 Luke 2:14. 44 Ps 84(85):12.
45 Luke 2:14. 46 See Luke 2:15.
47 Gregory refers to the *Protevangelium of James*.

mothers, which barren women could not share. In this regard she imitates also the stories about Samuel's mother.[48] She too came into the sanctuary of the holy ones and begged God, not because she had sinned in any way with respect to the law so as to fall out of the law's blessings, but that she might become a mother and offer the child to God.[49] Made capable by divine approval for the grace she had requested, she later bore the child and named her Mary so that through the name the divine bestowal of the grace might be indicated. And once the little girl had grown to the point that she no longer relied on the breast for her needs, they dedicated her to God, fulfilling the promise, and brought her to the sanctuary. For some time, the priests **[253]** – just like with Samuel – raised the child among the holy men, but once she had grown, they took counsel over what to do lest they cause that sacred body to sin against God. For on one hand it seemed most absurd to yoke her to the law of nature and to give her through marriage as a servant to a husband. After all, it was regarded an utter sacrilege for a person to become sovereign over what has been set apart for God, since by the law the husband was established as ruling over the wife. On the other hand, for a woman to be raised together with the priests within the temple and to be seen among the holy ones wasn't lawful and there was no reverence in it. As they were deliberating on these matters, counsel came from God to give her nominally in betrothal to a man who was the kind of person suitable to guarding her virginity. And thus Joseph was found, as the text demanded, from the same tribe and clan as the virgin. And, in accordance with the priests' counsel, he betrothed the child to himself. For the union went only as far as betrothal.[50]

[254] Then the virgin was initiated into the mystery[51] by Gabriel. The words of the mystagogy were a blessing. "Hail," he says, "blessed woman, the Lord is with you."[52] The address now comes to the virgin in a way completely opposite to the first utterance to a woman. That woman was sentenced to pains in childbirth on account of sin, but with this one, pain is cast out through joy. With that one, pains dominated childbirth, but here

48 See 1 Sam 1–2.

49 See *Protevangelium of James* 4.1, although in this text Anna offers her prayer in a grove of trees after her expulsion from the temple.

50 For the details of the narrative sketched by Gregory, see *Protevangelium of James* 7–9.

51 In Greek, *mystagōgeitai*; in the next sentence the noun *mystagōgias* is used.

52 *Protevangelium of James* 11.1; see Luke 1:28.

joy serves as midwife for the birth. "Do not be afraid," he says.[53] Since the prospect of childbirth brings fear to every woman, the promise of a pleasant childbirth casts out fear. He says, "You will conceive in your womb and will bear a son and you shall call his name 'Jesus.'"[54] And what did Mary do? Listen to the pure virgin's utterance. The angel declared the birth, and she clings to her virginity, judging incorruption to be nobler than the angelic appearance, and could neither disbelieve the angel nor abandon her judgments. She says, I have no experience of intercourse with a husband: "How will this happen to me, since **[255]** I have not known a husband?"[55] Mary's very utterance is proof of what is narrated in the apocryphal book. For if she had been taken by Joseph for marriage, how could she be totally astonished at the one who announced the birth to her if she was quite favorably disposed to becoming a mother according to the law of nature? But since the flesh that had been consecrated to God had to be kept inviolate like one of the holy dedicated things, this is why she says, "Even if you are an angel, even if you have come from heaven, even if the appearance was beyond human, still for a husband to know me is not possible. How will I become a mother without a husband? I know Joseph as a fiancé, but I have not known a husband." And what did Gabriel (the bridal escort) do? What sort of bridal chamber did he announce for the pure and undefiled marriage? "The Holy Spirit," he says, "will come upon you and the power of the Most High will overshadow you."[56] What blessed flesh that was, which through the abundance of its purity drew the goods of the soul to itself. For in the case of all other people a pure soul would scarcely receive the presence of the Holy Spirit. But here the flesh becomes a vessel of the **[256]** Spirit. But also "the power of the Most High will overshadow you." What does the text secretly reveal by this? "Christ is the power of God and wisdom of God," says the Apostle.[57] So then, the power of the Most High God, which is Christ, through the Holy Spirit's coming is given form in virginity. For just as the shadow of bodies assumes in outline the shape of the originals, in the same way the imprint and identifying marks of the Son's deity are brought to light by the child's power, and he is shown as image, seal, shadow, and radiance of the prototype through the wonder-working nature of his actions.

53 *Protevangelium of James* 11.2; see Luke 1:30.
54 *Protevangelium of James* 11.3; see Luke 1:31.
55 Luke 1:34.
56 Luke 1:35; see *Protevangelium of James* 11.3.
57 1 Cor 1:24.

But the angel's good proclamation calls us to return in our speech to Bethlehem and to peer into the mysteries in the cave.[58] What is this? A child wrapped in swaddling clothes, and laid to rest on a manger, the virgin after the birth, the incorrupt mother caring for her offspring.[59] Let us shepherds utter the prophet's saying, "As **[257]** we have heard, so we have seen in the city of the Lord of hosts, in the city of our God."[60] Is it therefore a matter of happenstance and coincidence that these things happened and are recounted in the story of Christ, there being no rationale for the account? What is meant by the Lord's descent into the cave, the lying on a manger, and becoming mixed with [human] life at the time of the tax-census? Isn't it obvious that, just as he who for our sake became a curse removed us from the law's curse[61] and transferred our stripes to himself so that "by his stripe we are healed,"[62] so too he also came as a tax-payment, to free us from wicked tributes to which humanity, levied by death, was subject? As you behold the cave in which the Lord is born, think of the dark, subterranean life of human beings, into which comes the one who appears to those seated in darkness and the shadow of death.[63] Bound in swaddling clothes is he who wrapped himself in the ropes of our sins.[64] The manger is the feeding-place of irrational beasts[65] to which the Word comes, so that **[258]** the ox might know its creator and the ass might know its Lord's manger[66] – the ox is the one yoked to the Law, the ass the beast of burden laden with the sin of idolatry. Now the nourishment appropriate to irrational animals is grass – "For he makes grass to spring forth for the beasts," says the prophet.[67] But the rational animal is nourished with bread. And so this is why it is in the manger, which is the irrational animals' hearth,[68] that the bread that comes down from heaven[69] is placed, so that the irrational beings, by partaking of rational nourishment, might come to be in reason. And so the Lord of both the ox and the ass mediates between them at the manger, so that when he destroys the wall of partition between them, he might make the two in himself into one new human

58 For the cave, see *Protevangelium of James* 18, 21. 59 See Luke 2:7, 12, 16.
60 Ps 47(48):9. 61 Gal 3:13. 62 Isa 53:5.
63 Luke 1:79; see Ps 22(23):4, 106(107):10; Isa 9:1, 42:7. 64 See Prov 5:22.
65 In Greek, *tōn alogōn*. Gregory will play on the double meaning of *alogos* here: those animals that lack reason (*logos*) and humans without the Word of God.
66 Isa 1:3. 67 Ps 103(104):14.
68 In Greek, *hestia*, which can have cultic connotations, referring to an altar.
69 John 6:50–51, 58.

being, removing the heavy yoke of the law from this one and unburdening the other one of the weight of idolatry.[70]

But let us gaze up at the heavenly marvels. For behold not only prophets and angels declare this good and joyous news to us **[259]**, but also the heavens proclaim the glory of the gospel through their own marvels.[71] Out of Judah our Christ rises, as the Apostle says,[72] but the Jew is not illuminated by the one who rose. The magi are strangers to the covenants of the promise[73] and aliens from the blessing of the fathers,[74] but in knowledge they preceded the Israelite people, recognizing the luminary in the heavens and not ignoring the king in the cave. They bring gifts; the others lay plots. They worship; the others persecute. They delight in finding the one they sought for; the others are distraught at the birth of the revealed one. For, it says, "when the magi saw the star above the place where the child was, they delighted with an overwhelmingly great joy."[75] But "when Herod heard the report, he was distraught and all Jerusalem with him."[76] They bring frankincense as if to God and honor the royal dignity with gold, while indicating by a certain prophetic grace the economy of the passion through the myrrh. **[260]** The others condemned all the youths to utter destruction, which seems to me to make them answerable not only for cruelty but also for their complete stupidity. After all, what do they wish to accomplish by the murder of children? And for what purpose do they risk incurring this kind of pollution that is for murderers? "It is because some new sign of heavenly marvels," he says, "has revealed the proclamation of the king to the magi." So what? Do you believe the revealed sign to be true or do you regard it as empty gossip? Indeed, if he is the sort of person who causes the heavens to be affected together with himself, then surely he is out of your hands! But if it is in your power to make him live or die, then it is pointless to fear such a person. For when you behave so as to make him become subject to your power, for what reason is he plotted against? Why is that dreadful decree handed down, the wicked judgment against the infants, that the wretched little ones be killed? Why harm them? What grounds for death and punishment have they provided against themselves whose only fault is that one charge: **[261]** being born and coming forth into the light? Was it really necessary for the sake of these executioners that the city be emptied and that the tribe of mothers and the clan of infants be assembled,

70 See Eph 2:14–15. 71 See Ps 18(19):2. 72 See Heb 7:14.
73 See Eph 2:12. 74 See Gal 3:14. 75 See Matt 2:9–10. 76 Matt 2:3.

since the parents were with them and presumably all the members of the family were brought to the suffering together?

Could anyone put the miseries into words? Could anyone descriptively bring before our eyes the sufferings – that comingled lament, the mournful song collectively of children, mothers, fathers, kinsfolk crying out in pity at the executioners' threat? How could anyone sketch a picture of the unsheathed sword as the executioner stands before the youth gazing sharply and murderously uttering such things, with one hand pulling the little one to himself and with the other extending the sword, while the mother from the other side pulls the child to herself and holds her own throat up to the tip of the sword, lest she see with her eyes the wretched child killed at the executioner's hands? **[262]** How could anyone tell the fathers' stories: their cries, their laments, their final embraces of the children, since many things of this sort happened at the very same time? Could anyone compose a tragedy out of this complex and manifold misery, the newborn's double birth-pangs, the bitter burners of her nature – how the poor little one was clinging to the nipple when it received the mortal wound in its vitals, how the wretched mother was holding her breast to the infant's mouth when she received the child's blood on her bosom? Perhaps in many cases given the force of his hand the executioner drove a single thrust of the sword through the child all the way into the mother and the stream of blood was single, mingled together from the blow to the mother and the child's fatal wound. But in Herod's murderous decree this point too was contained, that not only was the death-dealing sentence leveled at newborns. Rather, if anyone had grown even up to the second year, this one too was to be seized, for it is written, "From the second year and under."[77] So, the story presumably envisions yet another suffering, **[263]** since often in this interval the same woman has become mother of two children. So again what kind of spectacle was there in such cases, with two executioners working on one mother – the one pulling to himself the child at her side, the other tearing the nursling from her breast? What does the wretched mother suffer over these things, as she must have, with her nature split between two children, each of them equally kindling the flame in the mother's bosom, and her at a loss – which of the wicked executioners would she follow, the one on this side or the one over there, as they pull the infants to the slaughter? Does she run for the newborn who lets out a wail that is still without meaning and inarticulate? But she hears the other one, who has

77 Matt 2:16.

already made a sound and tearfully called out for the mother in a faltering voice. What does she suffer? Who should it be? Whose voice would she answer? To whose cry would she reply with tears of her own? Which death would she mourn, when she is tortured equally for both in the core of her nature?

[264] But let's bring our attention from dirges over the children and turn our minds to gladder things that are more appropriate to the feast, even though Rachel, according to the prophecy, drowns us out as she sorrows over the slaughter of the children.[78] For "on the feast day," as wise Solomon says, "there should be no mention of evils."[79] What could be more propitious than this feast of ours – when the "sun of justice"[80] radiates in its nature through this nature of ours, dispersing the devil's wicked, moonless night; when the fallen is raised up, the enemy is brought to terms,[81] the banished one is recalled, the one fallen from life returns to life, the one enslaved in captivity recovers the dignity of royalty, the languishing one fettered in death's bonds runs back to the land of the living? Now, in accordance with the prophecy, death's bronze gates are crushed, the iron bars are broken that used to keep the human race confined in death's prison.[82] Now is opened, **[265]** as David says, the door of justice.[83] Now the resounding voice of those keeping the feast is heard as in unison throughout the entire world. Through a human being came death; through a human being comes salvation.[84] The first fell into sin; the second restored the fallen one. The woman gave a defense on the woman's behalf. The first woman gave entrance to sin, but this one served the entrance of justice. That woman imbibed the serpent's advice, but this one provided the serpent's destroyer. That woman introduced sin through the tree; this one replaced it by introducing goodness through the tree. For the cross was a tree. And the always-blooming and never-fading fruit of this tree becomes life for those who taste of it.

And let no one think this kind of thanksgiving is fitting only for the Paschal mystery. For it should be considered that Pascha is the end-point of the economy. And how could the end-point have happened unless the beginning led the way? Which of the two is **[266]** prior? Obviously the birth is prior to the economy of the passion. Therefore, even the Paschal

78 Jer 38:14; Matt 2:17. 79 Sir 11:25. 80 Mal 3:20. 81 See Rom 5:10.
82 See Ps 106(107):16; Isa 45:2. 83 Ps 117(118):19.
84 See Rom 5:12–17; 1 Cor 15:21.

graces are part of the blessings surrounding the birth, and if one lists the kind deeds narrated in the gospels, and if he recounts healing marvels, feeding with limited resources,[85] bringing back the dead from their tombs,[86] the improvised cultivation of wine,[87] driving out demons,[88] changing various afflictions to health, the leaping of the lame,[89] eyes [restored] with clay,[90] divine teachings, acts of law-giving, leading to loftier mysteries through parables – all these are boons of the present day. For this day began the sequence of good things. Therefore, "let us be glad and rejoice in it,"[91] not fearing **[267]** people's reproach and not brought low by the disparagement, as the prophet exhorts,[92] of those who mock the account of the economy on the grounds that it is not fitting for the Lord to assume the nature of the body and to mingle himself with human life through birth. For you are not completely unaware of the mystery concerning this, how the wisdom of God contrived our salvation. We were willingly sold by sins, like purchased slaves we were enslaved to the enemy of our life. What could have been done by the Lord that would be more to your liking? Not to remove the miseries? Why do you bother about the means? Why do you legislate to the benefactor the form of the benefaction, just as if someone even accused a doctor for his beneficence because he performed treatment in this way rather than in that way?

But if in your meddling you are looking for the rationale of the economy, you only need to learn this much: that the divine is not some single one of good things alone, but all of them. Whatever is conceived of as good, the divine is this – powerful, **[268]** just, good, wise, and all names and concepts whatsoever whose meaning is fitting for God. Examine, then, whether all the things we mentioned (goodness, wisdom, justice, and power) coincided in what happened. Being good, he loved the one who had deserted him; being wise, he schemed the idea for the return of the captives; being just, he does not compel the captor, who had procured his purchase justly. Instead, he gives himself in exchange for those mastered, so that like a kind of guarantor who transfers the debt to himself, he might free the one who is detained from his masters. Being powerful he was not mastered by Hades nor did his flesh see corruption.[93] In fact, it was not possible for the "author of life" to be mastered by corruption.[94]

85 See Matt 14:13–21, 15:32–39; Mark 6:31–44, 8:1–10; John 6:1–13.
86 See John 11:44. 87 See John 2:1–12. 88 See, e.g., Mark 5:2–16.
89 See, e.g., Matt 9:2–8, 11:5. 90 See John 9:6–11. 91 Ps 117(118):24.
92 See Isa 51:7. 93 See Ps 15(16):10; Acts 2:27. 94 Acts 3:15.

But was it shameful to come into a human birth and to undergo the experience of the afflictions of the flesh? You mean the excess of the benefaction. For since it was not possible to remove humanity from evils in any other way, the king of all impassibility dared to exchange his own glory for our life. And purity came to be in our filth, but filth did not **[269]** cling to purity, as the gospel says, "Light shone in darkness and darkness did not grasp it."[95] For gloom is dispelled by the presence of sunlight; the sun is not dimmed by the gloom. Mortality is swallowed up by life, as the Apostle says; life is not consumed by death.[96] What is corrupted is saved by the incorruptible, but the corruption does not cling to incorruption. For these reasons, the common hymn of the entire creation arises as all send up in unison the doxology to the Lord of creation, with every tongue – those in heaven and on the earth and under the earth – crying out that Jesus Christ is Lord to the glory of God the Father and is blessed for ever and ever.[97] Amen.

95 John 1:5. 96 See 2 Cor 5:4. 97 See Phil 2:11; Rom 1:25, 9:5.

35

Theodore of Mopsuestia, *On the Incarnation of the Lord against the Apollinarians and Eunomians* (Fragments)

Introduction and Translation of Greek and Latin Fragments by Mark DelCogliano
Translation of Syriac Fragments by Ellen Muehlberger
Arrangement of Fragments and Appendix by Mark DelCogliano

INTRODUCTION

Theodore was a native of Antioch, where he was trained in rhetoric by Libanius before entering the ascetical school led by Diodore (later bishop of Tarsus). He was ordained a priest by Flavian of Antioch in 383 and then in 392 was consecrated bishop of Mopsuestia. In the course of his long episcopal tenure Theodore came to be regarded as one of the foremost theologians and exegetes of the pro-Nicene cause. In addition to numerous biblical commentaries on books of the Old and New Testaments, he produced a set of catechetical homilies explaining the Nicene Creed and the Lord's Prayer, polemical treatises such as *Against Eunomius* and *Dispute with the Macedonians*, as well as other works. Theodore's *On the Incarnation* was also polemical, according to the late fifth-century Gennadius of Marseilles:

> Theodore, presbyter of the Antiochene church, a man prudent in knowledge and skillful in speech, wrote fifteen books *On the Incarnation of the Lord against the Apollinarians and Eunomians*, containing as many as fifteen thousand verses, in which he showed by the clearest reasoning and by the testimonies of scripture that just as the Lord Jesus had the fullness of deity, so too he had the fullness of humanity. He taught also that a human being consists only of two substances, that is, soul and body, and that mind and spirit are not different substances, but inborn faculties of the soul

> through which it is inspired and is rational and makes the body capable of sensation. Moreover, the fourteenth book of this work is properly devoted to discussing the uncreated and alone incorporeal and all-ruling nature of the holy Trinity and also the rationality of creatures, which he explains insightfully on the authority of the holy scriptures. But in the fifteenth volume he confirms and strengthens the whole body of his work by citing the traditions of the fathers.[1]

According to Gennadius, then, Theodore wrote the massive *On the Incarnation* before his appointment as bishop while he was still a presbyter; thus his work represents a pro-Nicene Christological outlook of the 380s or early 390s. This was the period in which pro-Nicenes were actively confronting the Christologies of the Apollinarians and Heteroousians (also called Eunomians) as live options, such as was done by Gregory of Nazianzus and Gregory of Nyssa. And herein lies the importance of this work: it is a crucial non-Cappadocian witness to emerging pro-Nicene Christology as it developed in response to the perceived threats of Apollinarius and Eunomius but decades before dyophysite language became problematized through Nestorius. We see in Theodore, then, a Christology that is very much a work-in-progress as he attempts to work out the categories, concepts, and contours with which to articulate his understanding of Christ.

A few years after Theodore's death in 428, Cyril of Alexandria identified him, in spite of his reputation for unimpeachable orthodoxy during his lifetime, as a forerunner of Nestorius, an association that quickly tainted the legacy of Theodore. This eventually led to the condemnation of Theodore's person and writings as one of the so-called Three Chapters at the Council of Constantinople in 553.[2] Accordingly, some works of his, including *On the Incarnation*, survive only in Greek, Latin, and Syriac fragments, the latter due to the esteem in which Theodore was held by the Church of the East.

Fragments of Theodore's *On the Incarnation* survive in various treatises and collections. All the Greek fragments are preserved in Leontius of Byzantium's *Unmasking and Triumph over the Nestorians* from the early 540s.

1 Gennadius of Marseilles, *On Illustrious Men* 12 (PL 58: 1067–1068).
2 See *Acts of the Second Council of Constantinople*, translated in CEECW 4 on pp. 341–389.

There are Latin fragments in Facundus of Hermiane's *In Defense of the Three Chapters* from 550, as well as in the Acts of the fourth, the fifth, and the sixth sessions of the Council of Constantinople in 553. Syriac fragments are found in the fifth-century florilegium known as *The Blasphemies of Diodore, Theodore, and the Impious Nestorius* and in British Library Cod. Add. 14669, a mutilated sixth- or seventh-century manuscript that originally contained a complete Syriac translation of *On the Incarnation*. In most cases, the original location of the fragment is indicated, whether the book number or the section number or both. (It appears that, in addition to its division into fifteen books, *On the Incarnation* was also divided into sections, numbered sequentially from the beginning to the end of the treatise, and thus overlapped with the division into fifteen books.) Accordingly, the extant fragments below are placed in their original order as far as can be determined. Several fragments lack any internal indication of their original order, but sometimes the contents of a fragment offer clues to its approximate original location. In these cases a justification for where the fragment is placed in this translation appears in a footnote. In three cases no conjecture could be made about the original location of the fragment; these are simply placed after all the others. The original location of each fragment, if known, is indicated in the title of each fragment.

There are 73 unique fragments in total. Some are preserved in multiple languages. The translations below are always based on the original Greek if it is available. If a fragment is not extant in Greek, then the translation is based on the Latin version if one is available. Only in cases where neither the Greek original nor a Latin version is available is the translation below based on the Syriac. In a few cases fragments preserved in British Library Cod. Add. 14669 (whose Syriac translation of the original Greek is lacunose and difficult) can be presented with two columns, the left-hand column containing parallel fragments preserved in Greek, Latin, or a different Syriac translation. Whenever possible, the translators have made reference to the different language versions of the same fragment to gain insight from the ancient translators' interpretations.

With the exception of the Syriac fragments in British Library Cod. Add. 14669, the fragments of *On the Incarnation* were preserved by someone opposed to Theodore's views. Accordingly, since these fragments were selected and quoted precisely because they were deemed to reveal the most problematic aspects of Theodore's Christology, a reader must work carefully with these fragments and not interpret them through the polemical lens intended by those who preserved them. In the case of all the fragments, they are removed from their original contexts, which often makes reading them difficult – it is like hearing only a snippet of a wider conversation. They can seem cryptic, and a reader will have to work to reconstruct the questions or problems they are attempting to answer.

While it is difficult to summarize the Christological teaching of a treatise that survives in such a fragmentary state, certain repeated themes can be highlighted here. For Theodore, the purpose of the incarnation was soteriological, to undo the fallen human condition into which humanity sank in consequence of the sin of Adam. He insists that in Christ there is a union of two distinct, intact, and complete natures (humanity and divinity) in a single person. Against Apollinarians and Eunomians, he affirms that Christ had a human soul. In fact, he teaches that Christ struggled with desire in both flesh and soul yet overcame those temptations through the assistance of the indwelling divinity. Thus did the assumed human being achieve moral perfection. The union of humanity and divinity in Christ began at the moment of the conception of the assumed human being, enabling the human being to be preternaturally endowed with moral excellence. At the same time this union is presented as a reward for the assumed human being, whom God foreknew would make moral progress and advance to human perfection with the assistance of the indwelling Word. The precise details of this cooperation between the indwelling Word and indwelt human being remain somewhat fuzzy.

Theodore also spends considerable energy identifying the proper conceptual categories to use when trying to understand the incarnation. He speaks of it in terms of a "union," "conjunction," "assumption," or "indwelling," but he rejects "mixture." Theodore is known for speaking of God indwelling in Christ "by good pleasure" and that concept is also on display in these fragments. What he means by this is that God indwells in Christ according to the favorable disposition of his will, not by substance or activity. God also indwells the prophets, apostles, and saints by good pleasure, but not in the same way that he indwells in Christ by good pleasure. For in Christ God indwells by good pleasure "as in a Son" (Heb 1:2), by which Theodore means that there is a union of the indweller and the assumed human being, who thereby comes to share in every honor and title of God and becomes one person with him. Thus Christ can be called "Son of God" (by grace) because of his conjunction with the Word (who is Son of God by nature). Theodore resists the charge that his Christology implies that there are two sons. Likewise, the incarnate Word can also be called a "human being," though Theodore is clear that he is not a "mere human being."

The Greek and Latin fragments have been edited by Till Jansen, *Theodor von Mopsuestia De Incarnatione* (Berlin: De Gruyter, 2009),[3] and all the original language fragments of *On the Incarnation* by John Behr, *The Case against Diodore and Theodore* (Oxford: Oxford University Press, 2011). The following translations are based on Behr, with reference to Jansen when possible and to Brian Daley's edition of the works of Leontius of Byzantium (*Leontius of Byzantium: Complete Works* [Oxford: Oxford University Press, 2017]) in the case of the fragments preserved by him. See the Appendix to this translation for a table correlating our fragment numbers both to the codes that Behr assigned to each fragment and to Jansen's numbering of the fragments. The table also lists the internal indications of the original location of each fragment.

TRANSLATION

Fragment 1
From Book 1
(Translated from Syriac)

Since many have gone astray in various ways about the doctrine of the incarnation <...>

Fragment 2
From Book 1, Section 11
(Translated from Latin)

So then, just as Nathanael, by a confession such as this one,[4] is revealed to be lacking knowledge of his divinity (in hoping for such things, Jews and Samaritans were as far as possible from the knowledge of God the Word), so too Martha, by her confession,[5] is shown at that time to be lacking knowledge of his divinity, and moreover it is obvious that not even the

3 Jansen's Fragment II is omitted because it consists of excerpts from Theodore's homilies; it is not a fragment of *On the Incarnation*; see Richard Price, *The Acts of the Council of Constantinople of 553* (Liverpool: Liverpool University Press, 2009), 258 n. 147.

4 See John 1:49, "Rabbi, you are the Son of God, you are King of Israel."

5 See John 11:27, "You are the Christ, the Son of God, the one coming into the world."

blessed Peter [had knowledge of his divinity].[6] For until that point it was enough for those who received that revelation back then to understand that there was something exceptional and superior about him beyond the imagination of other human beings. But it was only after the resurrection, when they had been brought by the Spirit to knowledge, that they received perfect knowledge of the revelation. At that point they came to know that something exceptional had come to him beyond [that which comes to] other human beings, not in terms of some simple honor from God as is the case with other human beings, but through union with God the Word, through which participation in every honor is given to him after his ascension into heaven.

Fragment 3
From the Beginning of Section 33
(Translated from Syriac)

The Apostle said, "Just as sin arose in the world through one human being, and through sin, death,"[7] so too did grace abound for many through one human being, Jesus Christ.[8] In light of this it is normal that people ask about the implications of the words of the apostles even when they in fact know, and declare that they are persuaded by, the apostolic sayings. When they are not persuaded, though, asking us, "What is the answer to the problem?" we are happy to respond to this question, considering it our pride [to offer] a defense on behalf of the apostolic words. And so, we say: It was right that the human being had to find a solution, through his way of life, for his disobedience. But the mere human being was not able to conquer sin's power when he struggled with it, since it had been implanted in our very nature for such a long time. [Sin] possessed the soul, since [the soul] became easily subjugated to that which it had wanted to struggle with – for behold, it was conquered by fighting against it. The indwelling of God the Word became necessary, so that, with humanity's disposition to correct conduct preserved unharmed through the aid of God the Word who had made it fully capable, humanity might easily escape sin and find a solution to the disobedience that came about through the first of those formed like us.[9]

6 See Matt 16:16, "You are the Christ, the Son of the living God." See also Mark 8:29 and Luke 9:20.

7 Rom 5:12. 8 See Rom 5:14. 9 That is, Adam.

Fragment 4
From Section 35
(Translated from Syriac)

For our Lord's struggles were similar; they were not more useful than ours, though they were somewhat more noticeable. Even if it is not possible to say this, it is obvious that he took up a great struggle on our behalf against the passions of the soul. That struggle taken up against the passions of the flesh was less serious, given how much more it took to endure those of the soul. This is because the soul needed more healing. But it is obvious that, once he had taken up flesh and soul, he struggled in both and for both, mortifying sin in the flesh and subjecting its desires, making them easily conquerable by the superior reason of the soul. He was disciplining the soul, training it so it could subjugate its own passions and oppress the desires of the flesh. For when the divinity indwelled these things, it began to rule each of them. The grace of the Holy Spirit was also assisting with this, just as the blessed Apostle said too: "Great indeed is the mystery of godliness: he who was revealed in the flesh was also made righteous in the Spirit."[10] Because we ourselves are also going to receive the assistance of the Spirit to attain to the perfection of righteousness <...>

Fragment 5
From Section 36
(Translated from Syriac)

Since later he was going to give the assistance of the Spirit to human beings, who were going to need it for the fulfillment of perfect excellence,[11] first he gave it to the one who was assumed.

Fragment 6
From Section 36
(Translated from Syriac)

Like when he was speaking with his disciples about the gift of the Spirit, which was going to come to them, he said, "He will glorify me, for he will

10 1 Tim 3:16. 11 Alternatively, "virtue."

take what is mine and declare it to you."[12] He did not say "from me" but "from what is mine."

Fragment 7
From Section 37
(Translated from Syriac)

Yet he also said that he performs miracles by the Spirit of God. He said, "But if it is by the Spirit of God that I cast out demons … ."[13] So who is silly enough to say about God the Word that he casts out demons by the Spirit of God? Because this is a human thing: human beings do not have sufficient power of their own to perform miracles. It is proper, though, to speak this way of the one who was assumed.

Fragment 8
From Section 38
(Translated from Syriac)

The saying of our Lord – "Do not fear those who kill the body but are unable to kill the soul; rather, fear more the one who can destroy both soul and body in Gehenna" – also indicates this.[14] Thus their silly thought is proved wrong. For he who considers the will of the soul also thereby condemns the assumption of the flesh with the soul, which is superior to the flesh. They should not think this way! For excellence[15] is from the will, but the will also needs God's assistance for it, since it is drawn by inclination toward sin. Therefore, when our Lord assumed humanity, he gave it a great grace, namely, he removed the embedded sin from its flesh, and from its soul [he removed] the easy tendency toward the passions and the inclination toward sin. In this way he removed, on the one hand, the fervor of desire from the flesh where it resides, and on the other, he voided the grip of the passions on the soul. It was not that he removed the passions and impulses themselves, for [the body and soul] are still driven by both of them. But he has driven away their power and has given the soul suitable instruction by his own way of life. He made [the soul] invincible to its own passions, and by the superiority of good thoughts the attack of wicked [thoughts] will be repelled, so as to corral the desire of the flesh in the intention toward the good, being supported by the assistance of the Spirit.

12 John 16:14. 13 Matt 12:28. 14 Matt 10:28. 15 Alternatively, "virtue."

Fragment 9
From Sections 42–43
(Translated from Syriac)

By all means, the soul has rationality. For if mortal beings have natural movements in their own life, those which are immortal have it all the more, as their life is immortal. They have responsive and powerful minds. But maybe they'll say, "We didn't say that the soul does not have rationality." Well then, let them tell us why a third nature, which they call "mind," is required, and why they point to its sustenance, or why it assists and completes the human being. If the vitality of the body is administered by the soul, then the mind is also in [the soul], such that by it the divine nature is recognized; it also establishes all activity and administers all the guidance of the things that have been and those that will be – for these things all follow from the rational nature [that it has]. What then do the heretics say is the argument for the third nature that they invent and call "mind"?

The soul does not naturally have functions and activities like those of the body. Naturally, one calls the thing that sees "the eye," and naturally one calls the thing that hears "the ear," and naturally one calls the thing that is moved to make words "the tongue." Each of the members naturally has movements that move it. And if the soul in its turn is the same, it would require something else for its sustenance and vitality, just as these members also require the soul, by which they are sustained and are moved to the use of their actions. When the soul is removed, the remaining members of the body are not just voided, but they are truly destroyed; they [by themselves] were not sufficient for the form and sustenance of their soul.[16]

And as the soul is not so[17] – indeed, it is not, for it naturally lives in its hypostasis[18] by God's grace, administering life and sustenance for the body – then it is clear that it is immortal and does not have natural movements. Instead in the mind it turns to whatever it chooses.

But the heretics do not grant these things nor deem them fitting. What's more, they do not consider the teaching of the sacred books. Rather, for the demonstration of their position – that the human being is constituted from three natures – they summon for us a testimony from the blessed

16 The soul that inhabited them.
17 That is, requiring something else for its sustenance and vitality.
18 In Syriac, *qnoma*.

Paul, in which he said, "May the God of peace sanctify you entirely, and may all your spirit and soul and body be without fault until the coming of our Lord Jesus Christ."[19] [43][20] And this testimony, which they cite in order to question us, they "understand" foolishly.

And they summon another text, that Jesus "grew in stature and wisdom and in grace, before God and before human beings."[21] They are not Apollinarians, who deny the mind of the soul. Nor are they Eunomians, who like to inquire into and examine the assumption of the soul, similarly to those who reject that the soul was assumed. Both groups know that this testimony is contrary to their teaching. For if, according to [the second group's] position, he did not assume a soul, or, according to what [the others] say, he assumed a soul but not a mind – as if there is anyone who says that the soul of the human being can exist with no mind! – how then did Jesus "grow in wisdom"? If he says that it was the divinity that grew in wisdom – well, even they wouldn't dare to say this to us in their madness. And the body didn't "grow in wisdom," that much is clear. So, it seems obvious that he assumed a rational soul, for that is how it was possible that he could "grow in wisdom," namely in that he received by the mind the teaching of wisdom.

Yet persisting they also say that he visibly "grew" in the estimation of human beings, while not taking in that which was [actually] said, namely "in stature and wisdom and grace," and "before God and before human beings." If they confess about him that he truly "grew in stature and wisdom and grace," then obviously just as he really did grow in stature, not just in estimation, so also did he likewise truly grow in wisdom. The evangelist had prudently guarded his words and did not allow any opportunity to the wickedness of their craft, in that he said, "before God and before human beings." Let us think regarding their position that it was in estimation before human beings that he grew. Surely, it is not that he could grow in estimation before God. For if it was before God that he grew and increased, it is clear <...>

Fragment 10
From Sections 49–50
(Translated from Syriac)

<...> that it is, or that because he is not complete, he has not given him the designation "Son." Now, if they call God the Word "Son," that one is

19 1 Thess 5:23. 20 Section 43 begins here. 21 Luke 2:52.

something else apart from the divine nature. Whether the body alone or the body and soul, it is not worthy of being called "the Son of God," nor is it the perfected human being. What then should we say he is, according to their position? Quote for us a passage that is equal to these thoughts. If they say that the one who was assumed – whether they want to say it was the body, or the body with the soul – is conjoined and was complete in the one Son, how do they not grasp that this position is suitable and even agreeable to us? For we confess that the complete human being was assumed. After all, if the complete God the Word is by nature the Son of God, by birth he is from the Father. Thus, that which exists apart from that nature was not given its own personal name. Instead he is confessed by the name "Son of God" on account of his precise conjunction with God the Word.

Whatever is said regarding the Son of God obviously also applies to the one who was assumed, even as he was perfected. But we are not required to say "two sons" because of this, just as the two natures are soul and body, but are not the same as one another. This much is clear: even they confess this! For if the two natures which were assumed are not the same as one another, they are also not [the same as] God the Word who assumed them, nor do they constitute another person from them and for them, on account of their conjunction with God the Word. It is clear that not even the third nature – which is the mind, according to their position – does this, even if it is additional. For if there are two, body and soul, belonging to God the Word who assumed them, and he is truly the Son who is named and confessed to be with him according to the precise conjunction, it is obvious that even if this is a third nature, it does not in any way oppose our position in this matter. Just as these two natures are named and confessed with the name of the excellent nature – that is, of the one who assumed them – because of the precise conjunction, so too, even if there is a third nature, it is called "Son of God" and spoken of as though it is not separate from God the Word. And we do not concede anything else beyond "divine nature," that in his own person itself and for him is known and named the "Son of God." But by the name of "Son of God" we designate that one who was assumed, even if he is the one who is a complete human being. But if in their madness they say that "the mind is superior to the divinity of the Only-Begotten in that human being and it is right that from it, as from something superior, the other person of the human nature be named" – for such things are said to us – since we reject their position that "the mind is another nature beyond the soul and body," we have already demonstrated above with the aid of God that they are not so.

[50] But they say that neither is it right to apply to Christ the name of the "human being," nor is it fitting that he be called by this phrase.[22] The fact that they think this is a demonstration of their ignorance and of how poorly acquainted they are with the holy scriptures. For it is plainly known to all who wish to perceive it that we find this name in many places in the holy scriptures. For our Lord said to the Jews, "Why do you wish to kill me? I am a human being who speaks the truth to you."[23] And in a different place, when the Slanderer said, tempting him, "Make these stones into bread," he answered him, "It is written that the human being does not live by bread alone."[24] It is obvious that, if what was assumed was not a human being yet had a conflict with the Slanderer, [the Slanderer] would not fight with him to tempt him. For he thought that he was just what was visible and did not sense the divine nature that was residing in him. If he had known, he would not have dared to tempt him. Surely, strictly speaking, if he had sensed the divine nature, he would know also this: that he is above every temptation. Thus, he did not answer fittingly.

Fragment 11
From Section 50
(Translated from Syriac)

Just as death came through a human being, so too does the resurrection of the dead come through a human being. According to what is known, it is not fitting that resurrection be granted to humanity in any other way except by the one who is like in nature to the nature of the one who was the cause of death.[25] It is also right for him who is the cause of the resurrection to be the same.

Fragment 12
From Section 51
(Translated from Syriac)

For God is not said to wear flesh, for no one says, "God wears flesh." Let us say once more, "the human being in whom God dwelled." That is, it is not absurd for him to wear God, which is what they hasten to attack, as if it were clearly an absurdity. If he is said to be a human being, as we have

22 In Syriac, *bart qala*. 23 John 8:40. 24 Matt 4:4. 25 That is, Adam.

shown from the divine scripture, then it is in this one that God the Word dwelled. Whether "he is in him," or however they choose to say it, it is not absurd to say the human being "wore" God, the one who dwelled in him.

Fragment 13
From Section 51
(Translated from Syriac)

For they ask this especially: Is Christ one thing and the Son of God another thing? Or is this one Christ and the other one the Son of God? If anyone answers and says, "He is one and the same," then they immediately think their illness is upheld.

Fragment 14
From Book 5, Section 52
(Translated from Latin)

When someone distinguishes the natures, he necessarily finds one thing and another thing. And not even they,[26] I think, will object to this fact because we all agree that God the Word by nature is one thing and what is assumed is another thing, whatever it may be. At the same time, however, he is found to be the same as that [which is assumed] in terms of person, not by the natures being confused in any way but on account of the union that the assumed made with the assumer. For if we are honest when we agree that the latter is other than the former by nature, and it is clear that the assumed is not equal to the assumer, with neither the latter being similar to the former nor the assumed the same as the assumer, then it is clear that he will be found to be the same by reason of the union of the person. So then, it is appropriate to divide that which concerns Christ, for there is nothing contradictory in these divisions – after all, they are in utter harmony with the divine scriptures. In this way there will be neither a confusion of the natures nor a kind of wicked division of the person. For the principle of the natures must remain unconfused and it must be recognized that the person is undivided – the former by reason of the property of the nature, in that the assumed is distinct from the assumer, whereas the latter by reason of the union of the person, in that the nature, whether of the assumer or even that of the assumed, is accounted for in the single designation for the whole.

26 Presumably Theodore's opponents.

Accordingly, to use an example, as soon as we call upon God the Word using the designation "Son," at the same time we co-signify the assumed nature, whatever it may be, on account of the union that it has with him.

Fragment 15
From Book 6, Section 54
(Translated from Latin)

So then, though they[27] seem to be justified in calling us "human-worshipers"[28] because we call Christ a human being, prior to our saying this, scripture taught all human beings [the same] through those [passages] in which it does not refuse to call [Christ] a human being, just as we have shown above that in many passages Christ is called by this name. But it is fitting, they say, for those who call Christ a mere human being to be called human-worshipers. Now, this is a blatant lie, if they really should want to say this! For no one has ever heard us say such things, and I do not think that even they could pretend to allow such a blatant lie, not because they are unacquainted with lying but because they see that they can be refuted most easily – although if they should be careless, perhaps it would come even to this! For we ourselves think that to say this, that is, to deny the divinity of the Only-Begotten, is the height of madness. Otherwise, what reason now remains for why we are separated from the heretics? For what reason have we endured both such great and so many persecutions? Or who does not know that war is constantly waged against us by the heretics? Every mine and every deserted place is filled with our people on account of the doctrine of piety.[29]

Fragment 16
From an Unknown Book or Section[30]
(Translated from Syriac)

<...> many were taken up. And there was a slight diminishment of the danger that the whole mass of the people would perish in this error. The

27 Presumably Theodore's opponents. 28 In Latin, *hominicolae*.

29 That is, allies of Theodore have been sentenced to work in the mines or sent into faraway exile for their views.

30 Though this fragment has no internal indications of its original location, it is connected with Fragment 17, which also deals with Meletius of Antioch. Since Fragment 17 sums up the discussion of Meletius, it seems best to place this fragment before it.

entire East was confused with this opinion.[31] And some of those who were reckoned to have perfect knowledge of the faith in regard to the Son of God but whose understanding in regard to the Holy Spirit was not [yet] sound were only later confirmed and perfected in the knowledge of the truth.[32] At that time, the blessed bishop Meletius preached this faith with great boldness of speech, forsaking the honor that he had before the emperor or the magistrates. And even though he was aware that after his preaching he would be excluded from the honor and love of the emperor and the magistrates, he despised all this, and with bravery and excellence he preached the faith of the church. It is right that we accurately cite the words of his homily to explain and confirm what we are saying. For he said, "They are understood to be three, but we speak of them as one."[33] And immediately there was a great upheaval in the church and the uproar of the people kept getting louder and louder, for they were all amazed at the boldness of his doctrine, and the grace of God was established in the minds of all the people. But the enemies of the truth groaned very bitterly when they saw that all their schemes would be dissolved in a short time. For the bravery of his preaching and the boldness of his teaching were the confirmation of the fear of God[34] and a great rebuke of those who little by little were chipping away at the solid foundation of the faith. The words of his teaching could not be heard on account of the people's uproar. Not even if someone had used a horn would it have been possible to hear because of how loud the great uproar was. And then the blessed bishop Meletius fulfilled the function of the tongue with his holy hands, as he wished that all his members might become a mouth and that he might preach the truth through all of them.[35] And this blessed one was made holy by the confession of his

31 The "opinion" mentioned by Theodore is "Arianism."

32 Theodore is talking about some group active in the early 360s which later generations would call Pneumatomachians, Macedonians, or Homoiousians but which eventually adopted the pro-Nicene position. In the next sentence he appears to place Meletius in this group.

33 These words were spoken after Meletius preached the homily before Emperor Constantius II that is preserved in Epiphanius, *Panarion* 73.29–33; see Theodoret, *Ecclesiastical History* 2.31 and Sozomen, *Ecclesiastical History* 4.28. Theodoret preserves the original Greek of Meletius's words: *tria ta noumena hōs heni de dialegometha* (GCS n.F. 5: 172, 12–13 Parmentier/Hansen).

34 "Fear of God" here means "true piety."

35 As reported by Theodoret and Sozomen (see note 33 above), an "Arian" archdeacon attempted to stop Meletius from speaking by covering his mouth with his hand. Meletius

mouth, though before the confession of the church they[36] had been ruthlessly persecuted with the punishment of death, and they were not permitted to gather together for the service of prayer and the thanksgiving to the Lord God of all. For in Antioch of Syria, the emperors on many occasions had threatened and commanded that they be thrown in the river. For they used to assemble and gather at the river at that time. Our words do not suffice such as they are, but the deeds themselves already proclaim such words <...>

Regarding the blessed bishop Meletius (may his memory be a blessing!), who by his blessed way of life was [firmly established] in divine truth and who was much loved and greatly honored the emperor, why was he expelled from the city of Antioch and sent into exile?[37] Was it not the boldness of his preaching about the doctrine of the fear of God? For all the East was confused about the contents of the faith. Back then the heretics were not separated, but mixed together in one congregation were both those who with great care adhered to the teaching of faith in the fear of God and those who concealed the deceit of their error in their mind. Those of the right belief feared to preach the truth of their faith with boldness, since at that time the [heretics] were stronger than they were. [The heretics] knew that the crown and the magistrates belonged to the opposing opinion, and they were guided by the will of the emperor as if it were their own will, and also they subjugated their own opinion to that of many magistrates, [by accepting] abundant gifts for the provision of the church and all those who were ill in their opinions. For the people were not yet accustomed to understanding the blasphemy against the Son of God. For in this period when that wickedness began, they did not yet dare express their opinions openly but hid their deceitful error and little by little subtly dismantled the faith of the simple and drew them to the teaching that leads to perdition. And thus little by little this error <...>

then held up his own hand, showing three fingers, then one finger, thereby signaling the pro-Nicene doctrine of the Trinity.

36 That is, pro-Nicenes like Meletius.

37 Meletius was exiled from Antioch only a few months after becoming its bishop in consequence of the homily he preached before Emperor Constantius II. At the time, Meletius was not viewed as unmistakably pro-Nicene, but by the Council of Constantinople in 381 he was widely regarded as a leader of that alliance.

Fragment 17
From Book 6, Section 54
(Translated from Latin)

Now when the blessed Meletius endured all these things from the heretics, he first and then many others along with him throughout the provinces, the cities, and the countryside, what was the reason? Was it not because they were confessing that Christ was true God? Was it not because they were preaching that he was the true Son of God, begotten from the paternal essence, always existing simultaneously with the generating Father, adding also the pious confession about the Holy Spirit? And so, having suffered so much on account of this confession, how can we suffer calumny from them as if we called [Christ] "a mere human being," seeing that the facts themselves refute this patent calumny?

Fragment 18
From Section 56
(Translated from Syriac)

"We speak wisdom among those who are perfect."[38] By "wisdom" he refers to the whole preaching about Christ, in which all people have been educated, namely, that as God the Word indwelled, he directed all things in the human being. The crucifixion matters, then, not because of the nature of the passible one, but because of the power of the one who assumed him.

Fragment 19
From an Unknown Book or Section[39]
(Translated from Syriac)

<...> as also the arrival of the magi, which magnified and blessed the birth of the Messiah. They came from a distant place so that they might worship him according to the testimony of their words. [The birth of the Messiah] was revealed to many; the evangelist testified, saying, "Herod was disturbed

38 1 Cor 2:6.

39 Though this fragment has no internal indication of its original location, its content – the evidence that should have convinced the Jews to believe in Jesus Christ as God – indicates that it should be placed before Fragment 20, which implies a previous discussion of the same evidence.

and all Jerusalem with him."[40] And many other deeds were seen after "the testimony of John [the Baptist]."[41] First, our Lord performed miracles that were quite novel and wondrous. What's more, what his disciples performed in his name were clearly great miracles; he gave them the authority to do these when he said, "Cast out demons, cleanse the lepers, cure the sick; you have freely received, so give freely."[42] And the fact that the blessed apostles clearly accomplished these things in his name is even more impressive than what [John the Baptist] could do. For it does not seem that anyone could ever perform miracles in the name of a human being: Joshua son of Nun did not in the name of Moses, and Elisha did not in the name of Elijah. But in fact [Elisha] did receive the gift of his spirit in double [portion].[43]

Therefore, since all these things also made it known to the Jews that Christ was the Lord, inasmuch as he was greatly superior to Moses and all the prophets, they have no just excuse for their hardheartedness and their lack of obedience toward our Lord. It would have been right for them to obey him, since he was grander and greater than Moses and all the prophets who had come before. Because of the things he said, he was worthy of faith. [But] they abandoned the things that were necessary and thought of him in such a way as to crucify him, though there was no just cause of their hardheartedness. Yet what brought down the penalty upon them even more severely was that after the crucifixion and death of our Lord, the apostles had clearly performed signs before them, with even the shadow of the blessed Peter curing the sick before their eyes.[44] Despite all these things, the Jews abided in their evil opinion; though they had seen all these great wonders, they still subjected this apostle to shame and to imprisonment many times. But if they had wanted to repent after the crucifixion, their repentance would have been received. For we saw blessed Peter do this.[45]

And [when] all those in Judaea, the scribes, and the Pharisees together with Sadducees, and all the nation of the Jews [went out to John the Baptist],[46] he not only testified that [Christ] was manifest, but he also confessed that he was much greater than him: "He is so much greater that I am not worthy to loosen the straps of his sandals."[47] It is not that the testimony of John was received without any doubt; rather, John, who made his faith abundantly known to the Jews in all his testimony, testified about [Christ] without any

40 Matt 2:3. 41 John 1:19. 42 Matt 10:8. 43 See 2 Kgs 2:9.
44 See Acts 5:15. 45 This must refer to Peter's repentance for denying Christ.
46 See Matt 3:5–7; Mark 1:5; John 1:19, 24. 47 Luke 3:16.

doubt. It would have been right for them to have faith in him and obey him. And it was not only a question of John's testimony, but after this a pronouncement of the Father from heaven clearly confirmed John's testimony. It said, "This is my Son, my beloved, in whom I am well pleased."[48] And in the descent of the Spirit that testimony was made abundantly manifest and confirmed – the Spirit which clearly came in the likeness of the dove.[49] What greater testimonies than these could be needed? From human beings, John testified, he who was greater than all human beings of that era.[50] From heaven, [there are the testimonies of] God, whom the Jews acknowledged as Lord of all, and the Holy Spirit, who was described as God in the Old Testament and who gave the gift of prophecy to all the prophets.

Even the events before these were not insignificant.[51] For before John, Zechariah his father was informed by the angel about John's birth, which was also revealed to the whole nation of the Jews in its impiety. This was said to him about John: "He will be great in the sight of the Lord, and he will be filled with the Holy Spirit; he will go before him in the power and the spirit of Elijah the prophet to prepare for the Lord a perfected people."[52] It is clear that these words bring a great understanding about Christ to light. For inasmuch as John was excellent and great in the eyes of the Jews, the fact that he was testifying about our Lord, namely that he was greatly and immeasurably superior to him,[53] clearly confirms his testimony about our Lord. And along with all these things the angel also testified about the birth of our Lord when he appeared to the shepherds and said, "Today is born to you a Savior who is Christ the Lord."[54] And the shepherds quickly came to the city and told everyone.[55] And it was clear that these things were being reported throughout all of Judaea, for new things are wont to be reported and recounted by many mouths.

Fragment 20
From the Ending of Book 6
(Translated from Syriac)

<…> in it,[56] their faith and their repentance were acceptable. Now, because of all these things judgment is deservedly assigned to the [Jews], and the

48 Matt 3:17. 49 See Matt 3:16; Mark 1:10; Luke 3:22; John 1:32.
50 See Matt 11:11; Luke 7:28.
51 That is, the events before the testimony of John the Baptist.
52 Luke 1:15–17, with omissions. 53 That is, Jesus was superior to John.
54 Luke 2:11. 55 See Luke 2:15–18. 56 Or, "in him."

punishment equal to their presumption has been prepared for them, as they persisted in a rigid opinion through all of them. They were persuaded neither by the great wonders, nor by the appearance of the angels,[57] nor by the arrival of the magi, who had come from a foreign country and a distant land and would not have been aware of our Lord's birth if they had not been informed by a star and a revelation.[58] Nor were they persuaded by the voice of his Father, the Spirit's arrival, or John's testimony,[59] let alone the great miracles that our Lord clearly performed, along with those that his disciples performed in his name, before the crucifixion and after it, and all the great signs that happened at the time of the crucifixion. These things validate their condemnation and punishment even more, [a punishment] which in a little while <…> And what's more, in their perversity they used sizeable bribes to persuade the Romans guarding [the tomb] to conceal his resurrection and to act treacherously by saying, "the disciples came; they stole him in the night."[60]

All these things should have been enough to bring them to the faith that was superior to that of Moses and all the prophets. It would have been good for them to believe the things that he said, and if they had followed his faith they would have been brought little by little to understanding and knowledge of God the Word, like the apostles and the rest who had faith in him. All these things by which the Jews were not persuaded were insignificant to the heretics, and because of that, they rightfully receive the decree of judgment and great punishment for their guilt. Neither by Moses nor by the rest of the prophets, and after Moses not until the coming of our Lord, do we find such things as these performed by which Christ our Lord is clearly manifest, who is beyond comparison with Moses and superior to all the prophets.

The wicked <…> except those who in their ignorance about this do not see any of these things. But they say, "If they crucified a human being, they are not condemned to judgment. Just as those who killed someone wicked are not condemned, so too those who inflicted shame on the blessed apostles are not going to receive punishment." We learn from Christ our Lord clearly that those who insult and cause the blessed apostles distress receive the same punishment as anyone who offends our Lord. They receive

57 See Matt 1:20–24; Luke 1:11–20, 1:26–38, 2:9–15. 58 See Matt 2:1–2 and 9–12.
59 Matt 3:13–17; Mark 1:9–11; Luke 3:21–22; John 1:29–34.
60 See Matt 28:13.

punishment and censure; likewise, whoever honored the Lord receives a good reward. Accordingly, those who received the apostles sent by him and honored them receive the wages and good reward [of what they have done], as he clearly says, "He who receives you also receives me, and he who receives me receives the one who sent me."[61] And in another place he says, "Whatever you have done to one of the least of these who have faith in me, you have done it to me, and what you have not done for one of the least of these, you have not done it for me."[62] <...> "[Amen, I say to you, it will be more tolerable] for Sodom and Gomorrah on the day of judgment than for them."[63] If [we are talking about] the ones who contemned and dishonored those who had faith in him, this fitting punishment has been prepared for them, which it is right for those who contemned him to receive.

How, then, does the one who sins against a human being [receive] judgment and condemnation and punishment? The heretics say that if the Jews crucified a human being, there is no condemnation or punishment for them. But the truth of what has been said is clear. We have sufficiently shown that, even though they did not have knowledge of God the Word, and even though they did not perceive the divine nature that was dwelling in the human being, the Jews rightly received a punishment that was equal to their presumption. They could have come to knowledge of the truth and to faith in Christ by means of so many things. But they scorned and were not willing to be persuaded. For this reason they have no excuse for the wicked things they did in their presumption <...>

End of the Sixth Book.[64]

Fragment 21
From Book 7
(Translated from Greek)

For if we can learn how the indwelling comes about, we shall also know the manner [of the indwelling] and how that manner [of indwelling] is distinct. Now some have claimed that the indwelling happened by substance, whereas others claim it was by activity. Let us, then, examine whether one of these is true. But first let us come to agreement on this point, whether or not [God] indwells in all people. Well, it is clear that he does not indwell

61 Matt 10:40. 62 Matt 25:40, 45. 63 Matt 10:15.
64 Italicized rubrics in this translation are part of the fragment.

in all people. For God promises this as something special to the saints, or in general to those whom he wants to be dedicated to him. Otherwise, why did he ever promise, as though he were going to grant them something special, "I shall indwell in them and I shall walk among them, and I shall be their God and they shall be my people,"[65] if all human beings really share in this collectively? Therefore, if he does not indwell in all (for this is clear) – I do not mean in [all] beings only, but not even in [all] human beings – then there must be some distinctive principle of indwelling, according to which he is present only in those in whom he is said to indwell.

So then, to say that God indwells by substance is utterly inappropriate. For either his substance would necessarily be confined only to those in whom he is said to indwell and he will be outside all others – which is absurd to say about the infinite nature that is present everywhere and circumscribed by no place. Or else, if we were to say that God is present everywhere by reason of his substance, then all things would participate in his indwelling too, not only human beings but also even irrational creatures and lifeless things, if indeed we should say that he makes his indwelling by substance. Now both of these are clearly inappropriate. For saying that God indwells all things is recognized as sheer absurdity, and to circumscribe his substance is inappropriate or rather impious. Therefore, it would be utterly silly to say that the indwelling happens by substance.

And one could also say the same thing in regard to activity. For again, either his activity would necessarily be limited only to those [in whom he indwells], and [in this case] how would we uphold the principle that God foresees all things and arranges all things and works in all things that which is proper? Or else, if all things participated in his activity – now this is fitting and suitable, since all things are empowered by him to exist, each of them, and to act according to their proper nature – then we would be saying that he indwells all things. Therefore, it is impossible to say that God makes his indwelling either by substance or by activity.

So then, what's left? What principle shall we use that is regarded as preserving the distinctive [manner of indwelling] in these cases? Clearly, then, it is appropriate to speak of the indwelling as happening by good pleasure.[66] Good pleasure refers to the best and noblest act of will that God can make when he is pleased with those striving to be dedicated to him

65 Lev 26:11–12, which is quoted in 2 Cor 6:16. 66 In Greek, *eudokia*.

based on his good and noble opinion of them. This [understanding of good pleasure] is derived from scripture according to its customary usage and lies within it. So the blessed David speaks in this way, "His delight shall not be in the strength of the horse, nor his good pleasure in the legs of a man, but the Lord's good pleasure is in those who fear him and in those who hope in his mercy."[67] By this [David] means that [the Lord] refuses to work with some and declines to assist others, but does [work with and assist] those "who fear him," as he says. These he holds in high regard, these he has decided to assist and come to the aid of. This is the proper way, then, to speak of the indwelling. For being infinite and uncircumscribed by nature he is present to all, but by good pleasure he is far from some and near to others. In line with this idea it is said, "The Lord is near to the broken-hearted and those whose spirit is crushed he will save."[68] And elsewhere, "Do not cast me away from your presence nor deprive me of your Holy Spirit."[69] By means of intention[70] he is near those worthy of this nearness and in turn far from sinners: it is not by nature that he is separated and not by nature that he is brought closer, but he makes both happen by the disposition of his will.[71] So just as he is near and far by good pleasure (now it is quite clear from what's been said what we mean by good pleasure; that's why we discussed the meaning of the term with complete precision), so too by good pleasure he accomplishes the indwelling, not by circumscribing his substance or activity in those [whom he indwells] while being separated from all others, but rather by being present to all by substance while being separated from the unworthy by the disposition of his will. For in this way is his limitlessness better preserved, when it is made plain that he is not enslaved by some necessity to the limitlessness of his nature. For if it were the case that, because he is present everywhere by substance, he is also present everywhere by good pleasure, he would be found enslaved to necessity differently because he would no longer bring about his presence by his will but by the infinitude of his nature, having his will dragged along. But since he is present by nature to all and separated from those whom he wants [to be separated from] by his will, and since none of those who are unworthy benefits from God being present, the limitlessness of his nature

67 Ps 146(147):10–11. 68 Ps 33(34):19. 69 Ps 50(51):13.

70 In Greek, *diathesei*.

71 In Greek, *tēi schesei tēs gnōmēs*, which in the ancient Latin version of Fragment 69 is translated *secundum adfectum voluntatis*.

is preserved true and inviolate for him. In this way, then, by good pleasure he is present to some and separated from others, just as if he was with them by substance but separated from the rest.

Just as the indwelling comes about by good pleasure, so too does the good pleasure modify the manner of the indwelling. For that which brings about God's indwelling and that which makes it known that the one who is present everywhere by reason of his substance also indwells in a very small number of all the people – the good pleasure, I mean – this surely leaves its mark also on the manner of the indwelling. For just as he is present in all by substance without being said to indwell in all but [only] in those to whom he is present by good pleasure, so too, even if he is said to indwell, the circumstances of the indwelling are surely not identical but the manner of indwelling will also be consistent with the good pleasure. So when he is said to indwell in the prophets or in the apostles or in the righteous generally, he brings about the indwelling because he is well pleased[72] with the righteous, because he is satisfied, as is appropriate, with the virtuous. In [Christ], however, we do not say that the indwelling came about in this way – may we never be so insane! – but "as in a Son."[73] For that is the way he indwelt [in him] when he was well pleased[74] [with him]. But what does "as in a Son" mean? That he who indwelt united to himself the whole of the one assumed and caused him to share along with him in every honor in which the indweller himself, being Son by nature, participates, with the result that he effects one person by way of the union with him, and shares all his rule with him, and in this way accomplishes everything in him so that even the judgment and examination of all will be performed through him and his presence, even though the difference in their natural characteristics is clearly recognized.

Fragment 22
From Book 7, Section 59
(Translated from Greek)

As for us, then,[75] even though we will be perfectly governed by the Spirit in both body and soul in the age to come, nonetheless we now have a kind

72 The Greek participle *eudokōn* is cognate with *eudokia*, "good pleasure."
73 See Heb 1:2.
74 The Greek participle *eudokēsas* is cognate with *eudokia*, "good pleasure."
75 Reading *toinun* with Jansen and Daley instead of Behr's *toinēn*.

of partial first fruits of this, as it were, according to which by the aid of the Spirit we are under no compulsion to succumb to the disturbances of the soul. In the same way too the Lord, even though after these things[76] he had God the Word fully and wholly active in himself, with every activity of his inseparable from him, nonetheless even before this[77] he had him as much as possible accomplishing in himself most of what was required: in the period before the cross he was allowed, because of his need, to achieve virtue for our sake by his own intention,[78] but even in these matters he was supported by him and strengthened so that he could completely fulfill all the necessary things.

For right from the start, at the construction[79] in the womb, he had union with him. And when he reached the age at which discernment between what is good and what is not good naturally develops in human beings – rather, even before that age – he demonstrated a power to discern such things far more quickly and swiftly than the rest of human beings. In regard to the rest of human beings, the power of discernment does not develop in everyone in the same way at the same time: some grasp what is right more swiftly by greater intelligence, whereas others acquire this over a longer period of time by training. But this [power of discernment] came to him, in comparison to the rest, extraordinarily sooner than the typical age for human beings. It makes sense that he should have had something extra in human terms since he had not been born according to the nature typical of human beings, from the coupling of man and woman; rather, he was constructed by the divine action of the Spirit. In addition, he had an extraordinary propensity toward the good through his union with God the Word, of which he was deemed worthy by foreknowledge when God the Word from on high united him to himself. And so, because of all these things, along with discernment he immediately possessed a great hatred toward evil, and because he had conjoined himself to the good with irrepressible affection and received assistance from God the Word proportionate to his own intention, he was then preserved unaltered from any change for

76 That is, after the saving events of the economy.
77 That is, before the resurrection.
78 The Greek term here is *prothesis*, translated as "intention" when it appears in the Greek fragments. In one case "intention" translates *diathesis*: see note 70 above.
79 The Greek term *diaplasis*, "construction," refers to the seed's development into the embryo; it was regarded as the first stage of fetal development after conception.

the worse. This is the way he maintained [his own] will, and this is the way his intention was preserved by the assistance of God the Word.

And furthermore he pursued the most exacting form of virtue with the greatest ease, whether in keeping the law before his baptism or in pursuing a life in grace after his baptism; in this he provided us with a pattern, presenting himself as a kind of path for us in this regard. So, finally, after his resurrection and assumption into heaven, having shown himself worthy of the union on account of his own will – though he had received this union even before this, at his very construction [in the womb], by the good pleasure of the Master – finally he provides an exact demonstration of [what] the union [means], that no activity of his is separated or severed from God the Word and that he has God the Word accomplishing all things in himself through the union with himself. Accordingly, then, prior to the cross we see that he is hungry, we know that he is thirsty, we learn that he is afraid, and we discover that he is ignorant, since his intention for virtue comes from himself.[80]

And the prophet Isaiah is a witness to what has been said, saying, "For before the child knows good or bad, he refuses evil in order to choose the good."[81] Clearly, it is by discernment that he hated the former and loved the latter. For surely a choice happens by discerning what is worse. So then, how does he accomplish this "before the child knows"? Here's how: before he reached that age at which it is customary for the rest of human beings to acquire discernment between courses of action, he had something extra and exceptional in comparison to the rest of human beings. For if even among us we often find children of that age who give proof of great conscientiousness, such that they provoke wonder in onlookers because they display an innate intelligence superior to their age, by how much more must that human being[82] have surpassed all the human beings of his time.

Fragment 23
From Book 7, Section 59
(Translated from Greek)

"And Jesus progressed in age and in wisdom and in grace before God and human beings."[83] For he progressed "in age" as time marched on, and "in

80 Literally, "since he contributed to his intention for virtue from himself."
81 Isa 7:16. 82 That is, Jesus. 83 Luke 2:52.

wisdom" by acquiring conscientiousness with the passage of time, and "in grace" by pursuing virtue in a way consistent with his conscientiousness and knowledge. Because of this God's grace increased within him. And in all these [ways] he "progressed before God and human beings," with the latter observing his progress and the former not only observing [his progress] but also testifying to it and assisting with [all] that happened. This much is clear, then, that he achieved virtue with more precision and with greater ease than was possible for the rest of human beings inasmuch as God the Word, due to his foreknowledge of what sort of individual he would be, united him to himself right at the start of the construction[84] and supplied him with greater assistance from himself for the accomplishment of what was right, arranging all that concerned him for the salvation of all. And he urged him on to more perfect things while relieving him of the greater part of his toils, whether of soul or of body. And in this way he prepared for him a greater and easier achievement of virtue.

Fragment 24
From Book 7, Section 60
(Translated from Greek)

For the one assumed according to foreknowledge was united from the beginning to God, having received the commencement of the union at his very construction[85] in the womb. Because he had already been judged worthy of the union, he received all things that[86] it made sense for a human being united to the Only-Begotten and the Master of the Universe to receive. And being judged worthy of greater things in comparison to the rest by far, the exceptional [gift] of the union came to him. Indeed, compared to the rest of human beings he was the first to be judged worthy of the indwelling of the Spirit and of this he was judged worthy in a way unlike the rest. For he received in himself the whole gift of the Spirit, but to others he gave a partial share in that whole Spirit. And in this way it came to pass that the whole Spirit was active in him. So then, what spoke, in relation to the utterance of sound, was a human being, but the force of what was said was something great and distinctive.

84 See note 79 above on "construction."
85 See note 79 above on "construction."
86 Reading *hosōn* with Jansen and Daley instead of Behr's *hoson*.

Fragment 25
From Section 60
(Translated from Syriac)

When we speak [about him] as about God the Creator of all and as same-in-substance with the Father,[87] who is glorified with him according to natural affinity, we signify the nature of the Word. But when [we speak] about him as limited, as one who exists now beyond the heaven and is coming here at the end for a terrible transformation, then we signify the human being, who in union with [the Word] receives honor from all. He was indeed worthy of all this praise and is coming as judge of the whole world.

Fragment 26
From Book 7
(Translated from Latin)

Now the union of the person can be recognized because he accomplished all things through him – this union happened by the indwelling that is according to good pleasure. Thus, when we say that the Son of God will come as judge, we understand it to be a coming from heaven of both the human being and God the Word simultaneously – not because God the Word is conveyed according to nature like the human being, but because he is united with him in every way by his good pleasure, wherever he is, because he accomplished all things through him.

Fragment 27
From Book 8
(Translated from Greek)

"The glory that you have given me I have given them."[88] What kind [of glory] is this? Participation in adopted sonship. For he received this according to his humanity, first of all when he was baptized in the Jordan, where our baptism was prefigured in him. And the Father's voice testified to the rebirth taking place [there] when he said, "This is my beloved Son, with whom I am

87 Literally, "as a child of the Father's nature," which is one of the regular Syriac translations of *homoousios*.
88 John 17:22.

well pleased."[89] Once the Spirit descended, it remained upon him, just as we too would participate in this[90] in baptism. But this very thing came to him in an exceptional manner in comparison with us, since he participated in what the Son has by nature through his union with God the Word.

Fragment 28

From an Unknown Book or Section[91]

(Translated from Syriac)

<...> is greater than these. Along with that which indwells, the manner of indwelling is also known. It would be good for them to know that just because the term "indwelling" is common, it does not also indicate the specific manner of indwelling. Not in this instance alone do we find this to be the case. Rather, there are many things that have common names, and their specific features are known to be different. For even though the human being shares the name "living being" with the donkey, the bull, the sheep, the lion, the wolf, and the reptile, it is not the case that it actually participates with them.[92] It appears with its own distinctive features, but the principle of the distinctive features of each of them is yet still preserved. For these have "being" and "irrational" in common, but each is separated from its neighbor in terms of the distinctive features that each of them has.

Why are these minor examples necessary for strengthening our argument, when we have a major example for the refutation of their ignorance? For they think that it is certainly possible to know what similarity everything has by means of that which is common to everything – namely, the [phrase] "it is," which is common to God and to everything that exists. We say that God "is," and we say everything that exists "is," but we are not going to enumerate each one of them. Nor because God "is" are we saying that others are not. And it is not in the fact that we say "they are" as he is[93] <...>

89 Matt 3:17. The Greek verb *eudokēsa*, "I am well pleased," is cognate with *eudokia*, "good pleasure."

90 That is, the Spirit.

91 Though Fragments 28 and 29 have no internal indications of their original location, their contents indicate that they should be placed before Fragment 30, the ending of which indicates a recently completed discussion of the suitability of the concepts of "indwelling" and "mixture" – the subject of these two fragments.

92 That is, is simply an animal like them in all respects.

93 The lacunose nature of this fragment makes the point of this sentence unclear, though it is probably something like: "And even so [i.e. even though we say that they are], we do not say they are as he is."

If something has a name in common with another, [that name] does not signify its distinctive features. Instead, the opposite: many things are distinct from one another in terms of nature and rank. And they are distinguished in the same way that allows a distinction between God and his creation; there is no distinction that is greater than this. They are together under a common word, but we learn their precise glory from their distinctive features. So it is too with the word “indwelling”: it is common, but each one has its own manner of indwelling; it is not the name “indwelling” that reveals equality but the species that reveals equality. The opposite is also found in questions regarding words. For when they are distinguished according to the expression “indwelling,” a simple word <…>

<…> teaches us. For our Lord commanded that when we fast, we should wash [our] faces and anoint [our] heads,[94] and to the one about to pray, he said, “Go inside and pray by yourself.”[95] And we do not see that this was taught at all by those who came before, neither to those who fasted nor to those who prayed. If this had been the custom among those who prayed, the assembly of the church would be superfluous. Furthermore, our praying all together in a group would invalidate the command “to go into your inner chamber and pray,”[96] and the command that a person should anoint his head when he fasts[97] contradicts the command, “Take nothing.”[98] For where did he get the oil from, if <…>

Fragment 29
From an Unknown Book or Section[99]
(Translated from Syriac)

Now it is impossible for these natures to come to be in opposition to one another in this way. So the Lord caused the natures to be separate from one another, placing fire above in the heights and the earth below, and he enclosed the waters with sand acting like a city wall. And he separated them from each other, ordering that “the waters be gathered together into one place,”[100] so that the water would not mingle with the nature of earth. For [if they were mingled] they would be annulled and their natures would be obliterated by their contact in this [mixture]. [The waters] could not

94 See Matt 6:17. 95 See Matt 6:6. 96 See Matt 6:6. 97 See Matt 6:17.
98 Luke 9:3, “Take nothing for your journey, no staff, nor bag, nor bread, nor money; and do not have two tunics.”
99 See note 91 above. 100 Gen 1:9.

be received into the earth and would overrun it, since [the earth's] density would be depleted. And since [the waters] are stronger than fire, they would consume its nature, but earth would not conquer the fire in such a way that it carries it within itself <...> the earth and to allow it to germinate fruits. If the heat is strong, fruits will fail even more than dry sticks. Fruits wither from [both] hot and cold winds, since each of them has this activity, but the moisture of the winds easily rots them. Thus too if seeds are immersed in [too] much water, they fail in the ground. But if great heat is added to them, germination [happens too] rapidly, and their utility brings no benefit to the farmer, since the plant is incapable of being established in the depth, as something that rightly participates in the earth, so that it may be fixed in it. And if the cold is harsh, the generation of the seeds falters and fails. Thus, then, it is impossible for these natures to oppose one another. Previously <...>

Thus we say that heat is mixed with cold, or water with wine, and often we say that air is "mixed." When coolness is joined to heat, it mixes and the mixture becomes balanced. No one would say oil mixes with oil, or water with water, or dryness, or heat, or cold on the grounds that their activities result in different effects. So this word – "mixture" – is employed rightly. We even find that the divine scripture uses "mixture." For the blessed David said, "There is a cup in the Lord's hand, and it is full of mixed, turbid wine."[101] In other words, it is mixed. The wise Solomon said, "Wisdom built herself a house; she has slaughtered her sacrifice; she has mixed her vessels of her wine."[102] In these passages we find the word "mixture" in the scriptures.

We also use it. For how often do we use "mixture" in reference to a human being? That which has come to be from the commixture of the four elements is what constitutes the body. It is not that the earth that is in it is visible as earth, nor that the air that is known to be in it can be dissipated, nor that the water [that is in it] can flow. But when the activity of these elements [is] mixed, the constitution of the body is accomplished for us. For the effect of their activities is mixed – that is, the heat and the cold and the dryness and the moisture, according to the wisdom of their mixer. They are established for the protection of the body. And we say that the offspring of every species are established in the same way too, but these natures of

101 Ps 74(75):9. 102 Prov 9:1–2, with omissions.

fire and earth and air and water are not mixed. If this did not occur, the elements would disappear from them every time – [those very elements] which from part of their natures received constitution. Therefore, it is impossible for these natures to be opposed to one another because their activities are in opposition to one another. But if they are in a commixture, the result would be that they disappear <...>

Fragment 30

From Book 8, Section 62 and Book 9, Section 63

(Translated from Syriac and Greek)[103]

Angels said to the disciples of the one who was taken up to heaven, "Galilean men, why are you standing there and gazing at heaven? This Jesus, who was taken from you up to heaven, will come in the same way that you saw him ascend to heaven."[104]

Greek[105]

In every way, then, it is clear that the concept of "mixing" is terribly inappropriate and unsuitable since each of the natures remains by itself without dissolution. But it is perfectly clear that the concept of "union" is fitting, for through it, the natures are brought together to constitute one person according to the union. Accordingly, what the Lord said in reference to the man and woman – "so they are no longer two but one flesh"[106] – we too might also plausibly say in virtue of the principle of the union: "so they are no longer two persons but one," of course, as long as the natures are distinguished. For just as in the former case calling them "one flesh" does not do away with their being two

Syriac

Now from all these things it is very clear that the doctrine of mixture is superfluous, neither useful nor fitting. Rather, there is a union in which the natures remain undissolved. In this [union], the natures are joined and made one person, just as our Lord said regarding husband and wife, "so they are no longer two, but one flesh."[107] We have said the same thing about the doctrine of the union, that they are no longer two but one. It is clear that, though the natures are different, just as their being said to be one flesh is not at all marred by the number two – for how they are said [to be one flesh] is clear – so also here the union of the person is not corrupted by the difference between the natures. When we

103 The translation follows the Syriac of BL fol. 10. Where the original Greek is extant, it is placed to the left of the Syriac. Another fragment preserves a different Syriac translation of the same material; this parallel appears in the left-hand column at the appropriate place.

104 Acts 1:11.

105 This is the Greek of LT6.

106 Matt 19:6.

107 Matt 19:6. See Origen's similar Christological use of this same verse in *On First Principles* 2.6, translated in this volume on p. 192.

Greek

in number – for it is perfectly clear in what respect they are called "one" – so too in the latter case the union of the person does not do away with the distinctiveness of the natures. For when we distinguish the natures, we say that the nature of God the Word is complete and his person is complete (for it's impossible to speak of a hypostasis without a person), and moreover that the nature of the human being is complete and his person likewise. But when we turn our attention to the conjunction, then we say there is one person.

Syriac

consider the natures, we perceive the divine nature in its hypostasis and the human nature. When we observe the conjunction, we say one person and one hypostasis.

Syriac[108]

Also in the case of the human being: when we distinguish the natures, we say that the nature of the soul is one thing, and that of the body another – a single hypostasis of the one and a single [hypostasis] of the other. Thus we know they are different, namely, when the soul is distant from the body, it is its own dwelling[109] and exists in its own person. Therefore, each one of them is spoken of in its own person, in accordance with the doctrine of the nature. In fact, this is also the case with "the inner human being" and "the outer human being," as designated by Paul: each one is worthy of the name of the common whole. It is obvious, though, that with the addition of the "inner" and the "outer," he does not understand the whole together by a loose phrase or by a diminution of the name, inasmuch as he joins that which is said to the two of them together.[110]

Syriac

For just as when we distinguish the nature of the human being, we say the nature of the soul is one thing and that of the body another, recognizing that each of them has a hypostasis and nature, and just as we are convinced that, when the soul is separated from the body, it abides in its nature and in its hypostasis and each of them has a nature and hypostasis, so also do we learn from the Apostle that the same [applies] to the inner human being and the outer human being. We name their oneness by something common [to both], then add "inner" and "outer," so as not to name them simply with a phrase. For as we say about them that they are conjoined in one hypostasis and one person, we designate the two in one.

108 This is the Syriac of BT17b. 109 Literally, "place."

110 That is, when one specifies "inner" or "outer," one seems to limit the thing being referred to, but Theodore wants to make the point that having a phrase like "the inner human being" does not void the larger category "human being."

Greek[111]

In the same way also in this case, we say that the substance of God the Word is his own and that of the human being is his own. For the natures are distinguished, but one person is constituted by the union. Thus, in this case, when we attempt to distinguish the natures, we say that the person of the human being is complete and that of the divinity is complete, but when we focus our attention on the union, we proclaim that both the natures conjointly are one person, with the humanity receiving honor from [all] creation by the divinity and the divinity accomplishing all that is right in the humanity.

Syriac

In the same way also in this case we say that there is a divine nature and a human nature. And while we recognize the natures, there is one person of the union. And thus, when we wish to perceive the natures, we say that the human being is complete in his hypostasis. We also say that the divinity is complete. For what unity do we wish to perceive? We proclaim one person and one hypostasis for the two natures. As we know, humanity receives honor from creation because of the union with divinity and divinity performs all things in it.

The Beginning of Book Nine[112]

63. How the heretics use "the Word became flesh"[113] against us.[114]

64. How the heretics use "he took the form of a slave"[115] against us.

65. That it is impossible, according to the doctrine of the heretics, for God the Word with a human body to be called a human being.

Book Nine

In what we have already said, we have shown the might and magnitude of the church's teaching. We sufficiently demonstrated from the words of scripture we previously rehearsed that "indwelling" is fittingly said, and we demonstrated from the scriptures that we rightly employ the word "union" and abstain from the word "mixture." Although we have already addressed our position on these things well, we should not allow whatever they put forward to abolish the two of them.[116]

They say they have two firm witnesses that suffice to establish their novel fables. Here they are: from the evangelist, "the Word became flesh,"[117] and from the Apostle, "he emptied himself and took the form of a slave."[118] Oh, what an abundance of folly! How do they not realize that what seems

111 This is the Greek of LT7.
112 Italicized rubrics in this translation are part of the fragment.
113 John 1:14.
114 Book 9 begins with a list of the sections it contains.
115 Phil 2:7.
116 That is, the words "indwelling" and "union."
117 John 1:14.
118 Phil 2:7.

agreeable to them, which they often repeat, actually opposes them? How can "became flesh" be similar to "he took the form of a slave"? For that's how these passages would have to be understood according to their opinion. It is clear that something that is "becoming" is not anything else alongside what it "became" but it is whatever it is said to be "becoming," since it is known that that which is "becoming" in the hypostasis has "become." But the one that takes is said to be something else beyond what it takes, just as God in this way fashioned the body from <...>

Fragment 31

From an Unknown Book or Section[119]

(Translated from Syriac)

<...> himself. "Look, I have *become* a fool, because you have forced me [to it]."[120] It is not we who say that the Apostle was a fool, but this was said by him because of the boasting of those who are ignorant of the purpose of boasting. He did not say it so that he might engage in boasting himself, but in order to abolish boasters.

On the topic of Christ, [he said], "Christ redeemed us from the curse of the law by *becoming* a curse for us, as [is written], 'Cursed is he who by decree of the law is hung on the tree.'"[121] Since he accepted that he would be hung on a tree, our Lord is said to have become a curse – not as if he is changed into a curse, but [that he is changed] in the estimation of others. For the Apostle said, "Christ redeemed us from the curse of the law and *became* a curse for us," and after that, he quotes, "It is written that 'cursed is everyone that is hung from a tree.'" Thus he was a "curse" in the estimation of others because he accepted the punishment which the law stipulated for debtors – death – so that by [doing so] he might dissolve the curses upon us. He was estimated as a curse by those who failed to grasp the greatness of the [divine] economy and by the sinful Jews.

119 Though Fragment 31 has no internal indications of its original location, its contents – a discussion of the word "became" from John 1:14 – indicate that it should be placed after Fragment 30, which introduces the discussion of John 1:14, and before Fragment 32, which sums up a previous discussion of John 1:14.

120 2 Cor 12:11. In this fragment, Theodore discusses several scriptural passages which in Greek contain some form of the verb *ginomai*, which appears in John 1:14 as *egeneto* ("became"). Here the forms of this verb are italicized for clarity, even if they cannot always be translated with some form of "become."

121 Gal 3:13, quoting Deut 21:23.

According to the meaning[122] which is in the passage where Joshua the son of Nun says to his warriors, "Look, you will surround the city, and do not *be* very far from the city"[123] – for they were not surrounding it[124] and were very far from it – it is in this sense, then, that the Apostle said about our Lord, that "he *came to be* in the likeness of a human being."[125] For it was in the meaning when it was said that "he dwelled with the saints," as if [to say] "he was among them in love" and he was not very far [from them] in nature.

["Became" is also used] in reference to the receiving of children, as when it says, "Abraham was one hundred years old when Isaac *became* his son."[126] It is used in reference to the acquisition of wealth, as when it is said about Isaac, that "there *came* to him bulls and sheep and many workers."[127] It is used in reference to equality in honor, as in what was said about him, "The Lord blessed him, and the man grew rich and he continued to become strong until he *became* very great."[128] And it is used in reference to health, as when it said that "it *became* a corrupter of the flesh."[129]

So then, this [word], "became," has been used in many ways in the scriptures. It is also used in many ways according to our customary way of speaking. At times it is used in reference to activities, at times in reference to passive experiences. It is used in reference to changes in activity and in ways of thinking. And even now it is used as something thought by those who do not adhere to the truth of the literal [interpretation], as a [signal] for meaning. It is said in reference to the assumption <...> or in reference to the acquisition <...> or <...>.

It is also said in reference to the hypostasis, and thus many come to an accurate understanding of it. For by "hypostasis" is implied the two persons, whether they are as they were from the beginning or as [they have been] changed into other things. [It is used] in reference to activity, as when it is said, "The Lord *became* my helper and place of refuge and my salvation."[130] And in another place, "The Lord *became* for me a place of refuge and my God a helper"[131] – God has become a helper and Savior, not by changing, but by pitying and helping. This is something literal. Thus also in the Acts of the Apostles the blessed Peter said, "Men and brothers, it was fitting

122 Alternatively, "the understanding." 123 Josh 8:4.
124 Literally, "they were at a distance [from it]." 125 Phil 2:7.
126 Gen 21:5. 127 Gen 26:14. 128 Gen 26:12–13.
129 Citation unknown. 130 Ps 7:2. 131 Ps 93(94):22.

that the scripture be fulfilled, which the Spirit spoke beforehand through the mouth of David about Judas, who *became* the guide of those traitors."[132] This is said literally because he literally became a leader.

"Became" is also said in reference to passive experiences, "I have *become* like a deaf man in whose mouth there is no admonition."[133] And also, "I have *become* a byword to them."[134] It is not that there was an actual change into a deaf person but that as a result of much adversity he now became like one who was deaf. Thus, because of the many adversities of his passion it is said that he was like a deaf man.

["Became" is also said] in reference to a change in activity or in ways of thinking, as when it says about the Messiah that "he *came to be* under the law so that he might redeem those who were under the law."[135] It is said that "he *came to be* under the law" because it dictated his conduct, and he fulfilled everything in his life on its behalf. And again, "*Become* imitators of me."[136] And it is clear that this also refers to a change in lifestyle, as is thought by many in accordance with the non-literal interpretation. As for what he says about <…>

Fragment 32
From Book 9
(Translated from Greek)

In these circumstances, then,[137] we have found that "he became" cannot have been said in any other way than in the sense of "he appeared." In our statements above we taught that it is quite precisely this very thing that is said in the divine scripture and by others especially in regard to the Lord. For "the Word became flesh"[138] [means] he appeared, but appeared not in the sense that he did not take real flesh but in the sense that he did not become [real flesh]. For when he[139] says, "he took,"[140] he says it not in the sense that he [only] appeared [to take flesh] but in the sense that he really [took flesh]. But when [he[141] says] "he became," then [he says it] in the sense that "he appeared." For he was not changed into flesh. So then, one must

132 Acts 1:16. 133 Ps 37(38):14. 134 Ps 68(69):12. 135 1 Cor 9:20.
136 1 Cor 11:1.
137 Reading *toinun* with Jansen and Daley instead of Behr's *toinēn*.
138 John 1:14. 139 That is, Paul. 140 Phil 2:7.
141 That is, the author of the Gospel of John.

attend to the evangelist's meaning, for in this way shall we understand the meaning of his words.

Fragment 33
From Book 9
(Translated from Latin)

In any case, if the statement, "The Word became flesh," is said in a way indicating some alteration, how ought "he indwelt"[142] be understood? For it is obvious to everyone that what indwells is different from what is indwelt. For "he indwelt among us" when he assumed our nature and dwelt [in it] and arranged in it all things for our salvation. Therefore, how did the Word of God become flesh by indwelling? It is obvious that he was neither altered nor transformed, for then he could not be said to indwell.

Fragment 34
From Book 9
(Translated from Greek)

For what is said in our case in relation to our spatial disposition [is said] in God's case in relation to the disposition of his will.[143] After all, just as in our case we say, "I came to be in this place," so too in God's case [we say], "He came to be in this [place]." For what movement enacts in our case, willing does in God's case, since by nature he is present everywhere.

Fragment 35
From Section 66
(Translated from Syriac)

So, both from the testimonies they advanced and from the things said afterward, it is demonstrated that the human being, God the Word enfleshed, cannot be honored except if the human being is a living thing like this <…>

142 John 1:14. The verb in Latin is *inhabitavit*, which is normally translated, "he dwelt." But in order to bring out Theodore's point, a translation that highlights the *in* prefix is needed.

143 In Greek *kata tēn [schesin] tēs gnōmēs*, which in the Latin of Fragment 69 is translated *secundum adfectum voluntatis*.

Fragment 36
From Section 66
(Translated from Syriac)

Therefore, they are guilty on every count of talking very foolishly, since God the Word enfleshed is not known by the title of "human being." Obviously, when scripture mentions the title "human being" with respect to Christ, it always indicates the nature of the human being, which was assumed complete by him for our salvation. It is that one which scripture customarily calls by this title.

Fragment 37
From Book 10, Section 70
(Translated from Latin)

For just as we are taught the difference between natures by such words from the divine scripture, so too we declare the union as often as [scripture] combines the properties of both natures into one thing and so speaks of one particular thing. For this is to show both the different natures and the union of the person simultaneously: from the difference between the things said, the difference between natures is understood, but when they are connected in one thing, we recognize the clear union. And so, the blessed evangelist John said, "The next day he saw Jesus coming toward him and said, 'Behold, the Lamb of God! Behold, the one who takes away the sins of the world. This is the one of whom I said, "After me comes a man who ranks before me, because he was before me and I did not know him."'"[144] For in saying this – "He saw Jesus coming toward him and said, 'Behold, the Lamb of God!'" – it seems to me that he clearly signifies the humanity. For that which John the Baptist saw was that which underwent death, namely, the body that was offered for the whole world. But what follows – "the one who takes away the sins of the world" – is surely not in any way applicable to the flesh. For it was not the work of the flesh to take away the sin of the whole world, but this was unquestionably the work of the divinity.

144 John 1:29–30.

Fragment 38
From Book 10
(Translated from Greek)

"Then an angel from heaven appeared to him, giving him strength. And being in agony, he prayed more earnestly, and his sweat became like drops of blood falling down upon the ground."[145] We learn from these words, then, that Christ clearly endured the agony and no ordinary one at that.

Fragment 39
From Book 10
(Translated from Greek)

What sort of coherence is there between the phrases "the one who descended from heaven" and "the one who is in heaven"?[146] For the one eliminates the other: "descending from heaven" by "being in heaven" and "being" by "descending." But he "descended" by indwelling in the human being, whereas he "is in heaven" by being present to all through the limitlessness of his nature.

Fragment 40
From an Unknown Book or Section[147]
(Translated from Syriac)

<…> that are said. As the Apostle also said, "We speak the wisdom of God in secret, that which was hidden, which God first set apart before the foundations of the world for our glory. None of the rulers of this world knew it, for if they had, they would not have crucified the Lord of glory. But, as it is written, 'no eye had seen, nor ear heard, nor had it arisen in a human heart what God has prepared for those who love him.'"[148] This glory in the human being, which is superior to and has surpassed the entire human nature, was revealed to them. They did not acquire accurate

145 Luke 22:43–44.
146 John 3:13.
147 Though this fragment has no internal indications of its original location, its contents – an interpretation of Ps 8:1–3 – indicate that it is connected with Fragment 41, which interprets Ps 8:5–7 and should be placed before it.
148 1 Cor 2:7–9.

knowledge of him, something that we see even the apostles acquired at the end. It was important at that time that thenceforth the nature of the human being be revealed – but it was not possible for it to come forth, because of the profundity of the things that were spoken of among others. He recalled the greatness of glory; he was at that time silent about those things that were superior to the nature. And he rehearsed while speaking humbly about him, "You have made him a little lower than [the angels]"[149] <...> so that those, insofar as they were able, might at that time receive what was said, but those who came afterwards, after advancing to the limit of things that pertain to knowledge, would receive the truth from the miracles that were performed at that time and from the testimonies that were spoken beforehand, since these last activities would give them accurate knowledge.

But why am I saying these things when it is easy for us to make our demonstrations from scripture as we promised? The sense of the psalm is clear to everyone: it is right for us to reflect on its first words in reference to the only-begotten Son of God, God the Word, namely, "Lord, our Lord, how glorious is your name in all the earth?," and, "Your glory is higher than the heavens," and, "From the mouth of the child you have established your glory," and, "I see your heavens, the work of your hands," and, "the moon and the stars which you established."[150] And it is clear that we learn from our Lord [as well], as the book of blessed Matthew the evangelist has transmitted to us. For it narrated how in accordance with the word of prophecy the Lord sat upon the ass[151] and entered the city, and how <...>

Fragment 41
From Book 10
(Translated from Latin and Greek)

"What[152] is the human being that you keep him in mind, or the Son of Man that you visit him?"[153] So[154] let us investigate who the human being is about whom the prophet is amazed and astonished, that the Only-Begotten

149 Ps 8:6; Heb 2:7. 150 Ps 8:1–3.
151 Matt 21:5, alluding to Isa 62:11 and Zech 9:9.
152 The translation begins with the Latin. 153 Ps 8:5.
154 The translation switches to the Greek here.

should deign to keep him in mind and make a visitation. But that this is not said <about every human being> has been shown in the remarks above. That it is not about just one random individual – this too is quite clear. So let us put aside everything, let us accept the apostolic testimony, which is most trustworthy of all. For[155] when the Apostle writes to the Hebrews, he tells them about Christ and confirms his person, which was not acceptable to them, saying, "It has been testified somewhere, 'What is the human being that you keep him in mind, or the Son of Man that you visit him? You have made him a little less than the angels; with glory and honor you have crowned him and set him over the works of your hands; you have subjected all things under his feet.'"[156] And after quoting this testimony he added an interpretation of it, "Now by putting everything in subjection to him, he left nothing that was not subjected. But now we do not yet see everything subjected to him."[157] And then he teaches us who the human being is, since doubt was voiced about this by the blessed David, adding, "But we see Jesus made a little less than the angels, crowned with glory and honor because of the suffering of death."[158] Therefore, if we have learned from the gospels that it was in reference to the Lord that the blessed David spoke everything in this psalm – "you keep in mind" and "you visit" and "you have made less" and "you have subjected" and the rest – and if we are taught by the Apostle that it is Jesus of whom David was speaking when he said that he kept him in mind and visited him, and also that he subjected everything to him, when he made him a little less than the angels, then it is high time to put aside your shamelessness, even if it is difficult, in full awareness of what is proper. For you see, you who are most wicked of all human beings, how great the difference between the natures is, because there was amazement over [the Only-Begotten] deigning to keep the human being in mind, to visit him, and to make him share in the rest of the things in which he made him share, while on the contrary there was astonishment over [the human being] meriting to share in such great things surpassing his nature. The former is marveled at because he gives a promotion and bestows great things that surpass the nature of one who obtained the promotion, whereas the other is marveled at because he obtains the promotion and receives from him things that are greater than he deserves.

155 The translation returns to the Latin here. 156 Heb 2:6–8, quoting Ps 8:5–7.
157 Heb 2:8. 158 Heb 2:9.

Fragment 42
From Books 10 and 11
(Translated from Syriac)

And some things are applied to the two – some chrysolite and some fire. From Isaiah, "garments worn" and "reddened by the blood of [our] enemies."[159] And it is at another point, when he is in a human body and sitting on the throne, that he is surrounded by seraphim.[160] Forced, then, by such sights we might go as far as to think that they did not have human bodies, but rather were novel [bodies] created by uncommon means, since they have wings and feathers on the wings. And we say that the body that was assumed by God the Father is one thing, that assumed by the Son is another, and both are different and separate from the angels, because in fact, to Balaam he appeared as a human being, a sword clasped in his hand,[161] and to Joshua he appeared in the form of someone armed.[162] Lest we put forward too many words about these things, let us just say, "many bodies," if we are led along by such visions to think they are accurate. But if this is not possible (that these visions appear for the sake of their utility, to aid those who see them), it is clear that even Abraham received a vision that appeared to him suitably from God <...>

The End of Book Ten.[163]

The Sections of Book Eleven

Those who ask, "Is he the one saving or the one being saved? The one who conferred a benefit or the one who received a benefit?"

Those who say, "It is obvious that our Lord [does] not [have] a soul, and he comes to us in the mysteries [as] body and blood."[164]

<...>

<...> that the words he prepared

<...> that are said now

<...> the division of the natures, the union of the person; rightfully in these things

<...> said above.

We have employed sufficient proofs about the soul and the mind to confirm the truth of the required things. Here, we seek to demonstrate

159 Isa 63:1. 160 Isa 6:1–3. 161 Num 22:23. 162 Josh 5:13.
163 Italicized rubrics in this translation are part of the fragment.
164 The remainder of the section titles are quite fragmentary.

this alone, but we will also demonstrate something more: that we learn from the scriptures not merely the difference between the natures, but also the sign of the body and the rational soul, from which it is manifest that he is a complete human being. As a consequence, let us grasp on to what the orderly arrangement of the doctrine demands. These people raise many different questions to us to [try to] nullify the truth. Sometimes they say, "If we say [there are] two complete, then we must say two sons." And at other times, "It is not right to say one and the other." And also, "It is right to say that God the Word was crucified, for he is the Messiah and not something else." We have fittingly responded to such questions and promised to make known the truth of the church by an exposition. Because we did not lie with our promise, we have replied to the question in full, and we are compelled to do so with the words spoken in the accurate testimonies. First of all <...>

Fragment 43
From Book 11, Section 73
(Translated from Syriac)[165]

Did he assume, or was he assumed? Is he the form of God or the form of the human being? Do you not say it was the form of God that assumed, but the form of the slave that was assumed? Why do you need the artifice of asking questions now, and why don't you draw their distinction from the divine scriptures and impress knowledge of the fear of God on your pure minds? In what way is he who assumed similar to that which was assumed? Or what equality is there between God and the human being? Or between the slave and the Lord? Between the form of God and the form of the slave? See how greatly he has demonstrated to us the distinction between the natures, calling the one "the form of the slave" and the other "[the form] of God,"[166] the one who assumed and the one who was assumed. He put these distinctions together in one place and made us understand the union of the person. For he said, "Rather, he emptied himself and took the form of a slave, and came to be in the likeness of human beings."[167]

165 The translation follows the Syriac of BL fol. 12–13. Two fragments preserve a different Syriac translation of the same material; these parallels appear in the left-hand column at the appropriate place.

166 See Phil 2:6–7. 167 Phil 2:7.

And after mentioning his corporeality,[168] he turned toward the humanity, making known by his revelation its conjunction with God the Word. For he says, "He humbled himself and became obedient unto death, even death on a cross."[169] And clearly these things correspond to the nature of the human being, who was fastened with nails to the cross and accepted death according to his nature. What indicates the conjunction was the fact that he "humbled himself," not that he was human when he accepted death for himself. He who endured the decree of God upon his nature from the beginning[170] "humbled himself and became obedient unto death, and all the more [death] on a cross."[171] This is the one who was assumed by God the Word. And he became capable of overcoming death because of his conjunction. By his will, on behalf of our salvation, he endured suffering and he continued to speak things that are fitting and appropriate for human nature. In connection with these things, he said, "Because of this God highly exalted him and gave him the name above every name."[172] And what do we say was exalted? God the Word? If so, how did the one who was the form of God, the likeness of God, accept being taken up to the heights? For it is not possible that this was a kind of "participation" by theft; rather, it must be something that was appropriate to his nature, even though he knew full well that he was equal with his Father, and even though he was well pleased in his will that his glory be hidden and that he appear in the form of a slave for our salvation. This is what Paul said about him; is there anything greater than what has been said? He accepted [death] and was exalted. Otherwise, how did God elevate one who was equal to himself – or indeed one who made himself greater than God? It is vile to say this, but it is required if they are equal. When one remains within [a certain] measure, but the other is elevated beyond that measure of equality, then equality goes away. In this case, then, it is clear that he would be great [and] would have had actual equality from the start. And how, among these equals, is one able to give grace and the other to need it? And what [could be] given to him? In fact, we also see this: it says "the name." And what is that [name]? "At the name of Jesus, every knee will bend, in heaven and on earth and under the earth, and every tongue confess that Jesus Christ is Lord, to the glory of God his Father."[173] And [on their view] the Maker of

168 Presumably a reference to verse just quoted, Phil 2:7. 169 Phil 2:8.
170 A reference to punishment given to Adam and Eve in Gen 3.
171 Phil 2:8. 172 Phil 2:9. 173 Phil 2:10.

all received this grace [of the name] after death, even though by his hand everything was created and without him nothing of what exists would have even been established.[174]

For if someone says that this [name] was granted to him, that is, to God the Word, as many have wickedly said, they have turned to something other than knowledge of the truth and worshiped it. And [if this is true] it is clear that even the Father received this grace [of the name]. There were many who spoke wickedly in this way, but after the coming of Christ they turned to knowledge. However, according to their doctrine, it is right to say precisely the Father received the grace [of the name] all the more. For he who in the coming and in his suffering made it so that every person might be brought to knowledge of the Father, namely

Syriac[175]

Now, our Lord himself said, "I have made your name known to humanity."[176] It is obvious, then, that he said these [words] about the one who was assumed, the one who was glorified by all creation and [received] the confession of [his] lordship and veneration from all, "from those in heaven, those on earth, and those under the entire earth."[177] For this is the grace that the one who was assumed has taken up.

Syriac

our Lord, said to his Father, "I will make your name known among human beings."[178] It is clear then that these things were said about the one who was assumed, the one to whom glory was given from all creation, and the confession of [his] lordship and worship "from all in heaven and earth and under the earth."[179] It was he who was assumed that assumed this grace, not while he was simple and by himself but in union with God the Word.

For every glory is owed to the only-begotten God the Word from his creation, because all came into being through him. Those who offer worship to this one, even though they know that the form of the slave who was assumed is one with him, when they give glory also worship the form of the slave that was assumed, being aware of the union of the form of the slave with God the Word. So if anyone wants to say "God" about God the Word as the one who exalted him, it seems to me that he has spoken well. And this understanding is fitting also for the doctrine of the Word. For he assumed the form of a slave and in his union with him he exalted and elevated him, and allowed him to be worshiped by all creation. So then, where do we go

174 See John 1:3. 175 This is the Syriac of BT20. 176 John 17:6.
177 Phil 2:10. 178 John 17:6. 179 Phil 2:10.

from here? Did he assume, or was he assumed? Is he the form of God or the form of a slave? Is he the Maker of all, or has he received worship by grace? May every blaspheming tongue be silent! Let the blessed Apostle teach us, clearly, what the distinction between the natures is, and what the glory of the nature that assumed is, and whether he is the one who was assumed, and whether this one is the form of God and that one is the form of a slave, and how he allowed himself in his mercy to be brought down from his glory. By grace he was assumed by him and by grace he is worshiped by all creation.

And [the Apostle] adds to those things while teaching us about the union. He teaches this by gathering [the phrases] together in one place. For while he spoke about God the Word, [saying] that "he who was in the form of God"[180] and the rest, and that "he came to be in the likeness of human beings and was found in the form of the human being,"[181] he also added that "he humbled himself and became obedient to death, even death on a cross"[182] – which was a demonstration of humanity. He also said, "because of this God exalted him,"[183] and all those things that he thereafter also said about him. It appears that they were opposed, but I am amazed at the accuracy of the words of the Apostle, that first he said about him that he assumed and then about the other that he was assumed. He called the former the form of God and the latter the form of the slave. And after he distinguished the natures accurately, then he mentioned also his corporeality and death on a cross, and also the things that happened to him after death – namely, the glory he received from all creation – and in all these things he makes the union apparent. For in that assumption [there was] that which assumed and that which was assumed. And by the fact that the former was the form of God and the latter the form of the slave we distinguish the natures, but we understand the union of the person by the glory that makes God the Word participate in death and in the cross. But they do not want to give any heed to the things that were said, and they scorn learning the truth from the scriptures,

Syriac[184]	**Syriac**
So sometimes they ask, "Is he one thing and another thing, or is he one and the same?" and sometimes, "Is he the one saving or the one being saved, the one conferring a benefit or the one receiving a benefit?"	so they sometimes ask, "Is he one thing and another thing? Or is he [one and] the same?" And also, "Is he the one saving or the one being saved? Is he the one conferring a benefit or the one receiving a benefit?"

180 Phil 2:6. 181 Phil 2:7. 182 Phil 2:8. 183 Phil 2:9.
184 This is the Syriac of BT21.

Latin

What we have said in regard to such [questions] is indeed sufficient, where we showed both the difference between the natures and the union of the person, and that with respect to the natures, this one received a benefit, but the other conferred a benefit, since there is a firm union that results in honor being paid inseparably by the whole creation.

Syriac[185]

What we have already said about such questions is sufficient: we showed both the difference between the natures and the union of the person. And with respect to the natures, this one received a benefit, but the other was found to confer a benefit, since there is an obvious union that results in honor [being paid] inseparably from all completed creation.

Syriac

For these things that have been said are sufficient, in which we showed the difference between the natures and the union of the person. And it is manifest in terms of nature that the one received a benefit and the other conferred a benefit, since there is an obvious union of the two of them that results in worship being received from the whole creation.

Let us demonstrate this even more accurately from the words of the blessed David. For Paul witnesses to those things that were said or were explained by him and which were taken up by our Lord and by the apostles. In fact, they are from the Lord since he is the one who was speaking in the Apostle. The blessed David saw first in the grace of the Holy Spirit the whole economy that was going to happen, that God the Creator of all would be willing to dwell in a human being for our salvation, and to assume the form of a slave, and to make it one with him and let [this form] rule in union with him over all. He wondered at his mercy and was amazed by the magnitude of the glory of human beings, that [God] made us worthy of this glory, so that he might dwell in our nature. He knew this beforehand by the revelation of the Spirit, so that all people might be aware of God the Creator of all, and that in creation his name might be praised and everyone might know his Maker, who was not known to them before. He marveled about these two as one: first, about the fact that [God] would turn those inclined to evil to the good, and second, that he would perform this activity in a human being as if in a vessel, which he assumed as though the first from our race, and he prepared everything in him for the salvation of our lives, and that there be subjected to him <…>

185 This is the Syriac of BT21.

Fragment 44
From an Unknown Book or Section[186]
(Translated from Syriac)

<...> that it might be useful for the distinction between the natures. They ask us, "Is he the one saving or the one being saved? The one conferring a benefit or the one receiving a benefit?" And they continue on, putting this bitter and scheming question to those who are upright, having no care for what might be agreeable and suitable for the teachings of the church. Therefore, it is right to demonstrate these things from the divine scripture, even if it was already possible to demonstrate [them] from what was mentioned above. Different properties necessarily follow from different natures. When they want to inquire rationally into the natures, it is because of their stubborn disbelief; they ask unusual questions so as to propound novelties.

So let us add this: it is quite obvious that one conferred a benefit and the other received a benefit. We have already learned this from the gospel. For when our Lord came to Jerusalem and started to drive out from the temple those selling doves and sheep, he said to them, "This house is for prayer and not to be set up for business."[187] And they asked him for a sign, that he might demonstrate his greatness and thereby confirm that he could order the long-held custom to be stopped. But he did not show them this sign. Instead, he said to them, "Destroy this temple and in three days I will raise it up"[188] – in explanation of this the evangelist said, "He was talking about the temple of his body."[189] They continue on and say to us (for it is lovely to use their own words against them), "Is he the one who raises or the one who is raised? Is he the one who raises the one who was destroyed, or is he the one who receives the destruction?" Now these in fact do not fit with one another. For the one who is destroyed needs the one who raises him, who is beyond suffering and by his authority raises the one who is destroyed. Tell us then! What is right to say regarding this question? But we respond very easily and say we have sufficient knowledge

186 Though this fragment has no internal indications of its original location, its contents – a discussion of the questions, "Is he the one saving or the one being saved? The one conferring a benefit or the one receiving a benefit?" – indicate that it is connected with the similar discussion in Fragment 43, and should be placed before Fragment 45, which sums up the discussion of these questions.

187 See John 2:13–16. 188 John 2:19. 189 John 2:21.

of this from scripture. One is destroyed, the other raises. One is the temple that receives destruction; the other is the one who raises it, namely God the Word, who promised to raise his destroyed temple. How do they fail to learn the distinction between the natures from these things, and [arrive at] the knowledge of the truth? Instead they launch assaults with crafty questions to confuse the simple.

Fragment 45
From Section 73
(Translated from Syriac)

So as not to drag out the discussion too long, these topics – the natures and the subject of our demonstration, namely, that it is clearly shown from the divine scriptures that one confers a benefit and the other receives a benefit – have been covered sufficiently.

Fragment 46
From Section 77
(Translated from Syriac)

And now because of this, we must move on from these matters. For it will be demonstrated, with God's assistance, that the human being who was assumed is something other in nature than God the Word, as has been shown to us by the things said explicitly.

Fragment 47
From Book 12
(Translated from Greek)

For this reason he did not say, "He has spoken to us in *the* Son," but "in a Son."[190] Since this is said without qualification, it can signify both by the same [wording]: it principally signifies the true Son (and by "true Son" I mean the one who acquired sonship through a natural begetting) and secondarily along with this it also allows in its meaning the one who truly participates in the dignity [of sonship] through his union with him.[191]

190 Heb 1:2. 191 That is, with the true Son.

Fragment 48
From Book 12
(Translated from Greek)

At long last, then, will they end this shameful wrangling and abandon[192] this pointless quarrel, respecting the obvious meaning of the words? For he says, "bringing many sons to glory."[193] See, then, it is clear that the Apostle includes the assumed human being among the "many" in the category of sonship: he does not participate in sonship in a similar manner as them, but in a similar manner nonetheless, in that he received sonship by grace since divinity alone possesses natural sonship.[194] Now this much is perfectly clear, that the exceptional status of sonship is peculiar to him[195] in comparison to the rest of human beings, through his union with him.[196] Accordingly, he is conceptually understood to be included in the term "Son." But they concoct the argument against us that if we speak of two complete things, we will surely also be speaking of two sons. But note that in scripture "son" is mentioned by itself, with no reference to the divinity, when he is being classified with the rest of human beings, and we do not actually speak of two sons. The Son is rightly confessed to be one, since the difference between the natures ought necessarily to remain and the union of the person be preserved indivisible. And when he says, "bringing many sons to glory," he adds, "to make the pioneer of their salvation perfect through sufferings."[197] See how clearly he says that God the Word perfected the assumed human being "through sufferings," whom he also called "the pioneer of salvation" because he was the first to be deemed worthy of this and became the cause [of this] for others.

192 Reading *apostēsontai* with Jansen and Daley instead of Behr's *apostēsonta*.

193 Heb 2:10.

194 The insertions and omissions to this sentence suggested by Behr, Jansen, and Daley seem unnecessary, as sense can be made of the passage without them.

195 The Greek here is *tēs huiotētos autō … prosesti to exaireton*. The ancient Latin translation of this fragment goes as follows: *filiationis gloria … inest ei praecipue*. The difference is perhaps indicative of a corruption in the Greek as we have it. This led Jansen to conjecturally prefix <*hē doxa*> to these words. The Latin version translated would be: "Now this much is perfectly clear, that the glory of sonship is peculiar to him in an exceptional manner in comparison to the rest of human beings, through the union with him."

196 That is, with the Word.

197 Heb 2:10.

Fragment 49
From Book 12
(Translated from Greek)

For according to our interpretation, they continue to apply the name "son" to all who are such. For since what has been said reflects a more human way of speaking, they thought that it was right to use this term, which also happened to be his title, and that the name "Jesus" was the proper name of the one assumed, as "Peter" and "Paul" (or whatsoever one is mentioned) is that of the apostles, and he was called this [name] after his birth from Mary.

Fragment 50
From Book 12
(Translated from Greek)

But in response to this they say that the name "Jesus" means "Savior." So how, they say, might a human being be called "Savior"? They have forgotten that the son of Nun was also called "Jesus."[198] And the truly amazing thing is that he was not called this through some chance turn of events at his birth, but rather he had his name changed by Moses.[199] Now it is clear that he would not have tolerated this [name] being giving to[200] a human being if it were really indicative of the divine nature in every case.

Fragment 51
From Book 12
(Translated from Greek and Latin)

"In[201] many and various ways long ago God spoke to the fathers in the prophets, but in these last[202] days he has spoken to us in a Son."[203] For here it is clearly indicated that by "in a Son" he means "in the human being." "For[204] to which of the angels did he ever say, 'You are my Son, today I have begotten you'?"[205] He is saying that he made none of the angels a sharer in the dignity of the Son. When he said, "I have begotten you," as if thereby

198 That is, Joshua. 199 See Num 13:16.
200 Reading *ep'* with Jansen and Daley instead of Behr's *ap'*.
201 The translation begins with the Greek.
202 Reading *eschatōn* with Jansen and Daley instead of Behr's *eschatou*.
203 Heb 1:2. 204 Here the translation switches to the Latin.
205 Heb 1:5, quoting Ps 2:7.

bestowing a share in sonship, it is entirely and explicitly clear that what was said has nothing to do with God the Word.

Fragment 52
From Book 12
(Translated from Latin)

In response to this, however, the blessed Apostle tries to show how he[206] is a sharer in divine honor and that he enjoys this, not because of his own nature, but because of the indwelling power.

Fragment 53
From Book 12
(Translated from Greek)

Accordingly, [Paul] not only calls [Jesus] "Son" to distinguish him from God the Word, but he is also proven to be classifying him in the category of sonship along with the rest of those who participate in sonship. For he participates in sonship by grace, having not been begotten naturally from the Father, even though he has a preeminence in comparison to the rest because he has come to possess sonship through his union with him, which fact graces him with a more authoritative share in the reality.

Fragment 54
From Book 12
(Translated from Greek)

"And you will call his name Jesus. He will be great and will be called Son of the Most High."[207] See, then, how when [Gabriel] announces the good news of the birth from Mary (I mean the one according to the flesh), he orders that he be called "Jesus" but foretells that he will be called "Son of the Most High." It makes sense that he orders the former to be given as the proper name of the one being born but foretells that he will be called the latter, since the name was a symbol of the honor which eventually his share in the reality would confirm.

206 That is, Jesus. 207 Luke 1:31–32.

Fragment 55
From Book 12
(Translated from Greek)

It is clear that in making a distinction between the natures we must never lose sight of the fact that God the Word is said to be Son because of his natural begetting [from the Father] and the human being enjoys[208] the dignity of the Son, being much greater than what he is in himself, through his conjunction with him.

Fragment 56
From Book 12
(Translated from Latin)

But if someone should want to ask what I would say Jesus Christ is, I say that he is God and Son of God.

Fragment 57
From Section 77
(Translated from Syriac)

"It is fitting that he through whom and for whom all things [exist]" – obviously, this refers to God the Word – "in bringing many children to glory" – he means those worthy of adoption as children – "should perfect the pioneer of their salvation through suffering" – [this refers] to the human being who was assumed by him.[209]

Fragment 58
From Section 77
(Translated from Syriac)

Therefore, on the basis of these things it has also been demonstrated sufficiently that the human being assumed by God the Word is said to be "Son of God" because of him and in relation to him.[210]

208 Reading *apolauei* with Jansen and Daley instead of Behr's *apolauein*.
209 Heb 2:10. 210 That is, God the Word.

Fragment 59
From Sections 77–78
(Translated from Syriac, Latin, and Greek)[211]

<...> he did this. For it is also fitting that it was said, "of the Holy Spirit,"[212] but it is not fitting that the divinity was formed. And next he relates what the angel said to Joseph: "Joseph, son of David, do not fear to take Mary as your wife, for what has been conceived in her is from the Holy Spirit."[213] And one can find similar things [related] by the blessed Luke. For after he stated how the angel came to Mary and warned her that she was pregnant, saying, "Behold! You will conceive and you will bear a child," etc.,[214] and Mary doubted these things, saying, "How will this come to be, since I have not known a man?"[215] [Luke] said the angel responded to her, saying, "The Holy Spirit will come and the power of the Most High will rest upon you. Thus, what is born from you will be holy; he will be called the child of the Most High."[216] It is clear that not one of the things said here refers to the divinity.

[78] In addition to these things, let us now discuss the birth. What follows is similar: he was the one who acted according to the law, and he was diligent to keep it with full accuracy. We learn [this] sufficiently from the divine scriptures, when the evangelist says, "The child grew and became powerful in the Spirit, as he was being filled with wisdom and the grace of God was upon him."[217] In another [passage], "He went down with his parents, came to Nazareth, and was obedient to them."[218]

Latin and Greek

The Apostle also says something that agrees [with this], "And great indeed is the mystery of our piety: he[219] who was manifested in the flesh was also made righteous in the Spirit."[220] He says that

Syriac

And the Apostle said, "Great indeed is this mystery: he who was manifested in the flesh was also made righteous in the Spirit."[221] Now he says "made righteous in the Spirit" in reference to him because

211 The translation follows the Syriac of BL fol. 17. There are two fragments that preserve the same material, one Greek and the other Latin (the opening sentence of the Latin fragment preserves a sentence that is absent in Greek; otherwise, they are identical). These parallels appear in the left-hand column at the appropriate place.

212 Matt 1:18. 213 Matt 1:20. 214 Luke 1:31. 215 Luke 1:34.

216 Luke 1:35. 217 Luke 2:40. 218 Luke 2:51.

219 The translation from Latin ends with "piety," and the translation from Greek begins with "he."

220 1 Tim 3:16. 221 1 Tim 3:16.

Latin and Greek	**Syriac**
he "was made righteous in the Spirit" either because before his baptism he kept the law with the appropriate accuracy or because even after that he fulfilled the life of grace with great accuracy by the assistance of the Spirit.	either before his baptism he kept the law with all accuracy or after that he perfected the law through his graceful way of life of the Spirit and through his diligence.

Let us also proceed to the baptism. It is fitting to bring [this] to mind in snippets, so as not to extend our discussion …

Fragment 60
From Book 13
(Translated from Greek)

For not even what is said by John to him – "I need to be baptized by you and you come to me?"[222] – not even this will invalidate the fact that the one being baptized is the human being. For this would be appropriate for him even by reason of his humanity since in terms of virtue itself he was greatly superior to John, and on account of the nature of the divinity indwelling in him, he was rightly acknowledged as having a dignity not only surpassing John, but also surpassing all human beings and indeed even surpassing creation.

Fragment 61
From Book 13
(Translated from Greek)

Therefore, the Lord, wanting to demonstrate his endurance and philosophical character during his fast, did not ask for this to happen.[223] And showing that he cares little for food and that nothing is more valuable to him than virtue, he says to [the devil], "A human being shall not live by bread alone, but by every word that comes from the mouth of God."[224]

Fragment 62
From Book 13
(Translated from Greek)

For this is what the devil was eager to do: to persuade him that God cared nothing at all for him. And therefore he said, "If you are the Son of God,

222 Matt 3:14. 223 That is, that the stones become bread. 224 Matt 4:4.

do this"[225] – that is, "Do something to show that God cares for you." And he also made great promises so that by the former[226] he might separate him from God and then by the promises make him his own. And in the first temptation he put bread before him, enticing him with pleasure to succumb to the temptation.

Fragment 63
From Book 13
(Translated from Greek)

Therefore, the Lord bestowed upon us the victory over [the devil] by defeating him in the three [temptations]. For when he refused to ask that bread come from God, he showed that he was immune to pleasure. And when he refused to hurl himself down, he despised renown, persuading everyone that this was of no concern to him. And when he remained immune to the world's advantages in the course of the third [temptation], he showed that he kept himself undefeated by all of them on behalf of piety.

Fragment 64
From Book 13
(Translated from Latin)

It would be good, especially at this point, to draw a conclusion about the thrust that these statements have: that he lived among us, was baptized, was crucified, died, was buried, and rose again. We do not make these statements as if we were applying them to some mere human being. For each time we explain these statements we do not hesitate to add this (lest we give calumniators an occasion for speaking evilly): the indwelling by God the Word happens from the very construction[227] in his mother's womb, and indeed this indwelling does not happen in the way an indwelling ordinarily happens nor by way of that grace known to be in many, but in a certain exceptional way, according to which we also say that both natures are united and one person is effected by way of this union.

225 See Matt 4:3 and 4:6.
226 That is, by daring Jesus to do something.
227 The Latin word here is *plasmatio*, undoubtedly a translation of the Greek *diaplasis*; see note 79 above on "construction."

Fragment 65
From Book 14
(Translated from Greek)

Accordingly, then, such great honor has come to be associated with the human being who was deemed worthy of divine indwelling, of sitting at the right hand of the Father, and of being worshiped by all creation. For God would never have assumed a human being and united him to himself so simply and without good reason, preparing him to be worshiped by all creation, nor would he have judged it right for intellectual natures to worship him, if what had come to be associated with him were not a common benefit for all creation.

Fragment 66
From Book 14
(Translated from Greek)

We shall rightly say the same in the case of the Lord too, that God the Word, because he knew his virtue – and this according to foreknowledge right from the beginning at the start of his construction[228] – and because he was well pleased[229] to indwell [in him] and united himself to him by the disposition of his will,[230] bestowed upon him a certain greater grace, since the grace given to him would be given to all human beings after him. Accordingly, [God the Word] kept his[231] intention[232] for the good intact. For we should not say that the human being lacked any intention but that he preferred the good, or rather that he had in his intention an intense affection for the good and hatred for its opposite. And the inviolateness of his intention was preserved in him from the beginning by divine grace since God knew precisely what sort of individual he would be and in fact in order to support him provided him with great assistance by his own indwelling for the salvation of us all. Accordingly, one should not speak of injustice in regard to the human being assumed by the Lord having received something exceptional in comparison to all.

228 See note 79 above on "construction."
229 The Greek participle *eudokēsas* is cognate with *eudokia*, "good pleasure."
230 The ancient Latin version of this fragment translates the Greek *tēi schesei tēs gnōmēs* as *affectu voluntatis*.
231 That is, Jesus's.
232 In Greek, *prothesin*.

Fragment 67
From Book 14
(Translated from Latin)

He holds the place of an image[233] in two senses. For people very often set up images of their loved ones after they die thinking that this provides enough consolation for their death, and they think they see the one who is neither seen nor present by beholding him, as it were, in the image, and in this way they quench the fire and the intensity of their longing. And furthermore people who have images of the emperors throughout their cities are seen to honor, by the cult and adoration of these images, those who are not present as if they were present and visible. Now both of these [functions of image] are fulfilled by him.[234] For all who are with him, and pursue virtue, and have been prepared by repaying the debts owed to God, love him and honor him very much, and the divine nature, though it is not seen, fulfills love for him in the one who is seen by all, and thus everyone supposes that they are seeing him through him[235] and are always present to him. And in this way they pay every honor [to him] as if to an imperial image since it is as if the divine nature is in him and is seen in him. For even though it is the Son who is said to indwell, nonetheless the Father is also with him and it is believed by every creature that he is with the Son inseparably in every way. And the Spirit too is not absent, seeing that he functions as the anointing for him and he is always with the one who has been assumed. And we ought not marvel at this, since the Father is also said to be with the Son in all people who pursue virtue: "For the Father and I will come and make our home with him."[236] It is clear to all that the Spirit is also inseparable from such people.

Fragment 68
From Book 15
(Translated from Latin)

On account of this each one is justly called "Son," since there exists one person which the union of the natures produces.

233 See Col 1:15. 234 That is, Jesus. 235 That is, seeing the Son through Jesus.
236 John 14:23.

Fragment 69
From Book 15[237]
(Translated from Latin and Greek)

Let[238] no one be deceived by the wiliness of their questions. For it is truly disgraceful to put aside "so great a cloud of witnesses,"[239] as the Apostle said, and having been deceived by their crafty questions to join with the party of our opponents. So what is it that they ask with such cunning? Is Mary the Anthropotokos or the Theotokos? Who was it that was crucified, God or a human being? But in fact the answer to such questions is clear as well from our previous remarks in response to their questions; nonetheless, right now let us repeat the appropriate response briefly so that they may have no further occasion for craftiness. So[240] when they ask, "Is Mary Anthropotokos or Theotokos?" let it be said by us, "Both" – the one by the nature of the reality, the other by relation. For she is Anthropotokos by her nature since the one in the womb of Mary, who also proceeded from it, was a human being. Yet she is Theotokos, since God was in the human being that was born, not that he was circumscribed in him by nature but that he was in him according to the disposition of his will.[241] And[242] so, there is justification for saying both, but not according to a similar rationale. For it is not the case that just as the human being received a beginning in order to exist in the womb, so too did God the Word, since he was before every creature. And so, there is justification for saying both and each of them according to its own rationale. Moreover, the same response ought to be given if they ask, "Was it God that was crucified or a human being?" It is both, but not according to a similar rationale. For the latter was crucified in that he underwent the suffering and was nailed to the tree and was arrested by the Jews, but the former because he was with him according to the reason previously stated.

237 The ancient Latin versions of this fragment identify its source as Book 12, but the Greek fragment notes that it is from Book 15. Here the Greek text is prioritized.

238 The translation begins with the Latin of C5T3.

239 Heb 12:1.

240 Here the translation switches to the Greek of LT28.

241 The ancient Latin version of this fragment translates the Greek *kata tēn schesin tēs gnōmēs* as *secundum adfectum voluntatis*.

242 Here the translation returns to the Latin of C5T3.

Fragment 70
From Book 15
(Translated from Latin and Greek)

For[243] the Lord was troubled by and struggled with the passions of the soul more than with those of the body, and he subdued pleasures through his superior power of reasoning, unquestionably because the divinity acted as the mediator and assisted him in the achievement of this. Therefore,[244] the Lord is seen engaged especially in the struggle with these. For having been neither deceived by craving for money nor tempted by desire for glory, he gave nothing to the flesh, since he could not be conquered by such things. Now if he had not received a soul and it was the divinity that conquered these things, the gain from those things he accomplished would in no way at all redound to us – for what similarity is there between the divinity and the human soul when it comes to perfection of conduct? – and the Lord's struggles would seem to have had a gain that does not redound to us but to have been for the sake of some charade. But if it is not possible to say this (since it is certain beyond a doubt that these things have been accomplished for our sake), and if he engaged in a greater struggle with the passions of the soul and a lesser one with those of the flesh, then however much it used to happen that those [passions of the soul] troubled him intensely and acutely, so much was there something that acutely stood in need of an intense remedy. In other words, in assuming both flesh and soul he used to struggle in both on behalf of both, not only mortifying sin in the flesh and calming his sensual desires and making them easily controllable by superior reason of the soul, but also instructing and training his soul both to conquer its own passions and to bridle the sensual desires of the flesh. For he did these things through the indwelling divinity; indwelling, this [divinity] acted as mediator for both of them.

Fragment 71
From an Unknown Book or Section[245]
(Translated from Syriac)

Because of this they are outside the church of God. The fathers were right to cut them off like putrid members from a healthy body. But I would also

243 The translation begins with the Greek of LT29.
244 Here the translation switches to the Latin of C4T27.
245 This fragment has no internal indications of its original location, but it may belong to Book 15, which according to Gennadius cited "the traditions of the fathers"

like to offer a demonstration of these things: whether the fathers also spoke like this, or had the habit [of using] the name "human being." We find this usage among many, so necessarily I wish to corroborate my argument with their testimonies and I [want to] look at the issue from all sides: from the importance of their deeds to the uprightness of their thoughts; from the proof of the scriptures to the common usage of those who have been brought to faith in Christ. [But] those who quarrel with us in their blasphemy will, contrary to all these things [I will raise], approve their [own] teachings, which they have established with something that is distinctly new and not mentioned in doctrine; and they also honor their weakness more than all their illness, while they tempt others everywhere to turn aside from the truth.

The first testimony that is appropriate for proving what I am saying comes from Hegesippus, who lived in the time of the apostles. For in his fifth book he included the words of James, the brother of our Lord Christ, and told the story of his death and how the Pharisees killed him.[246] Then he related what his manner of life was, how he conducted himself, what garments he wore, what many thought of him on account of the excellence of his ways,[247] and how he exhorted many Jews to have faith in Christ.[248] And he said that on the day of the Passover many Jews gathered in the great city, along with the scribes and the Pharisees, and they said to him, "There are many who go astray in regard to the Messiah. But you, because all the people are persuaded by you on account of the excellence of your ways, go and get up on the pinnacle of the temple and turn every person away from

(see p. 421 above). Perhaps the testimonies from the apostle James, Hegesippus, and Eusebius of Caesarea discussed in this fragment were some of these "traditions." Alternatively, since Theodore attempts to demonstrate by appeal to patristic authorities the propriety of calling the incarnate Word as "human being," this fragment could stem from one of the earlier sections of the book that deal with this topic (see Fragments 10, 12, 15, 17, 20, and 36).

246 Here Theodore begins to summarize the fragments of Hegesippus preserved in Eusebius, *Ecclesiastical History* 2.23.4–18.

247 See Eusebius, *Ecclesiastical History* 2.23.4–7.

248 See Eusebius, *Ecclesiastical History* 2.23.8–9 (GCS 9/1: 168, 2–8 Schwartz/Mommsen): "Certain individuals from the seven sects which are among the people … tried to learn from him what the 'gate' of Jesus was [see John 10:1–9], and he said that he was the Savior. Some of them came to believe that Jesus was the Christ, but the aforementioned sects did not believe in either the resurrection or that he is coming to repay each according to their works [see Rom 2:6]. Now as many as came to believe did so through James." The translation of Eusebius here and in the following notes is by Mark DelCogliano.

this opinion."[249] I will set down his own words; this is what he said, "The scribes and the Pharisees made James stand upon the pinnacle of the temple, and they called to him and said, 'O just one, whom it is right for all of us to obey, since the people go astray after Jesus who was crucified, teach us what is the "gate" of Jesus?' And he said to them with a loud voice, 'Why are you asking me about Jesus, the Son of Man?'"[250] With these words he showed there is another besides God the Word, which he called "Son of Man." And he replied in reference to that one who was crucified, adding, "He sits in the heavens at the right hand of the great power, and he will come on clouds of heaven."[251] For no one says that the divinity will arrive upon the clouds since it exists in every place. Rather, it is fitting that it is the human being that will come upon the clouds, even if it is not separate from the divinity. For this does not in any way detract from its union with the humanity. Eusebius of Caesarea quoted this account by Hegesippus in the book *Ecclesiastical History* that he wrote. Thus, as was said, there are three witnesses for this: the blessed and great James who is the brother of our Lord, Hegesippus who told his story in his book, and Eusebius who included the verbatim testimony of Hegesippus. If there were any doubt about this, namely, that it is fitting for the apostles to think like this, he would not have quoted it verbatim. He told his story because <...> it was appropriate that the one spoke it and the other told the story of the one [who spoke it].

It is acceptable, too, that in the history also Justin <...> was.[252] He said that it was from those who called our Lord a mere human being that Simon

249 Eusebius, *Ecclesiastical History* 2.23.10–11 (GCS 9/1: 168, 8–20 Schwartz/Mommsen): "Therefore, since many authorities were also believers [see John 12:42], there was an uproar among the Jews and scribes and Pharisees, who were saying, 'The whole people is in danger of thinking that Jesus is the Christ.' So when they gathered, they said to James, 'We exhort you, restrain the people, for it has gone astray to Jesus, as if he were the Christ. We exhort you to persuade all who come for the day of the Passover in regard to Jesus. For all of us are persuaded by you since we testify about you, as does all the people, that you are righteous and that you show no partiality [see Luke 20:21]. Therefore, persuade the crowd that they not go astray in regard to Jesus. For indeed the whole people and all of us are persuaded by you. Stand, then, on the pinnacle of the temple, so that you may be manifested on high and your words may be easily heard by the whole people. For on account of the Passover all the tribes have gathered, along with the Gentiles.'"

250 Eusebius, *Ecclesiastical History* 2.23.12–13 (GCS 9/1: 168, 20–25 Schwartz/Mommsen). The question is about the "gate" to the sheepfold in John 10:1–9.

251 Eusebius, *Ecclesiastical History* 2.23.13 (GCS 9/1: 170, 1–2 Schwartz/Mommsen). Hegesippus echoes the language of Matt 26:64, which itself echoes Dan 7:13.

252 Justin mentions Simon and Menander in *First Apology* 26 and 56, but the information recounted here is not found in Justin. What follows seems to be based on Eusebius, *Ecclesiastical History* 3.26, which quotes Justin, *First Apology* 26.

and Menander after him, the magicians, received their origin, but not because they called him a mere human being. After discussing Menander,[253] [Eusebius] said that the "evil demon" attempted to "detach" Christians from "their devotion" to God; he chose to approach "the Ebionites whom the first Christians named in view of the poor and mean opinions" they confessed "about Christ."[254] "For they regarded him as a mere human being only declared righteous" in an ordinary way.[255] Previously he called them "heretics"[256] not simply, but to narrate those things about Simon and Menander, who nullified the corporeality of our Lord by saying that he appears as in illusions.[257] Rightly he calls them "heretics" since they are fools when it comes to the Lord's corporeality. They also deny his divinity. For they preach that he is a mere human being, because of which Eusebius finds fault with them when <...>

Fragment 72
From an Unknown Book or Section
(Translated from Syriac)

And again, in regard to the difference between the natures that we confess <...> since it is right in the case of the rest, even as many of them <...> human beings doubted them in their perversity. For it is clear from this which things are fittingly said about the humanity and which things differ from the divinity in their distinctions, while they coincide in the unique conjunction of all those things said about our Lord and Savior

253 See Eusebius, *Ecclesiastical History* 3.26.

254 See Eusebius, *Ecclesiastical History* 3.27.1 (GCS 9/1: 254, 24–256, 3 Schwartz/Mommsen): "But there were others whom the evil demon was unable to detach from their devotion to the Christ of God, yet he found them liable to being snared in another way and so won them over: these are the Ebionites whom the first [Christians] suitably named in view of their poor and mean opinions about Christ."

255 See Eusebius, *Ecclesiastical History* 3.27.2 (GCS 9/1: 256, 3–4 Schwartz/Mommsen): "For they regarded him as ordinary and common, a human being declared righteous by progress in character, this alone, and born of the coupling of a man and Mary."

256 In Syriac, *gvyy achrnyatha*, literally, "those who elect the alternate." It is possible that this phrase is an odd rendering of the Greek *hairetikoi*, "sectarians" or "heretics." The title given to chapter 27 at the beginning of Book 3 of the *Ecclesiastical History* is "On the heresy (*haireseōs*) of the Ebionites" (GCS 9/1: 184, 7 Schwartz/Mommsen). Perhaps that is what Theodore means when Eusebius "previously" referred to the Ebionites as "heretics." All this, however, remains speculative.

257 It is unclear what passage of Eusebius Theodore is referring to here. Theodore appears to connect Eusebius's words about Simon and Menander with a discussion of doceticism.

Jesus Christ. For when the natures are investigated separately in terms of what they indicate, there are some things that are fitting for the one nature and some for the other, as far as the rank of what is said about each of the natures is concerned. But when they are conjoined together in the union of the person, the two of them are spoken of in whatever way is fitting for this one [person] because of the union. For in this way too something that is separate in nature is manifested as spoken of jointly because of the union of the person <...>

<...> to whom and from whom was he born? And whose is he? In the narrative of the generations, it comes to David and from there it goes in the sequence of the succession until it finally arrives at Christ, when it says, "Matthan begot Jacob, Jacob begot Joseph the husband of Mary, from whom Jesus was born, who is called Christ."[258] Now these words clearly demonstrate that it is about Christ in the flesh that he writes, and [the evangelist] even speaks of him as born from Mary. Since he was not writing about the divinity, it was necessary to show that the Messiah was born from Abraham's seed. And lest Christ also be understood to have been born in the same sequence, he separates him from the three divisions containing fourteen [generations] each, saying, "Now the birth of the Messiah took place in this way: when Mary his mother had been betrothed to Joseph, even though they had not yet known each other, she found herself pregnant from the Holy Spirit."[259]

Fragment 73
From an Unknown Book or Section
(Translated from Greek)

Made known by the foreknowledge of the Word, the human being born from the Virgin without seed was not separated from the Word, being conjoined to him by an identity of will,[260] according to which, having been well pleased[261] [with him] he united him to himself and showed him to be indistinguishable from him in terms of activity[262] and to possess undividedly

258 Matt 1:15–16.
259 Matt 1:18.
260 In Greek, *tautotēti gnōmēs*.
261 In Greek, *eudokēsas*, a participle cognate with *eudokia*, "good pleasure."
262 Here I follow the emendation of *kai tēn energeian* to *kata tēn energeian* suggested by Richard Price, *The Acts of the Lateran Synod of 649* (Liverpool: Liverpool University Press, 2014), 355.

the same sovereignty and authority and also a worship that, by the law of equality, cannot be distinguished.

APPENDIX

ST = Fragments preserved by Severus of Antioch in various works

LT = Fragments preserved by Leontius of Byzantium, *Unmasking and Triumph over the Nestorians*

FT = Fragments preserved by Facundus of Hermiane, *In Defense of the Three Chapters*

C4 = Fragments preserved by *Acts of the Council of Constantinople* in 553, Fourth Session

C5 = Fragments preserved by *Acts of the Council of Constantinople* in 553, Fifth Session

C6 = Fragments preserved by *Acts of the Council of Constantinople* in 553, Sixth Session

BT = Fragments preserved in *The Blasphemies of Diodore, Theodore, and the Impious Nestorius*

BL = British Library Cod. Add. 14669

Jansen = Jansen's numbering

|| = parallel fragment (whether partial or full)

CEECW	Book	Section	Behr	Jansen
1.	1	–	BT (Syriac)	–
2.	1	–	C4T25 (Latin)	I
	–	11	|| BT1 (Syriac)	–
3.	–	33	BT2 (Syriac)	–
4.	–	35	BT3 (Syriac)	–
5.	–	36	BT4 (Syriac)	–
6.	–	36	BT5 (Syriac)	–
7.	–	37	BT6 (Syriac)	–
8.	–	38	BT7 (Syriac)	–
9.	–	42–43	BL fol. 4 (Syriac)	–
10.	–	49–50	BL fol. 7 (Syriac)	–
11.	–	50	BT8 (Syriac)	–
12.	–	51	BT9 (Syriac)	–

CEECW	Book	Section	Behr	Jansen
13.	–	51	BT10 (Syriac)	–
14.	5	52	FT17 (Latin)	III
15.	6	54	FT18 (Latin)	IV
16.	–	–	BL fol. 15 (Syriac)	–
17.	6	54	FT19 (Latin)	V
18.	–	56	BT11 (Syriac)	–
19.	–	–	BL fol. 5 (Syriac)	–
20.	6	–	BL fol. 6 (Syriac)	–
21.	7	–	LT1 (Greek)	VI
	7	–	‖ C4T30 (Latin)	–
22.	7	–	LT2 (Greek)	VII
	–	59	‖ BT12 (Syriac)	–
	–	–	‖ ST4 (Syriac)	–
	–	59	BT13 (Syriac)	–
23.	7	59	LT3 (Greek)	VIII
	–	59	‖ BT14 (Syriac)	–
24.	7	–	LT4 (Greek)	IX
	–	–	‖ ST1 (Syriac)	–
	–	60	‖ BT15 (Syriac)	–
25.	–	60	BT16 (Syriac)	–
26.	7	–	C4T31 (Latin)	X
27.	8	–	LT5 (Greek)	XI
28.	–	–	BL fol. 2 (Syriac)	–
29.	–	–	BL fol. 1 (Syriac)	–
30.	–	62–63	BL fol. 10 (Syriac)	–
	8	–	‖ LT6 (Greek)	XII
	8	–	‖ C4T29 (Latin)	–
	–	63	‖ BT17 (Syriac)	–
	8	–	‖ LT7 (Greek)	XIII
31.	–	–	BL fol. 3 (Syriac)	–
32.	9	–	LT8 (Greek)	XIV
33.	9	–	FT25 (Latin)	XV+XVI
34.	9	–	LT9 (Greek)	XVII
35.	–	66	BT18 (Syriac)	–
36.	–	66	BT19 (Syriac)	–
37.	10	70	FT20 (Latin)	XVIII

CEECW	Book	Section	Behr	Jansen
38.	10	–	LT10 (Greek)	XIX
39.	10	–	LT11 (Greek)	XX
40.	–	–	BL fol. 8 (Syriac)	–
41.	–	–	C5T1 (Latin)	XXI
	10	–	‖ LT12 (Greek)	XXI
42.	10–11	–	BL fol. 11 (Syriac)	–
43.	11	–	BL fol. 12–13 (Syriac)	–
	–	73	‖ BT20 (Syriac)	–
	–	73	‖ BT21 (Syriac)	–
	11	–	‖ C6T1 (Latin)	XXII
44.	–	–	BL fol. 9 (Syriac)	–
45.	–	73	BT22 (Syriac)	–
46.	–	77	BT23 (Syriac)	–
47.	12	–	LT13 (Greek)	XXIII
48.	12	–	LT14 (Greek)	XXIV
	–	–	‖ C5T2 (Latin)	–
	–	–	‖ C4T48 (Latin)	–
49.	12	–	LT15 (Greek)	XXV
50.	12	–	LT16 (Greek)	XXVI
	12	–	‖ C4T49 (Latin)	–
51.	12	–	LT17 (Greek)	XXVII
	–	–	‖ C5T5 (Latin)	XXVII
52.	12	–	C6T3 (Latin)	XXVIII
53.	12	–	LT18 (Greek)	XXIX
	12	–	‖ C4T50 (Latin)	–
54.	12	–	LT19 (Greek)	XXX
55.	12	–	LT20 (Greek)	XXXI
56.	12	–	FT21 (Latin)	XXXII
57.	–	77	BT24 (Syriac)	–
58.	–	77	BT25 (Syriac)	–
59.	–	77–78	BL fol. 17 (Syriac)	–
	13	–	‖ C4T55 (Latin)	XXXIII
	13	–	‖ LT21 (Greek)	XXXIII
60.	13	–	LT22 (Greek)	XXXIV
61.	13	–	LT23 (Greek)	XXXV
62.	13	–	LT24 (Greek)	XXXVI

CEECW	Book	Section	Behr	Jansen
63.	13	–	LT25 (Greek)	XXXVII
64.	13	–	FT3 (Latin)	XXXVIII
65.	14	–	LT26 (Greek)	XXXIX
66.	14	–	LT27 (Greek)	XL
67.	14	–	C4T17 (Latin)	XLI
68.	15	–	FT22 (Latin)	XLII
69.	12	–	C5T3 (Latin)	XLIII
	15	–	‖ LT28 (Greek)	XLIII
	–	–	‖ ST2 (Syriac)	–
	12	–	‖ C4T45 (Latin)	–
70.	15	–	C4T27 (Latin)	XLIV
	15	–	‖ LT29 (Greek)	XLIV
71.	–	–	BL fol. 14 (Syriac)	–
72.	–	–	BL fol. 16 (Syriac)	–
73.	–	–	–	XLV (Greek)

36

Augustine of Hippo, *On Eighty-Three Different Questions. Number 80: Against the Apollinarians*

Introduction and Translation by Andrew Radde-Gallwitz

INTRODUCTION

The conversion of Augustine of Hippo (354–430) to catholic Christianity in 386 is a famous story. After he was baptized in Milan, he abandoned his post as professor of rhetoric in that city, and he and his friends formed a small, quasi-monastic circle devoted to the philosophical life of study and asceticism. After the group moved to Augustine's native North Africa in 388, he composed a series of responses to questions posed by his confrères, writing his answers up in the style of the question-and-answer tradition of Greek and Latin literature. Upon becoming bishop in 396, Augustine had the various answers collected and circulated as a single work, with numbers for easy reference. Presented here is number 80 of the series, in which Augustine engages with the views of the Apollinarians.[1] It is unclear how he came to know their ideas. In his *Confessions*, which he started writing around the time of the collection of *On Eighty-Three Different Questions*, he mentions that during the time immediately prior to his baptism his friend Alypius had held essentially the Apollinarian view of Christ without at the time knowing its source (*Confessions* 7.19.25). In the work translated here, Augustine presumes that the group attached great weight to John 1:14 ("And the Word became flesh and dwelt among us"). Augustine argues that the evangelist's reference to flesh is not intended to deny that Christ also had a human soul, a point he demonstrates by various references to the gospel portrait of Christ's psychological experience, that is, passages

1 Several writings of Apollinarius are translated in this volume on pp. 301–347.

that show him thinking and feeling sorrow, hunger, strong emotion, and the like. For Augustine, the denial of a human soul (with its full range of capacities and experiences) is the central tenet of Apollinarianism, and it is the one he is at pains to refute here. Augustine maintains that just as there are certain things a subject cannot experience without a body (such as being born), so too there are other things one cannot experience without a soul (such as feeling exhausted). Augustine's general term for "experiences" is *affectiones*. Many cases of the second type of experience – those for which soul is a necessary condition – are recorded for Christ in the gospel, in passages that are meant to be read literally. This fact demonstrates that he had a soul.

This translation is based on the critical edition in Almut Mutzenbecher, *Sancti Aurelii Augustini: De diversis quaestionibus octoginta tribus; De octo dulcitii quaestionibus*, CCSL 44A (Turnhout: Brepols, 1975), 232–238.

TRANSLATION

1. Certain heretics, who are said to be called Apollinarians after one Apollinarius, their founder, claimed that our Lord Jesus Christ, insofar as he saw fit to become a human being, did not have a human mind. Some people, attaching themselves to them and listening earnestly to them, are pleased with this perversity, by which he diminished the human being in God, saying that he did not have a mind, that is, a rational soul whereby a human being differs in intelligence from the beasts.[2] But then they worked out for themselves that, if this is so, it is necessary to confess that the only-begotten Son of God – the wisdom and Word of the Father, through whom all things were made[3] – is believed to have assumed something bestial with the shape of a human body. They were dissatisfied with themselves, and yet it did not lead to correction such that they would return to the way of truth and confess that a complete human being was assumed by the wisdom of God without any diminishment of nature. Rather, employing a still greater audacity, they deprived him of even that soul and the entire vital power of a human being and claimed that he assumed only human flesh. While citing a testimony from the gospel – yet without understanding its meaning – in their perversity they dare to contend against the catholic truth, saying that

2 "Mind" renders the Latin *mens*; "soul," *anima*; and "intelligence" or "intellect," *animus*.
3 See John 1:1, 3.

it is written, "The Word became flesh, and dwelt among us."[4] For under cover of these words, they wish the Word to be joined to and fused with flesh in such a way that not only was there no mind between [the Word and the flesh] in this case but also no human soul.

2. In responding to them, one must first say that that verse is placed in the gospel as it is because that assumption of human nature by the Lord occurred all the way to the visible flesh, and in that entire unity of the assumption, the leading part is the Word, while the last and least is the flesh. And so the evangelist, wishing for our sake to commend the love of the humility of God who humbled himself, and expressing just how far he humbled himself, mentioned Word and flesh, passing over the nature of the soul, which is inferior to the Word but superior to the flesh. For he more strongly commends humility by saying, "The Word became flesh," than he would have had he said, "The Word became a human being." You see, if these words are closely scrutinized, another person – no less perverse – can accuse our faith on the basis of these words for saying that the Word itself was transformed and changed into flesh and ceased being Word, since it is written, "The Word became flesh," just as human flesh, when it becomes ash, is not both flesh and ash, but ash comes from flesh, and according to the more usual custom of speaking, whatever becomes what it had been ceases to be what it was. Yet we do not understand these words in this way. But even these people understand them as we do, such that, while the Word remains what it is, "the Word became flesh" is said because it assumed the form of a slave,[5] and not because it is transformed into the other form by a kind of change.

Finally, imagine if every time flesh was mentioned and soul passed over we had to understand each case in such a way that we believe no soul exists there. Thus those people would not have a soul about whom it is said, "And all flesh will see the salvation of God,"[6] as well as the verse in the psalm, "Hear my prayers; to you all flesh shall come,"[7] and the verse in the gospel, "Just as you have given him power over all flesh, so that all that you have given him may not be lost but have eternal life."[8] From these examples it is understood that human beings are customarily indicated through the mention of flesh alone, so that according to this way of speaking that verse too can be understood. Thus, when it is said, "The Word became flesh," nothing else is

4 John 1:14. 5 See Phil 2:7. 6 Isa 40:5; Luke 4:6. 7 Ps 64(65):3.
8 John 17:2.

said but "The Word became a human being." For just as when the soul alone is mentioned, from the part the human being as a whole and completely is understood – as it is in that verse, "So many souls went down to Egypt"[9] – so too in turn when flesh alone is mentioned, from the part the human being as a whole is understood, as in those passages that we have cited.

3. Therefore, we respond to this objection of theirs, which they cite from the gospel, in such a way that no person would be foolish enough to think these words compel us to believe and confess that the mediator between God and human beings, the human being Jesus Christ,[10] did not have a human soul. So too I ask how they respond to our very clear objections, in which we show through countless places in the gospel writings the evangelists relating about him that he shared in experiences that cannot exist without a soul. Indeed, I'm not putting forth my own claims, but things the Lord himself mentioned on so many occasions: "My soul is sorrowful unto death,"[11] and, "I have power to lay down my soul and to take it back up again,"[12] and, "Greater love no one has than to lay down his soul for his friends."[13] Now, a stubborn disputant can say to me that these were said by the Lord figuratively, just as he clearly said many things in parables. But even if those [parables] are not of this sort, there is no grounds for dispute where we have the evangelists' narratives, through which we recognize that he was born from the Virgin Mary, seized by the Jews, flogged and crucified and killed, and buried in the tomb – and no one can understand any of these to have happened without a body. Neither will anyone, unless he is demented, say that these narratives are to be taken figuratively, since they are recounted by those who narrated the events as they recalled them. Therefore, just as those narratives testify that he had a body, so too do those experiences, which cannot exist except in a soul, show that he had a soul. And we no less read of them in the same gospel narratives: Jesus was astonished[14] and angry and grieved[15] and glad[16] and countless many others. Similar too are those that display joint functions of soul and body together, such as that he was hungry,[17] that he slept,[18] that he sat down exhausted from his journey,[19] and others of this kind. Now, they can't say: in the old books[20] too anger[21] and joy[22] and several motions of this kind are said of

9 Gen 46:27. 10 See 1 Tim 2:5. 11 Matt 26:38. 12 John 10:18.
13 John 15:13. 14 Matt 8:10. 15 Mark 3:5. 16 John 11:15.
17 Matt 4:2. 18 Matt 8:24. 19 John 4:6.
20 That is, in the Old Testament. 21 See Num 16:46. 22 See Deut 28:63.

God, and yet it does not follow from these that we must believe God has a human soul. For these are said by way of prophetic imaginings, not to recount a narrative. After all, body parts are ascribed to God too: hands,[23] feet,[24] face,[25] and the like. Just as these do not indicate that he has a body, neither do those indicate a soul. Now, just as any narrative where hands of Christ and head and so forth are mentioned indicate his body, so too that which is mentioned concerning experiences of the intellect in the same narrative context indicates his soul. But it's daft to believe the evangelist when he narrates that Christ ate and not to believe him that he was hungry. For, granted that it doesn't strictly follow either that everyone who eats is hungry (for we also read that an angel ate,[26] but we do not read that it was hungry) or that everyone who is hungry eats (perhaps that person is prevented by some other task or lacks food and the means to eat). Regardless, given that the evangelist narrates both [hunger and eating], one must believe both, since like a witness to the events he wrote both as real occurrences. Now, just as one cannot understand his eating if he didn't have a body, so too his hunger couldn't have occurred without a soul.

4. Neither does that vacuous and silly cavil frighten us, which they say as they obnoxiously resist: "He was therefore subject to necessity, if he had these true experiences of the intellect." Actually, our response is easy: "He was therefore subject to necessity, since he was seized, flogged, crucified, and died." So let them finally understand without obstinacy, if they are willing, that he in his good pleasure assumed the passions (that is, the experiences) of the intellect by a willingness for the economy and yet they were true passions, in the same way as he assumed passions of the body by the same willingness for the economy without any necessity. Just as we do not die willingly, so too we are not born willingly. But he exhibited both willingly, as was fitting, and yet he exhibited both completely truly. Therefore, just as no one by using the word "necessity" tears either us or them away from believing in a completely true passion, through which his body is shown, so too no one using this word "necessity" deters us from believing in a completely true experience, through which we recognize his soul. Nor should it deter them from agreeing to the catholic faith, provided that they are not deterred by being fatally ashamed of changing an opinion that, though false, they have nonetheless defended for so long and with rashness.

23 See Ps 94(95):5. 24 See Ps 98(99):5. 25 See Exod 33:23.
26 See Gen 18:2–9.

37

Augustine of Hippo, *Letter* 137

Introduction and Translation by Andrew Radde-Gallwitz

INTRODUCTION

The surviving body of writings from Augustine includes a large corpus of letters, most from his time as bishop of Hippo in his native North Africa. The letters, which include briefs to as well as from Augustine, cover a remarkable range of topics. *Letter* 137 is part of a fascinating dossier of letters from around 412 between Augustine and the talented young aristocrat Rufus Antonius Agrypnius Volusianus. Volusian, as we will call him, was the son of the famous Christian patroness Melania the Elder, but not himself a Christian. He did not hesitate to share his doubts about Christian teaching with Augustine, who must have been his senior by at least thirty years. At one particular meeting of young aristocrats, which Augustine mentions in *Letter* 137, Volusian encountered objections to the Christian doctrine of the incarnation, which he vowed to forward to Augustine for a reply.[1] The main issue Volusian notes is the seeming incongruity in the doctrine, which posits that the ruler of heaven was confined in the tiny body of an infant and underwent the ordinary experiences of a human being. What's more, the miracles ascribed to Christ are attested for other people as well; driving out evil spirits, healing the sick, even raising the dead – these are all "small potatoes" for a god. Marcellinus, a mutual friend of Volusian and Augustine and a Christian, also wrote to Augustine, describing the same meeting; he makes clear that Volusian himself stood behind these objections, and he urges Augustine to pay special attention to the objection that Christ's miracles did not exceed those attested for men like Apollonius and Apuleius.[2] In *Letter* 137 we see Augustine's defense and exposition of belief in the incarnation, in which the Word assumed a human being. Contrary

1 Augustine, *Ep*. 135. 2 Augustine, *Ep*. 136.

to Marcellinus's wish, Augustine spends the bulk of his time (2.4–3.12) on the incongruity problem, asserting that the question, as posed, reflects a mistaken materialism. In his typical fashion, he counters by urging his addressee to reflect on the nature of human perception and thought, through which one can come to know at first hand the compatibility of incorporeal (mental) and corporeal realities. He then tackles the "small potatoes" problem and argues that the deeds Christ performed were appropriate for a human being. What's more, Augustine notes, if we try to imagine an act that would putatively be appropriate for Christ to perform as God – say, creating another world while inhabiting this one – this would have been not only odd but also logically incongruent. Augustine argues that Christ's deeds were appropriate for his twofold aim in becoming incarnate: that of *teaching* and *helping* the human race.

This translation is based on the critical edition in Al. Goldbacher, *Sancti Aureli Augustini Hipponiensis Episcopi Epistulae, Pars III*, CSEL 44 (Vienna and Leipzig: Verlag der Österreichischen Akademie der Wissenschaften, 1904), 96–125.

TRANSLATION

To his honorable lord and justly distinguished and most excellent son, Volusian, Augustine sends greeting in the Lord.

1, 1. I have read your letter, in which I saw a sample – packaged in an admirably concise manner – of some lengthy dialogue. I ought, therefore, to respond rather than to offer some excuse for my delay. For it conveniently happens that I have a little break from outside business. Indeed, I have postponed various other replies I had determined to spend this leisure time dictating, since I judged it to be in no way right to postpone even for a little while answering someone whom I had urged to ask. But which of us who administer Christ's grace to the best of our abilities, when he reads your words, would desire for you to be instructed in Christian teaching only as much as suffices for your own salvation – not the salvation of this life, which the divine word took pains to warn us is rather like a mist appearing for a little while and immediately vanishing and perishing,[3] but that salvation that we become Christians in order to obtain and hold

3 See Jas 4:14.

eternally? For us, you see, it is a minor thing for you to be instructed only to the extent necessary for liberating *you*. For your intelligence and your singularly superior and splendid eloquence ought to be of benefit to others as well. Against their sluggishness or perversity the dispensation of such a great grace[4] must be defended in a completely appropriate way, a dispensation totally discounted by proud little souls who pretend they can do quite a lot of things yet can do nothing to heal or even curb their own vices.

2. So then, you ask whether the Lord and master of the world filled the body of the chaste woman; whether the mother carried him for ten months' long weariness and yet was a virgin after giving birth in the usual way of childbirth with her virginity subsequently remaining inviolate; whether the one to whom the universe can scarcely be thought equal was hidden within the tiny body of a crying infant, endured the years of boyhood, grew up, and matured into a young man; whether this ruler was away from his throne for so long and his management of the whole world was transferred to one tiny body; also, you ask whether he relaxed in slumber, was nourished by food, and felt all the affections of mortals; and [you say] the proofs of [his] great majesty do not make the matter clear with any adequate signs, since, if we consider other people also,[5] driving out spirits, healing the infirm, and restoring life to the dead are small potatoes for a god. You write that this question was raised at a gathering of friends by one of the many people present, but the rest of you stopped the questioner from asking more and the gathering broke up and you deferred to the merits of one with greater expertise, lest these hidden matters be rashly and recklessly treated and the harmless error turn to something blameworthy.

3. You then turn the focus of your letter to me, and after this admission of ignorance you admonish me to understand what is being demanded from our side. You even add that my reputation is at stake in whether you come to know what you're looking for, since even though a lack of expertise is tolerated in other priests with no harm to divine worship, when it comes to me as a bishop, whatever I happen not to know, I must read up on. So then, I first ask that you set aside this opinion you have too readily taken up about me, that you release and abandon this sentiment you have

4 In Latin, *tantae gratiae dispensatio*. Augustine's term *dispensatio* can function like the Greek *oikonomia* to refer generally to divine providence and particularly to Christ's incarnate economy.

5 That is, if we compare Jesus Christ with other people who have performed similar feats.

too charitably formed towards me, and that you believe what I say about myself more than what any other person does – if you return my affection. For the depth of the Christian scriptures is so great that, had I set out to learn them alone from early youth all the way to decrepit old age with total leisure, the greatest attention, and abilities greater than I have, I would still be making daily progress in them. The difficulty is not as great with those matters that are necessary for salvation, but although someone might hold the faith in those matters, without which they cannot live piously and rightly, nonetheless for those making progress there remain many things to be understood that are darkened with multiple shadows of mysteries, and the depth of wisdom is so profound not only in the words by which they are expressed but also in the realities that are to be understood – so they are seized with the oldest, sharpest, and most burning desire for learning, as scripture itself describes somewhere, "When a human being has finished, then she is just beginning."[6]

2, 4. But why say more on this? I must instead come to the matter about which you asked. In the first place, I want you to know that Christian doctrine does not hold that God was poured into the flesh in which he was born from the Virgin in such a way that he abandoned or let slip his governing care for the universe or that he transferred it in a so-to-speak restrained or compressed form to that little body. This is the opinion of people who are capable of thinking of nothing except bodies, whether those that are denser as water and earth are or finer like air and light. Nonetheless these are bodies, and no body can be everywhere as a whole, since even if it has countless many parts, it is necessary that it have one part here and another there. And however great or small the body is, it occupies the place where it is and fills the same location in such a way that it is not in any part of it as a whole. Therefore, to be thickened and thinned, to be contracted and expanded, to be depleted into something tiny and grown into a massive bulk – these states belong to nothing but bodies. Vastly different is the nature of the soul than that of the body – how much more so is the nature of God, who is creator of both soul and body! God is not said to fill the world[7] as does water or air or even light, such that he fills a smaller part of the world with a smaller part of himself and a larger part with a larger part. He knows how to be everywhere and to be contained in no place; he knows how to arrive

6 Sir 18:6(7). 7 See Jer 23:24.

without leaving where he had been; he knows how to leave without deserting the place to which he had come.

5. The human mind marvels at this and, because it does not grasp it, perhaps it does not believe it. The examining mind should first marvel at itself. It should first raise itself a little, if it can, out of the body and out of those things that it typically senses through the body, and should see for itself what it is that uses the body. But perhaps it cannot, for, as someone said, "It takes great genius to summon the mind away from the senses and to lead one's thoughts away from what is customary."[8] Therefore it must examine the very senses of the body somewhat more attentively than usual. Without doubt, the body's senses are five in number. They cannot exist without the body or without the soul, since nothing can have sense perception unless it is alive, and this belongs to the body from the soul, and since we do not see, hear, or use the other three senses without bodily instruments and, as it were, equipment and organs. This rational soul should notice that it does not take the body's senses into consideration by the body's senses but by the mind itself and by reason. Without doubt, a human being cannot have sense perception unless she is alive; but she lives in the flesh, until the two are separated at death. So then, how does the soul perceive the things that are outside its flesh, when it does not live except in its flesh? But aren't the stars in heaven a very long way away from its flesh? Doesn't it see the sun in heaven? Or is seeing not a kind of perceiving, although among the five senses vision is more excellent than the others? Does it also live in heaven, given that it perceives in heaven and there cannot be sense perception where there is no life? Or does it perceive even where it doesn't live since, although it lives only in its flesh, it perceives even those places containing things beyond its flesh, which it touches by sight? Don't you see how obscure this matter is even for a sense faculty as conspicuous as the one called vision? Take hearing as well. After all, it too somehow spreads itself outside the flesh. For on what basis do we say, "There's a noise outside," unless we are perceiving at the place where the noise is? Therefore, in this case too we live outside of our flesh. But can we perceive and not live at that place, since it is not possible for a sense to exist without life?

6. The other three senses perceive in their own location, although this point can perhaps be doubted concerning smell. But concerning taste and

8 Cicero, *Tusculan Disputations* 1.16.38.

touch there is no controversy, since we perceive what we taste and touch nowhere else than in our flesh. Accordingly, let these three senses be excluded from consideration. Vision and hearing raise a wondrous question – either the soul somehow perceives where it does not live, or it somehow lives where it is not. For it does not exist except in its flesh, but it perceives even beyond its flesh. Surely it perceives wherever it sees, since to see is to perceive; it perceives wherever it hears, since to hear is to perceive. Therefore, either it lives at this place and therefore also exists here or it perceives without also living there or it lives without existing there. All of these alternatives are extraordinary: none of them can be affirmed without some sort of absurdity and we are speaking of a sense organ that is liable to death. So then, what is the soul itself, which considers these things beyond the sense of the body – that is, in its mind? For it does not make judgments about these bodily senses with a bodily sense. And yet we reckon something incredible is said to us concerning the omnipotence of God, when it is said that the Word of God, through whom all things were made,[9] assumed a body from the Virgin and appeared to mortal senses in such a way that it did not defile its immortality, did not alter its eternity, did not diminish its power, did not desert its administration of the world, and did not withdraw from the "bosom of the Father,"[10] that is, from the hidden place where it is with him and in him![11]

7. Don't understand the Word of God, through whom all things were made, in such a way that you think some part of it passes away and changes from being future to past. It remains exactly as it is and is everywhere as a whole. But it "comes" when it is made manifest and "departs" when it is hidden. Nonetheless it is present whether hidden or manifest, just as light is present to the eyes both of someone who sees and of a blind person; but to the one who sees it is present as something there, while to the blind person as something lacking. And a voice is present to the ears that hear and present to deaf ears – but to the former it is clear and to the latter it doesn't appear.[12] Yet what is more marvelous than what happens when our voices and words sound – something that obviously passes by so rapidly? For when we speak, there is clearly no place for the second syllable unless the first one stops resounding, and yet, if one listener is present, he hears all that we say, and if two are present, both hear just as much, because it is

9 John 1:3. 10 John 1:18. 11 See John 10:38.
12 Augustine employs a rhyme here: in Latin, *sed illis patet, istis latet.*

a whole even to each individual. And, if a silent crowd hears, they do not break up the sounds among themselves into pieces like bits of food. Rather, every sound is both whole to all and whole to each. Accordingly, then, wouldn't it be more incredible if the abiding Word of God did not have the effect on things that a human being's transitory word has on the ears, given that just as the human word is in some way simultaneously heard as a whole even by individuals, so too the Word of God is simultaneously everywhere as a whole?

8. Therefore, we shouldn't be afraid of the infant's little body, as if so great a God might appear to have suffered from confinement in it. For it is not in bulk but in power that God is great – God who gave a sense that somewhat resembles foresight more to little ants and bees than to asses and camels; who creates the fig tree's humungous size from the tiniest grain of seed, even though many smaller things grow from much larger seeds; who enriched the pupil, little though it is, with the power of vision, which, when it shoots forth through the eyes, surveys nearly half of the heaven in a moment of time; who from a single point and so to speak the center of the brain spreads out all five senses distinctly; who from the heart, a member so small, dispenses vital force through all the body's parts – in these and like instances, that which is not something small in small things, secretly achieves great things from the littlest ones. For the very magnitude of his power, which feels no constriction in narrow straits, made the virginal womb fecund not with another's but with her own offspring; it joined to itself a rational soul and through it also a human body – and the entire human being was completely changed for the better, while it was in no way changed for the worse – graciously assuming from it the name of humanity, while generously giving to it the name of divinity; through the mother's inviolate, virginal womb the very power brought out the child's members, which it later brought in through a closed door as members of a man.[13] Thus, if an explanation is sought for this thing, it will not be wondrous; if a comparison is demanded, it will not be unique. Let us grant that God can do something that we concede we cannot investigate. In such matters, the entire explanation of the deed is the power of the doer.

3, 9. Now, the very fact that he relaxed in slumber, was nourished by food, and felt all human affections proves to human beings that he in no

13 See John 20:19, 26.

way destroyed but rather assumed a human being.[14] Look, such are the facts, and yet certain heretics, perversely marveling at and praising his power, altogether refuse to recognize in him human nature, where dwells the whole assurance of grace, by which he saves those who believe, containing in himself deep treasures of wisdom and knowledge and imparting faith to minds so that he might lead them to the eternal contemplation of unchanging truth. Suppose that, being omnipotent, he had created a human being that was formed somewhere other than from its mother's womb, and had instead all of a sudden brought it into view. Suppose that the human being had not advanced in age from childhood to youth, had taken no food and no sleep. Would this not have confirmed the erroneous opinion that makes it impossible to believe that he took up a true human being in any way, and that, while granting all those deeds that are marvelous, takes away those things he did out of mercy? But in fact he appeared as a mediator between God and human beings in such a way that, by joining both natures in a unity of person,[15] he might elevate ordinary things with extraordinary ones and temper extraordinary things with ordinary ones.

10. But in all the motions of creation does God do anything that is not marvelous, even though they become devalued because of their routine familiarity? Indeed, look how many customary things are trampled upon, which upon consideration leave one speechless! Take, for instance, the very power of seeds: who can penetrate mentally, who can disclose in speech their variety, their vitality and efficaciousness, their latent powers, and their bringing about great things within a small frame? Therefore he who made himself a human being without seed is the same one who in the genesis of things[16] also made seeds without seeds. He who in his own body obeyed the variety of times and the measures of years is the same one who without changing through any mutability on his part weaves the sequence of the ages. For this body discerned objects temporally because it came to be at a certain point of time. But the Word in the beginning, through whom all times were made,[17] chose the time in which he would take on flesh and did not yield to time so that it could be changed into flesh. After all, it is the human being that draws near to God, not God that recedes from himself.

14 Augustine plays on words: *non consumpsit utique, sed adsumpsit.*
15 In Latin, *in unitate personae copulans utramque naturam.*
16 In Latin, *in rerum natura.* 17 See John 1:1–3.

11. But indeed certain people demand that an explanation be given to them of how God is mixed with a human being such that in Christ there was a single person, though necessarily this happened just once. They make this demand as if they themselves were capable of giving an explanation of something that happens every day, namely, how a soul mixes with a body such that in a human being there comes to be a single person. For just as in a single person a soul uses a body to make a human being, so too in a single person God uses a human being to make Christ. Therefore, in the former case the person is a mixture of soul and body, while in the latter case the person is a mixture of God and human being, provided that the listener leave aside the tendency of bodies whereby two liquids mix in such a way that neither retains its integrity, though actually even in bodies themselves light mixes with air without being corrupted. Therefore, the person of a human being is a mixture of soul and body, while the person of Christ is a mixture of God and human being; for when the Word of God mixed with a soul-having-a-body, he at once took on both soul and body. The former happens all the time for the propagation of human beings, while the latter occurred just once for the liberation of human beings. But yet the commixture of two incorporeal things ought to be more easily believed than that of one incorporeal thing and another corporeal thing. For if the soul is not mistaken about its own nature, it comprehends that it is incorporeal. How much more incorporeal is the Word of God, and therefore the intermixture of the Word of God and the soul ought to be more credible than that of the soul and the body. But the latter we know by experience in our very selves, the former we are commanded to believe in Christ. Now if both were enjoined upon us to believe, but they were equally unfamiliar to us, which of the two would we believe more readily? How could we not accept that two incorporeals can be mixed more easily than can one incorporeal and another corporeal, provided at any rate that the name "mixing" or "mixture" is not unworthily applied to these incorporeals because it is customarily used for corporeal things whose natures and origins are extremely different?

12. Therefore,[18] the Word of God – the same one who is Son of God, co-eternal with the Father, and the same one who is "power and wisdom of

18 Nearly all of section 12 forms a single periodic sentence, which imitates to some extent the formulae of creeds. To convey the effect of the original Latin, I have largely retained this punctuation, following the printed editions by breaking the sentence with half-stops, though I have inserted two breaks.

God"[19] – who reaches from the utmost end of the rational creation to the lowest end of the corporeal creation mightily and arranges all exquisitely,[20] is present and hidden, is nowhere enclosed, nowhere divided, nowhere extended but everywhere as whole without bulk; in some manner that is quite different than that by which he is present to other creatures, he took to himself a human being and in him made the one Jesus Christ; he is mediator between God and human beings,[21] equal to the Father according to the divinity but lesser than the Father according to the flesh,[22] that is, according to the human being; the same one is uniquely immortal according to the divinity that is equal to the Father,[23] and both mutable and mortal according to our congenital weakness; at that time which he had known to be most appropriate and had arranged before the ages, Christ came to human beings as *teaching* and *help*, so that they might attain eternal salvation.

Now, he came as *teaching* so that his authority, which was exhibited in the flesh, might confirm those truths that had previously been spoken profitably not only by the holy prophets, whose every word was true, but even by those philosophers, poets, and authors of every kind of literature, whom no one doubts mixed many truths with falsehoods, and he did all this on behalf of those people who were incapable of grasping or discerning those matters in their inner truth; and even before he assumed the human being, he himself was this truth for all who had been capable of participating in him; but, above all, by the example of his incarnation, he offered healing persuasion on this point: namely, since most human beings in their desire for divinity had through the heavenly powers, which they thought to be gods, enjoined upon themselves various rites containing illicit and sacrilegious (rather than sacred) petitions to God, doing so rather out of pride than of piety, by which attitude the demons, with a pride that is akin, substitute themselves for those holy angels, and with this being so, in order that human beings might come to know that the God to whom they had been making petition through interposed powers as if he were positioned far away is so close to human piety that he deigned to take up a human being and to become united with it in such a way that the whole human being might be joined to him as body is to soul, though without the condition of mutability: in this condition, which we observe that both body and soul possess, God is not changed.

19 1 Cor 1:24. 20 See Wis 8:1. 21 1 Tim 2:5. 22 See John 14:28.
23 See 1 Tim 6:16.

But he also comes as *help*, because without the grace of faith, which comes from him, no one can conquer wicked longings, nor can one who does not vanquish some residue of them be cleansed by a remitting pardon. Now, as to that point which pertains to his teaching, is there today a simpleton so low or a silly woman so base that he or she does not believe in the immortality of the soul and the life to come after death? Long ago, when Pherecydes the Syrian first discussed this point among the Greeks, he converted Pythagoras of Samos, who was moved by the novelty of that man's argument, from being an athlete to a philosopher.[24] So now, as Maro[25] said and we all see, "the Syrian shrub grows everywhere."[26] But this relates to the help of grace, which is in Christ, who himself is for all people,

> With him as guide, any remaining traces of our crime
> Shall be wiped out, and earth shall be released from endless dread.[27]

4, 13. "But," they say, "there are no proofs of his great majesty to make the matter clear with adequate signs, since, if other people are taken into consideration as well, driving out spirits, healing the infirm, and restoring life to the dead are small potatoes for a god."[28] Now, we too agree that the prophets did such deeds. After all, among these signs, what is more excellent than the dead living again? Elijah did this,[29] Elisha did this.[30] As to the miracles of magicians, the question of whether they too raised the dead, those people will have to declare their opinion – I mean those who tried to "convict" Apuleius too of the charge of magic, though not by accusing but by praising him, even though he defended himself at length against the accusation of practicing the magical arts.[31] We read that Egyptian magicians, who were most expert

24 Augustine's source is Cicero, *Tusculan Disputations* 1.16.38.
25 That is, Publius Vergilius Maro, known commonly as Virgil.
26 Virgil, *Eclogues* 4.25. 27 Virgil, *Eclogues* 4.13–14.
28 See above, section 1.2, where this question is first raised.
29 See 1 Kgs 17:17–22. 30 See 2 Kgs 4:18–35.
31 Apuleius of Maudaros (ca. 123–ca. 170) was a poet, a Platonist philosopher, and a professor of rhetoric, who is best known for his work the *Metamorphoses*, also known as *The Golden Ass*. Some light can be shed on Augustine's oblique reference to Apuleius here by comparing his discussion of Apuleius's *Apology for himself*, also known as *On Magic*, in *City of God* 8.19. In the Roman law of Apuleius's day, the practice of magic was illegal, and Apuleius had been accused of violating this prohibition. Instead of accusing the laws of being unjust while admitting the fact, Apuleius, in his defense, denies the fact. Apuleius's accusers evidently praised his character, even while lobbing the accusation of magic at him. When Augustine refers to those who "convict" Apuleius with praise rather than accusation, the point appears to be that even those predisposed both to praise Apuleius and to view him as capable of performing magical arts must deal with the fact that he himself denied the latter.

in these arts, were outdone by Moses, God's servant: when they performed the same wonders by nefarious arts, he, by invoking God alone, would overturn all of their schemes. But Moses himself and the other completely true prophets prophesied the Lord Christ and gave him great glory, and they foretold about him coming not as their equal, nor as their superior in the same miraculous power, but clearly as the Lord God of all, who became a human being for the sake of human beings. Therefore, he wished to perform the same sorts of deeds, lest there be a discordance if he would not himself do the very things he had done through those men. But nonetheless he also had to do something that was unique to him: to be born of a virgin, to rise from the dead, to ascend into heaven. If someone thinks *this* to be small potatoes for a god – I don't know what more he might be looking for![32]

14. Indeed, I think the kinds of things demanded of him are inappropriate for someone playing the part of a human being to do.[33] For "in the beginning was the Word and the Word was with God and the Word was God and all things were made through him."[34] Do you think that when he had assumed the human being he ought to have made another world, so that we might believe him to be the one through whom the world was made? But it would have been impossible for a world that is greater or equal to this one to come into being in this world. And had he made one inferior below this one, then this too would similarly have been considered small potatoes. Therefore since it was not fitting for him to make a new world, he made things new within the world. For a human being born of a virgin and raised from the dead to eternal life and exalted above the heavens is perhaps a mightier work than a world. Here they would likely reply that they do not believe that this happened. What, then, can be done with people who look down upon lesser deeds and do not believe greater ones? So, that life has been given back to the dead is believed, since others did it – and this is small potatoes for a god. That his own flesh is made from a virgin and raised from death to eternal life above the heaven is not believed, since no one has done it – and this befits a god. Accordingly, "what each person

32 As a sign of the letter's early circulation, part of this paragraph – from "But Moses" to "looking for!" – was quoted with approbation by John Cassian in *On the Incarnation of the Lord against Nestorius* 7.27. Selections from this work (though not 7.27) are translated in this volume on pp. 593–622.

33 Here, I am following modern editions, including the CSEL, which conjecture a *non* (whence, *in*appropriate) that is not present in the manuscripts.

34 John 1:1, 3.

thinks it easy for himself" not "to do" but to grasp, "this he readily accepts. Whatever goes beyond this, he considers as contrived, if not false."[35] I beg you not to be like those people.

15. These matters have been argued at great length and every twist and turn of the necessary questions have been laid bare to examination and discussion.[36] But faith opens a door for the intellect; faithlessness closes it. Who would not be moved to believe by the very sequence of events, which from the beginning is so wondrous, and by the very connection among ages, which gives faith concerning the present through the past and gives confirmation of what is earlier through what comes later, of what is ancient through what is more recent? One person, preeminent in his completely faithful piety, was chosen from the Chaldean nation; to him were revealed the divine promises, which, after the very long line of centuries, were fulfilled in the latest times – namely, those that foretold that in his seed all nations would find blessing.[37] Thus, worshiping the one true God and creator of the universe, the old man begat a son from his wife, who had been utterly deprived of the hope of childbirth by barrenness and old age. From that son there grew a most numerous people, which multiplied in Egypt where the divine governance, with frequent promises and fulfillments, had sent that offshoot from the eastern regions. It was brought out of Egyptian slavery a powerful nation, and, as the impious nations were struck with dreadful signs and miracles, it was led into the land of promise and was raised even higher when its kingdom was established. Later, when sin came to prevail – with outrageous acts of sacrilege the people routinely offended the true God who had conferred such wondrous gifts on them – the nation was stricken with various disasters and consoled with successes until it was led to the incarnation and announcement of Christ. It is this Christ – Word of God, Son of God, God who would come in the flesh, who would die, would rise, would ascend into heaven, would by his almighty name possess those peoples dedicated to him among all nations, and in whom remission of sins and eternal salvation would come to those who believe – that all the promises given to that nation, all the prophets, priests, sacrifices, the temple, and all the sacraments whatsoever express.

35 Sallustius, *On the Catiline War* 3.2. Sallust is speaking about the reader of history who only accepts stories of deeds that he thinks he himself could do, and therefore suspects stories of great men's deeds.

36 Augustine refers to another work.

37 See Gen 12:1–7, 15:5, 17:7, 18:8, 24:7; Rom 4:18; Gal 3:16.

16. Christ comes, and all the prophets' proclamations are fulfilled in his birth, life, deeds, words, sufferings, death, resurrection, and ascension. He sends the Holy Spirit and fills the faithful who were gathered in a single home and hoping in prayer and longing for this very promise.[38] And, filled with the Holy Spirit, they at once speak in the languages of all the nations; they boldly expose errors; they preach the most salutary truth; they exhort to repentance for the sinful living of one's past; they give assurance of pardon by divine grace. Suitable signs and miracles follow upon the preaching of piety and true religion. Cruel disbelief is stirred up against them; they endure what had been foretold; they hope for what had been promised; they teach what had been commanded. Few in number, they are spread throughout the world; with wondrous ease they convert peoples; among enemies, they increase; in persecutions, they advance; through dire straits, they expand to the very ends of the earth. Starting out as uneducated, lowly, and few as possible, they are illuminated, ennobled, and increased. The most distinguished abilities, the most elegant expressions, and the most wondrous expertise of the keen, the eloquent, and the learned – they bring these into submission to Christ and convert them to preaching the way of piety and salvation. As adverse events alternate with successful ones, they vigilantly practice endurance and self-control; as the world nears its end and in its weariness confirms that its last age is come, they ever more boldly look for the eternal happiness of the heavenly city, because this too is foretold. And in all these circumstances, the impious Gentiles' faithlessness rages against the church of Christ; it overcomes them by suffering and by confessing the unshaken faith amidst the savagery of her opponents. When that sacrifice which reveals the truth long veiled in hidden promises had replaced those sacrifices by which it had been prefigured, they were done away with by the destruction of the temple itself. The very nation of the Jews, being rejected on account of its faithlessness, was uprooted from their homes and dispersed through the entire world, so that it might carry the holy books everywhere, and thus is the prophetic testimony by which Christ and the church were foretold borne by these very enemies so that no one thinks it had been made up by us at that time. In the testimony, it is even foretold that they would not believe. Temples, images of the demons, and sacrilegious rites were toppled gradually one after another, as the

38 In the opening sentences of this paragraph, Augustine summarizes the Acts of the Apostles, beginning with the descent of the Spirit in Acts 2:1–12.

prophets had predicted. Heresies sprouted contrary to the name of Christ, though under the veil of Christ's name, so that the holy religion's doctrine would be trained, as had been announced before. All of these are read as predictions and seen as fulfillments, and based on so many great instances already seen, those that remain are expected to be fulfilled. Truly, what mind that longs for eternity and is disturbed by the brevity of the present life can contend against the light and eminence of this divine authority?

5, 17. Which arguments or writings of any of the philosophers, which laws of any city, can in any way be compared to the two precepts on which Christ says all the law and the prophets depend? "You shall love the Lord your God with all your heart and with all your soul and with all your mind, and you shall love your neighbor as yourself."[39] Here is physics, since all causes of all natures are in God the Creator; here is ethics, since the good and honorable life is not fashioned from any other source than when those whom one must love – namely, God and the neighbor – are loved as they are to be loved; here is logic, since there is no truth and the light of the rational soul other than God; here too is the praiseworthy security of the state, for the best city can neither be built nor be maintained except on the foundation and bond of faith and sturdy concord, when the common Good is loved, because it is the highest and most true God, and in him human beings love one another most sincerely since they love one another on account of him to whom they cannot hide the very mind by which they love.

18. As to that style of speaking in which holy scripture is written – how approachable it is to all, though it is penetrable to so few! Its more open contents, like an old friend, speak without ornamentation to the heart of both the learned and the unlearned; but in the parts it veils in mystery, it does not put on airs with haughty eloquence, which a slower and less learned mind might not be confident to approach, like a poor man approaching a rich one, but rather, it invites all with a humble speech, and not only feeds them with plain but also trains them with hidden truth, being consistent in both its open and its secret parts. But lest the open parts arouse disdain, the same truths are once again sought as hidden,[40] and being sought somehow makes them fresh, and being refreshed they become the heart's delight. Hence in a salutary way crooked minds are righted, small ones nourished,

39 Matt 22:37, 39, 40.

40 There is a play on words in Latin between the antonyms "open" (in Latin, *aperta*) and "hidden" (*operta*).

and great ones cheered. The mind that is an enemy to this doctrine is the one that either in its error does not recognize that the medicine is most salutary or in its sickness disdains it.

19. You see what a long letter I have written! So then, if any problem disturbs you and you would value us hashing it out, don't think you must observe the brevity of typical letters, for you know very well what lengthy letters the ancients tended to write when they were tackling something that they could not explain briefly. And if the custom of authors writing other sorts of letters is different, among our authors an authority more worthy of imitation has been given to us in this matter. So take note of the method of the apostolic epistles or even of those who have commented upon that divine eloquence, and don't let it vex you either to propose many questions, if many things bother you, or to dwell at considerable length on what you ask, so that it is possible – insofar as it can be for such as we are – that no cloud of doubt remain to obscure the light of truth.

20. For I know that Your Excellency is enduring the totally stubborn objections of certain people who think, or want it to be thought, that Christian doctrine is not conducive to the welfare of the state, because they prefer the state to stand not on the solid base of the virtues but on impunity for vices. No, with God it is not as it is with a human king or with some prince of a city, that whatever sin many people commit is left unpunished. But his mercy and grace, preached to human beings through the human being Christ, though bestowed through God and the Son of God, the very same Christ, does not forsake those who live by his faith and worship him piously. Whether they are enduring the evils of this life with patience and fortitude or using his goods with mercy and moderation, in either case they will receive an eternal reward in the heavenly and divine city, where hardship is no longer borne with distress nor lust restrained through diligence, but all that remains, without any difficulty and with perfect liberty, is the love of God and neighbor. May God's most merciful omnipotence keep you unharmed and ever happier, noble lord and rightly distinguished and most excellent son. I dutifully greet your holy mother, who is justly honored in Christ – may God hear her prayers on your behalf, as you merit. My holy brother and fellow bishop Possidius sends warm greetings to Your Excellence.[41]

41 Possidius (ca. 370–ca. 440) was bishop of Calama and a longtime companion who wrote Augustine's biography after his death in 430.

38

The Leporius Dossier

Introduction and Translation of Leporius, Statement of Amendment by Mark DelCogliano
Translation of Augustine, Letter 219 by Andrew Radde-Gallwitz
Translation of John Cassian, On the Incarnation of the Lord against Nestorius Book 1 by Mark DelCogliano

INTRODUCTION

In the late 410s or early 420s, in an epistle that is no longer extant, a monk in Gaul named Leporius, motivated by a desire to avoid attributing change and the human condition to God in the incarnation, wrote that he was disinclined to confess that God was born of a woman. Instead, he preferred to say that a perfect human being was born along with God rather than as God. The epistle sought to demonstrate this basic point and related Christological consequences through the interpretation of several key passages of scripture. But the form of Christological dualism that he advocated soon came to be deemed aberrant. When he refused to recant his views, Proculus, bishop of Marseilles, and Cillenius, a bishop of an unknown see in southern Gaul, formally rebuked Leporius in circumstances that remain unclear and expelled him from Gaul. Along with two disciples named Domninus and Bonus, he took refuge in North Africa with Augustine.

Under the influence of the bishop of Hippo he recanted his earlier Christological opinions. Leporius then authored a *Statement of Amendment* (*Libellus emendationis*), which was addressed to Proculus and Cillenius and signed by Leporius, Domninus, and Bonus. This is the first document of the dossier translated below. Here Leporius demonstrates his abandonment of his earlier Christological opinions by admitting that, though motivated by genuine piety, he had erred through ignorance. He also outlined his corrected Christological views and articulated his reasons for holding them. He admitted that his former views had the unintended consequence of positing two Christs and adding a fourth person to the Trinity. He now viewed the incarnation as a mixture of divinity and humanity without confusion or detriment to either nature, a mixture in which the properties of each nature are shared by the one Christ, the incarnate Word, who is the subject of all the human experiences of Jesus in respect of his humanity. He returned to several of the key scriptural texts he had used to support his earlier position and reinterpreted them in the light of his new understanding. Many scholars take Augustine himself to be ultimate source of Leporius's revised Christological opinions.

Leporius presented and read the *Statement of Amendment* in Carthage in the presence of Augustine and three other bishops: Aurelius of Carthage, Florentius of Hippo Dhiarrytus, and Secundus of Aquensis in Numidia. All of them signed the document, signaling their approval. The four bishops then forwarded the *Statement of Amendment* to Proculus and Cillenius, along with a cover letter, which has been preserved in Augustine's epistolary corpus as *Letter* 219. This is the second document of the dossier translated below. Here Augustine and his fellow bishops affirmed Leporius's repudiation of his former views, testified to his Christological orthodoxy, and urged the Gallic bishops to welcome him back into the church of Gaul.

Nonetheless, Leporius remained in Africa, where he was ordained a presbyter.[1] It is not clear why Leporius never returned to Gaul, especially since in the first book of his *On the Incarnation of the Lord against Nestorius*, written in late 429 or early 430, John Cassian reported that the *Statement of Amendment* had been received favorably in Gaul. The entirety of this first book is translated below as the third document in the dossier. Here Cassian depicted Leporius as a kind of Nestorius before Nestorius, attributing his Christological errors to his adherence to the teaching of Pelagius. Because of the confluence of Christological dualism and Pelagianism – whether real or imagined – in both Nestorius and Leporius, Cassian found in the latter not only a Western precursor to the Eastern heresiarch but also a powerful example of a heretic who had repudiated his errors in an admirable way, an example which Cassian suggested Nestorius himself should follow. In his treatment of Leporius, Cassian quoted four passages from the *Statement of Amendment*, indicating its early reception in Gaul and its importance for Cassian's

1 See Cassian, *On the Incarnation* 1.4.2–3. A presbyter named Leporius is mentioned by Augustine in *Sermon* 356 and *Letter* 223. It is not certain that this Leporius should be identified with the Leporius from Gaul, but it seems likely.

interpretation of Nestorius. The four passages of the *Statement of Amendment* that Cassian quoted are marked within the translation of the *Statement* itself, with superscript angle brackets (< >) indicating the beginning and end of each quotation. The four passages are labeled A, B, C, and D.

The translation of Leporius's statement is based on the critical edition of R. Demeulenaere in *Foebadius, Victricius, Leporius, Vincentius Lerinensis, Evagrius, Ruricius*, CCSL 64 (Turnhout: Brepols, 1985), 111–123. The translation of Augustine's letter is based on the critical edition of Al. Goldbacher, *S. Aureli Augustini Operum Sectio II: S. Augustini Epistulae*, CSEL 57 (Vienna: F. Tempsky, 1911), 428–431, with reference to Demeulenaere's edition in CCSL 64, 104–106. The translation of the first book of John Cassian's *On the Incarnation* is based on the critical edition of Michael Petschenig, *Iohannis Cassiani Opera, Pars I*, CSEL 17 (Vienna: F. Tempsky, 1888), 237–245.

TRANSLATION

Leporius, *Statement of Amendment*

To the most blessed lords and most venerable priests of God, Proculus and Cillenius, from the lowly Leporius.

1. [A<]I do not know what I should accuse in myself first, O my venerable lords and most blessed priests. I cannot discover what I should make excuses for in myself first. So strongly had pride born of inexperience, so strongly had foolish simplicity with harmful convictions, so strongly had zeal with immoderation, so strongly (to speak more truly) had a weak faith that was withering away, so strongly had I allowed all these to flourish in me simultaneously, that it is at the same time an embarrassment to have succumbed to such and so many [vices] and an overwhelming joy to have been able to cast them from my soul.[>A]

Therefore, I acknowledge my offense and I am willingly my own accuser. But I hope for mercy since I acted out of ignorance. For indeed it would be indefensible for me to make a case for the sin if I should have eagerly done something intentional in full knowledge of the fact. "I call on God as a witness against my soul,"[2] I believed my error to be the truth and considered the darkest gloom to be the purest light. "Zeal for God but without knowledge"[3] deceived me, being as I was incautious. But now, as I wandered in

2 2 Cor 1:23. 3 Rom 10:2.

rough places and rambled through tangles of thorns, his mercy has called me back to the straight path – which we believe will be pleasing to Your Beatitude. And therefore the crooked ways in me have been made straight and the rough places turned into smooth paths.[4] And so, having been instructed by my fathers, your fellow priests and brothers, the darkness has already been scattered and I understand in what way I was partially blind. And thus recognition of this truth makes me a humble supplicant.

I confess that I erred out of ignorance. And I overstepped the rule of truth on certain points, though it seemed to me that I was maintaining it perfectly. My inexperience is obvious. Indeed it is all the more burdensome to me because I attempted to uphold, at the cost of giving scandal to many, something which, as is now clearer than light, I had presumed by an error of human judgment rather than through the reasoning of faith that one must defend. But what else could have happened except that my own foolishness would live in me, since as a disciple I had myself as my own teacher! And surely humility has shattered that presumption of mine which lack of knowledge animated. But woe is me, for I was found both rash and proud at the same time! But with your permission I am already moving on from these matters and I shall not hesitate to do what must be done. I shall hasten to cure the wounded whom I injured when they were healthy. There will be no embarrassment in taking medicine because no precautions were taken to preserve good health. Where discord was born, there let peace grow.

2. To this end, that epistle, which became the source of scandal and the obstacle to charity, was previously written by me in simplicity, but on certain points, as I now acknowledge, I put things in a way opposed to the faith. Thus, I beg, in the light of the profession in this epistle and the authority of Your Sacredness, that you locate the relevant section [of the original letter] where claims were made that ought to be trampled on and obliterated and ideas opposed to the truth were argued out of ignorance so that it may be known and made patently clear to all through a just judgment that what was zeal for the faith contrary to the truth has been cut out of the body of the same epistle and condemned.

I confess, O my lords, that certain brothers with better insight into interior matters raised complaints, but we ourselves groped about with more external matters, and having been trapped in our own fog we blamed our

4 See Isa 40:4; Luke 3:5.

blindness on those who perceived things more accurately. But now, since by the Lord's favor our eyes have been opened, we see the true light along with them. We have regained our sight in the same grace of light, the healing mud having been put on our eyes by the true physician.[5] With the clearest possible vision we gaze upon Jesus Christ the Lord, not in the mistaken way as we did earlier, but as is the truth. In accordance with the truth of the symbol,[6] we now confess with unwavering steadfastness that which we were reluctant to say in our previous definition, when we were seduced not by any impiety but by error, namely that God was born of Mary. Although we did not deny, even then, that Christ the Son of God was born of the holy Mary, as you yourselves remember, we were nonetheless inattentive to the mystery of the faith and said that a perfect human being was born *along with* God, not that God himself was born *as* a human being, precisely because we were afraid of attributing the human condition to the divinity. Oh, foolish wisdom! As if God would not despise being born *along with* a human being, and yet in anticipation of that status he himself would spurn being born *as* a human being – as if he could do the former, but there was no chance of his doing the latter.

3. I firmly believe only one thing is impossible for God: what he does not want to do. If what God wanted was that he wanted to be born, without any question I believe that he could do it.[7] For the status of God can never be in danger. Having become a human being for our sake, he did not consider it unworthy to be produced from a human being. For he also did not deem it unworthy to make the female human being[8] from whom he was born as a human being.

[B<]If, therefore, we fail to perceive this power of God and we think about such matters according to our own understanding and our own reasoning, and if because of this we seek to avoid God seeming to do something beneath himself by claiming that the human being was born along with God, thereby letting us give only to God alone what belongs to God and attribute only to the human being alone what belongs to the human being, then we are obviously introducing a fourth person into the Trinity and out of the one Son of God we are beginning to make not one but two Christs. May Christ himself our Lord and God preserve us from that!

5 See John 9:6. 6 That is, the creed.

7 See Tertullian, *On the Flesh of Christ* 3.1, translated in this volume on pp. 147–148.

8 In Latin, *ipsam hominem*.

Therefore, we confess that Jesus Christ our Lord and God, the only Son of God, who was born from the Father before the ages, in these last days was born of the Holy Spirit and the ever-virgin Mary and became God the human being. And while we confess the twofold substance of the flesh and the Word, with the pious belief of faith we accept one and the same God and human being to be indivisible. And we claim furthermore that from the moment of his taking on flesh, just as everything which belonged to God passed over to the human being, so too everything that belonged to the human being came to God. It is in this sense that "the Word became flesh,"[9] not that he began to be what he was not by some change or transformation, but that by the power of the divine economy the Word of the Father, though never parted from the Father, deigned to become a human being in the proper sense of the term. Indeed, the Only-Begotten became incarnate through that hidden mystery that he alone knows. For indeed it is ours to believe, his to know! And so, just as God the Word himself, by taking on everything that belongs to the human being, is a human being, [so] too the assumed human being, by receiving everything that belongs to God, can be nothing other than God. Yet just because he is said to be incarnate and mixed,[10] we ought not to hold that there is any diminishment of his substance. For God knows how to be mixed without any detriment to himself and yet to be truly mixed. He who knows how to give the whole of himself without suffering any loss also knows how to receive into himself without growing by addition.

4. Therefore, we should not think that when God and the human being were mixed together some sort of body was produced as if through a confusion of flesh and Word. For this would be to make conjectures, as is necessitated by our weak understanding according to the visible proofs of our experiences, based on the way equal created things enter mutually into one another. Heaven forbid that we should believe such a thing, that we should think that two natures are reduced to one substance in some conflated way! For that kind of commixture is a corruption of both parts. For God, who contains but cannot be contained, who enters into but cannot be entered into, who fills but cannot be filled, who is at once everywhere in his entirety and spread out everywhere, through an infusion of his own

9 John 1:14.

10 In Latin, *immixtus*. This term can mean either "mixed" or "unmixed." That it means the former here seems indicated by what follows.

power is mixed with the human nature out of mercy,[>B] but the human nature is not mixed with the divine nature. Therefore, the flesh profited from being in the Word, but the Word did not profit from being in the flesh. And nonetheless it is true as true can be that "the Word became flesh."[11] But as we said, this happened only specifically in terms of the person, not in terms of the nature [shared] with the Father or with the Holy Spirit. For the only-begotten God, the true God who is one in nature with the Father and the Holy Spirit, is distinct in person. For we do not say that the Father is who the Son is, nor again do we say that the same Son is who the Father is, nor in turn do we call the Holy Spirit "Father" or "Son." Rather, we distinguish the persons by their distinctive properties, naming God the Father specifically "Father," calling God the Son specifically "Son," and confessing God the Holy Spirit to be specifically "Holy Spirit." And even though we say God, God, God three times, we do not believe in three gods but in one who is perfect in the Trinity of his own omnipotence.

5. [C<]Therefore, God the human being, Jesus Christ, the Son of God was born to us specifically of the Holy Spirit and the ever-virgin Mary. And so, Word and flesh became one, each in the other,[12] so that, while each substance remains naturally in its own perfection, both what is divine shares in the humanity and what is human participates in the divinity without either suffering any disadvantage to itself. Nor is it the case that God is one and the human being another, but that same God who is also the human being, and in turn the human being who is also God, is called and truly is Jesus Christ, the one Son of God. And accordingly we must always act and believe in such a way that we do not deny that the same God who became a human being is, from the moment he took on flesh, the Lord Jesus Christ, Son of God, the true God, whom we confess is always with the Father and equal to the Father before the ages. Nor do we believe that he became God as it were gradually over time, in possession of one state before the resurrection and of another after the resurrection, but that he was always in possession of the same fullness and power.[>C]

6. Furthermore, because he bore all our infirmities,[13] that is, the infirmities of our nature, he also truly took our experiences into himself according to the flesh to prove that he was a true human being. Since our mortality likewise ran its course in him, "he advanced," as the evangelist says, "in age

11 John 1:14. 12 In Latin, *in alterutrum unum fit Verbum et caro.*
13 See Isa 53:4.

and in wisdom,"[14] by power, not by necessity. He became hungry, thirsty, and tired; he was scourged and crucified; he died and arose again. Accordingly, he was not changed from the nature of the divinity. For we have already stated above that the nature of the divinity is unchangeable, immutable, and impassible. [D<]But because God the Word graciously descended upon a human being by taking on a human being, and because the human being ascended to God the Word by taking on God, God the Word in his totality became a human being in its totality. For it was not God the Father who became a human being, nor the Holy Spirit, but the Only-Begotten of the Father. Accordingly, we must accept that there is one person of the flesh and the Word, so that we may faithfully believe without any doubt that one and the same indivisible Son of God, who has also always been called "the giant of twin substance,"[15] "in the days of his flesh"[16] always truly bore everything that belongs to the human being and also always truly possessed what belongs to God, "since even though he was crucified out of weakness, yet he lives by the power of God.[>D]"[17] On account of this, we should no longer be afraid of saying that God was born of a human being, that according to the human being God suffered, God died, and so forth. Rather, we should glory in saying that God was born and that the same God suffered according to the human being. "For I am not ashamed of the gospel," says the Apostle, "for it is the power of God that leads to salvation for everyone who believes."[18] For "everyone who believes,[19] the power of God that leads to salvation" is believing that God suffered according to the human being. For those who do not believe, however, refusing to believe that God was crucified according to the flesh is reckoned "the weakness of God"[20] that leads to perdition. For this reason the same Apostle says again, "But we proclaim Christ and him crucified" and "the power of God and the wisdom of God. For God's foolishness is wiser than human wisdom, and the weakness of God is stronger than human strength."[21]

For to those who do not believe, what would seem as foolish and as weak as when they hear that God, the Son of God, was crucified? But "it pleased God through the foolishness of what we proclaim to save those who believe."[22] For our faith consists especially in this, that we believe that the only

14 Luke 2:52. 15 This is the line from Ambrose's hymn, *Intende qui regis Israel.*
16 Heb 5:7. 17 2 Cor 13:4. 18 Rom 1:16.
19 Here we read *omni credenti* instead of *utique.* 20 See 1 Cor 1:25.
21 1 Cor 1:23–25, with omissions. 22 1 Cor 1:21.

Son of God is not adopted but God's very own, that he is not an illusion but true, that he is not temporal but eternal, that he endured everything on our behalf according to the flesh, that he struggled not for himself but for us, and that it was not for his own sake but for ours (since we lay dead) that he came out of mercy from the heights to the depths. For as the Apostle says, "though he was in the form of God, he did not count equality with God a thing to be grasped, but emptied himself, taking the form of a slave," and so on.[23]

7. Could anything be clearer than recognizing the mystery of so great an economy in this testimony? For who is in the form of God but God? Let us see how the source of fullness emptied itself. Wasn't it by the form of God accepting the form of the slave? Though he was Lord principally, didn't he graciously assume those things that belong to the slave? Out of kindness and pity for us the Word made flesh[24] emptied [himself] qua person of what he possessed qua nature by bearing or rather by doing what was beneath him. Having entered into the true condition of humanity[25] by being obedient in the human being, he, in himself through his humility and obedience,[26] restored to our nature what we lost through disobedience in Adam.[27] Though he died in the flesh, he lives forever, giving life to all things along with the Father in the Spirit, and he will never again die in the time that remains, having been raised by the Father in the same flesh [in which he lived and died]. He who is the Only-Begotten of the living God and has been alive since before the ages becomes for us "the firstborn of the dead."[28] He who for our sakes experienced poverty in time and need in the human being receives on our behalf that which he always has for himself in abundance in the Father. "Oh, the depth of the riches and wisdom and knowledge of God! How unsearchable are his judgments and how inscrutable his ways!"[29] Everything he receives is given to him for our sake. But he bestows it upon all because God, the bestower of all things, makes himself known as God in the giving and makes himself known as a human being in the receiving, "so that at the name of Jesus every knee should bend, in heaven and on earth and under the earth, and every tongue confess that Jesus Christ is Lord, to the glory of God the Father."[30]

This is our faith, and "this is the change effected by the right hand of the Most High"[31] in amendment for the better. So we believe; so we

23 Phil 2:6–7. 24 See John 1:14. 25 See Phil 2:7. 26 See Phil 2:8.
27 See 1 Cor 15:22 and 45. 28 Col 1:18. 29 Rom 11:33.
30 Phil 2:10–11. 31 Ps 76(77):11.

maintain. "And this is not our doing, for it is the gift of God."[32] It is not something earned by our own wisdom, lest we glory in ourselves. "For we are his handiwork, created in Christ"[33] a long time ago, but now once more with the apostolic men bringing us to birth in the light, we are born in the same Christ. Therefore, honor and glory be to him always.[34]

8. Let us next take up what we expounded in that epistle so foolishly, though out of ignorance, and which we now confess to be execrable. We judged those things which are fitting to Christ (toil, devotion, merit, and faith) to be so thoroughly incompatible with the Son of God that, when we call to mind what we said, we credit our stupidity with the most profound blindness and we see clearly how certain individuals were roused against us with good reason. It is as if we made Christ almost like one of the saints – though we never had this in our heart. Ascribing to him "who is God over all"[35] that which is characteristic of a simple and bare mortality, we numbered him in a certain way among all the other [saints]. Although he is called "the head of the body" and truly is "the head of the body, the church,"[36] and although according to the flesh he is from the same lump from which the entire human race descends (though it is known that he came without sin),[37] nonetheless he who is unique should not be counted with all the others. Furthermore, those things which can have a limit should not be ascribed to him, for it was said to him, "For God does not give the Spirit according to limit."[38] After all, where there is fullness of deity,[39] there is neither limit nor measure. He knows nothing of attaining the goal of good deeds through toil, devotion, faith, and merit, for he is infinite and does everything through his unbounded power. Indeed, he becomes a human being and is truly born a human being according to the flesh, but he does not cease to be God. He is nourished, makes progress, grows up, reaches maturity, and, "like a lamb that is dumb before its shearer,"[40] he endures abuse and is scourged. "The author of life"[41] comes to the flesh and does not reject accursed death. But he does not accomplish all these things out of necessity as one of us. Rather, "having the power to lay down his soul and having the power to take it up again"[42] he graciously and willingly endured all these things.

32 Eph 2:8. 33 Eph 2:10. 34 See Rom 16:17; 1 Tim 1:17.
35 Rom 9:5. 36 Eph 5:23; Col 1:18. 37 See Heb 4:15. 38 John 3:34.
39 See Col 2:9. 40 Isa 53:7; Acts 8:32. 41 Acts 3:15. 42 John 10:18.

9. I think that we ought not fail to mention another point I included in that same epistle when I strayed through a similar error, namely that Christ our Lord fulfilled everything connected with his sufferings in such a way that, as a perfect human being, he was not in the least assisted by the help of his divinity. What I mean is that I wanted to designate a perfect human being in Christ, so that I could also assert that the Word of the Father was a stranger to these sufferings. I tried to prove that the human being alone by himself had experienced all these things through the capacities of his mortal nature, without any assistance from the deity. How truly blind I was since I confessed that the human being was received into God but refused to let anything connected with the human being be received into God! In regard to this issue, without any question, God definitely received into himself the whole human being so that the human being alone did not by himself experience those things which we through natural judgment consider unworthy of God, but God accomplished them through the human being and in the human being, having himself become a human being for us by the power and mystery of the divine economy. Then, lest any of my stupidity should go unmentioned, I, being an exceptionally erudite writer who corroborates misunderstandings using still more misunderstandings, thought that what we set out above would be best understood if I tried to confirm this very thing by that testimony in which it is written, "God, my God, why have you forsaken me?"[43] And thus [I argued that] "the Lord of glory"[44] had let out the words of this cry on the cross in order to demonstrate that the suffering accomplished by the human being in such great anguish occurred without any assistance from the deity. Therefore, if he let out this cry when he was in anguish to demonstrate that the suffering was human, then, in order to demonstrate the same suffering, he also ought to have cried out with the same words at the time when he was struck; he also ought to have uttered the same words at the time when he was mocked with that crown of many wounds, which has as many pains as thorns. Or perhaps the latter were easier for Christ to bear, while the first was harder? I think that he who deigned to have one will to undertake all these things also had one and the same strength to endure all these things.

Therefore, he cried out, as is written, and while hanging on the wood of the cross he let out this cry at the moment of death, not so that he might

43 Ps 21(22):1, cited in Matt 27:46 and Mark 15:34. 44 1 Cor 2:8; Jas 2:1.

demonstrate that the human suffering was accomplished in himself, which is shown without the testimony of this cry by the incidents themselves and by the clear facts, but rather so that he might truly and unmistakably show that the Son of God was about to die according to the flesh. And using, as it were, the voice of this flesh, he spoke in the past tense instead of the future tense because his death on the cross would inevitably result in his earthly body being abandoned by God for a time – and not only by God but also by his own soul that remained united with God. Thus, as he was dying he provided us with testimony of it before it actually happened. For the dead flesh would not have been able to utter this cry after his spirit had been given up.[45] Otherwise who would believe that Christ was really dead?

God did not [forsake] the human being in the midst of his sufferings but rather the body in the state of death, since he deigned to suffer in the human being according to the flesh. And according to the law of human death, the divinity, along with the soul united to it, did not abandon the crucified human being to punishment, but rather it deserted the lifeless flesh for a time. And as Christ, the Son of God, at the time of his death was laid in the tomb, so the same Christ, the Son of God, descended into hell, as the blessed Apostle said, "In saying, 'He ascended,' what does it mean except that he first descended into the lower parts of the earth? He who descended is he who also ascended above all the heavens."[46] Surely our Lord and God himself, Jesus Christ, the only Son of God, who descended with his soul into hell, ascended with his soul and body to heaven. Accordingly, both now and in the future let us venerate the God and human being together, the perfect and same one as Son of God, who is true God for eternal ages.

10. Therefore, just as I believe and confess in accordance with the great mystery of piety, that my Lord and God was born in the flesh, suffered in the flesh, died in the flesh, was raised in the flesh, was lifted up in the flesh, and was glorified in the flesh, so too do I believe that he himself specifically in the same flesh will come to pass judgment upon the living and the dead, and each will receive from the same one the everlasting reward for what each deserves.[47]

And moreover, so that going forward I may leave no excuse for anyone to suspect me [of heresy], I said back then [in the epistle], or rather I said in response to objections, that our Lord Jesus Christ was ignorant according

45 See John 19:30. 46 Eph 4:9–10. 47 See 2 Tim 4:1; 1 Pet 4:5.

to the human being. But now, not only do I not presume to say such a thing, but also I anathematize my prior statement precisely because we cannot say that the Lord of the prophets was ignorant even according to the human being. But we have dealt with the issues arising from all the rest of the allegations either in lecture or in preaching or in conference with the brothers. In these contexts, we may have expressed disagreement in terms of our understanding rather than over the faith itself, and since it would take too long to go through each one in accordance with the faith laid out in this epistle, let us confess most sincerely that we either accept or reject all those [teachings] precisely as the regulations of the catholic church hold. We call upon Christ the Lord as our witness that we do not profess one thing publicly and hold another thing in our heart. And to be sure, the disgrace of every heresy must be condemned by us, because with a pure conscience we always recognize ourselves as catholics on the basis of catholics. We utter an anathema against all the heretics: Photinus, Arius, Sabellius, Eunomius, Valentinus, Apollinarius, Manichaeus, and all who have stood against sound doctrine. For even if we slipped with our tongue or understanding, we stayed true in our will and heart, as is written, "There is one who slips with his tongue but not from his heart. For who has not sinned with his tongue?"[48]

11. Indeed, my most venerable lords and most blessed priests, as far as it has been possible for me I have become "a son of peace."[49] Because I did not offend in small matters but in those of the greatest consequence, in line with the Apostle's statement, "For whoever shall have kept the whole law but will offend in one point has become guilty of all of it,"[50] I made myself guilty of all of it in the whole of my heart. But in this matter I have shown that those who pursued me (admittedly without pleasure) had perfect charity, because I have changed for the better upon receiving the fullness of their love as quickly as they pursued me with perfect intention and zeal when I had lost my way. But with God as my witness I declare that I wish for and desire nothing more than peace. The only thing left for us to do now is ask again and again: grant pardon by forgiving us and bring it to completion by praying for us. I wish you, my fathers, life in the Lord.

12. I, Leporius, have dictated this statement according to my understanding. Therein I wanted to give the fullest possible expression of my

48 Sir 19:16–17. 49 Luke 10:6. 50 Jas 2:10.

faith which, God willing, I will hold even unto death. After reading it out in the presence of the holy bishops in the church of Carthage I have signed it.

I, Domninus, hold this faith and confess it and have signed this statement.
I, Bonus, hold this faith and confess it and have signed this statement.

The subscription of the bishops who acted as witnesses:

I, Aurelius, bishop of the church of Carthage, signed the statement presented to us and read out by Leporius.
I, Augustine, bishop of the church of Hippo Regius, signed the statement presented to us and read out by Leporius.
I, Florentius, bishop of the church of Hippo Dhiarrytus, signed the statement presented to us and read out by Leporius.
I, Secundus, bishop of the church of Aquensis or Magarmeltana, signed the statement presented to us and read out by Leporius.

*
* *

Augustine, *Letter* 219

To our most beloved lords and honorable brothers and fellow priests Proculus and Cillenius, Bishops Aurelius, Augustine, Florentius, and Secundus send greeting in the Lord.

1. When our son Leporius, having been rightly and properly rebuked by Your Sanctity for the impertinence of his error, came to us after his expulsion from there, we received him in a state of salutary agitation and in need of correction and care. For just as you obeyed the Apostle's decree to "rebuke the disorderly," likewise we his decree to "console the fainthearted and take in the weak."[51] For when "the man was carried away in some fault"[52] – not some trivial matter, but one that concerns the only-begotten Son of God – he lost his sense for what is right and couldn't perceive what is true: that "the Word was in the beginning and the Word was with God and the Word was God,"[53] but when "the fullness of time had come,"[54] "the Word became flesh and dwelt among us."[55] He

51 1 Thess 5:14. 52 Gal 6:1. 53 John 1:1. 54 Gal 4:4. 55 John 1:14.

denied that God became a human being, no doubt to avoid the consequence of an unworthy mutation or corruption of the divine substance, by which [the Word] is equal to the Father.[56] Nor did he notice that he introduced a fourth person into the Trinity, which is quite foreign to the sound faith and to the truth of the catholic symbol. So to the best of our abilities and with the Lord's help, we have instructed him in a "spirit of gentleness,"[57] especially because when the "vessel of election"[58] noted this, he added, "examine yourself, lest you too be tempted."[59] And so, lest such people rejoice that they have already come so far in their spiritual progress as to think that now they can't be tempted like human beings are, he added, most beloved and honorable brothers, a salutary and irenic instruction, that we each "bear one another's burdens because in this way we fulfill the law of Christ; for whoever considers himself to be something when he is nothing deceives himself."[60]

2. Yet we would have probably been entirely unable to carry out his correction if you had not previously condemned his faults. Therefore, the same one who is our Lord and healer, using us as his implements and ministers, through you pierced the swelling and through us soothed the pain, as he said, "I will strike and I will heal."[61] The same one who is caretaker and provider of his own house through you destroyed what was badly built and through us raised up what was in need of construction. The same one who carefully tends his own land through you pulled up what was unfruitful and harmful and through us planted what is useful and fecund. Let us not, then, give the glory to ourselves but to the mercy of him who holds us and our words in his hand. And just as our humility has praised your ministerial care for our aforementioned son, so too may Your Sanctity rejoice in our ministerial care. Accordingly, with the heart of a father and a brother, receive the one corrected by us with the leniency of mercy as we received the one rebuked by you with the severity of mercy. For though different roles were played by you and by us, yet by both of us a single love achieved what is necessary for our brother's salvation. Therefore, the one God achieved it, since "God is love."[62]

3. Hence just as he has been received by us in person, so too may he be received by you through his letter. In fact, we have seen fit to subscribe to his letter in our own hand testifying that it is his. Indeed, when he was

56 See John 5:18; Phil 2:6. 57 Gal 6:1. 58 Acts 9:15. 59 Gal 6:1.
60 Gal 6:2–3. 61 Deut 32:39. 62 1 John 4:8, 16.

admonished, he easily grasped that God became a human being, since "the Word became flesh"[63] and "the Word was God."[64] The Apostle taught him that the Word became this not by losing what he was but by assuming what he was not; for "he emptied himself," not letting go of the "form of God" but "taking the form of a slave."[65] So this was his concern when he did not want to confess that God was born from a woman, that God was crucified and endured other human weaknesses: that we not believe the divinity to have changed into a human being or to have been corrupted by mixture with a human being. A reverent fear, but a reckless error: he reverently saw that divinity cannot change but recklessly presumed that the Son of Man can be separated from the Son of God, such that the two are different and that there is no other Christ than these or rather that there are two Christs. But afterwards he recognized that the Word of God, that is, the only-begotten Son of God, became Son of Man in such a way that neither of the two turned into the other; rather, with each remaining in his own substance, God in a human being underwent human things in such a way that he preserved the divine things integrally in himself. He confessed Christ to be God the human being without any fear and he had greater fear of adding a fourth person in the Trinity than of any diminishment of the substance of the divinity. We scarcely doubt that Your Charity will freely accept this as his correction and will make note of it to those for whom his error was a scandal, since also those persons who came with him to us have been corrected and restored with him, as was made clear by their subscriptions, which they made in our presence. It remains that you, made glad by the salvation of a brother, deign to gladden us in return with a reply from Your Blessedness. We wish you, most beloved and honorable brothers, to fare well in the Lord as you remember us.

*

* *

John Cassian, *On the Incarnation of the Lord against Nestorius*, Book 1

1, 1. The tales of the poets relate that long ago the hydra grew stronger by sustaining injuries, springing up again after its numerous heads had been cut off. Thus, owing to a new and bizarre miracle, loss was a kind of gain for

63 John 1:14. 64 John 1:1. 65 Phil 2:6–7.

the monster, which multiplied every time it was killed. Its horrific fecundity produced two more of everything that the sword of the decapitator sliced off, until the man who was assiduously seeking to mow down that monster, toiling and sweating, his strength fading in the face of exertions so persistently ineffective, bolstered his courage for battle with the art of strategy, and by the application of fire, as they tell us, he cut off with a burning sword the multiplying brood of that hideous body, and with the inward parts thus seared, and the rebellious throbbings of that ghastly fecundity cauterized, at long last those monstrous births ceased.[66]

2. Now heresies in the churches bear a resemblance to that hydra which the fables of the poets invented. For they too hiss against us with deadly tongues, they too spit lethal poison, and they too spring up again when their heads are cut off. But because medicine should not be lacking when sickness returns, and because the more serious the illness the more quickly the remedy should be applied, our Lord God is able to bring it to pass that, in the church's battles, the truth can accomplish what the fictions of the pagans invented about the death of that hydra, and furthermore the fiery sword of the Holy Spirit can cauterize, in the new heretical offspring needing to be destroyed, all the inward parts of that most dangerous birth, so that at long last its horrific fecundity may stop arising from the throes of its death.

2, 1. For these shoots of that monstrous seed are no new thing in the churches. The harvest of the Lord's field has always endured burrs and briars, and in it the shoots of choking weeds have incessantly sprung up.[67] For hence have sprouted the Ebionites, hence the Sabellians, hence the Arians, hence too the Eunomians and Macedonians, hence the Photinians and Apollinarians, and all the other thorns and thistles of the churches that destroy the fruits of good faith.

2. The first of these was Ebion. In his excessive focus on affirming the Lord's fleshiness[68] he robbed it of its conjunction with the divinity. After him, in reaction to the just-mentioned heresy, there broke out the schism of Sabellius. By contending that there was no difference between the Father, Son, and Holy Spirit, he mixed together the persons of the sacred and ineffable Trinity, as far as was possible, in a blasphemous confusion. What

66 Cassian recounts here the second labor of Heracles. In most retellings he is assisted by Iolaus who cauterized each neck when Heracles decapitated it.

67 See Matt 13:24–30.

68 In Latin, *incarnationem*.

followed next after this man whom we have just described was the impiety of Arius's perverseness. In order to avoid the appearance of mixing the sacred persons, he said that there were different and dissimilar substances in the Trinity. Eunomius came after him, it is true, but he very much subscribed to the same wickedness as him. Though he affirmed that the persons of the divine Trinity were similar to each other, yet he also contended that they differed from each other, and so while admitting their likeness he denied their equality.

3. And there is also Macedonius, who blasphemed against the Holy Spirit with an impiety that cannot be forgiven.[69] Though he said that the Father and the Son were of the same substance, he nevertheless called the Holy Spirit a creature. Thus he was guilty of sinning against the entire divinity because no harm can come to anything in the Trinity without injuring the entire Trinity. As for Photinus, though he said that Jesus who was born of the Virgin was God, yet he erred in imagining that the beginning of God coincided with the beginning of the human being. But Apollinarius, giving no careful thought to how the human being was united to God, mistakenly believed that he did not have a human soul. For it is no less an error to add to the Lord Jesus Christ what does not belong to him than it is to rob him of what does belong to him. After all, anything said of him that deviates from what he actually is, even though it may seem to be honoring him, is actually an insult.

4. And so, each one gives birth to a heresy that is unlike other heresies: they all differ from one another, it is true, but all of them nevertheless think in a manner contrary to the faith. And recently too, that is, in our own days, we witnessed a poisonous heresy spring up from the greatest city of the Belgae.[70] Its error is certain but its name is uncertain because there is still doubt whether it ought to be called old or new, given the fact that it arose with a fresh head from the ancient stock of the Ebionites. For it is new in terms of its advocates, but old in terms of its errors.

5. Indeed, putting forth the blasphemy that our Lord Jesus Christ was born as an ordinary human being,[71] it asserted that his subsequent attainment of the honor and power of God was due to his human merit and not his divine nature, and that because of this he did not always have deity

69 See Mark 3:28–29; Matt 12:31–32; Luke 12:10.
70 The city is Trier and the heresy is that of Leporius.
71 In Latin, *solitarium hominem.*

itself in virtue of the property of the divinity united to himself, but rather merited it subsequently as a reward for his toil and suffering. Surely since it puts forward the blasphemy that our Lord and Savior was not born as God but was assumed by God, without question it borders on this heresy which has just now appeared[72] and is, as it were, its sibling and kin, in harmony with the Ebionites as much as with these new heretics.[73] Indeed it arrived at a time between both of them, but it is nonetheless conjoined with both of them in perverseness. Although there are several others like those which we have mentioned, it would take too long to recount them all. For it is not our task at present to enumerate those that have died out, but to refute those that are new.

3, 1. It is very much our opinion that this one fact should not be omitted, a fact which was peculiar and particular to that heresy mentioned above,[74] which descended from the error of Pelagius: that when they said that Jesus Christ had lived as an ordinary human being without any contamination of sin, they went even further to declare that human beings could also be without sin if they liked. For they supposed that if Jesus Christ, as an ordinary human being, was without sin, then it followed that all human beings could, without the assistance of God, also be whatever he could be as an ordinary human being who lacked fellowship with God. And so they made no distinction between every human being and our Lord Jesus Christ, since any human being could by exertion and diligence surely merit just the same as Christ had merited by his effort and toil.

2. In consequence of this it happened that they rushed into an even greater and more monstrous madness and said that our Lord Jesus Christ had come into this world not to bring redemption to humankind but to give an example of good works – that is, so that, by following his teaching and advancing by the same path of virtue, human beings might arrive at the same reward of virtue. Thus they nullified, insofar as they could, the entire gift of his sacred advent and the entire grace of divine redemption when they said that human beings could, by their own manner of living, attain just the same as God had accomplished by dying for human salvation.

3. They added too that our Lord and Savior became Christ after his baptism, and God after his resurrection, connecting the former with the

72 Here Cassian alludes to the heresy of Nestorius, against whom the entirety of *On the Incarnation* is directed.

73 That is, Nestorius and his supporters.

74 That is, the heresy of Leporius.

mystery of his anointing and the latter with the merit of his passion. Accordingly, when in the present day this new author of a not-new heresy[75] contends that our Lord and Savior was born as an ordinary human being, he is turning toward saying the exact same thing as what the Pelagians said previously. And it follows from their error that he who claims that our Lord Jesus Christ lived entirely without sin as an ordinary human being is not only putting forward the blasphemy that all human beings can of their own accord be without sin, but also denying that our Lord's redemption was necessary for the example he gave since human beings can (as they say) reach the heavenly kingdom by their own exertions alone.

4. And there is no doubt about this, as the affair itself shows without question. For this is why he encourages the complaints of the Pelagians by interceding for them and advances their cause in his writings,[76] namely because he cleverly or (to be more accurate) cunningly acts as their patron and with ghastly affection favors their ghastly teaching which is akin to his own. For he knows very well that he is of the same mind and of the same spirit. And therefore he is pained that a heresy akin to his own has been unjoined from the church, as he knows that it is altogether conjoined with his own in perverseness.

4, 1. But, nonetheless, because those who descended from this stock of pestilent thorns[77] were previously healed by divine help and affection, we too, since the earlier heresy is in harmony with this new one on certain points, should now pray to our Lord God, that he would grant a similarly happy ending to those who had a similarly bad beginning.[78]

2. For Leporius, then a monk and now a presbyter, who descended from the teaching or rather from the wickedness of Pelagius, as we said above, and was among the first and greatest advocates of the aforesaid heresy in Gaul, was admonished by us and corrected by God, and he so splendidly condemned his ill-conceived opinion that his correction was admired almost no less than the unimpaired faith of many. For the best thing is never to fall into error at all; the second best thing is to repudiate it well.

75 That is, Nestorius.

76 Cassian here refers to the fact that several Pelagians who had been condemned in the West had fled to Constantinople where Nestorius took up their cause, going so far as to write to Pope Celestine requesting that he forward the relevant evidence so that Nestorius could reassess their condemnation. See Nestorius's *Three Letters to Celestine of Rome*, translated in this volume on pp. 585–592.

77 That is, the Pelagians.

78 Here Cassian encourages Nestorius to renounce Pelagianism as Leporius had done.

3. Therefore, returning to himself he confessed his error with as much grief as he was without shame, not only in Africa, where he was then and is now, but he also gave to all the cities of Gaul his tearful letter of confession and lamentation, unquestionably so that where his previous deviation was already known there his amendment might also be made known, and that those who had formerly been witnesses of his error might also afterwards be witnesses of his correction.

5, 1. And from his confession or rather his lamentation we have thought it a good idea to insert some passages here for two reasons: first, in order that their correction might be both a testimony to us and an example to those who are wavering, and that they might not be ashamed to follow the amendment of those whose error they were not ashamed to follow; and, second, in order that just as they suffered from a like disease so too they might be cured by a like remedy. Therefore, he acknowledged the perverseness of his views, and seeing the light of faith, he wrote to the bishops of Gaul, and began as follows:

> 2. I do not know what I should accuse in myself first, O my venerable lords and most blessed priests. I cannot discover what I should make excuses for in myself first. So strongly had pride born of inexperience, so strongly had foolish simplicity with harmful convictions, so strongly had zeal with immoderation, so strongly (to speak more truly) had a weak faith that was withering away, so strongly had I allowed all these to flourish in me simultaneously, that it is at the same time an embarrassment to have succumbed to such and so many [vices] and an overwhelming joy to have been able to cast them from my soul.[79]

And after a little he adds:

> If, therefore, we fail to perceive this power of God and we think about such matters according to our own understanding and our own reasoning, and if because of this we seek to avoid God seeming to do something beneath himself by claiming that the human being was born along with God, thereby letting us give only to God alone what belongs to God and attribute only to the human

79 Leporius, *Statement of Amendment* 1, 5–11 (CCSL 64: 111 Demeulenaere) = Passage A above.

being alone what belongs to the human being, then we are obviously introducing a fourth person into the Trinity and out of the one Son of God we are beginning to make not one but two Christs. May Christ himself our Lord and God preserve us from that! 3. Therefore, we confess that Jesus Christ our Lord and God, the only Son of God, who was born from the Father before the ages, in these last days was born of the Holy Spirit and the ever-virgin Mary and became God the human being. And while we confess the twofold substance of the flesh and the Word, with the pious belief of faith we accept one and the same God and human being to be indivisible. And we claim furthermore that from the moment of his taking on flesh, just as everything which belonged to God passed over to the human being, so too everything that belonged to the human being came to God. 4. It is in this sense that "the Word became flesh,"[80] not that he began to be what he was not by some change or transformation, but that by the power of the divine economy the Word of the Father, though never parted from the Father, deigned to become a human being in the proper sense of the term. Indeed, the Only-Begotten became incarnate through that hidden mystery that he alone knows. For indeed it is ours to believe, his to know! And so, just as God the Word himself, by taking on everything that belongs to the human being, is a human being, [so] too the assumed human being, by receiving everything that belongs to God, can be nothing other than God. Yet just because he is said to be incarnate and mixed, we ought not to hold that there is any diminishment of his substance. 5. For God knows how to be mixed without any detriment to himself and yet to be truly mixed. He who knows how to give the whole of himself without suffering any loss also knows how to receive into himself without growing by addition. Therefore, we should not think that when God and the human being were mixed together some sort of body was produced as if through a confusion of flesh and Word. For this would be to make conjectures, as is necessitated by our weak understanding according to the visible proofs of our experiences, based on the way equal created things enter mutually

80 John 1:14.

> into one another. 6. Heaven forbid that we should believe such a thing, that we should think that two natures are reduced to one substance in some conflated way. For that kind of commixture is a corruption of both parts. For God, who contains but cannot be contained, who enters into but cannot be entered into, who fills but cannot be filled, who is at once everywhere in his entirety and spread out everywhere, through an infusion of his own power is mixed with the human nature out of mercy.[81]

7. And after a little:

> Therefore, God the human being, Jesus Christ, the Son of God was born to us specifically of the Holy Spirit and the ever-virgin Mary. And so, Word and flesh became one, each in the other, so that, while each substance remains naturally in its own perfection, both what is divine shares in the humanity and what is human participates in the divinity without either suffering any disadvantage to itself. Nor is it the case that God is one and the human being another, but that same God who is also the human being, and in turn the human being who is also God, is called and truly is Jesus Christ, the one Son of God. And accordingly we must always act and believe in such a way that we do not deny that the same God who became a human being is, from the moment he took on flesh, the Lord Jesus Christ, Son of God, the true God, whom we confess is always with the Father and equal to the Father before the ages. Nor do we believe that he became God as it were gradually over time, in possession of one state before the resurrection and of another after the resurrection, but that he was always in possession of the same fullness and power.[82]

8. And again a little later on:

> But because God the Word graciously descended upon a human being by taking on a human being, and because the human being ascended to God the Word by taking on God, God the Word in

81 Leporius, *Statement of Amendment* 3, 7–4, 11 (CCSL 64: 113–115 Demeulenaere) = Passage B above.

82 Leporius, *Statement of Amendment* 5, 1–14 (CCSL 64: 116 Demeulenaere) = Passage C above.

> his totality became a human being in its totality. For it was not God the Father who became a human being, nor the Holy Spirit, but the Only-Begotten of the Father. Accordingly, we must accept that there is one person of the flesh and the Word, so that we may faithfully believe without any doubt that one and the same indivisible Son of God, who has also always been called "the giant of twin substance,"[83] "in the days of his flesh"[84] always truly bore everything that belongs to the human being and also always truly possessed what belongs to God, "since even though he was crucified out of weakness, yet he lives by the power of God."[85]

6, 1. This confession of his, then, which is the faith of all catholics, was approved by all the bishops of Africa (from where he wrote) and all the bishops of Gaul (to whom he wrote). Nor has there ever been anyone who found this faith unsatisfactory without being guilty of unbelief. For to deny approved piety is tantamount to professing impiety.

2. The agreement of all should already, therefore, be enough on its own for refuting heresy, because what has the authority of all manifests indisputable truth and the rationale is made perfect when no one disagrees with it. Accordingly, if anyone ventures to hold opinions opposed to these, we should first and foremost not so much listen to his assertions as immediately condemn his perverseness. For whoever resists the judgment of all announces beforehand his own condemnation, and whoever disturbs what has been stipulated by all is afforded no opportunity to be heard. After all, once the truth has been confirmed by all, whatever arises in opposition to it must be recognized at once as falsehood for this very reason, namely because it disagrees with the truth. And thus it is right that this alone suffices for the sentence of condemnation: that he departs from the judgment of truth.

3. But nevertheless, because an account of one's rationale does no damage to the rationale itself, and because truth always burns more brightly when fanned, and because it is better for those in error to be corrected by the healing balm of discussion rather than condemned by the severity of censure, for these reasons we should cure the old heresy present in these

83 This is the line from Ambrose's hymn, *Intende qui regis Israel.*

84 Heb 5:7.

85 2 Cor 13:4. Leporius, *Statement of Amendment* 6, 9–19 (CCSL 64: 117 Demeulenaere) = Passage D above.

new heretics, inasmuch as we can with divine assistance. Once they have recovered their health through the sacred mercy, our hope is that their healing may bear testimony to the holy faith instead of their condemnation providing an example of just severity. May only the truth itself be present to our discussion and account of it, and may it come to the aid of human errors with that piety with which God deigned to come to human beings. After all, it was especially for this purpose that he willed to be born on earth and among human beings, that there might be no place any longer for falsehood.

39

Theodoret of Cyrrhus, *Exposition of the Orthodox Faith*

Introduction and Translation by Vasilije Vranic
Revised and Edited by Mark DelCogliano

INTRODUCTION

Theodoret was born ca. 393 in Antioch to a prominent Christian family. As the only child of a devout mother, he was not only well educated in the classical sense but was also exposed to monastic spirituality and piety from an early age. While still a child he was ordained a reader in the church of Antioch. Later he moved to a monastery near Apamea (Syria Secunda), where he became a professed monk. At the age of thirty, around 423, he was elected bishop of Cyrrhus. As a bishop, Theodoret waged a theological war against numerous heresies he detected in his diocese. He wrote a number of treatises against Judaism and Hellenic paganism, and at least one significant exposition of the Christian doctrine of God and Christ. Theodoret's extensive learning, his extraordinary gift for oration, his impeccable literary style, and his numerous theological writings secured him a prominent place in the Christological controversies of the fifth century. He was the leading theologian among the Easterners (so called because they came from the Roman diocese of Oriens or "East") around the time of the Council of Ephesus, writing several works against Cyril of Alexandria, including the *Refutation of the Twelve Anathemas*.[1] While deposed at the second Council of Ephesus in 449 for "Nestorian" views, he was exonerated and rehabilitated at the Council of Chalcedon in 451 – a reinstatement that would be a cause of posthumous controversy.[2] He died at some point after

1 Translated in this volume on pp. 641–657. A selection from Theodoret's *Eranistes*, written around 447, is also translated in this volume, on pp. 747–758.
2 See *Acts of the Council of Chalcedon*, translated in CEECW 4 on pp. 49–116.

453, perhaps around 457 or even 466. About a century after Theodoret's death, the second Council of Constantinople in 553 condemned his writings against Cyril of Alexandria as one of the Three Chapters.[3] This cast a shadow of doubt on his Christological orthodoxy. Contemporary scholarship, however, has revised that polemical view and now sees his Christology as aligned with the later Chalcedonian position.

Since at least the seventh century his *Exposition of the Orthodox Faith* (*Expositio rectae fidei*) was erroneously attributed to Justin Martyr.[4] This misattribution went unchallenged until the eighteenth century when M. Lequien disputed its authorship, arguing that the author must be "crypto-Nestorian." Hence the *Exposition* was placed among the spurious works attributed to Justin. The breakthrough in the identification of the author came when J. Lebon and R. V. Sellers argued independently for Theodoret's authorship. Current scholarly consensus accepts Theodoret of Cyrrhus as the author of the *Exposition of the Orthodox Faith*, and sees it as an early work of Theodoret, written sometime between his ascent to the bishopric in 423 and the Nestorian schism in 431, around the same time as his *Against the Jews* (now lost) and *Cure of Pagan Maladies*. It was written to summarize and explain Trinitarian and Christological doctrine to "the sons of the church" and in its exposition uses several extended examples to illustrate the theological points.

Thus, this short doctrinal treatise is a pedagogical work, comprised of eighteen chapters. The first nine are dedicated to a concise explanation of the doctrine of the Trinity, against unnamed opponents, most likely "Arians" of his era, perhaps some sort such as Heteroousians. Here Theodoret recapitulates the central pro-Nicene teachings about the Trinity articulated in the fourth century and in particular by the Cappadocian Fathers: the oneness of God; the sameness of rank of the Father, Son, and Holy Spirit and their distinction by mode of existence; the oneness of their indivisible substance; their inseparable operations; and divine incomprehensibility. The last nine chapters are dedicated to the discussion of Christology, which Theodoret addresses from the perspective of the economy of salvation. He stresses the soteriological purpose of the incarnation and

3 See *Acts of the Second Council of Constantinople*, translated in CEECW 4 on pp. 341–389.

4 It is quoted in Sophronius of Jerusalem's *Synodical Letter* 3.15 from 634, and Sophronius speaks of the author of the text as a martyr, though without naming Justin. Sophronius's letter is translated in CEECW 4 on pp. 447–465.

the fact that it results in a single Son. While professing ultimate ignorance about the mode of union between the humanity and divinity, he expends much energy attempting to elucidate it to the extent possible, ultimately teaching that in the incarnation two different substances have been united in a conjunction to create a single new entity, which he calls a person. At the end of section 12 Theodoret seems to conclude his treatise, but in section 13 he launches into the problem of reconciling the omnipresence of the Word with the constraints of the human body assumed in the incarnation. Before offering his solution in section 17, he rejects Christologies that conceive the incarnation as a blending or confusion of the divine and human natures, or that speak of the Word changing into the body or the body becoming divine. As in the conclusion to the Trinitarian section, Theodoret confesses that the incarnation is ultimately a mystery beyond the capacities of human epistemology, memorably commenting, "We confess that we do not have a clear understanding of the truth – indeed, that is a significant part of the victory" (17).

This translation is based upon the critical text of the *Expositio rectae fidei* published by Johann Karl Theodor von Otto, *Iustini philosophi et martyris opera quae feruntur omnia*, 3rd ed., CACSS 3.1 (Jena: Fischer, 1880), 2–67.

TRANSLATION

1. Having offered sufficient examination of the [beliefs of] Jews and Greeks, it follows that we should expound the sound faith.[5] For after the demonstration of the truth, it is necessary to know going forward how we ought to think about it. It is not the mere glorification of the Father and the Son that brings us salvation, but the sound confession of the Trinity that grants to the pious the enjoyment of the prepared goods, since one can hear even the unlike-minded hymning the Father and the Son, but not offering worship in the true sense. Thus, it is necessary for us to undertake the required exposition, which leads those who encounter it to a pure comprehension of the truth.

2. Therefore, the divine scriptures teach us to worship one God, just as the teachings of the fathers instruct us to do. For there has to be one supreme source of all so that nothing from outside could encircle and destroy the

5 This opening sentence probably refers to Theodoret's works *Against the Jews* (which is no longer extant) and *Cure of Pagan Maladies*.

things that have come into being. And if anything in the beginning were outside of God, then it would certainly have to be confessed by necessity to be either God or some other power. But if anyone says that [such a thing is] God, he annuls the divine words which manifestly cry out, "I, God, am first, and I am after these things, and besides me there is no god."[6] Yet if [he says such a thing is] not God, clearly then he is referring to angels and powers. But in that case he would be denying the scriptures, which affirm that even these [angels and powers] come from God: "Praise God from heavens; praise him in the heights! Praise him, all his angels; praise him, all his powers!"[7] And what follows: "He spoke and they came to be; he commanded and they were created."[8] Thus, if we agree that in the beginning nothing coexisted with the God of all, then it has been shown that everything has been brought into being by him. Therefore, the God of all is truly one, known as the Father, Son, and Holy Spirit. For from his own substance the Father begot the Son, and from the same [substance] he brought forth the Spirit; if they participate in one and the same substance, with good reason are they worthy of one and the same divinity.

3. So then, if that which begets is different from that which is begotten, and that which proceeds is different from that from which it proceeds (for the unbegotten Father is the one from whom both the Son has been begotten and the Spirit came forth), then one might ask, "How are the Father, the Son, and the Spirit identical?" Because "unbegotten," "begotten," and "proceeding" are not names for the substance, but are modes of existence. The modes of existence are indicated by these names. The substance is signified when the name "God" is used, so that the difference between the Father, the Son, and the Spirit is a question of the mode of existence but their sameness a question of the formula of the substance. For insofar as the first has being in an unbegotten manner, the second in a begotten manner, and the third by way of proceeding, it is possible for their differences to be contemplated, but as for the substantial being of the hypostasis of each one being signified, this is revealed by the common name of divinity. My point shall become clearer in what follows.

The one who looks into the existence of Adam, how he was brought forth into being, will find that he was not begotten, since he is not from some other human being, but was fashioned from the divine hand. But the fashioning reveals the mode of existence; it signifies how it happened.

6 Isa 44:6. 7 Ps 148:1–2. 8 Ps 148:5.

Again, similarly, the mode of existence indicates the fashioning, because it also reveals that the one fashioned has come into existence. If you seek his substance by which he is joined in common to those from him, you will find the underlying substrate to be human. Therefore, just as the fashioning reveals the mode of existence, and the mode of existence indicates the fashioning, and the formula of substance shows the underlying substrate to be human, so too we will find it in the case of God the Father. For if you seek his mode of existence, seeing that he has not been begotten of anyone, you will designate him "unbegotten." And if you look upon the designation "unbegotten," you will discover the explanation of his mode of existence. And if you wish to know his substance, by which he is joined in common to the Son and the Spirit, you will reveal it by using the name "God." Thus, unbegottenness and the modes of existence give knowledge of one another, while [the name] "God" reveals their substance. For just as Adam, even though not subject to a begetting, was joined in common to those begotten from him in terms of identity of substance, so too there can be no reason, on account of the unbegottenness, for dividing the commonality of substance that the Father has with the Son and the Spirit. As a result, unbegottenness, begottenness, and procession are not revelatory of substance, but are indicative of the hypostases. For it suffices for us to distinguish the persons and to point individually to the hypostasis of the Father, the Son, and the Holy Spirit. When "unbegottenness" is said to us it is like an imprint that immediately defines the hypostasis of the Father. And again, hearing the designation "begotten" is like receiving a sign by which we gain understanding of the Son. Likewise, through the indication of "proceeding" we are taught the proper person of the Spirit. And this is a sufficient proof that the unbegottenness, begottenness, and procession do not reveal the substance itself, but are indicators of the hypostasis, and in addition to this, signify the mode of existence.

4. It remains now to show how the substance of the Father, Son, and Holy Spirit is one. Well then, we see that by common custom those who are begotten are of the same substance as those who have begotten them. Rather, let's begin over again, so that no random concern brought up in the middle of our discourse should disrupt its continuity. And let us first of all make a distinction between beings. For we will find everything divided into the [categories of] created and uncreated. If a thing has a place among beings, its nature is either uncreated or created. While the uncreated is dominant and free from every necessity, the created is submissive

and subject to the laws of the dominating [nature]. And while the former does and is capable of doing whatever it wills by its own authority, the latter is capable of doing and fulfills only the task it has been given by the divinity. Thus, with this distinction in place, we need to adduce divine utterances for discussion and examine them with precision, to see how they teach us to rank the Son and the Spirit together. For when it comes to the children of the church, divine questions must not be settled by human deliberations; rather, an exposition of the Spirit's words must be offered for the purpose of instruction. And let David be the first to teach [us]. For when he composed a hymn to God on behalf of the entire creation, he put everything in heaven into one category, enumerated all the powers in heaven, and likewise made mention of earth and everything on it.[9] He did not include the Son and the Spirit in this doxology, as they are obviously conjoined to the divine nature. For if he had understood them to be of created substance, he would not have let only them go by unnamed [but] he would have mentioned them as principal and supreme among all the other powers. Likewise too the blessed Paul, who is possessed by the divine fire and displays the intense burning of his love for God and whose constancy of affection is acknowledged, says this: "For I am convinced that neither life, nor the world, nor death, nor angels, nor powers, nor rulers, nor things present, nor things to come, nor height, nor depth, nor anything else in all creation, will be able to separate us from the love of God in Christ Jesus our Lord."[10] After he enumerated the world, life, death, angels, powers, and rulers, things present and things to come, height and depth, he found nothing left in the created nature and because of this was held by an impulse to shout and bear witness, and he concludes his statement by adding a hyperbole, when he introduces "anything else in all creation." So then, having declared his longing for God to be unshakeable by means of the hyperbole in what he said, if he understood the Son and the Spirit to be of created nature, would he not have made mention of them together with the other [creatures]? But on the basis of these verses and others like them one must know that the Son and the Spirit are not conjoined to the created nature. It would be possible to adduce many more such testimonies. But since this discourse is [intended] for the sons of the church, and our object is to speak concisely, what was said I deem sufficient.

9 See Ps 148. 10 Rom 8:38–39.

5. It remains now to demonstrate that the Son and the Spirit are ranked together with the divine nature. And first of all we shall call to mind the most important thing. So then, our Lord Jesus Christ, after the resurrection from the dead and in anticipation of making his ascension into the heavens, instructed the apostles with a teaching about the nations and a doctrine about baptism: "Go, make disciples of all nations, baptizing them in the name of the Father, and of the Son, and of the Holy Spirit."[11] And when writing to the Corinthians, the blessed Paul adds at the end of his letter, as if setting a seal on his teaching, "The grace of our Lord Jesus Christ, and the love of God the Father, and the communion of the Holy Spirit be with you all."[12] And again, to the Ephesians he speaks thus: "With Christ Jesus himself as the cornerstone, in whom the whole structure is joined together and grows into a holy temple in the Lord, in whom you are also built together for a dwelling place of God in the Spirit."[13] You see how, while teaching the "structure in Christ," through which we become the Lord's temple, according to [the words], "I shall indwell in them and I shall walk among them, and I shall be their God,"[14] he introduces the three persons that are closely connected. For through such a teaching [Paul] instructs us that Christ and God and Spirit, the one divinity, dwells in us by activity when we are deemed worthy of grace. And this is also clear from what he says in another [letter]: "For this reason I bow my knees before the Father of our Lord Jesus Christ, from whom all fatherhood in heaven and on earth is named, that according to the riches of his glory he may grant to you that you be strengthened in the inner human being with power through his Spirit, and that Christ dwell in your hearts."[15] See, once again, while calling to mind the divine indwelling, [Paul] is shown to be thinking of the Father, Son, and Holy Spirit. And so, everywhere in his teaching he is seen to rank the three persons together. For when writing in the second epistle to the Corinthians he speaks thus: "It is God who established us with you in Christ and has anointed us, by putting his seal on us and giving us the Spirit in our hearts as first installment."[16] Clearly here too in his teaching he has conjoined the Father ("God"), the Son ("Christ"), and the Holy Spirit. And again to the Galatians [he wrote], "And because you are sons, God has sent the Spirit of his Son into our hearts, crying, 'Abba!

11 Matt 28:19. 12 2 Cor 13:13. 13 Eph 2:20–22.
14 2 Cor 6:16, quoting Lev 26:11–12. 15 Eph 3:14–17. 16 2 Cor 1:21–22.

Father!'"[17] Again, in like manner he handed down to us that the notion of the Father, Son, and Spirit is closely connected. And see how he lays out what gives knowledge of their supreme conjunction. For he did not merely say, "God sent the Spirit," but "[God sent the Spirit] of his Son," in this case joining [the Spirit] to the Son. But in other cases he links the Father with the ones he mentions:[18] "You have not received the spirit of the world, but the Spirit which is from God"[19] – that is, from the Father. And again, the Son himself calls the Spirit "of Truth"[20] because he is the Truth.[21] And again, [the Son] teaches that [the Spirit] is of the Father, since "he proceeds from the Father."[22] And so, since the divine scripture in every way and without qualification confirms [this] interpretation for us, you have ascertained that the notion of the Father, Son, and Holy Spirit is indivisible.

6. But the divine oracle did not instruct us that the activity of the Son and the Holy Spirit is separate from that of the Father in the creation of the universe. And let David be your teacher of this because he says, "At the beginning, O Lord, you founded the earth, and the heavens are works of your hands,"[23] including both the Son and the Spirit because of the meaning of "Lord." But nonetheless, for the sake of the uneducated, he also makes a distinction between the persons when he says, "By the Word of the Lord the heavens were established, and by the Spirit of his mouth all their power."[24] But we have not been taught by the divine scripture that the Son and the Spirit are lesser than the Father in authority. And how so? Listen to the scripture: "Our God is in the heavens," he says, "he does whatever he wills."[25] David says this about the Father. The Son demonstrates this [same] authority in the case of the leper: "I do choose," he says, "Be clean!"[26] The blessed Paul bears witness that the Holy Spirit too has this [same authority] when he writes these [words]: "All these are accomplished by the one and the same Spirit, who apportions to each one individually as he wills."[27] Well then, if one closely connected name of Father, Son, and the Holy Spirit is handed down to us in the teachings for the world, in the instructions about baptism, and moreover in the account of creation and their authoritative power, by what logic could the Son and the Spirit be deprived of their possession of the divine and blessed substance?

17 Gal 4:6. 18 That is, the Son and Holy Spirit. 19 1 Cor 2:12.
20 John 15:26; see also John 14:17 and 16:13. 21 John 14:6.
22 John 15:25. 23 Ps 101(102):26. 24 Ps 32(33):6. 25 Ps 113:11(115:3).
26 Matt 8:3; Mark 1:41; Luke 5:13. 27 1 Cor 12:11.

7. We will avoid the reproach that we promised one thing but delivered another, if having proposed to demonstrate the sameness of substance, we provide the proofs that the Son and the Spirit are conjoined to the Father. For giving an account of the conjunction communicates nothing other than the sameness of the substance of Father, Son, and Holy Spirit. And let my opponent, having taken into consideration their differentiation, search [the scriptures] scrupulously. For he will discover there the account of the substance to be fulfilled in the category of conjunction. Well then, above we divided beings into two [categories]: the uncreated nature and the created nature. And we confessed that the sure mark of the uncreated nature is that it is dominant and free from every necessity, and moreover it does and is capable of doing whatever it wills by its own authority, whereas conversely [the sure mark] of the created nature is that it is submissive and subject to the laws of the dominating nature, and moreover it is capable of doing and fulfills only the task it has been given by the divinity.[28] Thus, with this distinction in place, and with it being confirmed that there is nothing between the divinity and creation, everything that is different from creation is clearly not different from the divine [nature]. So then, if we have shown extensively that the Son and the Spirit are different from creation because they cannot be numbered with anything created but are conjoined to the Father everywhere, what utter folly would it be not to consider them to belong to the uncreated substance! For one of these two things will necessarily fail: to demonstrate that they belong to the created [substance] and to separate them from the uncreated [substance], or to show that they belong to the uncreated [substance] and necessarily to separate them from the created [substance]. But it is obvious that they are separate from the created [substance] and conjoined to the uncreated [substance]; it is confessed that there is nothing between them. It remains to add that they share in the substance whereby they are conjoined everywhere. For on the question of the Father, Son, and Holy Spirit, if we accept all that is said about them – now it is good to recall all this for the sake of a more complete demonstration – when it comes to the teachings for the world given by Christ, the instructions about baptism, and moreover when it comes to the divine teaching and the creation of the universe, and even more so [if we accept] their equality and identity[29] when it comes to their sovereign

28 See section 4 above. 29 In Greek, *paraplēsia kai tauta*.

authority, who would then be so stupid to dispute about their mutual sharing according to substance? Thus, it is befitting to confess one God, known in the Father, the Son, and the Holy Spirit: just as we know the Father and Son and Holy Spirit to be hypostases of the one divinity, so too we understand God to be the commonality of the hypostases according to substance. For Unity is understood in Trinity, and Trinity is known in Unity.[30]

8. And in what way this comes to pass, neither do I wish to inquire of another nor am I able to persuade myself to speak impudently about ineffable things with a tongue made of clay and polluted by flesh. For even if a pure intellect is established in us by which we often gain insight into the things above us, yet being burdened by the conjoined flesh it is incapable of the clear comprehension of superior things, since "the earthly tent weighs down the intellect full of thoughts."[31] In no way, then, would it be possible for mere human beings to reach that first and blessed substance. And what can I say about the divine substance? Not even those who are mystically initiated can do so. For "nothing of the divine is clear to human beings," as one of the Greek sages uttered.[32] Now I accept this statement as truth because I hear Paul, the chosen vessel,[33] who ascended to the third heaven,[34] who heard the unutterable words that human tongues have no right to pronounce,[35] who had a provider of words speaking in himself,[36] testify to the partial knowledge in himself and say: "Now I know in part; then I shall understand fully, even as I have been fully understood."[37] And again: "We know in part and we prophesy in part."[38] Accordingly, how can I believe that mere human beings have perfect knowledge of the divine? For if it was obscure and partial to those who attained Paul's measure (for seeing in a mirror and dimly[39] suggests obscurity), who would be so daring to the point of absurdity to declare having in himself the perfect knowledge of divine things? Therefore, we too, having come to know the limitlessness

30 A similar expression has fourth-century precedents: Epiphanius, *Anacoratus* 22.7 (GCS 25: 31, 22–23 Holl): "For we do not say 'henad and dyad' or 'unity and unity' but 'Unity in Trinity and Trinity in Unity'"; *Panarion* 62.3.3 (GCS 31: 391, 23–24 Holl): "We confess the Trinity, Unity in Trinity and Trinity in Unity"; Gregory of Nazianzus, *Oration* 25.17, 3–4 (SChr 284: 198 Mossay/Lafontaine): "Unity is worshiped in Trinity and Trinity in Unity"; and *Oration* 6.22, 18–19 (SChr 405: 176 Calvet-Sebasti): "Unity is worshiped in Trinity and Trinity is recapitulated in Unity."

31 Wis 9:15. 32 Euripides, *Hercules Furens* 62. 33 See Acts 9:15.

34 See 2 Cor 12:2. 35 See 2 Cor 12:4.

36 See 2 Cor 13:3; see also Rom 8:26; Matt 10:17–20; Luke 12:11–12.

37 1 Cor 13:12. 38 1 Cor 13:9. 39 See 2 Cor 12:2.

of the unutterable things, say together with David to the God of all, "Your knowledge is too wonderful for me, too strong, I cannot attain it."[40] But it is blessed to say these things and even more blessed to think them, since a pious and wise man surrenders to divine things.

9. Therefore, we understand in a way befitting God, to the extent that our investigation of divine things is conducted safely and to the extent that our worship is pious. For the complete incomprehensibility of the divinity does not mean that nothing beneficial comes from investigating it, but [the investigation] does require a lifetime spent in leisure. And moreover the inquiry must be undertaken diligently according to the measure of knowledge apportioned to each by the Lord, so that, convinced precisely that God is incomprehensible, we may conjoin ourselves to him through contemplation as far as we can. Well then, we understand the Son to be begotten of the Father, as light shining forth from light.[41] For the image suffices to communicate their co-eternity, their identity of substance, and the passionlessness of the begetting. After all, if he has shone forth, he has coexisted timelessly with the one who caused him to shine forth. By what interval of time could the shining of light have been disrupted? And if light is from light, it would reveal the same [light] as that of the one from which it has been begotten. And again, if the light was also that which was begotten, the begetting would also be passionless. For the shining of light happens through neither cutting nor flowing nor division, but it comes forth in a passionless manner from the substance itself. We possess the same knowledge about the Holy Spirit as well, that just as the Son is from the Father, so also is the Spirit, except that the mode of existence is different. For the [Son] has shone forth as light from light by begetting, but the [Holy Spirit], while also light from light, came forth by procession and not by begetting. Accordingly, he is co-eternal with the Father, has the same substance, and proceeded from him passionlessly. Thus, we understand Unity in Trinity and we know Trinity in Unity.[42]

Having perceived these things as far as we could and received this measure of knowledge from the Lord, we expounded what we comprehended to the sons of the church, urging them to think in this way until they are vouchsafed more perfect illumination of knowledge, seeing that it is

40 Ps 138(139):6.

41 Theodoret makes reference to a formula of the Nicene Creed that had long been traditional.

42 See note 30 above.

prudent to turn their attention diligently to what we have expounded. For we have not imagined our demonstration to be something clever, immoderate, or arrogant, but rather, having according to our abilities put together something that is pious and becoming to the true knowledge, we have expounded the knowledge of the one divinity in three perfect hypostases. And thus glorifying the holy Trinity, let us turn our discourse to the grace [that comes to us] from the economy of the Word. For the account of the economy is also ineffable, but again we can still investigate it according to our abilities.

10. When the Word became aware that the reformation of his own formations was necessary and that the debt of Adam's punishment, which he incurred by having transgressed, had to be repaid, at that very time he descended to us without absenting himself from the heavens. For the descent was not bodily, but a will of divine activity. He used the Virgin, who was descended from the Davidic race because of the promises made to him, as an intermediary for the purpose of the economy and entered her womb like some sort of divine seed, and thus he made a temple for himself, the complete human being, having assumed some part of that nature and given existence to the formation of the temple. Having entered it by way of utter unity, God and human being came forth simultaneously, and thus he accomplished the economy for us. Since Adam, having sinned, subjected the [human] race to death and made the entire nature liable to the debt, the Son, being God and human, repaired the transgression of Adam. Insofar as he was a human being, he lived blamelessly and accepted death voluntarily, destroying the transgression by fully living [a human life] and nullifying the debt by that death which was not owed. But insofar as he was God, he raised up that which was set free and entirely obliterated death itself. There is one Son, therefore, who is set free and raised up that which was set free. For insofar as he was a human being, he was set free, and insofar as he was God, he raised up. So when you hear contrary expressions about the one Son, divide the statements proportionately with the natures, ascribing anything great and divine to the divine nature and accounting anything little and human to the human nature, for thus you will avoid the dissonance of the expressions, with each nature receiving those things that are proper to it, and you will confess the one Son both before all ages and recently come according to the divine scriptures.[43]

43 This sentence is quoted in Sophronius of Jerusalem's *Synodical Letter* 3.15, translated in CEECW 4 on pp. 447–465.

11. And let no one ask me about the mode of the union. I will not be ashamed to admit ignorance, but on the contrary I shall boldly boast about it, since I believe in, and have been initiated into, ineffable realities which surpass the grasp of both reason and intellect. Accordingly, no one should hope to learn anything certain about [the mode of union] either from me or another. But if you should wish to know about it as far as is possible for our intellect, I shall not begrudge the children of the church and I shall add to what has been said only as much as I have made progress into comprehension to the extent of my abilities, since those attempting such an exposition need help and assistance from above.

So then, some people understand the union to be like that of the soul with body and declare it to be such. And in fact the example is fitting, if not entirely, at least partly. For just as the human being is one but has two different natures in himself, and according to one of these he plans but according to the other he actualizes the plan (for example, in the intellectual soul he plans the construction of a ship but executes the plan with his hands), so too the Son is one [entity] and two natures, and according to one of these he effected the signs of divinity and according to the other he accepted the lowly things.[44] For insofar as he is from the Father and is God, he performs miracles, but insofar as he is from the Virgin and is a human being, he voluntarily and naturally endures the cross, the passion, and suchlike. If someone accepts the illustration's implications up to this point, the image is a fine one; but should they compare [Christ] as a whole with the illustration as a whole, the points of difference will become plain. For even if a human being displays in himself a twofold nature, he is not two natures but *out of* the two [natures].[45] After all, just as the body is composed out of fire and air, water and earth, and you would not say that the body is fire or air or something else (for it is not identical with that out of which it is, because the definition of the composite is different from the definition of the constituent parts), so too, even if the human being is out of the soul and body, he is different from that out of which he is.

From what follows you will more clearly understand what I am saying. We build a house from different materials, but no one would say that the house is identical with the materials from which it is [made]. For the house is not simply the stones, the wood, or the rest. If it were so, then those

44 Part of this sentence is quoted in Sophronius of Jerusalem's *Synodical Letter* 3.15, translated in CEECW 4 on pp. 447–465.

45 In Greek, *ou duo phuseis estin, all' ek tōn duo.*

distinct materials could be justly called house even before the building of the house. But it is the assembling of those materials with each other that produces the house for us. Indeed, when the house gets demolished, the materials still remain, with each retaining its own proper definition, but we say that the house, which the conjunction of the same materials produced, has been destroyed. The same goes for a human being. Although he comes into existence out of soul and body, he is not to be identified with those things out of which he is, but he is something else, since that third thing produced out of the conjunction of the soul with the body is a human being.[46] And it is clear from this that when there is a separation of these things,[47] the body preserves its own proper definition (for it is three dimensional even when dead), and in turn the soul likewise remains rational, even if separated [from the body]. And the human being, which the conjoining of the two produced, is destroyed. But as for Christ, he was not produced out of divinity and humanity such that Christ is something different in comparison to the two, but he is each of the two, both God and human being: he is understood to be God through his performance of marvels and he is revealed to be a human being through his sufferings that are similar in nature [to ours]. And moreover the soul, being occupied with more than the sufferings of the body, often suffers before the body and suffers continually together with [the body], and it often appears to struggle in the separation from the body, to undergo change even before the body starts to suffer, and to endure no less pain after the separation. No pious person would dare to say or to accept this about the divinity of Christ. Thus, in the example of the human being certain things are acceptable, while the rest must be avoided.

12. Just before, we confessed that we have failed to attain a clear comprehension of this truth, and now we have no fewer qualms about confessing the knowledge according to the measure given to us, so much so that we are eager to take up [another] example for the purposes of a more pious, clear explanation, and we wish to compare the union not with some trivial and unimportant image, but with one that is magnificent and that is also befitting the begetting from the Father.

46 This comparison is the basis of Theodoret's Christological position. In humanity, two substances of entirely different qualities (i.e. soul and body) can be united into a close union (called a *synapheia*, "conjunction") as to create a new entity, a *prosōpon*. Theodoret draws a partial comparison with the two substances of entirely different qualities (i.e. God and human being) conjoined in Christ.

47 That is, the body and soul.

So then, since "light" – the Word – "came into the world"[48] and shone forth from the uncaused light, I wish to use light as the example of the union. So understand the Word as the primeval light that came into being at the first utterance of God through the Word himself.[49] And [understand] the human body, to which the Word was united in an ineffable way, as the body of the sun. And do not think of the sun as light that is different from the [light] brought into being initially, for the sun did not come into existence to meet a need, as if the first light was not up to the task of illuminating everything. For the Artificer is not such that he would neither provide something perfect nor create the ray of light for the purpose given to it by him. Therefore, the primeval light is one, and the body of the sun was created for it, and in it the light that in the beginning was scattered everywhere is gathered together and transported. With its body it also completes for us blamelessly the path of the hours of the day. For if it was not tied to its body and rather was entirely diffused in the air, it would neither define the measures of the day for us, nor show us orderly movement and [thereby] its Maker. And if you tell me that there were day and night even before the generation of the sun, first you will be admitting as well that the nature of light sufficed to illuminate everything, and then having searched for the reason for the generation of the sun you will find none other than that which we just stated. For initially the light, being entirely scattered in the air, moved about without regular movement and did not define the measures of the day, but gave way to the night by contracting itself. Accordingly, the light is one thing and the body of the sun that received [the light] is another.[50]

And so, given this [relationship] between the light and the body of the sun, consider now with precision what I am saying. For just as after the union of the primeval light with the body of the sun no one can divide them from one another, nor can one talk about the sun on its own and then mention its light separately, but the light together with its body are called one sun, so too in the case of the true light and the holy body one after the union cannot talk separately about the Son (the divine Word) and the Son (the human being), but will understand each as one and the same, as if one light and one sun, the light that was received and the body that received [the light]. Furthermore, just as the light is one and the sun is one, but two natures, with the one

48 John 3:19. 49 See Gen 1:4.

50 Theodoret adopts Basil of Caesarea's position on the initial light and the sun; see *On the Hexaemeron* 6.2–3.

[nature] being of the light and the other of the body of the sun, so too in this case, the Son, Lord, Christ, and the Only-Begotten is one, but two natures, with the one [nature] being beyond ours, the other ours. And still again, just as with the light no one would separate its activity from the body that received it, but by dividing them in thought one comes to know the nature to which the activity is proper, so too with the one only-begotten Son of God one should not separate the entire activity from the one Sonship, but should recognize what occurs by the principle of the nature to which it is proper.[51]

We have made this example of the divine union so that we could take refuge in a most pious concept: although we have not even come close to attaining the truth itself, at least we have put together an illustration that suffices for our purposes of pious inquiry. If you think that something else is closer to the truth than this [example], praise him who grants the measure of knowledge. And if you learn something more pious from someone else, again praise the Protector, because he who existed long ago effected it in that other [person]. Therefore, having expounded as best we could the orthodox confession in an adequate manner, we give our greetings to the sons of the church and confess our thanks to the giver of this abundant discourse, and putting this discourse to sleep, we shall live the rest of life in peace.

13. But I see that some are calling our discourse back in and are directing us to a racetrack for another inquiry, forcing us to run again. Perhaps they are somehow even trying to get us to give up on starting the last lap. Our discourse, however, imitates a spring that pours forth clearer water the more continuously it is drawn from. And the whole of our discourse is bent forward toward the track and is poised to emerge from the starting gates as soon as it hears the signal of the starter. And whenever you should wish to signal the subject of the inquiry, our discourse is ready to surge forward to overthrow unbelief, encircle the tongues that are fighting against God, and define precisely both what we should inquire about when it comes to divine topics and what we should believe about them. And thus by the law of the racetrack the victor will be determined.

How then, they ask, is the Word everywhere according to substance and also in his own temple? For if he is there in the same way that he is in all things,[52] then the temple contains no more of him than all other

51 Part of this sentence is quoted in Sophronius of Jerusalem's *Synodical Letter* 3.15, translated in CEECW 4 on pp. 447–465.

52 That is, if the Word is in the temple of his body in the same way or in the same sense as he is in all things.

things do. And what should we make of, "in him the whole fullness of divinity dwells bodily?"[53] If anyone were to think that more [of the Word] is present in the temple [than in all other things], then he is not present in everything according to substance – the very thing which is a distinguishing mark of God.

14. Saying "how" about God is a clear test of unbelief. For how [is God] the Creator of heaven, of earth and sea, of air and plants and all living beings, and even of you yourself, who are inquiring with precision into everything about God? You will undoubtedly say that he produced everything by the superabundance of his power. Well then, is it according to a contingent attribute or according to substance that the power of God is present in creatures? If according to a contingent attribute, then it was present in them, just as they exist now, even before they were brought into being, since the contingent attribute does not exist by itself but comes to exist in things that have already existed. If this is absurd, then the only option left is that his power is present in everything according to substance. Therefore, if his power is present in everything according to substance, then the aforementioned temple had no more of it than all others. The one explanation is perplexing and the other explanation is perplexing, but the solution to both is faith. Now you have seen how our discourse has charged ahead and overthrown unbelief; watch next the tongues that are fighting against God be encircled.

15. Tell us, you who make a pretense of honoring Christianity, who inquire into and allege such things for the destruction of the two natures, who busy yourselves with blending[54] and confusion,[55] with the changing of the body into divinity, and with similar perplexities, sometimes saying that the Word has become flesh, other times that the flesh took on the substance of the Word, and because of such perversions of your mind you have no clearly intelligible position whatsoever – so then, tell us how the Word did not leave the heavens when he became flesh. You will surely say that he became flesh while remaining God. But again, tell us how he became [one thing] while remaining [another thing]. For if he remained what he was, how did he become what he was not? But if he became what he was not, how did he remain what he was? You are perplexed over the solution; remain perplexed then over the mode of the union as well. But you believe

53 Col 2:9. 54 In Greek, *krasis*. 55 In Greek, *synchysis*.

that he became [one thing] while remaining [another thing]; believe also that the Word is present everywhere according to substance and that the Word is [present] in his own temple in an extraordinary way.

Once again, let us ask: how did the body become divine after the union? Either it was transformed into the substance of divinity, or the body remained a human body but because of its union with the Word continued on as incorruptible and immortal. But if this is the case, the body remained a body (for God is not a body), and it shared in the divine dignity, not by nature, but by the good pleasure of the Word.

If the Word changed the body into his own substance through the union, once again let us ask: how was the body changed into the substance of the Word? Did it add something to the [divine] substance when it was changed into the substance of the Word? But in this case [the divine substance] would have been incomplete before this, if it could receive an addition. But it received nothing from the [body], and thus that which was changed would be nothing. So how did nothing change into the divine substance?

But they say that the Word did not dissolve the body into his own substance, but that he transformed it into the divine [substance]. Once again, then, let them give us an answer: is the divine [substance] different from his [substance] or identical with his [substance]? If it is identical with his [substance], let us proclaim two divine substances of the Word, one which he has by being begotten from the Father and another according to which he made the body. But if [the divine substance] is different than his [substance], then they are saying that it is not divine but in fact created. For there can be nothing between divinity and creation. And [in this case] why would the change of the body be necessary, if it were changed into a created substance?

16. These perplexities are making you dizzy, and perhaps you somehow or other also fear that something said [here] undoes the account of our faith. But when I become perplexed in my inquiries, then I proclaim the wonder of the mystery of Christians, that it is beyond our intellect, beyond our reason, beyond our comprehension. And whenever you face a perplexity while investigating these topics, bring faith as the ready solution to the things being investigated, considering the fact that, wherever God [is in question], even if something said is incomprehensible, because of either the magnificence of the nature or the mode of the economy, no harm from this befalls those who cannot understand. And how can you not tremble completely in fear at the audacity of undertaking to settle questions about

divine topics? Or have you not heard the divine words, which, in order to deter us from such undertakings, applied to us the image of clay and potter, so that we might learn from this that we should not be pointlessly inquisitive and curious about divine things, but rather that we should yield to the divine will just as clay does to the potter?[56] In the final analysis, then, be careful, and make it your very modest resolution to put your deliberations to rest, and let faith alone provide the solutions to your inquiries. And furthermore tremble at the words, which are divine according to scripture, so that you may be made worthy of the divine descent and thus hear those blessed words of the God of all, who says, "To whom shall I look but to the one who is humble and silent and trembles at my words?"[57]

Therefore, with the tongues that fight against God encircled by these [efforts], our discourse presses on and runs to the explanation. But as for you, the sons of the church, who make this inquiry piously and are not attempting to propose novel questions but are seeking to learn as much as possible, at this point please prepare your intellect. The form of the divine teaching is manifold, but it is brought together as if by way of summary in the teaching and keeping of the commandments and in the knowledge and worship of God. Therefore, those who are lovers of piety are in no way tempted to ignore the keeping and teaching of the commandments and above all the worship of God. They will want to pursue the knowledge of divine things as much as possible, but when they grow tired let them worship what is unattainable, so that what pertains to our faith may not be rendered void.[58] And with us studying in this way what should be inquired into and what should be believed, let us then lead our discourse to contests of the racetrack and be eager to declare the victor. Descend now into the contests, O discourse!

17. We confess that we do not have a clear understanding of the truth – indeed, that is a significant part of the victory. Having investigated this question piously as far as is possible for human nature, I will resolve it for you. How, they say, is the Word in his own temple according to substance and in all beings in a similar way? And what will the temple have more of than other beings? Let us listen then to the word when it says that he "who is in the bosom of the Father"[59] is also indivisibly present in everything according to substance. But we are not claiming that he is in the Father in the same way that he is in all the rest: it is not through his substance being contained

56 See Rom 9:20–21. 57 Isa 66:2. 58 See Rom 4:14. 59 John 1:18.

in other things [that he is present in them] but through the ability of those who are receiving him, who are too weak to receive the divine. Thus, when we say that he is indivisibly [present] in his own temple and as it were profess that the fullness of divinity dwells [in him],[60] we are also saying that he is present according to substance in everything, but not in similar ways. For the body, being polluted, cannot receive the rays of divinity. And learn what is being said by this example – for I do not wish to shrink from the greatness of the question when piously discussing it with the sons of the church. The common sun is given to all of us individually, and it does not shine upon one less and upon another more, but sends forth its common activity equally upon all. But if someone has healthy eyesight, he receives more of the sun's rays, not at all because the sun as it were sheds more light on him than all the rest, but because of the strength of his own eyes. Whoever has weak eyesight, however, will not be able to look upon the very effulgence of the light because of the weakness of his eyes. So think about the matter in this way: the Sun of Righteousness[61] is, as God, present in everything equally according to substance, but all of us, like weak eyes barely able to see, are, because of the filth of our sins, too weak to receive the light, whereas his own temple, like the purest eye, admits the radiance of that whole light inasmuch as it was formed by the Holy Spirit and once and for all divided from sin. For just as the sun, although it reaches everything in a similar manner according to its activity, is not received by everything in a similar manner, so also the Word, although he is present in everything according to substance, is not present in his own temple and in all other things in a similar way.

18. You see how our discourse contended on the racetrack and has now been declared the victor. At long last, then, let it don the wreath, let it be escorted in a triumphal procession, let it be adorned by wreaths of victory, and let it celebrate the defeat of his adversaries! And as for us, let us sing the victory hymn of Christ as he leads the way; let us cry out, "You have fought the good fight, O discourse, you have finished the race, you have kept the faith, from now on there is reserved for you the crown of righteousness."[62] And even more so let us hymn the one who provided the victory, the most divine Word, "the true light, who shines upon every human being coming into the world,"[63] through whom all [exists],[64] the one in whom "we

60 See Col 2:9. 61 See Mal 4:2. 62 See 2 Tim 4:7–8. 63 See John 1:9. 64 See John 1:3.

live and move and have our being,"[65] the one through whom we are solving these logical puzzles, the Guardian, the Governor, the Benefactor, to whom we unceasingly offer a sacrifice of praise[66] and pour out, as it were, sincere supplications to God and to whom we offer the fragrance of [good] deeds, bringing him back to us, breathing him, considering him, devoting ourselves to him, hymning him in everything as the blessed hope and the bestower of the kingdom on high.

65 Acts 17:28. 66 See Heb 13:15.

PART IV

Controversy over Nestorius

40

Eusebius of Dorylaeum, *Protest*

Translation and Introduction by Vasilije Vranic
Revised and Edited by Mark DelCogliano

INTRODUCTION

Eusebius of Dorylaeum was a fifth-century bishop and a prominent theologian. Trained in legal practice, he became a distinguished rhetorician in Constantinople. His significant erudition earned him esteem at the imperial court. While still a layperson, Eusebius became the first person to contest Nestorius, the newly installed archbishop of Constantinople, in order to defend the title Theotokos for the Virgin Mary. When Nestorius challenged the theological propriety of the title, Eusebius confronted him in church. Cyril of Alexandria recounted the incident as follows:

> When [Nestorius] used novel and profane expressions in the midst of the church, a very talented and accomplished man, who was still among the laity and had moreover collected for himself an impressive education, was moved with fiery and God-loving zeal and said with a piercing cry, "The Word before the ages also endured a second birth, that which is according to the flesh and from a woman!" In response to this, pandemonium broke out among the people. Most of those with intelligence honored the man with immoderate praise as pious, extremely intelligent, and in possession of orthodox doctrines, but others raged against him. Sizing up the situation, he immediately indicated his approval of those whom [Nestorius] had brought ruin upon for teaching what he himself did and sharpened his tongue against the one who was refusing to consent not merely to his teachings but even to the holy fathers who had legislated for us the pious definition of the faith, "which we have as a sure and steadfast anchor of the soul,"

> according to what has been written.[1] "I am delighted," [Nestorius] said, "to see your zeal. But the refutation of the pollution uttered by this wretched man is self-evident. For if there are two births, there must be two sons. But the church knows one Son, the Master Christ."[2]

Years later, as bishop of Dorylaeum, Eusebius would also be among the first theologians to repudiate the miaphysite teachings of Eutyches when he indicted him at the Home Synod in Constantinople in 448.[3]

Sometime after 429 but before 431 – no doubt shortly after his outburst in church – Eusebius wrote a public denunciation of Nestorius's theology, known today as the *Contestatio Eusebii*, or *Protest*. It was posted anonymously in Constantinople at some point after Proclus, the bishop-elect of Cyzicus, delivered a sermon in 429 against Nestorius in defense of the title Theotokos. The authorship of Eusebius was universally accepted within a century of its composition, and it was ascribed to Eusebius in different collections of the acts of Ephesus. The majority of the pamphlet, similarly ascribed to Eusebius, also survives among the writings of Leontius of Byzantium.[4]

The *Protest* contains six theological statements in which the Christology of Nestorius is presented as strikingly similar to that of the third-century Paul of Samosata, who in the fifth century was regarded as the chief exponent of adoptionist Christology.[5] In addition to these sentences Eusebius includes his own brief interpretation of Nestorius's teaching. It also contains a small section of the Antiochene baptismal creed asserting that Christ was the incarnate Word. It appears that this selection of the creed was included to demonstrate the incongruence of Nestorius's teaching with that of the Antiochene Church. The *Protest* concludes with the proclamation of an anathema attributed to Eustathius of Antioch directed at those who divided the Word and Christ. Its purpose was to subject Nestorius to it.

1 Heb 6:19.
2 Cyril of Alexandria, *Against Nestorius* 1.5–6 (ACO 1.1.6: 25, 40–26, 13 Schwartz). The remark of Nestorius is *Fragment* 1h (*Nestoriana*: 352, 22–25 Loofs). Translation by Mark DelCogliano.
3 See the *Acts of the Home Synod at Constantinople*, translated in CEECW 4 on pp. 3–28.
4 Leontius of Byzantium, *Unmasking and Triumph over the Nestorians* 3.42. The quotation from the Antiochene Creed and the anathema attributed to Eustathius are not included.
5 Fragments from the writings of Paul of Samosata are translated in this volume on pp. 197–211.

This translation is based on the critical text of the *Contestatio Eusebii* in Eduard Schwartz, *Concilium Universale Ephesenum*, ACO 1.1.1 (Berlin: De Gruyter, 1927), 101–102.

TRANSLATION

Anyone who receives this document I adjure by the Holy Trinity to make it known to the bishops, priests, deacons, readers, and laypeople living in Constantinople, and furthermore to deliver the same to them as an accusation against the heretic Nestorius, that he is of like mind with Paul of Samosata, who was anathematized 160 years ago by our fathers the orthodox bishops. And here are the statements of both:

1a. Paul said: "Mary did not give birth to the Word."[6]
1b. In agreement Nestorius said: "O, best [of men], Mary did not give birth to the divinity."[7]

2a. Paul: "For she was not before the ages."
2b. Nestorius: "And they would prefer a temporal mother to the divinity, who is the creator of time."[8]

3a. Paul: "Mary received the Word and she is not older than the Word."
3b. Nestorius: "How then did Mary bear him who is more ancient then herself?"[9]

4a. Paul: "Mary gave birth to a human being that is equal to us."
4b. Nestorius: "A human being was born from the Virgin."[10]

5a. Paul: "In fact [he is] better in every way, because he is from the Holy Spirit and the grace upon him is from the promises and from the scriptures."
5b. Nestorius: "For he says, 'I saw the Spirit descending like a dove and remaining on him,'[11] granting him ascension – 'He was taken up,' it says,

6 The first five statements of Paul that Eusebius quotes here are part of Fragment 2. See p. 200.
7 Nestorius, *Sermon* 9 (*Nestoriana*: 252, 5–6 Loofs).
8 Nestorius, *Sermon* 8 (*Nestoriana*: 245, 18–19 Loofs).
9 Not edited in Loofs, but similar to Nestorius, *Fragment* 1a (*Nestoriana*: 351, 7 Loofs).
10 Nestorius, *Fragment* 1e (*Nestoriana*: 352, 1 Loofs).
11 John 1:32.

'after giving commands through the Holy Spirit to the apostles whom he had chosen.'[12] This [Spirit] granted such a great glory to Christ."[13]

6a. Paul: "So that the anointed one from David would neither be alien to the Wisdom nor would the Wisdom dwell in any other in this way. For it was also in the prophets, but even more so in Moses and in many lords, and even more so in Christ as in a temple." And elsewhere he says, "Jesus Christ is one and the Word another."[14]

6b. Nestorius: "Could it ever be possible for the one who was begotten before all the ages to be begotten as another all at once, and all this in his divinity?"[15]

Behold, it is clearly shown that the transgressor [Nestorius] says, "The one begotten of the Father was not born by Mary." Behold, he agrees with the heretic Paul, who says that the Word is one and Jesus Christ is another, and that he is not one as orthodoxy proclaims. Because of this, I will also note down for you, O zealous devotee of the holy faith, a portion of the teaching of the Antiochene church, from which in the beginning we received the name "Christians,"[16] because it does not know the Son of God as one and another, but as the one God from God who was begotten before all the ages from the Father, same-in-substance with the Father, and the same one was born from the Virgin Mary under Caesar Augustus. It was said:

True God from true God,
same-in-substance with the Father,
through whom both the ages were fashioned and all things came to be,
who for us came and was born of the holy virgin Mary
and was crucified under Pontius Pilate,
and what follows in the creed.

Also in agreement with[17] these things is the blessed bishop Eustathius of the same Antioch, one of the 318 bishops at the holy and great council [in Nicaea], who says this:

> [He is] not only a human being, but also God, just as prophet Jeremiah says: "This is our God; no other can be compared to

12 Acts 1:2. 13 Nestorius, *Sermon* 16 (*Nestoriana*: 293, 20–294, 2 Loofs).
14 The two quotations of Paul that Eusebius cites here are part of Fragment 3. See p. 201.
15 Nestorius, *Fragment* 1c (*Nestoriana*: 351, 23–24 Loofs). 16 See Acts 11:26.
17 Reading *sunainei* instead of *sunaidei*.

> him. He found out the entire way of knowledge and gave it to Jacob his son and to Israel his beloved. Afterward he was seen on the earth and lived among human beings."[18] But when did he live among human beings, if not when he was born with them among them from the Virgin and became an infant with them and grew with them and ate with them and drank with them and the rest?[19]

Therefore, if anyone should dare to declare that the Son, the Only-Begotten before the ages who was begotten from the Father, is one, and the one who was born of the Virgin Mary is another, and that the same is not one, the Lord Jesus Christ, let him be anathema!

18 Bar 3:36–38.
19 José H. Declerck, *Eustathii Antiocheni, patris Nicaeni, Opera quae supersunt omnia*, CCSG 51 (Turnhout: Brepols, 2002), 191, lists this passage among the "fragmenta dubia et spuria" of Eustathius of Antioch, as Fragment 132 (CPG 3389[1]). The fragment is identical to a passage in the Ps.-Athanasian *De incarnatione et contra Arianos* 22 (PG 26: 1024D–1025A Montfaucon). Martin Tetz, "Zur Theologie des Markell von Ankyra I. Eine Markellische Schrift 'De incarnatione et contra Arianos'," *Zeitschrift für Kirchengeschichte* 75 (1964): 215–270, has made a case that Marcellus is the actual author of this Ps.-Athanasian work. On this basis, Thomas Graumann, *Die Kircheder Väter: Vätertheologie und Väterbeweis in den Kirchen des Ostens bis zum Konzil von Ephesus (431)* (Tübingen: Mohr Siebeck, 2002), 310–11, claimed that the author of the passage quoted here was not Eustathius, but Marcellus of Ancyra. Nonetheless, the authorship of this passage remains contested.

41

Cyril of Alexandria, *Second Letter to Nestorius*

Introduction and Translation by Matthew R. Crawford

INTRODUCTION

In 412 Cyril became bishop of the church of Alexandria and all Egypt, succeeding his uncle Theophilus, whose episcopacy was famously marked by controversy with the Constantinopolitan church in the person of its bishop, John Chrysostom. Cyril carried forward his uncle's legacy by entering into a dispute with another bishop of Constantinople, Nestorius, within the first year of the latter's episcopal tenure in the Eastern capital. Soon after the start of Nestorius's episcopacy in 428, a local Christological dispute erupted between two groups in Constantinople regarding the propriety of the terms Theotokos ("bearer of God") and Anthropotokos ("bearer of the human being") for the Virgin Mary. Nestorius handled the situation by rejecting both terms and proposing that the word Christotokos ("bearer of Christ") be used instead, though this solution did little to quell the conflict. In early 429 Cyril, claiming that these rumblings in the imperial capital were beginning to cause distress and uncertainty in Egypt, decided to stake out a position in the growing debate by denouncing Nestorius's Christology in his *Festal Letter* 17 and *Letter to the Monks of Egypt*, though without naming Nestorius in either communication. Later in the same year he wrote directly to his Constantinopolitan counterpart (the *First Letter to Nestorius*), though this brief missive merely explained his reasons for composing the *Letter to the Monks of Egypt*, which had considerably annoyed Nestorius, and announced that Cyril's concern for Nestorius's orthodoxy was shared by Celestine, bishop of Rome. The present text, likely written in February 430 and known today as the *Second Letter to Nestorius*, represents Cyril's first direct and substantive engagement with his adversary in Constantinople over the issues at stake in the controversy. The spring of that year would be a profoundly productive period for the Alexandrian bishop, during which he would compose his *Five Tomes against Nestorius* and three *Orations* sent to the imperial court.

Cyril opens the letter in a defensive posture by addressing accusations being leveled against him by three laymen who, after being condemned by Cyril's judicial court in Alexandria, ended up in Constantinople. Attempting to go on the offensive against Rome and Alexandria, Nestorius had opened formal reviews of Celestine's handling of several Western bishops who had fled to the Eastern capital after being excommunicated as Pelagians, as well as of Cyril's treatment of these disgruntled persons from Egypt. This was clearly a power play meant to assert the authority of the bishop of Constantinople to act as a court of appeal for cases from elsewhere, and Cyril deftly dismisses the matter in the first paragraph of the letter by laying out the evidence against the three Egyptians. He then turns to address the theological controversy at hand by appealing to an authority he assumed both he and his counterpart would be willing to follow, namely the Creed of the Council of Nicaea from 325. By so doing he not only cast himself as the heir of Athanasius, defender of the Nicene faith against its detractors, but also sought common ground with Nestorius to serve as the basis for their debate. Two verbs from the Creed are chosen for special focus: to become incarnate (*sarkoō*), and to become human (*enanthrōpeō*). Cyril outlines two interpretations of these terms. On the one hand is a union "according to will or favor" or by the "assumption of a mere person (*prosōpon*)." The word "person" was Nestorius's preferred term to refer to the union of the divine Son and the human Jesus. Cyril, however, holds that the word refers merely to the observable aspect or outward appearance of a thing and so does not extend to its most fundamental metaphysical reality. He regards a union in terms of will, favor, or external appearance as something too occasional or impermanent, a sort of union in which the individual components might act independently of one another or even be separated. In contrast, he proposes that the Creed means that the union was "according to hypostasis" or "hypostatic." Here he introduces new technical terminology to the debate. The word "hypostasis" had been used in this sense by Apollinarians in the previous century but had since been dropped. Cyril, for example, nowhere uses it for the union of Christ prior to this letter, though from this point onward it becomes a standard component of his Christological discourse. What the term means for him here and elsewhere is that the union is a real union that results in one distinct subject or individual who acts and is the subject of predication. Hence, all the subsequent verbs of the Creed ("suffered … rose … ascended") refer to one acting individual and cannot be parceled out to the divine Word and the human being Jesus, as Nestorius proposed. As a result, Cyril argues, one cannot avoid saying the Virgin is Theotokos, since God the Word was united to the flesh she bore.

Unlike the *Third Letter to Nestorius*, the orthodoxy of this text was never seriously disputed, and it received synodal approbation at both the Council of Ephesus (431) and the Council of Chalcedon (451).[1]

The translation is based on the critical text of Eduard Schwartz, *Concilium Universale Ephesenum*, ACO 1.1.1 (Berlin: De Gruyter, 1927), 25–28. The *Second Letter to Nestorius* is *Letter* 4 within Cyril's epistolary corpus (CPG 5304).

TRANSLATION

To the most devout and God-loving fellow minister Nestorius, Cyril sends greetings in the Lord.

1. I have learned that certain persons are making wild assertions against my reputation in the presence of Your Reverence, and they are doing this often, taking advantage in particular of the opportunity afforded by the synods held by those in office. And in the hope that you would perhaps somehow appreciate such reports, they are sending your way reckless claims, even though these are persons who have in no way been wronged, but rather have been properly convicted: one was mistreating the blind and the poor, another brandished a sword at his mother, and another, together with a female slave, stole someone else's gold, always having had the kind of reputation that you would not wish to befall even your worst enemies. However, the word of such persons is of little concern to me, lest I should exaggerate my own insignificance as though it surpassed the Master and Teacher or the fathers. For it is impossible to escape from the perversities of such base persons, regardless of how one should choose to live one's life. 2. Those people, with "mouths full of curses and bitterness,"[2] will have to answer for themselves before the judge of all.

1 See the selections from *Acts of the Council of Ephesus* and *Acts of the Council of Chalcedon*, translated, respectively, in this volume on pp. 658–717 and in CEECW 4 on pp. 49–116.

2 Rom 3:14, quoting Ps 9:28 (10:7).

As for me, I will turn back to the task most appropriate for me and will now, as your brother in Christ, remind you that you should set forth before the laity with all caution both the standard of teaching and the way of reasoning about the faith. Consider, moreover, that causing even just one of the least of those who have believed in Christ to stumble brings about unendurable wrath.[3] So if there is a great multitude of people who have been disturbed, does it not require all our skill to prudently remove the stumbling-blocks and to correctly lay out the sound account of the faith to those seeking the truth? And the most correct way to do this will be to acquaint ourselves with the words of the holy fathers and earnestly hold them in the highest regard. We should then "test ourselves to see if we are in the faith,"[4] as it is written, thoroughly molding our mental conceptions to accord with their right and blameless views.

3. So then, the great and holy council said that the only-begotten Son himself, born from God the Father by nature, true God from true God, light from light, through whom the Father has made all things – he it was who came down, became incarnate, became human, suffered, rose on the third day, and ascended into the heavens.[5] We must follow both these words and these doctrines, by considering what the words "becoming incarnate" and "becoming human" reveal about the Word from God. For we do not say that the nature of the Word became flesh[6] by being transformed, nor that it was converted into a whole human being consisting of body and soul. Rather, we say that the Word became human by hypostatically[7] uniting to himself flesh animated by a rational soul in an ineffable and incomprehensible manner. He has accordingly been called the Son of Man, not according to mere will or favor, or as if by the assumption of a mere person.[8] Rather, though the natures brought together into a true union are different, there is one Christ and Son from both. This does not mean the difference between the natures was abolished as a result of the union;[9] instead, both divinity and humanity constitute for us one Lord and Christ and Son through their ineffable and mysterious concurrence into unity.

3 See Matt 18:6. 4 2 Cor 13:5.

5 A paraphrase of part of the Creed of Nicaea from 325. Cyril will next go on to consider two of the verbs from the creed in greater detail.

6 See John 1:14.

7 This is the phrase *kath' hypostasin* (literally, "according to *hypostasis*"), which entered into the controversy with this letter.

8 In Greek, *prosōpon*. See the introduction to this text for Cyril's understanding of this term.

9 This last phrase will be picked up in the Definition of Chalcedon.

4. It is in the following way that the one who existed and was born from the Father before all ages is also said to have been born from a woman according to the flesh: not as if his divine nature[10] received the beginning of its existence in the holy Virgin, nor as if his divine nature stood in absolute need of a second birth for its own sake, following the birth from the Father. For it is altogether rash and ignorant to say that the one who existed before all ages and was co-eternal with the Father required a second start to his existence. Rather, since "for us and for our salvation"[11] he united himself hypostatically to that which is human and so came forth from a woman, for this very reason he is said to have been born in a fleshly sense. For it is not as if a normal human being had first been born from the holy Virgin, and then the Word descended upon him. Rather, since the union occurred in the very womb itself, he is said to have undergone a fleshly birth, making his own the birth of his own flesh.

5. It is in the following way that we say that he both suffered and rose: not as if God the Word suffered in his own nature the beatings or the piercing of the nails or any of the other wounds, since that which is divine is impassible because it is also incorporeal. Rather, since the body that came into being as his own suffered these things, again he himself is said to suffer for us. For the impassible one was in the suffering body. We understand his death according to this same line of reasoning. For God the Word is, according to nature, immortal and incorruptible and life and life-giver. But, again, since his own body "tasted death by the grace of God for everyone,"[12] as Paul has said, he himself is said to have suffered death for us. This does not mean that he experienced death with respect to his nature, for it is madness to say or to think that. Rather, as I have just said, it means that his flesh tasted death. Similarly, when his flesh was raised up, again the resurrection is said to be his, not as if he had fallen into corruption – absolutely not! – but because his body had been raised again.

6. It is in the following way that we will confess one Christ and Lord: not as if we worship a human being along with the Word, lest we should give the impression of a division by saying "along with." Rather, we worship one and the same,[13] because the body of the Word is not alien to him. It is with

10 In Greek, *physis*. 11 Another allusion to the Nicene Creed.

12 Heb 2:9. Cyril, along with most early Christian exegetes, thinks Paul wrote Hebrews. Note that an important textual difference exists in the tradition on this verse. Both the readings "by the grace of God" and "apart from God" are attested, and the distinction played a role in the dispute between Cyril and Nestorius.

13 The phrase "one and the same" will be picked up in the Chalcedonian Definition.

this very body that he is seated with the Father, again not implying there are two sons seated with him, but one Son who is united to his own flesh. And if we were to reject the *hypostatic* union[14] as either impossible or unseemly, we would fall into speaking of two sons, and we then have no choice but to make a distinction and speak first of the human being who, on his own, had been honored with the appellation "son," and second of the Word from God who, on his own, possessed the title and reality of sonship by nature. For this reason one must not divide the one Lord Jesus Christ into two sons.

7. And it will in no way help to maintain the orthodox account of the faith if some people go on to speak of a union of persons.[15] For scripture has not said that the Word united to himself the person[16] of a human being, but that "he became flesh."[17] And to say that the Word became flesh is nothing other than to assert that, "in a manner akin to us, he partook of flesh and blood,"[18] he made a body like ours to be his own, and he came forth from a woman as a human being, not casting aside his existence as God and his birth from God the Father, but remaining what he was, even in his assumption of flesh. The account of the exact faith everywhere promotes this. We will also find that the holy fathers thought about it in these terms. For they had confidence to boldly say that the holy Virgin is Theotokos, not as if the nature of the Word, or his divinity, took the beginning of its existence from the holy Virgin. Rather, they affirmed that the holy body, animated rationally, was born from her, and that the Word, having hypostatically united himself to this body, is said to have been born according to the flesh.

I write these things now out of the love which is in Christ, exhorting you as a brother and solemnly urging you before Christ and the elect angels[19] to think and to teach these same things with us, in order that the peace of the church may be preserved and the bond of harmony and love may be maintained unbroken by the priests of God.

Greet the brotherhood with you. The brotherhood in Christ with us greets you.

14 Literally, "union according to *hypostasis*." 15 In Greek, *prosōpa*, the plural of *prosōpon*. 16 In Greek, *prosōpon*. 17 John 1:14. 18 See Heb 2:14. 19 1 Tim 5:21.

42

Nestorius of Constantinople, *Second Letter to Cyril*

Introduction and Translation by Matthew R. Crawford

INTRODUCTION

This letter, written in 430, represents Nestorius's reply to Cyril's *Second Letter to Nestorius*,[1] and so marks the first occasion in which the bishop of Constantinople directly set out his views on the topic of the debate to his Alexandrian counterpart. Although it maintains the degree of formality and graciousness expected of such communications, the letter exhibits a striking sarcasm over Cyril's long-windedness and a clear rebuke to his meddling in the affairs of the church in the imperial capital. The "actions" threatened at the outset of the letter likely refer to Nestorius's intention to consider the complaints against Cyril brought to him by the persons expelled from Alexandria who had fled to Constantinople for refuge, also referred to in Cyril's second letter.

This letter usefully sums up the main Christological points Nestorius repeatedly emphasized in his various letters and sermons throughout the controversy. "Accuracy" in theological statements is, in his view, critically important to avoid heretical predications. Accordingly, one must pay close attention to the precise names used in scripture and in the Nicene Creed, since some of these refer to the divine Son of God, some to the humanity of Jesus Christ, and some to both simultaneously. The premier name falling into the third category is "Christ," and Nestorius argues that, since this is the term used at the outset of the second article of the Nicene Creed as well as in the famous Pauline passage of Philippians 2, all the statements that follow refer not to the deity alone but instead to both the deity and the humanity together. This argument reveals that one of the main concerns driving Nestorius's Christology – perhaps *the* main concern – was to

1 Translated in this volume on pp. 564–569.

protect the transcendence of the divine nature from being implicated in such human affairs as birth, suffering, and death.

This letter also makes clear that Nestorius's conception of the unity of Christ's person (*prosōpon*) differed from that of Cyril. Whereas Cyril argued for a unification "according to nature" (*kata physin*) or a union brought about "hypostatically" (*kath' hypostasin*), Nestorius proposes that there is a "conjunction" (*synapheia*) between the humanity and the deity, a term that implies a looser sort of association than the unity of a single acting subject maintained by Cyril. And whereas Cyril emphasized the continuity of identity between the eternal Word and the incarnate Christ, repeatedly using divine names like "Son" or "Word" as the subject of verbs referring to the events of the earthly Jesus, Nestorius finds this kind of speech objectionable due to its lack of precision and potential to be interpreted along heretical lines. Moreover, when Nestorius concedes toward the end of the letter that the deity "appropriates what belongs to the temple," a statement that seems close to Cyril's own position, he then clarifies that this "appropriation" excludes the most offensive events of the incarnation. It is thus clear that Nestorius's theological scrupulosity ran counter to the sort of Christological piety propounded by Cyril, who thought that statements that in the view of some bordered on blasphemy (like calling the Virgin "Theotokos" or "bearer of God") were necessary to express the profound mystery of the incarnation.

This translation is based on the critical text of Eduard Schwartz, *Concilium Universale Ephesenum*, ACO 1.1.1 (Berlin: De Gruyter, 1927), 29–32.

TRANSLATION

1. To the most reverent and most God-fearing fellow minister Cyril, Nestorius sends greetings in the Lord.

I will pass over the insults against us contained in your marvelous letter, since they are worthy only of the patience required of a doctor and will soon enough be answered by actions. But there is one thing that will not endure silence, because if silenced it brings a great danger. Of this I will now, so far as I am able, attempt to give a concise account, not pushing myself to excessive wordiness, so as to avoid causing you any nausea from obscure and indigestible tediousness.[2] But I will begin from Your Charity's own all-wise words, citing them

2 A thinly veiled criticism of Cyril's long-winded style of discourse.

verbatim. Well then, what are the words of that marvelous teaching contained in your letter? "The great and holy council said that the only-begotten Son himself, born from God the Father by nature, true God from true God, light from light, through whom the Father has made all things – he it was who came down, became incarnate, became human, suffered, rose."[3]

2. These are the words of Your Piety, and you will perhaps recognize them as your own. But now listen also to our words, a brotherly exhortation on piety that the great Paul also solemnly enjoined upon his beloved Timothy: "Devote yourself to reading, to exhortation, to teaching. For by doing this you will save both yourself and your hearers."[4] Now, what is meant by the phrase "devote yourself"? Surely it implies that in superficially reading the tradition of those holy ones, you failed to recognize your mistake (understandable enough), since you thought that they were saying the Word co-eternal with the Father is subject to suffering. But examine, please, with exact attention to the precise wording, and you will find that the divine chorus of the fathers was not saying that the same-in-substance divinity was subject to suffering, nor that the divinity co-eternal with the Father was subject to a recent birth, nor that the divinity which raised the destroyed temple was itself raised. And if you will lend me your ears for the purpose of a fraternal healing, by setting forth for you the very words of the holy fathers, through them I will disprove your slander against them and against the divine scriptures.

3. Well then, they say, "I too believe in our Lord Jesus Christ, his Son, the Only-Begotten."[5] Observe how, by first using "Lord" and "Jesus" and "Christ" and "Only-Begotten" and "Son," they laid a foundation with the names common to the deity and humanity, and then they built upon it with the tradition about his becoming human and the resurrection and the suffering. By setting forth such names that are indicative of and common to both natures, they were intending that we should neither divide those things belonging to the sonship and those belonging to the lordship, nor run the risk of having those things belonging to the natures destroyed by being confused in the singularity of the sonship.

3 This is an exact quotation from Cyril's *Second Letter to Nestorius* 3 (ACO 1.1.1: 26, 20–23 Schwartz), translated in full in this volume on pp. 564–569.

4 1 Tim 4:13, 16.

5 Nestorius has in mind the Nicene-Constantinopolitan Creed from 381, whose wording he here echoes. Throughout the controversy Cyril consistently appealed to the Nicene Creed of 325 while Nestorius took the creed of 381 as authoritative.

4. Paul has been their instructor in this matter. For when he was recalling the divine humanification and was about to discuss the events of the passion, the first word he used was "Christ," which is the name common to the natures, as I just said, and then he introduced an account that is appropriate to both the natures. What does he say? "Have this mind among yourselves, which was also in Christ Jesus, who, although he was in the form of God, did not consider equality with God something to be grasped, but" (omitting all the particulars) "became obedient unto death, even death on a cross."[6] For since he was about to mention the death, to prevent anyone from supposing from this that God the Word was passible, he uses "Christ" as an appellation that signifies the impassible substance and the passible substance in the singular person. It is in this way that Christ may, without risk, be called both impassible and passible: impassible with respect to deity, but passible with respect to the nature of the body.

5. I could say many things on this topic, first of all the fact that when those holy fathers recalled what happened in the economy, they did not mention a birth, but rather a humanification. Yet I am conscious of my promise of brevity made in the introduction, which restrains my letter and moves us on to Your Charity's second section.

6. Here I applauded your distinction between the natures, in keeping with the rationale of the humanity and the divinity and their conjunction[7] into one person, as well as your affirming that God the Word had no need of a second birth from a woman and your confession that the deity is not capable of experiencing suffering. Such statements are truly orthodox and are opposed to all those heresies teaching heterodoxy about the Lord's natures. But as for the rest of your letter, only your exact mind can determine if it introduces some kind of concealed wisdom that is incomprehensible to the ears of your readers; to me, at least, it seemed to destroy the first things you said. For the one initially proclaimed as impassible and unable to receive a second generation is then introduced again – I know not how – as passible and recently created. It is as if those attributes belonging to God the Word by nature were destroyed by the conjunction with the temple, or as if some people thought it was insignificant that the sinless temple, which is inseparable from the divine nature, endured birth and death on behalf of sinners, or as if we shouldn't believe the Lord's voice when he cried out to

6 Phil 2:5–6, 8. 7 In Greek, *synapheia*.

the Jews, "Destroy this temple and in three days I will raise it."[8] He did not say, "Destroy my deity and it will be raised in three days"!

Again, although I would like to say more on this point, I am restrained by the recollection of my promise and must therefore speak with brevity. 7. All throughout the divine scripture, whenever mention is made of the Lord's economy, the birth and suffering for us are handed down as belonging not to the deity, but to the humanity of Christ, so that the holy Virgin is called, according to a more precise designation, Christotokos, not Theotokos.[9] Now listen to these passages from the gospels crying out, "The book of the generation of Jesus Christ, son of David, son of Abraham."[10] Here it is clear that God the Word was not a son of David. Or take another witness, if you like: "Jacob begot Joseph, the husband of Mary, from whom was born Jesus, who is called Christ."[11] Observe again another voice testifying to us: "The birth of Jesus Christ happened in this manner. For when his mother Mary was betrothed to Joseph, she was found to be pregnant from the Holy Spirit."[12] Who would ever suppose that this means the deity of the Only-Begotten was the creation of the Holy Spirit? And what should we say about the following passage: "The mother of Jesus was there."[13] And again: "with Mary, the mother of Jesus,"[14] and "that which is begotten in her is from the Holy Spirit,"[15] and "take the child and his mother and flee to Egypt,"[16] and "concerning his Son who came from the seed of David according to the flesh."[17] And once more, concerning the suffering: "God, by sending his own Son in the likeness of sinful flesh and for sin, condemned sin in the flesh";[18] and again: "Christ died for our sins";[19] and "Christ suffered in the flesh";[20] and "this is" – not my deity, but – "my body which is broken for you."[21] And there are countless other passages that testify to the human race that it is not the deity of the Son that is regarded as recent or as able to suffer bodily, but instead the flesh that was conjoined to the nature of the deity. It is for this reason also that Christ calls himself both Lord of David and Son. For he says, "'What do you think about the Christ? Whose son is he?' They said to him, 'The son of David.' Jesus answered and said to them, 'How is it then that David in the Spirit calls him Lord, saying, "The Lord said to my Lord, 'Sit at my right hand.'"'"[22] For he is certainly Son of David according to the flesh, but Lord according to the

8 John 2:19. 9 That is, "bearer of Christ" rather than "bearer of God."
10 Matt 1:1. 11 Matt 1:16. 12 Matt 1:18. 13 John 2:1. 14 Acts 1:14.
15 Matt 1:20. 16 Matt 2:13. 17 Rom 1:3. 18 Rom 8:3. 19 1 Cor 15:3.
20 1 Pet 4:1. 21 1 Cor 11:24. 22 Matt 22:42–44.

deity. Therefore, on the one hand, it is right and in keeping with the gospel traditions to confess that the body is a temple of the deity of the Son, a temple united according to a certain consummate and divine conjunction, with the result that the nature of the deity appropriates what belongs to the temple. But on the other hand, to say that this appropriation involves also the properties of the conjoined flesh – I mean the birth and suffering and death – brother, either this belongs to the misguided thinking of the Greeks, or it comes from a mind sick with the ideas of the brain-damaged Apollinarius and Arius and the other heresies, or something even more serious than them. For those persons who are carried away by this word "appropriation" would even have to say, on account of the appropriation, that God the Word took part in sucking at the breast, and experienced gradual growth and cowardice at the time of the passion, and was in need of angelic assistance. And I will not even speak about the circumcision, sacrifice, perspiration, and hunger, things which, if they are ascribed to the flesh, are revered as taking place for our sake, but, if attributed to the deity, are lies and the basis for our just condemnation as slanderers.

8. These are the traditions of the holy fathers. These are the precepts of the divine scriptures. It is in this manner that one should theologize about those things pertaining to the divine love for humanity and about those pertaining to the authority. "Meditate upon these things, immerse yourself in them, so that your progress may be evident to all," says Paul to everyone.[23] You do well by showing concern for those who have been scandalized, and thank you as well for your soul which is anxious about divine matters and also concerned for us. But you should know that it is you who have been deceived by those condemned by the holy synod here[24] for holding Manichaean opinions, or perhaps by the clerics in your own charge. For the affairs of the church are daily advancing, and by the grace of Christ the affairs of the people flourish to such a degree that those who see the multitudes cry out the words of the prophet, "The earth will be filled with the knowledge of the Lord as far as the waters cover the sea."[25] The imperial court is overjoyed as the doctrine is illuminated, and, to be brief, with respect to all the heresies that fight against God and against the orthodoxy of the church that saying is daily found to be fulfilled among us, "The house of Saul went and became weaker and the house of David went and became stronger."[26]

23 1 Tim 4:15. 24 That is, the local synod of Constantinople. 25 Isa 11:9.
26 2 Sam 3:1. Probably a reference to Nestorius's actions against the Novatians in Constantinople.

9. We give these words of advice as brother to brother. But "if someone is contentious," Paul has cried out to such a person through us too, "neither we, nor the churches of God have such a custom."[27] I and those with me send their heartiest greetings to all the brotherhood in Christ with you. May you continue in good health and in prayer for us, most honorable and pious lord.

27 1 Cor 11:16.

43

Proclus of Constantinople, *Homily on the Holy Virgin Theotokos*

Introduction and Translation by Andrew Radde-Gallwitz

INTRODUCTION

A gem of early Christian oratory, Proclus's first homily on the Holy Virgin draws on the emerging tradition of festal homilies such as we see in Basil of Caesarea's *Homily on the Holy Birth of Christ* and Gregory of Nyssa's *Homily on the Savior's Nativity*[1] and addresses the crises of his day. Proclus was bishop of Cyzicus in 430 when he proclaimed this homily in the presence of his archbishop, Nestorius, who had been installed by Theodosius II on the episcopal throne in Constantinople. The occasion, it appears, was the feast of the Virgin that had recently been instituted in Constantinople for December 26. Defying Nestorius, Proclus unequivocally defends the language of Mary as Theotokos, which for him safeguards what he calls here the "coupling of natures," divine and human, in Christ, the "incarnate God." To name Mary's role in effecting this union, Proclus draws on a trove of imagery at once exuberant and focused. Mary is, following the Cappadocians, the incarnation's "workshop," but also a bridge, a field, and a temple. She is the loom on which the economy is woven and her flesh is the thread, made of the wool of the skin-garments worn originally by Adam; it is his disobedience (or "mishearing") that she overturns by conceiving the Word through hearing Gabriel's announcement. To justify his two-nature theology, Proclus offers an argument reminiscent of Athanasius's *On the Incarnation* – and anticipating Anselm's *Why the God-Man?* (*Cur Deus Homo*) – for the necessity of a divine payment of humanity's debt incurred in Adam. In addition to speaking of humanity's debt, Proclus also uses a medical metaphor. He likens the state of humanity prior to Christ to a terminally ill

1 Translated in this volume, respectively, on pp. 354–365 and pp. 403–419.

patient whose malady has been diagnosed by doctors (in this case, the Hebrew prophets) who are incapable of healing them. Acknowledging their plight, they cry out to the heavenly doctor who comes in Christ with the remedy.

Proclus articulates his Christology by distinguishing it from various heretical positions, which he addresses in vocative statements. "O Jew," he says, Christ was not a mere man; "O Manichee," he continues, Christ truly had a body. He urges his hearers not to be disciples of Arius by severing Christ from the Trinity. In an apparent criticism of Nestorius, Proclus also chides anyone who would proclaim that there are two subjects in Christ. Christ and the Word are not *allos kai allos* – two distinct persons or subjects – since this would introduce a quaternity rather than a Trinity of hypostases.

The homily was included among the proceedings of the Council of Ephesus in 431. In 434, Proclus was installed as archbishop of Constantinople, where he would remain until his death in 446. His homily has enjoyed a brilliant liturgical afterlife. In the Orthodox churches it is read at the Feast of the Annunciation on March 25. This translation is based on the critical edition of the Greek text by Eduard Schwartz, *Concilium Universale Ephesenum*, ACO 1.1.1 (Berlin: De Gruyter, 1927), 103–107, as reprinted in Nicholas Constas, *Proclus of Constantinople and the Cult of the Virgin in Late Antiquity: Homilies 1–5, Texts and Translations*, Vigiliae Christianae Supplements 66 (Leiden: Brill, 2003), 136–147. The Greek text is on the odd-numbered pages.

TRANSLATION

Homily of Bishop Proclus of Cyzicus delivered with Nestorius seated in the Great Church of Constantinople

1. Today the Virgin's festival, brothers, calls the tongue to praise, and the present feast becomes a source of aid for those assembled. And this is completely right, for its subject is chastity, and what is celebrated is the boast of the race of women and the glory of what is female, because of her who is at once mother and virgin. A truly lovely meeting – for behold earth and sea attending to the Virgin: the one spreading its waves calmly beneath the ships, the other conveying travelers' footsteps unhindered. Let [human] nature leap for joy and let women be honored! Let

humanity dance and virgins be glorified! For "where sin increased, grace abounded still more."[2]

She who has convened us is holy Mary,[3]
undefiled treasure of virginity,
rational paradise of the Second Adam,[4]
workshop of the union of natures,
festival of the saving alliance,
bridal chamber where the Word weds the flesh,
living thorn-bush of [human] nature,
which the fire of the divine birth-pangs did not consume,
truly swift cloud[5]
who bodily bore the one [enthroned] upon the cherubim,[6]
bearer of purest rain from heaven,[7]
from whom the shepherd clothed himself with the sheep,[8]
servant and mother, Virgin and heaven,
sole bridge between God and human beings,
fearful loom of the economy,
on which the garment of the union ineffably was woven,
at which the loom-worker was the Holy Spirit;
the weaver, the overshadowing power from on high;[9]
the wool, the original sheepskin of Adam;[10]
the thread, the undefiled flesh from the Virgin;
the shuttle, the immeasurable grace of the wearer;
the craftsman, the Word who leaped in through the ear.

2. Who has seen, who has heard of God dwelling in a mother without circumscription? The one whom heaven cannot contain, the womb did not constrict, but rather he was "born from a woman"[11] not solely[12] God and not merely a human being. The one born rendered sin's ancient door as salvation's gateway. For where the serpent shot its arrow through

2 Rom 5:20.
3 Proclus here inserts a sort of hymn like those that appear in certain homilies of Gregory of Nazianzus and Gregory of Nyssa or, classically, in Agathon's speech in Plato's *Symposium* 197c5–e5.
4 See Rom 5:14; 1 Cor 15:21, 45.
5 See Isa 19:1.
6 See Ps 98(99):1.
7 See Judg 6:37–38.
8 See John 10:11; Matt 18:12–14; Luke 15:3–7.
9 See Luke 1:35.
10 See Gen 3:21.
11 Gal 4:4.
12 In Greek, *gymnos*. Proclus likens the Word's becoming human to putting on clothes; the adjective used here means literally "naked" or "stripped."

mishearing,[13] there the Word, having entered the temple through the ear, fashioned its shrine. From the place whence sin's first disciple Cain emerged, the redeemer of the race, Christ, sprouted unsown. The one who loved humanity was not ashamed of the woman's birth-pangs, for the objective was life. He was not tainted by inhabiting parts that he himself had crafted without embarrassment. Had the mother not remained a virgin, he would have been born as a mere human being and the birth would not be astonishing. But if she remained a virgin even after giving birth, he was born in an ineffable manner – he who also entered unhindered through locked doors,[14] and whose coupling of natures Thomas proclaimed when he said, "My Lord and my God."[15]

3. Do not be ashamed of the birth-pangs, O human being! For they became for us the starting point of salvation. Had he not been "born from a woman,"[16] he would not have died. Had he not died, he would not "have through death nullified the one who held power over death, that is, the devil."[17] There's no dishonor for a master craftsman to dwell in a house he built; clay does not taint the potter who repairs what he had fashioned. Likewise, proceeding from the virginal womb did not taint the undefiled one. For having fashioned it, he was not defiled; proceeding through it, he was not tainted. O womb in which the contract of the new liberty was ratified! O belly in which the death-fighting armory was forged! O field in which the farmer of [human] nature, Christ, sprouted unsown like a head of grain. O temple in which God became priest – not changing his nature, but through his compassion clothing himself with the one who is "according to the order of Melchizedek."[18] "The Word became flesh,"[19] even though the Jews do not believe the Lord who said this. God wore the form of humanity,[20] even though the Greeks mock the marvel. Indeed, for this reason "to the Jews," the mystery "is a stumbling-block, to the Gentiles, a folly,"[21] since the marvel is beyond reckoning. Had the Word not dwelt in a womb, the flesh would not have been seated on the throne. If it is a dishonor for God to enter into the mother, then it is also dishonor for the angels to minister to humanity.[22]

13 In Greek, *parakoēs*. This word, which includes the term for hearing or the ear (*akoē*), is often rendered "disobedience."
14 See John 20:19, 26. 15 John 20:28. 16 Gal 4:4. 17 Heb 2:14.
18 Heb 6:20, 7:11; Ps 109(110):4. 19 John 1:14. 20 See Phil 2:7.
21 1 Cor 1:23. 22 See Matt 4:11; Heb 1:14.

4. And so he who is by nature impassible through [his] compassion became many-sorrowed.[23] Christ did not become God by advancement[24] – surely not! – but rather through [his] compassion he became a human being, as we believe. We do not proclaim a deified human being; rather, we confess an incarnate God. To his own servant he gave the title of mother – he who in his essence is without mother and who in the economy is without father. Otherwise, how is the same one, in Paul's words, "without mother" and "without father"?[25] If he is a mere human being, he is not without mother, for he has a mother. If he is solely God, he is not without father, for he has a father. But in fact, he who is motherless is the same as the one who forms, and he who is fatherless is the same as that which is formed.[26]

5. Tremble also at the archangel's name. The one who proclaimed good news to Mary is called Gabriel. What does "Gabriel" mean? God and human being.[27] And so, since the one proclaimed by him is God and human being, the name was an anticipation of the marvel so that the economy might have confirmation. Learn the reason for the appearance and glorify the power of the one who became flesh. The human race owed a lot and couldn't pay the debt. Through Adam we had all signed ourselves over to sin.[28] The devil held us as slaves. He would bring forth our bills, using our many-sorrowed body for paper. The wicked forger stood firm, leaving us in debt and demanding that we give satisfaction. Therefore, one of two things had to happen: either that the satisfying death penalty be applied to all, since in fact "all have sinned,"[29] or that in exchange there be given such a person who had full justification to intercede. Now, no human being could save us, for they would be subject to the debt. An angel was incapable of buying him off, since it would lack the means to pay the ransom. One without sin had to die on behalf of sinners, for there remained only this dissolution of the malady.

6. What, then? The same one who had brought the whole nature into being, who in no way lacks the means of payment, won a most secure life for the condemned and a most fitting dissolution of death. And he became a human being in a way he alone knows, for words cannot explain the marvel. In what he became, he died; in what he was, he redeemed, according to Paul, who says, "In whom we have redemption through his blood, the

23 In Greek, *polypathēs*. "Impassible" is *apathēs*. 24 See Luke 2:52.
25 Heb 7:3. 26 In Greek, *plasma*. "The one who forms" is *plastēs*.
27 Proclus is offering an etymology of the Hebrew name. 28 See Col 2:14.
29 Rom 3:23.

remission of transgressions."[30] What an exchange! It was for others that he procured immortality, for he himself was immortal. In terms of economic function,[31] his like never existed, has not come into being, does not currently exist, and will not exist – none other than the only one born from a virgin as God and human being. He possesses a rank that does not simply counterbalance the multitude of the condemned but even surpasses all the votes of condemnation. As Son, he maintains indistinguishability with respect to the Father; as creator, he possesses unapproachable power; as merciful, he makes known his indomitable sympathy; as high priest, he bears credibility in making intercession;[32] none of which could ever be found in anyone else to an equal degree or even nearly so. So behold the love! Willingly condemned, he undid the death due to those who crucified him and turned the killers' crime into salvation for the criminals.

7. So, to save was impossible for a mere human being; for he too would have needed a savior, according to Paul, who says, "For all have sinned."[33] Sin brought us to the devil; the devil delivered us to death; we were in gravest danger. The solution was beyond our means, the doctors sent to us declared. What, then? Since the prophets saw that [to heal] the wound surpassed the abilities of human craft, they cried out to the heavenly doctor. And one of them said, "Incline your heavens and come down."[34] Another: "Heal me, Lord, and I will be healed."[35] Another: "Awaken your power and come to save us."[36] Another: "Will God really dwell with human beings?"[37] Another: "Let your mercies quickly seize us, for we have been greatly impoverished."[38] Another: "Woe, my soul! For the reverent one has perished from the earth and there is no one upright among human beings."[39] Another: "God, come to my help; Lord, speed to help me."[40] Another: "In a little while, the coming one will arrive and will not delay."[41] Another: "I have wandered like a lost sheep; seek out your servant who hopes in you."[42] Another: "God, our God, will appear openly and will not be silenced."[43] So the one who is by nature king did not long abandon [human] nature to tyranny; the merciful God did not forever leave it liable to the devil. No, he came – the one who is always present. And he laid down his own blood as ransom payment. To death he gave the body, which he had donned from the virgin, in exchange for our race. And he redeemed the world from the

30 Eph 1:7. 31 In Greek, *kat' oikonomian.* 32 See Heb 3:1. 33 Rom 3:23.
34 Ps 143(144):5. 35 Jer 17:14. 36 Ps 79(80):2. 37 1 Kgs 8:27.
38 Ps 78(79):8. 39 Mic 7:1–2. 40 Ps 69(70):1. 41 Hab 2:3; see Heb 10:37.
42 Ps 118(119):176. 43 Ps 49(50):3.

curse of the law, by death rendering death idle, and Paul cries out, "Christ redeemed us from the curse of the law."[44]

8. So the Redeemer was not a mere human being, O Jew; for the nature of human beings was enslaved to sin. But neither was he God stripped of humanity; for he had a body, O Manichee; for had he not clothed himself with me, he would not have saved me. But the one who appeared in the womb of the Virgin clothed himself with the condemned one and there the wondrous exchange occurred. While giving spirit, he received flesh. The same one is with the Virgin and from the Virgin: insofar as he overshadowed, with her; insofar as he was incarnate, from her. If Christ were one and God the Word another,[45] there would no longer be a Trinity, but a Quaternity. Do not rend the economy's garment, woven from above;[46] do not be a disciple of Arius. He impiously severed the substance. As for you, do not divide the unity, lest you be divided from God. Who is the one that "shone on those seated in darkness and in the shadow of death"?[47] A human being? Well, how? They, after all, dwelt in darkness, according to Paul, who says, "He who drew us out of the power of darkness,"[48] and again, "For you once were darkness."[49] So then, who shone? David instructs you when he says, "Blessed is he who comes in the name of the Lord."[50] Speak plainly, O David, "Cry out with strength and don't hold back; Lift up your voice like a trumpet."[51] Tell us, who is this? The Lord God of hosts. "The Lord is God, and he shone on us."[52] "The Word became flesh."[53] The natures came together and the union remained without confusion.

9. He came to save but had also to suffer. How were both possible? A mere human being did not have the power to save. God on his own was incapable of suffering. What then? The same one who was God became a human being, and through what he was, he saved, while through what he became, he suffered. For this reason, when the church saw the synagogue crowning him with thorns, she lamented the outrage and said, "Daughters of Jerusalem, come out and see the crown with which his mother has crowned him."[54] For the same one both donned the crown of thorns and undid the punishment of thorns.[55] The same one was "in the Father's bosom"[56] and in the Virgin's womb, in his mother's arms and "on the wings of

44 Gal 3:13.
45 In Greek, *allos* … *allos* (masculine singular pronouns). No noun is added to specify one *what* and another *what*.
46 See John 19:23–24. 47 Luke 1:79. 48 Col 1:13. 49 Eph 5:8.
50 Ps 117(118):26. 51 Isa 58:1. 52 Ps 117(118):27. 53 John 1:14.
54 Song 3:11. 55 See Gen 3:18–19. 56 John 1:18.

the winds,"[57] worshiped by angels[58] and at table with tax-collectors;[59] the seraphim would not look upon him[60] and Pilate interrogated him;[61] a servant struck him[62] and creation stood in wonder. To the cross he was nailed and his throne was not vacant. In the tomb he was shut and he spread out heaven like a curtain.[63] Among the dead he was counted and he despoiled Hades. Below he was accused of being an impostor[64] and above he was glorified as holy. O the mystery! I behold marvels and proclaim the deity; I see suffering and cannot deny the humanity. Though Emmanuel opened the door of our nature as a human being, as God he did not break the gates, but came forth from his mother just as he had entered through the ear: he was born just as he'd been conceived. He entered impassibly; he came forth ineffably, according to the prophet Ezekiel, who proclaims: "The Lord turned me around," he says, "on the way of the outer gate of the sanctuary, which faces east, and it was shut. And the Lord said to me, 'Son of Man, this gate shall be shut and shall not be opened. No one shall ever pass through it except the Lord God of Israel; he alone shall enter and exit, and the gate shall remain shut.'"[65] Look at this clear demonstration of the holy and Theotokos Mary. Hence let all contradiction be resolved, and let us be enlightened by the scriptures' teaching, so that we too might obtain the kingdom of heaven in Christ Jesus our Lord, to whom be glory for ever and ever. Amen.

57 Ps 103(104):3. 58 See Heb 1:6; Deut 32:43; Ps 96(97):7.
59 See Matt 9:10; Mark 2:15. 60 See Isa 6:2.
61 Matt 27:11; Mark 15:2, 4; Luke 23:3; see John 18:33, 37. 62 Mark 14:65; John 18:22.
63 Ps 103(104):2. 64 Matt 27:63. 65 Ezek 44:1–2.

44

Nestorius of Constantinople, *Three Letters to Celestine of Rome*

Introduction and Translation of First Letter by Matthew R. Crawford
Translation of Second and Third Letters by Mark DelCogliano

INTRODUCTION

The three letters that follow highlight the fact that the Nestorian controversy had as much to do with ecclesiastical politics as it did with theological debate. Indeed, these letters, despite their brevity, illustrate one of the main reasons why Nestorius lost his struggle against the bishop of Alexandria, namely, his failure to draw Bishop Celestine of Rome to his cause. The primary purpose of the first letter, probably written in late 429, was to seek from Celestine information about several clerical exiles who had come to Constantinople from the West. These bishops, including most prominently Julian of Eclanum, had, as a result of the efforts of Augustine of Hippo, been deposed for adhering to the views of Pelagius regarding sin and salvation. Nestorius's report to Celestine in the first letter hints at his intention to reopen their case, an action that he should have realized the bishop of Rome would not look kindly upon. This intention becomes more explicit in the second letter, written perhaps in early 430, as Nestorius complains of the lack of response from the Roman leader and insists that Celestine send him the dossiers used in the deposition of the Pelagian bishops.

This strategy was bound to fail. Presumably Nestorius was operating on the basis of the new status granted to the church of Constantinople at the council of 381, as possessing an "honor" second only to that of Rome, since the Eastern capital was a "second Rome." Celestine, however, would never have allowed his canonical decisions to be reconsidered by his Constantinopolitan counterpart. Moreover, the churches of Alexandria and of Rome had long been allies in theological controversies, stretching back at least to the 340s when Athanasius had fled to Rome in exile, so Celestine was, from the outset, more likely to side with Cyril than with the upstart Nestorius in Constantinople.

In the first and second letters Nestorius provides vague reports about his own struggle against the "heresy" he had discovered in Constantinople, not mentioning Cyril at all. Shortly after he took up his post in 428 a controversy erupted in the capital over whether it was proper to call Mary Theotokos, meaning that she is "God-bearer," or Anthropotokos, meaning "bearer of the human being." In the first letter to Celestine Nestorius suggests that those who use Theotokos adhere to some kind of "blending" of the humanity and divinity in Christ, which, he asserts, smacks of the fourth-century heresies of Arianism and Apollinarianism. At the end of the letter, almost as an afterthought, he concedes that the term could have an orthodox interpretation. Still, Nestorius seems to think it best avoided, since as he argues, "no one gives birth to someone older than herself," a line that would be sharply criticized by John Cassian, who prepared an assessment of Nestorius's Christology on behalf of the Roman see.[1] In light of this principle, Nestorius views the term Theotokos as "inferior" to the term Christotokos ("Christ-bearer"), which he prefers as a more accurate appellation for the Virgin since it avoided heretical extremes on both sides. In the second letter another common Nestorian theme emerges, namely that the humanity and the divinity of Christ are each worshiped or adored distinctly, though in unison or "together," a manner of speaking which Cyril attacked as necessarily implying a dual subjectivity.

The third letter is revealing of the state of Nestorius's mind in the run-up to the council in 431. In this letter he quietly drops all mention of the Pelagian bishops, and focuses entirely on his controversy with Cyril, presenting the debate over the term Theotokos as an attempt by his Alexandrian foe to draw attention away from the accusations being made against him. Accordingly, he tells Celestine that the primary purpose of the forthcoming ecumenical council is to assess these complaints brought against Cyril. Perhaps by this point Nestorius had become aware that Cyril was having success in his dealings with Celestine in contrast to the silence he had so far had to endure from the bishop of Rome. Whatever the case, it is clear that when he penned this letter he realized that his best chance of victory

1 John Cassian, *On the Incarnation* 2.2.1, 4.2.2, 5.1.3, and 7.2.1. Section 5.1.3 is translated in this volume on pp. 618–619.

in the widening conflict lay in his proximity to Emperor Theodosius II and in the council the emperor would soon summon.

This letter too, however, would go unanswered, as had the previous two. The first communication Nestorius would receive from Celestine was a letter dated August 10, 430, giving him ten days to recant his heretical views and comply with the faith set forth by the churches of Rome and Alexandria.[2] In it Celestine claimed that the reason Nestorius's letters had gone unanswered was because he had sent them in Greek, without having them first translated into Latin. Given the improbability that there was no one in Rome who could have translated the letters for Celestine, this claim only further illustrates the annoyance, and perhaps offense, that these letters aroused in him.

The original Greek versions of these letters are lost, but a fifth-century Latin translation survives. The translations here are based on the critical Latin text established by Eduard Schwartz, *Concilium Universale Ephesenum*, ACO 1.2 (Berlin: De Gruyter, 1925–1926), 12–15 and ACO 1.5 (Berlin: De Gruyter, 1924–1926), 182. Reference has also been made to the edition of Friedrich Loofs, *Nestoriana: Die Fragmente des Nestorius* (Halle: Niemeyer, 1905), 165–172 and 181–182.

TRANSLATION

First Letter to Celestine

1. We owe to each other brotherly dialogue, so that, with harmony prevailing between us in <a brotherly spirit>,[3] we might fight together against the devil, the enemy of peace. Why this preface? A certain Julian, Florus, Orontius, and Fabius, calling themselves bishops of the western regions, have frequently approached the most pious and most commendable emperor[4] and bewailed their situation, claiming that they are orthodox persons suffering persecution during these orthodox times. They have frequently made the same claim in our presence and have frequently been turned away, but they have not ceased making the same claim and continue day after day to fill the ears of everyone with tearful cries. We have replied to them using appropriate words, even while being ignorant of what is true and credible in their affair. But since we are in need of more explicit

2 ACO 1.1.2: 7–12 Schwartz.

3 This is Schwartz's proposed supplement to fill a small lacuna in the text.

4 Theodosius II.

information about their cases, lest our most pious and most Christian emperor have to endure repeated annoyance from these persons, and lest we, in ignorance of their cases, be pulled in two ways over the prosecution of the case, please deem us worthy to receive information about them. Otherwise certain persons might, in ignorance of true justice, cause trouble by showing them inappropriate compassion, or judge the canonical displeasure of Your Beatitude,[5] which was presumably sanctioned against them for heretical worship, to be something other than what it is. For the novelty of heresies calls for prosecution by true pastors.

2. This is the reason why, when we ourselves too had discovered no small amount of corruption of orthodoxy among certain persons here, day after day we made use of both anger and gentleness with those sick persons. For the sickness is not insignificant, but is related to the putrefaction of Apollinarius and Arius. For it is constantly muddling the Lord's appearance as a human being, resulting in some kind of confused blending, to such a degree that even certain clerics among us – some from inexperience, others from heretical deceit previously concealed within themselves (such as often happened also in the times of the apostles) – are sick like the heretics and openly blaspheme God the Word, who is same-in-substance with the Father, supposing that he received the beginning of his origin from the Christotokos Virgin, was fashioned along with his temple, and was buried with the flesh. And they say that after the resurrection his flesh did not remain flesh, but turned into the nature of the divinity. To be brief, they assign to the divinity of the Only-Begotten the same origin as that of the flesh that is conjoined with it and say it died along with the flesh. Moreover, they blasphemously claim that the flesh conjoined to the divinity turned into the divinity by means of the divinizing Word, which is nothing other than to destroy both. But they even had the audacity to treat the Christotokos Virgin as somehow divine along with God. For they have no qualms about calling her "Theotokos," even though those holy fathers at Nicaea who surpass all praise said nothing more about the holy Virgin than "our Lord Jesus Christ became incarnate from the Holy Spirit and the Virgin Mary."[6] And I pass over in silence the

5 Schwartz detects a small lacuna in the text here, but sense can be made of the wording without an addition.

6 Note that Nestorius cites a version of the Nicene Creed that accords with the one put forward at the Council of Constantinople in 381 rather than that from Nicaea in 325 which did not include the phrase "from the Holy Spirit and the Virgin Mary."

scriptures, which everywhere, both through angels and through apostles, proclaim that the Virgin is the mother of Christ, not of God the Word.

I suspect that a previous report has already informed Your Beatitude of the sort of conflicts we have endured for these matters. And you have heard too that our conflicts have not been in vain. For many of those who had been corrupted and separated from us have, by the grace of the Lord, been set aright, because,[7] properly speaking, that which is born is same-in-substance with the one who gave it birth, while that to which the Lord's appearance as a human being was entrusted is the creature of the Lord's humanity, which is conjoined to God [and which came] from the Virgin through the Spirit. Moreover, if someone suggests that the name "Theotokos" is used on account of the humanity that was born and is conjoined to God the Word, and not on account of the one who gave it birth, we reply that this term is inappropriate for her who gave birth. For a true mother must be of the same substance as that which is born from her. Nevertheless, this term can be allowed in light of the following consideration, namely, that this name is only given to the Virgin on account of the inseparable temple of God the Word that came from her, and not because she herself is the mother of God the Word. For no one gives birth to someone older than herself.[8]

3. I suspect that the earlier report has already informed you about these matters, but nevertheless we ourselves have recounted the events that have transpired, in order to show by [explaining] these matters that we wish to be informed about the case of the aforementioned persons[9] in a brotherly spirit rather than out of a desire born of crass curiosity, especially since we relate our affairs as brothers to brothers, disclosing to one another the truth about the heresies, so that the opening of my letter may be as true as can be. For when I began this letter I said we owe to each other brotherly dialogue. I and those who are with me send greetings to all the brothers in Christ who are with you.

7 Schwartz detected a lacuna here. He is certainly correct that it is an odd transition. He proposed that the omitted text said something like, "we refuse to use the word Theotokos with respect to the holy Virgin, for ..." But sense can be made of the text without any addition.

8 The last sentence of this paragraph is quoted several times in John Cassian, *On the Incarnation*, including at 5.1.3, which is translated in this volume on pp. 618–619.

9 That is, the Pelagian exiles from the West.

Second Letter to Celestine

1. I have often written to Your Beatitude on account of Julian, Orontius, and the others, who have usurped for themselves episcopal dignity, and made frequent appearances before the most pious and the most commendable emperor, and prostrated themselves in our presence with repeated lamentations, claiming that they were expelled from the West in orthodox times. But we still have not received from Your Worship any writings about them. If I had such documents, I would be able to respond to them and give a brief response to their weeping. As things stand, apart from the uncertain things they say, there is nothing to which one might turn, with some people calling them heretics and saying that for this reason they were expelled from the western regions, while they themselves swear that they are the targets of false accusations and have endured this trial for the sake of the orthodox faith as a result of surreptitious activity. Our lack of information about them is thus a heavy burden, whether their account is true or not. For it is a crime to commiserate with them if they are truly heretics, but it is harsh and impious not to commiserate with them if they are the targets of false accusations. Therefore, let Your Soul, most beloved by God, please deem us worthy to be informed [about them], since we are still pulled in two ways by the weight of each impulse, that is, toward hating them and having mercy on them. For we wish to learn what opinion we should hold about them. For day after day we defer giving a response to these men, disguising the fact that we still hope and wait on Your Beatitude.

2. For, as Your Supreme Worship knows, this is not an insignificant investigation of a pious faction, nor is the examination of those who do this a trifling matter. For we are also expending much energy here, striving to root out from the church of God that utterly foul impiety of the most harmful opinion of Apollinarius and Arius. For I do not know how some ecclesiastical persons have become diseased with the sickness of the aforementioned heretics, on account of their acceptance of a certain idea that the divinity and humanity of the Only-Begotten are blended. These heretics both have the audacity to make the bodily passions pour over into the divinity of the Only-Begotten and pretend that the divine immutability has turned into the bodily nature. They confuse both natures through the mutability that arises through the blending, even though both natures are adored through an unconfused conjunction of the highest sort in the single person of the Only-Begotten. Blind men! They do not remember the

exposition of those holy fathers that explicitly contradicts them: "We believe in one Lord Jesus Christ, the Son of God, who became incarnate from the Holy Spirit and the Virgin Mary."[10] For this statement [is made] with the title which signifies both natures, that is, Christ and <...>[11] same-in-substance with the divinity of the Father. But the humanity born in these latter times is from the holy Virgin; on account of its conjunction with the divinity, the humanity is worshiped by angels and humans together with [the divinity].

3. So then, have regard for the one here who is wearied by so many labors on behalf of doctrinal purity[12] and consider what he will unavoidably suffer again, if he should remain uninformed about the case of the people mentioned above and greatly afraid that out of ignorance he might make still more heretics in addition to those described here. Therefore, I ask that Your Holy Soul be diligent in every respect in giving information about the people mentioned above, especially since the most loyal carrier of the letter, the *cubicularius* Valerius, can give to Your Beatitude an explicit account of how they vex. I and those who are with me send the greatest number of greetings to all the brothers in Christ who are with you.

Third Letter to Celestine

I have learned that Cyril, the most distinguished bishop of the city of Alexandria, has been struck with terror because of the written complaints against him, which we have received, and is now hunting for subterfuges to avoid a holy synod taking place on account of these written complaints. In the meantime, he is devising some other subterfuges, namely, frivolous disturbances over terminology. He has fixed upon the terms "Theotokos" and "Christotokos" – the first he allows, but as for "Christotokos," sometimes he removes it from the gospels, and again sometimes he allows it, on the basis of what I believe is a kind of excessive prudence. In the case of the term "Theotokos," I am not opposed to those who want to say it, unless it should contribute to the confusion of natures in the manner of

10 This is a quotation from the Nicene-Constantinopolitan Creed of 381. Schwartz posits a small lacuna after it, but this seems unnecessary.

11 There is a small lacuna in the text here.

12 Here Schwartz's edition is followed, which reads *propter sectarum puritatem*. Loofs's edition reads *propter sectarum pravitatem*, which would be translated, "on account of heretical depravity."

the madness of Apollinarius or Arius. Nonetheless, I have no doubt that the term "Theotokos" is inferior to the term "Christotokos," as the latter is mentioned by the angels and the gospels. And if I were not speaking to Your Worship who is already so knowledgeable, I would need to give a very long discourse on this topic. But even without a discourse, it is known in every way to Your Beatitude that if we should judge that there are two heresies opposed to each other, the one using only the term "Theotokos," the other only "Anthropotokos," and each heresy draws [others] to what it confesses or, if they have not accomplished this, puts itself at risk of falling away from the church, it would be necessary to assign someone to such an affair should it arise. This person would exercise concern for both heresies and heal the danger of both parties by means of the term taken from the gospels that signifies both natures. For as I said, the term "Christotokos" <avoids>[13] the assertion of both parties,[14] because it both removes the blasphemy of Paul of Samosata,[15] who claimed that Christ the Lord of all was simply a human being, and also it puts to flight the wickedness of both Arius and Apollinarius. Now I have also written these very things to the most distinguished bishop of Alexandria, as Your Beatitude can tell from the copies I have attached to this letter of mine, as well as from the copies of what he wrote to us.[16] Moreover, with God's help it has also been agreed to announce a mandatory worldwide synod for the investigation into the other ecclesiastical matters.[17] For I do not think it will be difficult to investigate an uncertainty over words, and it is not a hindrance for a discussion of the divinity of Christ the Lord.

13 This is Schwartz's proposed supplement to fill a small lacuna in the text.
14 That is, advocates of Theotokos and adherents of Anthropotokos.
15 On Paul of Samosata, see his *Selected Fragments*, translated in this volume on pp. 197–211. Eusebius of Dorylaeum links Nestorius with Paul of Samosata in his *Protest*, translated in this volume on pp. 559–563.
16 That is, presumably, Nestorius's *Second Letter to Cyril* and Cyril's *Second Letter to Nestorius*, translated in this volume on pp. 570–576 and pp. 564–569.
17 This synod would eventually take place in Ephesus in 431. Nestorius wrote this letter prior to the formal announcement of an ecumenical council being sent out by Emperor Theodosius II. This statement is thus no doubt intended as a reminder to Celestine of Nestorius's proximity to the imperial court in Constantinople and his insider knowledge of palace affairs.

45

John Cassian, *On the Incarnation of the Lord against Nestorius* 3.1–16 and 5.1–4

Introduction and Translation by Matthew R. Crawford and Thomas L. Humphries

INTRODUCTION

John Cassian is more renowned for his seminal monastic writings than for his polemical tract against Nestorius. Around 380 Cassian traveled from the Roman province of Scythia Minor (modern-day Dobrudja) to Palestine, where he lived as a monk in Bethlehem for a few years. Around 385 he departed for Egypt to live among and learn from the Egyptian anchorites. In 399 or 400 he was forced to leave Egypt in the wake of a controversy that had reached violent proportions, when Origenist monks questioned the validity of Anthropomorphite theology. He accompanied the exiled Origenist monks through Palestine to Constantinople, where John Chrysostom ordained him to the diaconate. Toward the end of 404 the supporters of Chrysostom sent Cassian to Pope Innocent of Rome with information that exonerated the archbishop of some of the charges made against him. Chrysostom had been (falsely) accused of crimes ranging from excessive punishment and harassment of the clergy to gluttony and refusing to pray either inside or outside of the church.[1] Eventually Cassian settled in Gaul (France), near Marseille. Upon the request of the local bishop, in the 420s he wrote *The Institutes of the Coenobitic Monasteries and the Remedies for the Eight Principal Vices* (commonly called the *Institutes*) and the *Conferences* to help structure burgeoning monastic foundations in the region. While the *Institutes* deals with external matters (books 1–4) such as the canonical methods of communal prayer and the internal matters (books 5–12) of how to overcome the eight principal vices (gluttony, fornication, avarice,

1 Photius, *Bibliotheca* 59, details twenty-nine charges made against John Chrysostom at the Synod of the Oak, over which Theophilus of Alexandria presided in 403.

anger, sadness, acedia, vainglory, and pride), the *Conferences* are literary re-creations of discussions Cassian had on various aspects of the monastic life with the revered Egyptian anchorites.

Cassian then got involved in the controversy over Nestorius. In the course of their increasingly bitter doctrinal dispute, both Cyril of Alexandria and Nestorius of Constantinople wrote to Pope Celestine, seeking Rome's support for their cause. Nestorius indicated that he was reviewing the cases of several Latin theologians exiled for Pelagianism and requested that Celestine send materials for him to review.[2] Celestine understandably never responded to the request since it suggested that Constantinople could act as a kind of appellate judge over Rome. Cyril for his part wrote to Celestine seeking a judgment from Rome on the question of whether it was necessary to sever communion with Nestorius, and also provided a dossier of documents that included some of Nestorius's homilies and a florilegia of extracts from earlier writers.[3] Cyril was careful to have the dossier translated into Latin before it was sent to Rome. Whether as a result of Nestorius's attempt to have Constantinople supersede Rome or of Cyril's request for a formal decision from Rome, by mid-430 at the latest Celestine had taken action. Celestine deputized his archdeacon Leo (later himself pope) to request that Cassian, who was a respected theologian fluent in both Latin and Greek, examine the texts of Nestorius and produce a document to advise Celestine and the Roman church about the matter. Cassian quickly reviewed the material and firmly rejected Nestorius's position. The Roman synod which met under Celestine in August 430 formally condemned Nestorius. We possess only scant fragments from that synod, and the short letters Celestine wrote communicating the decision do not say much in the way of theology. Thus, it is not possible to form a judgment about the extent to which that Roman synod engaged Cassian's arguments. Nevertheless, as the first Latin text to assess Nestorius's theology, Cassian's *On the Incarnation of the Lord against Nestorius* was a key influence in setting the tone of what became a firm and longstanding opposition to Nestorian positions within Latin theology.

Cassian provides a consistent twofold critique of Nestorius. His first argument is that Nestorius has failed as a Christian to follow Christ. The second is that Nestorius has failed as an intellectual to understand scripture.

2 The three letters of Nestorius to Celestine are translated in this volume on pp. 585–592.

3 *Letter* 11.

The two are intimately related for Cassian. He thinks of Nestorius primarily as a fellow monk. A monk must have *studium* (zeal) in his pursuit of a Christ-like life.[4] Nestorius's failure to recognize the fullness of the incarnation and its implication is a failure of discipleship as well as a failure of intellectual pursuits. Even the harshest doctrinal condemnations of Nestorius's position leave open the invitation for him to return to the true faith, both as a disciple of Christ who belongs to the church and as an intellectual who must answer for his preaching and exegesis of scripture.

It will be helpful to summarize all seven books of *On the Incarnation* in order to situate the selections translated here. Before the first selection provided below, in Book 1 Cassian accuses Nestorius of "putting forth the blasphemy that our Lord Jesus Christ was born as an ordinary human being (*solitarium hominem natum*)" and asserting "that his subsequent attainment of the honor and power of God was due to his human merit and not his divine nature"[5] – a teaching he takes to be heretical. For Cassian, the catholic position accepts "one and the same God and human being" – Jesus – "to be indivisible" and that "from the moment of his taking on flesh, just as everything which belonged to God passed over to the human being, so too everything that belonged to the human being came to God."[6] Because Nestorius is willing to consider the human Jesus apart from the divine Jesus, especially at his birth from the Virgin Mary, Cassian argues that Nestorius falls prey to the error of the Ebionites (adoptionism). Nestorius must be thinking of the divinity of Jesus as something given later based on his merit as a human being; Jesus would be one human being among all the others whom God blessed in a unique way. Discussion of Jesus meriting divinity and being an example for Christians allows Cassian to articulate a theological link between Nestorianism and Pelagianism.[7] The fact that Nestorius wrote three letters to Celestine and appeared sympathetic to bishops deposed for their Pelagian theology gave political support to the theological connection between Nestorius's Christology and Pelagianism.[8] Thus, Nestorius's willingness to consider the "ordinary human being" apart from the divine opens him to critique

4 *On the Incarnation* 7.31; see also *Conferences* 1.7.

5 *On the Incarnation* 1.2.5 (CSEL 17: 239, 5–8 Petschenig). Book 1 of *On the Incarnation* is translated in this volume on pp. 525–534, as part of the Leporius Dossier.

6 *On the Incarnation* 1.5.3 (CSEL 17: 242, 23–243, 1 Petschenig), quoting the *Statement of Amendment* that restored Leporius to the catholic community, translated in this volume on p. 531.

7 See in particular *On the Incarnation* 1.2–3.

8 See n. 2 above.

from Cassian along several lines. Whereas Book 1 addresses the way Nestorius considers Christ an "ordinary human being," Book 2 addresses Nestorius's denial that Mary is the Theotokos or Mother of God. Cassian summarizes his second book as proof that "Christ is God, and Mary is the Mother of God."[9] Devoting particular attention to the Annunciation from Luke's gospel, Cassian argues that scripture consistently claims that the same Jesus who was born of the Virgin Mary is also God. Thus, scripture reveals that Mary is the Mother of God.

In the first selection below, which is the entirety of Book 3, Cassian uses exceptional rhetoric to put Nestorius on trial, as if the two were face to face in a courtroom. What is more, using the text of scripture, Cassian calls Paul, Martha, Peter, Thomas, and even the Lord himself as witnesses in the trial. As the drama of the argument unfolds, Nestorius is shown to contradict the testimony of apostles, saints, the incarnate Christ, and even the words and signs of the Father, Son, and Spirit. But Cassian wants Nestorius to convert and return to the true faith. He wants Nestorius "to stop fighting against the truth" (3.12.7) and to allow "these testimonies of the faith" to suffice (3.16.1). Book 4 makes the traditional argument that Christ was God even before the incarnation and demonstrates the union of God and humanity in the one incarnate Christ from multiple passages of scripture. The second selection is from Book 5, in which Cassian details his argument that Nestorius's Christology is subject to the same error as Pelagianism; it denies the necessity of Christ as Savior and cannot categorically separate the incarnate Christ from other holy men and women. Book 6 argues that Nestorius's position is inconsistent with the baptismal creed of his native Antioch and destroys catholic Christology and Trinitarian theology. Cassian also invites Nestorius to repent and return to true Christianity. Book 7 includes Cassian's arguments against Nestorius by replying to specific arguments Nestorius had made about the birth of Christ as a human being and further explains the relationship between the incarnate Word and the indwelling Holy Spirit. Cassian concludes the entire text with a series of selections from well-respected "fathers of the church" that further reveal Nestorius's errors.

The translation here is based on the critical edition of Michael Petschenig, *Iohannis Cassiani Opera, Pars I*, CSEL 17 (Vienna: F. Tempsky, 1888).

9 *On the Incarnation* 2.2.1 (CSEL 17: 247, 9–10 Petschenig).

TRANSLATION

Book 3

1, 1. When that divine teacher of the churches was writing to the Romans, arguing with – or rather weeping over – the faithlessness of the Jews, that is, his own brothers, he used these words: "I wished that I myself would be separated from Christ for the sake of my brothers, who are kin to me according to the flesh, who are Israelites, to whom belongs the adoption of sons, the glory, the covenant, the giving of the law, the worship, and the promises; theirs are the fathers, and from them according to the flesh is Christ, who is God over all blessed forever."[10] 2. Oh, the affection of the most faithful Apostle and most pious relative! He wants to die on account of his incomparable love, both as a kinsman for his relatives and as a teacher for his disciples. And what could possibly be the reason he wants to die? There is only one reason, that they might live. Moreover, in what did their life consist? In this, as he said, that they might know that Christ, who was born according to the flesh from their own flesh, is God. Therefore, the Apostle grieves all the more because they did not understand that he who was born from Israel, he who was brought forth from them, is the one they ought to love all the more.

3. "From them," he says, "according to the flesh is Christ, who is God over all blessed forever."[11] Now he says that the one born from them according to the flesh is Christ, who is God over all blessed forever. Surely you do not deny that Christ was born from them according to the flesh. But again, the same one who was born from them is God. How can you get around this? How can you evade it? The Apostle says that Christ, who was born from Israel according to the flesh, is God. Teach us when he was not.[12] "From them," he says, "according to the flesh is Christ, who is God over all."[13] You see, because the Apostle has brought this together into a single statement, "God" cannot be separated from "Christ" in any way. For just as the Apostle preaches that Christ is from them, so also he asserts that God is in Christ. You must either deny both or you must admit both. Christ is said to be born from them according to the flesh, but the same one is also

10 Rom 9:3–5. 11 Rom 9:5.

12 The ironic injunction here recalls the famous tagline of Arius, "There was when he was not," and is probably intended to color Nestorius with the taint of Arianism, an accusation that was also made against Pelagius and Pelagians.

13 Rom 9:3–5.

proclaimed to be "God in Christ" by the Apostle, as he says elsewhere, "For God was reconciling the world to himself in Christ."[14] In no way can one of these be divided from the other. Either deny that Christ came forth from them or confess that God in Christ came forth from the Virgin. For Christ, he says, "is God over all blessed forever."[15]

2, 1. The name "God" was, in fact, more than enough to indicate to the faithful the majesty of divinity. But he excluded the blasphemy of your deceitful assertion by adding "God over all blessed,"[16] so that none of the wicked, intending to denigrate the highest divinity of Christ, would assume that the term "God" is sometimes given even to humans by a temporary gift of divine privilege, and apply insulting comparisons to God,[17] such as when God says to Moses, "I gave you as a god to Pharaoh,"[18] or "I have said, you will be gods,"[19] since the meaning of these passages is clearly that only a name has been given. 2. For where he says, "I have said ..., " it is not a question of the name indicating that they have divine power but rather of God speaking in them when they speak.[20] But even that passage where he said, "I gave you as a god to Pharaoh,"[21] does not reveal the divinity of the recipient, but the power of the giver. For when he said, "I gave you," it is surely the power of the God who gave that is indicated rather than the divine nature of the one who received it. But when it comes to our God and Lord Jesus Christ, when it is said "who is God over all blessed forever,"[22] the reality itself is immediately evident in the words and the meaning of the words is demonstrated in the title. This is because the title "God" in the phrase "Son of God" is not an indication of an adoption that has been granted to him, but is the truth and property of his nature.

3, 1. Again, the same Apostle says, "From now on we know no one according to the flesh. Even if we once knew Christ according to the flesh, now we no longer know him in this way."[23] All the things written in the sacred word harmonize with one another well. In each and every part, even when they do not agree in the outer appearance of the words, they still

14 2 Cor 5:19. 15 Rom 9:5. 16 Rom 9:5.

17 Cassian is here drawing attention to the fact that Paul did not merely call Christ "God" but "God over all blessed," excluding the possibility of someone comparing Christ's possession of the name "God" with the two biblical passages mentioned in what follows, wherein the word is applied to human beings.

18 Exod 7:1. 19 Ps 81(82):6.

20 In Latin, *non tam nomen est potestatis quam sermo dicentis.*

21 Exod 7:1. 22 Rom 9:5. 23 2 Cor 5:16.

agree in the inner meaning. This is the case in that passage which says, "Even if we once knew Christ according to the flesh, now we no longer know him in this way."[24] For the testimony of the present passage is a confirmation of the one above, in which he said, "from them according to the flesh is Christ, who is God over all blessed forever."[25] 2. For in the first passage he put "from them according to the flesh is Christ," while in the second passage he put "even if we once knew Christ according to the flesh"; in the first he put "who is God over all," and in the second, "now we no longer know Christ according to the flesh." The plain appearance of these words is different, while their inner meaning is the same. The same one whom he proclaims in the one passage as God over all, born according to the flesh, he declares is no longer known according to the flesh. This is obviously right, for the one whom he knew was born in the flesh is the same one confessed to be God forever, and in this sense Christ is not known by him according to the flesh because he is "God over all blessed forever." Taking both of these passages together, whereas the first says, "who is God over all," the second says, "now we no longer know Christ according to the flesh"; and whereas the second affirms, "now we no longer know Christ according to the flesh," the first affirms, "he is God over all blessed forever."

3. Therefore, the preaching of apostolic teaching ascends in a way, as if to a higher level, and though both passages are in harmony with each other in terms of meaning, Paul nonetheless confirms the mystery of the perfect faith in an even more distilled sentence when he says, "Even if we once knew Christ according to the flesh, now we no longer know him in this way."[26] Of course, he said this because we first knew him as both a human being and God, but now only as God. For when the weakness of the flesh comes to an end, we no longer know anything in him except the power of divinity because the power in him belongs entirely to the divine majesty when the weakness of human frailty has ceased to exist. Thus, by the whole of this inner testimony he has explained the mystery of both the assumed flesh and the perfect divinity. 4. For by saying, "even if we once knew Christ according to the flesh," he spoke of the mystery of God born in the flesh. Moreover, by adding, "now we no longer know," he unfolded the significance of [Christ] having laid aside weakness. And through this he shows that knowledge of the flesh serves to indicate the human being, while not knowing the flesh serves to honor the divinity. That is why we

24 2 Cor 5:16. 25 Rom 9:5. 26 2 Cor 5:16.

say, "We knew Christ according to the flesh," only as long as what was known according to the flesh existed, but now that it has ceased to exist, "we no longer know him in this way."[27] 5. For the nature of the flesh was transformed into a spiritual substance, and that which formerly belonged to the human being was made to belong completely to God. We do not know Christ according to the flesh because nothing remained with the sacred body by which the weakness of the flesh could be recognized in it since bodily weakness was absorbed by the divine majesty. And for this reason, whatever had previously belonged to the twofold substance has come to belong to a single power, for there is no doubt at all that Christ, who was crucified out of our weakness, lives entirely by the divine majesty.

4, 1. What the Apostle proclaimed in the whole body of his writings, he formulated well to the Galatians: "Paul, an apostle, neither from human beings nor through a human being, but through Jesus Christ and God the Father."[28] You see how well he agrees with himself in the previous passages and in the present one. For in the former he says, "now we no longer know Christ according to the flesh," and in the latter, "neither from human beings nor through a human being, but through Jesus Christ." The same thing that he teaches above, he also teaches here. 2. For in saying that he was not sent "through a human being," he means "we do not know Christ according to the flesh." Therefore he wrote, "I was sent not through a human being, but through Christ," since "I was sent through Christ" means "I was not sent through a human being, but through God." The term "human being" no longer applies to the one whom divinity has completely claimed for himself. And, therefore, when he said that he was sent "neither from human beings nor through a human being, but through Jesus Christ," he rightly added, "and through God the Father." That is, he indicated that he was sent by God the Father and God the Son. 3. Concerning the Father and the Son, due to the mystery of the sacred and ineffable generation, it is indeed right that there are two persons, the begetter and the begotten, even though there is a single power of the God who sends. And therefore, the man who says that he was sent by God the Father and God the Son certainly revealed a duality in the persons, but taught a single power in the sending.

5, 1. "But through Christ Jesus," he says, "and God the Father, who raised him from the dead."[29] The illustrious and wonderful teacher, knowing that

27 2 Cor 5:16. 28 Gal 1:1. 29 Gal 1:1.

the Lord Jesus Christ must be proclaimed true God and also true human being, always proclaimed the majesty of divinity in him so that he would not in any way neglect the confession of the incarnation. With the reality of the incarnation he excluded the phantasm of Marcion, and with the perfect divinity he excluded the poverty of Ebion, lest someone should believe either extreme of blasphemy: either that the Lord Jesus Christ is a human being completely without God or God without a human being. 2. Thus, after correctly proclaiming himself sent both by God the Father and God the Son, the Apostle immediately added a confession of the Lord's incarnation in saying, "who raised him from the dead." Paul obviously taught that the true body of the incarnate God was raised from the dead, with these words: "Even if we once knew Christ according to the flesh," to which he rightly added, "yet now we know him no longer in this way."[30] 3. For he says that what he knows about him according to the flesh is that he was raised from the dead. However, he says that he does not know him any longer according to the flesh since he knew that, with the flesh's frailty having come to an end, Christ exists solely in the power of God. He who was corrected from heaven at the beginning of his calling is a believable and sufficient witness to the Lord's divinity, which must be proclaimed. It is clear that he not only believed with the faith of his mind, but he also confirmed the glory of our Lord Jesus Christ risen from the dead with the eyes of his body.

6, 1. For the same reason, while he was speaking before King Agrippa and the other judges of the world, he said, "When I was going to Damascus with the authority and permission of the chief priests, O king, I saw in the road at midday a light from heaven brighter than the sun shining around me and all who were with me at that time. And when we all fell to the ground, I heard a voice saying to me in Hebrew, 'Saul, Saul, why do you persecute me? It is hard for you to kick against the goad.' Then I said, 'Who are you, Lord?' And the Lord said to me, 'I am Jesus of Nazareth, whom you are persecuting.'"[31] 2. You can see that the Apostle was right to say that he no longer knew according to the flesh the one he saw in such radiant glory. For when he was lying prostrate and saw the radiance of that divine light which he could not endure, this voice came forth: "Saul, Saul, why are you persecuting me?" When he asked who it was, the Lord responded by revealing his identity: "I am Jesus of Nazareth, whom you are persecuting." You – you, I say, O heretic! – Now I ask! I am addressing you!

30 2 Cor 5:16. 31 Acts 26:12–15.

Do you or do you not believe what the Apostle said about himself? Or if you consider that insufficient, do you or do you not believe what the Lord said about himself? If you believe, the case is closed, for all that is necessary is that you believe what we believe.

3. We believe exactly as the Apostle: "Even if we once knew Christ according to the flesh, now we know him no longer in this way."[32] We do not hurl insults at Christ. We do not separate the flesh from God. And we believe that everything which Christ is exists in God. If you, then, believe the same thing that we believe, you must confess the same mystery of the faith. But if you disagree with us – if you believe neither the churches, nor the Apostle, nor finally even what God says about himself – then show us in what the Apostle saw which part was flesh and which part was God. I can separate nothing here. I see the ineffable illumination. I see the inexplicable brightness. I see the splendor that human frailty cannot endure. I see the inestimable majesty of God shining with a light beyond what mortal eyes are able to bear. What division is there here, what separation? 4. We hear Jesus in the voice; we discern God in the majesty. What else is left except that we believe that God and Jesus are one and the same substance? Nevertheless, I still want to say more to you about this same subject.

Tell me, please, whether what appeared to the Apostle who was at that time ignorant also appeared to you, who are currently persecuting the catholic faith. Did that brightness surround you when you were untroubled and least expecting it? Did the splendor of immeasurable light frighten you to the point of shock and terror? Were you thrown into the darkness of your own blindness and errors, a darkness which mental terror should have made more overwhelming and indescribable for you? 5. Tell me, I implore, when the fear of imminent death overwhelmed you and the terror of the threatening majesty pressed hard from above, did you, in such a confusion of mind, also hear that accusation that belongs to your faithlessness? "Saul, Saul, why do you persecute me?" And when you asked, "Who is it?" and the response came from heaven, "I am Jesus of Nazareth whom you are persecuting," what did you say? "I don't know. I'm still not sure. I want to think more about whom I consider you to be – you who speak from heaven, who crush me with the radiance of your divinity, whose voice I hear, and whose majesty I am unable to bear. 6. I must investigate this matter, whether or not I ought to believe you. Are you Christ or God? If you are God, are you

32 2 Cor 5:16.

God alone, or God in Christ? If you are Christ, are you Christ alone or Christ in God? I want this distinction to be exactly observed and carefully considered. What should we believe and what should we decide that you are? For I do not want to neglect any part of my duty so as to assign you some divine honor when I should look down upon you as a human being." If, then, you were lying prostrate on the ground like the apostle Paul was, and, overshadowed by the brightness of the divine light, you were gasping for breath, perhaps you would utter words like these; perhaps you would snarl with this tiresome, babbling chatter.

7. But what should we make of the fact that something else then occurred to the Apostle? When he had collapsed, shaking and half alive, he resolved not to hide any longer. Nor did he suppose that it should be deliberated any further. Rather, it was enough for him that after being admonished by the ineffable experiences, he came to recognize that the one whom he ignorantly believed to be a human being is God. He did not ignore it. He did not delay. Nor did he wickedly entertain some imagined error in a completely unfaithful deliberation. Rather, when he heard the name of Jesus his Lord from heaven, he answered with a voice as submissive as a slave, as frightened as someone who had been flogged, and as devout as a convert: "What am I to do, Lord?" 8. In this way, by his most resolved and devout faith, he immediately deserved never to be apart from the very one whom he faithfully believed. The very one in whose heart Paul had been transfixed, transfixed himself in Paul's heart, as the Apostle said about himself, "Do you seek proof of Christ who speaks in me?"[33]

7, 1. And concerning this passage, O heretic, I wish you would explain to me whether the one whom the Apostle says speaks in him is a human being or God. If he is a human being, how could the body of someone else speak in the Apostle's heart? If he is God, then Christ is not a human being, but God. For, since Christ spoke in the Apostle and no one could speak in him except God, then the Christ who spoke in him is God. You see, then, that there is nothing more that you can now say. Nor can there be any separation or division between Christ and God because all of God is in Christ, and all of Christ is in God. 2. No separation and no division can be admitted here. There is only one confession that is simple, only one that is devout, only one that is sound: to worship, to love, and to honor Christ as God.

33 2 Cor 13:3.

Still, do you want to know even more clearly and completely that there is no separation between God and Christ and that the same one who is Christ must be understood to be entirely God? Listen to what the Apostle said to the Corinthians: "For we must all appear before the judgment seat of Christ, so that each one may give an account of the deeds of his body according to what he has done, whether good or evil."[34] 3. Moreover, in another passage, when writing to the Roman church, he says, "We all will stand before the judgment seat of God, for it is written, 'As I live, says the Lord, every knee shall bend before me, and every tongue shall give praise to God.'"[35] Thus, you see that the one and the same judgment seat of God will belong to Christ. Understand beyond all doubt, then, that Christ is God. And, when you see that the substance of Christ and of God is inseparable, then acknowledge also that there is an inseparable person – unless, perhaps, since the Apostle said in one epistle that we must appear before the judgment seat of Christ, and in the other before the judgment seat of God, you make two judgment seats and suppose that some are judged by Christ and others by God. But these thoughts are silly, mad, and more insane than those who are crazy.

4. Therefore, acknowledge the Lord of all; acknowledge the God of the universe; acknowledge the judgment seat of God in the judgment seat of Christ. Love life; love your salvation; love the one who created you, and fear the one who will judge you. Whether you want to or not, you must appear before the judgment seat of Christ. Even if you set aside the blasphemy of impiety and the silly prattle of treacherous words, and you still think that the judgment seat of God is different from the judgment seat of Christ, you will come before the judgment seat of Christ and, based upon irrefutable evidence, you will certainly find that the judgment seat of God is the very same as the judgment seat of Christ. You will also find that all the glory of the Son of God and all the power of God the Father is in Christ, the Son of God.

5. "The Father does not judge anyone, but he has given all judgment to the Son, so that all may honor the Son just as they honor the Father."[36] For whoever denies the Father also denies the Son: "Everyone who denies the Son does not have the Father. Whoever confesses the Son has the Father."[37] Learn, therefore, that the honor of the Father and the Son is inseparable, that their dignity is inseparable, that it is neither possible for the Son to be

34 2 Cor 5:10. 35 Rom 14:10–11, quoting Isa 45:23.
36 John 5:22–23. 37 1 John 2:23.

honored without the Father, nor the Father without the Son. 6. Moreover, no one can honor God or the Son of God except in Christ, the only-begotten Son of God, since it is impossible to have the Spirit of the God who must be honored except in the Spirit of Christ, as the Apostle says: "But you are not in the flesh, but in the Spirit, if the Spirit of God dwells in you. If, however, someone does not have the Spirit of Christ, he does not belong to him."[38] And again: "Who will bring an accusation against the elect of God? It is God who justifies. Who is there who will condemn? It is Christ Jesus, who has died, or rather, who has risen."[39] Therefore, you see now, although you do not want to, that there is not any difference at all either between the Spirit of God and the Spirit of Christ or between the judgment of God and the judgment of Christ. Choose whichever you prefer, for the other follows necessarily, so that you will either come to understand through faith that Christ is God, or you will come to realize through damnation that God is in Christ.

8, 1. But let us see, nevertheless, the other passages that follow. Again, writing to the church of the Corinthians, the aforementioned Paul, the teacher of all the churches, said this: "The Jews demand signs, and the Greeks seek wisdom, but we proclaim Christ crucified, a stumbling-block to the Jews and foolishness to the Greeks, but to those who are saved, both Jews and Greeks, Christ the power of God and the wisdom of God."[40] Oh, what a steadfast teacher of the faith! Even in this passage when he was teaching the churches it did not seem sufficient to say that Christ is God without adding that he was crucified. It is obvious that he proclaims that the one whom he called "crucified" is the wisdom of God in order to make the doctrine of the faith most clear and firm. 2. This is why he did not use any subtlety or circumlocution of words. Nor was he ashamed of the phrase "the cross of Christ"[41] when preaching the gospel of the Lord. And, although it is indeed a stumbling-block to the Jews and foolishness to the Gentiles to hear of God being born, to hear of God being corporeal, to hear of God suffering, to hear of God crucified, nevertheless, he neither weakened the power of his piety on account of the impiety of Jewish stumbling nor diminished the strength of his faith on account of the infidelity of foreign foolishness. Rather, he preached plainly, resolutely, and boldly that the one whom a mother bore, whom people murdered, whom the

38 Rom 8:9. 39 Rom 8:33–34. 40 1 Cor 1:22–24, conflated with 2 Cor 2:15.
41 See 1 Cor 1:17; Gal 6:12; Phil 3:18.

spear pierced, whom the cross stretched out, was the power and wisdom of God, "a stumbling-block to the Jews and foolishness to the Gentiles." 3. But in fact, that which was a stumbling-block and foolishness to some was the power and wisdom of God to others. For with a diversity of people came a diversity of opinions. What foolish disbelief denied, lacking sound understanding and incapable of true good, wise faith perceived within the recesses of its soul to be sacred and saving.

9, 1. Tell me, therefore, you heretic, you who are the enemy of all people, but especially of yourself – tell me, you to whom the cross of the Lord Jesus is a stumbling-block along with the Jews and foolishness along with the Gentiles, you who spit out the mysteries of the true salvation because of the Jewish stumbling-block and do not savor them because of the Gentile stupidity – tell me, why was the preaching of the apostle Paul either foolishness to the pagans or a stumbling-block to the Jews?[42] Could it possibly have offended human beings if he had taught (as you assert) that Christ was an ordinary human being? For who would have found his birth, passion, cross, or death to be incredible or difficult? Would the preaching of Paul have had something new or unheard of in itself if it had said that Christ was a human being who suffered, something which the human condition has everywhere endured daily in human beings?

2. But what the foolishness of the Gentiles did not accept and what the Jewish faithlessness refused is surely what the Apostle said, namely that Christ, whom they and you thought of as an ordinary human being, is in fact God. Surely this is what the thought of those wicked people opposed, what the ears of the wicked could not bear. They could not understand that the birth of God is proclaimed in the human being, Jesus Christ; that the passion of God was revealed; that the cross of God was announced. Surely this is what was disagreeable. This was beyond belief, for what was never heard to have happened to the divine nature was unbelievable to human ears. 3. You, then, are "safe" in such an assertion and doctrine, since your preaching will never be foolishness to the Gentiles or a stumbling-block to the Jews. Nor will you ever be crucified with Peter by the Jews and Gentiles, stoned with James, or beheaded with Paul, for your preaching does not incite their indignation. You maintain that an ordinary human being

42 The English "mysteries" translates the Latin *sacramenta*, which is tied to the Greek *mysteria* in early Christian literature. The one term in Latin connects salvation, the incarnation, the liturgy, and the sacraments.

was born; you assert that an ordinary human being suffered. You need not be afraid that they will injure you by their persecution since you reassure them with your preaching.

10, 1. And yet, let us look into this issue further. According to the Apostle, then, Christ is "the power of God and the wisdom of God."[43] What can you say to this? How can you reply? You can neither escape this nor run away from it. Christ is the wisdom of God and the power of God. He, whom the Jews pursued, whom the Gentiles ridiculed, whom you together with them persecute – he, I say, who is foolishness to the pagans, a stumbling-block to the Jews, and both to you – he, I say, is the power of God and the wisdom of God. What can you do? Perhaps you can close your ears so that you cannot hear. The Jews did this when the Apostle was preaching. 2. But regardless of what you do, Christ is in heaven, is in God and with him; he is in the same one above in whom he also was when he was below. You can no longer persecute him with the Jews. And yet, you still do the one thing that you can do: you persecute him in the faith; you persecute him in the church; you persecute him with the spear of wicked opinions; you persecute him with the sword of perverse teaching. Perhaps you even do more than the Jews of old did. You persecute Christ now, after even those who persecuted him have come to believe in him. But perhaps you suppose this is a lesser crime since you cannot now strike him with your hands. I say it is not less: that persecution in which the wicked persecute him in his followers is no less serious.[44]

3. But the phrase "the cross of the Lord" offends you. This always offended the Jews as well. You shudder to hear that God suffered.[45] The Gentiles' error also ridiculed this. Therefore, I ask you now in what way you differ from them, since you agree with them in this perversity. I, on the other hand, not only do not diminish the proclamation of the sacred cross and the preaching of the Lord's passion, but rather exalt it as far as my devotion and nature allow. For I will preach not only that the one who was crucified is "the power and wisdom of God"[46] (than which nothing is greater), but

43 1 Cor 1:24. 44 See Acts 26:14–15.

45 At *On the Incarnation* 3.8.1 Cassian began his critique of Nestorius's problem with this phrase, "the cross of the Lord." The first part of his analysis compares Nestorius to non-Christians via 1 Cor 1:22–24. Cassian is convinced that Christianity involves following Christ by taking up our cross (see *Institutes* 4.34 and *Conferences* 1.22 and 7.5), and so Nestorius is simply a lackluster Christian and a poor monk. Here, Cassian turns to the theological argument behind Nestorius's objections, namely, the problem of a suffering God.

46 1 Cor 1:24.

also that he is fully Lord in divinity and majesty. I profess this because my way of speaking is the doctrine of God, as the Apostle said, 4. "We speak wisdom among the perfect, indeed not a wisdom of this age nor of the rulers of this age, which is passing away. Rather, we speak the wisdom of God in mystery, which was hidden, which God predestined before the ages for our glory, which none of the rulers of this age recognized. For if they had recognized it, they would never have crucified the Lord of glory. But, as it is written, 'What eye has not seen, nor ear has heard, nor has it risen in the human heart what God has prepared for those who love him.'"[47] Do you see how succinctly the apostolic expression says so much? He says that he speaks wisdom, but a wisdom which only the perfect know, a wisdom which the wise of this world do not know. For he says that the wisdom of God is that which is shrouded in divine mystery and predestined before all ages for the glory of the saints. Furthermore, for this reason it is known only to those who know God, but entirely unknown to the rulers of this age. 5. Moreover, he supplied the rationale which proves both points he had made when he added, "For if they had recognized it, they would never have crucified the Lord of glory. But, as it is written, 'What eye has not seen, nor ear has heard, nor has it risen in the human heart what God has prepared for those who love him.'"[48] Thus, you see that the wisdom of God, which is hidden in mystery and predetermined before the ages, was unknown to those who crucified the Lord of glory, but is known to those who accepted him. Furthermore, he rightly says that the wisdom was hidden in the mystery of God, since the human eye was never able to see, nor the ear to hear, nor the heart to consider that the Lord of glory would be born from the Virgin, would come in the flesh, or would be afflicted by all kinds of punishment and abusive suffering. 6. Rather, these teachings are gifts from God. Because no one is ever able to understand on his own when things are hidden in mystery, the one who learns what is revealed is blessed. Similarly, whoever does not recognize this fact must be counted among "the rulers of this age," while those who understand it are among "the wise of God."

Anyone who denies that God was born in the flesh will not recognize it. Since you deny it, you also do not recognize it. But whatever you do – no matter how wickedly you deny it – we will still believe the Apostle. And why do I cite the Apostle when we believe God even more? We believe

47 1 Cor 2:6–9, citing Isa 64:3. Cassian here has a variant which is not recorded anywhere else, indicating he is probably working from memory.

48 1 Cor 2:8–9, citing Isa 64:3.

him through the Apostle; we are certain that he spoke in the Apostle.[49] The divine word says that the Lord of glory was crucified by the rulers of this age, but you deny it. Those who crucified him also denied that they were crucifying God. 7. Those who confess it, however, have a place with the Apostle who confessed. It follows, then, that you have a portion with those who persecuted him. Therefore, what else can be said? The Apostle says that the Lord of glory was crucified. Change this, if you can. Separate Jesus from God now, if you wish. You cannot deny that Christ was indeed crucified by the Jews. But the one who was crucified is the Lord of glory. Therefore, you must either deny that Christ was fastened to the cross or confess that God was fastened to the cross.[50]

11, 1. But perhaps it offends you that all this time I have only or mostly talked about testimonies from the apostle Paul. He whom God chose is enough for me. God wanted him to be the teacher of the entire world, so I am not ashamed to have him as the witness for my faith. But nevertheless, perhaps you do not think I have other testimonies I can use. Allow me to indulge your wishes in this matter. Listen to Martha proclaim in the gospel the perfect mystery of human salvation and everlasting bliss. What did she say? "Yes, Lord, I believe that you are the Christ, the Son of the living God, who has come into this world."[51] Learn the true faith from this woman. Learn the confession of eternal hope. You still have a great consolation! You should not be ashamed to recognize the mystery of salvation from her whose testimony God did not refuse to accept.

12, 1. You should not be displeased with either the person or the sex of anyone who confesses the mystery and so becomes an authority, since, however insignificant someone's rank or position might be, the power of her faith cannot be diminished. Nevertheless, if, perhaps, the authority of a greater person would appease you, let us ask not just any young boy who is just starting out with a rudimentary education or a woman whose faith might seem to be nascent. Rather, let us ask that highest disciple among disciples, the highest teacher among teachers, who steers the helm of the Roman church. Just as he had leadership in the faith, so also he had leadership in the priesthood. 2. Tell us, therefore, Peter, prince of the apostles,

49 See 2 Cor 13:3.
50 This sentence puts the paradox of the incarnation in full view. Note that Cassian's argument already relies on the principle which later theology would articulate as the *communicatio idiomatum*, and in this respect he is in keeping with the kind of language that Cyril used throughout the controversy.
51 John 11:27.

tell us please how the churches should believe in God. For it is reasonable that you, who were taught by the Lord, should teach us and open for us the gate whose key you received.[52] Remove everything that undermines the heavenly home and turn away those who attempt to enter through secret passages and unlawful entrances. For it is certain that no one will be able to enter the doorway of the kingdom unless the key that was given to the churches through you opens it for him. 3. Tell us, then, how we should believe in Jesus Christ and confess a common Lord.[53] You will answer, without a doubt, "Why do you ask me how the Lord should be confessed when you can see how I myself confessed him? Read the gospel, and you will not ask me when you have my confession. Indeed, where you have my confession, you have me, for my authority is my confession itself, since I do not have authority without my confession." Tell us, therefore, evangelist, tell us that confession! Tell us the faith of the highest apostle. Did he confess that Jesus was only a human being or God? Did he say that there is only flesh in him, or did he preach that he is the Son of God?

4. When the Lord Jesus Christ asked the disciples whom they believed and confessed him to be, Peter, the first among the apostles, responded on behalf of them all. For the answer of the one was the same as the faith of them all, but it was fitting that the first apostle responded so that the order of response would be the same as the order of honor, and so that he who came before them in age would come before them in confession. What, then, did he say? "You are the Christ, the Son of the living God."[54]

5. I must use a simple and plain line of questioning to refute you, O heretic. Tell me, I ask, who was he to whom Peter responded? You cannot deny that he was Christ. Therefore, I ask, who is it that you call Christ? A human being or God? Without a doubt you will say that he is certainly a human being, for your entire heresy springs from this, since you deny that Christ is the Son of God. And for that reason you also say that Mary is Christotokos and not Theotokos, since she is the mother of Christ, but not of God. Thus, you assert that Christ is only a human being, not God,

52 See Matt 16:18.

53 The phrase *communem Dominum* appears to be unique to Cassian. There is a play here on at least two senses of "common." On the one hand, this could refer to Nestorius and Cassian confessing a *common* Lord together, which would require Nestorius to amend his position. On the other hand, this could also refer to a single Lord who is both God and human being, the *communion* of the two. It does not mean common in the sense of "everyday."

54 Matt 16:16.

and therefore that he is the Son of Man, not the Son of God. But how did Peter respond to these questions? "You are the Christ, the Son of the living God." 6. He testified that this Christ (whom you claim is only the Son of Man) is the Son of God. Whom do you want us to believe, you or Peter? I hope that you are not so shameless that you would dare to put yourself before the first apostle – although, what is there that you will not dare to do? Or rather, how could you, who have been able to deny God, not despise the apostle? He says, "You are the Christ, the Son of the living God."[55] Is there anything ambiguous here, anything hidden in this? This confession is nothing but simple and clear; it proclaims that Christ is the Son of God. Perhaps you deny that this was said, but the evangelist testifies that it was. Or are you saying that the apostle is lying? But accusing the apostle of deceit is an abominable lie. 7. Or do you, perhaps, contend that this was said about some other Christ? But this would be a new kind of bizarre falsehood. What, then, is left? Just this one thing, that when what was written is read, and what is read is true, you are bound finally either by force or by necessity to stop fighting against the truth, since you can no longer consider it false.

13, 1. But nevertheless, since I have used the testimony of the chief apostle, in which he, standing face to face with God, confessed that Jesus Christ is Lord, let us see how the one whom he confessed confirmed his confession. For if God himself praised this statement, it is worth much more than what the apostle said on his own. So, when the apostle said, "You are the Christ, the Son of the living God,"[56] how did the Lord and Savior respond? "Blessed are you, Simon bar Jonah, for flesh and blood did not reveal this to you, but the Spirit of my Father who is in heaven."[57] 2. If it does not please you to use the apostle's testimony, use God's. For by praising what was said, God added his authority to the apostolic saying such that even if the saying came out of the apostle's mouth, God made it his own when he confirmed it. He said, "Blessed are you, Simon bar Jonah, for flesh and blood did not reveal this to you, but the Spirit of my Father who is in heaven."[58] Thus, in the apostle's saying you see the testimony of the Holy Spirit, and of the Son who was present, and of God the Father. What more

55 Matt 16:16. 56 Matt 16:16.
57 Matt 16:17. Whereas most versions of this verse attribute Peter's revelation to "my Father who is in heaven," Cassian's citation has instead "the Spirit of my Father who is in heaven."
58 Matt 16:17.

do you need? What could even compare? The Son praised; the Father was present with them; the Holy Spirit revealed. 3. The saying of the apostle, therefore, is the testimony of the entire divinity, since this saying necessarily has the authority of the one from whom it originally proceeds. For this reason he says, "Blessed are you, Simon bar Jonah, for flesh and blood did not reveal this to you, but the Spirit of my Father who is in heaven."[59] If flesh and blood did not reveal this to Peter or inspire it, then you should consider who has inspired you. If the Spirit of God (who confessed that Christ is God) taught Peter, then you, who were able to deny this, should realize that you are taught by a demonic spirit.

14, 1. What else follows this saying of the Lord which praises Peter highly? "And I," he says, "say to you, 'You are Peter, and on this rock I will build my church.'"[60] Do you see that Peter's saying is the faith of the church? Therefore, whoever does not hold the faith of the church must be outside of the church. The Lord says, "And I will give you the keys of the kingdom of heaven."[61] 2. This faith earned heaven; this faith received the keys of the heavenly kingdom. Understand what waits for you. You will not be able to enter the gate that this key opens, for you have denied the faith that belongs to that key. "And the gates of hell," he says, "shall not prevail against you."[62] The "gates of hell" are the faith of the heretics, or rather their treachery. For the one who denies that Christ is God will be just as far from the one who confesses it as hell is from heaven. The Lord says, "Whatever you bind on earth will be bound in heaven; and whatever you loose on earth will also be loosed in heaven."[63] 3. The perfect faith of the apostle somehow received the power of the divinity, so that what he bound or loosed on earth would be bound or loosed in heaven. Therefore, since you, who oppose the faith of the apostle, see that you are now bound on earth, all that remains is that you understand that you are also bound in heaven. But to go through every detail is tedious, and together they would make this discussion lengthy and verbose, even if they were reviewed briefly and summarily.

15, 1. Nevertheless, I want to add one more testimony for you from an apostle so that you will understand that what was done before the passion of the Lord is consistent with what came after the passion. The Lord came when his disciples were gathered behind closed doors because he wanted to

59 Matt 16:17. 60 Matt 16:18. 61 Matt 16:19.
62 Matt 16:18. 63 Matt 16:19.

reveal to the apostles the reality of his body. The apostle Thomas, feeling his flesh, touching his side, and investigating his wounds, thoroughly verified the body which had been presented to him. What, then, did he cry out? 2. He said, "My Lord and my God!"[64] He did not say what you say, "Christ is a human being, neither God nor divinity," did he? Rather, he touched the body of the Lord himself, and he answered that he is God. He did not indicate any separation of human being and God, did he? Did he call that flesh *theodochos*,[65] as you say (that is, receiver of the Deity)? Or, following your custom of impiety, did the apostle Thomas mention that the one he touched should be venerated not on account of himself, but on account of the one whom he had received in himself?

Suppose the apostle of God did not know this subtlety of your discernment and did not have the elegance and distinction of your judgment. He was, after all, an inexperienced country bumpkin, ignorant of the art of dialectic and unaware of philosophical disputation. Without doubt the instruction of the Lord himself more than sufficed for him, and he knew nothing at all except what he had learned from the Lord's teaching. 3. Therefore, his words were heavenly teaching; his faith was divine instruction. He learned nothing about separating the Lord from his own body, as you do. He knew nothing about tearing God away from his inmost self. He was holy, genuine, and pious. He had skilled innocence, uninjured faith, and uncorrupted knowledge. He had common sense combined with understanding, and along with perfect simplicity he had wisdom unacquainted with any evil.[66] He was completely without corruption. He was totally immune to heretical perversity. He expressed in his own words the form of the divine teaching, but he taught exactly what he had learned. Thus, he who was an inexperienced country bumpkin, as you perhaps suppose, now shuts you up with a short answer and destroys you with his few words.

64 John 20:28.

65 The term *theodochos* is a Latin transliteration of the Greek for "something/someone who receives God," not to be confused with the much more well-known title for Mary, Theotokos. Nestorius argued that the flesh of Christ could be considered a kind of vehicle for or receptacle of the divinity, but not that the flesh and all its experiences belonged to the Word (as Cassian and Cyril argue). Nestorius used the term in *Sermons* 9 and 10 (see *Nestoriana*: 263, 12–13 and 276, 3–5 Loofs) and Cassian critiques it here and in several other passages of this treatise (*On the Incarnation* 5.2–5.4 and 7.8). He appears to have been the first person to comment on Nestorius's usage of this term for Christ, though in a letter to the clergy of Constantinople Cyril of Alexandria alluded to Nestorius's usage of the word for Mary (*Letter* 10).

66 It is difficult to capture Cassian's turn of phrase here. The terms we have translated "common sense" and "perfect simplicity" are a play on the Latin *simplex*.

When he approached to touch God, what, then, did the apostle Thomas touch? Without a doubt, he touched Christ. 4. And what did he cry out? He said, "My Lord and my God!"[67] Go ahead now, if you can, and separate Christ from God. Change this statement, if you are able. Give a dialectical debate. Produce worldly prudence and that foolish wisdom that comes with verbose craftiness. Turn yourself inside out and gather all your strength. Do whatever you can, whether by cunning or skill. Regardless of what you say or what you do, you cannot escape from this without admitting that what the apostle touched was God. And indeed, if you were at all able, perhaps you would want to change the proclamation of the gospel history so that it would read neither that the apostle Thomas touched the body of the Lord nor that he called Christ "Lord God." But what is written in the gospel cannot possibly be changed. 5. For "heaven and earth will pass away, but the words of God will certainly not pass away."[68] Behold, Thomas, the apostle who testified then, now also proclaims to you:

> Jesus, whom I touched, is God. It is God's limbs that I felt. I did not hold the incorporeal. I did not touch the untouchable. I did not contact a spirit with my hand, so that someone might believe that I said only about it that it is God. No, according to what my Lord said, "a spirit does not have flesh and bones."[69] I touched the body of my Lord. I felt flesh and bones. I placed my fingers into the wounds, and I proclaimed, "My Lord and my God!"[70] about Christ my Lord whom I touched. 6. I know nothing about making a distinction between Christ and God. I refuse to insert impious opinions between Jesus and God. I know nothing about tearing my God from himself. You who think differently or speak differently, get away from me, whoever you are. I know no other Christ besides the one who is God. This is the Christ I held with my fellow apostles. This is the Christ I passed on to the churches. This is the Christ I preached to the Gentiles, and about whom I again cry out to you, "Christ is God! Christ is God!" A healthy mind does not think otherwise. A healthy faith does not speak otherwise. Divinity cannot be torn away from itself. Thus, since without a doubt, whatever Christ is, he is God, nothing can be found in God other than God.

67 John 20:28. 68 Matt 24:35, slightly altered.
69 Luke 24:39. 70 John 20:28.

16, 1. What do you say now, heretic? Are these testimonies of the faith not sufficient, even for the greatest lack of faith? Or should still another be added? And what more could be added after the prophets or after the apostles, unless perhaps, as the Jews once demanded, you also require that a sign from heaven be given to you? But if you ask for this, the same response that was given to them then must be given to you: "A crooked and debased generation seeks a sign, but no sign will be given to it except the sign of the prophet Jonah."[71] 2. Indeed, this sign should have sufficed for you along with the Jews who crucified him, so that you, being taught by it alone, would also believe that our Lord is God. For even those who persecuted him came to believe by this sign. But nevertheless, because we made mention of the heavenly sign, such a sign from heaven which not even the demons ever opposed ought to be shown to you. Bound by the necessity of the truth, even though they recognized that Jesus was corporeal, they still clamored that he was God, which indeed he was.

What, then, did the evangelist say about the Lord Jesus Christ? "After he was baptized, he immediately came up from the water, and behold, the heavens were opened for him, and he saw the Spirit descending as a dove and coming upon him. And behold, a voice from heaven said, 'This is my beloved Son with whom I am pleased.'"[72] 3. Heretic, what do you say to this now? Is it the words or the person of the one speaking which bothers you? The meaning of the address certainly needs no interpretation. Nor does the dignity of the speaker need a kind of letter of recommendation. It is God the Father who spoke. What was said is clear. Surely you will not put forth a claim either so shameless or so sacrilegious as to say that one should not believe God the Father concerning the only-begotten Son of God, will you? Thus, he says, "This is my beloved Son in whom I am pleased."[73] But perhaps, supposing that this is madness, you will try to say that these words were said about the Word and not about Christ. In that case, tell me who it was who was baptized: the Word or Christ? The flesh or spirit? You cannot deny in any way that it was Christ.

4. That human being, therefore, who was born from a human being and from God, who was conceived by the descent of the Holy Spirit upon the Virgin and the overshadowing of the power of the Most High[74] and is thus the Son of Man and the Son of God, that same one was definitely baptized, as you cannot deny. If, therefore, he was baptized, he was also named,

71 Luke 11:29. 72 Matt 3:16–17. 73 Matt 3:17. 74 See Luke 1:35.

because the one who was named is the one who was baptized. It says, "This is my beloved Son with whom I am pleased."[75] Can anything at all be said that is more relevant or obvious? Christ was baptized. Christ came up from the water. The heavens were opened for the baptized Christ. The dove descended next to Christ. The Holy Spirit stood above Christ in a corporeal appearance. The Father called him "Christ." 5. If you dare to deny this saying about Christ, then all that is left for you to do is to assert that Christ was not baptized, that the Spirit did not descend, and that the Father did not speak. But the truth itself presses upon you and overwhelms you so that, even if you do not wish to confess it, still you cannot deny it. For what does the evangelist say? "After he was baptized, he immediately came up from the water."[76] Who was baptized? Surely Christ. "And behold," he says, "the heavens were opened for him."[77] For whom were they opened if not for the one who was baptized? Surely for Christ. "And he saw the Spirit descending as a dove and coming upon him."[78] Who saw? Surely Christ. Upon whom did the Spirit descend? Surely upon Christ. 6. And "a voice came from heaven saying" – talking about whom? Surely about Christ. For what follows? "This is my beloved Son in whom I am pleased."[79] So that it could be shown that all these things were done for his sake, the voice continued, saying, "This is my beloved Son,"[80] which is to say, "This is he for whose sake all these things have been done. This is my Son. For his sake the heavens were opened. For his sake my Spirit came. For his sake my voice was heard. For this is my Son." Therefore, when he says, "This is my Son," whom did he designate? Surely the one whom the dove touched. Whom, then, did the dove touch? Surely Christ. Therefore, Christ is the Son of God.

7. I believe that my promise has been fulfilled. Surely you see, therefore, O heretic, the sign given to you from heaven – indeed, not just one, but many remarkable signs. For you have one in the opening of heaven, another in the descent of the Spirit, and a third in the voice of the Father. All of these things clearly declare that Christ is God, since the unlocking of the heavens indicates that he is God, and the descent of the Holy Spirit upon him proves that he is God, and the address of the Father confirms that he is God. For heaven would not have opened except for the dignity of the Lord himself. The Spirit would not have

75 Matt 3:17. 76 Matt 3:16. 77 Matt 3:16.
78 Matt 3:16. 79 Matt 3:17. 80 Matt 3:17.

descended in a corporeal form except upon the Son of God. Nor would the Father have declared him "Son," unless he was truly his Son. This is especially the case with these signs of the divine birth, which not only confirm the truth of pious faith, but also exclude the perversity of impious speculation.

8. After the Father, with the ineffable grandeur of a divine saying, had clearly and distinctly said, "This is my Son," he added what follows, "beloved,"[81] and even, "in whom I am pleased." Indeed, just as through the prophet he had proclaimed that he is "the mighty God" and "the great God,"[82] so also here he says, "my beloved Son in whom I am pleased." To the title "my own Son" the Father adds the title "beloved and pleasing Son" so that the addition of the titles would clearly signify the status of the divine nature, and so that what had never happened to any human being at all would uniquely indicate the honor of the Son of God. 9. And so, these distinctive and unique things happened to the person of our Lord Jesus Christ: the heavens were opened; and, in the sight of everyone, God the Father virtually touched him with his own hand through the dove that came and remained; and, as if pointing a finger at him, he said, "This is my Son." Therefore, being called by the unique names "beloved" and "pleasing to the Father" was also distinct and particular to him, so that by the addition of unique titles the unique significance of his nature might be revealed and so that the distinctive property evident in the names might also confirm the distinctive property of the only-begotten Son, which had already been established on the basis of the honor of the signs previously given.

10. But the end of this book has already arrived. For this saying from God the Father can neither be augmented nor equaled by human words. Concerning his Son, our Lord Jesus Christ, God the Father is a more than sufficient witness for us on his own. He testified, saying, "This is my Son." If you think these words of God the Father ought to be opposed, then you must contradict him who by the clearest possible announcement caused the whole world to recognize that this was his own Son.

*

* *

81 In the Latin text of Matt 3:17, *filius meus dilectus*, the adjective "beloved" (*dilectus*) does follow "my Son" (*filius meus*).

82 See Isa 9:6.

Book 5

1, 1. We said in the first book that the present heresy, which is a disciple and imitator of the Pelagian heresy, assaults and attacks the truth on all sides with the aim of fostering the belief that the Son of God, the Lord Jesus Christ, who was born from the Virgin, is only an ordinary human being. This heresy maintains that after living a pious and religious life and advancing along the way of virtue, he became worthy, through this holy lifestyle, of having communion with the divine majesty. Thus, by excluding from him the inner dignity of a divine origin, the only option left is that he was chosen solely on account of his merits. The heretics aimed and worked at this: they put him on the level of all people and lumped him together with the multitude of the human race in order to teach that everyone would be able, through a lifestyle of good deeds, to merit whatever he had merited by living well. This destructive and fatal assertion, which both takes away from God what truly belongs to him and makes a false promise to human beings, is on both accounts an impious and damnable lie, since it inflicts the wound of sacrilege upon God, and it leads men and women into the hope of a false presumption. By this most perverse and impious assertion, it gives to mortality what did not belong to it and takes from God what was his.

2. Therefore, this fresh heresy, which has now sprung up from that deadly and pernicious depravity, has fanned old cinders into new flames as if rousing ashes to new life, since it asserts that the Lord Jesus Christ was born as an ordinary human being. Why then do we need to investigate any further whether it is perverse in its inferences when it shares the same wickedness as its source? For it is superfluous to ask what kind of thing it will be in its conclusions when it already leaves nothing at all to anticipate in its premise. Is there any reason to explore whether, in keeping with the earlier heresy, it promises human beings certain things, by – and this is its most monstrous crime – taking those same things away from God? It is almost impious to ask about what follows when we see what comes first, as if someone who denies God could find grounds in the inferences to prove that he is not impious. 3. Therefore, the new heresy says, as we have already explained often enough, that the Lord Jesus Christ was born from the Virgin only as an ordinary human being, and therefore Mary ought to be called the Christotokos, and not the Theotokos, because she is the mother of Christ, and not the mother of God. Furthermore, it adds to this sacrilegious assertion arguments as depraved as they are frivolous, saying,

"No one gives birth to someone older than herself."[83] As if the birth of the Only-Begotten of God, which was foretold by the prophets and announced beforehand from the ages could be investigated or even assessed by human methods! Or, dear heretic, whoever you are, did the Virgin Mary herself, whom you slander for giving birth, accomplish and perfect what was done by her own ability, so that human weakness would be a reason to reproach such a great matter and such a great deed? But if in this matter the deed was accomplished through human agency, then you could look for human explanations. If, however, everything that was done belongs to the power of God, then why are you so focused on what is impossible for humans when you can see that the efficacy is divine? But we will say more about this later. Now let us follow up the topic that we began to address a moment ago, so that everyone will realize that you are looking for a flame in the Pelagian ashes and are trying to stir up the old cinders by blowing upon them with new sacrilegious utterances.

2, 1. You say that Christ was born only as an ordinary human being. We already showed plainly in the first book that this is nothing other than what the heresy of the Pelagian impiety preached: Christ was born only as an ordinary human being. But beyond this, you add that Jesus Christ, the Lord of all, should himself be called a "God-receiving form,"[84] that is, not "God," but "one who receives God." Thus, you suppose that he must be honored, not for his own sake because he is God, but because he received God into himself. Clearly the aforementioned heresy also affirmed this, that Christ should be revered, not on account of himself, namely, because he is God, but rather because he deserved to have God dwell in him because of his good and holy actions. 2. You now see that you are spewing forth the Pelagian poison, that you are hissing like a Pelagian serpent.[85] Thus, it is fitting in your case that you appear not as one who will be judged, but as one who has already been judged, since when you belong to the same error you must

83 Cassian here quotes a line from Nestorius's *First Letter to Celestine* 2, translated in this volume on pp. 588–589. He cites the same line at *On the Incarnation* 2.2.1, 4.2.2, and 7.2.1.

84 In Latin, *theodochon imaginem*. Cassian here alludes to a passage from Nestorius, either *Sermon* 9 (*Nestoriana*: 263, 12–13 Loofs) or *Sermon* 10 (*Nestoriana*: 276, 3–5 Loofs), both of which say, "we ascribe divinity to the God-receiving form (*tēn theodochon morphēn*) along with God the Word." The latter adds, "but we do not ascribe divinity to the God-receiving (*theodochon*) Virgin along with God." On the term *theodochos*, see note 65 above.

85 At *On the Incarnation* 1.1 Cassian opened with the extended metaphor of heresy as a hydra, which he references again here.

also be consigned to the same condemnation. Moreover, I have not even mentioned that by comparing God to an imperial statue[86] you have rushed forth into such great sacrilegious impiety and blasphemy that you rightly seem in this madness to surpass by far even Pelagius himself, who had surpassed nearly everyone else in his impiety.

3, 1. You say that Christ should be called a "God-receiving form," in other words, that he is to be honored, not on his own account because he is God, but because he has received God into himself. Therefore, in this way you assert that there is no difference between him and all the other people who were holy because surely everyone who was holy had God within them.[87] For indeed we are not ignorant of the fact that God was in the patriarchs and God spoke in the prophets! 2. In brief, we believe that everyone – I have in mind not only the apostles and martyrs but also all the saints and servants of God – has the Spirit of God within themselves, just as the passage says, "For you are the temple of the living God, as God has said, 'I will dwell within them,'"[88] and again, "Do you not know that you are the temple of God because the Spirit of God dwells within you?"[89] For this reason they all are also "God-receiving,"[90] and so in this respect you should say they all are perfectly similar to Christ and equal to God. 3. But let us cast away the impiety of this odious error that considers the Maker equal to what he has made, the Lord equal to his servants, and the God of heaven and earth equal to earthly frailty. To claim that because he deemed a human being worthy to be his dwelling he himself is therefore only a human being is an insult to his own goodness.

4, 1. On the contrary! There is between him and all the saints the same difference that lies between the dwelling place and the one who dwells there. For certainly the fact that it is inhabited does not derive from the dwelling place but from the one who dwells there, for he is the one who decides both to build the dwelling place and to use it. In other words, he can either make it a dwelling place when he wants to do so or can deign to

86 Cassian has in mind the fact that Nestorius referred to Christ's humanity as a *morphē*, which he translated into Latin as *imago* (see note 84). *Imago* could be used to refer to a statue, as Cassian here suggests. However, Nestorius's use of *morphē* was almost certainly an allusion to the classical Christological passage in Phil 2:5–7.

87 This argument is parallel to the one put forward by Cyril of Alexandria in his *Letter to the Monks of Egypt* 10–11, namely that all Christians are "christs" since they are all anointed by the Holy Spirit, with the consequence that something more must be found to distinguish Jesus from everyone else. It is possible that Cassian may have had Cyril's letter as a part of the dossier Cyril had prepared and sent to Celestine.

88 2 Cor 6:16. 89 1 Cor 3:16. 90 In Latin/Greek, *theodochi*.

dwell there once he makes it. Thus the Apostle says, "Or do you seek proof that Christ is the one who speaks in me?"[91] And elsewhere he says, "Do you not know that Jesus Christ is in you, unless, of course, you fail the test?"[92] Again, he says, "Christ dwells within you through faith in your hearts."[93] 2. You see what lies between the apostolic teaching and your blasphemy. You say that God dwells in Christ as in a human being. But Paul testifies that Christ himself dwells in human beings, something that, as you yourself admit, flesh and blood certainly cannot do. And so, by the very proof you offer to deny that he is God, you actually prove that he is God. Since you do not deny that whoever dwells in a human being is God, we must believe that the one whom you think dwells in human beings is definitely God. Therefore, all of the patriarchs, prophets, apostles, martyrs, and even all of the holy men and women had God within themselves, and all were made children of God and all were God-bearing,[94] though for diverse and varied reasons. 3. For all those who believe in God are children of God through adoption, but only the Only-Begotten is Son by nature. The one who is begotten from the Father is not from some kind of matter since all things and even the matter from which all things are made exist through the only-begotten Son of God. The only-begotten Son is neither from nothing, since he is from the Father, nor is he born by separation,[95] since nothing in God is empty or changeable. Rather, in a manner ineffable and beyond reason, God the Father begot his Only-Begotten in those things which are unbegotten in him. And so, the Son is only-begotten, most high, and eternal since he is from the Father, who is unbegotten, most high, and eternal. He must be held to be in the flesh the same as he is held to be in spirit. He must be believed to be the same in the body as he is believed to be in majesty. For when he was about to be born in the flesh he did not create some sort of division or separation in himself as if one part of him could be born from another part which was not born, or as if some portion of divinity which had not been in him when he was born from the Virgin later came upon him. 4. For "the entire" – according to the Apostle – "the entire fullness of divinity dwelled bodily in Christ."[96] This is not because

91 2 Cor 13:3. 92 2 Cor 13:5.
93 Eph 3:16–17. 94 In Latin/Greek, *theodochi*.
95 Cassian uses the Latin term *partus* here, which refers to birth by departure or separation in the material, animal way. A child is separated from its mother's body at birth, but the Son's birth from the Father is not material.
96 Col 2:9.

sometimes it would dwell in him and sometimes it would not, nor because this was true of him at a later point and not previously. Otherwise, we would sink back into that impiety of the Pelagian heresy, claiming that God only dwelled in Christ from a certain time, namely when he came upon him, since it was from that point onward that he, by his life and morals, deserved to have the power of the divinity dwelling in him. 5. Therefore, these things belong to human beings, not to God, but to human beings: as far as human frailty allows, they should humble themselves before God, submit themselves to God, make themselves a dwelling place for God, and deserve to have God as their guest and indweller through faith and piety. To the extent that anyone has become suitable for the gift of God, divine grace is given to him. To the extent that anyone is regarded as worthy of God, he enjoys God's presence, in accordance with the Lord's promise: "If anyone loves me, he will keep my word, and my Father and I will come to him and make our dwelling with him."[97] 6. But in the case of Christ "in whom the fullness of divinity dwells bodily,"[98] the matter and its cause are very different. He has the fullness of divinity dwelling in him, so he gives generously to everyone out of his fullness. Having the fullness of divinity dwelling within him, he dwells in each of the saints insofar as he determines that they are worthy of his indwelling. Thus, he grants to everyone from his own fullness while continually maintaining that same fullness in himself. Therefore, even when he was on earth in his body, he was also within the souls of all the saints. Heaven, earth, sea, and the entire universe were filled with his infinite power and majesty, and yet he was so completely within himself that the entire universe could not contain him, since no matter how great and ineffable are the things he made, they are certainly not capacious or vast enough to be able to contain their Maker himself.

97 John 14:23. 98 Col 2:9.

46

Cyril of Alexandria, *Third Letter to Nestorius*

Introduction and Translation by Matthew R. Crawford

INTRODUCTION

This letter was delivered by a delegation of four Egyptian bishops to Nestorius in his residence after the morning service in Constantinople on Sunday, November 30, 430. Cyril had spent the past year building a solid coalition of support for his case against the bishop of the Eastern capital, by sending letters to various bishops in the East, and, most importantly, by sending to Rome a dossier including extracts from Nestorius's sermons. After ordering the archdeacon Leo (the future pope) to undertake an investigation, Pope Celestine called a synod to meet in Rome in August, which condemned Nestorius's teaching. He then wrote to Cyril deputizing him to order Nestorius to retract his errors and embrace the common faith of Rome and Alexandria, while leaving somewhat vague the precise contours of this common faith. In November Cyril thus held his own synod in Alexandria that likewise condemned Nestorius's views and produced the following letter, intended to spell out in greater detail the Christological dogmas to which the bishop of Constantinople must adhere. Hence, far from being a merely personal communication, this letter was intended to reflect the consensus that had formed against Nestorius's views, though scholars continue to debate whether Celestine and his party would have been willing to subscribe to all of the Christological propositions put forward by Cyril. Whatever the case, as far as Cyril and Celestine were concerned, the authoritative assessment of Nestorius's teachings had been carried out and a binding mandate had been issued, though the tables would soon turn when, in the period between Cyril's writing of this letter and its delivery to Nestorius, the emperor announced that there would be a universal council to consider the controversy.

As in Cyril's *Second Letter to Nestorius*,[1] so here again the Nicene Creed is taken as the standard of orthodoxy, although Cyril now admits that it is not enough for Nestorius merely to confess the Creed, since he gives it his own unorthodox interpretation. Hence, in sections 4–6 of the present letter Cyril provides his interpretation of the Creed, along much the same lines as he had already done in the previous letter. As before, he argues that it teaches a hypostatic union, a union resulting in one personal subject, rather than a merely external joining of two individuals who can be separated and act independently. The former is a true "union" (*henōsis*) while the latter is a "conjunction" (*synapheia*), the term that Nestorius preferred. After completing his interpretation of the Creed, from section 7 onward Cyril turns to consider briefly several other related issues that he had dealt with at greater length in his *Five Tomes against Nestorius* written earlier in the same year, including the Eucharist, the division of Christ's sayings in the gospels, and the role of the Spirit in the life of Jesus. Finally, Cyril argues that the hypostatic union means that one must confess the Virgin to be Theotokos, the disputed question that had set off the entire controversy some two years prior. The Twelve Anathemas that conclude the letter summarize his reading of the Creed and the additional points made in the letter, stating Cyril's position as forthrightly as possible in order to avoid any dissimulation on the part of Nestorius.

Although the positions Cyril sets out in this letter are entirely in keeping with what he had already stated in the *Second Letter to Nestorius*, here he does go further in terms of specificity and in extending his argument to related topics. It may be that, if he had not done so, he would have more easily secured either Nestorius's recantation or condemnation at the council several months later. For example, after learning of Celestine's decision, John of Antioch had been counseling Nestorius to conform to the verdict of the Roman synod, but he changed his mind when he read Cyril's letter. As it turned out, this letter, and particularly its Twelve Anathemas, became the main focus of the controversy in the lead-up to the council, with Andrew of Samosata and Theodoret of Cyrrhus writing separate rebuttals,[2] to which Cyril responded with two defenses, along with a third defense written during his forced stay in Ephesus in 431. At the Council of Ephesus the letter was read out, but was not formally approved,[3] and at the rival

1 Translated in this volume on pp. 570–576.
2 Theodoret's *Refutation of the Twelve Anathemas* is translated in this volume on pp. 641–657.
3 See *Acts of the Council of Ephesus*, session of June 22, section 50.

council convoked in Ephesus by Nestorius's allies (including John of Antioch) it was condemned as tainted by the heresies of Arius, Apollinarius, and Eunomius.[4] The letter and its attached anathemas finally received synodal affirmation at the second Council of Constantinople in 553.[5]

This translation is based on the critical text of Eduard Schwartz, *Concilium Universale Ephesenum*, ACO 1.1.1 (Berlin: De Gruyter, 1927), 33–42. The *Third Letter to Nestorius* is *Letter* 17 within Cyril's epistolary corpus (CPG 5317).

TRANSLATION

1. To the most reverent and God-loving fellow minister Nestorius, Cyril and the synod of the diocese of Egypt gathered in Alexandria send you greetings in the Lord.

Since our Savior clearly said, "The one who loves father or mother more than me is not worthy of me, and the one who loves son or daughter more than me is not worthy of me,"[6] what penalty would we incur when Your Reverence demands that we love you more than Christ, the Savior of us all? Who will be able to help us on the day of judgment? Or what sort of defense will we find if we place such a high value on a prolonged silence in the face of the blasphemies against him that are coming from you? Now if you were only doing wrong to yourself by thinking and teaching such things, we would not be as concerned. But since you have scandalized the entire church and have spread among the people the leaven of a bizarre and alien heresy – and not only among those there, but also among those everywhere, since the books of your expositions have been disseminated – what sort of answer would suffice for our continued silence? How could we not recall the saying of Christ, "Do not think that I have come to bring peace upon the earth, but a sword. For I have come to set a man against his father and a daughter against her mother."[7] For when the faith is being injured, let reverence for parents be done away with as vain and misleading, let even the law of affection toward children and brothers be set aside, and henceforth let the pious prefer death to life, in order that "they may attain a better resurrection,"[8] as it is written.

4 See *Acts of the Council of Ephesus*, session of June 26, sections 11 and 15, translated in this volume on pp. 698–700.

5 See the selections of *Acts of the Second Council of Constantinople*, translated in CEECW 4 on pp. 341–389.

6 Matt 10:37. 7 Matt 10:34–35. 8 Heb 11:35.

2. Accordingly, together with the holy synod that has met in Great Rome,[9] presided over by our most holy and God-fearing brother and fellow minister Bishop Celestine, we are solemnly warning you now with this third letter, advising you to dissociate yourself from the extremely crooked and perverse doctrines you both hold and teach, and to embrace instead the orthodox faith handed down to the churches from the beginning by the holy apostles and evangelists, who "were both eyewitnesses and ministers of the word."[10]

And unless Your Reverence does this by the date appointed[11] in the letters of our aforementioned fellow minister Celestine, the most holy and God-fearing bishop of the church of the Romans, know that you have no clerical standing with us, nor any place or status among the priests and bishops of God. For we cannot simply stand by watching churches being thrown into a tumult and people being scandalized and the orthodox faith being rejected and the flocks being torn asunder by you who should be saving them, if you ever were, like us, an adherent of orthodoxy, following the religion of the holy fathers. As for us, we all are in communion with all those laity and clergy who have been excommunicated or condemned by Your Reverence on account of the faith. For it is not right that those people who are wise enough to hold orthodox views should be wronged by your decrees simply because they did what was right by speaking out against you, as you yourself pointed out in the letter you wrote to Celestine, our most holy fellow bishop of Great Rome.[12]

And it will not be sufficient for Your Reverence merely to confess with us the symbol of the faith which was expounded in the Holy Spirit by the holy and great synod assembled in time past at Nicaea. (For you have not understood and interpreted it in an orthodox sense, but rather in a twisted manner, even if you have verbally confessed the words.) Consequently, you must also confess in writing and by oath that, on the one hand, you anathematize your own abominable and profane doctrines and, on the other hand, that you hold and teach the same as all of us, the bishops and teachers

9 This is probably intended as a reminder to Nestorius that Constantinople was merely "second Rome."

10 Luke 1:2.

11 Ten days from Nestorius's receipt of the letter from Celestine.

12 Cyril has apparently seen at least one of the letters Nestorius wrote to Celestine. Probably Celestine forwarded it to Cyril as evidence against him, following the synod in Rome that condemned Nestorius. Nestorius's three letters to Celestine are translated in this volume on pp. 585–592.

and leaders of the people in both the West and the East.[13] Moreover, both the holy synod in Rome and all of us here have agreed that the letters written to Your Reverence from the churches of Alexandria are orthodox and blameless.[14] And we have attached to this letter of ours what it is that you must think and teach as well as those things from which you must separate yourself.[15] For this is the faith of the catholic and apostolic church, which all of the orthodox bishops in both the West and in the East agree upon.

> 3. We believe in one God, Father, almighty, maker of all things both seen and unseen; and in one Lord, Jesus Christ, the Son of God, begotten from the Father only-begotten, that is, from the substance of the Father, God from God, light from light, true God from true God, begotten, not made, same-in-substance with the Father, through whom all things came to be, both those in heaven and those on earth, who for the sake of us human beings and for our salvation came down, and became incarnate and became human, suffered, and rose again on the third day, ascended into the heavens, and is coming to judge the living and the dead; and in the Holy Spirit. Now as for those who say: There was a point when he did not exist, and before he was begotten he did not exist, and that he came to be from nothing, or from a different subsistence or substance, claiming that the Son of God is either changeable or mutable, these people the catholic and apostolic church anathematizes.[16]

We follow in every point the confessions the holy fathers made with the Holy Spirit speaking in them, and we stick to the intent of their thoughts, keeping, as it were, to the Royal Road. Therefore, we affirm that the only-begotten Word of God himself, begotten from the very substance of the Father, true God from true God, light from light, the one through whom all things came to be, both those in heaven and those on earth, came down for our salvation and descended into self-emptying.[17] He thus became incarnate and became human, that is, he took flesh from the holy Virgin and made it his own such that he endured a birth like ours from his mother and came forth as a human

13 Cyril's grand claim of ecclesial unity in East and West is based on his assumption that the two most important sees – Rome and Alexandria – have spoken on the issue in agreement.
14 This must be a reference to the first and second letters sent by Cyril to Nestorius.
15 A reference to the Twelve Anathemas at the end of the letter.
16 The Creed of Nicaea in 325.
17 See Phil 2:7.

being from a woman. He did all of this not by ridding himself of what he was. Rather, even though he assumed flesh and blood, he still remained what he was – God by nature and in truth. And we affirm that neither was the flesh turned into the nature of the divinity nor was the ineffable nature of God the Word changed into the nature of flesh.[18] For the one who abides eternally, according to the scriptures,[19] is entirely unchanging and immutable, so that even when he is seen as an infant in swaddling clothes in the lap of the Virgin who bore him, he was still filling the entire creation as God, enthroned with the one who begot him. For what is divine is unquantifiable and without extension, and it admits of no boundaries.

4. So confessing that the Word was united[20] with flesh hypostatically,[21] we worship one Son and Lord, Jesus Christ. We neither separate nor divide human being and God, as if they were conjoined[22] with one another by a union of dignity or authority (for this is nothing but foolish nonsense). Nor do we specify the Word from God as Christ and likewise the one from the woman as another Christ. Instead, we know only one Christ, the Word from God the Father with his own flesh. For it was at that point that he was anointed[23] as human along with us, even though he also "gives the Spirit without measure"[24] to worthy recipients, as the blessed evangelist John says. But we do not assert that the Word from God dwelled in an ordinary human who was born from the holy Virgin, lest Christ should be regarded as a God-bearing human being. For even though it has been said that "the Word dwelt among us," and also that "all the fullness of the deity dwelt bodily"[25] in Christ, still we recognize that it was by becoming flesh[26] that he undertook this indwelling. By this we do not mean that the indwelling occurred in him in the same way that he is said to have dwelled in the saints, but rather that, by being united naturally to flesh, though not changed into it, he undertook the kind of indwelling that the soul of a person may be said to have with its own body.

18 With this line Cyril seeks to distinguish his position from Apollinarianism, of which Nestorius and others suspected him. It also distinguishes his position from the extreme view of his later supporter Eutyches, whose teaching provoked the second Council of Ephesus in 449 and the subsequent Council of Chalcedon in 451.

19 See Mal 3:6; Heb 13:8.

20 In Greek, *hēnōsthai*.

21 In Greek, *kath' hypostasin*, literally, "according to hypostasis."

22 In Greek, *sunēmmenous*, from *synaptō*.

23 The linguistic connection is not apparent in English, but Cyril assumes here that to say someone is "christ" (*christos*) means that he or she has been anointed (*kechristai*). Hence the connection between the previous sentence and this one.

24 John 3:34.

25 John 1:14 and Col 2:9.

26 John 1:14.

5. Therefore, there is one Christ and Son and Lord, not as if a human being simply had a conjunction with God, as though it were a union of dignity or authority, since equality of honor does not unite natures. Surely both Peter and John each have the same amount of honor as the other insofar as both are apostles and holy disciples, but these two are not one. We do not regard the manner of the conjunction in terms of a juxtaposition (for this is not enough to produce a natural union), nor in terms of a relational participation in the way that "we also are joined to the Lord and so are one spirit with him," as it is written.[27] Rather, we reject the word "conjunction,"[28] as insufficient to signify the union. And we do not call the Word from God the Father either the "God of Christ" or the "Master of Christ" for the obvious reason that we would then be cutting into two the one Christ and Son and Lord, and in this way fall under the charge of blasphemy by making him God and Master of himself. For, as we have already said, the Word of God, having been united to flesh hypostatically, is God of all and Master over everything, and he is neither slave nor master of himself. For it is absurd – or rather, profane – to think or say such things. He did indeed say that the Father is his "God,"[29] although he is God by nature and from his substance, but we nevertheless do not overlook the fact that, in addition to being God, he also became a human being subject to God, in keeping with the law proper to the nature of humanity. But how could he become the God or Master of himself? Therefore, inasmuch as he was a human being and experienced what was appropriate to the limitations of his self-emptying, he declared himself to be subject to God along with us. In this way he also was born under the law,[30] even though he himself, as God, spoke the law and is the lawgiver.

6. Now we reject this statement about Christ: "I venerate the one who is worn because of the wearer. I worship the one who is seen because of the one who is unseen."[31] It is shocking then to add to this, "The one who has been assumed shares the name 'God' with the one who has assumed him."[32] For the one who says these things again severs him into two Christs, setting up successively a distinct human being and similarly a

27 1 Cor 6:17. 28 In Greek, *synapheia*. 29 See John 20:17.
30 See Gal 4:4. 31 Nestorius, *Sermon* 9 (*Nestoriana*: 262, 3–4 Loofs).
32 Nestorius, *Sermon* 9 (*Nestoriana*: 262, 11–12 Loofs). See Cyril's fuller discussion of these passages in his *Five Tomes against Nestorius* 2.12–13. They were also included in the dossier of texts presented at the Council of Ephesus as evidence for Nestorius's condemnation: see *Acts of the Council of Ephesus*, session of June 22, section 60.15, translated in this volume on pp. 689–690.

God. For such a person is unquestionably denying the union that ensures we do not "co-worship" or call "God" one along with another but instead understand that Christ Jesus, the only-begotten Son, is one, he with his own flesh being honored by one worship. And we confess that the same Son and only-begotten God, begotten from God the Father, although being impassible according to his own nature, "has suffered in the flesh"[33] on our behalf, according to the scriptures, and was in the crucified body, impassibly making his own the sufferings of his own flesh. And "by the grace of God he tasted death on behalf of all,"[34] offering his own body to death, even though he was life according to nature and is himself the resurrection.[35] For by his inexpressible power he trampled on death, so that he, in his own flesh, might be the first one to become "the firstborn from the dead" and the "first fruits of those who have fallen asleep,"[36] and might blaze a trail for human nature to return to incorruptibility. Thus, as we just said, "by the grace of God he tasted death on behalf of all," and after three days came to life again, having despoiled Hades. Therefore, even if it is said that "the resurrection of the dead" came to pass "through a human being,"[37] we understand this to mean that the Word from God became a human being and that the dominion of death was destroyed through him. And he will come at the due time as one Son and Lord, in the glory of the Father, in order to "judge the world in righteousness," as it is written.[38]

7. We must deal with the following too.[39] In proclaiming the death, according to the flesh, of the only-begotten Son of God, that is, Jesus Christ, and in confessing his return from the dead to life and his ascension into heaven, we perform the bloodless worship in the churches and approach the mystical blessings,[40] and we are sanctified, becoming thereby participants in the holy flesh and "precious blood"[41] of Christ the Savior of us all. We do not receive it as if it were normal flesh – God forbid! – nor indeed as if it were the flesh of a man sanctified and conjoined to the Word in a union of dignity or as if he merely possessed a divine indwelling. Rather, we receive this flesh as being truly life-giving and the very Word's own flesh. For being life by nature, qua God, and since he has become one with

33 1 Pet 4:1. 34 Heb 2:9. 35 See John 11:25. 36 Col 1:18 and 1 Cor 15:20.
37 1 Cor 15:21. 38 Acts 17:31.
39 This sentence signals that Cyril has completed his interpretation of the Nicene Creed and is now moving on to other matters.
40 "Blessing" is Cyril's usual term for the Eucharist. 41 1 Pet 1:19.

his own flesh, he has declared it to be life-giving. So even if he says to us, "Amen, I say to you, unless you eat the flesh of the Son of Man and drink his blood,"[42] we do not regard it as the flesh of a human being like one of us – for how could the flesh of a human being be life-giving according to its own nature? – but as flesh which has truly come to belong to the one who has, for our sake, become the Son of Man, and was so called.

8. Now as for the sayings of our Savior in the gospels, we do not divide them either between two hypostases or indeed between two persons. For the one and only Christ is not twofold, even if he is understood as having been brought together from two different things[43] into an indivisible unity, just as, for instance, a human being is also understood as consisting of soul and body, and yet is not twofold, but one from both. So, holding the correct view, we will be inclined to think that both the human sayings as well as the divine ones were spoken by one. For when he says about himself, speaking in a manner appropriate to God, "The one who has seen me has seen the Father," and "I and the Father are one,"[44] we think of his divine and ineffable nature, according to which he is one with his own Father on account of their identity of substance, and he is the image and "imprint and radiance of his glory."[45] But because he did not disdain human limitation, when he says to the Jews, "But now you are seeking to kill me, a human being who has spoken to you the truth,"[46] again we no less acknowledge him as God the Word in his equality and likeness with the Father and [speaking] from his human limitations. For if it is incumbent upon us to believe that, though being God by nature, "he became flesh"[47] (in other words, a human being animated by a rational soul), what reason could anyone have for being ashamed of the fact that these sayings of his are expressed in a manner appropriate to a human being? For if he rejects words proper to a human being, who was it that compelled him to become a human being like us? But if he has lowered himself for our sake into a voluntary self-emptying,[48] why would he then reject those words that are proper to the self-emptying? Therefore, all the sayings in the gospels must

42 John 6:53.

43 Cyril here uses the word *pragma* ("thing"), which was the most generic way of referring to something, implying that he is deliberately avoiding giving a specific term to designate the duality in Christ, unlike the Council of Chalcedon two decades later, which would codify the phrase "two natures" to refer to the humanity and deity in Christ.

44 John 14:9, 10:30. 45 Heb 1:3. 46 John 8:40.

47 John 1:14. 48 See Phil 2:7.

be ascribed to one person – the one incarnate hypostasis of the Word.[49] For "there is one Lord Jesus Christ," according to the scriptures.[50]

9. Now if he should be called "the apostle and high priest of our confession,"[51] because he acts as a priest to God the Father and ministers the confession of faith which is offered from us both to him and through him to God the Father, and also indeed unto the Holy Spirit, again we affirm that he does so as the only-begotten Son who comes from God by nature, rather than assigning the title and reality of priesthood to another alongside of him. For he has become "a mediator between God and human beings,"[52] a mediator for peace, offering himself up as "a fragrant offering" to God the Father.[53] This is why he also said, "'Sacrifices and offerings you have not desired, but you have fashioned a body for me. In burnt offerings and sin offerings you did not delight.' Then I said, 'Behold, I have come, O God, to do your will, as it is written of me in the roll of the book.'"[54] For he has offered his own body as a fragrant offering on our behalf and certainly not on his own behalf. For what sort of offering or sacrifice would he have needed on his own behalf, since as God he is greater than all sin? For if "all have sinned and fallen short of the glory of God,"[55] in the sense that we became prone to going astray and human nature has become afflicted with sin, while he is not like this, which is why we are inferior to his glory, how could anyone doubt that the true lamb has been sacrificed for our sake and on our behalf? To say that he has offered himself both on his own behalf and on our behalf would by no means escape the accusation of impiety, since in no way did he go astray, "nor did he commit any sin."[56] Therefore, what sort of offering did he need, in the absence of the sin which would have required such an offering?

10. Now when he says about the Spirit, "That one will glorify me,"[57] we understand this in an orthodox manner, and so we say that the one Christ and Son did not take glory from the Holy Spirit as if he was in need of glory from someone else, because his Spirit is neither greater than him nor above him. Rather, it is because he used his own Spirit to perform

49 Note that here Cyril says "the one incarnate *hypostasis* of the Word." Following the Council of Ephesus he would have to deal at length with some of his supporters who preferred to say "the one incarnate *nature* of the Word." See his two letters to Succensus, translated in this volume on pp. 731–739 and pp. 740–746.

50 1 Cor 8:6. 51 Heb 3:1. 52 1 Tim 2:5. 53 Eph 5:2.

54 Heb 10:5–7, citing Ps 39(40):6–8. 55 Rom 3:23.

56 See 1 Pet 2:22. 57 John 16:14.

magnificent deeds as a demonstration of his own deity that he says he has been glorified by the Spirit, just as one of us might say about his innate ability or some special skill, "They will glorify me." For even if the Spirit exists in his own hypostasis and indeed is understood as distinct, inasmuch as he is Spirit and not Son, still he is not alien to the Son. For he has been named the "Spirit of truth"[58] and Christ is the truth,[59] and the Spirit goes forth from Christ just as he does of course also from God the Father. Therefore, when the Spirit also performed miraculous deeds through the hands of the holy apostles after our Lord Jesus Christ ascended into heaven, he glorified Christ. For it is believed that he is God according to nature, and so he himself works through his own Spirit. This is the reason that he said, "He will take from what is mine and proclaim it to you."[60] And in no way do we claim that the Spirit is wise and powerful by participation, since he is pure perfection and does not lack anything good. But since he is the Spirit of the Father's "power and wisdom"[61] (that is, the Son), he is absolute wisdom and power.

11. Now since the holy Virgin brought forth in a fleshly manner God united hypostatically to flesh, for this reason we also say that she is Theotokos. We do not say this in the sense that the nature of the Word began to exist from the flesh (for he was "in the beginning," and "the Word was God," and "the Word was with God,"[62] and he is the maker of the ages, co-eternal with the Father and fashioner of all things). Rather, we call her Theotokos because, as we have already said, he hypostatically united to himself that which is human and endured a fleshly birth from her womb. He did not need, out of necessity or for his own nature, a temporal birth in the last times of the age. Rather, he did all this in order to bless the very beginning of our existence, so that, with a woman having begotten him united to flesh, the curse against the whole race which sends our earthly bodies to death might finally cease. Thus the sentence, "in sorrow you shall bear children,"[63] was abolished through him, and he demonstrated the truth of what was said through the voice of the prophet, "Death prevailed and swallowed them up, and God has again removed every tear from every face."[64] We say that it was for this reason that he, in keeping with the economy, also himself blessed marriage, and, when he was invited, went to Cana in Galilee with the holy apostles.[65]

58 John 16:13. 59 See John 14:6. 60 John 16:14. 61 See 1 Cor 1:24.
62 John 1:1. 63 Gen 3:16. 64 Isa 25:8. 65 See John 2:1–2.

12. We have been taught to think in this way by the holy apostles and evangelists, as well as by all the inspired scripture, and on the basis of the true confession of the blessed fathers. Your Piety must also agree with and affirm all these things without any deceit. And what Your Piety must anathematize is appended to our letter here.

[The Twelve Anathemas]

I. If anyone does not confess that Emmanuel is God in truth and for this reason that the holy Virgin is Theotokos (for she gave birth in a fleshly manner to the Word from God who had become flesh), let him be anathema.[66]

II. If anyone does not confess that the Word from God the Father was hypostatically united to flesh, and that he is one Christ with his own flesh, that is, the same one is simultaneously God and human being, let him be anathema.

III. If anyone divides the hypostases in the one Christ after the union, conjoining them by a conjunction[67] merely in terms of dignity or authority or lordship and not instead by a coming together[68] in the sense of a natural union, let him be anathema.

IV. If anyone distributes the sayings in the evangelical and apostolic writings to two persons or two hypostases, whether those things said by the saints about Christ or those said by him about himself, and if he attributes some of them to a human being thought of separately alongside the Word from God but others exclusively to the Word from God the Father because they are appropriate for God, let him be anathema.

V. If anyone dares to say that Christ is a God-bearing human being and does not instead say that he is God in truth because he is the one Son and this by nature, insofar as the "Word became flesh"[69] and "partook like us of flesh and blood,"[70] let him be anathema.

VI. If anyone says the Word from God the Father is the God or Master of Christ, and does not instead confess that the same one

66 Unlike the section enumeration throughout the earlier part of the epistle, these anathemas are numbered sequentially in Cyril's original text.

67 In Greek, *synapheia*. 68 In Greek, *synodos*.

69 John 1:14. 70 Heb 2:14.

is simultaneously God and human being, since according to the scriptures the Word became flesh,[71] let him be anathema.

VII. If anyone says that Jesus was acted upon by God the Word as a human being would be, and that the glory of the Only-Begotten was attached to him as though he were another alongside the Only-Begotten, let him be anathema.

VIII. If anyone dares to say that the human being who was assumed ought to be worshiped together with, glorified together with, and named God together with God the Word, as if he were one with another (for the continual addition of "together with" requires us to think this), and if he does not instead honor the Emmanuel with a single worship and ascribe to him a single glorification, insofar as "the Word became flesh,"[72] let him be anathema.

IX. If anyone says that the one Lord Jesus Christ has been glorified by the Spirit, making use of the power that came through the Spirit as if it belonged to someone else and receiving from the Spirit the ability to work against unclean spirits and to accomplish divine signs among humanity, and if he does not instead say that the Spirit through whom he performed the divine signs is his very own, let him be anathema.

X. The divine scripture says Christ became "the high priest and apostle of our confession,"[73] and that he "offered himself on our behalf as a fragrant offering to God the Father."[74] Therefore, if anyone says that the Word from God did not himself become our high priest and apostle when he became flesh and a human being like us, but another alongside him did so, a human being apart from him, "born of a woman,"[75] or if anyone says that he brought an offering on his own behalf too and not instead solely on our behalf (for the one who knew no sin needed no offering), let him be anathema.

XI. If anyone does not confess that the Lord's flesh is life-giving and is the very own flesh of the Word from God the Father, but [says] that it belongs to someone else alongside him who is connected with him in terms of dignity or who merely has a divine

71 John 1:14. 72 John 1:14. 73 Heb 3:1.
74 Eph 5:2, altered. 75 Gal 4:4.

indwelling, and does not instead confess, as we have already said, that his flesh is life-giving because it became the very own flesh of the Word who is able to give life to all things, let him be anathema.

XII. If anyone does not confess that the Word of God suffered in the flesh, was crucified in the flesh, tasted death in the flesh, and became the firstborn from the dead,[76] insofar as he, as God, is both life and life-giving, let him be anathema.

76 See Col 1:18.

47

Nestorius of Constantinople, *Letter to John of Antioch*

Introduction and Translation by Matthew R. Crawford

INTRODUCTION

This letter comes from a crucial moment in the Nestorian controversy and partially accounts for why the attempted ecumenical council in Ephesus in July 431 was so fractious. The letter was penned at some point after November 30, 430, when Nestorius had received a letter from Celestine calling for him to recant his Christological views, and prior to Nestorius's sermons in the cathedral on December 6 and 7, since these are referred to in the postscript added later. It was written in response to a letter from John of Antioch, sent earlier in November 430, in which John had distanced himself from Nestorius's views and encouraged him to comply with the summons from Celestine and Cyril to confess that Mary was Theotokos, "bearer of God." In other words, although John is usually portrayed as an ally of Nestorius, and eventually became such, at this point he was effectively siding with Celestine and Cyril, leaving the bishop of Constantinople isolated among the powerful sees of Christendom.

Nestorius's strategy in response was to once more present himself as the reconciler of warring factions, proposing the title Christotokos ("bearer of Christ") for Mary in order to bring together those who insist on Anthropotokos ("bearer of the human being") and those who hold to Theotokos. As John had encouraged, following the injunction of Celestine, Nestorius in this letter affirms the term Theotokos, though he once again points out what he takes to be the heretical potential inherent to the word. Moreover, he makes clear that he realizes his only hope for exoneration lies in the ecumenical council to be summoned by the emperor, which would provide a forum for contesting the synodal decisions of Rome and Alexandria. Finally, he recalls the past interferences of the bishop of Alexandria in the affairs of the capital city, probably referring to the deposition and exile of

John Chrysostom and thereby presenting Cyril's present actions as a continuation of the unpopular tactics of his uncle Theophilus.

It was at this moment that Nestorius executed what was perhaps his first strategically clever move since the controversy began two years earlier.[1] When John had written his letter to Nestorius, he had not seen Cyril's *Third Letter to Nestorius* and its attached Twelve Anathemas, and Nestorius realized that these latest texts to emerge from Alexandria had the potential to break up the alliance that had formed against him. Thus, when he sent the present letter to John, he included with it Cyril's third letter as well as his own sermons preached on December 6 and 7. Nestorius's instinct proved correct, for once John had seen Cyril's *Third Letter to Nestorius*, he began writing to other Eastern bishops (so called because they came from the Roman diocese of Oriens or "East"), rallying those in his area of influence against Cyril's Twelve Anathemas. Hence, when everyone finally arrived at Ephesus in the summer of the following year, the battle lines had clearly formed, with Rome and Alexandria on one side and Antioch and Constantinople on the other.

The original Greek of the letter is lost, but a Latin translation survives. This translation is based on the critical edition of the Latin text by Eduard Schwartz, *Concilium Universale Ephesenum*, ACO 1.4 (Berlin: De Gruyter, 1922–1923), 4–6.

TRANSLATION

1. Nestorius, to the most beloved of God and most holy fellow minister John.

I would have sooner thought that people could bring malicious charges against me on any other grounds than that I did not understand the piety of the faith, since I have been delighted by the many thousands of enemies rising against me on account of the war I have until now waged against all the heretics. Nevertheless, it is necessary to endure even this trial with joy, because it too, if we should prove most vigilant, is able to produce for us great confidence in our piety. But what has happened to us has also accomplished another thing: it has highlighted the degree of interest Your Godliness has for our welfare.

1 Up to this point in the controversy Nestorius's maneuvers had resulted in a series of political miscalculations: he alienated Celestine by reopening the cases of the Pelagians; he alienated himself from parts of the imperial household; and he underestimated Cyril's support outside Egypt.

2. For the things that you recently wrote to us and to our most excellent son Irenaeus, friend of Christ, as well as to the bishops Musaeus and Helladius, beloved of God, clearly proclaimed like a trumpet the genuine esteem Your Godliness has for us, and also what great concern you have for the peace of the entire universal church. We also have a special concern for this peace and would regard it as a matter of utter madness and fraternal hatred for us alone, in opposition to everyone else, somehow to arrogate to ourselves authority over the matters that have been stirred up. For we are well aware that the word "Theotokos"[2] that is used to refer to her is taken by many heretics as their own word, and we bear in mind that some of those here who recklessly affirm this term have under its influence fallen into ideas that are heretical and far from pious, particularly those of the impious Arius and Apollinarius.

3. Therefore, recognizing in what you have written, as I said, the benevolence Your Godliness has for us and your appropriate concern for the churches of God, through this letter of mine on the issue that has been stirred up I have hastened to settle the dispute for your God-beloved soul. Meanwhile I also wanted to make this known, that even before Your Godliness's letter, I myself had settled it (in a manner of speaking). Basing myself on the deliberations of us all, I considered that it was proper to explain in one voice and unanimously the term "Theotokos"[3] that is used to refer to her. I did this not in order to delay in the slightest my own confession of the term, but in order not to allow any of those who least understand the things of God to use this as an occasion for seizing upon our words and creating a schism in the church.

4. For I think Your Godliness is also aware that as soon as we arrived here[4] we discovered that some here who belonged to the church were opposed to one another in divisive disagreement: some of them called the holy Virgin only "Theotokos," while others called her "Anthropotokos."[5] Accordingly, diligently trying to effect a reconciliation between the factions without disdaining any of the sheep lest one be lost (as we observe the Lord of all himself did),[6] we called her "Christotokos,"[7] since this term clearly signifies both, that is, God and human being. In regard to the terms used in the gospel, I also conceded to those so inclined that they could call

2 In Latin, *theotocos*, a Latin rendering of the Greek *theotokos*.
3 In Latin, *dei genetrix*, another way that the Greek *theotokos* was rendered in Latin.
4 That is, when Nestorius became bishop of Constantinople in 428.
5 The Latin here is *genetrix hominis*, no doubt translating the Greek *anthrōpotokos*.
6 See Luke 15:3–7.
7 The Latin is *genetrix Christi*, a rendering of the Greek *Christotokos*.

the Virgin "Theotokos"[8] or "Bearer of God"[9] in a pious manner, in other words not in the sense intended by either Apollinarius or Arius, but also not as if the divinity of the Only-Begotten received its beginning from the holy Virgin, but rather on account of the union that occurred the very moment the angel began to speak about the conception.[10]

5. Therefore, I ask that, as you enjoy a respite from such concerns about the case at hand and knowing that by God's grace we hold and have always held the same positions as you in matters pertaining to the piety of faith, pray as you usually do that both in this matter and in everything else we may obtain help from Christ the Lord and prove worthy of conversing with one another. For it is clear that if we should see one another, assuming that God grants us this synod that we hope for, we will settle this matter without any scandal and with concord, as well as whatever else needs to be done for the correction and help of the universal church. And the intended outcome is that they will accept as worthy of belief everything prescribed in a joint and universal verdict, leaving no opportunity for anyone to object, even if they should be altogether disposed to doing such a thing. But Your Godliness must not be shocked by the extreme audacity regularly shown by Egypt since you have such a plethora of examples of this behavior from the past. But in a short while, God willing, our judgment on this matter will be praised.

I and those who are with me send greetings to all the brothers with you. May you, who are most beloved of God and worthy of all honor, continue in good health and in prayer for us.

After the subscription to the letter:

In view of <the battle that> seems to me <soon to occur>[11] against those who are looking for one, we are using another means that is more expedient. For after receiving the letter of Your Godliness, we have, through that teaching we gave publicly in the church,[12] drawn to our side, by God's grace, even more clergy, people, and imperial courtiers.

8 In Latin, *genetricem dei*. See note 3 above.

9 In Latin, *partricem dei*. This seems to be a Latin gloss on the Greek *theotokos*.

10 See Luke 1:26–38.

11 The bracketed words are a conjectural emendation by Schwartz filling in a presumed lacuna in the textual tradition.

12 That is, the two sermons preached on December 6 and 7, 430, which Nestorius appended to the present letter sent to John, along with Cyril's *Third Letter to Nestorius*.

48

Theodoret of Cyrrhus, *Refutation of the Twelve Anathemas of Cyril of Alexandria*

Introduction and Translation of the Refutation of the Twelve Anathemas by Vasilije Vranic
Revised and Edited by Mark DelCogliano
Translation of the Twelve Anathemas by Matthew R. Crawford
Translation of the Letter of Theodoret to John of Antioch by Mark DelCogliano

INTRODUCTION

On November 30, 430, Cyril of Alexandria, acting on behalf of the churches of both Rome and Alexandria, had his *Third Letter to Nestorius* delivered to Nestorius, openly accusing him of heresy.[1] To this letter Cyril appended the Twelve Anathemas, Christological propositions threatening with excommunication everyone who did not subscribe to them. Being thus threatened with excommunication by Rome and Alexandria, Nestorius swiftly wrote a letter to his friend and compatriot John of Antioch, asking for advice.[2] John then asked two prominent bishops from the Antiochene milieu, Theodoret of Cyrrhus and Andrew of Samosata, to respond in writing to Cyril's Twelve Anathemas.

Theodoret responded to John's request in a letter (*Ep.* 150) to which he appended his *Refutation of the Twelve Anathemas*, twelve Christological counter-statements.[3] In the letter Theodoret denounced the Twelve Anathemas as a "heretical" and "blasphemous" revival of the "impious" teaching of Apollinarius. In the official text of the *Refutation of the Twelve Anathemas*, however, his tone was much more moderate. Here he does not make harsh,

1 Cyril's *Third Letter to Nestorius* is translated in this volume on pp. 623–637.
2 Nestorius's *Letter to John of Antioch* is translated in the volume on pp. 637–640.
3 On Theodoret, see his *Exposition of the Orthodox Faith* translated in this volume on pp. 535–555.

direct, or personal accusations of heresy against Cyril; he simply argues that Cyril's Christology is theologically unsound.

In the Twelve Anathemas, Cyril attacked Nestorius's criticism of the title Theotokos. Nestorius had argued that the title is inadequate since the Virgin Mary did not give birth to Christ qua God, but to the human element in Christ. Cyril argued in turn that any division of the divine and human elements in Christ would jeopardize the oneness of Christ with the divine Word. Cyril chose to speak of the union of the divine and human elements of Christ as the "hypostatic" or "natural" union of the two natures in Christ. The language of "one nature" (*mia physis*) of Christ after the incarnation put Cyril into a close association with the condemned teaching of Apollinarius, who proclaimed that God the Word was "one hypostasis" (*mia hypostasis*) with his own flesh and that the Virgin Mary is properly called Theotokos, since she gave birth to the Word. This similarity between Cyril's proposition and Apollinarius's theology did not escape the eye of Theodoret of Cyrrhus, who drew parallels between the two theologies in his *Refutation*.

This translation of the *Letter to John of Antioch* and the *Refutation of the Twelve Anathemas* is based on the critical texts in Eduard Schwartz, *Concilium Universale Ephesenum*, ACO 1.1.6 (Berlin: De Gruyter, 1927), 107–46. The translation of the Twelve Anathemas is the same as that found in the translation of Cyril's *Third Letter to Nestorius* in this volume on pp. 623–636.

TRANSLATION

The Letter of Theodoret to John of Antioch (*Letter* 150)

1. I suffered quite grievously when I read the anathematisms[4] you sent, urging us to refute them in writing and to expose their heretical ideas to all. I suffered because a man chosen to be a shepherd and entrusted with such an enormous flock and appointed to heal the weak among his sheep is himself quite sick and indeed very much so, and he attempts to infect his lambs with his sickness and treats his flock more cruelly than wild beasts do. For while they destroy the flock by scattering it and then snatching away the ones that have become separated, the one in their midst considered to be their savior and defender surreptitiously inflicts harm on those who have trusted him. Now one can defend against an open attack, but one finds that

4 An "anathematism" (*anathematismos*) is the expression of an "anathema" (*anathema*).

no defense is possible against a treacherous attack made under the pretense of friendship, and harm comes in easily. Therefore, traitors from within are far worse than foes from without. It distressed me even more that in the name of piety and under its pretense and in his position as shepherd he lets loose heretical and blasphemous statements and revives the teaching of Apollinarius, which is simultaneously ridiculous and impious and was stamped out long ago. And in addition to this, he not only champions these [teachings] but also dares to anathematize those who have not been persuaded to share in his blasphemy. All this assumes that this letter is genuinely his and was not composed in his name by one of the enemies of truth, who has thrown an apple in our midst, as the story goes, to stir up the flame of discord as high as possible.

2. Well then, whether he himself composed the letter or someone else did so in his name, I have refuted it as best I could with the amount of ability granted me by God, being helped in the investigation of this heretical heterodoxy by the light of the all-holy Spirit bestowed upon me. I have set against it the teachings of the evangelists and apostles, and I have shown just how strange his doctrine is. I have also made it clear how much [his letter] is in discord with the divine teachings by comparing it with the statements of the divine Spirit and by showing how it is out of harmony with and foreign to the divine [teachings]. In response to the inordinate recklessness of his anathematisms let me observe that Paul, that herald of the truth with the loudest possible voice, anathematized those who corrupted the teachings of the evangelists and apostles, even daring [to anathematize] the angels,[5] but not those who remained within the bounds laid down by the theologians. For these he fortified with blessings, saying, "As for those who walk by this rule, peace and mercy upon them and upon the Israel of God."[6] So then, let the author of these remarks enjoy, in the way the Apostle's curse dictates, the rewards of his own labors and the harvest of his heretical seeds, while we ourselves remain within the teaching of the holy fathers.

I have appended the counterarguments to this letter of mine, so that you can read them and decide whether we have provided an effective refutation of his problematic and heretical statements. I have set down each of his anathematisms individually and then added the counterargument, so that my readers may easily understand and the refutation of his doctrines may be clear.

5 See Gal 1:8. 6 Gal 6:16.

Refutation of the Twelve Anathemas

> I. If anyone does not confess that Emmanuel is God in truth and for this reason that the holy Virgin is Theotokos (for she gave birth in a fleshly manner to the Word from God who had become flesh), let him be anathema.

1. Inasmuch as we follow the teachings of the gospels, we say that God the Word did not become flesh by nature, nor was he transformed into flesh, since that which is divine is unchangeable and immutable. For this reason David the prophet says, "You are the same, and your years will not end."[7] Paul, that great herald of the truth, taught in the [epistle] to the Hebrews that this was said in reference to the Son.[8] And elsewhere God says through the prophet, "I am *I am*, and I do not change."[9] So if the divine is unchangeable and immutable, it does not admit change or transformation. And if it is impossible for the unchangeable to be changed, then God the Word did not become flesh by changing [into it], but assumed flesh and dwelt among us, as the gospels say.[10] And the most divine Paul makes this clear when he says in the [epistle] to the Philippians, "Let this same mind be in you that was in Christ Jesus, who, though he was in the form of God, did not regard equality with God a thing to be grasped, but emptied himself, taking the form of a slave."[11] Now these verses make it clear that the form of God was not changed into the form of a slave, but rather it remained what it was and took the form of a slave. So then, if God the Word did not become flesh but rather assumed living and rational flesh, then he was not born by nature from the Virgin, after having been conceived, constructed, or formed,[12] nor did he who existed before the ages and was God and was with God and existed with the Father and is known and worshiped together with the Father receive the beginning of his existence from her, but rather he constructed a temple for himself in the Virgin's womb and existed together with what was constructed, carried [in the womb], formed, and born. For this reason we call that holy Virgin Theotokos, not because she gave birth to God by

7 Ps 101(102):28. 8 See Heb 1:12.

9 Mal 3:6. The Greek here is *egō eimi egō eimi kai ouk ēlloiōmai*. Theodoret has replaced the first part of the verse in the Septuagint, *egō kurios ho theos* ("I am the Lord your God"), with the divine name from Exod 3:14.

10 See John 1:14. 11 Phil 2:5–7.

12 The sequence here is precise: conception (*sullēphtheis*) is followed by construction (*diaplastheis*) or the seed's development into the embryo, then formation (*morphōtheis*) or the articulation of the embryo into a recognizably human fetus, and finally birth.

nature but because [she gave birth to] a human being united to the God who constructed him. But if it was not a human being that was constructed in the womb of the Virgin but rather God the Word who is before the ages, then God the Word is something made by the Spirit. For Gabriel says "that which is begotten" in her is "of the Holy Spirit."[13] But if the only-begotten Word of God is uncreated and same-in-substance and co-eternal with the Father, then he is not something constructed or created by the Spirit. If the Holy Spirit did not construct God the Word in the womb of the Virgin, then all that remains is to understand that it was the form of the slave that was by nature constructed, formed, carried, and born. Now since it was not stripped of the form of God but was a temple that had God indwelling [in it], as Paul says, "For in him the whole fullness of the divinity was pleased to dwell bodily,"[14] we call the Virgin not [only] Anthropotokos but also Theotokos, with the former title referring to what was constructed, formed, and carried, and the latter [title] to the union. For this reason too the baby that was born is called Emmanuel, as he is neither God separated from human nature nor a human being stripped of divinity. For Emmanuel means "God with us," as the gospels say,[15] and "God with us" both reveals that he was taken from us for our sake and proclaims that God the Word is the one who assumed him. Therefore, the baby is Emmanuel because of God who assumed [the human being], and the Virgin is Theotokos because of the union of the form of God with the form of the slave that she conceived. For God the Word was not changed into flesh, but the form of God took the form of the slave.

> II. If anyone does not confess that the Word from God the Father was hypostatically united to flesh, and that he is one Christ with his own flesh, that is, the same one is simultaneously God and human being, let him be anathema.

2. Persuaded by the divine teachings of the apostles, we confess one Christ and we call the same one both God and human being because of the union. But we are completely unfamiliar with "the hypostatic union," as it is foreign and alien to the divine scriptures as well as to the fathers who have interpreted them. And if the coiner of this expression means to suggest by "the hypostatic union" that a mixture[16] of flesh and divinity has occurred, then we will oppose him with all fervor and refute his blasphemy. For confusion[17] necessarily follows upon mixture and once confusion is introduced

13 Matt 1:20. 14 A conflation of Col 1:19 and 2:9. 15 Matt 1:23.
16 In Greek, *krasis*. 17 In Greek, *synchysis*.

it removes the distinctive feature[18] of each nature. After all, things mixed together do not remain what they were before. It would be the height of absurdity to say this about God the Word and the one from the seed of David. Rather, we ought to be persuaded by the Lord, who showed that there were two natures when he said to the Jews, "Destroy this temple, and in three days I shall raise it up."[19] If a mixture had occurred, then neither would God have remained God nor would the temple have been recognized as a temple, but the temple would have been God by nature and God the temple by nature (for this is what the definition of mixture requires). And thus it would have been superfluous for the Lord to have said to the Jews, "Destroy this temple, and in three days I shall raise it up." For he should have said, "Destroy me, and in three days I shall be raised up," if some sort of mixture and confusion had really occurred. But instead he shows that there is a temple to be destroyed and God who can raise it up again. So then, "the hypostatic union" is superfluous, and I think it is being proposed to us as a subterfuge for mixture. It is enough to say "union," which both indicates the distinctive features of the natures and teaches us to worship the one Christ.

> III. If anyone divides the hypostases in the one Christ after the union, conjoining them by a conjunction merely in terms of dignity or authority or lordship and not rather by a coming together in the sense of a natural union, let him be anathema.

3. The meaning of these words is unclear and obscure, yet their meaninglessness is clear to those who are pious. For to whom is it not entirely clear that there is no difference at all between a "conjunction" and a "coming together"?[20] A coming together is a coming together of things that are separate and a conjunction is a conjunction of things that are divided. But this cleverest author of these words has presented these synonyms as opposites. For he says we ought not conjoin the hypostases by a conjunction, but by a coming together, and by a *natural* coming together at that. Perhaps he speaks in ignorance, or else he is blaspheming in full knowledge of the fact. For nature has to do with unavoidable things and involuntary needs; for instance, we hunger naturally, in that we do not choose to experience it but it comes upon us inevitably. No doubt those who live in poverty would be released from begging if they could choose not to be hungry! We thirst naturally, we sleep

18 In Greek, *idiotēs*. 19 John 2:19. 20 In Greek, *synapheia kai synodos*.

naturally, we breathe air naturally – all of these are involuntary, as I have said. After all, anyone who does not undergo these by necessity has reached the end of life. Well then, if the union of the form of God and the form of the slave had been *natural*, then God the Word would have been forced by some necessity to be conjoined to the form of the slave and would not have acted out of his love for humankind, and the universal lawgiver would turn out to be a follower of the laws of necessity. But this is not what the blessed Paul taught us; on the contrary, he said that "he emptied himself, taking the form of a slave."[21] The phrase "he emptied himself" indicates that he did so voluntarily. So then, if he was united to the nature he took from us intentionally and voluntarily, then the qualification of the word "natural" is superfluous.

Accordingly, it is sufficient to confess the union, namely, a union understood to be of things previously divided. For without a division between things it is impossible to imagine how there could be a union. So whoever assumes a union presupposes a division. How then can he say that hypostases or natures ought not to be divided? And he says this knowing full well that the hypostasis of God the Word was complete before the ages, and that the form of a slave taken by it was complete – this is precisely why he says "hypostases" and not "hypostasis." Thus, if each nature is complete, and both came together into the same thing, namely, when the form of God takes the form of a slave, it is pious to confess one person and likewise one Son and Christ. Yet at the same time it is not out of place but actually logically consistent to speak of two united hypostases, or indeed of two united natures. For if in the case of a single human being we divide the natures, and the mortal one we call "body" and the immortal one "soul," but both together are a human being, how much more reasonable is it to acknowledge the distinctive features of the two natures, the nature of God who assumes and the nature of the human being who is assumed? We also find the blessed Paul dividing one human being into two human beings. For on one occasion he says, "As much as our outer human being wastes away, so much is the inner one renewed."[22] And on another occasion, "I delight in the law of God, in my inner human being."[23] And again, "that Christ may dwell in the inner human being."[24] If the Apostle divides the natural conjunction of the two contemporaneous natures, how can this man, who teaches mixture though he uses different words for it, charge us with impiety for dividing the distinctive properties of the two natures,

21 Phil 2:7. 22 2 Cor 4:16. 23 Rom 7:22. 24 Eph 3:16–17.

namely, the nature of the God who is before the ages and the nature of the human being who was assumed "in these last days"?[25]

> IV. If anyone distributes the sayings in the evangelical and apostolic writings to two persons or two hypostases, whether those things said by the saints about Christ or those said by him about himself, and some of them he attributes to a human being who is thought of separately as alongside the Word from God but the others exclusively to the Word from God the Father because they are appropriate for God, let him be anathema.

4. These remarks are like the previous ones. For supposing that a mixture has taken place, he wants no distinction to be made among the sayings in the sacred gospels or the apostolic writings, and he boasts that these remarks equally confront Arius, Eunomius, and the rest of the heresiarchs. Well then, let our meticulous teacher of divine doctrines tell us how he is arguing against the blasphemy of heretics by attributing to God the Word those sayings uttered humbly and appropriately by the form of the slave. For the heretics make God the Word an inferior thing, a creature, something made, and a servant, and they teach that the Son of God is from nothing. So then, given that we think the opposite of them and confess that the Son is same-in-substance and co-eternal with God the Father, and that he is the fashioner of the universe, maker, orderer, governor, and ruler, that he is all-wise and all-powerful (or rather that he is power itself, life itself, and wisdom itself) – to whom should we attribute the sayings, "My God, my God, why have you abandoned me?"[26] and, "Father, if possible, let this cup pass from me,"[27] and, "Father, save me from this hour,"[28] and, "But of that day and hour no one knows, not even the angels of heaven, nor the Son of Man,"[29] and all other such humble sayings that he himself and the apostles have said and written about him? To whom should we ascribe the hunger and the thirst? To whom the fatigue and the sleep? To whom the ignorance and the fear? Who was it who needed the help of angels? If all this should be attributed to God the Word, how was Wisdom ignorant? How could someone suffering from ignorance be called "Wisdom"? How could he have been speaking truthfully when he said that all the Father had was his[30] but at the same time he did not have the Father's knowledge? For "only the Father,"

25 Heb 1:2. 26 Matt 27:46. 27 Matt 26:39. 28 John 12:27.
29 Matt 24:36. 30 See John 16:15.

he says, knows that day.[31] How could he be the indistinguishable image of his begetter without having everything that belonged to his begetter?

So then, if he is telling the truth when he says that he does not know, one should accept this about him. But if he knows the day and is intentionally concealing it and says that he does not know it, behold to what kind of blasphemy the conclusion leads! For either the truth is speaking falsehoods or it cannot reasonably be called truth since it contains something of the opposite. But if the truth does not speak falsehoods, and God the Word is not ignorant of that day which he himself made and which he himself appointed as the day on which he would judge the world, and rather as the Father's indistinguishable image he has the Father's knowledge, then the ignorance does not belong to God the Word, but to the form of the slave which at that exact time knew only as much as the indwelling divinity had revealed to him. The same ought to be said about the other similar passages too. For how else would it make sense for God the Word to say to the Father, "Father, if possible, let this cup pass from me; yet not as I will, but as you will."[32] Again, many absurd things would follow from this, above all that the Father and Son are divided in mind, with the Father willing one thing and the Son another, since he says, "yet not as I will, but as you will." And in this case, we would once again see great ignorance in the Son since he would be found ignorant of whether or not it is possible for the cup to pass from him. But to say this about God the Word is the pinnacle of impiety and blasphemy. For the one who came for this very reason, who assumed our nature willingly, who emptied himself,[33] knew precisely how the mystery of economy would be fulfilled. This is why he could foretell it to the holy apostles, "Behold, we are going up to Jerusalem, and the Son of Man will be delivered to the hands of the Gentiles to be mocked and scourged and crucified, and he will be raised on the third day."[34] So then, how could he who clearly knew everything that would happen wish for these things not to happen, especially since he had announced these things beforehand and reprimanded Peter for wishing for these things not to happen?[35] How absurd would it be for Abraham to have seen his day many generations before and rejoice,[36] and for Isaiah likewise to have foretold his saving sufferings, as did Jeremiah and Daniel and Zechariah and the entire choir of the prophets too, but he himself did not know them, begged to get

31 See Matt 24:36. 32 Matt 26:39. 33 See Phil 2:7.
34 Matt 20:18–19. 35 See Matt 16:22–23. 36 See John 8:56.

out of them, and wished for what was going to happen for the salvation of the world not to happen?

Therefore, these sayings do not belong to God the Word but to the form of the slave, which feared death because death had not yet been destroyed. God the Word allowed the form of the slave to say these things, having granted it an opportunity to show fear, so that the nature of what had been received could be made manifest and so that we would not consider what was from Abraham and David to be an appearance or illusion – by entertaining such ideas the mob of impious heretics gave birth to this blasphemy.[37] Therefore, all that was said and done in a manner fitting for God we should attribute to God the Word, but all that was said and done humbly we should assign to the form of the slave. In this way, then, we avoid becoming diseased with the blasphemy of Arius and Eunomius.

> V. If anyone dares to say that Christ is a God-bearing human being and does not rather say that he is God in truth because he is the one Son and this by nature, insofar as the "Word became flesh"[38] and "partook like us of flesh and blood,"[39] let him be anathema.

5. We say that it was through his union with blood, flesh, and an immortal soul that God the Word "partook like us" of such things. At the same time, however, not only do we deny that God the Word became flesh by any sort of change, but also we charge with impiety any who say this. This can be seen as the opposite of what the words of this verse mean. For if the Word has changed into the flesh, then he did not partake with us of flesh and blood. But if he partook of flesh and blood, then he partook of them as someone different alongside them. And if the flesh is something different alongside him, then he was not changed into flesh. Thus, by using the word "partaking" we worship as the one Son both that which assumes and that which has been assumed, yet we acknowledge the difference of the natures. In addition, we do not reject the expression "God-bearing human being," as it was said by many of the holy fathers. One of them is Basil the Great, who used it in his treatise *On the Holy Spirit to Amphilochius* and in his commentary on Psalm 59.[40] We call him a "God-bearing human being," not because he received some partial divine grace, but because he possessed

37 The "blasphemy" here is docetism, in which Jesus only appears to be a human being.

38 John 1:14. 39 Heb 2:14.

40 *On the Holy Spirit* 5.12 and *Homily on Psalm 59* 4. Basil actually calls Christ's flesh "God-bearing" rather than speaking of a "God-bearing human being."

the entire united divinity of the Son. This is what the blessed Paul was explaining when he said, "See to it that no one makes a prey of you by philosophy and empty deceit, according to human tradition, according to the elemental spirits of the universe, and not according to Christ. For in him the whole fullness of divinity dwells bodily."[41]

> VI. If anyone says the Word from God the Father is the God or Master of Christ, and does not rather confess that the same one is simultaneously God and human being, since according to the scriptures the Word became flesh,[42] let him be anathema.

6. The blessed Paul called that which was assumed by God the Word the "form of a slave." But because the assuming took place before the union, and because the blessed Paul was discussing the assuming when he called the nature that was assumed the "form of a slave,"[43] it follows that once the union has taken place, it is no longer appropriate to use this term of slavery. For if the Apostle was writing to those who believed in Christ when he said, "so you are no longer a slave but a son,"[44] and if it was to his disciples that the Lord said, "No longer do I call you slaves, but friends,"[45] then so much more is he who is the first fruits of our nature, he through whom we ourselves were deemed worthy of the grace of adopted sonship, set free from the name of "slave." So then, we confess that even the form of a slave is God because the divine form was united to it, and we are confident that the prophet is right when he calls the baby "Emmanuel"[46] and the child that was born "Messenger of Great Counsel, Wonderful Counselor, Mighty God, Ruler, Prince of Peace, and Father of the Age to Come."[47] Nonetheless, even after the union the same prophet proclaims the nature of what was assumed and calls the one from the seed of Abraham a "slave," speaking in this way, "You are my slave, Israel, and in you I will be glorified,"[48] and again, "Thus says the Lord, who constructed me from the womb to be his slave,"[49] and soon thereafter, "Behold, I have given you as a covenant to nations, as a light to the Gentiles, so that you may be for salvation to the ends of the earth."[50] Thus, that which was constructed in the womb was not God the Word, but the form of the slave. For God the Word did not become flesh by changing into it, but he assumed flesh which had soul endowed with intellect.

41 Col 2:8–9. 42 John 1:14.
43 Throughout this section "slave" translates the Greek *doulos*. 44 Gal 4:7.
45 John 15:15. 46 Isa 7:14. 47 See Isa 9:6. 48 Isa 49:3.
49 Isa 49:5. 50 Isa 49:6.

> VII. If anyone says that Jesus was acted upon by God the Word as a human being would be, and that the glory of the Only-Begotten was attached to him as though he were another alongside the Only-Begotten, let him be anathema.

7. If it is the nature of the human being to be mortal, and God the Word is life and life-giving, and he resurrected the temple that was destroyed by the Jews and took it up to heaven, then how has the form of the slave not been glorified through the form of God? For if the form of the slave, even though mortal by nature, became immortal through the union with God the Word, then it received what it did not have. It was by receiving what it did not have and being thus glorified that the form of the slave has been glorified by the one who has given him the glory. It is for this reason that the Apostle exclaims, "according to the working of his great might which he accomplished in Christ when he raised him from the dead."[51]

> VIII. If anyone dares to say that the human being who was assumed ought to be worshiped together with, glorified together with, and named God together with God the Word, as if he were one with another (for the continual addition of "together with" requires us to think this), and does not rather honor the Emmanuel with a single worship and ascribe to him a single glorification, insofar as "the Word became flesh,"[52] let him be anathema.

8. As I have said many times, there is one glorification that we offer to Christ the Master and we confess the same one to be simultaneously God and a human being, since the definition of the union teaches us this. However, we shall not deny the distinctive features of the natures. For neither has God the Word received a change into flesh, nor again has the human being lost what it once was and been transformed into the nature of God. Therefore, affirming the distinctive attributes of each nature, we worship the one Christ the Master.

> IX. If anyone says that the one Lord Jesus Christ has been glorified by the Spirit, making use of the power that came through the Spirit as if it was another's and receiving from the Spirit the ability to work against unclean spirits and to accomplish divine signs among humanity, and does not rather say that the Spirit through whom he performed the divine signs is his very own, let him be anathema.

51 Eph 1:19–20. 52 John 1:14.

9. Here it is clear that he has dared to anathematize not only those who are pious now, but also those ancient heralds of truth, both the very authors of the gospels and the company of the sacred apostles, and in addition to these, Gabriel the Archangel! For he was the first to announce even before the conception that Christ according to flesh would be born of the Holy Spirit, and after the conception he taught Joseph. In reply to Mary who asked, "How shall this be, since I have no husband?,"[53] he said, "The Holy Spirit will come upon you, and the power of the Most High will overshadow you; therefore the child to be born will be called holy, Son of God."[54] And to Joseph he said, "Do not fear to take Mary your wife, for that which is conceived in her is of the Holy Spirit."[55] Moreover, the evangelist says, "When his mother Mary had been betrothed to Joseph, she was found to be with child of the Holy Spirit."[56] And as for the Lord himself, when he entered the synagogue of the Jews and took up the prophet Isaiah, he read the passage in which is said, "The Spirit of the Lord is upon me, because he has anointed me"[57] and the rest, and then he continued, "Today this scripture has been fulfilled in your hearing."[58] The blessed Peter said the same thing when speaking to the Jews: "God anointed Jesus of Nazareth with the Holy Spirit."[59] And many generations before him Isaiah foretold this: "There shall come forth a shoot from the stump of Jesse, and a branch shall grow out of his roots. And the Spirit of the Lord shall rest upon him, the spirit of wisdom and understanding, the spirit of counsel and might, the spirit of knowledge and the fear of the Lord,"[60] and again, "Behold my servant, whom I uphold, my chosen, in whom my soul delights; I have put my Spirit upon him, he will bring forth justice to the nations."[61] This very testimony the evangelist also put into his own writings,[62] and the Lord himself says to the Jews in the gospels, "If it is by the Spirit of God that I cast out demons, then the kingdom of God has come upon you."[63] Also, John [the Baptist] says, "He who sent me to baptize with water said to me, 'He on whom you see the Spirit descend and remain, this is he who baptizes with the Holy Spirit.'"[64] Therefore, [Cyril] anathematized not only the prophets and apostles, nor has this astute examiner of the divine dogmas anathematized only Gabriel the Archangel, but he also extended the blasphemy to the Savior of all himself! For we have shown on the one hand

53 Luke 1:34. 54 Luke 1:35. 55 Matt 1:20. 56 Matt 1:18.
57 Luke 4:18, quoting Isa 61:1. 58 Luke 4:21. 59 Acts 10:38.
60 Isa 11:1–2. 61 Isa 42:1. 62 See Matt 3:17.
63 Matt 12:28. 64 John 1:33.

that after reading the passage, "the Spirit of the Lord is upon me, because he has anointed me,"[65] the Lord himself said, "Today this scripture has been fulfilled in your hearing,"[66] and on the other hand that to those who claimed he was casting out the demons by Beelzebub he said that he cast demons out by the Spirit of God.[67] We are not saying that God the Word, who is same-in-substance and co-eternal with the Spirit, was formed and anointed by the Holy Spirit, but rather that the human nature was, which was assumed "in these last days."[68] If [Cyril] speaks of the Spirit as being of the same nature and proceeding from the Father, then we shall confess together with him that the Spirit is the Son's own, and this statement we accept as pious. But if [he means] that the Spirit is from the Son or has existence through the Son, then we reject this as blasphemous and impious. For we believe the Lord who says, "the Spirit who proceeds from the Father,"[69] and the most divine Paul who likewise states, "We have received not the spirit of the world, but the Spirit which is from the Father."[70]

> X. The divine scripture says Christ became "the high priest and apostle of our confession,"[71] and that he "offered himself on our behalf as a fragrant offering to God the Father."[72] Therefore, if anyone says that the Word from God did not himself become our high priest and apostle when he became flesh and a human being like us, but another alongside him did so, a human being apart from him, "born of a woman,"[73] or if anyone says that he brought an offering on his own behalf too and not rather solely on our behalf (for the one who knew no sin needed no offering), let him be anathema.

10. The unchangeable nature was not changed into a nature of flesh, but it assumed human nature and it appointed this nature over the normal high priests. This is just what the blessed Paul teaches when he says, "For every high priest chosen from among the people is appointed to act on behalf of the people in relation to God, to offer gifts and sacrifices for sins. He is able to deal gently with the ignorant and wayward, since he himself is beset with weakness. Because of this he needs to offer sacrifice for his own sins as well as for those of the people."[74] And a little further on he explains this when he says, "Just as Aaron was, so also was Christ."[75] Then in order to prove the weakness of the assumed nature he says, "In the days of his flesh, he offered

65 Luke 4:18. 66 Luke 4:21. 67 See Matt 12:28. 68 Heb 1:2.
69 John 15:26. 70 1 Cor 2:12, slightly altered. 71 Heb 3:1.
72 Eph 5:2, altered. 73 Gal 4:4. 74 Heb 5:1–3. 75 Heb 5:4–5.

up prayers and petitions, with loud cries and tears, to the one who could save him from death, and he was heard because of his reverence. Though he was the Son, he learned obedience through what he suffered; and when he had been made perfect, he became the source of eternal salvation to all who obey him, having been designated by God as a high priest according to the order of Melchizedek."[76]

Therefore, who is this who was made perfect by the toil of virtue and was not perfect by nature? Who is this who learned obedience through trials and did not know it before the trials? Who is this who lived reverently and offered petitions with loud cries and tears, who could not save himself but begged the one who could save him and pleaded for deliverance from death? It was not God the Word, who is immortal, impassible, and incorporeal! The remembrance of him, according to the prophet, brings joy and deliverance from tears: "For he wiped away every tear from every face."[77] And again the prophet says, "I remembered God and I rejoiced."[78] It is he who crowns those who live with him reverently, who knows all things before they come to be, who has all that belongs to the Father[79] and is the indistinguishable image of his begetter, who shows the Father in himself.[80] But that which was assumed by him from the seed of David is something mortal, passible, and afraid of death, even if later it destroyed the power of death because of its union with the one who assumed it. It was this that walked in all righteousness and said to John, "Let it be so now; for thus it is fitting to fulfill all righteousness."[81] It was this that took on the title of the high priesthood according to the order of Melchizedek.[82] For this was beset with the weakness of our nature, not the omnipotent God the Word. For this reason, a little before this the blessed Paul said, "For we do not have a high priest who is unable to sympathize with our weaknesses, but one who in every respect has been tempted as we are, yet without sin."[83] It was the nature assumed from us on our behalf that experienced our sufferings without sin, not the one who assumed this nature for the sake of our salvation. And at the beginning of this chapter he again teaches the same thing when he says, "Consider Jesus, the apostle and high priest of our confession. He was faithful to him who appointed him, just as Moses also was faithful in God's house."[84] No one who promotes orthodoxy would call God the Word a creature, as he is uncreated, unmade, and co-eternal with

76 Heb 5:7–10. 77 Isa 25:8. 78 Ps 76(77):4. 79 See John 16:15.
80 See John 14:9. 81 Matt 3:15, slightly altered. 82 See Heb 5:10.
83 Heb 4:15. 84 Heb 3:1–2.

the Father, but the human being assumed from us can be called that. God the Word from God was not himself ordained as our high priest, but the one from the seed of David was, he who became our high priest and our sacrificial victim because he was free from all sin. He offered himself to God on our behalf, clearly because he had within himself God the Word from God united and inseparably connected to him.

> XI. If anyone does not confess that the Lord's flesh is life-giving and is the very own flesh of the Word from God the Father, but instead [says] that it belongs to someone else alongside him who is connected with him in terms of dignity or who merely has a divine indwelling, and does not rather confess, as we have already said, that his flesh is life-giving because it became the very own flesh of the Word who is able to give life to all things, let him be anathema.

11. It seems that he cultivates obscurity – deliberately, I think – in order thereby to conceal his heterodoxy and to have it go unnoticed that his doctrine is the same as the heretics. But nothing is more powerful than the truth, which clears away the clouds of falsehood by its own beams of light. Enlightened by this, we shall establish that his faith is clearly unorthodox. First, nowhere has he mentioned that [Christ's] flesh is rational, nor has he confessed that the one who has been assumed is a complete human being, but he everywhere says "flesh," following the doctrines of Apollinarius. Next, among his arguments he sows the notion of mixture, though without using the actual term. Here he clearly says that the flesh of the Lord is soulless. For he says that if anyone confesses that the Lord's flesh is not the very own flesh of the Word himself from God the Father, but instead belongs to someone else alongside him, let him be anathema. From this it is evident that he does not confess that God the Word assumed a soul, but only flesh, and that God the Word takes the place of the soul for the flesh. But we say that the Lord's flesh, which possesses a soul and is rational, is life-giving on account of the life-giving divinity united to it. He also unintentionally confesses the difference between the two natures by talking about flesh and God the Word, and calling the flesh "his very own." Therefore, God the Word was not changed into a nature of flesh, but he has the flesh that he assumed as his very own and by the union he has made it life-giving.

> XII. If anyone does not confess that the Word of God suffered in the flesh, was crucified in the flesh, tasted death in the flesh, and

became the firstborn from the dead,[85] insofar as he, as God, is both life and life-giving, let him be anathema.

12. The passions belong to the one who is passible. For the impassible one is high above the passions. Thus, it was the form of the slave that suffered, of course with the form of God being together with it. The latter allowed the former to suffer because salvation is born of sufferings, whereas the latter appropriated the sufferings through the union. Therefore, it was not God who suffered, but the human being who was assumed from us by God. For this reason, the blessed Isaiah cried out, foretelling that he would "be a human being in affliction, and knowing how to bear infirmity."[86] And Christ the Master himself asked the Jews why "you seek to kill me, a human being who has told you the truth."[87] It is not life itself that is killed, but the one who possesses a mortal nature. And teaching this to the Jews on another occasion the Lord said, "Destroy this temple, and in three days I will raise it up."[88] Therefore, the one who is from David was destroyed, while the only-begotten God the Word, who was begotten impassibly from the Father before the ages, raised up the one who was destroyed.

85 See Col 1:18. 86 Isa 53:3. 87 John 8:40. 88 John 2:19.

49

Acts of the Council of Ephesus (June–October 431): Selected Proceedings

Introduction and Translation by Mark DelCogliano

INTRODUCTION

The Council of Ephesus was the culmination of two years of machinations on the part of Cyril of Alexandria to isolate Nestorius of Constantinople both theologically and ecclesio-politically.[1] This required a high degree of coordination between the sees of Alexandria and Rome as well as with Emperor Theodosius II. But from start to finish the Council of Ephesus unfolded in a way that no one could have anticipated, as highhanded maneuvering and factionalism destroyed any possibility of collaborative deliberations. A counter-council even met in opposition to the majority council. In the end Nestorius was deposed, but Cyril himself was too, at least for a time, and temporarily placed under house arrest in Ephesus. Furthermore, the council did not resolve the Christological issues that had pitted Cyril and his allies against Nestorius and his supporters; rather, the council only exacerbated the divisions. It would take nearly two years for a compromise to be reached, in 433, when the Formula of Reunion was issued.[2] Accordingly, the Council of Ephesus is best seen as initiating a long process of Christological debate within the Christian churches and as setting the broad parameters of those debates, without offering or even attempting to offer a permanent solution to them.

1 For the course of the controversy over Nestorius in the years 429–430, see the introductions to the letters exchanged in these years between Cyril of Alexandria, Nestorius of Constantinople, Celestine of Rome, and John of Antioch, in this volume on pp. 564–576, 585–592, and 623–640.

2 Cyril's *Letter of Reunion to John of Antioch*, translated in this volume on pp. 718–725, quotes the Formula of Reunion. The introduction to this letter summarizes developments after the Council of Ephesus until 433.

The massive documentation for the council records the ecclesio-political maneuvering of the factions and preserves some substantive Christological debate. There is a superabundance of fascinating material: not only are the minutes of nine sessions of the majority council and counter-council preserved, but also many letters and homilies from the key players involved and a wealth of other documents issued by or associated with both councils. The excerpts from the synodal acts translated here have been chosen to give a sense of the theological issues at stake as well as the contention between the factions. In order to contextualize these extracts, what follows is a summary of the sessions, and what happened between the sessions, that indicates which selections have been translated. The translation includes extensive selections from the sessions on June 22, June 26, and July 22, as well as some letters and homilies.

The Prelude (June 7–22, 431)

On November 19, 430 Emperor Theodosius II sent a sacra (imperial letter) to all Eastern metropolitans announcing the convocation of the Council of Ephesus on June 7, 431, the day of Pentecost that year, to resolve the controversy roused over Nestorius.[3] As the time for the convocation approached, Theodosius sent another sacra to the yet-to-be-assembled council announcing that he had appointed Candidianus, the count of the sacred palace officials (the captain of the imperial bodyguard), to keep public order in Ephesus during the council, to oversee the conciliar proceedings without involving himself in ecclesiastical business, and to ensure that the council completed its work before adjourning.[4] The reading of this sacra would formally open the council. But when the day of Pentecost came, the only delegations to have arrived in Ephesus were those of Nestorius (with sixteen bishops) and Cyril (with fifty bishops). Memnon of Ephesus was of course already present, along with the bishops he had assembled from his diocese and from nearby Pamphylia (fifty-two bishops in total), but not enough bishops had arrived to open the council.

So they waited. Juvenal of Jerusalem and the Palestinian delegation arrived on June 12, and around the same time so did Flavian of Philippi

3 *Collectio Vaticana* 25 (ACO 1.1.1: 114–116 Schwartz).
4 *Collectio Vaticana* 31 (ACO 1.1.1: 120–121 Schwartz).

and the Macedonian delegation. Celestine of Rome had not planned to attend the council, but sent three proxies (the bishops Arcadius and Projectus, and the presbyter Philip), whom he instructed to align themselves with Cyril.[5] The papal delegation from Rome would not arrive until July 10. But the most consequential absence was that of John of Antioch and the "Eastern" delegation (so called because they came from the Roman diocese of Oriens or "East"). Many of them suspected Cyril of Apollinarianism because of the content of the Twelve Anathemas or Twelve Chapters he had appended to his *Third Letter to Nestorius* and understood the upcoming council to be an opportunity to examine the views of both Nestorius and Cyril.[6]

The delay in opening the council resulted in the bishops who were already present forming alliances and lobbying those also already there, but who were still neutral, in order to win their support. An anti-Nestorian coalition soon formed under the leadership of Cyril, which included Memnon, Juvenal, Flavian, and their respective delegations. As tensions rose between the bishops and among a populace deeply invested in the controversy, Candidianus had to summon reinforcements to keep the peace. As the bishops waited, public debates were held at the lodgings of Nestorius between him and Theodotus of Ancyra, and then between him and Acacius of Melitene. Both were friends of the Constantinopolitan bishop who were attempting to persuade him to tone down his dual-subject language when speaking of Christ. But Nestorius refused and eventually alienated his friends, who promptly joined ranks with Cyril and Memnon. Though bishops were continuing to trickle into Ephesus, John of Antioch and the Eastern delegation had still not arrived two weeks after Pentecost, further delaying the opening of the council. It is at this point that Cyril made a fateful decision.

On the morning of June 21 Cyril received a letter from John, brought by an advance party that included Alexander of Apamea and Alexander of Hierapolis. In the letter John apologized for the delay and gave assurances that he was traveling as quickly as he could and had only "five or six staging-posts" to go – a journey of less than a week.[7] This letter is translated below. Along with the letter John sent a verbal communication to Cyril via the two Alexanders, who told Cyril, not once but repeatedly, Cyril reported,

5 *Collectio Veronensis* 8 (ACO 1.2: 25 Schwartz).
6 Cyril of Alexandria's *Third Letter to Nestorius* is translated in this volume on pp. 623–636.
7 *Collectio Vaticana* 30 (ACO 1.1.1: 119, 14 Schwartz).

to proceed with the business of the council if he was further delayed.[8] The message the two Alexanders conveyed, according to Cyril, was this: "He commanded us to tell Your Godliness, if he should be delayed even longer (*kai eti bradunai*), not to defer the synod but rather to do what was necessary (*ha dei*)."[9] The statement is admittedly ambiguous. John probably meant that Cyril should open the council if he were delayed "even longer" than the week he already anticipated. Cyril, however, took the statement to mean, whether innocently or tendentiously, that John was ceding him the right to open the council immediately in view of his absence.[10]

On the afternoon of June 21 Cyril announced that the council would finally convene under his own presidency, sending summonses to the bishops already present in Ephesus. Protests were immediately issued by sixty-eight neutral bishops who wanted to wait for the Eastern delegation to arrive, as well as by Nestorius and his seventeen episcopal supporters.[11] Candidianus was appalled by Cyril's move and tried to stop him, claiming it was contrary to the imperial will, pleading for a delay of four days so that John of Antioch's Eastern delegation could arrive, and threatening to annul any conciliar decisions transacted without them, but all to no avail. On the evening of June 21 Cyril arranged for a formal summons to be sent to Nestorius, that he was to appear the next day at the council. Nestorius gave a diplomatically evasive reply, neither refusing nor accepting.

Session 1 (June 22, 431)

The Council of Ephesus opened on the morning of June 22, presided over by Cyril, with neither Nestorius nor John of Antioch, nor their respective delegations, present. It appears that the council first concerned itself with

8 *Collectio Vaticana* 82.3–4 (ACO 1.1.3: 6, 11–30 Schwartz).
9 *Collectio Vaticana* 82.3 (ACO 1.1.3: 6, 20–21 Schwartz).
10 In *Collectio Vaticana* 82 (ACO 1.1.3: 5–9 Schwartz), Cyril lays out his interpretation that John's delay was calculated. John actually had the best claim to the presidency of the council, as Nestorius was under canonical censure and thus technically a defendant and the Easterners intended the council to examine Cyril for suspected Apollinarianism in his Twelve Anathemas, or Twelve Chapters, though he had not been formally charged. In the absence of John and the Roman delegation, however, Cyril's claim for the presidency was strong, since Celestine of Rome had essentially deputized Cyril to act on his behalf, and he had the support of the local hierarch Memnon – and now John had seemingly ceded him the presidency.
11 *Collectio Casinensis* 82 and 83 (ACO 1.4: 27–31 Schwartz).

the canonical requirement that a defendant should be given three summonses to appear before it imposed penalties. Nestorius had been summoned for the first time the night before, so a second summons was sent. His reply through intermediaries was that he would not appear until all the bishops were present. Did he mean until all the bishops already in Ephesus were present, or until the Eastern delegation was present? Either is possible.

After the second summons, the sixty-eight protesting bishops led by Theodoret of Cyrrhus descended upon the council, accompanied by Candidianus and a military escort, to lodge their complaint formally. Candidianus then ordered the council to disband, saying it contravened imperial orders and was thus illegal. At this point Cyril outmaneuvered Candidianus. While Cyril was confident that he was canonically authorized to open the council, he knew that no imperial approbation would be given to the council unless the emperor's sacra had been read out, which would officially open the sessions. So when Candidianus ordered the council to disassemble, Cyril and his supporters demanded to hear the sacra read out to determine if the council was really contrary to the imperial will. Candidianus did so, and inadvertently gave imperial and legal sanction to the council. It was now formally in session. Since the sacra had expressly stipulated that Candidianus was not to involve himself in ecclesiastical business, the bishops kicked him out, along with his military detachment.[12] Theodoret left in disgust. Some of the sixty-eight dissenting bishops stayed. By this time it was late morning, and a third summons was sent to Nestorius. He did not even bother to send a reply through intermediaries. He would be tried *in absentia*.

It was late afternoon when the bishops sent to summon Nestorius for a third time returned, and the formal proceedings now began. Substantial portions of these proceedings are translated below. First, the secretary read out a summary of the epistolary exchange between Cyril, Nestorius, and Celestine in the years 429–430, which had resulted in Nestorius being given by Celestine ten days (from November 30, 430) to recant his views or be deposed. Since he had not done so, in the eyes of Rome and Alexandria and their supporters Nestorius was to appear at the council as a defendant whose case had to be heard before any rehabilitation. And such is how

12 Candidianus narrated these events in the solemn protest he issued after being driven from the council: see *Collectio Casinensis* 84 (ACO 1.4: 31–32 Schwartz).

those in control of the council's agenda treated him. Next, the three groups of bishops who were sent to summon Nestorius gave reports of their visits to the Constantinopolitan bishop. In the case of the second and third summonses, the bishops related that they had been unable to see Nestorius, as he was sequestered in his lodging and guarded by soldiers bearing clubs. In the case of the third, they had even been manhandled by the soldiers.

The council then turned to establishing that the views of Nestorius were contrary to the Nicene faith. The Nicene Creed, Cyril's *Second Letter to Nestorius*, and Nestorius's *Second Letter to Cyril* were read out. The council judged the former to be in accord with the Nicene Creed and the latter opposed to it. At this point all the bishops collectively anathematized Nestorius. Then Celestine's *Letter to Nestorius* and Cyril's *Third Letter to Nestorius* were read out, the former of which gave Nestorius ten days to repudiate his views or be deposed. The reading of these letters thus entered into the record the formal judgments against Nestorius by the Roman and Alexandrian churches.[13] After the reading of these two letters, the Egyptian bishops who had delivered them to Nestorius in Constantinople on November 30, 430 testified that they had been properly delivered, indicating that Nestorius was well aware that he needed to recant his views or be deposed. To demonstrate that Nestorius had persisted in his teaching until the present day, Theodotus of Ancyra and Acacius of Melitene provided reports about their debates with Nestorius a few days earlier, both confirming that Nestorius had not altered his views.

The case against Nestorius, however, was not yet concluded. A florilegium of sixteen excerpts from Western and Eastern patristic authorities was read out, chosen to demonstrate that Cyril's teaching had the approbation of tradition while Nestorius's did not. After this, a florilegium of twenty-five excerpts from the sermons and writings of Nestorius was read out to prove his heresy. This was followed by the reading of a letter from Capreolus the bishop of Carthage, who explained why he had not been able to attend the council but offered his support for its decisions.

Now the case against Nestorius was concluded. He was deemed guilty of obstinacy for disobeying the three summonses to appear and for holding and preaching impious opinions, and a verdict against him was issued, deposing him. It was signed by nearly 200 bishops, including about forty

13 Note that Cyril's *Third Letter to Nestorius*, to which he appended the Twelve Anathemas, was not formally judged by the council, but simply entered into the record.

of the sixty-eight bishops who had formally objected to the opening of the council earlier in the day. Only about thirty bishops were still ready to support Nestorius. The long first session ended well after sunset. But the council was far from over.

The Arrival of the Easterners and the Conciliabulum (June 23–29, 431)

The day following the first session was consumed with disseminating and reacting to the previous day's proceedings. The council formally notified Nestorius of his deposition, and similar notifications were sent to clergy and laity of Constantinople.[14] Nestorius and the sixteen bishops of his delegation sent a report to Theodosius, protesting his treatment and requesting either that another council be held, this time licitly and according to proper procedure, or to let them all return home.[15] Cyril sent letters to the Alexandrian church,[16] as well as to his agents in Constantinople,[17] informing them of the previous day's events. He also sent a similar report to Theodosius, though the missive did not reach the emperor until early July.[18] Candidianus formally protested the deposition of Nestorius.[19] He also informed the council that the previous day's session had been illegal and instructed them to await until the Eastern and Roman delegations arrived.[20] Candidianus also sent a report to the emperor.[21] Nestorius, Cyril, and Candidianus were, therefore, each attempting to shape the imperial perception of the first session according to their own agendas.

Finally on June 26 John of Antioch and the Eastern delegation arrived. After being caught up on all that had transpired, John decided to convoke a counter-council that very afternoon with only the supporters of

14 *Collectio Vaticana* 63, 65, and 69 (ACO 1.1.2: 64–65 and 70 Schwartz).
15 *Collectio Vaticana* 146 (ACO 1.1.5: 13–15 Schwartz).
16 *Collectio Vaticana* 28 (ACO 1.1.1: 117–118 Schwartz). This is *Letter* 24 within Cyril's epistolary corpus.
17 *Collectio Vaticana* 67 (ACO 1.1.2: 66, 10–68, 11 Schwartz). This is *Letter* 23 within Cyril's epistolary corpus. Within a week the addressees of this letter sent a memorandum back to Ephesus detailing the reaction to the deposition of Nestorius in Constantinople: see *Collectio Vaticana* 66–67 (ACO 1.1.2: 65–69 Schwartz). (Cyril's letter is embedded in this memorandum.)
18 *Collectio Vaticana* 81 (ACO 1.1.3: 3–5 Schwartz).
19 *Collectio Casinensis* 85 (ACO 1.4: 33 Schwartz).
20 *Collectio Casinensis* 86 (ACO 1.4: 33 Schwartz).
21 This does not survive but is mentioned in other documents issued on June 23.

Nestorius and the Eastern delegation in attendance. Astoundingly, Candidianus endorsed this move in spite of protesting a far less partial council fewer than five days previously. The session, which came to be called the conciliabulum ("little council"), began with Candidianus reading the imperial sacra, formally opening and giving legal sanction to the proceedings.[22] John then interviewed him about what happened on June 22. Candidianus claimed that Cyril's council on June 22 had met illicitly and was thus invalid, and that Nestorius had been deposed without a proper hearing. After Candidianus left in accord with the imperial sacra, the conciliabulum turned to ecclesiastical business. The bishops accused Cyril and Memnon of a host of misdeeds including mistreatment of Nestorius and his allies, threatening bishops, causing general confusion and chaos, contravening canon law, and preventing an examination of the Twelve Chapters, which they claimed agreed with the teachings of Arius, Eunomius, and Apollinarius. Deeming them guilty of transgressing imperial and ecclesiastical law, the bishops excommunicated and deposed Cyril and Memnon. Their allies at the first session were provisionally excommunicated until they anathematized the Twelve Chapters and confessed the Nicene Creed. The decree was signed by John and fifty-three other bishops. The proceedings of this session are translated in their entirety below.

Putting the decree of the conciliabulum into effect was another question. The next day, a Saturday, John asked Candidianus to enforce the decree by keeping Memnon, Cyril, or any of their clergy from celebrating the liturgy on Sunday, June 28. Cyril and Memnon simply ignored the demand and Candidianus was powerless to stop them. On Sunday morning, as Cyril prepared to preside at the liturgy in the Church of St. Mary, Candidianus showed up and repeated his demand, again to no avail. At this liturgy Cyril preached a triumphant homily against Nestorius.[23] The same day the Eastern delegation attempted to seize control of the Church of St. John and consecrate Memnon's replacement, but they failed and only increased tensions.[24] Shortly after this the Eastern delegation held a second session of their conciliabulum at which Candidianus reported his efforts to hinder Cyril and Memnon from celebrating the liturgy,[25] and they sent a letter to

22 The minutes of this session survive: see *Collectio Vaticana* 151 (ACO 1.1.5: 119–124 Schwartz).

23 *Collectio Vaticana* 80 (ACO 1.1.2: 102–104 Schwartz).

24 *Collectio Vaticana* 101 (ACO 1.1.3: 46–47 Schwartz).

25 *Collectio Casinensis* 95 (ACO 1.4: 43–44 Schwartz).

the supporters of Cyril and Memnon, upbraiding them for their continued contravention of their excommunication.[26]

On June 29 Emperor Theodosius sent a letter to the council via the imperial courier Palladius, declaring Cyril's council on June 22 invalid and ordering that no bishop should leave Ephesus until his original instructions were carried out.[27] Palladius returned to Constantinople on July 1 with a plea from Cyril's council, which defended proceedings on June 22 as canonical and accused Candidianus of bias toward Nestorius and also of misleading the emperor. It also charged John with acting out of favoritism toward Nestorius, not with a true concern for piety. The minutes of the proceedings on June 22, now ready, were included to prove that Nestorius had received a fair trial.[28] But for the moment everyone remained stuck in the summer heat of Ephesus as they awaited further instructions from the emperor.

The Arrival of the Roman Delegation and Further Sessions (July 431)

On July 10 the Roman delegation finally arrived. That same day Cyril's council held its second session.[29] The main business of the session was the reading out of a letter from Pope Celestine to the council (written on May 8, 431), requesting confirmation of the Roman condemnation of Nestorius the previous year. After this, the Roman delegates requested a copy of the proceedings so that they could inform themselves about what had transpired before their arrival. The third session was held the next day.[30] Having now read the acts, the Roman delegation formally signed them. The June 22 decree condemning and deposing Nestorius was read out, and the three Roman delegates each in their own way affirmed the decision. After these two sessions a letter was sent to the emperor requesting approval of the proceedings on June 22, making it clear that the Roman delegation

26 *Collectio Vaticana* 152 (ACO 1.1.5: 124 Schwartz).
27 *Collectio Vaticana* 83 (ACO 1.1.3: 9–10 Schwartz). It appears that Theodosius had received the reports of Candidianus and Nestorius, but not that of Cyril. Nor does Theodosius's letter evince awareness of John's arrival and the conciliabulum.
28 *Collectio Vaticana* 84 (ACO 1.1.3: 10–13 Schwartz).
29 The minutes are preserved: see *Collectio Vaticana* 106.1–24 (ACO 1.1.3: 53–59 Schwartz).
30 The minutes are preserved: see *Collectio Vaticana* 106.25–39 (ACO 1.1.3: 59–63 Schwartz).

supported them as well. The letter also suggested that the work of the council was complete and therefore the bishops should be sent home and a new archbishop for Constantinople be chosen.[31]

But the decision to return home was not the bishops' to make, so they remained in Ephesus awaiting instructions from the emperor. In the meantime a further two sessions of Cyril's council were held, both concerned with retaliating against John and the Eastern delegation for convening the conciliabulum and excommunicating Cyril and Memnon. A fourth session was held on July 16.[32] It began with the reading out of a plea from Cyril and Memnon defending the legitimacy of the session on June 22, accusing John of holding the conciliabulum contrary to imperial and ecclesiastical law, and requesting that John be summoned to the council for examination. The same day two summonses were sent to John, who was barricaded in his lodging protected by clerics and a detachment of soldiers with unsheathed swords. He gave no reply to the first summons, but in response to the second he let it be known that he refused to sit in session with excommunicates. A fifth session on July 17 began with Cyril asserting that the charges of heresy the Easterners had made against him were slanderous, and he demanded that his opponents answer for this.[33] So a third summons was sent to John, but the message was not even received. The council then went on to declare John's proceedings against Cyril and Memnon on June 26 uncanonical and concluded by excommunicating John and thirty-three other bishops.

A sixth session was held on July 22 that largely reiterated the work of the session on June 22, again reading out the Nicene Creed, the same florilegium of sixteen excerpts from Western and Eastern patristic authorities, plus four additional ones, and the same florilegium of excerpts from the writings of Nestorius. These were not discussed anew. But this session did deal with a new item: the plaint of Charisius, a presbyter of Philadelphia in Lydia, who brought to the council's attention a matter connected with Nestorius. In his plaint he reported that some Lydian Christians, hoping to return to orthodoxy from the Quartodeciman and Novatian sects, had been tricked by local supporters of Nestorius into signing an exposition

31 *Collectio Vaticana* 107 (ACO 1.1.3: 63–64 Schwartz).

32 The minutes are preserved: see *Collectio Vaticana* 87–89.12 (ACO 1.1.3: 15–21 Schwartz).

33 The minutes are preserved: see *Collectio Vaticana* 89.13–21 and 90 (ACO 1.1.3: 21–26 Schwartz).

of faith in the form of a "Nestorian" creed instead of the Nicene Creed. When Charisius confronted the church leadership in Philadelphia for duplicitously spreading what he considered heresy, he was excommunicated. He asked the council to resolve the matter and affirmed his orthodoxy by reciting a version of the Nicene Creed. The "Nestorian" creed was then read out, along with the statements of the signatories who had been duped. This "Nestorian" creed is translated below.

Cyril would later report that this creed should be attributed to Theodore of Mopsuestia.[34] The same creed was also entered into the record at the Council of Chalcedon in 451, when selections from the acts of the Council of Ephesus in 431 were read out at the first session (section 921). At the Council of Constantinople in 553 it was read out at the fourth session (section 81) and attributed to Theodore of Mopsuestia, no doubt because of Cyril's letter. Whatever its origin, the creed reflects the Christology that was associated with Nestorius. It stresses that the human nature of Christ, conceptualized as a distinct subject conjoined to God the Word, shares in the titles of Son and Lord, as well as the honor and worship properly belonging to them, in virtue of his conjunction with God the Word. The creed also includes a short commentary on 1 Corinthians 15:45–48, explaining why Christ is called "the second Adam" and "the second human being" by Paul. Accordingly, this creed provides an accessible summary of "Nestorian" Christology.

Following this, the council issued what has come to be known as Canon 7. It prohibits the production and composition of any new creed in view of the sufficiency of the Nicene Creed, and imposes severe penalties for any who venture to do so. In its original context, the prohibition applied to creeds professed by converts to orthodox Christianity from paganism, Judaism, or heresy. At subsequent councils, however, much appeal was made to Canon 7 by those opposed to any new formulations or definitions of faith besides the Nicene Creed, not just creeds to be professed by converts. A translation of Canon 7 is included below.

Throughout the council Cyril had agents in Constantinople working to advocate for his cause with high-ranking ecclesiastical and imperial officials (and was in constant contact with them by letter). At some point in July these agents, as part of the campaign to sway the emperor to their side, convinced Scholasticus, who as the eunuch chamberlain of the imperial

34 *Ep.* 91.

palace had the ear of Theodosius and could greatly help their cause, that Nestorius continued to reject the term Theotokos. This was reported to the Easterners in a letter to them from Count Irenaeus.[35] Nestorius replied to the slander in a letter to Scholasticus himself. Here he reiterates his acceptance of the term Theotokos, as long as it is paired with Anthropotokos, and rails against Cyril's Christology because it attributes change, suffering, and even death to God the Word. He complains that Cyril has refused and continues to refuse to meet with him in Ephesus, suggesting that he has done so to avoid being condemned for the Twelve Chapters that Nestorius deems heretical. At the end of the letter he promises to resign the episcopacy and return voluntarily to his monastery if orthodoxy is restored to the churches – an offer that Theodosius took him up on less than six weeks later, though without orthodoxy, as Nestorius understood it, being restored to the churches. This letter is translated below in its entirety.

From the Arrival of Count John to the Dissolution of the Council (August to October 431)

In early August John, the count of the sacred largesses (the imperial treasurer), arrived in Ephesus to deliver a new sacra from Theodosius and take control of the situation in the emperor's name. He convened both parties in spite of vociferous protests from each side that the bishop(s) it had excommunicated – whether Nestorius or Cyril and Memnon – should be excluded. (This was the only time in Ephesus that the two factions met.) John then shocked the assembly by announcing that Theodosius had decided to validate the decrees of both the majority council and the counter-council and thus confirm the depositions of Nestorius, Cyril, and Memnon. All three were put under house arrest and the rest of the bishops were ordered to return home.[36] This set off a flurry of written protests and negotiations, each side lobbying the emperor to overturn his decision in its favor, lasting until the end of August. Translated below is the Eastern delegation's letter to Theodosius in response to the sacra. Here we have a

35 *Collectio Vaticana* 164 (ACO 1.1.5: 135–136 Schwartz).

36 The sacra accepting the depositions: *Collectio Vaticana* 93 (ACO 1.1.3: 31–32 Schwartz). John's report of his delivery of the sacra: *Collectio Atheniensis* 45 (ACO 1.1.7: 67–68 Schwartz). The responses to the sacra by each party: *Collectio Vaticana* 94 (ACO 1.1.3: 32–33 Schwartz) [Cyril's party] and *Collectio Atheniensis* 48 (ACO 1.1.7: 69–70 Schwartz) [Easterners].

rare glimpse into the Christology of those opposed to Cyril as they pressed their case with the emperor. Though the Easterners were willing to make Christological affirmations that amounted to a repudiation of Nestorius, they were unwilling to drop the charge that Cyril's Twelve Chapters were tainted with Apollinarianism and thus contrary to the Nicene Creed. They pleaded with Theodosius to issue a decree against them. The Christological statement included in this letter was the basis for the Formula of Reunion in 433.[37]

In the midst of all this, a seventh session of the council met on August 31 dealing with jurisdictional issues. No one realized it at the time, but this would turn out to be the last session of the council. On September 3 Theodosius reconfirmed the deposition of Nestorius, who was then released from house arrest so that he could return to his monastery in Antioch with a military escort. Nestorius would remain in Antioch until 435, when he was exiled by Theodosius to the Great Oasis of Hibis in Egypt, where he died at some point after 450. After the Council of Ephesus Nestorius the person ceased to be a factor in the Christological debates, even as "Nestorianism" became the subject of much theological anxiety.

In early September 431 eight-person embassies from both factions went to Chalcedon for five debates before the emperor beginning on September 11, each attempting to convince Theodosius of the rightness of its cause. (Cyril and Memnon remained under house arrest in Ephesus.) The Cyrilline embassy included Celestine's proxies Arcadius and Philip, Firmus of Caesarea, Theodotus of Ancyra, and Acacius of Melitene, with the latter as the leading theologian in the group. The Eastern embassy was headed by John himself and Theodoret of Cyrrhus was the chief theologian. The Cyrilline embassy was charged by the council not to accept communion with John of Antioch and his assembly, who were described as refusing to depose Nestorius and continuing to defend him, unless they subscribed to the deposition of Nestorius, anathematized his doctrines, and restored Cyril and Memnon.[38] Similarly, the Eastern embassy was told not to sign any conciliar decree of reconciliation unless Cyril's Twelve Chapters were rejected and anathematized.[39] In letters back to their faction in Ephesus the Eastern embassy reported some initial success in theological debate with

37 Cyril of Alexandria's *Letter of Reunion to John of Antioch*, translated in this volume on pp. 718–725, quotes the Formula of Reunion.

38 *Collectio Vaticana* 95 (ACO 1.1.3: 33–36 Schwartz).

39 *Collectio Vaticana* 96 (ACO 1.1.3: 36–39 Schwartz).

the Cyrilline embassy, but in the end neither side could convict the other of heresy and they remained at an impasse over the Twelve Chapters. Around this time the Eastern embassy wrote a letter to Rufus of Thessalonica, a senior bishop long allied with Rome who had not attended the council, attempting to persuade him to support their cause. Their letter summarizes their case against Cyril and Memnon to justify their deposition and offers a summary of Cyril's aberrant (in their eyes) Christology. This letter is translated in full below. In the end, Rufus sided with the Cyrilline majority.

On October 25 Maximian was consecrated bishop of Constantinople to replace Nestorius. Soon after this Theodosius released Cyril and Memnon from house arrest, sent a sacra dissolving the council, and ordered everyone to return home. In essence, Theodosius had dismissed the charge that Cyril had fallen into Apollinarianism in the Twelve Chapters. Memnon resumed his episcopacy in Ephesus, and on October 31 Cyril departed Ephesus for Alexandria. Meanwhile in Chalcedon, before departing home, Theodoret of Cyrrhus and John of Antioch preached farewell homilies to their supporters. The homily of the latter is translated below. Here John praises his supporters for having fought for orthodoxy so resolutely and, bracing for future persecution, urges them to remain steadfast in the authentic Christological faith they hold, which John concisely summarizes and contrasts with his opponents' views.

The translations here are based upon the text of the acts edited by Eduard Schwartz, *Concilium Universale Ephesenum*, ACO 1 (Berlin: De Gruyter, 1922–1930). The translations are based on Greek where it is extant, with reference to the Latin versions; otherwise they are based on one of the Latin versions. More precise bibliographical information is provided in a note at the beginning of each excerpt from the acts translated below.

TRANSLATION

Letter of John of Antioch to Cyril of Alexandria[40]

(Received by Cyril on June 21, 431)

To my master the most God-beloved and most holy fellow minister Cyril: Greetings in the Lord from John.

40 *Collectio Vaticana* 30 (ACO 1.1.1: 119 Schwartz) [Greek]; *Collectio Casinensis* 21 (ACO 1.3: 49 Schwartz) [Latin]. This letter is translated in its entirety.

It pains me to no small degree that, while Your Sacredness has already arrived in Ephesus, I have been late for these few days. Indeed, it is yearning for Your Holiness more than necessity that pushes me to complete the journey swiftly. At any rate, through the prayers of Your Sacredness, I am finally at the gates after having suffered considerable hardship on the journey. For I have been on the road for thirty days (such is the length of the journey), never surrendering myself in any way, and some of my lords, the most God-beloved bishops, experienced sickness on the way and many animals collapsed from the swiftness of the journey. So then, pray, my master, that we travel and speed through these five or six staging-posts without incident and your holy and sacred head be embraced by us.

Paul and Macarius, who are in the company of my lord the most God-beloved bishop John, salute Your Sacredness.[41]

I and those with me heartily greet the entire brotherhood with you.[42] May you continue in good health praying for us, my most God-beloved and most sacred master.

*

* *

First Session[43]

(Held on June 22, 431)

33 After the consulship of our masters Flavius Theodosius for the thirteenth time and Flavius Valentinian for the third time, perpetual Augusti, ten days before the Kalends of July, the synod assembled in the metropolis of Ephesus by decree of the most God-beloved and Christ-loving emperors. And there were seated in the holy church called Mary's the most God-beloved and most godly bishops:

Cyril of Alexandria, also speaking in the place of the most holy and most sacred Celestine archbishop of the church of Rome;

41 Though the grammar of this sentence is unclear, it seems to have been written by the scribe, conveying the personal greetings of Paul of Emesa and Macarius of Laodicea, leading members of the Eastern delegation.

42 This and the following sentence seem to have been written by John in his own hand.

43 *Collectio Vaticana* 33–62 (ACO 1.1.2: 3–64 Schwartz) [Greek]; *Collectio Veronensis* 11–19 (ACO 1.2: 27–75 Schwartz) [Latin]. Omissions from the translation are noted.

Juvenal of Jerusalem;

Memnon of Ephesus;

Flavian of Philippi, also holding the place of Rufus the most reverent bishop of Thessalonica;

Theodotus of Ancyra in Galatia Prima;

Firmus of Caesarea in Cappadocia Prima;

Acacius of Melitene in Armenia ...[44]

* * *

34 Presbyter Peter of Alexandria the chancellor of the notaries said, "Already earlier, when the most reverent Nestorius had been ordained bishop for the holy church of Constantinople and not many days had passed, some people brought sermons of his from Constantinople which were troubling to those who read them, causing great uproar in the holy churches. When he learned of this, the most reverent bishop Cyril of Alexandria wrote a first and a second letter to His Reverence, full of advice and exhortation.[45] In response to them [Nestorius] wrote back, rejecting and rebuffing what had been sent. And in addition to these, when the same most reverent bishop Cyril learned that [Nestorius] had sent letters and books of his sermons to Rome as well, he took it upon himself to write to the most godly bishop Celestine of Rome through deacon Posidonius, enjoining him, 'If you discover that the books of his sermons and letters have been delivered to him, deliver my letter too; but if not, bring it back here undelivered.' He discovered that his sermons and letters had been delivered, so he was obliged to deliver [Cyril's letter].[46] And the most sacred and most godly bishop Celestine of the church of Rome wrote a sensible reply, containing a clear

44 At this point the names of 148 additional bishops in attendance are omitted from this translation.

45 This of course refers to Cyril's *First Letter to Nestorius* (from June 429) and his *Second Letter to Nestorius* (from February 430); the latter is translated in this volume on pp. 564–569.

46 In this letter of Cyril to Celestine (from the summer of 430) the Alexandrian bishop informs his Roman counterpart about Nestorius's recalcitrance in teaching what he considers blasphemy, and sends documentation drawn from Nestorius's own homilies and letters as evidence. Cyril also asks Celestine to advise him and the other Eastern bishops about whether communion should be maintained with him. This is *Letter* 11 (CPG 5310) within Cyril's epistolary corpus.

instruction.[47] Therefore, since by imperial and God-beloved command your holy synod has been convened here, we must inform you that we have the relevant documents at hand, ready to be supplied to Your Godliness."

35 Bishop Juvenal of Jerusalem said, "Let the God-beloved letter of the most pious and Christ-loving emperors written to each of the metropolitans be read out and let it be the first to shine in the record of our present proceedings."[48]

36, 1. Bishop Firmus of Caesarea in Cappadocia said, "Let it be confirmed by the most God-beloved and most holy bishop Memnon of the city of Ephesus how many days have passed since our arrival."

2. Bishop Memnon of the city of Ephesus said, "Sixteen days have passed since the time appointed in the pious and God-beloved letter."[49]

3. Bishop Cyril of Alexandria said, "This holy and great synod has patiently endured long enough waiting for the arrival of those most God-beloved bishops who are expected to attend. Since many of the bishops have fallen ill and some have even passed away, and since it is fitting to carry out right now what the decree requires and to wrestle with the matters of faith for the benefit of the whole world under heaven, let be read out in sequence the documents pertinent to the subject, especially since a second decree of the most God-beloved and Christ-loving emperors has been read out to the synod by the most magnificent and most glorious Candidianus the count of the sacred palace officials, which commands that matters of faith be examined and articulated without any delay."[50]

37 Bishop Theodotus of Ancyra said, "The reading of the documents will take place at the proper time, but now it is fitting that the most God-beloved

47 Celestine's letter to Cyril was sent on August 10, 430, the same day Celestine sent a letter to Nestorius. The "clear instruction" (in Greek, *typon phaneron*) referred to is Celestine's demand that Nestorius recant his views within ten days of receiving the letter or be deposed. In his letter to Cyril, Celestine authorized Cyril to act as his delegate in the matter. The letter was delivered to Nestorius on November 30, 430.

48 At this point the sacra of Theodosius convoking the synod was read out (*Collectio Vaticana* 31 [ACO 1.1.1: 120–121 Schwartz]). It was omitted from the Greek acts, but the Latin version included it in the minutes. The account here obscures the circumstances in which it was read out: see above, p. 662.

49 The sacra announcing the synod (issued November 19, 430) had designated June 7, 431 (on which Pentecost fell that year) as the opening date of the council: see *Collectio Vaticana* 25 (ACO 1.1.1: 114–116 Schwartz).

50 The "second decree" to which Cyril refers is the sacra (*Collectio Vaticana* 31 [ACO 1.1.1: 120–121 Schwartz]) that was read out earlier in the day but not recorded in the minutes. It is the "second" after the imperial letter of November 19, 430, that convoked the synod.

bishop Nestorius also attend the proceedings, so that what pertains to piety may be established by common decision and approval."

38, 1. Bishop Hermogenes of Rhinocolura said, "Your Godliness sent us yesterday to remind the most reverent Nestorius that he was obligated to participate in the synod, but he had been unaware of the day of this holy synod and said, 'I will think about it for a while, and if I need to come, I will come.'"

2. Bishop Athanasius of Paralus said, "Your Godliness sent us yesterday to remind the most reverent Nestorius to participate in this holy synod, and we visited him to remind him of this, but he declared, 'I will think about it, and if I need to come, I will come.'"

3. Bishop Peter of Parembole said, "Yesterday Your Godliness sent us to the most reverent bishop Nestorius to remind him that this holy synod would meet today, and he replied, 'Let me think about it, and if I need to come, I will come.' The most reverent and most godly bishops there were also reminded, about six or seven of them, and they too said, 'We are thinking about it, and if we deem it appropriate, we will come tomorrow.'"

4. Bishop Paul of Lappa said, "When your holy and blessed synod commanded us to go to the most reverent Nestorius and to remind him to come today to your holy and blessed synod, I also went with the holy brothers who have already given depositions and I reminded him to come and participate today in your holy synod. He said, 'If I decide to, I will come at that time.' We reminded not only him, but also some most reverent bishops whom we found with him. There were about six or seven bishops with him."

39, 1. Bishop Flavian of Philippi said, "Let some of the most reverent bishops go and remind him again to come and participate in the holy synod."

2. The holy synod sent bishop Theodulus of Elusa in Palestine, bishop Anderius of Chersonesus in Crete, bishop Theopemptus of Cabasa in Egypt, and Epaphroditus who is the lector and notary of the most reverent bishop Hellanicus of the city of Rhodes. They carried a message from the holy synod to the most reverent bishop Nestorius. These are the contents:

3. "Your Godliness needed to be reminded yesterday by the most reverent and godly bishops to hasten to the holy synod assembled today in the holy and catholic church [and] not to miss it. Since Your Sacredness did miss the convocation of the holy synod, out of necessity we again, through the most reverent and most godly bishops Theopemptus, Theodulus, and

Anderius, and through Epaphroditus the lector and notary of the city of Rhodes, summon you to come and not to miss the proceedings, especially since the most pious and God-beloved emperors commanded that we leave aside everything to achieve a confirmation of the faith."

4. When they returned, presbyter Peter of Alexandria the chancellor of the notaries said, "Since the most reverent and most God-beloved bishops sent by the holy synod are present, we require that they give depositions about what response they received."

40, 1. Bishop Theopemptus of Cabasa said, "When this holy and great synod sent us to the most reverent Nestorius, we went to his house. Seeing a throng of soldiers with clubs, we asked to be announced. But they stopped us, saying, 'He is taking a walk by himself, and we have been ordered to let no one in to meet him.' We said, 'We cannot leave unless we receive a response. For the holy synod has sent a message to him, bidding him to participate [in the synod] with them.' His clergy came out and gave us the same response as the soldiers. As we tarried, insisting that we receive a response, the sacred tribune Florentius came out, the associate of Candidianus the most magnificent and the most glorious count of the sacred palace officials, and he made us stay, as if he was about to get us a response, and so we waited. Later he came out with [Nestorius's] clergy and said to us, 'I have not been able to see him, but he told me to say to Your Godliness, "Once all the bishops have gathered, we will meet with them."' After calling on him, all the soldiers present, and his clergy to testify to this, we departed."

2. Bishop Theodulus of Elusa said, "I also heard the same and give the same deposition."

3. Bishop Anderius of Chersonesus in Crete said, "I also went there in accordance with the decree of your holy and blessed synod and I said and heard the same, just as the most God-beloved bishops with me flawlessly stated in their depositions."

41, 1. Bishop Flavian of Philippi said, "Since it is fitting to omit nothing that pertains to ecclesiastical procedure, and since it is clear that, even though he was reminded yesterday and a second time today, the most God-beloved Nestorius did not appear, he shall be reminded again by a third message. Let the most God-beloved fellow ministers bishop Anysius of Thebes in Hellas, bishop Domnus of the same Hellas, bishop John of Hephaestus in Augustamnica, and bishop Daniel of Darnis in Libya go and remind him in plain language for the third time."

2. They departed with Anysius, who is the notary and lector of bishop Firmus of Cappadocia, bearing a message. These are the contents:

3. "In this third invitation the most holy synod – obeying the canon and bestowing forbearance and patience toward you – summons Your Reverence. Deign even now at last to come and defend yourself before the ecclesiastical community in regard to the heretical doctrines you are reported to have said in the churches, knowing that if you do not come to vindicate yourself in response to the charges made against you orally and in writing, the most holy synod will be compelled to decree in your case what the canons of the holy fathers dictate."

42, 1. When they returned, presbyter Peter of Alexandria the chancellor of the notaries said, "Since the most reverent bishops who were sent have now returned, we require that they testify what response they received."

2. Bishop John of Hephaestus said, "When this holy and God-beloved synod sent us to remind the most godly Nestorius with a third message that he should now hasten at once to the holy synod so that his statements about the faith could be examined in the presence of His Godliness, in conformity with instructions of Your Godliness to us, we arrived at his lodging and when we reached the gateway we found a throng of soldiers with clubs standing in his very gateway. We asked them either to let us through the gate of the house where the same most godly Nestorius was staying or at least for them to inform him that the holy synod had sent us with a third message summoning him kindly and with all mildness to the holy synod. We tarried a long time and the soldiers, shoving us arrogantly, telling us to leave the place, and offering us no kind response, would not even let us stand in the shade. We persisted with our demands for a long time, saying, 'We are four bishops in number, who have been sent not for insolent purposes nor to do anything offensive or unbecoming, but following every procedure to remind him, even now, to come to this sacred church and participate in this holy synod.' Finally the soldiers sent us away, saying that we would receive no other response even if we waited at the gateway of the house until evening. They added this too, saying that they were standing at the gateway for this reason, so that they could prevent anyone from the synod from entering, having received these orders from him."

3. Bishop Anysius of Thebes said, "The deposition given by the most holy brother and fellow minister John is the truth. For while we stood for

a long time at the gateway of the most reverent Nestorius, that is what we saw and heard."

4. Bishop Domnus of Opus in Hellas said, "What the most holy and most God-beloved brothers and fellow ministers John and Anysius testified is what I too saw and heard."

5. Bishop Daniel of Darnis said, "The deposition given by the most godly bishops, that is what I heard and is the truth."

43 Bishop Juvenal of Jerusalem said, "Even though the ecclesiastical laws prescribe that a third invitation is sufficient for those summoned for a defense in regard to those things for which they would be prosecuted, we would be ready to go beyond this with a fourth message through the most godly bishops to call the most reverent Nestorius again. But since a company of soldiers surrounds his residence, as the most godly bishops who have just arrived stated in their depositions, not permitting anyone to enter, it is clear that in bad faith he is refusing to come to the holy synod. Therefore, let us proceed in accordance with what the canonical order dictates and whatever contributes to the preservation of our orthodox and pious faith. Let be read out in first place the faith expounded by the 318 most holy fathers and bishops gathered in Nicaea, so that, by comparing the statements about the faith[51] with this exposition, those that agree with it may be confirmed and those that differ from it may be rejected."

The symbol was read out as follows:

> The synod at Nicaea expounded this faith: We believe in one God, Father, almighty, maker of all things both seen and unseen; and in one Lord, Jesus Christ, the Son of God, begotten from the Father only-begotten, that is, from the substance of the Father, God from God, light from light, true God from true God, begotten, not made, same-in-substance with the Father, through whom all things came to be, both those in heaven and those on earth, who for us human beings and for our salvation came down, and became incarnate, and became human, suffered and rose again on the third day, ascended into the heavens, and is coming to judge the living and the dead; and in the Holy Spirit. Now as for those who say: There was a point when he did not exist, and before he was begotten he

51 As becomes clear from what follows, these "statements of faith" are Cyril of Alexandria's *Second Letter to Nestorius* and Nestorius's *Second Letter to Cyril.*

did not exist, and that he came to be from nothing, or from a different subsistence or substance, claiming that the Son of God is either changeable or mutable, these people the catholic and apostolic church anathematizes.

44, 1. When this had been read out, presbyter Peter of Alexandria the chancellor of the notaries said, "We have at hand the letter that the most holy and most godly archbishop Cyril wrote to the most reverent Nestorius, which is full of advice and exhortation, on the grounds that his opinions were not orthodox. If Your Holiness commands, I will read it out."

2. Bishop Acacius of Melitene said, "Since the most reverent and most godly presbyter Peter, who has initiated the discussion, has said that a certain letter was sent by the most God-beloved and most sacred bishop Cyril to the most reverent Nestorius on the grounds that his teaching was not orthodox, it follows that it should be read out too."[52]

* * *

4. After the letter was read, bishop Cyril of Alexandria said, "The holy and great synod has heard what I sent to the most reverent Nestorius in advocacy of the orthodox faith. And I am inclined to think that I am not caught for having in any way departed from the orthodox account of the faith or for having transgressed the symbol expounded by the holy and great synod that met long ago at Nicaea, and I urge Your Sacredness to state whether or not I have written these things in an orthodox manner, unassailably, and in a way that accords with that holy synod."

45, 1. Bishop Juvenal of Jerusalem said, "Now that the holy faith expounded at Nicaea and the letter of the most holy and most sacred archbishop Cyril have been read out, and the expositions of the holy synod have been found to be in accord, I agree and consent to these pious teachings."

2. Bishop Firmus of Caesarea in Cappadocia said, "Since Your Godliness has with subtlety and exactitude interpreted the statements made briefly and in summary by the holy synod at Nicaea, you have made the meaning of the expounded faith more clear and apparent to us, so that there is no ambiguity in your statements since they are all in harmony with one

52 At this point Cyril of Alexandria's *Second Letter to Nestorius* was read out. It is omitted from the translation here, but there is a translation in this volume on pp. 564–569.

another and the faith is confirmed. Therefore, since they are precise and unimpeachable and introduce no novelties, I too agree, having received the same opinion from my fathers the holy bishops."

3. Bishop Memnon of the metropolis of Ephesus said, "The letter of father Cyril the most holy and most God-beloved bishop that was just read out contains things that accord with the faith expounded by the 318 holy fathers gathered at Nicaea. We too agree and consent to them, finding nothing lacking, nothing discordant."[53]

* * *

46, 1. Bishop Palladius of Amaseia said, "It would be consistent that the letter of the most reverent Nestorius also be read out, which the most reverent presbyter Peter mentioned at the beginning, so that we may know if it accords with the expositions of the holy fathers at Nicaea."[54]

* * *

47, 1. After the letter had been read out, bishop Cyril of Alexandria said, "What does this holy and great synod think about the letter that was just read out? Does it seem to accord with the faith defined at the synod of the holy fathers that met long ago in the city of Nicaea, or not?"

2. Bishop Juvenal of Jerusalem said, "In no way at all does it accord with the pious faith expounded by the holy fathers at Nicaea, and I anathematize those who hold such beliefs. For it is in every way foreign to the orthodox faith."

3. Bishop Flavian of Philippi said, "All the contents of the letter just read out are in every way at war with and absolutely foreign to the faith expounded at Nicaea by the most holy fathers. I judge those who hold such beliefs to be foreign to the orthodox faith."

4. Bishop Firmus of Caesarea in Cappadocia said, "Even though he gives a semblance of piety at the beginning of the letter, as his account proceeded he was unable to conceal his thought in any way and exposed his thought stripped of any covering, which is discordant with and

53 At this point there are 122 more statements from bishops affirming, each in their own way, that Cyril of Alexandria's *Second Letter to Nestorius* is in accord with the Nicene Creed. These are omitted from the translation.

54 At this point Nestorius's *Second Letter to Cyril* was read out. It is omitted from the translation here, but there is a translation in this volume on pp. 570–576.

contrary to the faith of the 318 holy fathers and the letter of the most sacred bishop Cyril."[55]

* * *

8. Bishop Acacius of Melitene said, "The letter of the most reverent bishop Nestorius that was read out has shown that it was not without reason that he agonized with fear about coming to this holy and great synod. For it makes sense for the one who was fully aware that he twisted the divine scriptures and wrecked the teachings of the holy fathers to be seized by such fear that he would surround his house with a throng of soldiers. For his letter, which was read out, shows utterly plainly that by setting aside the statements about the only-begotten Son of God contained in the faith of the holy fathers, the 318 bishops, he attributes those things that pertain to the saving economy to the flesh alone, claiming that it was merely the temple of God that endured birth and death. And he has made false claims about scripture, as though it teaches that the birth and suffering do not belong to the divinity but to the humanity. And moreover he disparages the letter of the most holy and most godly bishop Cyril, as if it said that God was passible, which neither he nor anyone else with pious views has either conceived or dared to say. He has completely shown himself to confess the union of God with the flesh in name alone while denying it completely in reality, and he has convicted himself of employing a strange teaching by saying that the doctrines have now been brought to light by himself in this present time. I disavow all these things because they are foreign to the truth and contain great impiety, making myself a stranger to communion with those who utter such things."

* * *

13. Bishop Prothymius of Comana said, "I trust the letter expounded by Your Holiness and I anathematize the one who does not state that the holy Virgin is Theotokos."

* * *

55 At this point there are thirty-one more statements from bishops affirming, each in its own way, that Nestorius's *Second Letter to Cyril* is not in accord with the Nicene Creed; in some cases it is added that it is also not in accord with Cyril's *Second Letter to Nestorius*. These are omitted from the translation, except for the three statements that follow.

19. Bishop Fidus of Joppa said, "'What communion does light have with darkness? What agreement does Christ have with Belial?'[56] For the letter of the most reverent Nestorius that was just read out is far removed from the truth, but it is very much in agreement with the lawless opinion of Paul of Samosata.[57] Therefore, because of the blasphemies it contains it will be unacceptable to all."[58]

* * *

48 All the bishops exclaimed together, "Let anyone who does not anathematize Nestorius be anathema!" "The orthodox faith anathematizes him!" "The synod anathematizes him!" "The holy synod anathematizes him!" "Let anyone in communion with Nestorius be anathema!" "We all anathematize the letter and doctrines of Nestorius!" "We all anathematize the heretic Nestorius!" "We all anathematize those who are in communion with Nestorius!" "We all anathematize the impious faith of Nestorius!" "We all anathematize the impious doctrine of Nestorius!" "We all anathematize the impious Nestorius!" "The whole world anathematizes the impious worship concocted by Nestorius!" "Let anyone who does not anathematize him be anathema!" "The orthodox faith anathematizes him!" "The holy synod anathematizes him!" "Let anyone in communion with Nestorius be anathema!" "Let the letter of the most holy bishop of Rome be read out!"[59]

* * *

51 Bishop Fidus of Joppa said, "That he continues until today in the same teaching[60] can be verified also by the most godly bishops here present,

56 2 Cor 6:14–15.

57 Fragments of Paul of Samosata are translated in this volume on pp. 197–211. The connection between Nestorius and Paul of Samosata seems to have first been made by Eusebius of Dorylaeum in his *Protest*, translated in this volume on pp. 559–563.

58 The remainder of the statements from bishops affirming, each in its own way, that Nestorius's *Second Letter to Cyril* is not in accord with the Nicene Creed are omitted from the translation.

59 Sections 49–50 are omitted from the translation. Here two documents were read out: Celestine of Rome's *Letter to Nestorius* (dated August 10, 430) and Cyril's *Third Letter to Nestorius*, both of which were delivered to Nestorius on November 30, 430. (The latter is translated in this volume on pp. 623–636.) After the reading of these letters, the Egyptian bishops who had delivered these letters to Nestorius in Constantinople testified that they had been properly delivered.

60 In other words, Nestorius did not renounce his teachings after receiving the letters of Celestine and Cyril, which had urged him to do so.

Acacius and lord Theodotus, who had discussions with him even though these would put someone at risk. We summon and adjure them by the holy gospels set before us and in the presence of the trustworthiness of the minutes to state what they heard three days ago from Nestorius himself."

52 Bishop Cyril of Alexandria said, "Since our discussion is not about random matters but about an issue more important than all others, namely, faith in Christ, it is fitting that the most reverent and in all respects most God-beloved bishops Theodotus and Acacius, in accordance with the summons and adjurations imposed by the most reverent bishop Fidus, since they are lovers of truth and holy men, state what they heard [Nestorius] himself say in the city of Ephesus, when they initiated a discussion with him on behalf of the orthodox faith."

53, 1. Bishop Theodotus of Ancyra said, "I feel bad for my friend, but I value piety more than every friendship. Thus it is necessary for me, though utterly heartbroken, to tell the truth about what I am being asked. I do not think our testimony is needed when his thinking is clear from the letter to Your Godliness. For what he forbids saying about God there, namely the Only-Begotten, when he derides his human experiences is precisely what he said in our discussion here, that we should not say that God was fed with breastmilk or born from a virgin. Thus also here he said many times that a two- or three-month old baby should not be called God. All this not only we ourselves heard, but also many others too, when not many days ago he had a discussion with us in Ephesus."

2. Bishop Acacius of Melitene said, "Since the matter at hand is faith and piety toward God, it is necessary to put aside all affection. Accordingly, even though I had so much more love for the lord Nestorius than others and endeavored in several ways to rescue him, out of love for the truth it is now necessary to report what he said lest my soul be condemned for concealing the truth. As soon as I arrived in the city of Ephesus I conducted a discussion with the aforementioned man, and realizing that his views were unorthodox I endeavored in several ways to set him straight and get him to renounce his wicked views, and I saw him confess with his lips that he had changed from such an opinion. After an interval of ten or twelve days, when another discussion was initiated, I took up the true account and saw him oppose it, and I realized that he had fallen into two absurdities at the same time. First, during his questioning (which was absurd) he foisted upon his respondents the necessity of either denying altogether that the divinity of the Only-Begotten was humanified or confessing (and this was

impious) that the divinity of both the Father and the Holy Spirit became incarnate along with the Word – both of which in every way smacked of a sinister understanding that jettisoned the pious faith. Then, when a second discussion was initiated, one of the bishops who was with him took up the debate and said that the Son who undertook the suffering was one and God the Word was another. Being unable to subject myself to this blasphemy, I said goodbye to all and left. And another one of those with him charged the Jews with impiety not toward God but toward a human being."[61]

* * *

60 Presbyter Peter of Alexandria chancellor of the notaries said, "We also have [at hand] books of the blasphemies of the most reverent Nestorius, from one of which we have selected passages, which, if it pleases this holy synod, we shall read out." Bishop Flavian of Philippi said, "Let them be read out and entered into the proceedings."

From the book of Nestorius himself, Quaternion [62] *17, on doctrine*

> 1. When then the divine scripture is about to speak of either the birth of Christ from the blessed Virgin or his death, it appears that nowhere does it set down "God," but rather either "Christ" or "Son" or "Lord." For these three are indicative of the two natures, sometimes of this one, sometimes of that one, sometimes of both together, just as I have been saying. When the scripture narrates for us the birth from the Virgin, what does it say? "God sent his Son."[63] It did not say, "God sent God the Word," but instead it took the name that indicates the two natures. For since the Son is a human being and God, it says, "God sent his Son, born of a woman,"[64] so that, when you have heard "born of a woman" and then seen the name set down just before that indicates the two natures, you will say that the birth from the blessed Virgin is the Son's. For the Virgin Christotokos indeed gave birth to the Son

61 Section 54 is omitted from the translation. Here sixteen excerpts from Western and Eastern patristic authorities were read out, chosen to demonstrate that Cyril's teaching had the approbation of tradition while Nestorius's did not. Sections 55–59 are also omitted from the translation, as they properly belong to the session of July 22 (see ACO 1.1.2: 44 Schwartz, note on p. 45, 3).

62 In Greek, *tetras*. A quaternion is a quire with four folded sheets forming sixteen pages.

63 Gal 4:4. 64 Gal 4:4.

of God. But since the Son of God is twofold with respect to his natures, she did not give birth to the Son of God but she did give birth to the humanity, which is the Son because of the Son conjoined with it.[65]

Likewise, by the same, Quaternion 21

2. See what follows, heretic. I do not begrudge the Virgin Christotokos this expression,[66] but I know she is worthy of veneration who received God, through whom came forth the Master of the universe, through whom shone forth the sun of righteousness.[67] Again, I am suspicious of the applause. How have you understood "came forth"? For me "came forth" isn't interchangeable with "was born," for I do not so quickly forget what distinguishes them. I was taught by the divine scriptures that God "came forth" from the Virgin Christotokos, but nowhere was I taught that God "was born" from her.[68]

And after some other words

3. Well then, nowhere does the divine scripture say that God was born from the Virgin Christotokos, but rather Jesus Christ, Son, Lord. All this we acknowledge, for wretched is anyone who does not immediately accept what the divine scripture has taught. "Rise, take the child and his mother."[69] This is an utterance of the angels. Perhaps the archangels had a better understanding of the character of his birth than you. "Rise, take the child and his mother." It did not say, "Rise, take God and his mother."[70]

Likewise, by the same, Quaternion 24

4. So then, we were talking about, "Do not fear to take Mary your wife, for that which was born in her … "[71] Whether one letter nu or two is used,[72] the sense of the passage is not affected ("for that

65 Nestorius, *Sermon* 10 (*Nestoriana*: 273, 18–274, 17 Loofs).
66 As is clear from what follows, "came forth." 67 See Mal 4:2.
68 Nestorius, *Sermon* 11 (*Nestoriana*: 277, 19–278, 2 Loofs). 69 Matt 2:13.
70 Nestorius, *Sermon* 11 (*Nestoriana*: 278, 5–13 Loofs). 71 Matt 1:20.
72 The verb (participle) used in Matt 1:20 is *gennēthen*, "was born," which is from *gennaō*. Throughout antiquity the meaning of this verb and its cognates overlapped with those of *gignomai*, "to become, to generate," and given the similarities in spelling, pronunciation,

which is engendered in her is of the Holy Spirit"[73]), but it would be if we were to say that God the Word was born in her womb.[74] For there is a difference between being with the one being born and being born. "For that which was born in her," it says, "is of the Holy Spirit,"[75] that is, the Holy Spirit created that which was in her. Therefore, the fathers, being well versed in the divine scriptures, saw that if we were to put "was born" instead of "was incarnated," God the Word would turn out to be either the son of the Spirit or to have two Fathers, or, with one letter nu, God the Word would turn out to be a creation of the Spirit. Accordingly they avoided the term "born" and put "who came down for us human beings and for our salvation and became incarnate."[76] What is meant by "became incarnate"? Not that he was changed from divinity into flesh. With "became incarnate of the Holy Spirit,"[77] they followed the evangelist. For when the evangelist came to the humanification, he avoided speaking of birth in reference to the Word and put incarnation. Where? Listen: "And the Word became flesh."[78] He did not say, "The Word was born through the flesh." Indeed, wherever the apostles or evangelists mention the Son, they put that he was born of a woman.[79] Pay attention to what is being said, I beg you! Wherever they say the name "Son" and that he was born of a woman, they put that he "was born." But wherever they mention the Word, none of them ventured to speak of birth through the humanity. Listen: when the blessed evangelist John came to the Word and his humanification, listen to how he speaks; "The Word

and meaning (e.g., *genesis*, "becoming, generation," from *gignomai*, and *gennēsis*, "birth," from *gennaō*), they were often confused in manuscripts. Nestorius's point, then, is that whether the participle is spelled with two nus (from *gennaō* implying a birth) or with one nu (from *gignomai* implying a generation or creation), the meaning of the passage does not change.

73 Matt 1:20. Here Nestorius replaces *gennēthen* with *techthen*, a synonym that conveys "giving birth" without the ambiguity of the scriptural participle.

74 Here the Latin version reads "in the flesh" instead of "in her womb."

75 Matt 1:20. 76 Nestorius is speaking of the fathers who wrote the Nicene Creed.

77 These words are found only in the version of the Nicene Creed issued at the Council of Constantinople in 381, the version which Nestorius generally preferred to use.

78 John 1:14.

79 See Gal 4:4. The key phrase is *genomenon ek gunaikos*. The participle *genomenon* is derived from *gignomai*, and the reference here shows the equivalency of *gignomai* and *gennaō* in the mind of Nestorius.

became flesh," that is, he took up flesh, "and dwelt among us," that is, he put on our nature and indwelt among us, "and we beheld his glory," that of the Son.[80] He did not say, "We have beheld the birth of the Word."[81]

Likewise, by the same, Quaternion 15, on doctrine

5. So we give the name "God" also to Christ according to the flesh on account of his conjunction with God the Word, while recognizing what appears as a human being. Listen to Paul preaching both: "From the Jews," he says, "is Christ according to the flesh, who is God over all."[82] He acknowledges the human being first and then speaks of what appears in divine terms in virtue of his conjunction with God, so that no one would suspect Christianity of worshiping a human being.[83]

Likewise, by the same, Quaternion 27

6. But just as we say that the Creator of all is God, and that Moses is God (for it says, "I have set you as God to Pharaoh"[84]), and that Israel is Son of God (for it says, "My firstborn son is Israel"[85]), and just as we say that Saul is Christ (for it says, "By no means shall I put my hand upon him, for he is the Lord's Christ"[86]) and Cyrus likewise (it says, "Thus said the Lord to my Christ, Cyrus"[87]), and that Babylon is holy (for it says, "It is I who direct them; they have been made holy and I lead them"[88]), so too we say that the master Christ is God, Son, holy, and Christ. There is a similar sharing of names, but there is not the same dignity.[89]

Likewise, by the same, Quaternion 15

7. "Have this mind among yourselves, which was also in Christ Jesus, who, though he was in the form of God, emptied himself, taking the form of a slave."[90] He did not say, "Have this mind

80 John 1:14. 81 Nestorius, *Sermon* 14 (*Nestoriana*: 285, 24–287, 21 Loofs).
82 Rom 9:5. 83 Nestorius, *Sermon* 8 (*Nestoriana*: 248, 10–249, 1 Loofs).
84 Exod 7:1. 85 Exod 4:22.
86 1 Kgs 24:7, meaning, "for he is the Lord's anointed."
87 Isa 45:1, meaning "to my anointed, Cyrus." 88 Isa 13:3.
89 Nestorius, *Sermon* 15 (*Nestoriana*: 289, 6–15 Loofs).
90 Phil 2:5–7, with omissions.

among yourselves, which was also in God the Word, who, though he was in the form of God, took the form of a slave." Instead, using "Christ" as the designation that indicates the two natures, he calls him without any peril both "the form of a slave," which he took, and "God," with the expressions being assigned irreproachably to the duality of the two natures.[91]

Likewise, by the same, Quaternion 16

8. "So that at the name of Jesus," he says, "every knee should bend, in heaven and on earth and under the earth, and every tongue confess that Jesus Christ is Lord."[92] I venerate the one who is worn because of the wearer. I worship the one who appears because of the one who is hidden. God is inseparable from the one who appears. For this reason I do not separate the honor of the one who is not separated. I separate the natures, but I unite the worship.[93]

Likewise, by the same, Quaternion 17, on doctrine

9. For even before the humanification God the Word was Son and God and co-existent with the Father, but in the end times he took the form of a slave. But even though he was Son and was called such before this, after the assumption it is not possible for him to be called this separately, so that we do not teach two sons. Rather, since he is conjoined to that one who from the beginning is the Son (who is conjoined to him), it is not possible to accept a division in the dignity of sonship. I am saying: "in the dignity of sonship," not "in the natures." For this reason, God the Word is also named Christ, because he has a conjunction with Christ that is continuous.[94]

Likewise, by the same, Quaternion 15, on doctrine

10. Well then, let us keep the conjunction of the natures unconfused. Let us confess God in a human being. Let us venerate the human being who is worshiped together with almighty God in virtue of the divine conjunction.[95]

91 Nestorius, *Sermon* 9 (*Nestoriana*: 254, 5–12 Loofs). 92 Phil 2:10–11.
93 Nestorius, *Sermon* 9 (*Nestoriana*: 261, 20–262, 6 Loofs).
94 Nestorius, *Sermon* 10 (*Nestoriana*: 275, 1–11 Loofs).
95 Nestorius, *Sermon* 8 (*Nestoriana*: 249, 1–4 Loofs).

Likewise, by the same, Quaternion 6

11. Consider too what follows this immediately: "so that he might become," he says, "a merciful and faithful high priest in service of God. For because he himself has suffered and been tempted, he is able to help those who are tempted."[96] Therefore, the one who suffered is a merciful high priest. It is the temple that was able to suffer, not the life-giving God of the one who suffered.[97]

Likewise, by the same, Quaternion 27

12. So that you may learn, it means, how intense was the conjunction with the divinity, which was seen even in infancy of the master's flesh. For he was both an infant and master of the infant. You praised the saying but do not applaud it without due examination. For I said: The same was an infant and the inhabitant of the infant.[98]

Likewise, by the same, Quaternion 1

13. For the activities of the Trinity are shared and possess distinction only in the hypostases. So the glory of the Only-Begotten is attributed sometimes to the Father (for it says, "It is my Father who glorifies me"[99]), sometimes to the Spirit (for it says, "The Spirit of truth will glorify me"[100]), and sometimes to the sovereignty of Christ.[101]

Likewise, by the same, Quaternion 16

14. About the Son he says: He is the one who says, "My God, my God, why have you forsaken me?"[102] He is the one who endured a death that lasted three days. I worship him along with the divinity as co-worker of divine authority.[103]

And after other words

15. I venerate the one who is worn because of the wearer. I worship the one who appears because of the one who is hidden. God

96 Heb 2:17–18, with omissions.
97 Nestorius, *Sermon* 5 (*Nestoriana*: 234, 10–16 Loofs).
98 Nestorius, *Sermon* 15 (*Nestoriana*: 292, 1–6 Loofs).
99 John 8:54.
100 John 16:13–14, with omissions.
101 Nestorius, *Sermon* 5 (*Nestoriana*: 225, 13–18 Loofs).
102 Matt 27:46.
103 Nestorius, *Sermon* 9 (*Nestoriana*: 260, 4–7 Loofs).

is inseparable from the one who appears. For this reason I do not separate the honor of the one who is not separated. I separate the natures, but I unite the worship.[104] What was formed in the womb was not in itself God. What was created by the Spirit was not in itself God. What was buried in the tomb was not in itself God. For if so, we would obviously be worshipers of a human being and worshipers of the dead. Rather, since God is in the one assumed, then the one who has been assumed, as he is conjoined to the one who assumed him, shares the name "God" on account of the one who has assumed him.[105]

Likewise, by the same, Quaternion 3, against heretics, speaking about the Spirit

16. How could the one who works together with the Son and Father be a slave? Even if one were to inquire into the actions of the Spirit, one would find that they were in no respect deficient in comparison to those of the Father and the Son, not because the one divinity is divided but because the divine scripture divides what belongs to a single power according to each hypostasis, for a demonstration of the likeness of the Trinity. And consider with me a similar demonstration that originated in the works that occurred in time. God "the Word became flesh and dwelt among us."[106] The Father made the assumed humanity sit with himself, for it says, "The Lord said to my Lord: Sit at my right."[107] And the descending Spirit applauded the glory of the one assumed, for it says, "When the Spirit of truth comes, he will glorify me."[108]

Likewise, by the same, Quaternion 6, speaking of Christ

17. He was sent "to proclaim release to the captives,"[109] so the Apostle adds [to this] and says that he is the one who was made a high priest faithful to God[110] (for he came into being without

104 Up to this point the excerpt is identical with number 8, except for the quotation of Phil 2:10–11.
105 Nestorius, *Sermon* 9 (*Nestoriana*: 262, 3–12 Loofs). 106 John 1:14.
107 Ps 109(110):1.
108 John 16:13–14, with omissions. Nestorius, *Sermon* 2 (*Nestoriana*: 226, 14–227, 3 Loofs).
109 See Luke 4:18. 110 See Heb 2:17.

preexisting eternally). He is the one who advanced gradually to the dignity of high priest, you heretic! Listen to a statement that proclaims this to you even more clearly: "In the days of his flesh," it says, "[Jesus] offered up prayers and supplications to him who was able to save him from death, with loud cries and tears, and he was heard for his reverence. Although he was Son, he learned obedience from what he suffered, and being made perfect he became the source of eternal salvation to all who obey him."[111] That which advances gradually was made perfect, you heretic! On this subject John proclaims in the gospels, "Jesus advanced in age, wisdom, and favor."[112] Speaking in agreement with this Paul says, "Being made perfect he became the source of eternal salvation to all who obey him, being designated by God a high priest according to the order of Melchizedek."[113]

And after other words

18. He was called a high priest. Therefore, why do you misinterpret Paul by mixing the impassible God the Word with an earthly likeness and making him a passible high priest?[114]

Likewise, by the same, Quaternion 7

19. Therefore, holy brothers, who share in a heavenly call, consider the apostle and high priest of our confession, Jesus, who was faithful to the one who made him.[115]

And after other words

20. Therefore, since we have only this high priest who suffers together with us, who is akin to us and steadfast, do not turn back from faith in him. For because of the blessing promised us from the seed of Abraham, he was sent so that he might offer the sacrifice of his body on behalf of himself and his kin.[116]

111 Heb 5:7–9.
112 Luke 2:52. The Latin version contains a correction: "On this subject John elsewhere and Luke in the gospels cries ... "
113 Heb 5:9–10. Nestorius, *Sermon* 5 (*Nestoriana*: 235, 6–236, 6 Loofs).
114 Nestorius, *Sermon* 5 (*Nestoriana*: 236, 12–14 Loofs).
115 Heb 3:1–2. Nestorius, *Sermon* 5 (*Nestoriana*: 240, 1–4 Loofs).
116 Nestorius, *Sermon* 5 (*Nestoriana*: 240, 4–9 Loofs).

(Note that after confessing that every high priest requires a sacrifice and exempting Christ from this requirement, he says in these remarks that he offers the sacrifice on behalf of himself and his kin.)[117]

Likewise, by the same, Quaternion 4

21. Well then, listen attentively to the words. He says, "He who eats my flesh."[118] Recall that the statement is about the flesh and that I am not adding the word "flesh," lest I appear to them to misinterpret. "He who eats my flesh and drinks my blood."[119] Did he say, "He who eats my divinity and drinks my divinity"? [No, he said,] "He who eats my flesh and drinks my blood abides in me, and I in him."[120]

And after other words

22. Back to the subject. "He who eats my flesh and drinks my blood abides in me, and I in him."[121] Recall that the statement is about the flesh. "As the living Father sent me"[122] – the "me" is that which appears. But sometimes I may misinterpret, so let's listen to what comes next. "As the living Father sent me."[123] [My opponent] says [that the "me" is] the divinity; I say it is the humanity. Let's see who is misinterpreting. "As the living Father sent me." The heretic says that here it is speaking of the divinity; it says, "He sent me," [the "me" being] God the Word. "As the living Father sent me, and I" – according to them, [the "I" is] God the Word – "live because of the Father."[124] Next after this: "And he who eats me will live."[125] Whom do we eat, the divinity or the flesh?[126]

Likewise, by the same, Quaternion 16

23. And in general if you were to mine the entire New [Testament] altogether, you would not find anywhere that death is ascribed to God, but rather either to Christ or the Son or the Lord. For "Christ," "Son," and "Lord," which are taken from scripture as

117 This is an editorial comment, not the words of Nestorius.
118 John 6:56. 119 John 6:56.
120 John 6:56. Nestorius, *Sermon* 3 (*Nestoriana*: 227, 20–228, 3 Loofs).
121 John 6:56. 122 John 6:57. 123 John 6:57. 124 John 6:57.
125 John 6:57. 126 Nestorius, *Sermon* 3 (*Nestoriana*: 228, 4–16 Loofs).

relating to the Only-Begotten, are indicative of the two natures. And sometimes they signify the divinity, sometimes the humanity, and sometimes both. For instance, when Paul is writing a letter and declares, "While we were enemies we were reconciled to God through the death of his Son,"[127] he proclaims the humanity of the Son. Again, when the same Paul says to the Hebrews, "God has spoken to us in [his] Son, through whom he made the ages,"[128] he indicates the divinity of the Son. For the flesh is not the creator of the ages, seeing that it was created after many ages.[129]

And after other words

24. The divinity did not have James as its brother,[130] nor do we proclaim the death of God the Word when we eat the blood and body of the master.[131]

Likewise, by the same, Quaternion 23

25. I notice that our people possess great reverence and most ardent piety, but err because of ignorance of knowledge of God as it pertains to doctrine. Now this is not an accusation against the people, but (how can I say it nicely?) against teachers not having had the opportunity to communicate to you any of the more accurate teachings.[132]

Presbyter Peter of Alexandria the chancellor of the notaries said, "See how clearly he says in this remark that none of the teachers prior to him said to the people what he himself says."

Bishop Flavian of Philippi said, "Since these statements of Nestorius are terrible and blasphemous and our ears cannot bear to be defiled any longer, let each part of his blasphemy be entered into the proceedings as an accusation against the teacher of such things."[133]

* * *

127 Rom 5:10. 128 Heb 1:2, with omissions.

129 Nestorius, *Sermon* 10 (*Nestoriana*: 269, 14–27 Loofs). 130 See Gal 1:19.

131 See 1 Cor 11:26. Nestorius, *Sermon* 10 (*Nestoriana*: 271, 1–3 Loofs).

132 Nestorius, *Sermon* 14 (*Nestoriana*: 283, 2–8 Loofs).

133 The reading of the Nestorian florilegium was followed by the reading of a letter from Capreolus, the bishop of Carthage, who explained why he had not been able to attend the council but offered his support for its decisions. This letter also mentions that the invitation to attend the council sent to Augustine of Hippo did not reach him before he died.

Verdict pronounced against Nestorius, deposing him

61 The holy synod said, "Since in addition to other things the most honorable Nestorius neither wanted to obey our summons nor even received the most holy and godly bishops whom we sent, of necessity we proceeded to an investigation into his impieties and discovered from his letters and writings that were read out, as well as from his recent statements in this metropolis, for which testimonials have been given, that he holds and preaches impious opinions. Of necessity we are compelled by the canons and by the letter of our most holy father and fellow minister Celestine the bishop of the church of the Romans, after frequently shedding tears, to proceed to this sad decree against him."

[Decree]

62, 1. Our Lord Jesus Christ, having been blasphemed by him, has decreed through the present most holy synod that the same Nestorius is ousted from episcopal dignity and all priestly assembly.

2. I, Bishop Cyril of Alexandria, have signed, pronouncing with the holy synod.

3. I, Bishop Juvenal of Jerusalem, have signed, pronouncing with the holy synod.

4. I, Bishop Flavian of Philippi, have signed, pronouncing with the holy synod.

5. I, Bishop Firmus of Caesarea in Cappadocia, have signed, pronouncing with the holy synod.

6. I, Bishop Memnon of Ephesus, have signed, pronouncing with the holy synod.

7. I, Bishop Acacius of Melitene by the mercy of God, agreeing with the holy synod over the pronouncement recorded above, have signed.

8. I, Bishop Theodotus of the holy church of Ancyra, agreeing with the holy synod, have signed.[134]

*
* *

134 The remaining 189 signatures are omitted from the translation.

Session of the Counter-Council of the Easterners[135]

(Held on June 26, 431)

Minutes of the proceedings of the Eastern bishops in which they depose the most holy Cyril and Memnon and excommunicate all [the bishops participating] in the holy synod.

1. In the presence,[136] at his own residence, of the most holy and most God-beloved bishop John of the metropolis of Antioch in the diocese of the East and the holy synod with him, the most magnificent and most glorious Candidianus the count of the sacred palace officials said, "All that I wished for, in the presence of Your Godliness together with the whole synod gathered as one, was to deliver the letter of our masters and most pious emperors, so that, with the whole synod gathered, as I said before, their commands could then be carried out. But five days ago,[137] when the most reverent bishop Cyril and bishop Memnon of this city and their most reverent episcopal allies gathered in the holy church, I tried to stop them from assembling by themselves alone contrary to the decrees of our masters and most pious emperors, and I kept warning them to wait for the arrival of all of you. But they kept demanding that I read out the sacra. Even though I didn't want to do this, because Your Holiness wasn't present and many other bishops and metropolitans hadn't yet arrived, I was compelled by them because they claimed that they were unaware of what our masters had written. For this reason, then, since they had gathered I was compelled not to give any pretext for disorder, and I read out the sacra to them. Both when I was still there and when I was about to leave, I protested that they should do nothing rash, as many of the most holy bishops who accompanied me to them know. But unrestrained, they did whatever they pleased."

2. The most God-beloved bishop John said, "All that we wished for was to obey the pious letters. For we must not make conjectures about the issues, but advance to the truth itself and learn the pious objective of our God-beloved emperors, who expend all their efforts on the churches of

135 *Collectio Vaticana* 151 (ACO 1.1.5: 119–124 Schwartz) [Greek]; *Collectio Casinensis* 87 (ACO 1.4: 33–38 Schwartz) [Latin]. The acts from this session are translated in their entirety, except for the list of signatories to the decree.

136 Here the Latin acts open with the date: "In the consulship of Antiochus, six days before the Kalends of July, in the presence … "

137 Counting inclusively, so June 22.

Christ and prefer nothing to him. So then, let Your Magnificence inform us what happened next after you read out to them this most God-beloved letter."

3. The most magnificent count Candidianus said, "As the sacra was being read, they all applauded it, so that I thought that they would in fact comply with everything decreed by our pious emperors, and in turn I started to rejoice over this. But after the reading, when I exhorted them all to comply with the letter, no one would pay me any attention. Rather, with insults they expelled the most reverent bishops sent by the most holy bishop Nestorius and their allies. And though I exhorted them again at length, they expelled me from the meeting, on the grounds that I had no right to participate in their decisions. Besides this, they did not even allow the message sent to them by the most reverent bishops to be read out,[138] as the most holy bishops who were there with me know and can testify to the proper procedure I followed. All this we referred to the knowledge of the masters of the world, making it clear that we were waiting for the arrival of Your Holiness and the most holy bishops with you."

4. The most God-beloved archbishop John said, "Let the pious letter be read out also to us."[139]

5. Once the most holy bishops had stood up, the most magnificent count Candidianus read out the letter. When he was finished and the most God-beloved bishops had prayed for the [emperors'] pious rule, the most God-beloved archbishop John said, "The serenity of this pious letter was sufficient to induce them to follow every detail of the legal process, even if they were not of the priestly rank. But since, as Your Magnificence said, after the reading of the letter they filled everything with chaos and disorder and hurled insults at both the God-beloved bishops and Your Magnificence, we have come in accordance with the proper legal process and have heard the letter, and we are ready to put the objective of our most God-beloved

138 This refers to the formal complaint issued by the sixty-eight bishops who disagreed with opening the council before John and the Eastern delegation arrived: see *Collectio Casinensis* 82 (ACO 1.4: 27–30 Schwartz).

139 This refers to the sacra of Theodosius convoking the synod (*Collectio Vaticana* 31 [ACO 1.1.1: 120–121 Schwartz]), which Cyril had outmaneuvered Candidianus into reading on June 22. It was not entered into the minutes. Here the Latin has, "Let both the initial and subsequent pious letters be read out also to us, and may they be the first to shine in the record of our present proceedings," referring to the imperial letter of November 19, 430, announcing the synod and the letter mentioned in the Greek acts.

emperors into effect, God willing. But I entreat, if they commanded anything else, let us learn it from Your Magnificence."

6. The most magnificent count Candidianus said, "Since Your Holiness investigates everything with precision and according to proper procedure, it is right that I should relate the rest of what happened. The next day, when I was still completely ignorant of what had been transacted [the previous day], suddenly I heard that they had deposed the most holy bishop Nestorius. I withdrew the letter of deposition they had issued and after reading it I sent it to our most pious emperors. A little later I heard that the public criers were also going around the forum broadcasting the deposition of the aforementioned most holy bishop Nestorius. Once I became aware of this I sent them instructions to do nothing contrary to what had been commanded by our most pious emperors. And no less did I also demand of those most holy bishops who had not assembled with them to wait for the arrival of Your Holiness."

7. The most God-beloved archbishop John said, "Was it after discussion in the presence of all, in conformity with the canons and the ecclesiastical laws and the imperial letter, with the asking of appropriate questions and the obtaining of replies, that they proceeded to the deposition after having established proof, or did they condemn the man without any defense?"

8. The most magnificent count Candidianus said, "All the most godly bishops who were there with me know that they issued the verdict without any trial, inquiry, or investigation."

9. The most God-beloved archbishop John said, "Nor indeed was their behavior toward us according to proper procedure. For although those who have just arrived from so long a journey and are still covered with dust ought to be welcomed in a brotherly spirit, treated with courtesy, and refreshed with brotherly affection, they immediately came to us, causing us trouble and distress and displaying their customary disorder. Nevertheless, the holy synod currently joined with me did not even grant them a hearing. But the holy synod will decide in conformity with proper procedure what ought to be decreed against those who have disrupted everything in a manner so lawless and despotic."

10. With these exchanges completed, and once the most magnificent Candidianus the count of the sacred palace officials had departed after the reading of the pious letter and the recounting of events in the deposition he gave above, the most God-beloved archbishop John said, "Your Godliness has heard the pious letter of our most God-beloved emperors and the

deposition of the most magnificent count Candidianus, and has been informed of the objective of the most pious emperors, namely, exercising all foresight for the peace of the church, for the sound and unshakeable faith, and for the doctrines of the apostles, they assembled a holy synod here, commanding that it take place in a manner worthy of their God-beloved rule, so that everyone could be in the same place and examine the issues in a brotherly spirit and as befits priests, by way of proposition and resolution as well as by question and answer, without any disruption and absent of tumult, without anything else being investigated, neither a criminal nor a civil charge, before a precise examination and confirmation of the pious faith of the holy and blessed fathers who assembled at Nicaea in Bithynia. Well then, what does Your Godliness resolve should be done about such contempt for the pious letter?"

11. The holy synod said, "The most reverent bishop Cyril of Alexandria has been blatant, as has the most reverent bishop Memnon of the city here, who has cooperated with him in everything, as we have learned in precise detail by having come before Your Godliness and beheld, so to speak, all the effronteries perpetrated by him. For he shuttered the holy churches, the holy martyria, and the holy Church of the Apostle, not even permitting the holy [feast of] Pentecost to be celebrated by the God-beloved bishops. Gathering a mob of brutes, he disrupted the city, sending his own clerics to the houses of the God-beloved bishops and unleashing countless dire threats if they did not join the meeting lawlessly convoked by them. In bad conscience they have disrupted and confounded everything; they have made the affairs of the church teem with tumult; they have shown contempt to the pious letter; they have trampled upon the ecclesiastical laws – all this to avoid an examination of the heretical heterodoxy that we found in the chapters sent previously to the imperial city by the most reverent bishop Cyril, the majority of which agree with the impiety of Arius, Apollinarius, and Eunomius.[140] So then, it is necessary for Your Holiness and all of us to fight bravely on behalf of piety, lest anyone be ensnared by the heretical chapters of the most God-beloved bishop Cyril or the faith of holy fathers be corrupted, and to condemn the instigators of both the heretical beliefs and the lawlessness that surpasses all reason with a verdict worthy of their transgressions and to subject the most reverent bishops ensnared and captured by them to an ecclesiastical penalty."

140 The synod refers to the Twelve Anathemas or Twelve Chapters that Cyril appended to his *Third Letter to Nestorius*.

12. The most God-beloved bishop John said, "All that I wished for was that none of those ordained to the priesthood of God would be excluded from the body of the church. But since incurable members must be cut off for the health of the whole body, it is right that Cyril and Memnon be subjected to deposition, as instigators of the lawlessness that has occurred and the trampling upon the ecclesiastical laws and the pious decrees of our most pious emperors, and because of the heretical views of the aforementioned chapters. But those ensnared by them should be excommunicated so that, acknowledging their offense, they may anathematize the heretical chapters of Cyril and consent to abide by the faith expounded by the most holy fathers gathered at Nicaea, introducing nothing different to it or foreign to piety, and meet with us in accordance with the pious letter of our most God-beloved emperors, and conduct an inquiry into the issues in a brotherly spirit and confirm the pious faith."

13. The holy synod said, "Your Holiness has declared a sentence that is lawful and just. Now must the deposition of Cyril and Memnon and the excommunication of the rest be stated in a joint letter and ratified by the signatures of us all."

14. The most God-beloved archbishop John said, "What has been approved shall be done. I, John the bishop of Antioch, have so resolved."

Decree

15. The holy council assembled by the grace of God in Ephesus in accordance with the letter of our most pious and Christ-loving emperors has passed the following resolution:

We had wished that the synod had taken place peacefully in accordance with the canons of the holy fathers and in accordance with the letter of our most pious and Christ-loving emperors. But since you, employing defiance, lawlessness, and heretical intention, have met by yourselves, even though we were at the gates[141] in accordance with the letter of our most pious emperors, and since you have filled the city and the holy synod with every kind of disruption for the purpose of avoiding an examination of the chapters that agree with the heterodoxy and impiety of Apollinarius, Arius, and Eunomius, and since you did not wait for the arrival of the most

141 Here the Latin is more specific: "even though, with some of us already present, the rest of us were at the gates."

holy bishops who had been summoned from all parts by our most pious emperors, and since you did these things even though the most magnificent count Candidianus commanded you in writing and orally to venture no such thing but to wait for a combined meeting of all the holy bishops, for this reason know that you are deposed and ousted from the episcopacy – you, Cyril of Alexandria, and you, Memnon of this city – and you are ousted from every ecclesiastical ministry as instigators and leaders of all the lawlessness and transgression and as those who have caused the canons of the fathers and the imperial decrees to be trampled upon. But all the rest, who conspired with these men who acted lawlessly and transgressed the canons and the imperial decrees, you are excommunicated until you acknowledge your offense, repent, and accept the faith of the holy fathers assembled at Nicaea, introducing nothing different or foreign to it, and you anathematize the heretical chapters expounded by Cyril of Alexandria that are contrary to the teaching of the gospels and apostles, and abide by the letter of the most pious and Christ-loving emperors, which enjoins that matters of faith be examined quietly and with precision.

These are the signatories:

Bishop John of Antioch;

Bishop Alexander of the metropolis of Apamea ...[142]

*

* *

Sixth Session[143]

(Held on July 22, 431)

73 Minutes of the transactions by the holy synod at Ephesus for the confirmation of the symbol of the holy fathers at Nicaea and for the plaint

142 The remaining fifty-two signatories are omitted from the translation. The Greek acts list only forty-three signatories, whereas the Latin acts contain fifty-three. Theodoret of Cyrrhus is one of the signatories.

143 *Collectio Atheniensis* 73–79 (ACO 1.1.7: 84–117 Schwartz) [Greek]; *Collectio Casinensis* 46 (ACO 1.3: 119–140 Schwartz) [Latin]; *Collectio Palatina* 38 (ACO 1.5: 85–116 Schwartz) [Latin]. Omissions from the translation are noted.

delivered by presbyter Charisius. After the consulship of our masters Flavius Theodosius for the thirteenth time and Flavius Valentinian for the third time, perpetual Augusti, eleven days before the Kalends of August, which is Epiphi 28 according to the Egyptians, the synod assembled in the metropolis of Ephesus by decree of the most God-beloved and Christ-loving emperors. And there were seated in the episcopal residence of the most godly bishop Memnon the following most God-beloved and most godly bishops:

Cyril of Alexandria, also proxy for the most holy and most sacred Celestine archbishop of the church of Rome;

Juvenal of Jerusalem;

Memnon of Ephesus;

Flavian of Philippi, also proxy for Rufus the most reverent bishop of Thessalonica;

Firmus of Caesarea in Cappadocia Prima;

Theodotus of Ancyra in Galatia;

Acacius of Melitene ...[144]

* * *

A Copy of the Exposition of the Falsified Symbol

76, 4. Those who are now for the first time being instructed in the accuracy of the ecclesiastical doctrines or who want to switch from any heretical error to the truth must be taught and confess: We believe in one God, Father eternal, who did not begin to exist at some later point but who from the beginning has been eternal God, nor indeed did he become Father at some later point since he was always God and Father.

5. And we believe in one Son of God, Only-Begotten, who is from the substance of the Father, because he really is Son and of the same substance as the one whose Son he is and is believed to be.

144 At this point the names of 150 additional bishops are omitted from the translation. What follows (sections 74.1–76.3) is also omitted from the translation. Replicating the proceedings at the session on June 22, here the Nicene Creed and the same sixteen excerpts from Western and Eastern patristic authorities were read out, plus four additional ones. After this, the matter concerning Charisius was introduced (see the introduction for details) and his plaint was read out.

6. And [we believe] in the Holy Spirit, who is from the substance of God, who is not Son but God in substance, because he is of that substance of which the God and Father is, from whom he exists according to substance. For [Paul] says, "We have not received the spirit of the world, but the Spirit that is from God,"[145] setting him apart from all creation and conjoining him to God, from whom he exists according to substance, in a manner that distinguishes him from all creation,[146] which we consider to be from God not according to substance but by reason of its being created. And we consider [the Spirit] neither to be the Son nor to have received his existence through the Son.

7. And we confess that the Father is perfect in person and likewise the Son and the Holy Spirit in the same way, and so we preserve the formula of piety by considering the Father, Son, and Holy Spirit not as three different substances, but as one [substance] acknowledged in an identity of divinity.

8. And in regard to the economy which God the Master accomplished for our salvation in the economy according to Christ the Master, it is necessary to know that God the Word assumed a complete human being who was from the seed of Abraham and David, according to the declaration of the divine scriptures,[147] who was in nature that which those from whose seed he was were, [namely,] a complete human being in nature, composed of an intellectual soul and human flesh. This human being, who accords with us in nature, who by the power of the Holy Spirit was formed in the womb of the Virgin, who was "born of a woman and born under the law, in order to redeem" all of us from the slavery of the law, "so that we might receive the adoption as sons"[148] as was predestined long ago – it is this human being that [God the Word] ineffably conjoined to himself. He made him experience death in accordance with the law of human beings, "raised him from the dead," led him up into heaven and "seated him at the right hand of God," because of which he indeed is "above all rule and authority

145 1 Cor 2:12.
146 That is, Paul sets apart the Spirit with a phrase ("from God") that distinguishes the Spirit from all creation.
147 See Matt 1:1. 148 Gal 4:4–5.

and dominion and power and every name that is named not [only] in this age, but also in the one to come."[149] [This human being] receives worship from all creation because he has an inseparable conjunction with the divine nature, in virtue of his relationship to God and in the understanding of all creation as it renders worship to him.

9. And we do not speak of "two sons" or "two lords." For God the Word is one Son according to substance, the only-begotten Son of the Father. By being conjoined to him and partaking in sonship this [human being] shares the designation and honor of "Son." And God the Word is Lord according to substance. By being conjoined to him this [human being] shares the honor. And we do not speak of "two sons" or "two lords" for this reason too, because while Lord and Son clearly exist according to substance, the one assumed for our salvation, having an inseparable conjunction with him, is promoted to the name and the honor of the Son and the Lord. He is not like each one of us, a son in himself, which is why we are called "many sons" according to the blessed Paul.[150] Rather, he alone, being in possession of this special feature in virtue of his conjunction with God the Word and partaking in sonship and lordship, demolishes every notion of a duality of sons and lords, and in virtue of his conjunction with God the Word enables us to have all faith, understanding, and contemplation of him. Because of all this, in virtue of his relationship to God, he receives worship from all creation. 10. So we avow that the Son and Lord Jesus Christ is one, through whom all things came into being.[151] We consider the Son of God and Lord according to substance to be principally God the Word, but along with him we also give consideration to that which was assumed, "Jesus of Nazareth," whom "God anointed with spirit and power,"[152] because he shares in sonship and lordship in virtue of his conjunction with God the Word.

11. According to the blessed Paul he also is called "the second Adam"[153] because he is of the same nature as Adam and has

149 Eph 1:20–21. 150 Heb 2:10. 151 See John 1:3. 152 Acts 10:38.
153 1 Cor 15:45.

made known to us the condition to come. There is such a great difference between him and Adam: it is the difference between the one who bestows ineffable goods in the condition to come and the one who provided the origin of the present sorrows. In like manner he is also called "the second human being"[154] because he revealed the second condition. For while Adam, in whom we indeed received likeness to him, became the origin of the first condition, which was mortal and passible and brimming with many pains, Christ the Master makes known the second: when he has appeared from the heavens in the [age] to come he will lead us all into the proper communion with him. For "the first human being," [Paul] says, "was from the earth, made of dust; the second human being, the Lord, is from heaven"[155] – that is, he is going to appear again from there in order to lead all to imitation of himself. For this reason he adds, "As was the earthly one, so too are those who are earthly; and as is the heavenly one, so too are those who are heavenly. And just as we have borne the image of the earthly one, we shall also bear the image of the heavenly one."[156] At the time of this appearing and being seen by all who are about to be judged, the divine nature, which is unseen, will render judgment, according to the blessed Paul, who says, "For the times of our ignorance God overlooked, but now he commands all human beings everywhere to repent, because he has fixed a day on which he is going to judge the world in righteousness by a man whom he has appointed, and of this he has given assurance by raising him from the dead."[157]

This is the teaching of the ecclesiastical doctrines. And let everyone who holds views contrary to these be anathema. Let everyone who does not accept salvific repentance be anathema. Let everyone who does not keep the holy day of Easter according to the law of the holy and catholic church be anathema.[158]

* * *

154 1 Cor 15:47. 155 1 Cor 15:47. 156 1 Cor 15:48–49.
157 Acts 17:30–31.
158 Most of the Lydian Christians who signed this creed were Quartodecimans. Their statements and signatures (76.12–32) are omitted from the translation.

[Canon 7]

77 When this had been read out,[159] the holy synod stipulated that no one is permitted to produce or write or compose another faith beside the one defined with the Holy Spirit's help by the holy fathers gathered at Nicaea, and that those who venture to either compose or present or produce another faith for those who want to convert to the knowledge of the truth from either Hellenism[160] or Judaism or any heresy whatsoever, these very ones, if they are bishops or clerics, should be ousted, the bishops from the episcopacy and the clerics from the clergy, but if they are lay people they should be anathematized. In the same way, if any bishops, clerics, or laypeople are detected to hold or teach the views contained in the exposition presented by Charisius the presbyter about the humanification of the only-begotten Son of God, or the abominable and twisted doctrines of Nestorius, which are appended, let them be liable to the sentence of this holy and ecumenical synod, meaning that a bishop should be ousted from the episcopacy and deposed and likewise a cleric should be evicted from the clergy. If it is a layperson, however, he too should be anathematized as stated above.[161]

*

* *

Letter of Nestorius to Scholasticus the Eunuch of Emperor Theodosius[162]

(Sent late July 431)

1\. I admire your God-loving soul, and especially when it is firm and does not scatter itself in errors, which is how it gives approval to the fictions of the impure, who say of us that we have rejected the term "Theotokos."[163]

159 That is, the material connected with Charisius: his plaint, the "Nestorian" creed, and the signatures.
160 This term is frequently used in late antique literature to designate pagan worship.
161 The remainder of the proceedings from July 22 is omitted from the translation. After Canon 7, a florilegium of excerpts from the writings of Nestorius was appended, identical to the florilegium read out at the session on June 22, 431. Following this was a list of signatories to the deposition of Nestorius.
162 *Collectio Casinensis* 103 (ACO 1.4: 51–53 Schwartz) [Latin]. The original Greek is not extant. This letter is translated in its entirety.
163 The Latin *dei genetrix* no doubt renders the Greek *theotokos*.

This term, as you well know, we have often used, but we have used it so as[164] to prevent anyone from supposing that the Lord Jesus Christ is either a mere human being or God without humanity. For if these spawn of demons had done their job competently, surely they would have reported what we said in Constantinople, as Your Admirableness also knows. But at present there certainly has been no conversation at all between us. For how could this happen when we have not even seen one another? If they describe words exchanged between me and other bishops, which was done privately as a test of discipline, as our conversations with Cyril, surely they lie. Know that what I have often said to them, and what both they and I believe to be perfectly fine, is that the holy Virgin should be called both "Theotokos" and "Anthropotokos"[165] – "Theotokos," not as if God the Word took the beginning of his existence from her (for how could that be when he is the Creator of the Virgin?), but to prevent anyone from supposing that the one who was born was a mere human being; and "Anthropotokos," so that we do not reject the economy and our first fruits[166] like the Manichaeans do. This is what I said to the bishops as if in a preliminary practice[167] – and often we said it mutually to one another! And repeatedly both parties said that it was perfectly fine, so much so that they even praised this when they left. But Cyril has completely avoided and continues to avoid conversation with us, hoping by this to sidestep having the chapters he wrote be condemned for incontrovertible heresy.[168]

2. How then has Your Admirableness accepted such an accusation against us, when you must certainly remember that we used both terms even in Constantinople on account of the mystery of the economy and the ineffable union? Do not then, I ask you, give credence so easily to the accusations made against us. For we believe that the term "Theotokos," provided that it is used with the term "Anthropotokos,"[169] is the surest mark of piety. For when we say ["Christotokos," just as when we say][170] "Christ," "Jesus,"

164 Schwartz detects a lacuna here, but sense can be made of the passage without a conjectural addition.

165 In Latin, *dei partricem et hominis*.

166 See 1 Cor 15:20.

167 In antiquity and late antiquity, "preliminary practices" were widely used training exercises in rhetorical education, for which students would craft their words to fit with predetermined literary genres and styles in order to learn how to develop an argument or narrative.

168 Nestorius refers to the Twelve Chapters appended to Cyril of Alexandria's *Third Letter to Nestorius*.

169 In Latin, *hominis genetrix*.

170 Schwartz detects a lacuna here, to fill which he suggests these words.

"Son," "Only-Begotten," and "Lord," the name signifies both, but to those who disapprove of this term we have offered the phrase "Theotokos and Anthropotokos" because it indicates the two natures, which is to say, the divinity and the humanity. As a result, no one can hide from the fact that we cannot run into the error of either Manichaeus or Paul [of Samosata], being protected against both. For whoever says that what is same-in-substance with us was born from the Virgin full of inseparable divinity proclaims the whole mystery of the Lord's economy in all its integrity. But the denial of any of these is the abrogation of the whole economy. Those who reject it have had [their reproach][171] turned back against their own head and will soon have it turned back even more.

3. But what is altogether worse and especially harmful and provokes the great indignation of Christ the Lord and is worthy of a thousand lightning strikes and thunderbolts is to say[172] that the deity of the Only-Begotten is mortal, that God the Word died, that he needed to rest in the tomb, and that he merited resurrection together with the flesh. All these are foreign to ecclesiastical orthodoxy and will never be accepted by us. Perish the thought that we should think that the divinity, which gives life to our first fruits, was at some point deprived of life and needed to be given life by another who was greater! If anyone says that the divinity, whose flesh did not see corruption,[173] was corrupted together with the flesh, how is he not to be regarded as in league with a demon? For the divinity is incorruptible and not susceptible to any change in accordance with what God said through the prophet, "I am *I am*, and I shall not be changed."[174]

4. Now, Your God-Beloved Soul can take all the writings of the fathers and learn from them that what we proclaim is orthodox and what those despicable people hope for is to vanquish the word of truth by theft. For by using names that are homonymous with the orthodox fathers, they attempt to seduce the more simple-minded. For instance, there is a certain Basil of Ancyra,[175] a man who was one of the heretics, and there is Basil of Caesarea

171 An emendation proposed by Loofs based upon Neh 4:4 and endorsed by Schwartz is also adopted here.

172 Schwartz unnecessarily added a word here.

173 See Acts 2:31.

174 Mal 3:6.

175 Basil of Ancyra was involved in the Trinitarian controversies of the fourth century and became a leader of the Homoiousian alliance in the 350s. He is credited with the authorship of *The Synodal Letter of the Council of Ancyra*, translated in CEECW 1 on pp. 134–149.

in Cappadocia, one of those who endured many dangers for the faith.[176] There is also one Melito, the heretic, and another Melito, the orthodox.[177] There is one Vitalis, who was a bishop of the orthodox, and another Vitalis, who was ordained by the impious Apollinarius.[178] There are many other [heretics] who have the same name [as orthodox fathers], but I won't go through each one. Using [the name Basil], they present the shared name to the simple-minded and by means of the homonym they lead into perdition those who do not realize that there is also a Basil of Ancyra. And by many names of this kind those skilled in abusing homonyms for deceptive purposes easily set snares.[179] But I beseech you not to be duped by this, as you are a vessel of the orthodox faith in all its integrity and purity. Deign to put your efforts into eliminating a heresy that depends on repeated acts of deception. For God is my witness that, if the teachings that are now being proclaimed, I know not how, by those most impure people were to prevail in the churches, the outcome would be nothing other than that the churches would cultivate the teachings handed down by Arius, Eunomius, and Apollinarius.[180]

5. But the Lord of all will demand of me nothing more than to make this matter known to those who can keep it from happening. Having done this from the beginning even to the present moment, I have not rested from constantly making this matter known also to you, the servants of God, so that you won't be inattentive to the nobility of godliness while it is being destroyed. Accordingly, if what is pertinent to orthodoxy were to receive due confirmation through your zeal, I would, with God as my witness, most readily renounce the honor of episcopacy. Perhaps you think I am just saying this? So that you won't, if godliness is confirmed and orthodoxy

176 Some works of Basil of Caesarea are translated in this volume on pp. 348–365.

177 It is unclear to which figures named Melito Nestorius refers. Given that the other two pairs with shared names lived in the fourth century, one wonders if the Latin *Meliton* is a corruption or mistranslation of the Greek *Melition* or *Meletion* (the Greek of the letter is lost). If so, Nestorius might be referring to the early fourth-century Melitius of Lycopolis, who initiated the Melitian schism in Egypt, and Meletius of Antioch, who briefly presided over the Council of Constantinople in 381.

178 The first Vitalis was an early fourth-century bishop of Antioch. The second Vitalis was an Apollinarian priest of Antioch who went to Rome around 375 and received a letter of approval from Bishop Damasus. He was actually ordained by Meletius of Antioch, not Apollinarius.

179 The Latin of the previous three sentences is defective and the translation here incorporates and rejects some of the emendations of Schwartz.

180 Nestorius here echoes the Eastern bishops who saw Cyril's Twelve Chapters as expressing of the views of Arius, Eunomius, and Apollinarius.

restored to the churches, require of me that at that point I bid you farewell from here[181] by letter and return voluntarily to my previous way of life in the monastery. For nothing is more divine or blessed to me than stillness of this kind. But I could wish too that the reports which they have issued against us and the most godly bishops of the East would come for discussion in the presence of the most pious and Christ-loving emperor, with either myself present there too or with others sent there, so that these too might rouse you to expel those who are throwing everything into disorder by their falsehoods. For of all the things they have reported nothing at all whatsoever is true.

*
* *

Report of the Easterners Written in Response to the Sacra Delivered by Count John[182]

(Written early August 431)

1. One may with good reason deem people today to be more blessed than those who lived before our generation, since they are governed by Your Sovereignty. For even though Your Piety is beset by a myriad of cares for the world, you have chosen to focus on pious worship above all else. And Your All-Praised Sovereignty values the things of God more than all things upon earth because faith in him dominates your thoughts and deeds and accomplishes all good by virtue of Your Piety. That this is so we learn continually from what happens, but this has become especially clear at the present time. For when unanticipated disturbances have halted the business of priests, with everyone in conflict with everyone else, and the fellowship of our college [of priests] has been badly shaken, with the Egyptian[183] as usual having thrown the world into confusion, the decree of Your Piety issued through the, in all respects, most magnificent and most glorious John, the count of all the largesses, would prove sufficient to calm the senseless passions of everybody, should we wish to show some restraint.

181 That is, in Ephesus.
182 *Collectio Atheniensis* 48 (ACO 1.1.7: 69–70 Schwartz) [Greek]; *Collectio Casinensis* 105 (ACO 1.4: 55–57 Schwartz) [Latin]; *Collectio Winteriana* 10 (ACO 1.5: 362–364 Schwartz) [Latin]. This report is translated in its entirety.
183 Cyril.

2. What is more important than everything is the command of Your Sovereignty in the letter itself to rid the orthodox faith of the offensive things imported into it by certain people and to use, as rule and norm, the faith expounded long ago by the fathers at Nicaea. Having nothing either missing or superfluous, it provides salvation in summary, encompassing in a few words everything whatsoever that the divine scriptures have handed down to us about piety and banishing the opinions of those who wish to introduce novelties to us and have wandered into error. For this reason, when we received the letter of Your Piety and noticed that the objective of Your Sovereignty was consistent with the orthodox faith of the fathers, we became eager to reject the chapters recently expounded by Cyril against the teaching of the gospels and apostles, in which he ventured to anathematize all the saints, both those alive now and those who had ever lived in the past. At present, having found an opportunity in the current confusion among the bishops, he has attempted to ratify the chapters by synodal authority, taking as his task the exploitation of the masses' ignorance, and also the sickness of some, which formerly was hidden but has now been made manifest by his arrogant wheedling.

3. But as Your Sovereignty knows, our most God-beloved and most holy father and bishop Acacius[184] also informed the holy synod by letter that these chapters were consistent with the impiety of Apollinarius. This he knows with certainty, as he is a man who has lived for one hundred and ten years, having spent all his life in apostolic labors, attended many synods, and always been in close proximity to those who share the views of Apollinarius. Accordingly, he could easily detect that the previously mentioned chapters fall into that heterodoxy.

4. Together with the most magnificent and most glorious count John, we beseeched the bishops, who had already been deceived and agreed to subscribe to the chapters, to reject them and to hold them as alien to the orthodox faith and to join us in subscribing to the orthodox faith of the fathers who assembled in Nicaea. When we were unable to persuade them because their preconceptions had turned evil, by ourselves we had to confess that this orthodox faith was impeccable, to subscribe to it, and to reject in a written confession that needless exposition of the chapters brimming with heterodoxy. For the confession of those few words of the orthodox faith suffices for both the refutation of all heretical error and the teaching

184 Of Beroea.

of the truth to those who want it. For on the issue of the divinity of the Only-Begotten, the aforementioned faith of the fathers permits no waffling, but by proclaiming "same-in-substance" kept the minds of the faithful unshakeable and destroyed the Arian heresy. And it handed down the precise boundaries of the economy, teaching us the immutability and unchangeability of the divinity of the Only-Begotten and declaring its conviction that our Lord Jesus Christ was not a mere human being, but really Son of God – a statement that harmonizes with the divine and holy scriptures. Accordingly, following their lead, we neither add anything to nor take away anything from the faith and exposition of the confession, since the exposition of the fathers suffices for everything.

5. Since you have commanded us, Most Pious Emperors, after this assent to the inviolable faith, that we inform Your Unsurpassable Piety about the holy and Theotokos Virgin (for the most magnificent and most holy count John told us this), now we inform Your Piety what we have been taught from the divine scriptures, having requested God's help – for it is better to do this than to attempt such things through human effort alone. By confessing our own weakness we are shutting out those who want to attack us for considering matters that surpass human capacity.[185]

6. Accordingly,[186] we confess that our Lord Jesus Christ, the only-begotten Son of God, was complete God and complete human being, of a rational soul and body. With respect to his divinity he was begotten before the ages from the Father and with respect to his humanity[187] was begotten at the end of days from the Virgin Mary. The same one was same-in-substance with the Father with respect to his divinity and same-in-substance with us with respect to his humanity.[188] For there occurred a union of two natures, on account of which we confess one Christ, one Son, one Lord. In keeping with this notion of the unconfused union we confess that the holy

185 This sentence is replicated verbatim in the Formula of Reunion of 433, which is included in Cyril's *Letter of Reunion to John of Antioch*, translated in this volume on pp. 718–725.

186 This entire paragraph is replicated verbatim in the Formula of Reunion of 433, with one exception, which is mentioned in the next note.

187 The Formula of Reunion reads, "and the same one with respect to his humanity … "

188 This is the first occasion where the so-called double consubstantiality of Christ is explicitly stated, that Christ is same-in-substance (*homoousios*) with the Father in respect of his divinity and same-in-substance (*homoousios*) with all human beings in respect of his humanity. The affirmation of Christ's consubstantial humanity was intended to rule out Apollinarianism, of which Cyril was suspected by the Easterners.

Virgin is Theotokos due to the fact that God the Word became incarnate and became human, uniting to himself from the very moment of the conception the temple taken from her.

7. Having been taught these things by the theologians, evangelists, apostles, prophets, and those in their time who were teachers of the pious faith, we have given a summary exposition. We call upon and beg Your Sovereignty to defend, as you usually do, pious worship, which is in danger of destruction from the sickness coming to it from the Egyptian chapters, and to decree that the priests presiding over the holy churches should reject the chapters introduced by the aforementioned Cyril into the orthodox faith for the corruption of the churches and that they should subscribe only to the confession of the holy fathers who assembled in Nicaea. For it is otherwise impossible to maintain peace in God's churches except to reject that impious exposition.

*

* *

Letter of John of Antioch and Others to Rufus of Thessalonica[189]

(October 431)

To the most God-beloved and most sacred fellow minister Rufus: Greetings in the Lord from John, Himerius, Theodoret, and the rest.

We believe that piety and ecclesiastical peace have been greatly harmed by the absence of Your Holiness. For your presence would have put a halt to the confusion that has arisen and the disorder that has been ventured, and it would have battled alongside us [40] against the heresies that have been introduced into the orthodox faith and the teaching of the gospels and apostles, which children have always received from their fathers and passed all the way down to us. Yet we do not say this without reason, but because we have learned of another objective of Your Sacredness from what was written by Your Godliness to the most God-beloved and most holy Julian the bishop of Serdica. For the letter declared that it was necessary for the aforementioned most godly bishop to join in the battle for

189 *Collectio Vaticana* 97 (ACO 1.1.3: 39–42 Schwartz) [Greek]. There is no ancient Latin version. This letter is translated in its entirety.

the faith that was expounded by the blessed fathers assembled at Nicaea and not to allow a blotch to be introduced into those brief words which suffice to demonstrate the truth and refute falsehood. Your Sacredness gave this instruction rightly, justly, and piously, and the recipient of the letter followed the counsel of the letter. But many of those present at the synod "turned away," as the prophet says, and "become depraved,"[190] abandoning the faith they had received from the fathers and subscribing to the Twelve Chapters of Cyril of Alexandria, which are full of the heterodoxy of Apollinarius, and moreover they accord with the impiety of Arius and Eunomius and anathematize everyone who does not accept this blatant impiety. We who have assembled from the East and others from various dioceses have stood firmly opposed to this outrage against the faith so that the faith expounded at Nicaea by the blessed fathers may be confirmed. For as Your Holiness knows, it is in no way deficient for the teaching of the doctrines of the gospels and for the refutation of every heresy. We have continued to battle on its behalf, while at the same time holding all the pleasures and pains of life to be of little account, in order to preserve this ancestral inheritance intact.

For this reason, we have subjected Cyril and Memnon to deposition, the former because he is a heresiarch and the latter because he is his collaborator and fights for him in every way to get the chapters expounded for the ruin of the churches confirmed and established. And we have excommunicated those who dared to subscribe and assent to the doctrines that are contrary to piety until they anathematize them and return to the faith of the holy fathers who gathered at Nicaea. But our patience has profited them nothing. For up to the present day they fight on behalf of their corrupt doctrines. They have impaled themselves on the canonical rule that clearly stipulates that if any bishop deposed by a synod, or any presbyter or deacon deposed by his bishop, permits himself the liturgy without awaiting the synod's judgment, he no longer has the opportunity for defense, not even at another synod, but he and those in communion with him are entirely expelled from the church. Both those who were deposed and those who were excommunicated have broken this rule. For immediately upon learning that their deposition and excommunication had taken place they celebrated the liturgy together and continue to celebrate it, clearly as if

190 Ps 13(14):3.

they are unfaithful to one who said, "Whatever you bind on earth shall be bound in heaven."[191]

We considered informing Your Holiness of these things immediately, but because we expected some change in the distressing situation to happen we have waited until now. But our hope has proven to be false. For they have continued to fight on behalf of this impious heresy and show no respect even to the counsel of the most pious emperor. **[41]** For he has already met with us and them five times and commanded them either to reject the chapters of Cyril as contrary to the faith or to take up the battle on their behalf and demonstrate that they are consistent with the confession of the blessed fathers.[192] For we ourselves have proofs ready by which we can show that they are a direct attack on the teachers of orthodoxy and thoroughly accord with the teaching of the heretics. For through these very chapters the begetter of these wicked offspring teaches that it was the divinity of the only-begotten Son of God that suffered and not the humanity that he assumed for our salvation, obviously with the indwelling divinity appropriating the sufferings as being of his own body, but suffering nothing in his own nature. And in addition to this, he teaches that the result is one nature of divinity and humanity. For he has interpreted "The Word became flesh" in the sense that the divinity underwent a certain change and was transformed into flesh. In addition to this, he anathematizes those who distinguish the sayings about Christ the Master in the gospels and apostles and attribute the lowly sayings to the humanity and the ones appropriate for God to the divinity of Christ. This is precisely how the Arians and Eunomians think, who referred the lowly sayings about the economy to the divinity and contorted themselves in claiming that God the Word was a creature and something made and was different-in-substance from the Father and unlike him. Hence, if any blasphemy results, it is easy to spot. For it introduces a confusion of the natures and attributes [the following passages] to God the Word: "My God, my God, why have you forsaken me?"[193] and "Father, if possible, let this cup pass from me,"[194] and the hunger and the thirst,[195] and the being strengthened by an angel,[196] and the saying, "Now my soul is troubled,"[197] and "My soul is very sorrowful, even

191 Matt 18:18. Here John refers to the events on Sunday, June 28: see above, p. 665.
192 Here John refers to the meetings in Chalcedon: see above, pp. 670–671.
193 Matt 27:46. 194 Matt 26:39. 195 See Matt 4:2; John 19:28.
196 Luke 22:43. 197 John 12:27.

unto death,"[198] and all such things that happened to the humanity of the Lord. Anyone can see without any effort that such things clearly accord with the impiety of Arius and Eunomius. For those men, being unable to set "different-in-substance" on a solid foundation, attribute the sufferings and the lowly sayings to the divinity of Christ, as mentioned above. Let Your Godliness know that the Arian teachers currently teach in their churches nothing other than that those who teach "same-in-substance" currently share the beliefs of Arius and that after a long time the truth has appeared.[199]

But as for us, we abide by the doctrines of the blessed fathers who assembled at Nicaea and those after them who were well known for this teaching – Eustathius of Antioch, Basil of Caesarea, Gregory, John, Athanasius, Theophilus, Damasus of Rome, Ambrose of Milan, and those who taught the same as them – and we follow in their pious footsteps. For following the statements of the gospels, apostles, and prophets, they left behind for us a precise rule of orthodoxy, which all of us living in the East strive to keep unwavering and unshakeable, as do likewise those of Bithynia, Paphlagonia, Cappadocia Secunda, Pisidia, Dacia, Moesia, Thessaly, Europe, Rhodope, and many others from various provinces. And it is clear that the Italians also do not support this novelty. For the most God-beloved and most holy Martin the bishop of Milan sent a letter to us and forwarded to the most pious emperor a book **[42]** of the blessed Ambrose on the Lord's humanification, which teaches the opposite of these heretical chapters.[200]

Let Your Holiness know that it was not enough for Cyril and Memnon to commit outrages against the orthodox faith, but they have also trampled upon all the canons. For they immediately received into communion not only those who had been excommunicated by various dioceses and provinces, but also others charged with heresy who hold the same views as Caelestius and Pelagius (for they are Euchites, or Enthusiasts,[201] because of which they were excommunicated by the governor and metropolitan). De-

198 Matt 26:38.

199 In this polemical jab John claims that present-day Arians think that present-day pro-Nicenes (like Cyril) have finally espoused the Christology long held by Arians.

200 This work is likely Ambrose's *On the Mystery of the Lord's Incarnation*.

201 Christians who devoted their lives solely to prayer in order to arrive at union with God in ways considered contrary to norms were sometimes labeled Euchites (*euchetai* in Greek, meaning "those who pray"). They were also known as Enthusiasts and Messalians.

spising proper ecclesiastical procedure, then, they received all of these people into communion, gathering a multitude around themselves from everywhere, striving to issue doctrine more tyrannically than piously. For since they are denuded of piety, out of necessity they have concocted for themselves another means of influence, a human one, aiming to battle against the faith of the fathers with a flood of money.[202] But none of this will benefit them, since Your Sacredness is strong and defends piety as usual.

So then, we beseech you, Most Holy Master, to guard against communion with those who have ventured these things and introduce this heresy, and to inform everybody near and far that these are the chapters for which the thrice-blessed Damasus[203] deposed the heretics Apollinarius, Vitalis, and Timothy,[204] and that one must not automatically accept the letter sent by [Cyril], in which he obscures his heretical opinions and applies a veneer of pious doctrine. For in the chapters he laid his impiety quite bare, and here even dared to anathematize those with different beliefs, while in the letter he used cunning in his attempt to seduce the more simple-minded.[205] So Your Sacredness should not disregard this matter lest later, when you see that heresy has prevailed, you feel pain and are aggrieved to no avail, as you are no longer able to come to the aid of piety.

We have also sent a copy of the document which we presented to our most pious and Christ-loving emperor, which includes the faith of the holy fathers at Nicaea. In it we rejected the heretical chapters recently introduced by Cyril, judging them to be foreign to the orthodox faith. Since only eight of us have come to Constantinople, as the most pious emperor instructed, we have also appended the copy of the authorization we were given by the holy synod, to make known the provinces represented at it, which Your Sacredness can learn from the subscriptions of the metropolitans.[206]

We greet all the brothers with you.

*

* *

202 A list of the bribes Cyril gave to imperial officials survives in *Collectio Casinensis* 294 (ACO 1.4: 224–225 Schwartz).

203 Bishop of Rome, 366–384.

204 On the Apollinarian Vitalis, see note 178 above. Timothy of Beirut was another disciple of Apollinarius.

205 John notes a rhetorical discrepancy between the *Third Letter to Nestorius* itself and the Twelve Anathemas appended to it.

206 Both the documents John mentions here are extant: see *Collectio Vaticana* 96 (ACO 1.1.3: 36–39 Schwartz).

Homily of John of Antioch Delivered in Chalcedon after Theodoret Spoke[207]

(Preached late October 431)

It is a sacred law that fathers are to be given credit for what their children do. Well then, "Gilead is mine; Manasseh is mine,"[208] or rather not mine but God's, who gathered your sacred flock unto us and granted it steadfastness in piety along with other goods. But as for me, I have stood up in your midst as much to speak to you as to greet you and simultaneously to bid you farewell. For now we are leaving after having stayed with you, but we are still with you when we depart to your brothers. For it is the nature of love to spread everywhere without impediment. I greet you and exhort you to be at peace with God, you who were formerly faithful but now are also confessors. Everyone who is convinced that he has obtained something of great worth courageously fights for it and does not shrink from toiling for what he has acquired lest he surrender what he possesses. So then, let no one deprive you of the patrimonial faith, which we too must entrust to our children as an inheritance. Look to your ancestors: neither torture nor death nor anything else human could deprive them of genuine faith. In our case slight are the threats but great is the reward; slight are the sufferings but great are the crowns. Let no one rob you of the inheritance, I mean, precision in doctrines. Let no one persuade you to believe that the divinity is passible or that there is one nature of body and divinity. For the latter is the self-divine[209] substance, but the former he assumed. For this reason we proclaim conjunction and not confusion, union not mixture. The former is God because of the latter; the former is the Son because of the latter. The former is everything because of the latter. The former is worshiped together with the latter; the former has been glorified together with the latter. And being conjoined to the latter inseparably and always, the former is considered the first fruits of our nature. Guard these things, and the God of peace will be with you, defending you in the way that he himself knows. To him be glory forever. Amen.

207 *Collectio Atheniensis* 72 (ACO 1.1.7: 84 Schwartz) [Greek]; *Collectio Casinensis* 126 (ACO 1.4: 79 Schwartz) [Latin]; *Collectio Winteriana* 25 (ACO 1.5: 381 Schwartz) [Latin]. This homily is translated in its entirety.

208 Ps 59(60):9.

209 In Greek, *autotheia*.

50

Cyril of Alexandria, *Letter of Reunion to John of Antioch*

Introduction and Translation by Matthew R. Crawford

INTRODUCTION

The two rival parties that met in Ephesus in July 431, one led by Cyril and his allies and the other by Nestorius and John of Antioch, failed to reach an accord and instead each condemned the legitimacy of the other. Emperor Theodosius II then intervened by arranging for a smaller group of representatives from each side to have a series of meetings in Chalcedon under his personal supervision. With Cyril under house arrest in Ephesus and Nestorius deposed and sent into exile, it was hoped that the two sides could achieve reconciliation. Some of the Easterners (so called because they came from the Roman diocese of Oriens or "East"), including John of Antioch himself, were willing to agree to Nestorius's excommunication, but they continued to hold that Cyril's Twelve Anathemas (also called the Twelve Chapters) appended to his *Third Letter to Nestorius* were tainted with heresy (especially Apollinarianism) and so insisted that they too had to be condemned. As these negotiations stretched into October, it became evident that a resolution would not be achieved in the short term, so Theodosius finally released all the bishops to disperse to their sees, including Cyril who had already departed for Alexandria. Thus, the Council of Ephesus formally came to an end with the two parties of the Eastern church still in a state of disunion. By mid-432 Theodosius, prompted by a letter from Pope Celestine, began afresh the efforts at reunion, dispatching imperial officials to travel to Antioch and Alexandria, and enlisting the help of the two most respected ascetics at the time, Simeon Stylites and Acacius of Beroea. Initially the Easterners continued to demand that Cyril's Twelve Anathemas be condemned and that the only standard for orthodoxy should be the Nicene Creed and Athanasius's *Letter to Epictetus*, the latter thought to be an epistle directed against the Apollinarian heresy and thus at odds with Cyril's Twelve Anathemas.[1]

At this stage of the controversy Cyril notably shifted his strategy. Whereas he had been uncompromising on the deposition of Nestorius, he now sensed that the other Easterners did not maintain as extreme a Christological duality as had the former bishop of Constantinople and were, in their own terms, seeking to maintain the single subjectivity of Christ. As a result, he was open to reconciliation with the Easterners, and although he refused to recant the Twelve Anathemas, he went to great lengths to explain why they were not Apollinarian as the Easterners suspected. These negotiations carried on for months and were finally resolved when the Easterners agreed to the deposition of Nestorius, and Cyril agreed to sign a statement of faith provided by them, with the issue of the Twelve Anathemas being quietly dropped. The expression of faith that formed the basis for restored unity was a slightly revised version of the statement the Easterners had put forward in the meetings in Chalcedon from the previous year, including the addition of the words "the same," one of Cyril's hallmark Christological terms. The present letter, written in the spring of 433, is Cyril's announcement to John of Antioch that the peace of the church had been restored and cites at length the statement of faith produced by the Easterners, now known as the Formula of Reunion, which famously includes a statement of the double consubstantiality of Christ (the idea that Christ is both same-in-substance with the Father and same-in-substance with all humanity). This letter was read out at the Council of Chalcedon in 451, receiving approbation from all the bishops assembled there.

This translation is based on the critical text of Eduard Schwartz, *Concilium Universale Ephesenum*, ACO 1.1.4 (Berlin: De Gruyter, 1927), 15–20.

TRANSLATION

To the lord John, my beloved brother and fellow minister, Cyril sends greetings in the Lord.

1. "Let the heavens rejoice and let the earth exult."[2] For "the dividing wall of partition has been abolished,"[3] our suffering has come to an end, and all manner of discord has been taken away, since Christ, the Savior

1 Translated in this volume on pp. 279–290. 2 Ps 95(96):11. 3 Eph 2:14.

of us all, has awarded peace to his churches, and since our most pious and divinely favored emperors[4] have called us to this. For having become excellent and zealous followers of their ancestral piety, they are protecting the orthodox faith firm and unshaken in their own souls, and are exercising remarkable oversight toward the holy churches, so that they might also have glorious renown forever and demonstrate that theirs is a most illustrious empire. To them the Lord of powers himself distributes goods by his abundant hand, granting them rule over their opponents and gracing them with victory. For he who says, "As I live, says the Lord, the one who glorifies me I will glorify," cannot deceive.[5]

2. So then, when my lord Paul,[6] the most devout brother and fellow minister, came to Alexandria, we became filled with joy, and for good reason, with such a man acting as a mediator and choosing to undertake such difficult labors. For he came in order that he might conquer the envy of the devil and unite that which had been divided and, after removing the stumbling-blocks standing in the way, crown the churches – both those among you and those among us – with harmony and peace. It would be useless now to state the manner in which they had been divided; I believe we ought rather to reflect on and speak of what is suitable to the time of peace. And so, we were delighted by our conversation with that most devout man just mentioned, who had perhaps imagined that it would be no small struggle to persuade us that it is necessary to unite the churches in peace, and do away with the laughter of the heterodox and, what's more, to render dull the sharp point of the devil's perversity. But upon arrival he found us so ready for this that he undertook no trouble at all. For we had in mind the Savior who said, "My peace I give you. My peace I leave with you,"[7] and we have also been taught to say in prayer, "O Lord, our God, give us peace, for you have given us all things."[8] So, if someone should be a partaker of this God-given peace, he will lack nothing that is good.

4 A reference to Theodosius II, emperor in the East, along with his Western counterpart Valentinian III, though only the former had any role in bringing about the reunion of the churches.

5 1 Sam 2:30.

6 Paul, bishop of Emesa, had been dispatched by John of Antioch to travel to Alexandria with the imperial officials to lead the peace negotiations, bringing with him the statement of faith composed by John and Theodoret for Cyril to sign. After anathematizing Nestorius, he preached in the cathedral church of Alexandria on Christmas Day 432, calling the Virgin Theotokos, to the acclaim of the assembled crowd.

7 John 14:27. 8 Isa 26:12.

3. Now we had by this point become convinced that the dissension of the churches was unnecessary and without any foundation, when my lord, the most devout bishop Paul produced a document bearing an unimpeachable confession of faith and confirmed that this had been composed by both Your Holiness and the most devout bishops in the same place. And the document is now given word for word, inserted into this our letter:

> 4. Now what we think and say about the Theotokos Virgin and the manner of the humanification of the only-begotten Son of God – that which we hold, having received it from the beginning from both the divine scriptures and the tradition of the holy fathers – this we must state briefly, not as a supplement but in the form of an assurance, adding nothing whatsoever to the faith of the holy fathers expounded at Nicaea. For, as we have just said, it suffices for knowledge of all piety and the excommunication of every heretical false opinion. And as we speak, we are not striving for what is beyond our reach, but, by confessing our own weakness, we are speaking so as to shut out those who want to attack us for considering matters that surpass human capacity. 5. Accordingly, we confess that our Lord Jesus Christ, the only-begotten Son of God, was complete God and complete human being of rational soul and body. With respect to his deity he was begotten before the ages from the Father, and the same one with respect to his humanity was begotten at the end of days from the Virgin Mary for us and for our salvation. The same one was same-in-substance with the Father with respect to his deity and same-in-substance with us with respect to his humanity.[9] For there occurred a union of two natures, on account of which we confess one Christ, one Son, and one Lord. In keeping with this notion of unconfused union, we confess that the holy Virgin is Theotokos due to the fact that God the Word became incarnate and became human, uniting to

9 As in the report of the Easterners written in response to the imperial sacra delivered by Count John (translated in this volume on pp. 709–712), here the so-called double consubstantiality of Christ is explicitly stated, that Christ is same-in-substance (*homoousios*) with the Father in respect of his divinity and same-in-substance (*homoousios*) with all human beings in respect of his humanity. The affirmation of Christ's consubstantial humanity was intended to rule out Apollinarianism, of which Cyril continued to be suspected by his opponents, but it equally counters the doctrine of Eutyches which would emerge at the end of the following decade.

himself from the very moment of conception the temple taken from her. And as for the evangelical and apostolic sayings about the Lord, we recognize that the men of divine speech[10] have made some statements to be common, as referring to one person,[11] and have distinguished others, as referring to two natures, handing down the divinely fitting ones with respect to the deity of Christ and the lowly ones with respect to his humanity.

6. When we read these holy words of yours and found that we too think likewise (for "there is one Lord, one faith, one baptism"[12]), we glorified God the Savior of all, rejoicing with one another that both the churches among us and those among you hold the faith which agrees with the divinely inspired scriptures and the tradition of our holy fathers.

7. And when I learned that certain niggling persons, who are like fierce wasps buzzing around, spitting out fallacious words against me – as if I said that the holy body of Christ was brought down from heaven and did not come from the holy Virgin[13] – I thought it necessary to say a few things on this topic to these people. O foolish people who know only how to accuse falsely, how were you misled into this notion and how have you become sick with such stupidity? For clearly you must know that nearly our entire struggle on behalf of the faith has been waged with the insistence that the holy Virgin is Theotokos. But if we say that the holy body of Christ, the Savior of us all, was begotten from heaven and not from her, how would she be regarded as Theotokos? For in short to whom did she give birth, unless it is true that she has begotten the Emmanuel according to the flesh? So let those people be laughed at who are spreading such nonsense about me!

8. For the blessed prophet Isaiah is not lying when he says, "Behold the virgin will conceive and bear a son and they will call his name Emmanuel, which is translated 'God with us.'"[14] And surely the holy Gabriel also is speaking the truth when he says to the blessed Virgin, "Do not fear, Mary, for you have found favor with God, and behold, you will conceive in your womb and will bear a son and you will call his name Jesus."[15] "For he will save his people from their sins."[16] And whenever we

10 That is, the authors of "the evangelical and apostolic sayings about the Lord."
11 In Greek, *prosōpon*. 12 Eph 4:5.
13 A reference to Cyril's suspected Apollinarianism. Apollinarius was thought to teach that Christ's flesh came down from heaven, such that he was a "heavenly human being." See the writings of Apollinarius translated in this volume on pp. 301–347.
14 Isa 7:14, quoted in Matt 1:23. 15 Luke 1:30–31. 16 Matt 1:23.

say that our Lord Jesus Christ is from heaven and from above, it is not as if we say such things because his holy flesh was brought down from heaven above. Rather, we are following the divine Paul, who so clearly cried out, "The first human being was dust from the earth; the second human being, the Lord, is from heaven."[17] And we also bear in mind the Savior himself, who said, "No one has ascended into heaven except the one who came down from heaven, the Son of Man,"[18] yet surely he was, as I just said, begotten according to the flesh from the holy Virgin. And when God the Word descended from heaven above, "he emptied himself, taking the form of a slave,"[19] and he took the name "Son of Man" while remaining what he was, namely God (for he is according to his nature unchanging and immutable). And so, understood as already being one with his own flesh, he is said to come down from heaven and is also named "the human being from heaven,"[20] being complete in deity and the same one complete in humanity, and so perceived as one person.[21] For "there is one Lord Jesus Christ,"[22] even though we do not ignore the difference between the natures, from which we say that the mysterious union has been accomplished.

9. And as for those who say that there occurred a blending or confusion or mixture of God the Word with the flesh, let Your Holiness bid them to be silent. For it seems that such people repeat these things about me as though I thought or said them, but I am so far from thinking any such thing that I regard as mad anyone who in any way thinks that a "shadow of change"[23] could occur with respect to the divine nature of the Word. For it[24] remains what it is and "has never changed,"[25] nor would it ever change or be capable of admitting change. And, in addition, we all confess that the Word of God is impassible, even if he also, managing the mystery of the economy with all wisdom, is seen to be assigning to himself the sufferings that befell his own flesh. Indeed, the all-wise Peter also says, "Christ suffered on our behalf in the flesh"[26] and not in the nature of the inexpressible deity. For in order that he might be believed to be the Savior of all, he refers the sufferings of his own flesh to himself, as I said, in an economical appropriation. Something similar was spoken ahead of time through the prophet's voice,

17 1 Cor 15:47. 18 John 3:13. 19 Phil 2:7. 20 See 1 Cor 15:47.

21 In Greek, *prosōpon*. 22 1 Cor 8:6. 23 Jas 1:17.

24 The grammar of the sentence requires that the subject of the verbs must be the "nature" of the Word rather than the "Word" himself.

25 See Mal 3:6. 26 1 Pet 4:1.

as if in his person: "I gave my back for lashes and my cheeks for blows, and I did not turn my face away from the shame of spittings."[27]

10. So now let Your Holiness be assured – and let no one else doubt either – that we everywhere follow the opinions of the holy fathers, especially those of our father, the blessed and all-praised Athanasius, refusing to go beyond them in anything. I would have also adduced many passages from the fathers,[28] confirming my own words from theirs, except that I was concerned about the length of the letter, lest it should consequently become tedious. And in no way are we allowing the faith – or rather the symbol of the faith – defined by our holy fathers who once gathered at Nicaea to be shaken by anyone. Nor do we permit ourselves or anyone else either to change a word of what was laid down there or to go beyond one syllable, recalling the one who said, "Do not remove the eternal boundaries which your fathers have set."[29] For they were not the ones speaking, but rather the Spirit of God the Father,[30] who "proceeds from him,"[31] and yet is not alien to the Son according to the principle of substance. And on this topic the words of the holy mystagogues[32] provide confirmation for us. For in the Acts of the Apostles it is written, "When they had come through Mysia they tried to enter Bithynia, and the Spirit of Jesus did not permit them."[33] And the divine Paul writes, "Those who are in the flesh cannot please God. And you are not in the flesh but in the Spirit, if the Spirit of God lives in you. And if someone has the Spirit of Christ, he belongs to him."[34] So whenever one of those people who are used to perverting orthodoxy should distort my words in whatever way seems right to them, let not Your Holiness marvel at this, knowing that those from every heresy also collect

27 Isa 50:6. "Face" here translates the Greek *prosōpon*.

28 Cyril is alluding to the practice of appealing to authoritative figures of the past to support one's position, a tactic used in the fourth century by Athanasius and Basil of Caesarea. However, in the fifth century this developed into a more formal and even scholastic undertaking with the emergence of the florilegium genre, which consisted of a collection of extracts from earlier authors. Cyril prepared such florilegia himself, appending them to his anti-Nestorian treatises sent to the imperial household and deploying them as a part of the case against Nestorius at the Council of Ephesus.

29 Prov 22:28. The English translation obscures the fact that the word "boundary" (*horion*) in Greek is related to the word "defined" (*horizō*) used in the previous sentence to describe the actions of the fathers at Nicaea. Hence, Cyril understands this passage to be referring to boundaries in the specific sense of "definitions."

30 See Matt 10:20. 31 See John 15:26.

32 A favorite word of Cyril to describe those who provide instruction in divine truth, especially Trinitarian dogma.

33 Acts 16:7. 34 Rom 8:8–9.

from the divinely inspired scripture the material for their error, corrupting what was rightly spoken through the Holy Spirit by turning it to their perversity, thereby drawing down unquenchable flames upon their own heads.

11. Now since we have learned that some have caused injury to many by going as far as to publish a corrupted version of the orthodox letter that our father, the all-praised Athanasius, wrote to the blessed Epictetus,[35] we thought it useful, even necessary, for the brethren to send copies to Your Holiness from the ancient exemplars that have been preserved correctly among us.[36]

35 Athanasius's *Letter to Epictetus* (which may be found earlier in this volume on pp. 279–290) played an important role in the dispute surrounding the Council of Ephesus. An extract from the letter was included in the florilegium cited at the Council against Nestorius (ACO 1.1.2: 40 Schwartz). Nevertheless, Cyril's opponents also thought the letter supported their cause, since they suspected Cyril of being an Apollinarian, and the letter was understood to be directed against the Apollinarians. It is curious that he here suggests that corrupted copies of the letter have been deliberately circulated to support the cause of his opponents. No such version has survived, and it is unclear what sort of changes the supposed faulty version would have included. The corrupted version of the letter is also mentioned in Cyril's *First Letter to Succensus*.

36 Cyril here refers to the *antigrapha*, that is, the copies made when Athanasius originally wrote the letter, which were deposited in the ecclesiastical archive in Alexandria.

51

Ibas of Edessa, *Letter to Mari the Persian*

Introduction and Translation by Bradley K. Storin

INTRODUCTION

Ibas was the bishop of Edessa from 435 to 457. In 449 the second Council of Ephesus deposed him and several other bishops for their dyophysite ("Nestorian") views, but the Council of Chalcedon exonerated and reinstated him in 451. A century later he would gain infamy as the author of one of the Three Chapters – the letter to the otherwise unknown Persian cleric Mari translated here – that Emperor Justinian had condemned at the second Council of Constantinople in 553. Written in the mid-430s after Cyril of Alexandria and John of Antioch had agreed to the so-called Formula of Reunion, Ibas's *Letter to Mari* is important for its succinct narrative account of the Council of Ephesus in 431 and the reconciliation between Cyril of Alexandria and John of Antioch in 433, as well as for the window it provides on the Christological divisions within the Christian community in Osrhoene.

While a priest under Bishop Rabbula, Ibas attended the raucous Council of Ephesus in 431 that culminated in the deposition of Nestorius of Constantinople. He writes about it in this letter, but he also celebrates the cessation of hostility between Cyril and John without letting Cyril off the hook. Ibas criticizes him as an unsavory individual (initiating the council's proceedings early and bewitching everyone present with a magic spell) with an unsavory Christology ("one nature" of Christ) communicated in an unsavory text (the Twelve Anathemas contained in his *Third Letter to Nestorius*).[1] Only after Cyril anathematized his previous statements and those who abided by them, Ibas writes, did the Lord "soften his heart" and allow the reconciliation to occur.

Ibas also gives readers a sense of the local tensions in Edessa, an intellectually rich city at the eastern edge of the Roman Empire. He designates

1 Translated in this volume on pp. 623–636.

his episcopal predecessor Rabbula, known for his advocacy for Cyril's "one nature" Christology and his penchant for violence in the service of orthodoxy, as a "despot" who spoke ill of Theodore of Mopsuestia (ca. 350–428) and tried to round up all existing copies of his books in Osrhoene. Of course, as becomes clear in this text, Ibas rejected Rabbula's Christology and embraced Theodore as the orthodox source of his own Christological tradition.[2] By 489 Ibas's followers had dissociated themselves from the organization at Edessa, moving east to the frontier city of Nisibis.

The text from which this translation was made is Eduard Schwartz, *Concilium Universale Chalcedonense*, ACO 2.1.3 (Berlin: De Gruyter, 1935), 32–34. The paragraph breaks have been made by the translator for ease of reading.

TRANSLATION

A translation of a letter[3] written by the most pious Ibas, bishop of the city of the Edessenes, to Mari the Persian. After the epistolary opening, [the text begins:]

It is to Your Brilliant Intelligence, which can fully comprehend many things with [only] a few words, that we strive to succinctly inform you of what happened here [both] earlier and currently. For we know that by writing this to Your Godliness our claim will become known to everyone there through your effort, that the God-given scriptures have admitted no alteration.

I'll begin my account with narratives that you yourself know well. A conflict has broken out since Your Godliness was last here between these two people, Nestorius and Cyril, and they composed harmful arguments against each other, which caused those who heard them to stumble.[4] Indeed, as Your Godliness also understands, Nestorius said in his arguments that the blessed Mary is not Theotokos, and consequently many people considered him to belong to the heresy of Paul of Samosata, who said that Christ is a mere human being.[5] But in his desire to refute Nestorius's arguments, Cyril lapsed and was found to have fallen into the teaching of Apollinarius.[6] Yes, Cyril even wrote like Apollinarius, that God the Word himself became a human

2 The fragments of Theodore's *On the Incarnation* are translated in this volume on pp. 420–488.

3 This letter was originally written in Syriac.

4 See 1 Cor 8:9.

5 *Selected Fragments* of Paul of Samosata are translated in this volume on pp. 197–211. In his *Protest* Eusebius of Dorylaeum was the first to connect Nestorius with Paul, translated in this volume on pp. 559–563.

6 Several writings of Apollinarius are translated in this volume on pp. 301–347.

being in such a way that there was no difference between the temple and the one who dwelled within it. Indeed, he wrote in the Twelve Chapters,[7] as I would guess Your Godliness knows, that there is one nature of the divinity and the humanity of our Lord Jesus Christ, with the result that it isn't necessary, he claims, to distinguish the sayings that were said, either the ones the Lord spoke about himself or those the evangelists [spoke] about him. Even before we say it, Your Holiness will know the degree of impiety that these words have ginned up. For how can "In the beginning was the Word"[8] be taken to refer to the temple begotten from Mary, or how can "You have made him a little less than the angels"[9] be said about the divinity of the Only-Begotten? Indeed, as even Your Godliness understands, and was both taught and confirmed **[33]** by the divine teaching from the words of the blessed fathers from the beginning, the church speaks like this: two natures, one power, one person, who is one Son Lord Jesus Christ.

Because of that conflict, the victorious and pious emperors commanded that the leading bishops be convened in the city of the Ephesians, and the arguments of Nestorius and Cyril be judged by all. But before all the bishops who were commanded to be convened had come to Ephesus, the same Cyril took the initiative and preempted the trial of everything with a magic spell that blinded the eyes of the wise. He found a pretext in [his] hatred for Nestorius. Even before the most holy and God-beloved archbishop John arrived at the synod, they deposed Nestorius from the episcopate with neither trial nor investigation. Two days after his deposition, though, we came to Ephesus; when we learned that, at the deposition of Nestorius that they enacted, they referred to and confirmed the Twelve Chapters that Cyril had authored, which stood contrary to the true faith, and assented to them as if they were harmonious with the true faith, all the Eastern bishops[10] deposed Cyril himself and decreed an order of excommunication against the other bishops who had assented to the Chapters. And after this mess each returned to his respective city, but Nestorius could not return to his city[11] since it and its bigwigs hated him.[12] The Easterners' synod continued

7 The list of anathemas that Cyril includes at the end of his third and final letter to Nestorius, which is translated in this volume on pp. 623–636.

8 John 1:1. 9 Heb 2:7, quoting Ps 8:6.

10 So called because they were from the diocese of Oriens or "East."

11 That is, Constantinople.

12 Nestorius lived the rest of his life in exile, and in 435 Emperor Theodosius II ordered that his books be burned. He died sometime after 450, perhaps after the Council of Chalcedon in 451.

to refuse communion with those bishops who were in communion with Cyril. Because of these things, a great deal of misery arose between them, with bishops in conflict with bishops and faction with faction. In the deed, the scriptures were fulfilled: "Let a person's enemies be his housemates."[13]

From this point pagans and heretics issued many reproaches against us. Indeed, no one dared to travel from one city to another or from one place to another, but each persecuted his neighbor as an enemy. Many, who did not keep the fear of God before their eyes, or with the pretense of zeal that they had for their churches, strived to put into action the hatred concealed in their heart. One of these turned out to be the despot of our city[14] – even you are not ignorant about him! – who, under the pretense of faith, exacted vengeance not only on the living, but also on those who long ago departed for the Lord. One of these was the blessed Theodore, herald of truth and teacher of the church, who not only during his life pummeled heretics into his true faith, but even after death left to the church's children a spiritual weapon in his treatises, as Your Godliness also knows, you who kept his company and were persuaded by the works written by him. He who dared all these things dared publicly in church to anathematize him who not only turned his own city from error to the truth out of his zeal for God, but also educated faraway churches with his teaching. And concerning his books, an exhaustive inquiry took place everywhere, not because they were alien to the true faith (for, really, while [Theodore] was living, [Rabbula] would frequently praise him and read his books), but because of his concealed hatred that he had for him, since he rebuked him publicly in the synod.

While these evil things took place among them,[15] and each departed however he wanted, as it is written,[16] our venerable God, who in his loving-kindness is always concerned for the church, inspired the heart of the most faithful and victorious emperor to send a great and well-known courtier to compel the most holy archbishop of the East, lord John, to be reconciled with Cyril. For he had deposed [Cyril] from the episcopate. After receiving the emperor's letter, [John] dispatched the most holy and God-beloved Paul, bishop of Emesa; he wrote through him the true faith and commanded him to enter into communion with [Cyril], so long as Cyril assented to this faith and anathematized those who say that the divinity suffered and

13 Matt 10:36. 14 Rabbula, bishop of Edessa from 412 to 435.
15 That is, Cyril's supporters. 16 Passage unknown, but perhaps a reference to Joel 2:7.

those who say that there is one nature of the divinity and the humanity. But the Lord, who is always concerned for his own church that was redeemed with his own blood, chose to soften the Egyptian's heart too, so that even he assented to the faith without irritation, accepted it, and anathematized all those who believed outside of [the true church]. And once they entered into communion with each other, the conflict was taken from their midst; there was peace in the church and no longer did a schism remain in it, but peace was there as previously.

As to what the words were that the most holy and God-beloved archbishop John wrote, and as to how he accepted Cyril's response, I have sent to Your Sanctity the letters themselves as an appendix [to this letter] for Your Godliness so that, by reading them, you may know and proclaim to all our peace-loving brothers that the conflict has finally ceased, that the wall between enemies has come down, and that those who, with no discipline, came against the living and the dead now stand in shame, accounting for their shortcomings and teaching points contrary to their initial teaching.[17] For no one dares say that there is one nature of the divinity and the humanity; rather, they confess [their belief] in the temple and in the one who dwells in it, the one Son, Jesus Christ. I am writing these words to Your Godliness with the tremendous affection that I have for you, convinced that Your Holiness is training yourself in God's teaching, night and day, so that you might benefit many.

17 Cyril's *Letter of Reunion to John of Antioch* is translated in this volume on pp. 718–725.

52

Cyril of Alexandria, *First Letter to Succensus*

Introduction and Translation by Matthew R. Crawford

INTRODUCTION

The Formula of Reunion in 433 officially restored the peace of the churches but did not bring the Christological debate to an end.[1] The resolution had been achieved only through delicate and difficult negotiations, and further diplomacy was required to maintain the fragile peace. The leaders of each party had the unenviable task of selling the agreement to their followers, some of whom were disinclined to accept any settlement with the opposing side. Some of the Easterners (so called because they came from the Roman diocese of Oriens or "East"), such as Theodoret, insisted that Cyril's signing of the Formula of Reunion could only be interpreted as a departure from the position he had maintained earlier in the controversy, and they began pressing Cyril's supporters with hard questions on this point. Cyril's partisans then turned to the Alexandrian bishop to ask him to weigh in on the matter. One such person was Succensus, bishop of Diocaesarea in the province of Isauria, to whom Cyril penned two letters addressing the questions being posed by the Easterners and debated amongst his own followers.

The *First Letter to Succensus* was written sometime between 434 and 438, that is, after the reunion but before Cyril began writing explicitly against Theodore and Diodore. In several important respects, this letter and the accompanying *Second Letter to Succensus* set the stage for the ongoing Christological debate that would extend until the second Council of Constantinople in 553. First, it is now clear that not only Nestorius but also the sources of Nestorius's teachings are in question,

1 See the introduction to Cyril of Alexandria, *Letter of Reunion to John of Antioch*, on pp. 718–725.

namely Diodore of Tarsus and Theodore of Mopsuestia.[2] Cyril initially resisted condemning Theodore since he had died in the peace of the church, but by the mid-430s he realized this tactic would be impossible, and so began mounting a case against them, eventually composing three books *Against Diodore and Theodore* using the same method he had employed in his *Five Tomes against Nestorius*. The brief description of Diodore's Christology in the letter that follows demonstrates that by this point he already had some acquaintance with his writings. Second, for the first time in this letter the question of how one should speak of the "two natures" of Christ is directly addressed by Cyril. The Formula of Reunion spoke of a "union of two natures," which has surely prompted Succensus's question, since this admission of duality might be taken as undermining the single subjectivity of Christ that Cyril had fought so strenuously to maintain. In this letter he clarifies that this means the union occurred "from" two natures. By means of contemplation one can discern these two united natures, though this distinction exists only in terms of abstract thought. Third, the nature of Christ's flesh has become a topic of discussion. The two natures, Cyril argues, are united "unconfusedly" and "unchangeably" (both these adverbs were later picked up in the Chalcedonian Definition), such that any transformation of the humanity into divinity is precluded. Yet, even though the flesh remains flesh, it attains incorruptibility and can even be described as "divine," since it belongs to the Word. Finally, some of Cyril's supporters are now evidently questioning whether his acceptance of the Formula of Reunion represents a departure from the position he had earlier held when opposing Nestorius, an accusation he obviously denies. Each of these issues – the legacy of Diodore and Theodore, the proper way to speak of the "nature" or "natures" of Christ, the incorruptibility of Christ's flesh, and the interpretation of Cyril's own writings – would continue to be debated well into the sixth century.

This translation is based on the critical text of Eduard Schwartz, *Concilium Universale Ephesenum*, ACO 1.1.6 (Berlin: De Gruyter, 1928), 151–157. The *First Letter to Succensus* is *Letter* 45 within Cyril's epistolary corpus (CPG 5345).

2 See the fragments of Diodore of Tarsus and Theodore of Mopsuestia translated in this volume on pp. 366–387 and 420–488.

TRANSLATION

1. I have read the memorandum sent by Your Holiness. It gave me great joy that, although you are capable of benefiting us along with others owing to your great love of learning, you saw fit to urge us to write down what we have on our mind and what we have resolved to maintain. So then, when it comes to the economy of our Savior, we hold the same view as the holy fathers before us. For by reading their works we attune our own mind,[3] so that we may follow after them and not introduce anything novel to their orthodox doctrines.

2. Now since Your Perfection is inquiring whether or not, with respect to Christ, one should ever speak of two natures, it seems to me necessary to address this. A certain Diodore, who they say had been a fighter against the Spirit for a time,[4] came into communion with the church of the orthodox. Believing himself to have put off the stain of the Macedonian heresy, he then fell into another sickness. For he was of the opinion, which he put in writing, that the one born of David's seed from the holy Virgin was one distinct son, while the Word from God the Father was separately another son. And as if disguising a wolf in a sheepskin,[5] he pretends to speak of "one Christ," attributing the title[6] solely to the only-begotten Son, the Word who was begotten from God the Father, but also assigning the title to David's seed, as he says, "in the category of grace." And so he calls David's seed "son" since he is united, so he says, to the true Son, though not united in the sense that we understand it, but instead only in terms of dignity and authority and equality of honor.

3. Nestorius became a disciple of this Diodore, and with his mind darkened by his books he too pretends to confess one Christ and Son and Lord, but he also divides into two him who is one and indivisible, saying that a human being was conjoined[7] to God the Word by a shared name, by equality of honor, and by dignity. What's more, he divides the sayings about Christ in the evangelical and apostolic proclamations and says that some

3 This sentence highlights Cyril's consistent strategy throughout the Nestorian controversy, namely, to marshal the prior tradition as a witness against his opponent's presumed deviancy.

4 In the later fourth century those who opposed ascribing unqualified deity to the Holy Spirit were known either as Macedonians or Pneumatomachians ("Spirit-fighters"). Aside from this statement of Cyril there is no other evidence that Diodore was a part of the group.

5 See Matt 7:15. 6 That is, the title "Christ."

7 In Greek, *synēphthai*, the verb cognate to the noun *synapheia* ("conjunction").

ought to be applied to the human being (namely, the human ones), and others are appropriate only for God the Word (namely, those appropriate to God). And so, by making so many distinctions, he posits in succession the one born from the holy Virgin separately as a human being, and similarly he posits the Word from God the Father separately as a son. It is for this reason that he says the holy Virgin is not Theotokos but rather Anthropotokos.[8]

4. But as for ourselves, we hold that this cannot be the case. Rather, we have been taught from the divine scripture and the holy fathers to confess one Son and Christ and Lord, that is, the Word from God the Father. He was begotten from the Father before the ages in an indescribable and divinely befitting manner, yet the same one in the last times of the age was begotten from the holy Virgin according to the flesh for our sake. And since she has given birth to God made human and made flesh, for this precise reason we also name her Theotokos. Therefore, there is one Son, one Lord Jesus Christ, both before the incarnation and after the incarnation. For it is not the case that the Word from God the Father was one son, and the one from the holy Virgin was again another son, but rather our faith is that the very same one who was before the ages was also born from a woman according to the flesh. This does not mean that through the holy Virgin his deity started to exist or was called into being for the first time, but rather that, as I said, the Word who existed before the ages is said to have been born from her according to the flesh. For the flesh was his own flesh, just as, for example, each one of us too possesses his body as his own.

5. Now some persons are entangling us in the opinions of Apollinarius and assert, "If you say that the Word from God the Father, who became human and was made flesh, was one Son according to an exact and clenched union, then perhaps you imagine or have come to think that there was a confusion, a blending, or a mixture of the Word with his body, or maybe a transformation of the body into the nature of divinity?" On this point we astutely reject their chicanery and say that the Word from God the Father, in a manner inconceivable and unspeakable, united to himself a body animated by a rational soul and went forth from a woman as a human being,

8 *Anthrōpotokos* means "bearer of the human being." It was actually some of Nestorius's party in Constantinople who clung to the term *anthrōpotokos*. Nestorius himself preferred *Christotokos*, which he held to be the most accurate description of the Virgin, least open to heretical misinterpretation.

becoming like us not by a transformation of his nature, but rather by his good pleasure in line with the divine economy.[9] For he willed to become a human being not by rejecting his existence as God according to nature. Rather, even if he has condescended to our limitations and taken on the "form of a slave,"[10] still he has retained the preeminence of his deity and his lordly nature.

6. Therefore, in some inexpressible way that surpasses human understanding, we unite the Word from God the Father unconfusedly, unchangeably,[11] and without transformation to the holy flesh endowed with a rational soul. Thus, we confess one Son and Christ and Lord, the same one God and human, not one and another, but one and the same[12] is and is understood to be both things. Therefore, sometimes, as a human being, he discourses in human fashion in keeping with the economy,[13] whereas at other times, as God, he speaks with the authority proper to the deity. Moreover, we assert that by skillfully examining the manner of the economy with the flesh and carefully scrutinizing the mystery on all sides, we shall observe that the Word from God the Father both became human and became incarnate, and did not fashion that holy temple of a body from his own divine nature but rather took it from the Virgin. For otherwise how did he become a human being, unless he bore a human body? Therefore, as I said, when we consider the manner of the humanification, we observe that two natures have come together with one another unconfusedly and unchangeably according to an inseparable union. For the flesh is flesh and not divinity, even if it has become God's flesh, and likewise God the Word is also not flesh, even if he has made the flesh his own for the purpose of the economy. Therefore, whenever we consider this, we do no wrong when we say that the coming together into a unity occurred from two natures,[14] though, to be sure, after the union we do not divide the natures from one another nor do we take him who is one and indivisible and chop him into

9 In Greek, *eudokia oikonomikē*, referring to the divine *oikonomia*.

10 See Phil 2:7.

11 The last two adverbs in Greek are *asynchutōs* and *atreptōs*, which would be taken up in the Chalcedonian Definition approximately a decade and a half later.

12 In Greek, *ouk heteron kai heteron, all' hena kai ton auton*. The Greek uses masculine pronouns here, so it is the concrete "Son and Christ and Lord" that is "one and the same."

13 In Greek, *oikonomikōs*, literally, "economically."

14 In the later Christological controversies this would become a point of intense debate: did the incarnation occur merely "out of" or "from" (in Greek, *ek*) two natures or did the incarnate Christ persist "in" (in Greek, *en*) two natures, or were both expressions true and necessary?

two sons. Instead, we affirm one Son, and, as the fathers have said, "one incarnate nature of the Word."[15]

7. Therefore, insofar as it is a matter of contemplation and perceiving strictly with the eyes of the soul the manner in which the Only-Begotten became human, we affirm that there are two natures that were united but one Christ and Son and Lord, that is, the Word of God who became human and was incarnated. And now, if it seems good to you, let us take the example of our own composition, that which constitutes us as human beings. For we are composed from soul and body and thus we perceive two natures, one belonging to the body and the other belonging to the soul. Nevertheless, as a consequence of the union, there is one human being from the two, and the fact that we are composed out of two natures does not make one human being into two human beings, but rather, as I said, there is one human being as a consequence of the composition formed out of soul and body. For if we should repudiate the claim that the one and only Christ is from two different natures – albeit existing as indivisible after the union – then those who fight against orthodoxy will say, "If the entirety[16] is a single nature, how did he become human or what kind of flesh did he make his own?"

8. Now since I found in your memorandum an expression suggesting that, after the resurrection, the holy body of Christ, the Savior of us all, migrated into the nature of divinity, such that the entirety is only divinity, I deemed it necessary to speak also to this point. When the blessed Paul was explaining to us the reasons for the humanification of the only-begotten Son of God, at some point he wrote, "For what the law was unable to do, in that it was weak through the flesh, God has done by sending his own Son in the likeness of sinful flesh and because of sin. He condemned sin in the flesh, in order that the righteous requirement of the law might be fulfilled in us who walk not according to the flesh but according to Spirit."[17] And on another occasion he wrote, "For since the children have shared in flesh and blood, he himself has likewise partaken of the same things, in order that through death he might destroy the one who had the power of death, that is, the devil, and might set free all those who through fear of death were

15 See the discussion of this phrase in the introduction to the *Second Letter to Succensus* on pp. 740–741. As indicated by the way Cyril introduces the phrase here, he is quoting it from what he takes to be an orthodox source, unaware that it is actually Apollinarian in origin.

16 That is, the "entirety" of Christ.

17 Rom 8:3–4.

subject to lifelong slavery. For surely he is not concerned with angels, but is concerned with the offspring of Abraham. This is why he had to be made like the brothers and sisters in every way."[18]

9. Therefore, we affirm that, because human nature suffered corruption from Adam's transgression and because our thoughts are held under tyranny by pleasures or rather by the innate impulses of the flesh, the salvation of those of us upon the earth required the Word of God to become human. He did this in order that he might make his own the human flesh that is subject to corruption and sick from its love of pleasure, so that he, being life and life-giving, might abolish corruption in the flesh, rebuking its innate impulses – that is, its love of pleasure. For it was in this way that the sin in the flesh was put to death; we recall the blessed Paul who also called the innate impulse within us "a law of sin."[19] Therefore, from the moment the human flesh became the Word's own flesh, it has ceased to be subject to corruption, and, since he who appropriated the flesh and showed that it is his own knew no sin (since he is God), the flesh, as I said, has also ceased being sick from love of pleasure. And the only-begotten Word of God has not achieved this for himself (for he is what he is, always), but obviously did it for us. For if we have endured the evil consequences of Adam's transgression, surely also Christ's accomplishments will come to us, that is, incorruptibility and the putting to death of sin. Accordingly, he *became* a human being – he did not *assume* a human being, as Nestorius supposes – and to make us believe that he became a human being while remaining what he was, that is, God according to nature, it is said that he hungered and grew weary from traveling, and that he experienced sleep, agitation, grief, and all the other human passions that do not incur blame.[20] And again, in order to fully assure those who saw him that along with being a human he was also true God, he used to perform divine signs: rebuking seas,[21] raising the dead,[22] and accomplishing other wonders. And he even endured a cross, in order that, having suffered death (in the flesh and not in the nature of divinity), he might become "firstborn from the dead."[23] He also did so in order that he might pave the way for human nature to progress to incorruptibility and so that, by despoiling Hades, he might have mercy on the souls imprisoned within it.

10. And indeed after the resurrection, it was the same body that had suffered, albeit no longer possessing human weakness within itself. For we

18 Heb 2:14–17. 19 Rom 7:23. 20 See Matt 4:2; John 4:6; Matt 8:24, 26:38.
21 Matt 8:26. 22 For example, John 11:43. 23 Col 1:18.

assert that it was no longer susceptible to hunger, or weariness, or anything else of this kind, but was thereafter incorruptible and not only this, for it was also life-giving. For it is a body of life, that is, it is the body of the Only-Begotten, and it is illuminated by the glory proper to God and is understood to be God's body. Hence, even if someone should call it "divine," just as, for instance, you call a body that belongs to a human being, "human," such a person would not be deviating from appropriate logic. It was for this reason, I think, that the all-wise Paul too said, "Even if we knew Christ according to the flesh, now we no longer know him so."[24] For, to repeat my point again, the body existed as God's own body and thus surpassed all things human, though it is not possible for a body from the earth to undergo a transformation into the nature of divinity. For this is impossible, since in this case we would be accusing the divinity of being generated and receiving into itself something which was not proper to it according to nature. For it is just as absurd to say that the body was transformed into the nature of divinity as it would be to say that the Word was transformed into the nature of the flesh. For just as the latter is impossible (since he is immutable and unchanging), so also is the former. For it is not in the realm of possibility that one of the created things should be able to migrate into the substance or nature of the divinity – and indeed the flesh is a created thing. Therefore, on the one hand, we affirm that the body of Christ is divine, since it is also the body of God, resplendent with ineffable glory, incorruptible, holy, and life-giving. But, on the other hand, the idea that it was transformed into the nature of divinity was never thought or expressed by any of the holy fathers, and we do not intend to do so either.

11. I do not want Your Holiness to be unaware of this issue as well, that when certain individuals in his day were agitated, our father Athanasius, of blessed memory, formerly bishop of Alexandria, wrote a letter to Epictetus, bishop of Corinth, which is full of all orthodoxy.[25] And Nestorius was refuted by it, and those intent on holding the same views as him were put to shame when it was read by the defenders of the orthodox faith. As a result, his supporters, out of their dismay at the refutations it contained, devised a vindictive scheme worthy of their heretical impiety. For they corrupted the letter by publishing a version in which they had removed certain things and added others, so that it seemed that that famous man thought in harmony with Nestorius and his partisans. Therefore, in order to prevent certain

24 2 Cor 5:16. 25 Translated in this volume on pp. 279–290.

persons there from introducing the corrupted letter, it was necessary to get a transcript from the certified copies[26] we have and send it to Your Reverence. For when the most pious and reverent Paul, bishop of Emesa, came to Alexandria, he raised this issue, and we discovered that he had a copy of the letter that had been corrupted and falsified by the heretics. Hence, he too thought it was a good idea to have a transcript based on our certified copies forwarded to those in Antioch, and so we have sent it.

12. Following in every respect the orthodox views of the holy fathers, we have written a book against the teachings of Nestorius,[27] and also another against certain individuals who impugn the meaning of the Chapters.[28] I have sent these to Your Reverence, so that, if there should be any of our other brothers who, despite sharing our faith and being one in soul with us have nevertheless been beguiled by the nonsense of certain individuals and suppose that we have changed our mind about the things I have written against Nestorius, they may be reproved by reading and learning that we have fairly and properly rebuked him as someone who has gone astray, and that even now we are pressing no less hard against him, fighting everywhere against his blasphemies. Now Your Perfection, whose mental powers are greater still, will help us both by your writings and by your prayers.

26 See the conclusion to Cyril's *Letter of Reunion to John of Antioch*, where the corrupted version of Athanasius's letter is also mentioned.

27 That is, Cyril's *Five Tomes against Nestorius*, composed in 430 as he was building his case against the Constantinopolitan bishop. The treatise consists of a series of extracts from Nestorius, each followed by a refutation from Cyril.

28 The Chapters are the Twelve Anathemas appended to Cyril's *Third Letter to Nestorius*. Cyril wrote three defenses of the Twelve Anathemas or Chapters, two prior to the Council of Ephesus (one directed against Theodoret and one against Andrew of Samosata), and a further one while under house arrest in Ephesus in the summer of 431.

53

Cyril of Alexandria, *Second Letter to Succensus*

Introduction and Translation by Matthew R. Crawford

INTRODUCTION

The date of this letter is unknown, though it is later than the *First Letter to Succensus*. It could almost be regarded as the charter of the miaphysite movement that would crystalize after the Council of Chalcedon and persists to the present day. Here Cyril responds directly to a series of questions presented to Succensus by an unspecified person from the camp of the Easterners (so called because they came from the Roman diocese of Oriens or "East"), presumably in response to what he had written in the *First Letter to Succensus*. Notably all of the questions turn on the issue of what the words "flesh" (*sarx*) or "become incarnate" (*ensarkoō*) mean and what they imply about how one should use the language of "nature" (*physis*) with respect to Christ.

Singled out for particular focus is Cyril's usage of the phrase "one incarnate nature of the Word" (*mia physis tou logou sesarkōmenē*) in the previous letter to Succensus. Although this phrase became the hallmark of the miaphysite movement, which looked to Cyril as its foremost theological authority, it is actually used sparingly in his corpus, appearing only three times in all of his writings prior to the Formula of Reunion in 433. Moreover, two of these three occurrences are quotations from Apollinarius's *Letter to Emperor Jovian*, which Cyril took to be a work of Athanasius.[1] Hence, the key phrase can hardly be viewed as central to his Christology, and in fact it was not Cyril but his followers and opponents who turned the phrase into a matter of controversy in the years after 433. Based on his own usage, it seems that Cyril probably preferred the phrase "one incarnate hypostasis of the Word," which he had used in the *Third Letter to Nestorius*, but the

1 Apollinarius's *Letter to Emperor Jovian* is translated in this volume on pp. 311–313. Following his condemnation, Apollinarius's supporters circulated his writings under false authorship.

supposed Athanasian precedent for the term "nature" precluded the option of giving up on the controversial catchphrase.

In the present letter Cyril insists that even though only flesh is mentioned in the phrase (in the cognate verb *ensarkoō*, which literally means "to enflesh"), an entire human being with a rational soul is meant. To explain the sense of the word "nature" he turns to the well-worn analogy of the human person. Soul and body are not same-in-substance with one another, yet they form a single human "nature," whose constituent components may be distinguished merely in the realm of contemplation. So also, Cyril argues, the divinity and humanity of Christ come together to form a single, incarnate "nature." His fundamental point is the same as it was at the start of the controversy with Nestorius, that Christ is a single acting subject. He can be said to act "by" or "through" either his divinity or humanity, but the crucial point is that in every case there is one and the same Christ who acts. Cyril does not back away from reasserting one of the more shocking implications of this position which he had previously insisted upon in his twelfth and final anathema against Nestorius, namely that the Word himself suffered, albeit not "with respect to his divinity" but rather "with respect to his humanity." To deny this, he maintains, would be to undermine the whole purpose of the divine plan to save humanity.

This translation is based on the critical text of Eduard Schwartz, *Concilium Universale Ephesenum*, ACO 1.1.6 (Berlin: De Gruyter, 1928), 157–162. The *Second Letter to Succensus* is *Letter* 46 within Cyril's epistolary corpus (CPG 5346).

TRANSLATION

1. The truth reveals itself to those who love it, but I believe it hides itself from and tries to elude those with crafty minds. For they show themselves to be unworthy of beholding it with radiant eyes. And those who love the blameless faith "seek the Lord in simplicity of heart,"[2] as it is written. But those who proceed along twisted paths with "a crooked heart,"[3] as it is said in the Psalms, amass for themselves crafty pretexts for perverted thoughts with the aim of perverting the straight ways of the Lord and leading astray the souls of the simpler folk so that they inevitably hold wrong ideas. And I assert these things having read the memoranda from Your Holiness and finding in them certain

2 Wis 1:1. 3 Ps 100(101):4.

dangerous propositions put forward by those who – I do not know how – love the perversity of knowledge falsely called.[4] Now here they are:

2. He says, "If Emmanuel has been brought together from two natures, and after the union there is understood to be one incarnate nature of the Word, it will surely follow that one must say he suffered in his own nature."

The blessed fathers who decreed for us the sacred symbol of the orthodox faith[5] said that the Word from God the Father, who is from his substance, the Only-Begotten through whom are all things, became incarnate and was made human. Now of course we do not say that those holy ones were unaware that the body united to the Word was animated by an intelligent soul, so that even if someone should use the words "become incarnate," he is not confessing that the flesh united to him was without an intelligent soul.[6] Thus, I think – no, instead I boldly affirm – even the all-wise evangelist John did not say, "the Word became flesh,"[7] as though the Word was united to a flesh without soul (God forbid!), nor as though he was subject to change or alteration. For he remained what he was, that is, God by nature. Even while accepting existence as a human being, that is, being born like us from a woman according to the flesh,[8] still he remained one Son, although he was not without flesh as he was previously, that is, before the time of his humanification, but he was clothed as it were with our own nature too. But even if the body, which was indwelt by an intelligent soul and united to the Word begotten from God the Father, is not same-in-substance with the Word (for the mind imagines the natural difference between the things united), still we confess one Son and Christ and Lord, since the Word has become flesh.[9] And whenever we speak of "flesh," we mean "human being." What sort of necessity is it then that requires him to suffer in his own nature, if we should speak of one incarnate nature of the Son after the union? For if the principles[10] of the economy included nothing that naturally experiences suffering, they would have been correct in saying that, in the absence of something naturally inclined to suffer, the suffering would inevitably and unavoidably fall to the nature of the Word.

4 See 1 Tim 6:20. 5 That is, the Nicene Creed.

6 The need to make this point arises from the fact that the Greek word translated here as "become incarnate" is *sarkoō*, the verb cognate to *sarx* ("flesh"). So "become incarnate" literally means "become flesh" and Cyril has to stress that even though only "flesh" is mentioned, it is understood that the flesh is united to a soul to make a complete human being.

7 John 1:14. 8 See Gal 4:4. 9 See John 1:14.

10 In Greek, *logois*, dative plural of *logos*, translated "word, principle, reason."

But if, on the contrary, when we say "incarnate" we introduce the whole principle of the economy with flesh (for he became incarnate in no other way than by "laying hold of the seed of Abraham"[11] and "becoming like his brothers in every respect"[12] and "taking the form of a slave"[13]), then those who say that it absolutely must follow that he had to experience suffering in his own nature have spoken utter nonsense, since we are presupposing the flesh, which of course is understood to have suffering as an attribute, while the Word is impassible. Nevertheless, we do not for this reason rule out saying that he suffered. For just as the body became his own body, so also everything that belonged to the body, except sin alone, is said to belong to no one else except him, according to the economy of appropriation.[14]

3. He says, "If there is one incarnate nature of the Word, then there absolutely must somehow be a blending and a mixture, with the human nature in him being diminished and, as it were, suppressed."

Those who "pervert what is upright"[15] are again ignorant that there is, in actual fact, one incarnate nature of the Word. For if the Word ineffably begotten from God the Father, who afterwards in accordance with the assumption of flesh (not a soulless flesh but one animated with an intelligent soul) came forth as a human being from a woman – if this Word is truly by nature one Son, then he shall not for this reason be divided into two persons or sons. Instead, he has remained one, except that he is not fleshless or without a body, but has made the body his own according to an inseparable union. And whoever says this does not in any way at all signify a mixture, or a confusion, or anything else of this sort, nor indeed would this follow as a necessary deduction. Why? Because even though we say that the only-begotten Son of God, who became incarnate and became human, is one, this does not mean he has been jumbled together as they suppose, nor that the nature of the Word converted into the nature of the flesh, but neither does this mean that the nature of the flesh converted into the nature of the Word. Rather, while each of them remains in the particular property that it has according to nature and is understood as such (as we have just explained), nevertheless having been ineffably and indescribably united, he exhibited to us the Son's single nature, although, as I have said, it was one incarnate nature. For "one" is a word properly used not only for those things

11 Heb 2:16. 12 Heb 2:17. 13 Phil 2:7.

14 Cyril means "appropriation" (*oikeiōsin*) in the sense that the Word made everything belonging to the body to be his own. He refers here to what the later tradition would call the doctrine of *communicatio idiomatum*.

15 Mic 3:9 (LXX).

that are simple according to nature, but also for those things that are brought together through a combination, the sort of thing that applies, for example, in the case of a human being who is comprised of soul and body. For soul and body are in different classes and are not same-in-substance with one another. Yet they form one united nature of a human being, even though the natural difference between those things brought together into unity inheres in the principles of the combination. Hence, those people are wasting their words when they say that if there is one incarnate nature of the Word it must assuredly follow that there is a blending and a mixture, as if the nature of the human being were diminished and suppressed. For it is neither diminished nor, as they say, suppressed. For to say "he became incarnate" suffices as the most complete indication that he became a human being. For if we had let this fact go by unmentioned, then there would have been a pretext for their calumny, but since the claim that he became incarnate has been added, as necessity required, how is there any kind of diminution or duplicity?

4. He says, "If the same one is understood as 'complete God' and 'complete human being,' and is, on the one hand, 'same-in-substance with the Father with respect to the divinity' and, on the other hand, 'same-in-substance with us with respect to the humanity,'[16] where is the completeness if the human nature no longer subsists? And how is he same-in-substance with us if our substance, that is, our nature, no longer stands?"

The solution (or rather defense) in the previous section suffices also as an explanation for these questions too. For if when we said "one nature of the Word" we had stopped there, not adding the word "incarnate" (as if we were excluding the economy), then perhaps there would somehow be a plausible reason for them to feel justified in asking, "Where is the completeness of his humanity?" or, "How has the substance like ours subsisted?" But since both the completeness of his humanity and an indication that he has a substance like ours have been introduced when one says "incarnate," let them stop supporting themselves with this staff made out of a reed.[17] For if someone disregarded the economy and denied the incarnation, it would be just to charge them with stripping the Son of his complete humanity. But if, as I have said, to say "he became incarnate" is a clear and unambiguous confession of the fact that he became a human being, nothing any longer

16 The phrases in quotation marks in this statement are taken directly from the Formula of Reunion, which is contained in Cyril's *Letter of Reunion to John of Antioch*, translated in this volume on pp. 718–725.

17 See Isa 36:6.

prevents one from understanding that the same one, Christ, existing as one and only Son, is God and human being, just as complete in divinity as he is complete in humanity. And Your Perfection has expounded the rationale of the Savior's suffering most correctly and with great wisdom when you maintain that the only-begotten Son of God himself, insofar as he is understood to be and actually is God, did not suffer bodily things in his own nature, but rather that he suffered in his earthly nature. For it was necessary that both assertions must be preserved with respect to the one and true Son: both that he did not suffer with respect to his divinity and that he is said to suffer with respect to his humanity. For the flesh that suffered belonged to him. Again, however, these people think that with this statement we introduce what they call "theopaschism,"[18] and they do not take account of the economy, but with evil intent attempt to transfer the suffering to the human separately, foolishly pursuing a punishable piety.[19] Hence, the Word of God is not confessed as Savior, as the one who gave his own blood on our behalf.[20] Instead, Jesus, who is understood rather as a distinct human being by himself, is said to have accomplished this. But to think in this way is to rattle the economy with the flesh down to its very foundation, unambiguously reducing the meaning of our divine mystery to the worship of a human being. What's more, they do not realize that the blessed Paul said that the one who is from the Jews according to the flesh – the one who is the seed of Jesse and David – is "Christ" and "Lord of glory," and "God over all blessed forever."[21] Hence, Paul shows that it was the Word's own body that was nailed to the tree and that for this reason the cross is ascribed to him.

5. Now I understand that there is still another matter to discuss in addition to these: "So then, whoever says the Lord suffered in bare flesh makes the suffering irrational and involuntary. But if someone were to say that he suffered with an intelligent soul, so that the suffering would be voluntary, nothing prevents one from saying that he suffered in the nature of humanity. But if this is true, then how can we avoid conceding that two natures subsist undividedly after the union? Thus, if you say, 'Therefore Christ suffered for us in the flesh,'[22] this is nothing other than saying, 'Christ suffered for us in our nature.'"

18 In Greek, *theopatheian*, literally, "divine suffering." This is likely to be the first time the word is used, though it would become a matter of debate among miaphysites in the next century.

19 That is, these opponents remove suffering from the divine Son due to their excessive devotion to safeguarding his deity.

20 See Heb 9:12. 21 1 Cor 2:8; Rom 9:5. 22 1 Pet 4:1.

Again, this problem is just one more attack on those who say that there is one incarnate nature of the Son. Intending, as before, to show that such an idea is pointless, they are obstinately endeavoring at every turn to demonstrate that two natures subsist. But they have failed to realize that whatever things tend toward being distinguished at more than a merely theoretical level may definitely also withdraw completely from one another into the difference between two entirely independent things, one alongside another. Now let us take again the example of a human being like us. For in this case too we also perceive two natures: on the one hand, the nature of the soul and, on the other hand, the nature of the body. But even though we distinguish them in mere thought and accept the difference through subtle contemplation or by the mind's imagination, we are not positing two natures in succession, nor are we allowing someone to imagine a thorough severance of them. Instead, in so doing we are regarding them as belonging to one thing, such that the two are no longer two, but are constituted as one living thing through them both. Therefore, even if they should speak of a nature of humanity and of divinity in the case of the Emmanuel, still the humanity is now proper to the Word and so we understand one Son with the humanity. Now since the divinely inspired scripture says "he suffered in the flesh,"[23] it is better for us too to speak in this manner, rather than to say he suffered "in the nature of humanity," even though this statement would do no damage to the principle of the mystery, unless certain people should say it in a cantankerous way. For what is the nature of humanity except flesh animated with an intelligent soul? And we affirm that the Lord has suffered in the flesh. They are, therefore, splitting hairs when they say he suffered "in the nature of humanity," as if separating the humanity from the Word and setting it to one side on its own, in order that two may be understood and the incarnate and humanified Word from God the Father may no longer be one. Adding the word "undividedly" seems to be a sign that they are with us on the side of orthodoxy, but they do not understand it in this sense. For they take the word "undivided" in a different sense, in terms of the absurdity of Nestorius. For they say that the human being in whom the Word dwelt is undivided [from the Word] in terms of equality of honor, identity of will, and authority, with the result that they cite the words not straightforwardly but with a certain malice and deceit.

23 1 Pet 4:1.

54

Theodoret of Cyrrhus, *Eranistes: Epilogue*

Introduction and Translation by Vasilije Vranic
Revised and Edited by Mark DelCogliano

INTRODUCTION

The *Eranistes*, or the *Polymorphus*, is Theodoret's last extant Christological work, written in 447, shortly before the outbreak of the Eutychian controversy.[1] It thus represents a statement of Theodoret's mature Christological position. It is written in the form of dialogue between two anonymous characters, Orthodoxos and Eranistes. The main purpose of the work is to prove the real existence of both the divine and human natures in Christ after the union effected in the incarnation. It is clear from the text that Orthodoxos represents the doctrinal views of Theodoret, while Eranistes collects various "heretical" Christological opinions in his arguments – hence the name given to the imagined interlocutor, Eranistes, which in Greek means "beggar, collector."

The *Eranistes* is divided into three separate dialogues, each on a different Christological topic. The first dialogue deals with the immutability of the Word. The second is a debate about the manner of union between the Word and the human nature in Christ. The third dialogue argues for the impassibility of the Word *qua* God in the union of the two natures in the incarnation. After each dialogue, Theodoret provides a florilegium of patristic quotations on the topic, carefully chosen to support his argument.

Theodoret ends the work with an epilogue, translated here, which provides a concise summary of the arguments from the three dialogues. The summary of the first dialogue contains twelve syllogisms for the immutability of the Word. That for the second also offers twelve syllogisms whose purpose is to confirm that the union of the natures in Christ was

1 For a fuller introduction to Theodoret, see his *Exposition of the Orthodox Faith*, translated in this volume on pp. 535–555.

free of mixture and confusion and that each nature retains its properties in the union. The summary of the third dialogue contains sixteen syllogisms which argue for the impassibility of the Word in the incarnation. Thus, the epilogue provides a résumé of Theodoret's Christology laid out in forty theological propositions which were divided into three subjects.

The following translation of the epilogue is based upon the critical text of the *Eranistes* established by Gerard H. Ettlinger in *Theodoret of Cyrrhus, Eranistes: Critical Text and Prolegomena* (Oxford: Clarendon Press, 1975).

TRANSLATION

That God the Word is Unchangeable

1. We confessed that there is one substance of the Father, the Son, and the Holy Spirit, and have proclaimed in unison that it is unchangeable. Well then, if there is one substance of the Trinity, and it is unchangeable, then the only-begotten Son is unchangeable, since he is one person of the Trinity. If he is unchangeable, he surely did not become flesh by changing, but is said to have become flesh by taking flesh.

2. If God the Word became flesh by undergoing a change into flesh, then he was not unchangeable. For no one can reasonably call that which is changed unchangeable. But if he is not unchangeable, then he is not same-in-substance with the one who begot him. For how could one part of the simple substance be changeable while another is unchangeable? If we were to concede this, then we would certainly fall into the blasphemy of Arius and Eunomius. For they say that the Son is different-in-substance.

3. If the Son is same-in-substance with the Father, and the Son became flesh by undergoing a transformation into flesh, then the substance is changeable and not unchangeable. If anyone ventures this blasphemy, he will certainly extend it further with blasphemy against the Father. For he would surely call even him changeable, since he shares in the same substance.

4. The divine scriptures say that God the Word took both flesh and a soul, and the most divine evangelist said, "And the Word became flesh."[2] So then, we must do one of two things: either we must admit a change of the Word into flesh and reject all of divine scripture, both old and new, because

2 John 1:14.

it teaches falsehoods, or we must trust in the divine scripture and confess the assumption of flesh and expel change from our thoughts because we understand the gospel passage in a pious manner. We must do the latter, because we confess the nature of God the Word to be unchangeable, and we have countless testimonies to the assumption of the flesh.

5. That which dwells is another alongside that which is dwelt in. The evangelist called the flesh a dwelling and said that God the Word dwelt in it. "The Word," he says, "became flesh, and dwelt among us."[3] If he became flesh by changing, he did not dwell in flesh. But we have learned that he did indeed dwell in the flesh. For in another passage the same evangelist called his body a temple.[4] Thus, we must believe the evangelist who unfolded the passage and explained what seemed ambiguous to some.

6. If after writing "The Word became flesh"[5] the evangelist added nothing that could dispel the ambiguity, perhaps the dispute over the passage would have a reasonable pretext, namely, the obscurity of the text. But since he immediately added, "dwelt among us," then those who are quarreling over it argue in vain. For the words that follow explain the words that preceded.

7. The all-wise evangelist clearly proclaimed the unchangeability of God the Word. For after he said, "The Word became flesh and dwelt among us,"[6] he immediately added, "And we have seen his glory, glory as of the Only-Begotten from the Father, full of grace and truth."[7] If he had undergone a change into flesh, as stupid people claim, he would not have remained what he was. But if he was emitting rays of the Father's nobility while hidden in flesh, he surely has an unchangeable nature, and even in the body shines and sends out flashes of the invisible nature. For nothing can dim that light. For "the light shines in the darkness, and the darkness has not overcome it,"[8] as the most divine John says.

8. When the all-praised evangelist wished to explain the glory of the Only-Begotten but at that time could not complete the task, he hints at what it is by means of the commonality with the Father. For he says that [the Only-Begotten] has his existence from that nature. He acts like someone who sees Joseph serving, beneath his dignity, people ignorant of the eminence of his ancestry and tells them that Jacob was his father and Abraham his forefather. The evangelist has done something similar, saying that

3 John 1:14. 4 See John 2:19. 5 John 1:14.
6 John 1:14. 7 John 1:14. 8 John 1:5.

he did not diminish the glory of his nature by dwelling among us. "We have seen his glory, glory as of the Only-Begotten from the Father."[9] If it is clear that he remained what he was even after becoming enfleshed, then he remained exactly what he was and did not undergo a change into flesh.

9. We confessed that God the Word assumed not only flesh but also a soul. Well then, why did the divine evangelist say nothing about the soul here and speak only of the flesh? Or is it evident that by indicating the visible nature through it he also revealed the one joined to it by nature? For any reference to the flesh brings along with it the thought of the soul. For when we hear the prophet saying, "Let all flesh bless his holy name,"[10] we do not suppose that the prophet is exhorting soulless flesh, but we believe that through one part the whole is called to sing hymns of praise.

10. The passage "The Word became flesh" reveals his ineffable love for humankind, not a change. For the all-praised evangelist said, "In the beginning was the Word, and the Word was with God, and the Word was God."[11] And then he showed that he was the fashioner of the visible and invisible things,[12] and called him "life" and "true light,"[13] and said other things like this, and he provided a theological account in a way the human mind could comprehend and the tongue could suffice to express in language, and then added, "And the Word became flesh," as if he were surprised and astonished at the intensity of his love for humankind. Thus, though eternal, God, and eternally with God, though he made everything and is the source of eternal life and true light, he put a dwelling of flesh on himself for the salvation of human beings. But he was thought to be only that which was visible. For this reason there was no mention of the soul, but only of the perishable and mortal flesh. He said nothing about the soul as immortal in order to demonstrate the infinitude of his goodness.

11. The divine Apostle calls Christ the Master "seed of Abraham."[14] If that is true, and it is true, then God the Word was not changed into flesh but according to the teaching of the Apostle himself took hold of the seed of Abraham.

12. God swore to David that Christ would arise according to the flesh from the fruit of his loins, as the prophet said and the great Peter explained.[15] If God the Word was called Christ because he was changed into flesh, we shall never find truth in the oath. But we have been taught that

9 John 1:14. 10 Ps 144(145):21. 11 John 1:1.
12 See John 1:3. 13 John 1:4. 14 Heb 2:16.
15 See Ps 131(132):11 and Acts 2:30.

God does not lie, but is rather the truth itself. Therefore, God the Word did not undergo a transformation into flesh, but in accordance with the promise took the first fruit from the seed of David.

That the Union is Without Confusion

1. Those who believe that after the union there was one nature of divinity and humanity destroy the distinctive attributes of the natures with this idea, and the destruction of these is a denial of each nature. For the confusion of the united entities does not allow understanding the flesh as flesh or God as God. But if one can discern the differences of the united entities even after the union, then it was not confusion that occurred but a union without confusion. If this is the confession agreed upon, then Christ the Master is not one nature but one Son who reveals each nature unadulterated.

2. We say and they confess along with us that the union took place at conception. Well then, if the union mixed and confused the natures, how could the flesh be seen after the birth with nothing new? But it showed human features, preserved the limitations of an infant, put up with swaddling clothes, and nursed at its mother's breast. If these were accomplished in an illusory manner and by way of mere appearance, then we also have obtained salvation in an illusory manner and by way of mere appearance. But if even these people do not, as they claim, admit the illusory manner and mere appearance, then what was seen was truly flesh. If this is the confession agreed upon, then the union did not confuse the natures but each nature has remained unadulterated.

3. Those who concocted this diverse and multifarious heresy sometimes say that God the Word became flesh, while at other times they say that the flesh attained a transformation into the nature of divinity. Each statement is worthless, foolish, and full of lies. For if God the Word became flesh in the way they say, then why on earth do they call him God, and only this, and why are they unwilling to call him a human being in addition to this, but instead greatly criticize us for saying, along with our confession that he is God, that he is also a human being? But if the flesh was changed into divinity by nature, why indeed do they partake of the symbols of the body?[16] For when the original is destroyed, the symbol is superfluous.

16 Theodoret is speaking of participation in the Eucharist.

4. A nature that is incorporeal is not circumcised in a bodily manner. The phrase "in a bodily manner" is added because there is the spiritual circumcision of the heart.[17] Circumcision is surely done to the body. But Christ was circumcised; therefore, Christ the Master had a body. If this is the confession agreed upon, then the idea of confusion has been refuted.

5. We have learned that Christ the Savior actually got hungry and thirsty, and we believe that these things truly happened and that they did not happen by way of mere appearance. But these experiences do not belong to the incorporeal nature, but to the body. Therefore, Christ the Master had a body, and before the resurrection it was subject to the experiences of the nature. The divine Apostle also testifies to this when he says, "For we do not have a high priest who is unable to sympathize with our weaknesses, but one who in every respect is tempted as we are yet without sin."[18] For sin does not belong to the nature, but to the evil choice.

6. The prophet David said about the divine nature, "He sleeps not nor slumbers, Israel's guard."[19] The narrative of the gospels shows Christ the Master sleeping in the boat.[20] Sleeping is the opposite of not slumbering. The words of the prophet surely contradict those of the gospels, then, if Christ the Master is only God, as they say. But in fact these passages are not contradictory, since they both flow from the one Spirit. Therefore, Christ the Master had a body that was akin to other bodies, since it experienced the need for sleep. And thus the idea of confusion is proven false.

7. The prophet Isaiah has said about the divine nature, "He shall not be hungry nor grow weary," and so on.[21] And the evangelist said, "Jesus grew weary from his journey and sat down beside the well."[22] Not growing weary is the opposite of growing weary. Therefore, the prophecy contradicts the narrative of the gospels. But in fact these passages are not contradictory, since they both come from one God. Therefore, not growing weary pertains to the uncircumscribed nature since it fills all things, and moving is a distinctive trait of the body that is circumscribed. And when that which moves needs to walk, it is subject to the weariness that comes from a journey. So then, it was the body that walked and grew weary. For the union did not confuse the natures.

8. When the divinely inspired Paul was in prison, Christ the Master said to him, "Do not be afraid, Paul,"[23] and so on. But he who drove out

17 See Rom 2:29. 18 Heb 4:15. 19 Ps 120(121):4. 20 See Matt 8:23–24.
21 Isa 40:28. 22 John 4:6. 23 A conflation of Acts 23:11 and 27:23–24.

Paul's fear was so afraid of suffering, as the blessed Luke said, that he shed bloody drops of sweat from his entire body, saturated the ground underneath the body with them, and was strengthened only with the help of an angel.[24] But these passages are contradictory. For how can being afraid not be the opposite of driving out fear? But in fact these passages are not contradictory since the same one is God by nature and a human being. As God he encourages those who lack courage, but as a human being he receives courage through the angel. Yet even though both the divinity and the Spirit were present as an anointing, at that time neither the divinity conjoined to it nor the all-holy Spirit supported the body and encouraged the soul. Instead, they entrusted this service to the angel so that they might show the weakness of the soul and body and so that the natures of these weak things might be revealed through the weakness. This clearly happened with the consent of the divine nature, so that people in the future who believed in the assumption of the soul and the body would be confirmed in their belief by these proofs, while those who opposed them would be refuted by unambiguous testimonies. Well then, if the union was conjoined at conception, and if the union, according to what those people say, made two natures one nature, how could the distinctive attributes of the natures have remained unmixed? How could the soul have been in agony and the body sweated so much that it shed bloody drops from excessive fear? If the latter is characteristic of the body and the former of the soul, then one nature of flesh and divinity did not result from the union, but one Son is revealed, who shows in himself both divine and human attributes.

9. If they were to say that the body obtained a transformation into divinity after the resurrection, you should respond in the following way. Even after the resurrection the body was indeed seen as circumscribed, with hands, feet, and the other parts of the body; it could be touched and seen, and it had the same cuts and wounds as it had before the resurrection. Therefore, we must say one of two things: either we must ascribe these body parts to the divine nature, if the body was transformed into the divine nature and has these parts, or we must confess that the body remained within the limits of its nature. But the divine nature is indeed simple and uncompounded, while the body is composite and divided into many parts. Thus, it was not transformed into the nature of divinity, but after the res-

24 See Luke 22:43–44.

urrection it is also immortal, incorruptible, and full of divine glory, even though it is still a body with its own circumscription.

10. After the resurrection the Lord showed his hands and feet and the marks of the nails to the unbelieving apostles. Then, in order to teach them that what they saw was not some illusion, he added, "A spirit has no flesh and bones, as you see that I have."[25] Thus, the body was not transformed into a spirit. For it was flesh and bones, and hands and feet. Therefore, even after the resurrection the body has remained a body.

11. The divine nature is invisible, but the thrice-blessed Stephen said that he saw the Lord.[26] Therefore, the Lord's body was a body even after the ascension. For this is what the victorious Stephen saw, since the divine nature cannot be seen.

12. According to what the Lord himself said, all human nature will see the Son of Man coming on the clouds of heaven,[27] and again he said to Moses, "No one can see my face and live."[28] If both passages are true, then he will come back with the body with which he ascended into heaven. For that body is visible. And the angels said this to the apostles: "This Jesus, who was taken up from you into heaven, will come in the same way as you saw him go into heaven."[29] But if this is true, as in fact it is true, then there is not one nature of flesh and divinity. For the union is without confusion.

That the Divinity of the Savior is Impassible

1. We have been taught by both the divine scripture and the holy fathers who gathered at Nicaea to confess that the Son is same-in-substance with God the Father. And the nature teaches the impassibility of the Father and the divine scripture proclaims it. Therefore, we shall also confess that the Son is impassible. For the identity of the substance teaches this definition. So then, when we hear the divine scripture proclaiming the cross and death of Christ the Master, we say that the suffering belongs to the flesh. For it is impossible for the divinity that is impassible by nature to suffer in any way.

2. Christ the Master said, "All that the Father has is mine,"[30] and one of the "all" is surely impassibility. Therefore, if he is impassible as God, then he suffered as a human being. For the divine nature does not admit of suffering.

25 Luke 24:39. 26 See Acts 7:56. 27 See Matt 26:64. 28 See Exod 33:20. 29 Acts 1:11. 30 John 16:15.

3. The Lord said, "And the bread that I shall give is my flesh, which I shall give for the life of the world."[31] And again, "I am the good shepherd, and I know my own and I am known by my own, and I lay down my soul for my sheep."[32] Thus, the good shepherd gave his body and soul for the sheep that have bodies and souls.

4. The nature of human beings is composed of body and soul. But it sinned and needed a sacrifice that was entirely blameless. So then, the Fashioner took flesh and soul, kept them untouched by the stains of sin, and gave his body on behalf of bodies and his soul on behalf of souls. If this is true, and it is true (for these are the words of truth itself), then those who attribute the suffering to the divine nature are uttering foolishness and blasphemy.

5. The blessed Paul called Christ the Master "firstborn of the dead."[33] But the firstborn surely has the same nature as the ones of whom he is called the firstborn. Thus, he is the firstborn of the dead as a human being. For he first loosed the pangs of death[34] and gave the sweet hope of new life to all. And he suffered in the same way in which he was resurrected. Therefore, he suffered as a human being, but as wonderful God he remained impassible.

6. The divine Apostle called Christ the Savior "the first fruit of those who have fallen asleep."[35] And the first fruit has kinship with the whole group of which it is the first fruit. Therefore, he is not called the first fruit insofar as he is God. For what kinship is there between divinity and humanity? The former nature is immortal, whereas the latter is mortal. This latter is the nature of those who have fallen asleep, of whom Christ was called the first fruit. Thus, the death and the resurrection pertain to this nature. For we have the resurrection of this nature as the pledge of the general resurrection.

7. When Christ the Master wanted to persuade the doubting apostles that he had been resurrected and destroyed death, he showed them the parts of his body – his side, his hands, his feet – and the proofs of his suffering preserved in them. Therefore, this body was resurrected, for it was surely this body that was shown to them even though they did not believe. What was resurrected is in fact that which was also buried, and what was buried is that which had also died, and what had died is indeed that which

31 John 6:51. 32 John 10:14–15, with omissions. 33 Col 1:18.
34 See Acts 2:24. 35 1 Cor 15:20.

had also been nailed to the cross. Therefore, the divine nature remained impassible even though it was conjoined to the body.

8. Those who call the Lord's flesh life-giving make life itself mortal by such an idea. They should have understood that the flesh is life-giving only because of the life united to it. But if life is mortal, as they say, then how could the flesh, which is mortal by nature but becomes life-giving through life, remain life-giving?

9. God the Word is immortal by nature, while the flesh is mortal by nature. But after the passion the flesh also became immortal through participation in the Word. So then, is it not wicked to say that the giver of such immortality has shared in death?

10. Let those who insist that God the Word suffered in flesh be asked about what their statement means. And if they dare to say that the divine nature endured the pain of the body when it was nailed to the cross, let them learn that the divine nature did not fulfill the function of the soul. For God the Word assumed a soul together with body. But if they renounce this idea as blasphemous and say that the flesh suffered by nature while God the Word appropriated the suffering because it was his flesh's very own, they should not offer enigmatic and obscure explanations but clearly state what their confusing statement means. For they will have those who choose to follow the divine scripture as supporters of this interpretation.

11. In the catholic epistle the divine Peter said that "Christ suffered in the flesh."[36] But whoever hears "Christ" does not think of the incorporeal God the Word but of God the Word who became flesh. Therefore, the name of Christ reveals both natures. But the phrase "in the flesh" that is added to "suffered" signifies the nature that suffered, not both of them. For whoever hears that "Christ suffered in the flesh" understands that he is impassible as God and attributes the suffering only to the flesh. For again when we hear him saying that God swore an oath to David that he would raise up Christ according to flesh from the fruit of his loins,[37] we are not saying that God the Word obtained his beginning from the seed of David, but that the flesh which God the Word assumed was of David's line. In the same way, whoever hears that Christ suffered in flesh must realize that the suffering belongs to the flesh, and at the same time confess the impassibility of the divinity.

36 1 Pet 4:1. 37 Ps 131(132):11.

12. When Christ the Master was being crucified, he said, "Father, into your hands I commend my spirit."[38] The adherents of Arius and Eunomius say that the "spirit" here is the divinity of the Only-Begotten. For they think that a body without a soul has been assumed. But the heralds of truth say that the soul is being called the "spirit," arriving at this understanding because of the passage that follows. For immediately the all-wise evangelist added, "Having said this, he breathed his last."[39] In this way, then, did Luke report these events, and the blessed Mark similarly put that he "breathed his last."[40] But the most divine Matthew said that he "yielded up his spirit,"[41] while the divinely inspired John said that he "gave up his spirit."[42] Now they said all this according to human custom. For it is customary to say about those who die that "he breathed his last," "he yielded up his spirit," and "he gave up his spirit." Therefore, none of these expressions signify the divinity, but they do refer to the soul. And even if one were to accept the Arian understanding of the passage, it will nonetheless show, when taken this way, the immortality of the divine nature. For he commended his soul to the Father; he did not send it off to death. So then, in regard to those who deny the assumption of a soul and say that God the Word is a creature and teach that the Word came in the body in the soul's stead, if they say that he was not handed over to death but was commended to the Father, what kind of forgiveness could these people obtain? For they confess that there is one substance of the Trinity and let the soul be in its own immortality, but at the same time they dare to say without hesitation that God the Word, who is same-in-substance with the Father, tasted death.

13. If Christ is both God and a human being, as the divine scripture teaches and the all-praised fathers never ceased to proclaim, then he suffered as a human being, but remained impassible as God.

14. If they confess the assumption of the flesh and say that it was passible before the resurrection and proclaim the nature of the divinity to be impassible, why on earth do they leave the passible nature alone but impute the suffering to the impassible nature?

15. If the Lord and Savior, according to the divine Apostle, nailed our bond[43] to the cross,[44] then he nailed the body [to the cross]. For every

38 Luke 24:36. 39 Luke 24:36. 40 Mark 15:27.
41 Matt 27:50. 42 John 19:30.
43 In Greek, *cheirographon*, a document "written by hand." 44 See Col 2:14.

human being fixes the stains of sins, like letters, in the body. On behalf of sinners, then, he gave up the body that was free of all sin.

16. When we say that the body, or the flesh, or the humanity suffered, we are not separating the divine nature from it. For just as the divine nature was united to the nature that got hungry, thirsty, and tired, that even slept and struggled with the suffering, yet did not submit to any of these, and at the same time agreed to receive within it the passions of the human nature, so too was divine nature joined to the crucified nature and agreed with the suffering to be consummated to destroy death by suffering. It did not receive any pain from the suffering, but appropriated the suffering since it belonged to its own temple, namely the flesh united to it. It is because of this flesh that those who believe are called "members of Christ,"[45] and he himself has been named the head of those who have believed.[46]

45 1 Cor 6:15. 46 See Eph 4:15.

Suggestions for Further Reading

Bathrellos, Demetrios. *The Byzantine Christ: Person, Nature, and Will in the Christology of Saint Maximus the Confessor*. Oxford Early Christian Studies. Oxford: Oxford University Press, 2005.

Behr, John. *The Case against Diodore and Theodore: Texts and their Contexts*. Oxford Early Christian Texts. Oxford: Oxford University Press, 2011.

Brock, Sebastian P. "The 'Nestorian' Church: A Lamentable Misnomer." *Bulletin of the John Rylands University Library of Manchester* 78, no. 3 (1996): 23–35.

"Miaphysite, not Monophysite!" *Cristianesimo nella storia* 37, no. 1 (2016): 45–54.

Chesnut, Roberta A. *Three Monophysite Christologies: Severus of Antioch, Philoxenus of Mabbug, and Jacob of Sarug*. Oxford Theological Monographs. Oxford: Oxford University Press, 1976.

Daley, Brian E. *God Visible: Patristic Christology Reconsidered*. Changing Paradigms in Historical and Systematic Theology. Oxford: Oxford University Press, 2018.

Fairbairn, Donald. *Grace and Christology in the Early Church*. Oxford Early Christian Studies. Oxford: Oxford University Press, 2003.

Forness, Philip Michael. *Preaching Christology in the Roman Near East: A Study of Jacob of Serugh*. Oxford Early Christian Studies. Oxford: Oxford University Press, 2018.

Gavrilyuk, Paul. *The Suffering of the Impassible God: The Dialectics of Patristic Thought*. Oxford Early Christian Studies. Oxford: Oxford University Press, 2004.

Gleede, Benjamin. *The Development of the Term ἐνυπόστατος from Origen to John of Damascus*. Vigiliae Christianae Supplements 113. Leiden: Brill, 2012.

Gray, Patrick T. R. *The Defense of Chalcedon in the East (451–553)*. Leiden: Brill, 1979.

Grillmeier, Aloys. *Christ in Christian Tradition. Volume One: From the Apostolic Age to Chalcedon (451)*. 2nd rev. ed. Translated by John Bowden. Atlanta: John Knox Press, 1975.

Christ in Christian Tradition. Volume Two, Part One: Reception and Contradiction. The Development of the Discussion about Chalcedon from 451 to the Beginning of the Reign of Justinian. Translated by Pauline Allen and John Cawte. Atlanta: John Knox Press, 1987.

Grillmeier, Aloys, with Theresia Hainthaler. *Christ in Christian Tradition. Volume Two, Part Two: The Church of Constantinople in the Sixth Century*. Translated by John Cawte and Pauline Allen. London: Mowbray; Louisville: Westminster John Knox Press, 1995.

Christ in Christian Tradition. Volume Two, Part Four: The Church of Alexandria with Nubia and Ethiopia after 451. Translated by O. C. Dean, Jr. London: Mowbray; Louisville: Westminster John Knox Press, 1996.

Hainthaler, Theresia, in continuation of the work of Aloys Grillmeier, with contributions by Aloys Grillmeier, Theresia Hainthaler, Tanios Bou Mansour, and Luise Abramowski. *Christ in Christian Tradition. Volume Two, Part Three: The Churches of Jerusalem and Antioch from 451 to 600*. Translated by Marianne Ehrhardt. Oxford: Oxford University Press, 2013.

Hovorun, Cyril. *Will, Action, and Freedom: Christological Controversies in the Seventh Century*. Leiden: Brill, 2008.

Lietzmann, Hans. *Apollinaris von Laodicea und seine Schule: Texte und Untersuchungen*. Tübingen: Mohr Siebeck, 1904.

Loofs, Friedrich. *Nestoriana: Die Fragmente des Nestorius*. Halle: Max Niemeyer, 1905.

McGuckin, John A. *Saint Cyril of Alexandria and the Christological Controversy: Its History, Theology, and Texts*. Crestwood: St Vladimir's Seminary Press, 2004.

Menze, Volker L. *Justinian and the Making of the Syrian Orthodox Church*. Oxford Early Christian Studies. Oxford: Oxford University Press, 2008.

Meyendorff, John. *Christ in Eastern Christian Thought*. Crestwood: St. Vladimir's Seminary Press, 1987.

Michelson, David A. *The Practical Christology of Philoxenos of Mabbug*. Oxford Early Christian Studies. Oxford: Oxford University Press, 2014.

Pawl, Timothy. *In Defense of Conciliar Christology: A Philosophical Essay*. Oxford Studies in Analytic Theology. Oxford: Oxford University Press, 2016.

Price, Richard. *The Acts of the Council of Constantinople of 553 with Related Texts on the Three Chapters Controversy*. 2 vols. Translated Texts for Historians 51. Liverpool: Liverpool University Press, 2009.

The Acts of the Second Council of Nicaea (787). Translated Texts for Historians 68. Liverpool: Liverpool University Press, 2018.

Price, Richard, with contributions by Phil Booth and Catherine Cubitt. *The Acts of the Lateran Synod of 649*. Translated Texts for Historians 61. Liverpool: Liverpool University Press, 2014.

Price, Richard, and Michael Gaddis. *The Acts of the Council of Chalcedon*. 3 vols. Translated Texts for Historians 45. Liverpool: Liverpool University Press, 2005.

Price, Richard, and Thomas Graumann. *The Council of Ephesus of 431: Documents and Proceedings*. Translated Texts for Historians 72. Liverpool: Liverpool University Press, 2020.

Sellers, R. V. *The Council of Chalcedon: A Historical and Doctrinal Survey*. London: SPCK, 1961.
Torrance, Iain R. *Christology after Chalcedon. Severus of Antioch and Sergius the Monophysite*. Norwich: Canterbury Press, 1988.
Trostyanskiy, Sergey, ed. *Seven Icons of Christ: An Introduction to the Oikoumenical Councils*. Gorgias Handbooks. Piscataway: Gorgias Press, 2016.
Young, Frances M., with Andrew Teal. *From Nicaea to Chalcedon: A Guide to the Literature and its Background.* 2nd ed. Grand Rapids: Baker Academic, 2010.
Zachhuber, Johannes. *The Rise of Christian Theology and the End of Ancient Metaphysics: Patristic Philosophy from the Cappadocian Fathers to John of Damascus*. Oxford: Oxford University Press, 2020.

The study of early Christianity is continually expanding, with new perspectives emerging and replacing old ones. For the student who is interested in following the ongoing development of scholarship in this field, we strongly recommend consulting the regular publication of journals such as *Augustinian Studies*, *Church History*, *Hugoye*, the *Journal of Early Christian Studies*, the *Journal of Ecclesiastical History*, the *Journal of Theological Studies*, *Vigiliae Christianae*, and *Zeitschrift für Antikes Christentum (Journal of Ancient Christianity)*. Each of these journals contains scholarly articles and reviews of recent books in the field. Additionally, for up-to-date bibliography on topics in early Christianity and the ancient world generally, one can consult *L'Année philologique*.

Scriptural Index

Most of the verses cited in the index will be found in the footnotes of the given page(s).

Printed in the USA
CPSIA information can be obtained
at www.ICGtesting.com
CBHW051438291024
16558CB00003B/206